"*Gang of Five* is an intriguing chronicle of the human element behind the Right's successful, if hostile, takeover of much of American politics in the last twenty-five years. Scrupulously researched, stylishly written, *Gang of Five* grasps what most infuriates liberals about the ascendant Right: They have beaten the Left at its own game—exploiting the media, shameless self-dramatizing, and mixing guerrilla tactics with political polish.

In her appreciative dissection of five of the Right's most interesting and influential insurgents, Nina Easton reveals that the Right has made many of the same mistakes that led to the demise of the liberal establishment: insisting that a surfeit of ideology could compensate for a deficit of character, scorning compromise, overreaching, and pursuing power as a blood-sport.

Nina Easton does for the conservative movement that upended the dominant political and cultural order what Robert Timberg did for a generation of Annapolis grads who served in Vietnam in *The Nightingale's Song*—absent the selfless heroism of a John McCain or Jim Webb."

—Mark Shields, syndicated columnist,
political commentator, *The NewsHour with Jim Lehrer*

"What fun! A cross between *The Best and the Brightest* and *Revenge of the Nerds*. Nina Easton brings a strange and wonderful cast of characters to life in a book that is serious and often hilarious."

—Joe Klein, author of *Primary Colors*
and *The Running Mate*

"The rise of the political Right caught most journalists by surprise because they didn't take conservatives seriously. Nina Easton is a rare reporter who does. She rarely agrees with her five prominent profile subjects, but her illuminating book shows what they believe, why they believe it, and how they're succeeding."

—Paul Gigot, Pulitzer Prize–winning columnist,
The Wall Street Journal, and political commentator,
The NewsHour with Jim Lehrer

50¢

"*Gang of Five* is a lively and thoughtful narrative that tells the story of five fascinating baby boomers who have changed the course of American conservatism. Read Nina Easton's fine book if you care about where American politics is going. Read it if you want to know where you've come from. And, especially, read it if you enjoy an elegant page-turner of a biography that illuminates both individual lives and the important forces shaping our times."

—E. J. Dionne, author of *Why Americans Hate Politics*
and *They Only Look Dead*

"Nina Easton has written the definitive account of the next generation of conservative leaders. *Gang of Five* is an essential resource for anyone interested in the political Right and the direction this powerful movement will take in the post–Bill Clinton era. Easton has the insight and knowledge to pick five men who are at the center of the national debate, each of whom has already demonstrated the ability to shape and direct legislative policy and election strategy. The real value of this book is Easton's intelligent understanding not only of politics but of the competitiveness, ideological commitment, and personal struggles of each of her subjects."

—Thomas Edsall, *The Washington Post*, author of
Chain Reaction and *The New Politics of Inequality*

"This is a richly reported and elegantly written book about a little-known part of contemporary history: the rise of the baby-boom conservatives. If you want to understand better the movement that helped shape American politics in the past decade, read Nina Easton. *Gang of Five* is both a series of fascinating profiles of some of the major conservative activists of the day and a thoughtful analysis of what went right—and wrong—with their movement."

—Dan Balz, *The Washington Post*,
coauthor of *Storming the Gates*

"Finally, the 'back story' of how the United States moved rightward late in the twentieth century. Easton illuminates an essential historical truth—that a tiny handful of clever ideologues can change the world."

—Jonathan Alter, *Newsweek*

Also by Nina J. Easton

Reagan's Ruling Class: Portraits of the President's Top 100 Officials *(with Ronald Brownstein)*

GANG

Leaders at the Center of the

A TOUCHSTONE BOOK
PUBLISHED BY SIMON & SCHUSTER

NEW YORK   LONDON   TORONTO   SYDNEY   SINGAPORE

OF FIVE

Conservative Ascendancy

Nina J. Easton

To my family

 TOUCHSTONE
Rockefeller Center
1230 Avenue of the Americas
New York, NY 10020

Copyright © 2000 by Nina J. Easton
All rights reserved,
including the right of reproduction
in whole or in part in any form.
First Touchstone Edition 2002
TOUCHSTONE and colophon
are registered trademarks of Simon & Schuster, Inc.
For information about special discounts for bulk purchases,
please contact Simon & Schuster Special Sales:
1-800-456-6798 or business@simonandschuster.com
Designed by Edith Fowler
Manufactured in the United States of America

10   9   8   7   6   5   4   3   2   1

The Library of Congress has cataloged the Simon & Schuster edition as follows:

Easton, Nina.
  Gang of five : leaders at the center of the
conservative crusade / Nina J. Easton.
     p.   cm.
  Includes bibliographical references (p.   ) and
index. 1. United States—Politics and government—
1945–1989. 2. United States—Politics and
government—1989– 3. Politicians—United
States—Biography. 4. Republican Party (U.S.:
1854–)—Biography. 5. Politicians—United
States—History—20th century. 6. Conservatism—
United States—History—20th century. 7. Right
and left (Political science). I. Title.
E839.5 .E27 2000
320.52'092'273—dc21   00-040050

ISBN 0-684-83899-0
      0-7432-0320-8 (Pbk)

CONTENTS

INTRODUCTION

ON JANUARY 20, 2001, the most conservative new president in two decades took the oath of office. For those who thought that George W. Bush's loss of the popular vote and narrow electoral college win would enlighten him to the virtues of centrism, the Republican president's first months in office were a rude awakening. Acting with the ideological confidence of a landslide winner, President Bush quickly moved forward on his promised tax cut, the largest since Ronald Reagan's and a drop in federal revenue certain to limit the horizons of Washington's generous spenders. He revived a nuclear missile defense system and pursued a foreign policy suspicious of international protocol. He overturned popular environmental and workplace safety protections. He appointed a libertarian to run the Interior Department and a religious-right Pentecostal as attorney general. He cut off funds for organizations providing abortion services overseas and declared that the federal government should lend financial support to religious charities.

Among his many critics, confusion reigned: Hadn't candidate Bush portrayed himself as a unifier, not a divider, a former governor who had worked hand in hand with the Democrats in his home state of Texas? Wasn't this son of a president supposed to be above all a "Bush"—a man, like his father, more loyal to people (and popularity) than ideas? Wasn't he merely a politician talented at tailoring his message for his audience—drawing applause from moderate corporate chieftains one day, religious right enthusiasts the next, and mainstream educators the next? And wasn't Bush, after all, a president without a public mandate?

George W. Bush may be all those things. But he is also a true conservative, the product of one of the most important political movements of the late twentieth century. With Bush's razor-thin victory, the Right again emerged as a potent political force. The president balanced the moderates in his administration with a broad range of Rightists, from "compassionate conservatives" to antigovernment libertarians to foreign policy hard-liners. Conservatives outside the administration can count on a friend in the Oval Office for the first time since Reagan. And in sharp contrast to earlier generations of conservatives, the Rightists in and around the Bush administration are adroit at using political power to advance their agenda.

The world in which this conservative movement operated changed dramatically on September 11, 2001, when the country suffered the deadliest attacks ever on American soil and a war against terrorism was launched. When Bush first came into office, critics had derided his foreign policy as the "new unilateralism." The president's initial policies carried an unmistakable America-first cast, shaped by an implicit confidence that America was the embodiment of virtue on the international stage. After September 11, the president became a builder of international alliances in an attempt to create a global coalition against terrorism. He used the spending power of the federal government to boost the economy in dramatic ways that would have infuriated his conservative allies a month earlier. But even in this new state of emergency, conservatives and their ideas continue to compete for supremacy in national politics: internationally, on the question of how to conduct this war against terrorism, and domestically, in the ongoing struggle to balance the protection of the citizenry with the protection of civil liberties.

Whenever a new spirit of conservatism takes hold in American politics, outsiders are left asking all those questions that invariably accompany discussions about the ascendancy of the modern Right: Why the emphasis on injecting religion and judgments about private morality into public life? Why the disdain for international agreements and government regulation, even popular environmental protections? Why the reluctance to use public authority—through legislation or the courts—to reduce inequality in America? Why the unabashed scorn for liberalism and Democrats, and the habitual resort to bloody confrontation with political opponents? Why the frantic desire to wrestle the nation's plot line from liberal historians—an emotion evidenced in ongoing efforts to enshrine Ronald Reagan's name on airports and buildings and monuments in every county in the country?

The answers to these questions are part of a hidden history in American politics—the rise to influence of a new generation of rebels who form the core of today's political Right. These conservatives are baby boomers, and even today their personalities mark them as part of the Question Authority generation: They bring to their political battles much of the hubris and irreverence and impatience for change that once characterized their foes on the Left. But the "authority" against which these Rightists rebel is a prevailing liberal wisdom in academia, the media, and the nation's political institutions.

I call this a hidden history because so little is understood about the dynamics and roots of a political movement that has succeeded in nudging the country rightward over the past three decades. Unless they are making sufficient noise or threatening to gain political power, these "right-wingers" tend to be ignored, dismissed, and derided. Under Reagan in the 1980s, they were the cold warriors who stood in the way of the popular nuclear freeze movement. In the 1990s, the public caught glimpses of the Right as the "extremists" behind the Republican Revolution or the "vast right-wing conspiracy" against the Clintons. After Bush's election, the media rushed to rediscover conservatives and their ideas.

Yet the entrenchment of conservatives and their ideas in American political life is an ongoing reality. Bill Clinton understood this when he co-opted pieces of the conservative agenda, including welfare reform and spending controls, and built his first presidential campaign around such words as "personal responsibility." Eight years later, after an election that divided the nation evenly in half, an ideological conservative sits in the White House. In the new millennium, economic turbulence, a shifting international order, new technologies that both reinforce and disrupt our domestic comforts, and a widespread craving for renewed spirituality could very well create fertile ground for a new resurgence of the conservative mind.

TO UNDERSTAND TODAY'S MOST influential conservatives, it is necessary to trace the thread back to the 1970s. By then, the crushing 1964 defeat of Barry Goldwater had pushed most of the Right out of the Republican Party and into citizen groups—collectively known as the New Right—whose air of anger and defeat consigned them to the fringes of American politics. But during that same decade, a new generation of conservative activist was emerging on college campuses. Determined to see American prestige and power restored, these baby boomer rebels were well educated, cocky, doggedly certain of victory—and only too happy to borrow the Left's organizing tactics and strategy to achieve it.

The new generation of conservative insurgents brought to their cause an unprecedented level of political and media sophistication (not to mention the thrill of youthful insurgency). Refusing to remain on the outskirts of American politics, they played to win—the Republican Party became their vehicle and Ronald Reagan their hero. They graduated from many of the same elite universities as their liberal foes, carrying the weight of law degrees and Ph.D.s to the national debate. They shrewdly embroidered their distrust of government with enough liberal language and sensibility—using words such as "empowerment" and "grass roots"—to reach well beyond the traditional conservative base. President Bush's "compassionate conservatism" grew directly out of their efforts.

At their best, the Right's baby boomers were farsighted reformists. They understood far more clearly than liberals that bloated welfare rolls were creating a culture of dependency among the poor, consigning generations of children to poverty. They understood the role of marriage in reducing poverty—rejecting the liberal argument, popular in the 1980s, that the steep rise in babies born to single mothers should be accommodated rather than combated. Whether promoting stricter public school standards or vouchers for private schools, they stood foursquare against school bureaucracies that had embraced the lowest common denominator in education. During the cold war, they provided an important ballast against liberal naivete about the Soviets' intentions. Conservatives could speak to broad swathes of middle America during periods when Washington seemed remote and elitist and out of touch.

But the personalities who thrived in the modern Right were (like their generational peers on the Left) contrarian, edgy, eager to provoke. The campus activists of the 1970s began their political lives as insurrectionists against the legacies of the 1960s Left, and shared with the enemy all its potential and pockmarked idealism—but also all its excess. Too often they pursued their cause, in the words of their onetime mentor Newt Gingrich, as "war without blood." They had rebelled against the "political correctness" of liberals, but within the ranks of the Right a uniform orthodoxy likewise prevailed—and woe unto those who dared question hardcore conservative doctrine.

This thirty-year history of a political movement is as much social as political. And so I tell it through the intertwined lives and careers of five baby boomers at the center of the movement, a "gang of five," each of whom began political life on campus in the 1970s and came to Washington with the conservative tide that followed Reagan in the 1980s. Together with their peers, these men helped lay the intellectual foundations for the brand of modern conservatism that the Bush administration and fellow conservatives in Congress are determined to pursue. Their ideas will play out over and over again in the coming years—in policy debates, in pitched battles over Supreme Court nominees, in congressional elections, and ultimately in another race for the presidency.

By explaining these five men—their histories and motivations and their influence on political life—my intent is to provide a front-seat view of a provocative political movement that has changed the face of America.

* BILL KRISTOL, intellectual architect of the Right's moral crusades. For three decades, this Harvard-trained political philosopher and publisher of the magazine *Weekly Standard* has waged a determined war in defense of traditional values and against liberal humanism— and its emphasis on individualism, sexual freedom, and tolerance. Yet Kristol is also an elitist who has far more in common with his secular-liberal foes than they would ever suspect. He's made enemies in the movement by challenging the antigovernment dogma of fellow conservatives; he first set his moral compass by ancient Greek philosophy, not religious faith; and he is the son of neoconservatives, former socialists who turned rightward against the excesses of the sixties. Don't be lulled by the acerbic and contrarian wit he regularly displays on network TV: Kristol has a serious vision of an America where citizens lead lives of conservative and patriotic virtue, and the nation's leaders are democratic-minded statesmen who refuse to accommodate dictatorships (like China) abroad.

* RALPH REED, mastermind behind the ascendancy of the religious right inside the Republican Party. During the 1990s, Reed built the Christian Coalition into a potent political force, courted by congressional and presidential candidates alike. Even after his departure (Reed now chairs the Georgia GOP) and the group's institutional drift, the religious right as a whole continues to enjoy a place at the table of Republican politics. With Reed's help, religious activists were instrumental in helping Bush win the Republican nomination and re-

main a visible presence on the president's agenda. Like his generational peers on the Right, Reed was forced to move beyond his own hardball past to build a movement with elements of moderation, inclusion, and, most of all, respectability with the national press and political establishments. Part of his success was his strategic brilliance; and part of it was Reed's unnerving personal magnetism—which made conservatives flock around him like a rock star (and made Leftists think of goose-stepping troops).

• GROVER NORQUIST, the movement's resident "market-Leninist." To understand the hard-Right's antipathy toward government, the sanctity of private gun ownership, and the fear of taxation as "tyranny," it's important to understand this man's worldview. Shaped by the cold war, Norquist still divides the world neatly between Good Guys (conservatives and capitalists) and Bad Guys (liberals and socialists lumped together)—and is ever on guard for signs of disloyalty within his ranks. Norquist leads the foremost anti-tax insurgency in the country, and has convinced hundreds of state and national candidates to sign a pledge binding them to resist tax hikes. He worked on the massive Bush tax cut, and once that was passed, continued to press the administration for deeper cuts, hoping to eventually force Congress to cut the size of the federal government by half. He is also at the center of the "vast right-wing conspiracy" that so animates Washington liberals: Each Wednesday, dozens of strategists from the Right gather in his conference room to plot their latest offensives against Democrats, unions, and the Left.

• DAVID MCINTOSH, wonk behind the Right's campaigns to roll back health, safety, and environmental protections. If one piece of the Right's antigovernment crusade is tax cuts, the other is slashing federal regulation. This has been an uphill battle, and David McIntosh has been at its center—first in Bush Senior's White House and later as the leader of a band of ideological young freshmen elected to the House of Representatives in 1994. His antiregulatory work there helped lay the framework for George W. Bush's controversial opposition to the Kyoto treaty and other environmental causes. Bearing degrees from Yale and the University of Chicago, McIntosh was emblematic of those conservative leaders who gained their political footing in campus debate societies in the 1970s: brainy, articulate, and looking for a fight. To ascend, McIntosh (like the movement he represented) would struggle to find a more human face for all his bookish free-market theories. In the 1990s, he was one of the movement's young stars, but his loss in the election for Indiana governor in 2000 provided a harsh lesson in the limitations of the Right's antiregulatory crusades.

- CLINT BOLICK confounds his liberal critics because he is something that is not supposed to exist on the Right: an idealist. His propaganda war against affirmative action has landed him atop most liberal enemies lists. In fact, Bolick spends most of his time as a constitutional lawyer representing the urban poor. He sues bureaucracies on behalf of bootstrap entrepreneurs barred from business and represents poor parents whose children attended private schools on taxpayer-funded vouchers. School vouchers remain a hot-button issue (as President Bush has learned); critics charge conservatives with trying to drain money from the public schools. So Bolick's passionate commitment to the lives of inner-city children in failing schools offers a different perspective on this controversy. For a serious understanding of compassionate conservatism, Bolick's life is a good place to start. The lifelong mission of this University of California, Davis law graduate is to car-jack the phrase "civil rights" from the Left, redefining notions of racial fairness from a libertarian perspective.

The composition of this cast is not meant to suggest that white males are the only leaders of the conservative movement. The Right includes a substantial minority of women (though far fewer nonwhite activists), and many appear prominently in these pages. Rather than fill a race or gender box, I chose these figures for their centrality to the movement—each has helped to build an important institution—and their lasting impact on the national stage. And they stand in stark contrast to the sometimes popular view of the Right as paranoid militiamen, abortion clinic assassins, or any number of racist groups that attach themselves to the conservative fringe.

Taken together, moreover, these political figures cover the range of important ideas undergirding the Right, from the Chicago School's aversion to economic regulation to the Straussian philosopher's ideal of a virtuous citizenry, a pillar of the family values movement. The story of this movement also sheds light on the conflicts and tensions within the Republican Party over post–cold war foreign policy, as unilateralist sentiment and anticommunist sentiments compete with a capitalist-driven desire to engage even "red" countries. On China in particular, conservatives battle each other, often finding themselves in strange-bedfellow alliances with liberals.

But in the tempestuous struggles for political power that played out during the 1990s, conservatives demonstrated remarkable unity.

To understand today's Right—and its role in ideological wars that left Congress in gridlock and Washington leaders under a cloud of permanent investigation—it is necessary to trace the thread back to the campus culture of the 1970s, when conservatives were pariahs and liberalism set the parameters of political morality. Underlying all the counterculture swagger of today's Right is a social story: On campus in the 1970s, liberals were the intellectuals, the rational thinkers, the ones who cared about their fellow man (or so the story went). Conservatives were derided as unenlightened, brutish, and greedy, out to protect themselves and their own kind. Name it, and the young conservatives were called it: racist, elitist, fascist. Their views were ostracized, dismissed, or (worse) ignored. Part I of the book introduces each of these men against the backdrop of 1970s campus culture. Despite the rise of figures such as Reagan, the standing of conservatives in elite quarters hadn't altered appreciably since the 1950s, when political scientists purported to "prove" that conservatives were backward, fearful, uneducated, and exhibited lower IQs—that a conservative was "psychologically timid, distrustful of difference, and of whatever he cannot understand," as one study earnestly explained.

But the mainstream Republican establishment was just as wary of the Right, even with Ronald Reagan's election in 1980. Part II narrates the story of these young Rightists as they came to Washington behind a victor and, determined to bypass the "accommodationists" in their own party, established ideological vanguards both inside and outside the administration. The over-the-top antics of the College Republicans rankled GOP moderates; young activists toting their AK-47s into far-flung anticommunist guerrilla camps upset the careful designs of a more cautious Reagan State Department; the revolutionary rhetoric of young constitutional lawyers isolated Reagan's Justice Department.

Part III opens with the Right's multi-front war against Clinton and his administration. Clinton's health care plan was mortally wounded as GOP leaders adopted Kristol's piercing observation that "there is no health care crisis." Clinton's civil rights agenda was sullied by Bolick's campaign against a nominee he labeled a "quota queen." Norquist stirred up grass-roots anger over the president's first-year tax hike. McIntosh came to Congress in 1995 with the vaunted "Republican Revolution," aiming his crosshairs at the Clinton White House and later at his own party's leadership. When the conservative rebels failed to find the next Reagan to recapture the presidency in 1996, they ratcheted up the war against Bill and Hillary Clinton.

The Right's failed war against the Clintons had aspects of déjà vu: Who better than Bill and Hillary Clinton—unkempt private morality married to public self-righteousness—to remind the movement's true believers, daily, of the innumerable slights they had suffered at the hands of a liberal elite that seemed to coast through American culture with an unchallenged claim to the moral high ground? For all their electoral victories and success at shifting the political landscape, today's conservatives still cling to a self-image as an oppressed majority in American political life. Now, with a friend in the Oval Office, they've been handed a rich opportunity to become more than a counter-counterculture frozen in the act of revolt.

PART ONE

THE 1970S:
CAMPUS REBELS
WITH A CAUSE

CHAPTER 1

CONTRARIAN

I T WAS IN THE NATURE of the times to talk back. Oratory as ridicule, the language of 1960s activists, troubled the Harvard University administration nearly as much as windows smashed and buildings blockaded. Even in the fall of 1970, with the decade officially closed, anti-war demonstrations ebbing, and the media declaring the death of the New Left, caustic retort (in reply to the Establishment version of truth) remained a highly developed art form inside Harvard Yard. William Kristol, Harvard class of '73, patently rejected the political ethos of his generation. He was, nevertheless, a master of its style, a first-rate smart aleck.

He arrived that fall pumped full of trenchant ridicule for the anti-war activists who, just eighteen months earlier, had spilled blood on the steps of University Hall as four hundred helmeted police swinging nightsticks broke up their sit-in. Two-thirds of Harvard's students had protested the crackdown by boycotting class. But Kristol derided the "stupid, self-congratulatory" Leftists at Harvard and elsewhere who continued to attract attention and sympathy. Only seventeen, he wore the casual arrogance of a young man who had graduated at the top of his class from a rigorous Manhattan prep school and then qualified for an accelerated three-year track toward graduation from Harvard. He had playful eyes under a high forehead, and brows that seemed to carry on their own conversation as he issued barbed wit under his breath.

From his surefooted start, Kristol would go on to become an intellectual Brahmin of the modern conservative movement, as confident in the superiority of his own thinking as any "liberal elitist" scorned by his populist friends on the Right. Rare was the right-winger who could talk the language of the *New York Times* editorial board, but this was the vernacular of Bill's upbringing. By the 1990s, he would become a practiced translator, relaying the Right's message through the house organs of the media establishment—TV networks, eminent newspapers, foreign policy journals. He founded the *Weekly Standard,* an influential, and relentlessly irreverent, magazine. Behind the scenes, he helped shape some of the most important Washington policy battles of the era. But Bill's elite background also granted him license as an iconoclast inside a political movement that placed a premium on loyalty: He would confound and anger his loyalist allies on the Right, sometimes treating their cause (it seemed) with all the seriousness of a robust set of doubles.

By the time he reached Harvard that first semester in 1970, it was clear Bill Kristol would cut his own direction in life. He arrived at the peak of youthful revolt, without ever having rebelled against parents, authority, tradition. He never holed up at the Fillmore East, as his Manhattan prep school buddies did, smoking pot while Jimi Hendrix worked his guitar. He didn't, as his buddies did, indulge in the sexual revolution unfolding around him. But he was, like his buddies, a contrarian. The difference was that Bill Kristol's parents provided their son with a built-in outlet for his contrarian energies. Essayist Irving Kristol and historian Gertrude Himmelfarb were leading figures in an intellectual circle of ex-socialists who by the 1960s had turned their indignation from capitalist bosses to the counterculture then engulfing America's youth. Called "neoconservatives," these former Leftists would go on to provide intellectual heft to a conservative movement they once spurned.

Irving Kristol, who edited a journal of commentary, the *Public Interest,* had spent the entirety of his son's adolescence issuing forth scornful wit against conventional (that is, liberal) wisdom. Irving had been a socialist as a college student in the 1930s, but he couldn't stomach the radicals of his son's generation. He ascribed 1960s activism to motivations no more grand than boredom—"a radical mood in search of a radical program . . . the last, convulsive twitches of a slowly expiring American individualism."

Bill absorbed all of his father's salty opinions, so that by the time he arrived at Harvard, arguing with the Left came naturally. But not in a Republican/right-wing/Young Americans for Freedom sort of way. In fact, Bill didn't even know many conservatives; in 1970, right-wingers were still considered mostly philistines within his parents' intellectual orbit of Humphrey Democrats. Richard Nixon, Bill's father fretted in 1968, appealed to the wrong majority, whose dominant temper was "sullenly resentful" and "impulsively reactionary." Bill, a budding avatar of realpolitik, considered the Right practically irrelevant to American electoral politics; he recalled reading *National Review* columns as a twelve-year-old that unabashedly, and wrongly, insisted that a silent majority of conservative Americans would sweep Barry Goldwater into the White House in 1964.

In the self-conscious world of New York intellectuals, the Kristols had achieved a measure of fame, with Irving Kristol broadcasting his opinions through the *Atlantic Monthly* and the *New York Times*. So their world offered an attractive safe harbor for a young man making his way in rebellious times. Harvard's eminent and diverse government department, which Bill was about to enter in 1970, included a number of his parents' friends and colleagues. Among them were James Q. Wilson, who headed the much reviled committee meting out discipline to Harvard's protesters; department chair and foreign policy scholar Samuel P. Huntington, whose 1969 report to the State Department on how to prop up the South Vietnamese regime in a postwar coalition had provoked the ire of campus Leftists; and Edward C. Banfield, the urban scholar whose exploration of a "lower-class" culture entrapping the poor sparked student protest. And there were sociology professor and *Public Interest* co-founder Daniel Bell, government and sociology professor Seymour Martin Lipset, education professor Nathan Glazer, and government professor Daniel Patrick Moynihan—then Nixon's chief adviser on urban affairs and Bill's boss during a White House internship in the summer of 1970. Philosophy professor Harvey C. Mansfield had been to the Kristols' apartment for dinner, concluding that Bill's dismissive description of his toney prep school was a sure sign the young man would fit in with the Harvard elites.

Months after arriving, Bill signed on as contributing editor to a start-up conservative magazine aimed at a national college audience, the *Alternative*. Edited by R. Emmett Tyrrell Jr., the *Alternative* in the 1970s offered young conservatives reinforcement and a place to air their unpopular views. (Later, the magazine broadened its readership and took the name *American Spectator,* publishing some of the most controversial and savage sallies against the Clinton administration.)

Bill contributed a review to the magazine's November 1970 issue, castigating a book by Supreme Court Justice William O. Douglas as "more than stupid, more than cliché-ridden, more than simple minded, more than an insult to almost any reader's intelligence. . . . The book is, alas, neither serious nor humorous; it is merely pathetic." He compiled a droll holiday wish list asking for, among other things, "a few weeks of obscurity" for Spiro T. Agnew, "babies" for Women's Lib leaders, and "a success . . . some success . . . any success" for Richard Nixon. Later he wrote a column complaining that a purported Harvard-Radcliffe "charity" was in fact a solicitation for such political causes as the United Farm Workers and ethnic identity groups. That liberals would call this a charity, he wrote, was more evidence of their "facile ideological self-gratification."

On the Harvard campus itself that first year, leftist protests that might offer targets for Bill's poison pen were on the wane. Small groups of radicals still raised howls over American imperialism in front of the university's Center for International Affairs, the target of a violent Weathermen raid a year earlier. But the national Students for a Democratic Society, once the flagship of the New Left, had splintered internally into carping factions at Harvard and elsewhere.

During that first full academic year of the 1970s there was a sense that the winds had shifted, something was over. "As we rush off to the first day of classes this morning we might remember, if just for a moment, that this University is on strike. Remember . . . ?" pleaded one commentator in the *Harvard Crimson,* the campus newspaper. The previous academic year had ended with a student protest against the U.S. invasion of Cambodia, with demonstrations sparked by the deaths of four students at Kent State, with a tense meeting at Harvard's Sanders Theater where students overwhelmingly voted to support a university strike. "Remember?" the commentator begged his readers as Bill began his first term.

Despite the lull in protests, Harvard's student body remained predominantly liberal and left, with conservatives viewed as curiosities at best, warmongers at worst. In the 1972 presidential election, 75 percent of Harvard-Radcliffe students would favor George McGovern over Richard Nixon. The *Harvard Crimson,* which editorialized in support of Vietnam's Communist-backed National Liberation Front, was still a font of socialist wisdom. The faculty was more politically diverse, with a government department that served as a bastion of "neos," liberal and conservative. So Bill never felt constrained from offering his minority opinions in class. He took every chance he could to point out the "mindless conformism" of the Left: The kind of lazy thinking, for example, that would prompt the *Crimson* editors to make the leap from criticizing American military policy to supporting the Communists.

During Bill's first years at Harvard, conservative views frequently became the target of harassment by leftist radicals. The Harvard chapter of SDS, which had curbed its anti-war efforts, now picketed and stalked professors, such as Banfield, whose work was considered racist and reactionary. A pro-war "counter-teach-in," organized by Bill's friend Stephen Rosen under the guise of the Young Americans for Freedom, was cut short by hooting radicals. Kristol friend Jim Muller described to *Crimson* readers an encounter with an SDS activist who was urging fellow radicals to shout down supporters of Nixon's Vietnam policies. "I asked him whether or not he supported free speech, and here was his answer: 'I'm for it, as long as it isn't counterproductive.' " When Harvard President Nathan Pusey denounced the campus's leftist radicals as dangerous imitators of Joseph McCarthy, it struck a chord with broad segments of students, liberal and conservative.

Bill wasn't intimidated by the Left's pugilists. On the contrary, he sought them out. During his second year at Harvard, he would slip into his Spiro Agnew T-shirt and wander up to the Radcliffe campus to visit his former roommate Robert McTiernan. (Kristol didn't really like the crass vice president, but he couldn't resist promoting a politician who had dismissed anti-war leaders as an "effete corps of impudent snobs.") He'd take up a spot in McTiernan's dorm, or inside the dining hall, juicing casual talk into pointed political debate, his forehead crinkling, his eyes dancing in delight. Was Kristol kidding or not when he praised Nixon's 1972 bombing of the Haiphong Harbor, a wave of B-52 raids that set off another round of student strikes, as "one of the great moments in American history"? It didn't matter because the provocations had the intended effect, putting Bill at the center of the debate—the practiced warrior alone among flailing liberals.

On a campus where liberalism was equated with enlightenment, Bill's conservative opinions stood out as strange, farcical, or daring, depending on his audience at any given moment. Susan Scheinberg, the attractive freshman who lived next door to McTiernan, was part of the tiny audience of undergraduates who categorized Bill's politics as daring. She was on her way to becoming a rising star in the classics department, ultimately graduating with honors and an award as Radcliffe's most promising humanities student. Like a good classicist, Susan didn't think much about contemporary politics, though she called herself a liberal Democrat when she did. At the time, she didn't believe conservatives could be erudite; like most Harvard liberals, she assumed they were all golf-playing executives, racists, or just plain ignorant. Until she met Bill.

Susan and Bill struck up a courtship that eventually would lead to the marriage of the brash fast-talking Manhattanite to the shy, scholarly daughter of a neurologist from Scarsdale, New York. The pair shared a love of high culture, discovering opera together, and a disdain for a youth culture that blithely dismissed the wisdom of age and the ages. Susan's view of the world blended more shades of gray than did Bill's. But she was impressed by Bill's political stamina, his imperviousness to insult or denunciation. "Like water off a duck's back," she'd say (and would watch with bemusement years later as Bill counseled their three children to do the same whenever their feelings were hurt). He welcomed attack and delighted in the gamesmanship of fierce political debate. He was fast on his feet, quick with the comeback, and had the demeanor of a young man convinced he'd already heard it all.

As Bill began his final year as an undergraduate in 1972, a number of professors from Harvard and elsewhere, as well as his parents, signed onto an advertisement in the *New York Times* supporting Nixon's reelection. Student radicals loudly protested, calling for the firing of Harvard professors who had advertised their support for this "war criminal." That activists would react with such extremist rhetoric to the prospect of professors supporting an incumbent president confirmed in Kristol's mind the growing intolerance of leftist thought. Free speech and the free speech movement had been pillars of 1960s activism; this protest, he decided, revealed the radicals as supporters of free speech only for those who agreed with them.

Bill could barely contain himself.

Inside a Radcliffe dining hall, he provoked a vociferous argument with one of the protest's instigators. The two young men debated for hours, back and forth, thrust and jab, the activist denouncing Nixon for war crimes, Bill defending the Nixon administration and questioning his opponent's commitment to academic freedom. Susan stood in awe of her boyfriend, not for his forensic skills, but for his audacity: Bill harbored his own doubts about America's military policy in Vietnam. And he hadn't even supported Richard Nixon. In the spring of 1972, he'd been the chief Harvard organizer for the presidential primary bid of Senator Henry "Scoop" Jackson, a military hawk, but also a Democrat.

But he never let on.

□

ONE COULD MAKE THE CASE that Harvard's radicals, in their ardor and anger and grand certitude, were no different than Irving Kristol and his cadre of Trotskyist friends in the 1930s, gathering in Alcove 1 of New York's City College lunchroom to "argue the world" with the Stalinists in adjoining Alcove 2. One could assert that Bill was prematurely adopting the pose of a famous father who had drifted rightward to become a middle-aged crank, ignoring his own past to denounce the new generation of radicals as "a mob who have no real interest in higher education or in the life of the mind." Hadn't Bill sadly skipped a beat in his own development when he leapfrogged the progression from youthful utopianism to the mature skepticism that had shaped his father?

One could make that argument, and many a liberal adversary would. But it would miss the core of the Kristols: Like father, like son, and like mother and daughter, this was about as bourgeois a family as they come. Even in the days when twenty-two-year-old Irving and eighteen-year-old Bea Himmelfarb, the girl with the shiny brown eyes who would become his wife, were dutifully attending Brooklyn branch meetings of the Young People's Socialist League—Fourth International (where Trotskyists nourished the fanciful notion of organizing local blacks), radicalism was not a natural fit for Bill's parents. If there was such a thing as a conservative temperament, "cool and critical in respect of change . . . unadventurous, that has no impulse to sail unchartered seas" (to borrow the words of political theorist Michael Oakeshott), the Kristols embodied it. In the 1930s, with the world's economies in depression and fascism's shadow looming across Europe, "it was very easy to be radical, particularly if you were Jewish," recalled Irving Kristol. "The only question was what kind of radical you'd be." Along with fellow CCNY students such as Daniel Bell, Nathan Glazer, Irving Howe, Melvin Lasky, and Seymour Martin Lipset, Kristol opted for the Trotskyist brand, which had fewer sins to disguise than the Stalinists, who were forced to defend the Soviet Union's despotic leader.

The Kristols were drawn to socialism as much by the swirl of brainy energy behind the Trotskyists' relentless theoretical arguments as by the prospect of an egalitarian future. (Politics and study, Kristol once wrote, were outlets for the sexual energies of young men at the all-male City College.) "It was very stimulating intellectually to be a Trotskyist," Bea, who attended Brooklyn College, would later recall.

"They were simply the smartest people around." In their lunchroom debates, these radical polemicists learned what Howe would famously call the "uses of the appearance of a coherent argument."

There was nothing personally rebellious in the Kristols' short foray into socialism, nothing suggesting disdain for their parents, their professors, their communities or universities. As noted by historian Alexander Bloom, the immigrant world in the 1930s was full of radical literature; the city's socialist college students "planned to be emissaries from their parents' worlds, not exiles." What would horrify the Kristols three decades later was the passionate bad manners of 1960s activists who spurned their parents, violently stormed campus offices, and shouted down police officers as "pigs" and government officials as "war criminals." "Our objections to 'the system' focused on issues, not individuals," Himmelfarb insisted. Neither could the Kristols countenance a political movement as determined to upset society's social order—marriage and sex and gender roles—as its economic order.

Irving asked Bea to marry him after four dates (foreign movies only for these cafe radicals), and waited a year for her parents' consent, as he sought to assure them that his future was brighter than his $13.89-a-week apprentice machinist job. The pair was never tempted to pursue the Bohemian lifestyle that captivated some young radicals. Irving "wanted a girl to love and marry," not free love. Politically, what Irving Kristol aspired to, what most of these precocious Jewish sons of East European immigrants in the 1920s and '30s aspired to, was less to upend the American way of life than to become the social conscience of the nation's thinking elite. The college diploma, to New York's radicals in the 1930s, was a ticket to American nobility. They faced rampant anti-Semitism and the systematic exclusion of Jews at preeminent universities such as Harvard and Columbia, but remained convinced of their rightful place at the top of the American pyramid. They self-consciously titled themselves "intellectuals"—as if that were a career description—and busily started up journals and magazines aimed at a thinking elite.

Unlike the 1960s radicals, Irving Kristol didn't harbor a natural aversion to authority. In fact, he rather liked it. After he was drafted in 1944, seeing action as an infantryman in Europe, he gained new appreciation for "army vigilance," which, he asserted, was the only check on his fellow soldiers, who "were too easily inclined to loot, to rape, and to shoot prisoners of war." He was an unabashed urban elitist who once wrote of the group of midwestern soldiers in his unit, "I can't build socialism with these people. They'll probably take it over and make a racket out of it." (A generation later, his urbane son Bill would leave office colleagues snickering behind his back after regaling them with an awestruck description of a Texas truckstop—a thoroughly alien dining experience for him.)

Irving recalled that "it would never have occurred to us to denounce anyone or anything as 'elitist.' The elite was us—the 'happy few' who had been chosen by History to guide our fellow creatures toward a secular redemption." Even Irving's attraction to Bea bespoke an inclination toward *ancienne noblesse:* Both were children of immigrants—his father a garment subcontractor, hers the owner of a small glass manufacturing business. But Bea's quiet sophistication—she would later describe herself as an "unregenerate prig"—suggested an upbringing, in contrast with Irving's, of strong intellectual roots. Bea's grandfather had been a Hebrew teacher and her brother Milton became a leading religion commentator; her parents always expected her to attend both college and graduate school. Bea also attended the Jewish Theological Seminary as a college student and was trained in the faith's rigorous intellectual traditions. Moreover, like other learned New York Jews of the era, she had a keen interest in matters European, particularly British.

By age twenty-two, Irving Kristol was ready to leave the Trotskyists and nurse his ambition to become both an "intellectual" and a "writer." Like their comrades, the Kristols had opposed U.S. involvement in the "imperialist" war looming in Europe. Stalin's 1939 nonaggression pact with Hitler, freeing German tanks to roll across Europe, changed their minds. When Bea earned a fellowship to pursue graduate studies at the University of Chicago, Irving followed and took a part-time job as a railroad freight handler while awaiting the draft. He also attended classes at Chicago, and thus was introduced to a vibrant academic atmosphere that focused more on classics than radical politics. After the war, the Kristols' traditional marriage continued building on untraditional gender roles. When Bea was offered a scholarship to pursue a dissertation on Lord Acton in England, Irving again followed, busying himself with work on a novel. When they returned to New York in 1947, Irving joined *Commentary*—an anticommunist, culturally highbrow Jewish magazine—and within five years rose to managing editor.

Bea Kristol was, in the work she authored, Gertrude Himmelfarb. She kept her own name professionally, though insisting that this was no feminist statement; she was simply too lazy to change the paperwork. (Intimates, on the other hand, saw it as a calculated decision to maintain a voice independent of her more polemicist husband.)

Himmelfarb's attitude toward work would be something difficult to grasp for those in the modern feminist era: She never envisioned herself pursuing a "career" even though she went on to write nine books, becoming a leading Victorian scholar. "It never occurred to me that I might become a professor," she said later. "I went to the university not to become 'credentialed' but to get educated. I chose the University of Chicago because I was told it was intellectually exciting. I got my graduate degrees by default, as it were. In order to get fellowships, I had to do the right things—take courses, pass exams, write dissertations. In the process of doing those things, I somehow acquired the degrees."

The best way to understand Gertrude Himmelfarb is to place her in the same category as eminent Victorian women she studied, such as George Eliot or Charlotte Brontë, who opposed women's suffrage and thought it quite appropriate that men and women keep to their separate spheres in life. While Himmelfarb might not oppose the women's vote today, she became a vigorous critic of feminist politics in academia, and she defended the centrality of what multiculturalists deride as "Dead European White Males" in the curriculum. She criticized the feminist movement for promoting "equality rather than liberty" and "not the equality of opportunity for individuals but the equality of results for groups as a whole." Of modern women, she would say, "It's very sad, women who feel under this pressure to be a 'career' mom."

Himmelfarb was a working mother herself. But in her mind, she was merely pursuing her scholarly interests while tending her family. She worked at home, writing, and in university libraries, researching. When her two children, Bill and Liz, were born in the 1950s, she hired au pair girls to help out while they lived in London ("English girls from the countryside—Mind you, all my English friends had proper nannies, and thought it rather outré only to have an au pair") and a housekeeper when they moved back to New York. She didn't go "to work"—in the sense of having an outside-the-home job—until Bill was twelve and Liz was nine, when she became a professor at City University of New York's graduate school and began teaching a couple of courses each week.

Quiet in demeanor, meticulous in her work, ever fretful of saying something publicly that might be factually precarious or misconstrued, Gertrude Himmelfarb never achieved the high profile of the vocal polemicists who populated the neoconservative movement. Nevertheless her tiny voice in person could slash opponents in print. *New Republic* contributor Roy Porter once described her as a historian who "has made it her mission to lay bare the pretentions of the founding fathers of modernity; her forte is exploding their pretentions with deadly elegance." The work she produced from the 1940s on, particularly her controversial studies defending the Victorian era, would lay much of the scholarly foundation for the conservative "family values" movement in the 1980s and 1990s. (What other college kid would get the opportunity, as Bill did, to cite his mother's work in the footnotes of his senior thesis?)

Timing and bloodlines practically ensured that Bill would be born with the soul of a contrarian. In December 1952, the month he was born in a New York City hospital, his mother was outlining a book challenging conventional wisdom about Darwin's legacy, and Bill's father had just earned widespread notoriety as an apologist for Senator Joseph McCarthy. In the years following the war, Irving Kristol was still a liberal, but—like many other liberals of the era—he was also staunchly anticommunist. In 1952, as McCarthy was blindly accusing hundreds in government, Hollywood, and academia of Soviet sympathies, Kristol wrote an essay condemning not McCarthy, but liberals defending the civil liberties of his victims. Although he labeled McCarthy a "vulgar demagogue," what his readers would always remember was his defense of the demagogue: "There is one thing that the American people know about Senator McCarthy: He, like them, is unequivocally anticommunist. About the spokesmen for American liberalism, they feel they know no such thing. And with some justification."

Later, Kristol would express regret at not further disassociating himself from McCarthy. And, in fairness, Kristol was far from the only New York intellectual with a fuzzy position on McCarthy: Nathan Glazer later echoed regrets that he and other New York anticommunist liberals never articulated a respectable and moral position. But the McCarthy essay, Kristol's first serious plunge into political writing, set a pattern in the coming decades—a poison pen that would take a fabric of truth and stretch it, his critics asserted, beyond the tentpoles of supportable fact—just as he had in the McCarthy essay by ignoring widespread anticommunist sentiment among leading American liberals.

By the time Bill was five months old, the Kristols were back in England, where Irving co-edited *Encounter,* a start-up magazine funded by the Paris-based Congress for Cultural Freedom, a collection of anticommunist intellectuals. Their six years in London were intoxicating. By day, Bea wrote her study of Darwinism. By evening, both Kristols mingled with prominent literary lights. For the first time in their lives, they met elected politicians, mostly deeply learned liberal Members of Parliament and their conservative counterparts. The latter revealed to the Kristols another world to which they'd never been exposed: vibrantly intellectual conservatism.

Their circle of friends included homosexuals as well, such as poet W. H. Auden. No one, said the Kristols (who would later become open critics of the gay rights movement) made a fuss, or frankly paid much attention, to sexual orientation. "We knew [Auden] quite well," recalled Himmelfarb. "He was perfectly open about his homosexuality, very accepting of it for himself. But if you talked to him about it, he would say it's a great misfortune to be a homosexual." Their Manhattan friends were not immune to the changing cultural mores that troubled both Kristols and later emerged as major themes in their writings. But the Kristols were less judgmental of their friends than of society writ large. Widespread divorce, a few out-of-wedlock children, but "very few scandals" was how Himmelfarb described their circle.

The Kristols returned to Manhattan in 1959, renting an apartment on Riverside Drive, in a building overlooking the Hudson River. Within weeks of arriving in the States, six-year-old Bill had shed his British accent and was consuming baseball statistics like popcorn. The Kristols wanted their children to pursue old-fashioned classical educations, where respect, discipline, and Latin figured prominently. So when the rote lessons of the French Lycée proved insufficient, they enrolled Bill in the prestigious Collegiate School for Boys, a five-block walk from their West Side apartment.

Collegiate was, its granite facing explained, "A PLACE TO ATTEND TO YOUR SOUL"—Protestant style. With its accented masters determined to turn each year's crop of young boys into proper Renaissance men, Collegiate easily could be mistaken for a British school. In fact, it was Reformed Protestant Dutch, attached to the West End Collegiate Church. Bill went to a school with a glass crucifix overhanging one end of the Flemish-styled building (the church) and an American flag overhanging the other (Collegiate School). One morning a week, the schoolboys were ushered into the Christian chapel to hear a moral lesson from the pulpit.

Other Jewish boys attended this Protestant school, and some, as they grew older, were troubled that they had been schooled in a Christian atmosphere. Bill and his parents were not. "We had gone through public schools, we had sung Christmas carols, it didn't matter," recalled the senior Kristol. "We were so secure in our Judaism," added his wife. Secure enough, in fact, that Bill's mother saw to it that her son attended Hebrew school at the Orthodox Congregation Shearith Israel, which blended the traditions of Sephardic and Ashkenazic Judaism. As nonkosher Jews whose display of faith mostly consisted of observing the high holidays, the Kristols were not permitted to join the Orthodox temple. But Himmelfarb, attracted to its upper-class style and intellectual rigor, was determined that Bill pursue his bar mitzvah studies there.

As parents, the Kristols didn't issue rules so much as set standards that Bill rarely crossed. As a youngster, he fit comfortably into Collegiate School, which had impressed Irving because the students, neatly attired in jackets and ties, stood up whenever an adult entered the room. Eager to overcome its aristocratic reputation, the school offered scholarships to a few needy high achievers. Still, the culture of the A-team prevailed. "There was this code," recalled Bill's friend Mark Farrell, who attended Collegiate on scholarship, "like the students there knew they were part of the winner's circle." To a public school student like Farrell, it was the kind of place where you noticed the smell of new books, where you felt awkward at birthday parties that looked more like adult cocktail receptions, where the kids' banter sounded dauntingly sophisticated and worldly. In seventh grade, Kristol and two friends precociously borrowed from the Greek myth of Hermes in naming their satiric magazine *Turtle Scoops*.

Billy, as he was known to friends then, didn't qualify as the most popular kid in school, but he was best friends with the kid who did— Jimmy Warren, big shot athlete, student council president (and later a liberal-leaning TV pundit from his post as Washington bureau chief for the *Chicago Tribune*). Billy was a little too condescending, a little to smart-alecky with his under-his-breath comebacks to be a class favorite. "Cynical with a somewhat condescending edge that could turn people off," was how Warren put it. Ken Turner, a scholarship student who went on to become a firefighter, saw the same personality trait: "When you're as opinionated as him you could rub people the wrong way, but he's so damn smart." Ted Merritt, one of a pair of students who annually competed with Bill for the class's top academic spot, agreed: "He didn't suffer fools gladly, but I think he had a real respect for people achieving in other [than academic] ways, like sports." In fact, Bill was consumed by sports, and his cutting style was just as likely to be employed in an argument defending the Mets as it was debating the merits of the antiwar movement.

There was something remarkably self-sufficient about Bill, as if his parents set his rudder early and let him cruise at his own, predictable bearing. His parents were neither a visible presence at school, nor at Bill's sporting events. If there was daylight left after school and activities, Bill would play pick-up basketball with friends. (As an athlete, Kristol wasn't a star, but he was intense and determined, bulldoggish in the workmanlike position he played for the school's soccer team.) On weekends the boys would ride the New York subways on their own to see the Knicks or the Mets or the movies.

Bill had an early obsession with electoral politics that his parents—with no real interest in the gritty details of vote-stumping—never understood. "To us, Washington was a foreign country," his father recalled. But Bill studied party conventions and election outcomes with the same zeal that he applied to studying batting averages. When he was twelve, he rode in on the back of Pat Moynihan's truck, handing out flyers in support of his unsuccessful campaign for New York city council president.

At Collegiate, Kristol's academic achievements earned him a spot near the top of the forty-boy class. In his high school years, Billy was the kid who could conjugate French verbs better than anyone, who readily qualified for advanced placement in European history. But he wasn't the egghead either, tied as he was to Jimmy Warren and Collegiate's popular clique. There's a relic of the era, a hippie-esque short film made by his high school friends (even the title bespeaks the late 1960s culture—*No Tracks on the Ground but the Ones He's Making*) that opens with a scene of Collegiate students sitting in class, killing time while a teacher grades papers. As the classroom of scruffy-haired teenage boys erupts into loud chaos, a clean-cut Billy Kristol sits at his desk, neither part of the rowdies creating a ruckus, nor one of the loners absorbed in a book. What's striking is his awareness: He's watching the scene and the camera, connected but apart, seeing it all unfold even while he's in it (just as he would two decades later in the tumble of Washington politics).

In the late 1960s, Collegiate's other teenage boys weren't as immune as Bill from the counterculture sweeping the country. Their hair pushed the boundaries of Collegiate's above-the-collar rule; drugs and rock 'n' roll clashed with the Dutch Reform morals. Instead of meeting white-gloved girls at mixers, the most daring boys slipped off to smoky, slow-motion parties where they passed reefers to the strains of Hendrix and the Stones. They flashed each other peace signs and several banded together as a political party they called the SNOIDES, modeling themselves on the Dada art movement as they commented on "the boredom that infests this school like maggots on a fat pig." The Vietnam War, and the prospect of being drafted, weighed heavily on the minds of this set of Collegiate students, many of whom attended an anti-war moratorium in Washington. By contrast, Bill never went to Vietnam protests and didn't think much about the draft. (As it turned out, he didn't have to; his registration in December of 1970 came as the draft was winding down and few numbers were called.) His parents sheltered him from much of the unrest, once declining an offer of cheap rent on a Greenwich Village house because of that neighborhood's thriving counterculture.

As they neared graduation, Bill increasingly stood out from his classmates. His curly, ash-colored hair stayed short. He wore his camel-hair sports jacket to school without complaint. He didn't sneak off to drug parties or rock concerts. ("Bill's a baby boomer? Yeah, I guess he is, I never thought of him that way," his father would say in a telling remark twenty-five years later.) Bill's politics were at odds with his classmates', too. When several friends floated the idea of starting a group to foster pride among black and Hispanic students, Bill spoke out against it, arguing that Jewish students also faced discrimination but didn't organize for special recognition.

The boys at Collegiate knew Bill was different, too, because of the whispers about his father. In 1966, when Bill was fourteen, the *New York Times* revealed that in the 1950s the CIA had secretly funneled money into the Congress for Cultural Freedom and, by extension, the magazine *Encounter* that Kristol had co-founded in London. Irving Kristol denied any knowledge of the CIA connection. Nevertheless, in an era when the CIA was seen as the satanic arm of American imperialism, the rumors shaped his son's reputation as Collegiate's budding radicals passed the word that Irving Kristol was a reactionary mole. (Indeed, in the mouths of the teenagers, this *New York Times* report was contorted into a belief that the CIA financed Kristol's current magazine venture, the *Public Interest*.)

Shortly before Bill's graduation from Collegiate, Irving was invited to the school to give a lecture defending American policy in Vietnam. The students, long past the age when they jumped to their feet when an adult entered the room, asked questions that were skeptical, aggressive, even disrespectful. The elder Kristol grew visibly annoyed. One student stood up to say he hoped the domino theory was accurate and that communism would spread through Asia, rescuing its people from America's evil grip. Friends broke into applause.

Bill wasn't fazed by his classmates' abuse and would remain in political sync with his father. "We often wondered," said Stephen Rosen, one of Bill's closest Harvard friends, "why aren't we rebelling?

We had good relationships with our parents. As a result, we saw nothing inherently unjust about authority, about somebody telling you what to do."

THAT BILL SAW NOTHING unjust about authority—nor any of the traditional social orders that had incited the defiance of his generation—marked him as an ideal candidate for the Straussians, a school of political philosophy that one of its many critics has labeled "radical elitism." During his graduate studies at Harvard, from 1973 to 1978, Bill became a devoted follower of Leo Strauss, a twentieth-century philosopher who rejected the prevailing view that all thinking since the Enlightenment had, by definition, led to society's betterment. Strauss taught that "the beginning of wisdom—not the end, the beginning—is to take the ancients seriously again," wrote Bill's uncle, Milton Himmelfarb. Embracing science, technology, and liberal democracy, Americans considered their society a testament to human progress, looking backward from a vantage of superiority. But Strauss, wrote Gertrude Himmelfarb, taught that "great minds are great for all time, not only for their own time," and that "truth does not change, only beliefs do."

For Bill and other bright young conservatives on campus in the 1970s, Strauss held intuitive appeal. There was, first of all, the dizzying intellectual high of joining a small cadre of political philosophy students who considered themselves smart enough to mine the complex secrets of ancient thinkers such as Plato. There was, too, the Straussian language of morality—"good" and "evil," "character" and "virtue"—that offered a vivid counterpoint to liberalism's blurring of social and moral distinctions. And there was the thrill of pursuing a discipline that was so (to use a term that hadn't yet been invented) "unpolitically correct," brazenly tearing asunder modern America's assumptions about tolerance and equality and even democracy. For Straussian political theory was the black-diamond slope of scholarship—as dangerous as it was difficult.

Strauss, a German Jewish immigrant who fled Nazi persecution in the 1930s, taught for two decades at the University of Chicago before his death in 1973. Strauss's followers ranked him with the likes of John Locke and Edmund Burke. "There are many excellent teachers," Milton Himmelfarb once wrote. "They have students. Strauss had disciples." Strauss's widening circle of followers became influential (if widely reviled) on university campuses, where they settled into government or political science departments. Although dismissed by liberal colleagues, their courses were often popular because they were able to "address the souls of students," noted one adherent. Among the most prominent scholars associated with Strauss was Allan Bloom, whose critique of modern society, *The Closing of the American Mind,* became a best-seller on its release in 1987. Straussian graduate students from the 1970s, such as Bill, were second-generation disciples of the philosopher; in the 1980s and 1990s, as they moved into the upper echelons of academia and government, they would form an intellectual elite to counter a liberal elite's definitions of morality and justice.

The Straussians believed that the measure of a healthy society was how virtuous its citizens were—not how much personal freedom they enjoyed, nor how equal their standing. Indeed, they saw inequalities as a natural (and age-old) element of human life. The rot of modern thinking, Straussians believed, was evident in the presumptuous social engineering by twentieth-century courts and government in such matters as school busing and affirmative action. Straussians also regarded as dangerous the anything-goes ethos of the 1960s, particularly in sexual matters. They raised alarms about liberation movements that led to legal abortion, single motherhood by choice, and civil rights protections for homosexuals. Straussians were concerned with personal behavior, the character, of people—and, unlike liberals, they didn't shrink from judgment. They condemned the new tolerance underpinning public policies that offered sympathy and assistance, no questions asked, to poor women who continued to have children out of wedlock or homeless drug addicts who refused to seek treatment.

To be sure, this antimodernism of the Straussians was in keeping with a history of conservatism that resisted change (captured so concisely by William F. Buckley Jr.'s injunction to conservatives to "stand athwart history, yelling 'Stop!' "). But in contrast to other social conservatives—leading Catholic thinkers such as Buckley Jr. or, in later years, *Book of Virtues* author William J. Bennett—the Straussians arrived at their focus on old-fashioned virtue from a starting point devoid of religious faith. Indeed, like the liberal secular humanists they loathed, Straussians relied on human reason and generally lacked personal religious beliefs. Strauss, who believed his own Judaism to be a "heroic delusion" and "noble dream," wrote of the "incompatible claims of Jerusalem and Athens. . . ." Milton Himmelfarb described Jewish Straussians as distantly respectful of their faith. "In general they think religion to be a good thing—politically, of course, and for others: Strauss says that liberal education used to be for gentlemen and religious education for the masses. The philosopher's education began where the gentleman's left off."

Straussians believed that the ancient philosophers offered time-less truths that transcended the ages. These truths could be grasped by human reason and a life committed to a quest for true knowledge. Straussians drew a sharp distinction between these ancient truths and the changeable "opinions" guiding modern society's belief system. As modern Americans "it's so very hard for us" to respect the teachings of the past, explained Harvey Mansfield, Harvard's premier Strauss-ian and Bill's graduate professor. "Not only do we believe in democ-racy, but we believe in progress. We think we're on the edge of things and everything has led up to us. . . . You need a counterforce against the weight of present-day opinion."

As scholars, Straussians have drawn much criticism from univer-sity historians. Strauss believed that the writings passed down by classical philosophers contained timeless truths that could only be un-locked with rigorous and imaginative reading of their works. His method largely rejected the modern historical view that these writings were not just a product of great minds, but also should be studied in their context—time, place, and social and economic circumstance. Straussians approached texts like Talmudic scholars, reading pas-sages over and over, debating the author's true meaning and inten-tions, assuming that contradictions were there for a purpose. (A book or paper written by a Straussian, such as Bill's senior thesis, is laden with Ibid. footnotes, references almost solely to the work under con-sideration to the exclusion of comparative works or other analyses.) The most devoted Straussians also believe that ancient texts contain possible numeric codes: If there are seven chapters, is the author's true meaning found in Chapter Four, the precise middle of the text?

This "esoteric" reading of texts was based in part on the assump-tion that, historically, prophets of truth faced persecution: Socrates, for example, had been forced to drink the cup of hemlock after Athens's "mob-led, passion-ridden democracy" had convicted him of impiety. But Strauss also made a more controversial assumption— that the great classical thinkers knew, as he knew, that truth was dan-gerous to society and should not be broadly circulated. Truth should only be accessible to a democratic aristocracy, one that by intellectual ability, interest, and character had devoted itself to the quest for true knowledge.

The idea of dangerous truths—that philosophic truth might con-flict with political or social order—is not a new one, nor is it terribly offensive when one stops to consider the role that myths and manner play in civilized society. What led critics such as University of Calgary professor Shadia Drury to condemn the Straussians as "radical elitists" was their underlying assumption that they had a special claim on the truth. While Straussian philosophers, wise and good, could be entrusted to use their own reason, everyone else needed to live by moral codes as defined by traditional society, and by God. Straussianism, Drury argued, is "neither wise nor good. It is not wise because it cannot defend its beliefs before the tribunal of reason; it preaches only to the converted."

If Straussians considered religion a societal myth, they, unlike secular liberals, didn't believe this dangerous truth should be broadly circulated: Religion, with its clear moral standards, provided the life-glue to civilization. Straussians actively cultivated a deep and abiding respect for religion and those who practiced it; the clash between divine faith and philosophy, they believed, was a fruitful tension. "We Straussians always say that we're different from the other secularist academic types that infest our country because we take religion seriously," Mansfield explained. "But, on the other hand, you can wonder whether it's possible to take religion seriously without being religious."

As a graduate student, Bill shared his peers' belief that faith was for others, not himself. He wrote in his senior thesis: "Religion can, at least indirectly, cause democratic man to regulate his opinions and his tastes; by influencing men at home, it can moderate their public greed and restrain some of their passions. . . . Men need dogmatic beliefs, and religious beliefs are the most desirable of all." A decade later, after he and Susan had three children and were living in the Virginia suburbs, he would return to the synagogue, explaining (in opaque Straussian terms) that "a moral basis for modern society has to come out of the biblical tradition to some degree. You're not going to reinvent Athens."

The notion that society's health should be entrusted to a sort of democratic aristocracy, one whose membership rests on natural and cultivated intelligence and character—not wealth or family lineage—held a particular lure for young men who were Jewish or sons of immigrants. (There were few women among the Straussians.) For Bill and other right-leaning intellectuals like him, the right-wing Young Americans for Freedom, its roots with the aristocratic Buckley and Catholic social circles, wasn't a comfortable fit. The elitism of the Straussians was purely intellectual.

The Straussians offered "an invitation to join those privileged

ascended from the cave, gaze upon the sun with un-
ile yet mindful of those others below, in the dark,"
rab wrote. Bill's family had long ago ascended from
ve: Both of his parents, and his uncle, were deeply influenced by
the philosopher. But Bill had not truly begun his ascent from the
cave until his first semester at Harvard in 1970, when, once a week,
he pushed the elevator button at the Holyoke Center and traveled to
the eighth floor. There, in assistant professor Mark Blitz's office, he
and a handful of other students discussed and debated Plato's vision
of a just society, while down below in Harvard Square, boarded-up
shops tried to recover from the summer's spree of rioting by leftist
protesters.

Blitz, a leading protégé of the eminent Mansfield, was still in his
twenties when he taught those weekly sessions. He had a New
York–bred fast mind and faster tongue; Bill immediately clicked with
his instructor. What initially appealed to Kristol, and his friends Jim
Muller and Bob McTiernan in that same tutorial, was Blitz's Straussian
style of teaching. Never before had these young men read a single
text so carefully, assiduously peeling each layer of onion, missing
nothing. For Bill, it was like opening a window to a new world. He
and the other students spent an entire semester on Plato's *Republic,*
wrestling with troubling and fundamental questions about equality,
democracy, and justice. The following semester they embarked on
Nietzsche's *Beyond Good and Evil.*

To young men questioning the egalitarianism of the Left, the insights of the philosophers they studied offered fortitude, making the
case that the leveling of society would lead to a worship of mediocrity.
Certainly, this had its political implications, but there was also a personal attraction: The philosophers' acceptance of natural inequalities
as an inescapable fact of life was liberating to brainy young men who
had long ago looked around and realized that, No, everyone *wasn't* as
intelligent or gifted or driven—or as suited to political leadership. The
notion that truth could be dangerous, or at the very least politically
unacceptable, also rang true to students who had witnessed rising leftist orthodoxy on college campuses.

In his second year at Harvard, Bill enrolled in Mansfield's lecture
course, Government 106, a staple of budding Straussians that sur-
veyed political philosophy from Plato to Locke. Mansfield was a the-
atrical lecturer who spoke in hushed tones and riddles. He pitched his
lectures high, leaving sophomores scrambling to keep up but attracting graduate students to return for second go-arounds, knowing there
was always more to mine.

Bill and his friends were inspired by the professor's provocations. Mansfield wrote much about the weaknesses of American democracy: "Once democracy is established, the gravest danger may arise not from outside but from within. . . . Populism undermines democratic legitimacy by making the government timid and the people impatient." Those who had the most to gain from modern American democracy—principally women and minorities—were the students most ill at ease in his class. Mansfield needled the students with sexist remarks and was a staunch opponent of affirmative action. (Twenty years later, he still had his doubts about coed campuses, noting that male students had become less high-spirited, turning into "premature husbands" in the presence of female company.)

As a graduate student beginning in 1973, Bill became part of a bumper crop of Harvard Straussians with ambitions to change the world. The friendships he brought from his undergraduate years included Alan Keyes, later ambassador to the U.N. Economic and Social Council and far-right presidential candidate; Stephen Rosen, who became a Harvard professor of national security and military affairs; and Jim Muller, a scholar specializing in Winston Churchill's life. In graduate school, this group was joined by an even more devoted group of Straussians from Cornell University, where they had lived in Telluride House with Allan Bloom as their resident adviser. They included, among others, Francis Fukuyama, who later authored *The End of History,* asserting the universal triumph of capitalism and democracy; Stephen R. Sestanovich, a Soviet scholar who later served as ambassador at large in the Clinton State Department; and future author-professors Jeremy Rabkin, Arthur M. Melzer, and Robert P. Kraynak.

If the global issues facing these Harvard students in the 1970s weren't quite of the magnitude as those facing Irving Kristol and his friends at CCNY forty years earlier, you'd never know it. The Straussians were just as pugnacious, just as arrogant, just as certain that they held the nation's uncertain future in their hands. "It would never occur to anybody to say, 'Well, I don't think I'm really competent to pass judgment on something like that,' " recalled Eliot A. Cohen, who later chaired the Strategic Studies program at Johns Hopkins University's School of Advanced International Studies. Recalled Rosen, "We thought we were smarter than anybody else, full of piss and vinegar and testosterone."

Kristol was less intent on verbal conquest, more willing to listen to an opponent's arguments than the worst of his braggadocio friends. When he began teaching undergraduate courses, he was popular with his students. With fellow Straussian students, he eagerly shared access to the prominent figures in his family's life. If there were flashes of "famous father syndrome," rooted anxieties about measuring up to his last name, it could be glimpsed in one classmate's recollection: Bill would fill his lunch tray inside the student lounge and plant himself next to a fellow student who might be a friend, a competitor, or both. Then he'd offer this jarring conversation opener, "So who do you think, among the people we know, will become a legend in his own time?" But then, that story might have more to do with Bill's own internal drive, his propensity for networking and getting himself known, regardless of the fact that he had a father whose opinions appeared in the *New York Times*.

Kristol, Rosen, and Keyes roomed together in a cockroach-infested apartment during their first year of graduate school. (When the bikers upstairs noticed their neighbors' subscription to *National Review,* the trio could hear them ominously ranting about their uncontrollable urge to aim their shotguns at the "fascists" one floor below.) Between Kristol's barbed retorts to the latest stupidity on TV and Keyes's operatic voice pontificating on the devolving state of America, even Rosen could feel a little slow. They played touch football with the other Straussians on Saturday mornings, an outing open only to those who could present a coherent distinction between the moderns and the ancients (a test that typically unfolded something like this: "Oh, wow, let's see. . . . Well, the moderns argued that you can know what's best for politics without knowing what's best for men, whereas the ancients have to know what's best for men before they could put together a state." "Okay, fine, you play center.")

After Susan and Bill married in 1975, they moved into an apartment near Radcliffe that quickly became the social center of the Harvard Straussians. Their friends would come over for dinner, settling onto the couples' brown corduroy couches, plates in laps, to debate everything from welfare reform to Plato's views on justice. The verbal jousting usually began with an opener such as: "I heard someone say that until the last poor person in the world is fed, we have no right to any additional possessions." Then they'd rigorously work through the proposition, debating such questions as, "Do the poor have first claim over everybody else in society?" and "Would people actually be better off with such a redistribution of wealth?" Even if they never reached a conclusion, the debate would leave these young Straussians on an endorphin high from the exercise of their restless minds.

Bill's scholarly influences during those years extended beyond Strauss, and included neoconservative social scientist James Q. Wilson, as well as Daniel Patrick Moynihan, whose 1976 Senate bid gave Kristol his first real campaign experience. But mostly he was shaped by the Straussians, particularly Mansfield. The Straussians offered a rich intellectual vocabulary to counter liberal views that as a freshman Bill could only dismissively label "stupid" or "self-congratulatory." If the Left talked about the moral consequences of declining cities, the Straussians could change the subject to the moral consequences of broken families in those cities. If the Left's activists talked about the immorality of the Vietnam War, the Straussians could respond by asking about the morality of Communism, which destroyed not only lives, but the human spirit. Even in foreign policy they invoked the language of morality and virtue and—in sharp contrast to the Republican establishment—eschewed the popular diplomatic jargon of "game theory" and "spheres of influence," terms which they considered soulless.

If the post-Watergate 1970s were a period of rampant cynicism about national leaders, the Harvard graduate students found in Strauss a place to park their personal idealism. For Strauss considered political life a high moral calling, with the potential to shape a society, its economic health, even the character of its people. Straussians were taught to appreciate the "magnificence of statesmanship, and to worry abut the conditions that make it possible," said Mark Blitz. Abraham Lincoln was one model, a president whose determination to hew to a standard of right and wrong, independent of popular opinion, led him to define the nature of equality and liberty. Winston Churchill, who could single-handedly will a depleted nation to continue resisting the Nazis, loomed as another huge and inspirational figure. In 1974, Bill and his friends celebrated the former prime minister's 100th birthday the British imperial way—by roasting a pig.

Kristol would always harbor his own concerns about the dangers of the Straussian school promoting "a bunch of self-important jerks" by granting license to a democratic aristocracy. But he absorbed the alternative moral universe offered by the Straussians and put it to work in a political philosophy he would later label, "the politics of liberty, the sociology of virtue." His Straussian training would also provide a scholarly foundation to his opinion that educated elites have a civic duty to guide public opinion. As he would explain twenty years later: "I don't think 'all men are created equal' means everyone has the same judgment, capacity of judgment, or understanding. In a healthy society there would be elites that directly or indirectly shape the culture and people's understanding. . . . One of the paradoxes of being conservative in the late twentieth century is that you're supposed to be for the elites, but today the elites are more liberal [than the people], so you end up being for 'the people.' And that can degenerate into a kind of dumb populism."

For Kristol, the best hope for democracy lay in what he would later call "guided populism." He would continue to live by the words he first typed in his senior thesis, that it "is necessary for those who now direct society to educate democracy." If there was one thing that Mansfield wanted his students to take away from their education, it was the importance, especially in a democracy, of standing up to the vagaries of public opinion. Bill absorbed that lesson, and with it the Straussian emphasis on reasoned men controlling the passions of a less enlightened populace. As Mansfield put it: "We live in a democracy, so you need the people on your side, but there is a difference between the present majority and what the majority might be. Changing the majority [opinion] requires a kind of courage, taking a risk to lead people from what they now think to what they might think."

But Straussian political philosophy also posed conundrums for these American students on two fronts—religious faith and patriotism. Those students with strong religious beliefs tended to peel off and become "fellow travelers" who preferred to look to the Bible, rather than ancient Greece, for moral guidance. For a patriot (as American conservatives claimed to be), Strauss's critiques of liberal democracy posed a similar conflict: America was the embodiment of modernity, equality, democracy, and liberty to pursue one's own "happiness"—all the things that presumably troubled the Straussians. Critics such as Shadia Drury questioned the Straussians' commitment to American democracy. But historian Gordon S. Wood explained it another way: The Straussians, he wrote, attempted to overcome these inherent conflicts by lavishing their scholarly attention on America's founding documents and the statesmen who crafted them; the Straussians found "natural truths" in America's origins that harkened back to classical notions of governance in ancient Greece. It was the Straussians, not historians, Wood wrote, who first "appreciated the fact that republicanism . . . meant not just an elective representative government but the virtue of self-sacrifice and an antipathy to commerce. And they saw, sometimes more clearly than many historians, that the Founders' great republican faith in the people was limited by their fear of direct democracy or of interested majorities."

Those words certainly capture the themes of Kristol's own Straussian writings. In his senior thesis, Kristol used French writer Alexis de Tocqueville's description of the American settlers' cruel treatment of Indians to demonstrate democracy's shortcomings and the greed and acquisitiveness arising from the country's commercialism. Reflecting a Straussian's skepticism that virtue can arise from economic self-interest, he described the skillfulness of the American colonialists in "satisfying their desires at the expense of others," and their tendency to succumb to short-term passions. "It seems that the natural inclination of a democracy, if left unattended, is to degenerate at least into a society whose members vainly try to satisfy vulgar passions, at worst into a despotism," the Harvard student fretted.

Kristol's Ph.D. dissertation on the American judiciary is a condemnation of activist courts, which by the 1970s had become a sympathetic forum for liberals unable to obtain the laws they sought in legislatures. But most of the paper's 494 pages are devoted to a Straussian-style meditation on what the authors of the *Federalist Papers*—Alexander Hamilton, James Madison, and John Jay—intended when they made their case in support of the U.S. Constitution. Kristol emphasizes the "sacred maxim" of the Constitution's separation of powers, which modern judicial activists breached by making policy decisions originally intended for legislators. The Founders, Kristol argues, granted the judiciary a special role in curbing the public passions of the moment, and they expected judges to hew strictly to the Constitution, the original and fundamental expression of the people's will. This, he writes, is necessary "for the sake of the people's liberty."

Most, though not all, of the Harvard Straussians learned to live with the conflicts between their training and religious or patriotic beliefs. To the Harvard Straussians, contradictions and conflicts were a natural part of human life; only liberals, with their intellectually uninteresting earnestness, were naive enough to think conflict was unhealthy. "People never show their true face to the world," explained Rosen. "Hypocrisy is the tribute that vice pays to virtue. You pretend to be good even if you know you're bad. . . . It's a tribute to how powerful Good is. It's not dishonesty in the sense that you're living a lie, it's that this is the best you can do under the circumstances."

In 1977, when Billy Joel sang the line "We all have a face that we hide away forever" in his hit song "The Stranger," Kristol and his fellow graduate students joked that the singer must be a closet Straussian.

CHAPTER 2

WONK

"CAN CAPITALISM SURVIVE?" *Time* magazine asked America in the summer of 1975, when the unemployment and inflation rates seemed to be running a two-legged race toward the 10 percent mark, when the word "business" was modified by "big" before being stapled to images of closed-down auto plants and dead rivers catching fire and rusty steel drums leaking poison into the water supply. David McIntosh was a good Democrat at a time when good Democrats didn't believe that a free market, left to its own devices, would produce a livable America. That he would go on to become one of the Republican Party's leading defenders of unfettered capitalism says something about the shifting political tides of the late 1970s, and the quiet but growing intellectual appeal of conservative ideas to brainy young people looking for a fight. For David McIntosh was raised to excel in the art of argument, and at Yale University he found the most adventurous debates on the Right—challenging the prevailing authority of liberalism.

David came to Yale in the fall of 1976 by way of a small Indiana town and a widowed mother who trained him for the lofty political career he dreamed of pursuing. At the McIntosh dinner table, you were expected to defend your assertions with clean, crisp reasoning—or face withering rebuke. This intellectual tough-mindedness was a family trait passed down through his mother's side of the family, the Sloughs, where the most able of its verbal sparrers were known as "Slough slayers." David was a slight young man, almost comically unathletic, with dark eyes under bushy brows and crooked lips that sometimes gave the mistaken appearance of a sneer. Forensics was his sport, and he was tenacious and unforgiving in its practice.

Fifteen years after his graduation from Yale, when David was a U.S. congressman from Indiana, leading a brigade of rightist freshmen in ideological warfare on the Clinton White House, he would face the first crisis of his political career, a headline that blared, "Rep. McIntosh charged with assault and battery." The facts of the case were far less dramatic than the charges suggested. Nevertheless, the event stood out as a symbol of the youthful obstinance that plagued David as he made his way in national politics.

McIntosh had arrived at a USAir gate at National Airport in May of 1996, running late but determined to catch his plane. When a pair of attendants closed the doors minutes before departure time and refused to seat him, he defiantly started down the jetway anyway, bags in each hand, and bumped into attendants trying to block him. The USAir employees accused McIntosh of assault and made use of a provision in Virginia law to file a citizen's warrant for his arrest. Apologies ensued, and charges were dropped. Leave aside the question of who was at fault (and McIntosh would insist that the employees were rude and abrasive, not he). More telling was that those who knew David as a child saw something strikingly familiar in the incident: His propensity to barge through, even if the obstacles in his path might be reasonable ones. It was a trait shared by other smart young lawmakers on the Right in the 1990s, as they pushed their no-holds-barred strategy of confrontation, even when their standing with the public flagged.

There was a compassionate side to David, one that would reveal itself in teaching his dyslexic little brother how to read, or leading a church youth group in building shelters for homeless Mexican families. But he didn't traffic in emotion easily. The boy whose kindergarten year was shaken by his beloved father's death would grow up to be the man who counseled his wife: "Put your faith in ideas, not people. Ideas won't let you down." He could, and did, use his considerable intellect like a steamroller: "If you were not quite thinking at his speed, you'd get run over," his sister recalled.

McIntosh wasn't the only young sophist to find his way toward the Right in the 1970s. In an era when America was in a funk of malaise and dysfunction, its place as world leader shaken (and too many politicians accepting this as a necessary reality), conservative ideas, particularly anticommunism, appealed to growing numbers of young people. With liberals often dominating campus newspapers and student government, debate societies provided a forum for expressing these ideas—and trained a generation of ideological warriors.

Unlike liberals, budding conservatives on campuses had to defend themselves against a prevailing assumption that they were wrong; forced to justify their positions, they became brilliant debaters, assuming intellectual airs expressly designed to make their liberal foes look sloppy-minded and ill-informed. They studied (so they could quote, it sometimes seemed) John Locke and James Madison and Edmund Burke. They memorized the U.S. Constitution, could recite the Bill of Rights, built arguments out of prose from the *Federalist Papers*. They combed out of Western thought their own standards of idealism—of freedom and individual liberty—to counter liberal ideals of social justice and equality. At Yale in the 1970s, the Political Union was a breeding ground for all manner of Rightists—Straussians, libertarians, traditionalists, free-marketers, aspiring constitutional lawyers. Through this campus debate society, David would begin an exhilarating intellectual journey, taking him from left to right as he completed a history degree and went on to be baptized into the faith of the free market at the University of Chicago law school.

This journey of the mind would take him far away from the daily hum of his Indiana town, where he worked summers in a foundry, blasted by the heat of molten iron, wary in the knowledge that he had replaced a worker struck by a falling brick. To rise in politics, he would struggle to connect all his free market textbook theories to the lives of average Americans like his fellow foundry workers—a challenging, and often elusive, goal for David and other smart young conservatives. This helped explain why David's generation was so enthralled with Ronald Reagan—and spent so much energy trying to recreate the Gipper's visceral connection to middle America.

When he entered Yale that fall, there were certain truths that eighteen-year-old McIntosh, midwestern and middle class, could cling to as he crossed tracks with the heirs of senators and chief executive officers and trust-funded yachtsmen. One was that he deserved to be there, even if he was the son of a widowed nurse from the tiny Indiana town of Kendallville (and even if he had decided to apply to Yale because Thurston Howell had promoted it during a *Gilligan's Island* episode). David Martin McIntosh didn't have a Roman numeral following his name—though his mother made it a point always to call him "David," never "Dave." To join the Ivy League he had to piece together student loans, scholarships, and money saved from the foundry job. But he never questioned his right to be there: He had always competed, and usually won, when the competition involved intellect.

It wasn't just the quantity of facts he accumulated, but how he used them that made McIntosh stand out. He had a mind bent on logic and rational discourse that could argue circles around an unsuspecting stepfather or an academic competitor. He liked his arguments orderly, words toting up as neatly as numbers on a balance sheet. Even after a high school year abroad in Switzerland had loosened him up, he carried into Yale the unmistakable demeanor of teacher's pet (which he was), Eagle Scout (which he was), church choirboy (which he was).

But there was more to his makeup, because David had spent a fatherless youth helping his mother raise three young children. The ten-year-old who arbitrated fights between sisters or could coax little brother out of a tree had grown into an eighteen-year-old with an uncanny ability to get people to do what he wanted (often getting them to think it was what *they* wanted). Opponents who later wrote him off as a single-minded ideologue, a kind of political Mr. Spock, invariably underestimated McIntosh and his shrewd political instincts.

The other truth David carried with him to Yale was a certainty that this college experience would prepare him for the soaring political career he had been plotting since he was eight years old. He intended to pursue that career as a Democrat, the party label handed down through his mother's side. He considered himself a liberal—partly because he thought of himself as someone open to change, and conservatives as antiquarians who stood in its way. But at Yale, he would see how much his small-town upbringing had made him a traditionalist, and how, on an elite campus in the 1970s, being a traditionalist made you a rebel.

Months after America elected Jimmy Carter, who promised a government "good and honest . . . and idealistic and compassionate," David stepped into the Gothic halls of the Yale Political Union to join the Progressives, one of five political parties that formed the debate society. The Progs, as they were known, portrayed themselves as "unwilling to give up" on society's complex problems. "We are convinced that something can be done, even if it means changing the 'system,' " the party's literature proclaimed. Although he had joined a leftist party, David's ideology was still uncertain. The teenage boy eager to step up to any verbal match in high school initially hung back in the intimidating aura of Yale.

The Political Union was the center of political life on campus, and modeled itself after the Oxford and Cambridge debating societies, opening its sessions with the offer of a resolution for debate ("Resolved: Private charity should replace public welfare"). McIntosh's Progressive Party was the farthest to the left, sponsoring speeches by peace activists Daniel Ellsberg and Daniel Berrigan, and social democrat Michael Harrington. The Progs also strategized with local Leftists, including the head of the New Haven Communist Party. "In our search for alternative community and political structures we talk with people who possess innovative, progressive outlooks on society," the party stated in YPU literature from the period.

The Progs were Leftists to be sure, but there was more to this political picture than labels. Like the parties to the right, the Progs were mostly rebels against the entrenched Liberal Party, which controlled nearly half the votes and all of the union's leadership positions during the 1970s. An ambitious young man like David who aspired to be president of the union, and was not in the Liberal Party, would need to build some unlikely alliances. In the fall of 1978, his junior year, David began plotting with the conservative parties to oust the Liberals, thus beginning his rightward swing.

Out of that alliance came three close friends—Steven G. Calabresi of the Independent Party, Peter D. Keisler of the Tory Party, and Lee Liberman of the Party of the Right. Together with David, this foursome of pre-law students gained control of the Yale Political Union. In law school, they went on to build one of the most influential institutions in the modern conservative movement, the Federalist Society.

The slight and scholarly Calabresi, son of Humphrey Democrats whose uncle later became Yale Law School dean and then a federal appeals judge, drifted rightward against the background of the Carter administration's seeming unwillingness to stand up to Communist aggression. Steven would later clerk for federal judge Robert Bork. Keisler's Tory Party, which attracted Yale undergrads who considered themselves Anglophiles, described itself as a party that frowns "upon the extreme and closed-minded both on the left and the right." Peter would sit at Bork's side during his explosive nomination hearing for U.S. Supreme Court justice. Liberman, a stalwart conservative from her first days at Yale, pulled the foursome farthest to the ideological edge from her position inside Yale's Party of the Right—home to the movement's original right-wing rebel, William F. Buckley. Lee would become a key architect behind Clarence Thomas's narrow confirmation to the U.S. Supreme Court.

Except for the charismatic Keisler, this was hardly the most suave group of undergraduates. But watching their considerable intellects at work was a sight to behold. Liberman, oblivious to social graces, known to trip down stairs while her mind was on something else, could quote pages of Shakespeare without missing a "thou." Calabresi, a young man remembered for turning white with fear at the thought of jumping off a river raft for a swim, carried an encyclopedic grasp of law and philosophy and could weave both together seamlessly. Keisler, the most persuasive public speaker of the bunch, had such a brainy reputation that his friends were unfazed when they heard he received an 800 score on his LSAT. Together these three worked a powerful influence on the small-town kid from Indiana.

During his early months at Yale, David engaged in the usual undergrad life—toga parties, late-night games of Euchre with his roommates, beer sessions that once left him drunk enough to fall into a moat on campus. But as his interest in the YPU and his union friends grew, his interests began to shift. Liberman introduced David to opera; Calabresi was his partner in long talks on political philosophy that sometimes ended as the rising sun was peeking over the top of Sterling Library. And when they weren't talking about the meaning of life, liberty, and the pursuit of happiness, the foursome was plotting a takeover of the Political Union. While David was well-liked inside the union, he joined his friends in earning a reputation as an ambitious schemer. Several students ribbed him with a personalized version of the song "Mac(k) the Knife."

In the fall of 1978, this plotting by the four-party alliance broke the Liberal Party stronghold; Calabresi was elected YPU president, Keisler as speaker, and McIntosh as vice president for programs. Liberman served as chair of the all-powerful Rules Committee. One year later, in the fall of 1979, it was David's turn to serve as union president. He rode smoothly into office on the same alliance of progressives and conservatives, and quickly earned respect for his energy at organizing union events.

While the allied parties spanned an ideological spectrum, they were united in their conviction that the dominant Liberals (not to mention the alleged keepers of the First Amendment at the *Yale Daily News*) were dulled in their sense of righteousness, pat in their stands, fearful of real debate. Because it issued invitations to big-name speakers, the Yale Political Union was an inviting target for activists protesting views that they found abhorrent.

Yale's struggle with the question of free speech and academic freedom dated back to 1950, when Buckley's *God and Man at Yale* attacked the liberal orthodoxy he encountered as an undergraduate. Ironically, Buckley at the time argued that the university was too open to too many points of view, lending equal weight and respect to leftist doctrines at the expense of inculcating its students with the value of religious faith and individual liberty. Nevertheless Buckley—like the conservative students of the 1970s—argued that there was an "orthodoxy" (in modern parlance, political correctness) among establishment liberals that could not be breached from the right.

In 1975, Yale historian C. Vann Woodward chaired a committee that reported "signs of declining commitment to the defense of freedom of expression in the University." In 1963, the *Yale Daily News,* among others, had vociferously objected when the political union revoked an invitation to Alabama Governor George Wallace, calling the action a threat to the "basic duty of a free University." But a decade later, the Woodward report noted, criticism was muted when the threat of violence by antiwar protesters prevented General William Westmoreland, and later Secretary of State William Rogers, from speaking. In 1974, when Stanford University physicist William Shockley was invited to debate his explosive views on race and intelligence with Roy Innis, the black chairman of the Congress of Racial Equality (the debate was Innis's idea), an outpouring of protest prompted the Political Union to cancel the debate. Months later, the Yale chapter of the Young Americans for Freedom organized a debate between Shockley and William Rusher, publisher of the *National Review,* that was shut down by "derisive applause, insults chanted at Shockley, and shouted obscenities."

The invitation to Shockley, whose proposals included government cash incentives for low-IQ individuals to have themselves sterilized, would test any university's tolerance for free expression. But Woodward's report stressed the importance of the university as a forum for "unfettered freedom, the right to think the unthinkable, discuss the unmentionable, and challenge the unchallengeable. . . . The banning or obstruction of lawful speech can never be justified on . . . grounds the speaker is deemed irresponsible, offensive, unscholarly or untrue." The report recommended disciplinary measures for disrupters.

Despite this official blessing of free expression, protests erupted during David's tenure at Yale when the South African ambassador was invited to speak on campus. And when the Political Union convened to debate the question "Resolved: That Yale should abolish affirmative action," black student groups protested that "we are not debatable." (Though in the latter case, one union officer recalled that the episode unfolded with both sides acting appropriately: The protesters were invited in to give their position, which they did, before peacefully departing.)

In more subtle ways, conservatives looking for pointed debate at Yale felt claustrophobic within the moral confines set by their liberal peers. The erudite Keisler captured their frustrations in a fictitious dialogue he penned between "Vincent and Socrates" over the morality of crossing a picket line: "What is the essential form of morality which makes all moral actions moral?" Socrates asked. "That which is more pleasing to the liberals is moral. . . ," Vincent answered. As president of the union, the more earnest McIntosh issued a plea for free expression: "The censors adopt a paternalistic stance which denies that people here at Yale are adults. . . . This attitude reflects a deeper fear, a fear that society's beliefs . . . might be wrong. Only by confronting [opposing views] can an understanding of the truth be reached."

In this atmosphere, the Party of the Right captured the imagination of McIntosh, as well as that of his friends Keisler and Calabresi. Even on sensitive issues, even at the risk of being labeled undemocratic or racist, the members of the Party of the Right dared to tread where no others would go. "They were intellectually adventurous," explained Calabresi. Every other year, the Party of the Right sponsored the debate "Resolved: That democracy is the best form of government," in which members (some of them with the same Straussian views as Kristol's academic circle) criticized the "excesses" of modern democracy. The party's ranks included some of the smartest and best-read minds on campus; its members wore a kind of flashy intellectualism, sprinkling their remarks with quotes from Plato or the *Federalist Papers* or obscure British monarchs. (There was a story making the rounds about one student, overheard defending a Party of the Right chairman against a liberal critic with the remark, "You know, he's *really* intelligent." The liberal retorted: "Yes, but it's an evil intelligence—")

While the liberal parties debated issues from the day's headlines, Party of the Right members tackled philosophical questions such as, "When does life begin?" and "What is the nature of the Good Life?" They sponsored debates that harkened back to days when minds were trained to learn and articulate the ideas of great thinkers, not *Time* and *Newsweek*. If the typical liberal was drawn into politics to help the needy or make society more just (and might likely spend his or her Sundays working in a New Haven soup kitchen), the typical conservatives on campus were drawn to the intellectual calisthenics of the process (and would more likely spend their Sundays reading and debating the *Republic*).

David didn't formally join the Party of the Right, but he became a regular presence. His roommate Andrew Zydney recalled that David was especially drawn to the social side of the Party of the Right. It was a party hidebound in tradition—ritual for ritual's sake, and ritual observed to annoy liberals. Unlike their blue-jeaned, T-shirted counterparts on the Left, the members of the Party of the Right dressed with the formality of elites-in-training, the chairman wearing around his neck a Charles I medal, in honor of the British monarch whose struggle for supremacy with the Parliament led to the English Civil War. Each year, the chairman would recite by memory Charles's "scaffold speech" before his beheading, a thoroughly libertarian (and thoroughly undemocratic) intonement: "Freedom and liberty consists in having government under those laws by which their lives and their goods may be most their own. It is not in having a share in government, sirs." Each year, too, the Party of the Right held a spring picnic culminating in the ceremonial burning of a biography of Charles I's nemesis Oliver Cromwell, a consciously inflammatory act designed to needle liberals who blanched at the thought of anyone burning any book for any reason.

McIntosh was intrigued by the Party of the Right, and increasingly persuaded by Liberman's argument that his strong Christian faith and embrace of individual liberty made him a prime candidate for the conservative camp. By the spring of 1980, as David neared graduation, his political label at Yale remained Progressive, but he had determined to tie his political fortunes to the polemicists of the Right.

WHEN HIS FATHER DIED, five-year-old David McIntosh took on the weight of the world, or at least his mother's piece of it. She insisted she didn't drop the burden onto her eldest son's small shoulders (and others in the family backed her up on this claim—Jean McIntosh really didn't demand that he grow up as fast as he thought he should). It seemed to them that it was David who, stoically and alone, decided he had a larger job in life than just being a kid.

Or, maybe, it went like this: When tragedy struck at that fragile age, an age when nothing is figurative and everything is literal, David took to heart the counsel of the well-meaning adults who patted him on the head during the dark days after his father's death and told him that now *he* would have to be the man of the house. His father died on January 4, 1964, when the family was living near San Francisco; the surgeons had closed him up the day before Christmas, saying the stomach cancer would devour him inside of six months. A blood clot in his cancer-ridden liver killed him ten days later. For months after, through that chilly winter and into the spring, David refused to utter a single word about the event that had left a gaping hole in his young life. Then, near the last day of kindergarten, during show-and-tell, he stood up because he had something to "tell." "My father died," the little boy blurted out, "so now I have to be the man of the family."

The family was five: Four children born in five years to a thirty-seven-year-old nurse, smart and independent-minded, harboring high ambitions for her brood. Jean Slough McIntosh had left her small Indiana town as a teenager, made her way to Chicago to complete her training in psychiatric nursing, set her sights on the big cities farthest east and farthest west, and finally settled on San Francisco over New York. She readily passed California's state exams and landed a position at a neuropsychiatric institute at age twenty-four.

David's mother carried the telltale traits of Indiana's German-Anglican Slough family: Ambitious, focused, and hard-driving. Jean was valedictorian of her high school and had every intention of becoming a lawyer—until her father refused to pay for a girl's law school education and suggested she find a more feminine occupation. She opted to specialize in psychiatric nursing so she could be on a closer par with doctors. "In those days, if a doctor said, 'Sit,' you sat," she recalled. "But in psychiatrics, nurses played a bigger part in treatment [and designing protocols for patients]. It wasn't just changing bed pans."

She met Norman McIntosh at the San Francisco hospital where she was caring for patients and he was visiting as a pharmaceuticals sales rep. Norman was from the Central Valley town of Stockton, where his parents had divorced and his father worked in the family lumber business. He had served in the Navy in World War II, worked in construction for the federal Civilian Conservation Corps in Alaska, and attended college in Stockton. But mostly his was an entrepreneurial mind. He was an outgoing, friendly man, slow to anger and eager to give everyone the benefit of the doubt—a healthy balance to Jean's intensity. "He'd settle me," she recalled.

They married in 1956 and David was born two years later, when she was thirty-two and Norman was thirty-seven. In short order, Beth Ann, Lilian, and Malcolm followed. Norman died just as he was about to open up a steakhouse in San Francisco called the Top Hat, a life's dream of a man who loved to cook, and wanted to be his own boss. This wasn't young David's only painful loss. After her husband's death, Jean moved her family back to Indiana, settling in Kendallville so she could raise her children alongside the families of her two brothers, both of them doctors. Uncle Dick in particular became a father figure to young David, and soon the boy was a fixture at his uncle's side, learning the Indiana country life of boating and fishing. Two years after he came into young David's life, Dick was dead, too, the victim of a massive heart attack at age thirty-two.

Under the tutelage of his grandmother in the years following these deaths, David became a deeply religious young boy. That was not a trait shared by all of the Sloughs, first and foremost among them Jean. Even as she ushered her family into the pews of Kendallville's Methodist church each Sunday without fail, Jean harbored her own spiritual doubts, which she shared with her daughter Beth Ann many years later. "She said, 'I wanted you to have the opportunity to understand enough to make a choice, even though I didn't believe it,' " Beth Ann recalled. The weekly religious rituals had mixed results with the four children; with David, it fired his inner core.

Indiana has been called an older America (and in recent decades one of the nation's most reliable territories for Republican presidential candidates). Its roots were white and Protestant; people born there stayed there, living in small towns and on farms where life was often as provincial as it was secure. Despite the growth of factory towns and the influx of southern blacks and immigrants, that small-town sensibility remained. Decades later, David McIntosh would be elected the Congressman from Muncie, site of the famed sociology study on "Middletown" in the 1920s and '30s. But his hometown of Kendallville, about a hundred miles to the northeast, probably resembled Middletown more than modern Muncie. Kendallville was a days-gone-by place: The town's clapboard houses had porches—whether screened or open, wrap-around or stoop—and folks used them, sitting out front to assess the languid world rolling by. Families went to church every Sunday, supported the Elks and Rotary Club, and meant it when they waved American flags on Independence Day.

Locally, Democrats were as strong as Republicans. But growing up in Kendallville also meant being exposed to the fringes of American politics. Indiana had been a Ku Klux Klan stronghold early in the century, home to its imperial wizard and a powerful political machine. Largely destroyed in the 1920s, the KKK stirred in the 1960s and '70s, and Kendallville's kids were well aware of the town secret that a local chapter was listed in their phone book under the heading "Kayotts-Kutts-Kutts." (Jean McIntosh's children remember well her outrage at the thought of the Klan being active in town.) Also, families driving along the highway to reach the closest big city, Fort Wayne, would pass a farmer's sign reading "Get Out of the United Nations" on one side and equating taxation with thievery on the other. "Take our firearms, and they'll be after our farms next," was a common sentiment, recalled David's friend, Scott Stroman.

But Jean McIntosh was a dyed-in-the-wool Democrat. She had grown up in a nearby town that embraced the New Deal and its aid to struggling farmers. Her father owed his appointment as town postmaster to the state's Democratic patronage machine. As a young woman in San Francisco, she had once climbed a fence just to hear Adlai Stevenson speak, a man she considered one of the few great statesmen. "His problem," she crisply asserted, "is that he talked over the heads of most people." In the McIntosh household, FDR practically qualified for sainthood and Richard Nixon was, if not quite the devil, at least a bad guy. But David was also a Slough, and as such he was expected to articulately challenge received wisdom, and so he would.

During David's youth, Kendallville's population stretched both ends of the category "middle class" but rarely spilled out. The town's social and economic pecking order was defined by what jobs parents held in the small factories that ringed the town—Kraft Foods, Flint & Walling air pumps, foundries, tool and die shops, concrete manufacturers, electrical and roofing companies. (Town motto: "The World Takes What Kendallville Makes.") But the town wasn't big enough to hold neighborhoods delineating status, so everybody got jumbled together along neat criss-cross streets, as flat as the land around the town and the land after that. David and his cousins lived out childhood fantasies in an old mansion built by a refrigerator magnate in the 1920s, and purchased by his uncle in the 1960s. They'd slide down the curving staircase of the grand foyer, toss stones in the backyard pond, dance in the third-floor ballroom.

In his own modest home, David served as his widowed mother's aide-de-camp, arbiter of any fights that broke out between his three younger siblings, disciplinarian and safety patrol in his mother's absence. Jean's nurse's salary was supplemented by her husband's veteran's benefits and Social Security for widows (the kind of government aid criticized by many of the Right). The children never felt financial strain, though their mother made clear early on that they would go to college, and that they would do so on scholarships, loans, and money saved from summer jobs.

Jean McIntosh and her eldest son ran a tight ship. "He liked to control the situation and control us," Beth Ann recalled. For the most part, the kids were well-disciplined, focused, expected to act respectful toward adults. As a child, David would stay in the house and read while the others in the neighborhood played outside. The thin boy was terribly uncoordinated: If he dribbled a basketball, he'd invariably bounce it off his ankle and out of bounds. "He was *so* bad," his friend Richard Thrapp, who played high school football, laughingly recalled. Behind his back, neighborhood boys called David "Mr. Spock," which evolved into "UniMac" when, as a teenager, he taught himself how to operate the mainframe computer in the office where he worked summers. (He even programmed the thing to play tic-tac-toe—and this in the days when computer programming involved more than clicking a mouse.)

What his classmates didn't always see was that David knew exactly what he wanted to do with his life, and was progressing meticulously through the steps to get there. He told his cousin Jim Slough at age eight that he planned to run for political office (and Jim, like a good Slough, told McIntosh he planned to be a doctor; he, too, stuck with his youthful designs). "David had a burning desire to be a politician," said his stepfather Nelson Harrod. By high school, David had it all planned out: He told his mother he planned to run for U.S. House, stay there six years, then on to the Senate, stay there for a period, then on to the White House. "He enjoyed politics," said his sister Lilian, "there's a power to that—being able to come up with rules and regulation and governance, to have something go smoothly, to have it all come together, where an end can be achieved."

Jean McIntosh expected her children to be articulate, well-spoken, and authoritative in their opinions. "If you had a view you had to be able to back it up with airtight reasoning," recalled Lilian. "Otherwise you could get laughed off the table." David often annoyed his friends with his smart-guy talk. High intellect friends such as Scott Stroman sought him out for a worldliness that eluded other teenagers. But they also knew that David refused to back down and might storm off in a huff if he lost an argument, though he'd always regroup and come back for more. He was drawn to a good debate and in high school always knew exactly what he thought about issues (his papers, his teachers noted, were pungently written, a joy to read).

Scott Stroman, Mark Kimpel, and McIntosh—a trio who became friends during advanced math in junior high—emerged as leaders of an interdenominational Bible group in high school. But even this religious endeavor became a forum for their debate skills. "I've done youth groups on a large scale since then and I've never come across anything like it," Stroman recalled twenty-five years later. "We had high-powered debates about biblical semantics, the meaning of scripture, how literally the scripture should be interpreted. We all had Bible concordances and we were cross-referencing each other. We fed off each other. It was serious intellectual competition. All of the other kids were out of their depth." Soon, local church leaders were complaining that many youngsters didn't want to attend; anyone who was quiet, or new to Bible studies, or simply not on an intellectual par was intimidated. When the sessions did turn to the sharing of innermost feelings and fears, David gave nothing. He was self-assured, not given to displays of warmth, not open to shows of passion or weakness.

But David was devoted to the little tribe of children that he helped raise. Even when he was twelve or thirteen years old, he didn't mind taking his sister Beth Ann to the fair, so she wouldn't have to go alone, strolling through the booths with her, hand in hand. He pushed his dyslexic brother Malcolm to pursue an advanced degree when everyone else assumed trade school was his only future. This was the nurturing side of David's personality, which would reveal itself many years later in his extensive Muncie garden, where he'd go in his overalls to lose himself after a strenuous week on Capitol Hill, lovingly pruning his roses and clipping herbs to dry and send to friends. (But even this passion, characteristically, took on shades of a science project, with floodlights installed so he could work at night, and a little mechanism he carried to test the pH balance of the soil.)

David's mother intended to let nothing get in the way of her eldest son's ambitions. Her other children were accomplished, too: Malcolm would become an electro-optical engineer with a masters degree in applied physics, working on the design of optical instruments for spacecraft. Beth Ann would graduate from Vanderbilt University and pursue a career as a mechanical and chemical engineer. Lilian would attend Syracuse University before settling down to raise her own children and pursue an artist's life as a glassblower. But everyone operated in David's shadow. He was the star, especially in his mother's solar system. "She and David very much connected," said Lilian. "Philosophically, their views of life were similar, the goal orientation, what they viewed as success."

It grated on the nerves of some of the Kendallville mothers all those years, hearing Jean McIntosh boast about "David-this" and "David-that," one friend recalled. Despite her pride, his mother also worried: Her eldest was too serious, too focused. Everything he did had to have a purpose. He resisted her entreaties to invite friends over for play. Once, she found him sitting on his bed, one sock on, the other still sitting in his hand, staring off into space. "What are you thinking about?" she asked. "Oh," he stuttered, "I'm working out a math problem." In high school drama, he let his hair down a bit. (Memorable yearbook picture: David McIntosh, dressed as Carol Channing for the annual variety show, complete with artificial chest, false eyelashes, drop earrings, and curly wig.) But even that activity seemed part of a larger plan—to build an eye-popping resumé that also included Eagle Scout, foreign exchange student, honor student, sousaphone player, pianist, and statistician for his Hoosier town's basketball team.

David's accomplishment-filled life, and his mother's pride in it, was part of the problem when Nelson Harrod came along as his stepfather. Jean McIntosh married Nelson when her eldest son was on the brink of adolescence. Harrod ran his own company in Kendallville, installing roofing, insulation, and siding. He was a guy's guy, the kind of stepfather who liked to toss a baseball with a kid or teach him how to fix a car. His relationship with David was rocky from the start. "He always resented me," recalled Harrod, who also described David as "smart, a hell of a student." Decades later, as his political career took off, David would portray Harrod as an avuncular figure, someone who came into his life and led his Boy Scout troop and took him camping. In fact, it was a turbulent time, marked by conflict and shouting, with David stomping upstairs to his room and his stepfather stomping out of the house for days at a time.

One intimate said the problem was that Jean was overprotective of her eldest son, a view that reinforced Harrod's version of events. "His mother set it up so you couldn't criticize David. David was special," the stepfather recalled. Others said the problem was that Harrod was not David's intellectual equal—and David, even as an eleven- and twelve-year-old, understood this dynamic and how to exploit it. David always had a knack for sizing up people, and once he sized up Harrod, he wasn't going to back down. "David was smarter than him," said his cousin Jim Slough. "David scared him. Nelson couldn't win an intellectual argument with him."

Jean McIntosh described the problems in her marriage to Harrod as rooted in his frustration over the attention lavished on the successes of her own children, especially David (Harrod had two grown children from a previous marriage). "He became very critical of the kids, to the point where they said, 'We don't want to come home from college,' " she recalled. "David would get very very hurt. I remember going up to his bedroom and saying, 'You have to understand, you can't be responsible for someone else's behavior. You can only learn the good things from them and figure out the bad things.' "

Another strain in Jean's second marriage was her own political career. From 1970 until 1978, she served as city judge, an elected position. Kendallville, like other Indiana towns at that time, had a judgeship that was filled quadrennially by a layperson who mostly handled such cases as public loitering and drunk driving. Jean's first campaign for city judge offered David an indelible lesson in how perseverance and a dollop of chutzpah can propel even a neophyte into an odds-defying victory. Running as a Democrat, Jean campaigned door to door, sending David and a friend to pass out brochures. She told voters that she intended to get tough on public drinking and drunk drivers, and was rewarded with a solid victory, becoming the first female city judge in the state.

In office, Judge McIntosh was no-nonsense in dishing out punishment; she was also determined to help many of the defendants in her court stay sober by assigning them to treatment programs. "My philosophy was always that people needed to be responsible for their behavior," she recalled. "A lot of this came from my psychiatric training. I felt that when people didn't take responsibility for their bad behavior, they repeated it and hurt themselves." This was her philosophy toward raising teenagers, too, and she told them that if they were ever caught breaking a law, she wouldn't bail them out. Once, when Nelson was ticketed for a vehicle inspection violation, she made news by refusing to waive the fine.

But Jean's judgeship lent her a prominence that overshadowed her husband. "We'd go out and people would say, 'I'd like to meet the judge,' and they'd look across Nelson. It was too much for him," she recalled. Between this and the stepfather's tensions with David, the marriage crumbled: Eight years after they married, Jean McIntosh and Nelson Harrod were divorced.

For the fatherless David, Judge McIntosh would remain his role model—and in politics he would prove just as fearless and single-minded as his mother. But at the time no one outside his closest friends and family expected him to seek a position in the public eye.

For all his obvious love of politics and history, David didn't seem eager for the spotlight. If his teachers predicted a political career for their star student, they saw him behind the throne, not in it.

But his mother could see it. So could Beth Ann. And it came as no surprise to either woman when he shed his Democratic label and declared himself a Republican. They had never viewed David as anything but conservative, because of the way he looked at life, and the way he lived his own. "His ideas about life," Beth Ann explained, "are very conservative: You progress through your life very logically—you go through school, you acquire the means, you get married, you have children. If a wrench gets thrown in, it will fall off balance." And it came as no surprise to Scott Stroman that his old friend would be drawn to anti-authority libertarians at the University of Chicago: "He very much had the mentality of being angry over being imposed upon, having his personal space encroached upon."

REVOLT HUNG in the corridor air of the modernish University of Chicago Law School in the fall of 1980, conservative revolt, active resistance to the smug intellectual complacency that (as the Chicago professors saw it) had hopelessly infected liberal academia. "If there's a position that everybody thinks is right and is happy with, then they're probably wrong," explained Richard Epstein, one of the school's most outspoken professors. "And the reason they are probably wrong is that they spend too much time on self-congratulation instead of attacking each other." To the restless high minds who inhabited the law school's sixth-floor faculty offices, contemporary liberalism had become a nationwide exercise in self-congratulation. Professor Epstein, a key influence on David's political thinking, recalled criticizing compulsory union membership during a talk at Yale and being dismissed with haughty disdain. He concluded right then and there that rigorous intellectual debate had shifted to the Right, while all the "narrow thinking, all the ad-hominems, all the anti-intellectualism and partisanship came from the Left."

By the time David enrolled that fall, the Chicago law school was the engine of what had become known as the "law and economics" movement, which expounded the view that the country's legal system could and should promote economic efficiency. The Chicago philosophy rejected the prevailing conventional wisdom that the free market needed government guidance and regulatory checks. A law student could choose to breathe Chicago's air of revolt, or not: There were plenty of students in the early 1980s, unable to see past the $70,000 salaries awaiting them inside some glassy Manhattan skyscraper, who ignored it. But David breathed deep. If he was seen as a conciliator at Yale, he would take on the garb of ideologue at Chicago, piping up in class with increasingly hard-right opinions.

The Chicago law school shared a campus with the famed economics department, the "Chicago School," which had churned out Nobel laureates Milton Friedman and George J. Stigler, along with a host of other prominent economists. Their revolt against Keynes, and their faith in the free market, carried over to the law school, producing, by the time McIntosh arrived, a studied aversion toward antitrust law (embodied in Chicago alumnus Robert Bork's 1978 book, *The Antitrust Paradox*); a disdain for regulation (which Epstein theorized as an infringement on constitutional property rights); and a presumption that law should work to promote "wealth maximization" (a theory most notably set forth in Chicago professor Richard Posner's 1972 text *Economic Analysis of Law*).

Theirs was a view of the world infused with clean, cool, controlled rationalism. In a different era, minds like that (and like Dave McIntosh's) might have been drawn to Robert McNamara and his whiz kids, dubbed the "best and brightest," accomplished young men convinced that applied intelligence, devoid of passion and emotion, could control a messy Indochina war (just as McNamara had managed the messy business of the auto industry). But this was the early 1980s, not the early 1960s: Bureaucrats were seen as inefficient meddlers, not skilled technocrats shaping wars and economies. The great and logical minds at Chicago were determined to un-manage, de-plan, free the free market from the bureaucrats so it could operate in its inherently rational fashion. Their theories clicked with David's logical mind.

There wasn't much tolerance in this rational atmosphere for words like "fairness" or "justice"—"terms which have no content," Posner once said. Or, in Epstein's view, words that were important in private matters, values to inculcate in children, but not useful as underpinnings of constitutional law. If the high-minded rhetoric of liberal legal scholars focused on justice and equality, that of the Chicago professors focused on free association—no manager should be forced to hire a minority, no worker should be forced to join a union—and the constitutional supremacy of personal property.

This focus on economic relationships, rational self-interest, and wealth maximization left the Chicago law school's many critics cold, conjuring up images of Bedford Falls transformed into Pottersville because Jimmy Stewart wasn't there to stop the advance of greed. To its critics, Chicago School devotees viewed the world through a prism of sterile economic determinism, Marx-like, without reference to a greater moral or national good, and based on a questionable assumption that people always act in their rational economic self-interest. "They would genuinely welcome a politics that permits no distinction between human workplaces and sweatshops, that shrugs before the great gaps between rich and poor, and that puts health care on exactly the same moral level as vacation homes," complained the liberal *American Prospect* journal in a critique of Posner and Epstein.

There was another aspect to the Chicago law school that troubled liberals: its resolute rejection of the prevailing view that the U.S. Constitution should be adapted to a more tolerant and egalitarian-minded twentieth century. Their opinions about the best way to interpret the Founders' documents ranged, but the Chicago law professors stood united in their belief that judges should adhere strictly to the original words of the Constitution. They argued that liberal judges had invented rights nowhere found in the Constitution—chief among them "privacy," the underpinning of the 1973 *Roe* v. *Wade* abortion decision that served as a call to arms for the conservative movement.

If David McIntosh was plotting a career in politics, he couldn't have picked a better place at a better time to start paving the path. He entered law school the same season that Ronald Reagan was elected, a president who would raid Chicago's economics and law schools for federal and judicial appointments. Most of Reagan's top economic advisers hailed from Chicago, and his appellate court appointments were heavily laden with such Chicago names as Posner, Antonin Scalia, Danny J. Boggs, Frank H. Easterbrook, Bernard H. Siegan, and Ralph K. Winter. The president would treat Scalia to a Supreme Court appointment in 1986, and a year later, he would name Bork as well, only to be blocked by the Senate after a bloody confirmation battle.

As always, David's mind was on politics when he moved into his Hyde Park apartment in the fall of 1980, after graduating from Yale. Epstein complained that the twenty-two-year-old law student would be better off thinking less about politics and more about scholastics: David readily won election to the law student association and closely followed the doings of the new Reagan adminstration in Washington. But he also found intellectual inspiration in Epstein's property rights theories.

Epstein was a pariah in most legal circles, too controversial to receive any of the judicial appointments the Reaganites were doling out to his colleagues in the early 1980s. But students were enthralled by the wide-ranging intellect of this wild man at the lecture podium. "The more outlandish (in liberal eyes) the position he is arguing, the more rapid-fire his delivery becomes," one writer observed in an apt description of Epstein. "Working up to the clincher of an argument, he quite literally spits forth concepts drawn from ancient philosophers and Roman jurists, frothily mixing them with the street-corner aphorisms of Epstein's native Brooklyn."

The root of the "outlandish" position that built his notoriety was his interpretation of the Takings Clause of the Fifth Amendment to the Constitution: "Nor shall private property be taken for public use, without just compensation." Historically, courts interpreted that clause to mean that when the government literally "takes" property—as in eminent domain—the owner should be compensated. Epstein preferred a sweeping interpretation, arguing that most regulations, from zoning to pollution controls, and nearly all federal transfer payments such as welfare, were "takings" of someone else's property and therefore required compensation. "The liberal philosophy of government," he once said, "reminds me of Leo Durocher's famous challenge, 'Let's him and you fight.' What the liberal is really saying is: 'I'll distribute your money to him.' " Epstein's theory would become the driving engine behind a burgeoning property-rights movement on the Right during the 1980s.

Epstein acknowledged that his position would invalidate most twentieth-century law (as well it should, he added). And even many thinkers on the Right rejected Epstein's interpretation as a stretch. But his ideas appealed to David and would enshrine in this law student's mind a belief in the supremacy of individual property rights. Epstein's teachings inspired David's career course—first in the Bush White House, later in Congress—as a leading enemy of federal health, safety, and environmental regulations.

During their second year of law school, McIntosh and Liberman, at Chicago, and Calabresi, at Yale Law School, began brainstorming on a project that would grow in influence beyond anyone's expectations—the Federalist Society. In the 1980s and 1990s, the society would become central casting for the biggest names in Washington's ideological wars—Robert Bork, Clarence Thomas, Kenneth Starr. Yet it started with more modest ambitions: Young law students who were seeking an intellectual forum for conservative views they felt were shut out by the overwhelmingly liberal cast of law school faculties and the American Bar Association. Law schools, they believed, were producing graduates who hadn't been exposed to conservative ideas, nor, often, to the fundamental precepts of the U.S. Constitution.

In 1981, the threesome decided to organize campus-based student groups at their own law schools as conservative alternatives to the leftist National Lawyers Guild. (Though at the University of Chicago, where the guild had collapsed, one student commentator quipped that the Liberman/McIntosh chapter would be "one of the few reactionary groups with nothing to react against.") Obtaining funding from the Chicago's law student association—which had routinely funded organizations with clear liberal leanings—wasn't easy; student leaders fretted about giving money to a group pursuing a conservative agenda. So a rider was attached to a $170 authorization, giving the twenty-five-member chapter seed money but only to support "the discussion of ideas."

It was left to Bill Kristol's father to step forward with real money. By the spring of 1982, the Chicago group had sister chapters at Harvard and Stanford. The Harvard connection was key, bringing in E. Spencer Abraham, a law student and future U.S. senator (and close friend of Bill Kristol) who was editing the influential *Journal of Law and Public Policy*—which similarly had been denied university funding because it was considered too political. That year the journal linked up with the Federalists, and the full name the law students finally adopted—The Federalist Society for Law and Public Policy Studies—reflected the importance of the Harvard faction. The Institute for Educational Affairs, which Irving Kristol had co-founded with former Treasury Secretary William Simon to influence new generations of elite students, kicked in $25,000 for a founding conference. Kristol senior would continue to be an important funding adviser to the group, while his son would become a regular speaker at Federalist Society gatherings.

At Yale, professors Bork and Ralph Winter encouraged Calabresi in his efforts and, at the University of Chicago, Scalia agreed to serve as faculty adviser to McIntosh and Liberman. In March 1982, the University of Chicago chapter kicked off its speakers series with an Epstein talk on the takings clause, followed by lunch at a Chinese restaurant. The next month, more than two hundred students and professors from twenty universities (and a handful of interested academics from other disciplines, including Bill Kristol) poured into New Haven to hear the conservative legal world's most prominent names pontificate on the subject of "legal and political ramifications" of federalism.

The Federalist Society tapped a responsive chord with conservative-leaning law students. Notices and coverage of the group in the *National Review* magazine prompted an outpouring of letters from students who wanted to start their own chapters. Inside his Hyde Park apartment, McIntosh, together with Liberman, began typing out instructions on how to organize Federalist Society chapters on other campuses. Their booklet stressed the need to organize debates, rather than lectures: "You are more likely to convince people of your viewpoint if they feel the other side has been given a fair hearing." And they suggested that membership would be broader if chapters avoided explosive topics: "[T]here are some topics that tend to be viewed in very emotional terms, where adopting deliberately controversial rhetoric may close minds further rather than opening them a crack."

Three years earlier, conservative legal scholar Michael Horowitz had exhorted the Right's funders to stop wasting time and money on small, obscure colleges where their ideas flourished, and to redouble their efforts on capturing the minds of the brightest students at the best law schools. With the birth of the Federalist Society, shrewd strategists on the Right quickly saw its potential to do just that. The treasuries of the Right's foundations opened, and money poured in to the Federalist Society from Pittsburgh billionaire Richard Mellon Scaife, the Olin Foundation, the Bradley Foundation, the Smith Richardson Foundation. The Federalists hired an executive director, Eugene B. Meyer, son of Frank Meyer, a key voice of conservatism in the early years of *National Review.*

During the 1980s, with the Republicans in control of the White House, the society quickly transformed into a clearinghouse for federal appointments and clerkships for the expanding ranks of conservative judges. It became the most important national forum for conservative legal thought. But the Federalist Society was also becoming much more—a cultural harbor, a place where aggrieved Rightists could come and lick their wounds after bloody battles with the liberal establishment. David initially stayed out of Washington's political fray; after graduating in 1983, he accepted an offer to practice law in the Los Angeles office of Sidley & Austin, which gave him a chance to pay off student loans, and to toy with the idea of launching his political career from his father's home-state. But he continued to organize Federalist Society chapters on college campuses and, three years later, when the call came with an offer to join the Reagan Revolution, David was out the door.

CHAPTER 3

HARD-CORE

TALK ABOUT impeccable timing: Harvard University released Grover Glenn Norquist into the world, if only temporarily, at
the peak of the 1970s taxpayer revolt. California voters were issuing
a war-cry called Proposition 13, threatening to lop their property
taxes in half. Republican leaders were traversing the country in a Boe-
ing 727 nicknamed "The Republican Tax Clipper" promising to cut
federal taxes by a third. Even Democrat Jimmy Carter would soon
sign a series of tax breaks, though fearing as he did so that his signature would favor the rich. In the spring of 1978, Grover couldn't wait
to join this unfolding bourgeois revolt. Halfway through his graduation party he apologized to his parents, slipped behind the wheel of
his loaded U-Haul, waved goodbye, and zipped down Interstate 95
from Boston to Washington to start his life as an antitax crusader.

A zeal for tax cuts, even those forced on politicians by rebellious
citizens, might seem a stuffy preoccupation for a young person. But
Grover was no ordinary young person. He considered himself a revolutionary—on behalf of a worldwide free market. What else but the
promise of overthrowing the established order could spark such passion in a twenty-one-year-old kid who couldn't muster the same intensity for romance or friendship, music or even sports? (He had
never even read a sports page when his *Harvard Crimson* editor as-

signed him a baseball game to cover.) Grover would go on to find his own version of romance—in a self-styled war on liberals and the welfare state they defended, in his forays to the African bush to aid "freedom fighters' " against encroaching communism, in late-night strategy sessions with leaders of the 1995 Republican Revolution in Congress.

Grover was an ideologue, and one could find versions of his personality on the Left as well as the Right—activists who view society as the interaction of systems rather than human personalities. "He has an intellectual appreciation for people more than a need for emotional contact," explained his friend Amy Moritz Ridenour. "He likes people, but he's more interested in them in groups—groups of activists, groups of gun lovers, groups." As Grover evolved into his role as one of Washington's premier Rightists in the 1990s, he would utter his lengthy proclamations like one of those old-fashioned carnival fortune tellers: Drop in a nickel, pull the lever, and the face—a place-saver for matching copper beard and glasses—would come to life in a robotic monologue about the ceaseless struggle between Right and Left, Good and Evil, "our team" and "their team," Liberty and Tyranny.

Grover's mechanistic views were reinforced by his upbringing as the son of a safety engineer who often acted as if life was a piece of machinery to be hard-wired. Warren Norquist was not a man to leave the turns of life in the hands of Fate, or anyone else for that matter. He chose his wife by making a list of characteristics he considered essential to a future bride: She had to be smart, Protestant, a Republican. She had to have an angular face and couldn't smoke. He then pulled out his University of Michigan yearbook and turned to the page with the photo of the women's honors society. Examining the picture with an engineer's precision eye, he jotted down the names of four women who might pass inspection. His first call was to the woman who would become Grover's mother, and after a lengthy conversation he was able to check off at least fifteen items on his list. Carol had a round face, not angular, he recalled, but she met just about all the other criteria. They were married on a Saturday, the day after graduation.

But as the son of an engineer, Grover was also eminently practical. "He says the darndest things. He gives the impression of being over the top, but he runs a fairly disciplined operation," his longtime associate James Lucier later said of Grover's organizing efforts. Even as an adolescent, Grover believed that the Republican Party would prosper by adopting tax cutting as its name-brand theme, like buying Coke at the 7-Eleven—you'd always know which fizz you were getting. So in the 1980s he devised an antitax pledge, and convinced hundreds of GOP candidates to sign his promise forswearing tax hikes.

In the 1990s, this market-Leninist would shepherd a nationwide vanguard of hard-core ideologues who exerted relentless pressure on Republicans in Congress to remain purist. Even as they moved closer to the country's power center—with conservative lawmakers running the U.S. House and Grover's longtime friend Newt Gingrich as speaker—these activists would stand guard against any signs of weakness in their ongoing insurrection against the liberal establishment. Grover and his allies called themselves "hardcore," and they labeled as "squishes" those who defected from the party line.

AS A STUDENT at Harvard, Norquist's fixation with tax cuts was actually a gateway to a far more radical worldview. He discerned in the 1978 tax revolt the golden thread of a popular uprising to defrock America's government. It was proof (as if he needed any more) that he was on the right side of history: The voters were throwing tea into Boston Harbor; revolution was afoot ("revolution" being one of those jarring nouns Grover liked to borrow from the far Left). "No one wore war paint or carried tomahawks, but on December 7 [1977], Massachusetts began another taxpayers' revolt," he wrote in the pages of a shoe-string libertarian newspaper called the *Harvard Chronicle,* which he and like-minded friends published on campus.

Most analysts, of course, interpreted the '78 tax revolt in less radical ways: The American people had soured on swelling bureaucracies that produced surly clerks and long lines. Middle-class families, watching as their yearly tax bill grew to nearly one-third of their paychecks, had reached their limit; the salary raises they eked out of a stagflated economy merely bumped them into higher and more onerous tax brackets. In California, the revolt was surgically specific: Skyrocketing home prices had produced huge property tax bills, nearly doubling the levy in some neighborhoods.

But to Grover, the tax revolt was more than an argument over the size of one's annual IRS check: Tax-and-spend government was a slippery slope toward socialism, something the liberal establishment behind Big Government was too witless to recognize, or too deceptive to admit. This hard-core ideology was almost fully formed by the time Grover arrived at the gates of Harvard in 1974, in the way it might be for a bright, intense teenager who consumed books, mastering just enough history early in his life to convince himself he saw truths that others didn't, particularly on the subject of Communism versus Freedom. Norquist considered himself well-equipped to stand up to what he saw as the weak-mindedness of his professors, the distortions of his liberal and leftist peers at college, the lies of the liberal media.

The skinny kid with big glasses was hardly a towering presence on the Harvard campus. Grover's peers at Harvard would recollect him as a kind of social misfit; in memory, they'd want to button the top button of his shirt, even if he never buttoned it; they'd want to put a plastic pocket protector on his front pocket, even if he didn't wear one. The "before" version of the old Charles Atlas body-building ads, with the nerd getting sand kicked in his face, was the image offered up by former *Harvard Crimson* editor Nicholas Lemann. Norquist attended Harvard during the same period that Bill Kristol was pursuing his Ph.D. with the Straussians. But Grover, son of an introverted engineer, was a natural outsider. Kristol, son of renowned New York intellectuals, was a natural insider. Decades later, their two factions would collide, threatening to fracture the unity of the Right. But at Harvard in the 1970s, they operated in separate worlds.

Grover didn't wear the effortless polish of a young man raised in the womb of the country's social power structure; nor was he blessed with a sixth sense for how to merge into it. Still, he managed to get himself elected to the business side of the prestigious *Harvard Crimson,* drew some grudging respect from liberal up-and-comers like Lemann and Jonathan Alter (who admired his chutzpah and saw in him a very smart, though not terribly nuanced, mind), and attached himself to a tiny band of conservatives. By the mid-1970s, the liberalism of the campus had become complacent, even lazy; Alter, later a *Newsweek* columnist, remained convinced this flabbiness of leftist thought hardened Norquist's ideology.

The radical chic crowd then dominated the *Crimson*'s shabby editorial offices: Political monologues by New Deal liberals such as Alter were booed. During the 1976 presidential race, Democrats Jimmy Carter and Morris Udall were considered sellouts, but leftist Democrat Fred Harris was admired for his keen understanding of American class conflict. The campus paper, which not long before had lent editorial support to the communist-backed Vietcong, was still billed by staff radicals as a leading socialist voice. Critics nicknamed the *Crimson* "the Kremlin."

But the *Crimson*'s leftism wasn't always oppressive; the radicals tolerated their opponents, and a fair range of views made it into the pages of the paper. Norquist didn't feel particularly persecuted, but he did feel superior. During one editorial meeting, when the *Crimson*'s prep school radicals were promoting armed struggle in the third world, Norquist interjected: "Do any of you have guns?" Of course, none of them did—what Harvard undergraduate stocked firearms? "Well I do," Grover prodded with his hyena's grin. "And my friends do, so if you want to borrow them for your revolution, just let us know."

In the handful of Marxists on an elite campus otherwise drained from a decade of political activism, Grover could find sustenance for his view that America's power structure was dominated by Leftists arrogantly running roughshod over the lives of true Americans. And when he graduated cum laude with a degree in economics in 1978, he could pour more concrete around his already impregnable ideology by drawing on the promise of the tax rebellion erupting throughout the country. All around him, from Massachusetts to California, he saw a popular uprising against bureaucracy and socialist creep.

"Get rid of the Soviet government," he would say, "and I don't really have much use for ours." He was convinced that the adults behind this tax revolt saw what the prep-school radicals at Harvard couldn't, or wouldn't: The struts and supports of America's sprawling government were producing weak and dependent people. (And with the lessons in self-sufficiency that infused Grover's childhood, he didn't harbor much tolerance for weak, dependent people.) Government had the pernicious power to steal money from the strong and corrupt the weak with handouts. Government was communal, which meant other people (bureaucrats who weren't as smart, otherwise they wouldn't be bureaucrats) telling people like him what to do. The government used taxpayer dollars to create all kinds of mischief.

As he drove into the nation's capital after his graduation, Grover was sickened by the sight of the imposing federal buildings, by the very idea that bureaucrats had forcibly taken money from the people to build those marble halls. "Neo-American fascism," he called blocks of federal buildings, "stuff that looks like Albert Speer designed it."

THE IMMODERATE YOUNG MAN who looked at Washington and saw Berlin was raised the son of Rockefeller Republicans. Carol and Warren Norquist voted for Nelson Rockeller in 1968. They voted for Gerald Ford in 1976. Anything much farther to the right would have stood out in Weston, Massachusetts, a suburb of doctors, lawyers, corporate executives, and other professionals who could afford to settle in this exclusive enclave twenty miles west of Boston. If his parents were squishes (temporarily, since Grover later would steer them rightward), his Swiss grandmother was hard-core. Grandmommy Norquist from St. Louis, Missouri was the one who explained to Grover that he should support Nixon and stay away from both Reagan and Rockefeller because they were divorced. She was the one who passed on her copies of *Human Events,* which introduced him to the concept of "totalitarian liberals," the "leftist bias in academia," threats posed by Big Labor, and American weakness in the face of encroaching "Red tyranny."

But family opinions go only so far in explaining Grover's worldview. A more telling clue lies in the life lessons that Warren and Carol Norquist assiduously nurtured in all four of their children: Be prepared for any contingency; don't go looking for—or expect to find—help outside yourself and your family; always stay one step ahead of everyone else. Grover's parents left him with a confident righteousness about the world and how to maneuver in it. In doing so they raised a supremely confident young man, but one who seemed to his friends strangely incapable of connecting with others. "He's not a fellow who is motivated by or particularly needs a whole lot of human warmth or interaction," explained one friend.

Grover would later have trouble understanding, coping with, or even deciphering flaws in those around him. While friends insisted he had a strong moral compass for his own actions, the nuances of human personality in others often eluded him. Friends and allies worried: Grover would embrace a bad apple, based on a precariously built certainty that the person was an ideological loyalist. Just as readily, he'd turn against an ally, based on an equally dubious conclusion that the person was (or would be, or might be) a betrayer to the cause. He remained intensely private about his own personal life; good friends who confided in him about romantic troubles were surprised that he never reciprocated with revelations about his own life.

Politically, this overcharged sense of self-sufficiency produced in Grover an intolerance for the view that people might turn to government for help as an arbiter, an equalizer of society's power imbalances. People were best off left alone; a coddling, meddling government could only sap reservoirs of individual strength. From his upbringing, too, came a natural empathy for the survivalist rhetoric of the gun crowd and the antigovernment themes of Western libertarians. Raised in a chic Northeastern suburb, Norquist would increasingly sound like a man spawned from the individualist West. "I've always thought," he would explain later, "that it is part of the American ideology, the American worldview, that people should be left alone to take care of themselves, and other people shouldn't tell you what to do."

In 1961, when Grover was five, the Norquists settled into Weston, which was well on its way to becoming the highest per-capita-income town in the state of Massachusetts. Carol gave up her job as a fifth grade teacher to raise her four children; Grover, the eldest, had been followed by a sister and two brothers. Meanwhile, Warren began a long and successful climb up the corporate ladder at the nearby offices of Polaroid. He rose to head of manufacturing for four-by-five photos, then chief of quality control. He developed a theory of zero-based pricing, to squeeze the costs of inflation out of transactions, that landed him on the cover of *Purchasing Magazine*.

The family enjoyed a prosperous and happy home life. In 1963, they built a sprawling white clapboard house for $28,000 on a wooded lot that cost $9,000, later recounting in detail the money they had saved by building from scratch, since completed homes in that neighborhood were going for close to $50,000. The children picked blueberries in the summer, and played in the acres of woods in their backyard. As they grew older, Warren saw to it that his children were never idle, and they helped with painting or electrical work in the basement. For years, there was no TV in the house. When they finally did buy one, the parents made sure it didn't induce idleness in their progeny: If Carol saw one of her children sitting in front of the tube, she'd hand over an iron and some handkerchiefs.

The Norquists had a vigorous recreational life—and one that, like Warren's courtship, left nothing to chance. Warren wanted his children to learn that no matter how difficult the situation, they could get themselves out without seeking outside help. The family would tow their twenty-four-foot aluminum power boat for outings off Cape Cod or on lakes in New Hampshire or Maine. Warren would make sure there were two batteries hooked up, and two others along as back-up. He'd bring four anchors. The boat had a main motor and an auxiliary motor. He'd carry in his car an extra towing strap. When they flew on airplanes, each of the Norquists would take an aspirin to prevent blood clots. When they went skiing, the children were the only ones on the slopes wearing helmets.

Always rely on redundancy, Warren Norquist would counsel his children. And when, as occasionally happened, they were caught in rain on the Cape or snowstorms on the slopes, the Norquist family was always prepared, and didn't need to seek help. These layers of preventive measures also meant that the Norquist family could, and did, do as they please—taking risks that others wouldn't, ignoring the pleas of safety patrols, snickering at the ski-lift operator who emerged from his hut, mid-blizzard, to castigate Warren for taking children out in such dangerous conditions (just as young Rightists might scoff at the health and safety warnings of government bureaucrats).

Warren Norquist turned even board games into life lessons. When he played chess or checkers with one of his young children, who invariably fell behind, he put off defeat by turning the board around and starting over. When you're stuck, he'd remind them, there's always another chance. Lessons in economics also were woven into the family rituals: On mountain trips, a favorite game was calculating the actual cost of each ski run. When the children went for ice cream at the neighborhood Dairy Joy, their father would steal bites from his kids' cones with lessons in taxation. "This the federal tax." One bite gone from Grover's cone. "This is the state tax." A bite from sister Lorraine's. "This is the city tax." Brother Alan would lose a chunk. And on it would go. Grover's mother was elected chairwoman of the town's board of tax assessors in 1977, where she recalled gaining a new appreciation for the fact that a bureaucrat's power lay in his ability to say "no."

Actually, high property taxes and onerous regulations made Weston a remarkably attractive setting in which to raise a family, with its high-income homeowners watching their property values soar. Weston was, and is, considered one of the Boston area's "trophy towns." Its taxes and per-capita budget were among the highest in the state, funding elite police and fire departments, and nationally recognized schools. By the mid-1990s Weston's high school students enjoyed the highest S.A.T. scores in the state. Strict zoning required each home to sit on at least one and a half acres; Grover's home, at the crest of a circular driveway reaching into the woods, was surrounded by neighbors with property that comfortably fit their swimming pools and tennis courts. Weston's commercial zoning produced a charming New England town rather than a suburb overrun by fast-food joints and chain stores. None of this suggested to Grover any benefits of government: Later, when asked about Weston's zoning laws or taxes, he merely retorted that just because he drove on public roads didn't mean he believed in them.

The Norquists weren't hunters, but they built a target range in the basement, aiming .38-caliber pistols at a heavy metal bullet trap (Grover liked to joke that they'd hang their least favorite teachers on the wall). After a neighbor's son was shot on Boston's Memorial Drive while trying to protect his girlfriend, Grover resolved never to be left at the mercy of criminals. He went down to the basement every day to practice shooting. "He must have fired three thousand rounds or so," his father recalled. "He got very good." For Grover, the experience would feed his political disposition that one's fate should not be left in the hands of others, least of all government. "If only the government and the criminals have guns," he decided, "then you're completely at the mercy of the police and the criminals. You have no ability to protect yourself."

Years later, the Washington cognoscenti would look at Grover and see a burly, bearded man. But in his youth, he was clean shaven and rail thin, keeping in good physical condition with soccer, skiing, and almost daily runs. He also excelled at school. While he never actually enjoyed math, he was good at it and qualifed early for advanced placement. (His sister Lorraine and brother Alan would become the ones to follow in their father's engineering footsteps.) Despite the blond straight hair that reached to his shoulders, causing organizers at one GOP fund-raiser to balk at his offer to volunteer, Grover was a straight kid. He didn't challenge his parents. He and his friends were close enough to their high school teachers that they could get away with playing harmless pranks on them, like hiding the chalk.

At the homogeneous Weston High, there wasn't much trouble anyway—a few kids who looked tough, and some rumors that the French exchange students were into LSD, but no rampant drug scene. Grover's claim to fame was organizing "junior skip day" in which all the students in his junior class (with their parents' permission) skipped school and spent the day on a Cape Cod beach. His classmates thought enough of him by senior year to pile on the "mosts"— "most likely to succeed," "most intelligent," "most studious," "most responsible," "most ambitious."

Under their senior yearbook photos, members of the class of '74 offered quotes from favorite thinkers, writers, and artists, ranging from Socrates and William Blake to Kahlil Gibran and Joni Mitchell. Grover crafted his own: "A dictatorship is like a machine with a warranty—it works well for a while. A democracy has no guarantees and as such needs to be constantly maintained, nurtured, even pampered, lest the people allow her to rust and begin to cast covetous glances at her more expedient rival."

THE 1970s were supposedly years of youthful political apathy, so what accounts for this seventeen-year-old's passionate prose in defense of democracy, and his angular and intense description of it? The answer can be found inside the pages of the landmark book *Witness,* an autobiography of onetime Communist spy Whittaker Chambers, who went on to become an evangelist for freedom and God—and a hero to budding young Rightists such as Grover. *Witness* recounted Chambers's undercover life as a spy, his tortuous 1948 decision to accuse prominent American diplomat Alger Hiss of being a communist operative, and his undoing at the hands of powerful figures who rallied to Hiss's side. The Chambers-Hiss case came at the beginning of an anticommunist crusade by Congress that ended with the downfall of Senator Joseph McCarthy, but not before ripping the seams of a nation.

Witness inspired generations of prominent conservatives, starting with William F. Buckley Jr., who befriended the author in his twilight years. For activists such as Grover, coming of age in the 1970s, the book was their Rosetta stone, unlocking a language that would give order and meaning to a murky world seemingly controlled by liberals. The enduring influence of *Witness* may seem mysterious to outsiders, but the book needs to be understood as far more than one man's story, for it offered young people on the Right a powerful paradigm for explaining their own underdog standing in modern America.

Because of a statute of limitations, Alger Hiss didn't face espionage charges, but he was convicted of perjury and sentenced to five years in jail after Chambers produced microfilm of classified government documents—the famed "Pumpkin Papers"—which apparently had been typed or handwritten by Hiss and turned over to Chambers in the mid-1930s. In the 1980s, historian Allen Weinstein, who initially intended to prove Hiss's innocence, instead sided with Chambers—a conclusion backed a decade later by the release of KGB cables and files from Hungarian and Czech archives.

But Hiss steadfastly maintained his innocence—and for decades this was an article of faith in many liberal quarters, where his perceived persecution stood as a testament to the dangers of right-wing extremism. Hiss's many defenders portrayed Chambers as paranoid and emotionally unstable, possibly pursuing Hiss because of an unreciprocated homosexual passion. In the early 1970s, when Grover read *Witness*, Hiss enjoyed the ACLU's legal counsel in securing a government pension, and was a popular speaker on college campuses, where he was greeted as a hero against the dark forces of the Right.

Grover escaped to the cool of his basement one especially hot summer in high school to lose himself in Chambers's eight-hundred-page sermonizing thriller. For him, Chambers's poetic drama (often verging on melodrama) was life-shaping. Later, Grover recalled: "I realized then that whenever you'd hear somebody explain that Hiss was innocent, you knew they were either a liar or an idiot." More than that, *Witness* convinced him—and thousands of young conservatives like him—that reality was not what it seemed, certainly not what the liberal media proclaimed it to be. How could it be (they asked) if a cunning Soviet spy like Hiss could be defended by the likes of Eleanor Roosevelt, much of the foreign policy establishment, and the most influential liberal newspaper columnists of the time? How could it be if Hiss sat at the right hand of FDR at Yalta in 1945 (where, the young activists would point out, the president ceded half of Europe to Stalin) six years after Chambers told a State Department official that Hiss was an underground communist? How could it be if Chambers revealed to government authorities in 1939, and again in the 1940s, that the man entrusted with America's postwar monetary policy, Harry Dexter White, was part of that same underground? "Grover," his mother later remarked, "never takes kindly to people who push out as truth that which isn't true."

For Grover and like-minded young people on the Right, the Chambers case provided a clear dividing line between those willing to write the "true" accounting of American history and those who accepted the "whitewashing" provided by the media and the liberal elite. As a teenager, Grover even viewed the local library's used-book sale through this prism: He asserted that the conservative histories on sale there—which he could pick up for just a quarter—proved that liberal librarians were eager to "censor" their shelves of right-leaning analysis. As an adult, Grover would become a self-styled historian, offering his own rightist version of central events such as the Great Depression and the postwar division of Europe. Because the telling of American history was dominated by liberals, he repeatedly counseled fellow activists, conservatives needed to rewrite the past in order to explain both the present and the future.

Whittaker Chambers predicted an inevitable Armaggedon between the West and communism. Even as a teenager, Grover never embraced that pessimism. But he did accept Chambers's argument that the inner drift of liberalism "was prevailingly toward socialism." And he adopted Chambers's neat divide of history—God-fearing freedom fighters on one side; Godless communists, socialists, and well-intentioned but easily duped liberals on the other. Grover's mind shut out the gray nuance of history, as his stated enemy became the liberal elite crowd that Chambers described as "impeccably pedigreed, socially and culturally poised . . . staggering under M.A.'s and Ph.D.'s," the same crowd who "howl[ed] for my head." Chameleon-like, despite his Harvard degree and privileged upbringing, Grover would adopt a populist pose to attack what he called "the Establishment Left" and "the elite," this "serious enemy, not lightly conquered." He would make warlike reference to the "savage defense the Washington establishment put up to defend the spoils of empire." Norquist became, as Lionel Trilling once said of Chambers, a man "whose commitment to radical politics was meant to be definitive of his whole moral being, the controlling element of his existence."

For the generation of conservatives who emerged on campus in the 1970s—and onto the national scene in the '80s and '90s—the personal connection with Chambers was visceral. Any one of them could have stepped into the shoes of this "little fat man," with his unfashionable anticommunism, conducting a brave but lonely struggle against an elite "conspiracy of gentlemen." Any one of their ideological opponents might serve as a stand-in for the elegant Alger Hiss, with his impeccable Ivy League credentials, his position as a pillar of an entrenched liberal establishment, and his ultimate duplicity. Start with the moralistic put-downs a young Rightist likely endured at the hands of campus liberals in the 1970s, and wind through subsequent years of pitched battle against liberal groups that enjoyed easy popularity with the press and political establishments: In the 1990s, didn't the unpopular conservative prosecutor Kenneth Starr fit the first role? Didn't the popular liberal (and, to the Right, duplicitous) Bill Clinton fit the second?

In the 1980s, Grover would join an informal club called the Pumpkin Papers Irregulars, named for the hollowed-out pumpkin on Whittaker Chambers's Maryland farm that served as a hiding spot for crucial microfilm evidence. Surrounded in pumpkin decor, sipping pumpkin soup, and nibbling pumpkin pie, these Rightists would gather yearly to immerse themselves in the internecine business of ferreting out real and would-be Hiss supporters. They conducted "Traitors Tours" of Georgetown, site of Hiss's home, and handed out the annual "Victor Navasky Prize," named for the editor of the leftist *Nation* magazine, whom they ridiculed "as the most outrageous and steadfast defender of the unrepentant Soviet spy Alger Hiss." * Sympathetic journalistic investigators would share the latest KGB cable or file describing Hiss. Then the guests would find brotherhood in lam-

---

* Recipients of the Navasky Prize over the years included Jane Fonda for being Jane Fonda; journalist Bob Woodward for *Veil,* his exposé on the CIA; Occidental Petroleum chief Armand Hammer, friend to many Russian leaders, for "lifetime service to Soviet Union"; Warren Beatty for the pro–Bolshevik revolution movie *Reds;* investigative reporter Seymour Hersh for "destructive jihads against the American intelligence operations"; movie director Oliver Stone for "American celluloid lies"; Energy Secretary Hazel O'Leary for declassifying nuclear-related documents; and Clinton CIA director John Deutch for a variety of sins.

basting "the apotheosis of that type of American liberal who spent the Cold War inventing excuses for the Soviets that even the Soviets weren't willing to offer," as conservative publisher Al Regnery put it one year.

From the Pumpkin Paper Irregulars, Grover earned an award as a "revolutionary hero."

AFTER HIS 1978 GRADUATION from Harvard, Grover set up shop in Washington as the National Taxpayers Union's resident whirling dervish, talking to local activists on two phones at the same time, pacing his office, eyes intense behind thick glasses, shifting stacks of piles back and forth, at work until all hours of the night. (Grover never could sit still: In restaurant meetings, his hands transmitted the electric charge when his body couldn't, as he moved salt shakers to and fro, picked up sugar packages to shake, switched the catsup with the mustard—leaving one wondering what would happen if he was forced to sit at a table cleared of condiments.) When Grover went on the road, he likewise operated like a fidgety young operative on a time-sensitive mission. In Las Vegas on one trip, he stayed up all night at a casino, cramming strategy sessions into the fifteen-minute breaks of a blackjack table manager who also happened to be a tax activist. In between, he killed time shooting video game tanks.

NTU had been at the forefront of national efforts to aid Howard Jarvis's Proposition 13 campaign in California. The group's next audacious moves included helping Jarvis take the initiative nationwide and pushing for a balanced budget amendment to the U.S. Constitution. Twelve states had already endorsed the idea of a constitutional convention to craft an amendment. With the mundane title of associate director, one of Grover's first assignments was to help bring that number to the constitutionally required thirty-four, a challenge that proved a good outlet for Norquist's hyperactivity.

Three months into the NTU job, Norquist was promoted. That gave him a chance, as spokesman, to try out his hard-core rhetoric on the Washington press corps, which he did with youthful exuberance. "Two shibboleths have been smashed," the twenty-two-year-old counseled a *Washington Post* reporter writing about the taxpayer revolt. "One said that paying taxes to government was like giving to the United Way, and the other said that you get it all back in services. The facts are that government is not a benevolent charity—the poverty program didn't help the poor, it helped the bureaucrats—and government is not providing services efficiently. You go to city hall or the post office and what do you see? Bureaucrats pushing papers, drinking coffee, and harassing people." Nothing but constitutional amendments, he argued, could stop tax-hiking legislators, "those slimy sons of guns that they are" who "drive their Sherman tanks through the loopholes" of tax legislation.

Grover and his peers, who found their political footing on campus in the 1970s and early 1980s, formed a third generation of postwar American conservatives. The first was primarily a generation of intellectuals—such as Friedrich A. Hayek, Richard M. Weaver, James Burnham, Russell Kirk, and William F. Buckley Jr.—and was highlighted by the founding of the magazines *Human Events* in 1944 and *National Review* in 1955. The second generation was activist, dating back to the Draft Goldwater movement of the early 1960s. By the time Grover first arrived in Washington, these second-generation leaders were already ensconced on the national scene with a network of well-financed lobby groups known as the New Right.

The New Right had attitude and dollars to blow. Its bank-rollers included the names that would become familiar nemeses to liberals—Colorado beer brewer Joseph Coors; Vicks Vaporub heir H. Smith Richardson Jr.; Fred C. Koch, the oil magnate whose political tastes ran to purist libertarian causes; former Treasury Secretary William Simon, who ran the John M. Olin Foundation and (with Irving Kristol) founded the Institute for Educational Affairs to fund conservative agitprop; Richard Viguerie, who introduced his rightist friends to the allure of direct mail fund-raising; and Richard Mellon Scaife, the reclusive publisher who earned his notoriety with a 1981 *Columbia Journalism Review* profile in which he accused the reporter of being an ugly communist with bad teeth, a smear he laced, for good measure, in vivid obscenity.

In the late 1970s, when the mainstream press first awoke to its size and scope, the New Right was a behemoth to behold. The Heritage Foundation, founded by Paul Weyrich and Coors in 1973, was on its way to prominence and lasting influence, particularly during the Reagan years. Weyrich's Committee for the Survival of a Free Congress was credited with helping elect key New Right allies to Congress. (The committee labeled a third of House members as leftist "radicals.") Terry Dolan's National Conservative Political Action Committee was raising millions to defeat liberal candidates, with shrill fundraising letters he admitted were designed to "stir up hostilities." Viguerie and Howard Phillips's Conservative Caucus were trying to coordinate the activities of a booming network of "home and family" groups. Phyllis Schlafly was closing in on her life goal of killing the Equal Rights Amendment. And a fundamentalist preacher from Lynchburg, Virginia, named Jerry Falwell had just founded the Moral Majority to enable Christian conservatives to muscle their way into Washington.

Later, groups such as NCPAC and the Moral Majority collapsed, driven under by the same expensive direct mail campaigns that had built their membership lists. But in the 1970s, the New Right was brimming not only with cash but also with shock troops activated by the liberal drift of America since the 1960s, especially the Supreme Court decisions permitting abortion, protecting the rights of criminals, outlawing school prayer, and lending First Amendment protection to pornographers. By the middle of the decade, children were being bused to schools outside their neighborhoods to achieve court-mandated goals on racial makeup. Women were throwing tradition to the wind and pouring into the workforce, loudly demanding equal standing with men. More and more parents were divorcing, while their kids were inhaling mind-numbing smoke and pills, their bodies gyrating to the rhythms of rock and, worse, each other. Fear has always been a terrific political motivator, and in the 1970s the New Right leaders viscerally understood its explosive potential.

Howard Phillips told one writer that the only answer for America's ills was to "resort to biblical law." In Congress, legislators on the Right forced roll-call votes designed to put liberals on the defensive over such flagship issues as abortion and school prayer. Homosexuality was a popular bugaboo. In Florida, Anita Bryant attracted the Right's support with her campaign against the "evil influence" of homosexuals. In California, state senator John V. Briggs sponsored a referendum to bar homosexuals from teaching in public schools, a proposal that Reagan refused to endorse on civil libertarian grounds. Phil Crane's name appeared on a NCPAC fund-raising letter carrying the message: "Our nation's moral fiber is being weakened by the growing homosexual movement and the fanatical ERA pushers (many of whom publicly brag they are lesbians)." (A few years later, NCPAC's founder, Terry Dolan, who hid his life as a gay man, would die of complications related to AIDS.)

Seeing nothing but trouble in these divisive issues, the National Taxpayer Union brass counseled its staff, including Grover, to steer clear of the New Right. Fund-raising was hard enough: Taxpayer groups always struggled, partly because they represented citizens who didn't like to hand over money to anyone, even lobbyists on their behalf, and partly because of the defeatism of citizens who believed that death and taxes really *are* inevitable. Allying the tax movement with social conservatives would risk splitting a broad, if fragile, donor base. Besides, the NTU officials wanted to leave enough wiggle room in their lobby work for alliances with liberals—including environmental groups and the ACLU—on such projects as killing the Clinch River Breeder Reactor and devising a taxpayers' bill of rights.

But Grover had his own ideas, and his own agenda. He would never last long inside any organization, other than one of his own design, and NTU was no exception. When he arrived in states to organize for the balanced budget amendment, he reached out not only to libertarians, but also to social conservatives around the country. He befriended outspoken moral police such as Schlafly, who opposed NTU's drive for a constitutional convention to balance the budget, fearing such a session would give liberals a chance to sneak in an Equal Rights Amendment. In Washington, Norquist made it a point every Friday morning to attend Paul Weyrich's Kingston meetings, a strategy session of New Right activists.

Like Grover, the New Rightists divided the world into Good Guys and Bad Guys. Like Grover, the New Rightists saw themselves as outsiders, revolutionaries, battling a staid and corrupt liberal establishment, one that also infested the Republican Party. "The Good Guys," wrote Alan Crawford, a close observer of the period, "are those individuals who are untainted by liberalism or moderation; they oppose it to the last corral, shooting it out like some Wild West sheriff holding off the outlaws of liberalism. . . . The New Rightists show their greatest contempt not for liberals but for individuals who are reluctant to ride the plains alone, who have adjusted to national politics."

From the New Rightists, Grover would borrow the word "squish," their term of art for yellow-bellied conservatives who couldn't muster the courage of their convictions, who caved in the face of a craving for broader public support. Washington insiders such as Senator Howard Baker, William Brock, and Senator Robert Dole topped the squish list. But even Barry Goldwater, who supported super-squish Gerald Ford in 1976, provoked the ire of many in the New Right. To some hard-core activists, Ronald Reagan was a squish in the mid-1970s; his 1976 campaign had attracted the professional class, eager to swap political stands for votes, and he had picked moderate Senator Richard Schweiker as a running mate. To Grover, Reagan was too old, too soft. The young activist was far more attracted to the talk of "confiscatory taxation" by the harder-edged Philip Crane, the youthful Illinois congressman and former chairman of the American Conservative Union who, like Reagan, was a contender for the 1980 GOP presidential nomination.

Still, as a libertarian who wanted government to stay out of all aspects of people's lives, Grover was not a precise fit with much of the New Right. He didn't think much about social issues such as abortion or homosexuality that so inflamed these second-generation conservatives. He supposed, if pressed, that he was "reasonably pro-life" (though one friend was left with the impression that he was pro-choice in those days). If asked in private, he might offer a put-down of homosexuals by saying he never knew any who were "truly gay." But he didn't see the point in enforcing sodomy laws, or issuing rhetorical attacks on the gay community. He couldn't abide by government-enforced affirmative action programs, but was perfectly comfortable working beside blacks or women or anyone else who cared to join the Good Guys team. He was bemused that "swarthy-looking" immigrants (as he called them) made so many New Right leaders nervous; personally he didn't have any problems throwing open America's borders, as long as government handouts weren't the lure.

He was raised Methodist, and remained a believer, but he was not a regular churchgoer and he had no interest talking about religious issues in the political arena. He hewed to the standard libertarian line that making drug use a crime caused more problems than the drug war (though he wasn't going to make an issue out of it while the welfare state was still around, forcing people to pay for others' mistakes). Mostly, in Norquist's mind, there wasn't much that should be entrusted to the government, other than fighting communists—and even that, in the 1970s, Washington seemed to be making a mess of. He didn't get caught up in the New Right's sky-is-falling frenzy over the Panama Canal treaties, though he appreciated the political symbolism of it—a weakened America giving up control of a strategic asset to some tinhorn dictator. Instead, he worried about the gains the Soviets were making globally, especially in Africa.

Baby-boom activists such as Norquist, products of the campus wars of the 1970s, detected a subtle difference between themselves and the older New Rightists. There were fewer old-fashioned moralists (like Weyrich) among them. They were coming of age just as free market economist Milton Friedman was enjoying celebrityhood, with a best-selling book and TV show. His antigovernment message connected with a reality that voters could grasp, and the young activists sensed it. "The Post Office was inefficient, the potholes didn't get fixed, taxes kept going up," Friedman recalled. "People got disillusioned." Friedman was one of the figures who offered these young people a way to avoid addressing divisive social issues: Blame the government, where aggressive liberal policies had forced these matters into the public arena. Make the argument that if you take judges and bureaucrats out of the business of social hall monitor, these issues wouldn't cause such turmoil. School prayer, he insisted, wouldn't be an issue if schools were in private hands, and parents could shop for academic and religious preferences.

If the younger generation allied themselves with the New Right's politics of resentment, they also infused it with more confidence. They didn't carry with them the stench of decades of defeat. Norquist was in elementary school when the Right's hero, Barry Goldwater, was crushed by LBJ, a defining moment for the old guard. While Grover was certain that the country's institutions of influence—the media, academia, government—were held captive by the Left, he always believed that most Americans agreed with him. It never occurred to Grover that he might be representing a minority position, or that he wouldn't eventually win. By the time Grover arrived on the national political scene, Ronald Reagan was on his way to victory, and vociferous lawmakers on the Right were shaking the halls of Congress. More to the point: The Carter administration had an uncanny ability to make liberalism look crusty, inept.

The baby-boom Rightists were certain of victory and hungry for power. Grover's winsome confidence that he could build a movement that might one day lop the federal government by half, or more, provoked some smirks. "The conventional wisdom was that there's no way—he'll never be able to do the stuff he wants to do," said Republican activist Ann Stone. "Poor Grover thinks all this stuff is possible." Like his peers, Grover was also instinctively more inclusive than the older crowd. He intended to give voice to the voiceless, though in his world the voiceless weren't poor urban ethnics, but rural and suburban religious fundamentalists who initially confounded and discomfited some of the old-line conservatives. Grover met his first fundamentalist, his friend Peter Ferrara, at Harvard, and by the time he reached Washington he saw this crowd as a valuable ally.

The Goldwater generation saw American popular culture as something alien, frightening, dangerous. But the twenty-something activists who flooded Washington in the late 1970s and early 1980s frequented action thrillers, tuned in to *Saturday Night Live*, listened to rock and roll, were imbued with a *National Lampoon* sense of humor. Grover, in what seemed to be a determined attempt to relieve himself of his nerdish image, listened to Janis Joplin and had a brief foray as a Grateful Dead fan; he was puzzled by the panic that rock music set off with the older crowd. His approach to moral issues was to keep them out of the discussion ("no sex please," he would tell friends in strategy sessions). He figured if he didn't wave a red flag by bringing up social issues, no one would charge.

Despite these generational distinctions, the New Right represented the pure, undiluted expression of the free-market, anticommunist dogma that made Norquist's life a political calling. What he saw when he looked at the New Right were comrades-in-arms who hated government, hated taxes, hated gun control. (Actually, Grover believed that guns were more important than taxes: "Once they get our guns, they don't have to argue with you about taxes anymore.") Just as important, they set off ear-piercing alarms within the liberal-leaning media and political establishments. Grover figured they must be doing something right.

Norquist's mission, forged in the late 1970s, was to stitch together an antigovernment coalition to take over the Republican Party, and then Washington. But before he could take on these grand ambitions, Grover had to satisfy his father's wishes and return to Harvard to earn his MBA (where, of course, he sparred with his Keynesian professors). That done, he returned to Washington after Ronald Reagan's election to wage an eight-year battle with the "squishes" controlling the Republican Party.

CHAPTER 4

WHITE MALE

Race, that El Niño of American politics and culture, roiled college campuses in the 1970s, disrupting, overturning, confusing social codes. If the great divide of campus activism in the 1960s was between student and administration, rebel and establishment, young and old, by the late 1970s it had opened between student and student, white and black, bilingual and "monolingual elitist," to borrow one militant term of art. The first wave of liberal-activist baby boomers had organized themselves around ideology and cause—civil rights, free speech, the Vietnam War, social democracy; the second wave found common cause in personal traits—being female, being gay, being black, being Latino.

This was not a friendly environment for a law student who was a fervent proselytizer of individualism, a white male who openly criticized any attempt to level the playing field by roping off reserved sections for women and minorities. Clint Bolick would have encountered resistance to his libertarian philosophy at any number of topnotch law schools (all of which would soon be under order by the American Bar Association to adopt race-based affirmative action programs). But in 1979 he chose one of the most hostile settings around: the ten-year-old Martin Luther King Law School at the University of California, Davis, just a brisk walk from the medical school that had been the target of Allan Bakke's famed "reverse discrimination" lawsuit.

It was tempting to slap the label "angry white male" on this young man, cloaked as he was in righteous certainty that neither his gender nor his skin color had conferred any special privileges. His welder father died when he was twelve, leaving the family in precarious financial standing, and Clint had financed his undergraduate studies by patching together scholarships, loans, and work in the local Shop-Rite grocery store. He was the product of a working-class New Jersey town, part of an Anglo minority that shared neither ethnic identity nor an immigrant's experience. With the nation's employers and colleges embracing affirmative action in the 1970s, Bolick, Bakke, and other less-than-privileged young men bitterly concluded they now were forced to play a game of Life in which the dice were tossed before they could take their place at the table.

But with Bolick, the angry-white-male box wasn't an exact fit. This was a young man with a goofy sense of humor, a wicked talent for mimickry, a reputation as an incurable romantic, and aspirations to write the great American novel. His face, and his voice, were doughy soft. Years later, when he was one of the Right's leading constitutional lawyers, seen pleading his cases before high courts, one could just as easily picture him in costume at a kids' birthday party (maybe as a clown, with his hairline receding into character), and the kids pulling at his cheeks (because he had that kind of face, fleshy and pliable). Even in court, he talked in story narrative, his characters heroic figures struggling against the cold calculations of self-interested bureaucrats.

The word "idealist" in modern American parlance is generally reserved for those of liberal persuasion—the college student who joins the Peace Corps to help the poor, the environmentalist determined to save the rain forest. Young people on the Right are supposed to be too hard-headed, too accepting of man's original sin, too skeptical of altruistic claims for remaking society to earn such a label. But Bolick would become (if one conceded that such a creature might exist) a right-wing idealist, an intensely ambitious but determined crusader whose motives always confounded his liberal foes. Although he would gain a reputation in the 1990s as a militant anti–affirmative action activist, most of his legal work was on behalf of poor minority clients in antiregulatory and school voucher cases. As a boy, he was weaned on the casual bigotry of a father he adored; as a man, he would attempt to cast himself as the Right's version of civil rights crusader.

But behind this idealism was also an intense, almost desperate, desire to be noticed, and liked. His hunger for acceptance often helped his work, and he broadened the movement by constantly seeking unlikely allies on the Left. That hunger, however, also revealed an inner demon, for Bolick was also, at times, an intensely insecure man. Setbacks and attacks—whether against him or a pair of father-figure mentors in his life that included Clarence Thomas—didn't roll off easily. Politics for Bolick wasn't a game (as it sometimes was for Kristol); it wasn't war (as it always was for Norquist), it was, rather, a personal mission, a test of his own metal. When he fell, he fell hard. "More than anyone I've ever known," said one friend, "Clint goes into complete despair and depression. He feels like a failure. He can't put a loss in perspective."

If, in the 1990s, Clint Bolick appeared the rabid right-winger, the bane of the Clinton Administration's civil rights team, it had much to do with deeply felt scars left by earlier ideological battles.

AS A YOUNG MAN completing his undergraduate studies, Clint opted to "save the world" through constitutional law rather than politics after a summer internship on Capitol Hill revealed the less savory side of American politics. He was drawn to the bar by a two-semester constitutional law course he took as a senior at New Jersey's Drew University, and by the landmark Supreme Court decision in *Brown* v. *Board of Education*. That 1954 decision not only ended segregation in public schools, but also set the stage for overturning the color bar on beaches and in bathhouses, on municipal golf courses and in public transportation. To the impressionable young Bolick, the decision represented a "triumph of the principle of equality," a momentous judicial action that, literally overnight, ushered in sweeping social change.

That Bolick would find lifelong inspiration in a court case revered by progressives hinted at a recurring theme in his future career, in which he would draw on liberal verities (the goal of a color-blind society) for the express purpose of undermining liberal verities (support for affirmative action). He sent out his applications to half a dozen law schools, presumptuously hoping for a career that might one day lead him up the steps of the U.S. Supreme Court to argue a constitutional case of similar import.

Bolick didn't fully understand it yet, but he was about to learn a hard lesson: He was swimming upstream in the public opinion wars on college campuses, where the enlightened view held that discrimination was so pervasive in America that persons of color could never reach an equal footing without special treatment. As Supreme Court Justice Harry A. Blackmun explained in his written opinion on the Bakke case: "In order to get beyond racism, we must first take account of race. There is no other way. . . . In order to treat persons equally, we must treat them differently."

By the time Clint settled on law as a career in 1979, affirmative action was deeply embedded in the economy. The U.S. Census had been recording ethnic origins for a decade. Washington agencies enforced employment diversity in government contracts and on universities that received federal funding—virtually all of them. None, certainly not U.C. Davis, admitted to using quotas, reserving a set number of slots for applicants based on skin color or sex. But if minorities and women were to make progress, and if progress was to be measured, numbers had to be used. Corporate officers studied the ethnic makeup of labor pools to establish numerical targets; universities compared the racial composition of their enrollment figures to that of high-school graduation classes. In the late 1970s, California officials fretted that only 27 percent of the students in the state's university system were minorities, compared to 37 percent of high school graduates in the state.

The Supreme Court's 1978 Bakke decision, one of the most eagerly awaited of the decade, upheld the prospective medical student's contention that he had been a victim of reverse discrimination. But it also affirmed the right of colleges to consider race as one of many factors in admissions. In other words, the Davis medical school's admissions policy, based on a system that looked suspiciously like quotas, went too far. But short of that, the court considered affirmative action a legal way to give minority students an extra leg up.

On September 26, 1978, in the wake of that ruling and one year before Clint entered the U.C. Davis law school, Allan Bakke shouldered his way through a crush of reporters and protesters to attend his first day of medical school. The quiet, publicity-shy man was trailed by forty local and national reporters and greeted by about a hundred protesters marching and carrying such signs as FIGHT NATIONAL OPPRESSION. A law student addressing the protesters called the Bakke decision "the symbol of the new racist trends in housing and employment against minorities."

Six months later, during spring break in 1979, Clint visited the Davis campus for the first time and settled on King Hall as his top-choice law school. The politics of race were not uppermost on Bolick's mind that lovely spring week. He didn't hear the shouts of protesters or read the accusations of racism against the university filling the school's student newspaper. What he heard in the air was the meditative click-click-click of bikes, scores of them, as they criss-crossed the town and campus, ferrying students through seemingly blissful daily lives. Bike paths were everywhere, jutting through the pines that arched lushly and fragrantly above the university's green lawns, hugging roads that stretched through the farmlands surrounding Davis, a view as flat and endless as an Iowa horizon. To the twenty-one-year-old Bolick, it was all so idyllic, promising a pastoral break from the miserable eastern winters that had been haunting New Jersey.

He was accepted and enrolled in U.C. Davis's King Hall along with 22 Asians, 9 blacks, 16.5 La Raza (the current appellation for Latino), .5 Native American, 3 Filipino, and 3 students listed as "other," a minority population that comprised 26.2 percent of the class. Half-points were accorded students from mixed marriages. These were the best numbers King Hall had seen in years, and the dean declared this minority enrollment a "delightful improvement," though his efforts had been aided by his decision to expand the entering class from the usual 200 to 206 students.

Bolick had watched the controversy over Bakke unfold from afar. Now he was about to get his first taste of the lawsuit's bitter legacy: In the year since Bakke entered the medical school under police escort, this liberal university community had become prickly and defensive over questions of race, anxious to prove its commitment to ethnic diversity. Bolick would become part of an intriguing racial subplot at the law school—one that would harden his own position, and foreshadow future strains in the nation's widely accepted proposition that a just society should seek "not just equality as a right and a theory, but equality as a fact and a result," as President Lyndon B. Johnson declared in 1965.

Shortly before the fall session opened, Clint stashed his belongings inside a roof carrier on his Volkswagen Dasher, and, with his girlfriend on the passenger side, headed west across the country. The trip may have been an omen of the tough times to come: The VW kept breaking down, and Bolick's cash supply dwindled as he reached into his wallet for repairs. In Reno, Nevada, the couple celebrated their last night of travel by spending most of the money they had left, splurging on a night out on the town. When Clint went to retrieve his car from the hotel valet the next morning, it was gone. The VW, along with the roof carrier full of his belongings, had been stolen.

Driving a rental car, Bolick made it to Davis in time for the start of classes. Late summer heat had settled in along the Sacramento Valley, turning the lush greens of spring into a lifeless brown as a scorching autumn approached. West of Sacramento and surrounded by farmland, the college town of Davis was frying in its own political heat—the fallout from Bakke.

Before Bakke, no one had questioned Davis's commitment to progressive politics. During the 1960s, the town had imported bits and pieces of youth counterculture—the bong shops and natural food stores, the smell of incense and talk of oppression—leaving the more violent radical action to its cousin campus ninety minutes away, U.C. Berkeley. In the 1970s, Davis students picketed alongside farmworkers, and Tom Hayden's leftist Campaign for Economic Democracy ran competitively in municipal elections.

With the Bakke ruling, however, Davis risked earning the image as a bastion of angry white males. In the months following the Bakke ruling, Davis's minority students routinely accused the university of pervasive racism—in the composition of its faculty and student body, in admissions policies that employed standardized test scores, in everyday "subtle racisms" and "patronizing attitudes," as one student leader asserted at the time. The "token" inclusion of minorities in governing bodies on campus was condemned as racist. When the university eliminated funding for a Chicano dance troupe, three dozen activists seized the student newspaper offices to protest the alleged racism of the act.

"Welcome Back to King Hall" proclaimed the first issue of the *King Hall Advocate* that Clint picked up from a newspaper bin on his way to the first day of class. But the story that filled the front page of the law school's student newspaper was less hospitable. Under the headline "Those Summertime Blues," the article recounted how, the previous spring, eight law students had been "disqualified"—expelled, to use a less bureaucratically vague term—because they had failed to maintain at least a C average.

"King Hall holds the dubious distinction of leading the U.C. law schools in the number of students disqualified," the article ominously asserted. Students who had appealed their fate at an August hearing had been accompanied by protestors rallying under the banner: CHANGE THE PROCEDURES. LAWYERS FOR COMMUNITIES, NOT CORPORATE PROFITS. The pressure had some affect: On the day of the hearing, six of the eight students were reinstated.

Like so much else at Davis that year, this story was really about race: Most of the students expelled each year had been admitted under the school's affirmative action program, which granted bonus points to minority applicants in an attempt to diversify a mostly white student body. Some of the affirmative action students who entered Davis with lower undergraduate grades and test scores couldn't keep up. Those whose grade point averages dropped below a 2.0 received a springtime letter from the dean informing them that they should not make plans to continue in the fall. Despite the appeals process outlined in each dispatch, the letters typically ended with the dean's admonition, "If I may speak candidly, I do not encourage you to petition."

This system of expelling students, which offered no probationary period or second chances, was a tactless annual ritual, discomforting for everyone involved. Law school professor Ed Rabin described the system as "the best possible way to create anger and civil unrest." After receiving this crushing letter, the "disqualified" student could petition for reinstatement by showing up before the entire faculty for a ten-minute appeal, showing that "extraordinary circumstances" had prevented him or her from performing up to par. "They'd come in with their excuses—they were sick, there was an illness in the family, whatever—and the faculty was supposed to decide which ones were valid," recalled Rabin. Invariably, as the hearings convened each summer, the sound of protesters accusing the faculty of racism filled the air outside.

The process was equally disturbing to much of the faculty, especially because those expelled were usually minorities, and the law school was having enough trouble keeping up respectable minority enrollment numbers. Student leaders estimated that one-quarter to one-third of all affirmative action students who enrolled each year were expelled within twelve months, and questioned whether King Hall deserved to bear the slain martyr's name.

Few questioned the validity of race-based admissions policies, or, if they did, they didn't volunteer that opinion. The law school had its own Bakke case, filed by a white male named Glen DeRonde, who claimed he was unfairly passed over because of King Hall's race-conscious admissions policy. The student paper treated him as a villain in this ongoing drama. (In 1980, the California Supreme Court rejected DeRonde's claim, and the U.S. Supreme Court let that decision stand.) Law school officials responded to allegations of racism by releasing more numbers and more recruitment plans to prove their commitment to diversity. Professor Rabin, a liberal who in 1968 pushed forward the student proposal to name Davis's law school after Martin Luther King, recalled learning early on that it was unwise to advertise his own "moral opposition" to racial preferences, so he kept quiet. Another liberal, California Supreme Court

Justice Stanley Mosk, who wrote the state-level ruling upholding Bakke's challenge (before it was appealed to Washington), was the target of vociferous protest when the law school invited him to deliver a commencement address. Recounting the experience to two chroniclers of the Bakke case, Mosk remarked, "I have been harassed a good deal by the Third World Coalition. I see no difference between their position and that of George Wallace. They both want race to be a factor, and I don't."

It was clear that Clint would be virtually alone in voicing doubts about race-based preferences. He entered law school just as King Hall's Law Student Association was adopting its own minority recruitment plan, declaring that "diminishing minority representation among students is the most significant problem facing King Hall." The student president, a white male, outlined a plan to send teams of law students to nearby colleges to help minority candidates with "unimpressive GPA's and LSAT's to qualify for affirmative action with strong personal statements and letters of recommendation. . . . We're helping marginal candidates get into the group of accepted students."

Clint was charmed by the wrongheadedness he was convinced he saw around him. As an undergraduate at Drew, he had spent most of his political energy combating student apathy. But here at Davis, meaty discussions about race and politics filled the columns of the newspaper and the corridors of King Hall, spilling out onto the tree-covered terrace adjoining the student lounge. Clint saw three happy years stretching out before him: By day, provoking good-natured arguments designed to show his leftist peers the errors of their ways; by night, feasting on wines from nearby Napa Valley, the centerpiece of his chosen new life as an epicure. "He was on fire. He was on fire with all of this," fellow student Luis Cid said of Clint's budding political passions.

Two weeks after arriving in Davis, Clint did what he always did when he had something to say: He ran for office, seeking a position on the law school's Faculty Recruitment Committee. Bolick advertised his candidacy in a statement arguing that the hiring of "high-quality educators" should be the committee's primary goal. In a thinly veiled criticism of the law school's emphasis on diversity, he added, "Any other goals must be subordinated to this fundamental one." Each of the other four candidates, however, made racial and gender diversity of the faculty their top priority. "The school currently has only one faculty member who is a member of a minority group," as one candidate wrote. "There are only five women. . . . We should and must give a high priority to creating a truly diverse faculty."

When the votes were tallied, Clint's fate at the law school came sharply into focus: Each of the candidates who had promoted efforts to diversify the faculty won. Clint alone lost.

The electoral loss was hardly life-altering, but it did signal the start of Clint's isolation from King Hall life. "See, they didn't dislike Clint," Cid said later of his friend. "They thought he was silly and ridiculous. . . . He was a little bit of a pariah. People made jokes about him. I was more interested in getting dates and just surviving. I'd say, 'Look, I think [the liberal positions are] all stupid and disgusting as well, but who are we? We're just two little law students. Why waste the time? Let's go have a beer.' Clint was more drawn into the debate and more willing to endure people's nasty remarks than I was. I just didn't want to draw attention to myself."

DONALD BOLICK had a deep Southern drawl and firm opinions on matters of race. His two sons would remember him as an early prototype of Archie Bunker, a comparison that fit, right down to his ratty armchair of a throne and his one black friend from work, which somehow proved that he wasn't a bigot, just a realist. It wasn't only blacks that Clint's father had problems with. Poles, Italians, Catholics, you name it (and there was his eldest son Jerry, always rebelling by falling in love with some Italian or Polish Catholic girl). In the refinery town of Linden, New Jersey, the Bolick family was part of a white minority who didn't share an ethnic identity; 13 percent of the town's residents were nonwhite and 40 percent, according to the 1970 census, were foreign-born or children of foreign-born parents. The town's European émigrés clung to their roots and language, its main street a mishmosh of Italian delis and Polish travel agencies advertising their wares and services in their native tongues.

Linden provided more than these displays of ethnic pride to feed his father's racial views: When his youngest son Clint was nine, Newark, the hub city just a twenty-minute bus ride away, exploded in one of the most destructive race riots of the century. On July 12, 1967, a black driver was pulled over for a traffic violation, a scuffle with police ensued, and unfounded rumors that the man had been killed touched off violence. By that summer, the pattern already had become familiar in its broad outlines during the previous "long hot summers" of racial violence in America's cities. In Newark, two years after the

Watts riots, twenty-six people died, all but two of them black, and 1,500 were injured. Police sealed off a third of the city, and barbed-wire barricades sealed Newark off from surrounding suburbs such as Linden. Some racial violence did spill over into Linden, but Newark's nervous neighbors mostly watched the drama unfold on TV. The shopping sprees to Newark's big-city department stores once enjoyed by Linden's working class, black and white, suddenly ended. Overnight, Newark became a city to avoid, a blight on the New Jersey landscape.

Donald Bolick had voted for Goldwater in 1964, but thereafter he was a George Wallace man, through and through. Short but compact, with wavy dark hair, a winning smile, and a fierce temper, Donald was a commanding presence in his modest household. He was a man of few words, but those few were sharp—and not to be challenged. "He was real tough physically," recalled his son Jerry. "I got hit as a kid, and wow—he could hit hard! I never felt like I was abused or anything like that, but I got hit if I got out of line. He had a big personality, and he ruled the house. I was afraid of him, yes, I was afraid of him." But, then, Jerry insisted, that seemed to be the case with most of the kids in their neighborhood of longshoremen and assembly line workers. "We were scared of each other's fathers," said Jerry. "They ruled the house, and you always went to Mom." Donald Bolick expressed his love not in words but in the swingsets he built for the kids in the backyard, or in the playrooms he carved out of the basement.

Jerry, the eldest, rebelled in the way many frustrated young men do against domineering fathers. He dropped out of college, joined the Marine Corps, and never came back. After the military, he settled in the Haight-Ashbury section of San Francisco with his new Filipino wife, appalling his father with the prospect of mixed-race—and Catholic—grandchildren. In contrast to Jerry's angry silence, his little sister Diane stood her ground and fought her father at every turn, and ended up staying close to home. Clint, the accidental third child, wasn't born until Jerry was nearly out of the house and Diane, at twelve, was moving into adolescence.

The strains between the two older children and their father thrust Mrs. Bolick into the role of peacemaker, "the one you could always count on," as Jerry put it. "My Rock of Gibraltar," said Clint. A slight woman, Emily Bolick had rarely been outside her hometown of Rahway, just a short drive from Linden, before she met Donald. She didn't learn to drive until after Clint was born. In between raising her three children, she looked forward to grabbing a cup of coffee with a friend at the local Woolworth coffee shop. She did what, and went where, her husband dictated. "Today, you would call her browbeaten," Jerry recalled of those early years.

Like father, like son. Donald Bolick, too, had rebelled against a strict upbringing. His runaway attempts as a teenager were legendary in the small North Carolina town where he was raised. Even after marrying and settling into a job as a factory welder in Linden, Clint's father remained restless. He would fix up one house and then decide he wanted to move into another, not five minutes away. "He loved change," said Mrs. Bolick. When Clint was eight, his father, attracted by higher factory wages, moved his family back to North Carolina. Clint noticed that his father had a friendly, easy relationship with the southern black families he knew; Donald Bolick just happened to believe (in that tortured way that Wallace Democrats made their racist case) that there was a "natural order of things." The move south lasted only a year: Clint's father decided to return to Linden, and his union, when the South's right-to-work labor conditions proved intolerable.

Clint had it easier with his father than did Jerry or Diane. By the time his youngest child came along, Donald Bolick was thirty-eight years old and considerably more mellow. Rather than fearing him, Clint remembers his father as romantic, imaginative, even silly at times. "I always thought they had this kind of magical relationship," said Jerry. Still, as he had with the first two children, Mr. Bolick had firm ideas about what Clint should do with his life. In his mind, the bright and talkative little boy—who would correct his mother's pronunciation when she read storybooks ("Mom, it's 'Mopsy, Flopsy, and Ag-a-MEM-non'"!)—was going to be somebody.

It didn't seem to bother his father that Clint was not athletic; he didn't try to toughen him up, as he had with Jerry, by putting boxing gloves on him and forcing him to learn how to punch. He was proud of his youngest boy's academic achievements, and let him know. Donald would hand his son a crisp five-dollar bill every time he brought home straight A's; he boasted about his son to his factory friends; he stretched the family finances far enough to move into a white-collar neighborhood so Clint could attend a better school, one with a name instead of a number. (Clint was certain he caught the neighbors looking askance at his father's workman overalls.)

Then, one nightmarish night when Clint was twelve, Donald Bolick was seized by a cerebral hemorrhage. His father collapsed in the wee hours of the morning with a cry of pain so awful it would forever ring in his son's ears. An alarmed Mrs. Bolick tried unsuccessfully to reach the family doctor, then called the police. Officers arrived within minutes, took her husband's pulse, and got the family doctor on the phone. Then came that sick, sinking feeling as Mrs. Bolick watched the physician who had delivered Clint walk up to the house and knock on their door—without his medical bag in hand. Only minutes had passed since she first called for help, but the officers had already declared her husband dead. Only Clint's closest friends would ever hear him talk about that terrible night, and even then he didn't say much; the memory was too wrenching.

Diane Bolick is convinced her little brother would have rebelled, just as she and Jerry did, if his father hadn't been stolen away from him that horror-filled night. Instead, Clint and his mother would have to focus on the business of just getting by. Donald Bolick hadn't left behind much in the way of savings. Clint's mother filed for survivor's benefits from the Social Security Administration, for herself and for Clint, and went back to work, as a cashier at Woolworth's. A few months later they headed west to be close to Jerry, settling in a garden apartment in Daley City, California, a working-class community just south of San Francisco. Mrs. Bolick took an office job with a travel agency.

That year in California provided Clint with his first introduction to politics. At Benjamin Franklin Junior High School, his eighth grade government teacher, Robert Lasley, opened the year with lessons in parliamentary procedure, then turned his students into the "U.S. Senate," as they introduced bills, debated, and engaged in power plays. "It was the last class of the day, and we lived for it," recalled classmate Jim Rogan, who went on to become a U.S. congressman and key leader of the impeachment effort against Bill Clinton.

Lasley also encouraged his students to volunteer for political campaigns, and they signed on with the nearby offices of the two rivals for California governor, Ronald Reagan and Jesse Unruh. Later, Bolick would tell fellow conservatives that he had worked on Ronald Reagan's 1970 gubernatorial campaign. In fact ("in classic brown-nosing fashion," he admitted), he was neglecting to mention that he also worked on Unruh's race.

A year later, Clint and his mother returned to New Jersey to care for his ailing grandmother, initially renting an apartment in Linden until Emily Bolick found an affordable house in the neighboring town of Hillside, a small but noticeable step down on the socioeconomic ladder. Clint worked as a box boy for the local Shop-Rite to help make ends meet. With his thick glasses and saggy shoulders, his polyester flares and printed shirts, Clint could hardly claim a place inside the cool crowd at Hillside High School. "As a guy who wasn't a nerd in high school, I can say that Clint was a nerd," recalled his brother Jerry. "He was somebody you would beat up on—smart, opinionated, could cut you down with a couple of sentences." Clint and his high school friend Lennie Clark entertained themselves by replaying Gothic horror scenes (in this town of ethnic loyalties "we were the only two Englishmen," Clark recalled in mild exaggeration) and episodes of *Dark Shadows,* the campy horror soap opera. Their idea of getting into trouble was smoking lettuce cigarettes under the train bridge late at night, which made them both miserably sick.

Politics, the art of smart talk, would lend Clint the kind of stature he couldn't find in sports or social life. Politics would give him a place in the spotlight, an outlet for his overwhelming energies. It would also lead him to a new father figure who would give shape to his vague political ambitions. Although he lived in the town next door, Clint was soon drawn back to Linden's vibrant political life. During election season, campaign signs multiplied like weeds in the town's front yards. The Linden City Hall was an imposing granite presence on the main shopping street, an excessive display of power for a suburban town of 41,000. Inside, the hall demanded the hushed respect of a church, with its wooden pews and walls trimmed in red and gold.

Clint had first met the town's charismatic mayor, John T. Gregorio, when he was eight years old and the politician was campaigning door to door. So upon his return from California, nursing a newfound ambition to be a politician, Clint tried to volunteer for the powerful Democratic mayor. But he couldn't get his foot in the door. So he instead made the life-altering decision, at age thirteen, to call upon Joseph P. Locascio, the lone Republican on the Linden town council and the man who represented the ward where Clint grew up.

Locascio called himself a Republican; in fact, this Sicilian was an iconoclastic reformer whose political philosophy could be summed up in his oft-used adage, "When you vote for the elephant or the donkey, that's what you get." "Joe" to his voters, "Mr. Locascio" to Clint, the councilman was a lonely warrior against a Democratic machine, controlled by Gregorio, that ruled Linden largely unchallenged. Mr. Locascio openly asserted that his town was ruled by a despotic political machine of protection and patronage, run for the privilege of the mayor and his cronies. Locascio's unyielding battles for term limits on city officials and for an elected—rather than a mayor-appointed—board of education were constant thorns in the side of local Democrats. He was a colorful figure who embarrassed his opponents by fighting the pay hikes they voted for themselves, and attempting to make public their closed-door meetings. "The majority is not silent," he would say. "The government is deaf."

One night, Clint and his friend Lennie Clark knocked on the front door of Locascio's home. The ninth-graders were lured by no more than the thrilling prospect of joining a political campaign; only later would they appreciate the purity, and danger, of Locascio's reform efforts. Locascio opened the door, cigar in hand, greeted the boys warmly, and waved them into his dining room. His wife filled the table with Italian pastries while Locascio and the boys talked long and lustily about the business of Linden politics. The meeting became a familiar ritual over the next four years, cementing Clint's lifelong relationship with Mr. Locascio, a father of four grown boys who, it seemed, had room for one more.

Locascio weakened Clint's Republican leanings, teaching him to put principle above party loyalty. Locascio's battles were not so much partisan conflicts as an ongoing personal siege against entrenched power. It was from Locascio that Clint first heard of something called "term limits." It was from Mr. Locascio that Clint began to appreciate populist rhetoric and grass-roots advocacy. Locascio prided himself on knowing the names of just about every voter in Ward 2, as well as those of their children. To Clint, Locascio was "one of the greatest statesmen I ever met."

At Hillside High, Clint formed the Linden-Hillside Teenage Republican Club, a motley assortment of about a dozen kids who met in Clint's basement bedroom and recruited Locacsio as their "adviser." Clint's public relations skills as an adolescent were precocious, and uncanny. The local newspaper covered, in detail, the doings of the tiny teenage Republican club (which, when all was said and done, was mostly a platform for Clint). The paper published stories when the club members endorsed candidates—and when they failed to endorse. Each year, it reported the youth club's annual "man of the year" awards honoring local officials. Even the club's disbandment earned a sizeable story in the paper. "After a colorful history spanning three years, the Linden-Hillside Teenage Republicans disbanded on Election Night," the paper reported in 1976. Clint was quoted as saying the group couldn't attract enough members. "Young people today are terrribly apathetic," he complained.

Clint's name also appeared in the local paper when he was admitted to the National Honor Society, when he was named Boy of the Month by the Hillside Lions Club, when he received an internship with Senator Orrin Hatch in Washington, when he took part in a student trip to the Soviet Union, and when he was hit by a car and slightly injured while working in the Shop-Rite parking lot. (Clint relayed the whole story to the news reporter, noting that the women who hit him dismissed the whole episode with a snide "Well, ya ain't dead!" before driving off.)

But mostly Clint's name appeared in the letters-to-the-editor pages. Providing a glimpse into his evolving, and varied, political views, his letters were written in the adult-speak of an overly mature adolescent. He submitted letters on how to spice up the high school's English classes ("boredom leads to frustration; frustration leads to trouble"); on the decision by Hillside's sole movie theater to feature a pornographic film ("an insult to both the youth and to clean-minded adults who don't want to waste money on 'garbage' "); on pay raises for New Jersey state cabinet officials ("in my opinion, the $41,000 they now receive is more than sufficient"); on the arrogance of local police ("seems to me we should be talking about pay cuts, not increases, and about firing some of the obnoxious officers").

Clint spent hours each week with Mr. Locascio, at his dining room table, in his office, in Clint's basement during teen Republican meetings. He took up Locascio's white-hat cause of reforming city politics with a vengeance. Opposition to the Democratic machine in Linden was slight. The Republican Party was "dormant at best, utterly bankrupt at worst," as Clint later recalled. The Democratic mayor and his allies were quite popular: They kept taxes low, and services efficient and extensive. Patronage, exercised through service clubs and ethnic organizations, cemented the mayor's broad reach.

In 1974, when he was seventeen, Clint witnessed the political destruction of his mentor and father figure. The months leading up to the incident were difficult ones for the town's mayor. A handful of the mayor's officials were indicted on charges of running an illegal lottery, extortion, and other abuses of office. Mayor Gregorio himself was the target of an investigation by a state-appointed prosecutor that would later result in an indictment on charges of extortion and perjury. (Gregorio, who would later be acquitted, asserted he was the victim of a conspiracy against him.) Meanwhile, Locascio, seeking reelection for the fourth time, stepped up his attacks on the entrenched Democrats.

In December, after his reelection victory, Locascio's name hit the headlines: He stood accused of receiving unwarranted disability payments from the federal Department of Health, Education, and Welfare for a psychotic illness. HEW, alleging that Locascio had lied about his mental health, was suing him to recover the money. In fact, Mr. Locascio did suffer from an undisclosed psychological condition, which had been successfully controlled with medication. He had been in a long-running dispute with HEW over the payments and the nature of his disability.

But the disclosure about his mental health ruined his public reputation, and he had no choice but to resign from office. "I want you to know," he told Linden's voters in an emotional goodbye, "I have done nothing wrong. . . . I believed that my personal problems were private and should rest and remain with myself and my family."

Clint remained convinced that the leak against his beloved mentor was the vicious doing of Linden's Democratic machine. If other young people in that post-Watergate era saw Democrats as reformers, Clint saw Linden's Democratic Party as an entrenched, and corrupt, power structure. At Drew University five years later, he would use his senior thesis to vindicate Joe Locascio, condemning the Linden Democratic machine for preying on the "apathy, ignorance, and impotence of the citizenry." Twenty years later, Mr. Locascio lived alone in an assisted-care facility for the elderly, and John Gregorio was still mayor of Linden.

FROM LINDEN, it was a natural progression from Clint's contempt for official power to libertarianism, a philosophy rejecting collective control over individuals. As an undergraduate at Drew University, he discovered the macho individualism of Ayn Rand when he devoured her influential novel *Atlas Shrugged*. At the time, the acerbic writer-philosopher was enjoying a revival, especially on college campuses. She preached a "new morality of rational self-interest," insisted the concept of God was "morally evil," and proclaimed capitalism as the only moral economic system. Seduced, Clint declared himself an atheist and took to wearing a dollar-sign around his neck.

He discovered another political hero in Thomas Paine, the rootless revolutionary propagandist who transformed the philosophy of limited government into "common sense" in order to rally colonialists against the English throne. In many ways, Paine was a strange idol for a modern political conservative. (Political allies would later scold Bolick for constantly quoting him.) A one-time tax collector, Paine owned no property, claimed no family, called no place home, had a reputation as an indolent freeloader, was disdainful of wealth, and supported the French Revolution. But Bolick was captivated by Paine's denunciation of slavery, his courageous and near-traitorous attacks on King George, and his unshakable distrust of power: "Society in every state is a blessing," Paine wrote, "but government even in its best state is but a necessary evil; in its worst state an intolerable one." Perhaps no remark better summed up the libertarian label that Clint feverishly adopted.

In their desire for a radical downsizing of government power, modern American libertarians reflected an unlikely marriage of Left (stop the draft, end most overseas military interventions) and Right (eliminate public highways, cut federal agencies). As libertarian writer David Boaz has explained the philosophy: "Libertarianism proposes a society of liberty under law, in which individuals are free to pursue their own lives so long as they respect the equal rights of others." The purists adored its consistency: End welfare to individuals—and corporations. Keep the government out of our wallets—and our bedrooms.

So, when Clint openly opposed U.C. Davis law school's affirmative action program, he brought to his case something quite different from straight conservative politics, or even white male anger. But his class peers weren't interested in the nuance. By Thanksgiving of 1979, his first semester in law school, Clint—desperately lonely and struggling with his studies—was thinking seriously about dropping out. The atmosphere at King Hall was intensely competitive, made more so because those who could not maintain a 2.0 grade point average faced expulsion. The work was hard and tedious; even Clint, normally an A student, wasn't doing well. He also had trouble learning to think like a lawyer. Law students were expected to argue a case from every side; but Clint saw just two sides—right and wrong. Law students were expected to ferret out a dozen courses of action; Clint could see just one. His grades dropped to B's and C's.

Luis Cid convinced his friend to put aside his fantasies about becoming a teacher and remain in law school. Clint made it through the holidays, only to be stricken by mononucleosis in early 1980. By the spring, though, he was recharged, and decided to run for a California state assembly seat on the Libertarian Party ticket. The party was then at its peak, with Ed Clark running for president and his running-mate, energy mogul David Koch, bringing a million dollars to the effort. The pair ran on a platform of cutting taxes, equal rights for women and homosexuals, legalizing drugs and prostitution (to libertarians, these were "victimless" crimes and police crackdowns only exacerbated inner city problems), and removing the government from energy planning, education, Social Security, and a host of other areas of life.

Clint's unofficial campaign consultant was a journalism student at nearby Sacramento State University, John Fund, who would later become one of Grover Norquist's closest friends and a key voice for baby-boom conservatives as an editorial writer at the *Wall Street Journal*. Fund, a walking encyclopedia of political and media gossip, steered Clint toward useful contacts. They raised $7,500 and crafted a stump speech rich in the anticorporate rhetoric that endeared the libertarians to much of the leftist press that year, attacking such corporate goodies as import tariffs and business subsidies. "The real scoundrel in society is not the poor welfare recipient but the rich welfare recipient," Clint proclaimed. Clint and his family—like David McIntosh and his—had benefited from the same government largesse that libertarians denounced. He had been able to afford law school because he chose a publicly funded university; once he established residency, his costs were minimal. That, however, didn't stop Clint from running for office with a promise to institute a new tuition system that would free California's taxpayers from the burden of educating the state's "elite" students.

Clint crafted his campaign to appeal to young people who were economically conservative but socially liberal. He offered a detailed plan to cut state spending, but to Davis's liberal student audiences in particular he emphasized his support for drug decriminalization and ending the military draft registration that President Carter had recently reinstated. "I felt like I had a noose around my neck when I saw friends busted for drugs and kids being registered for the draft," he told one campus audience.

Running against an incumbent Democrat, Clint lost in the same November 1980 election that sent Ronald Reagan to the presidency, but not before collecting 7.1 percent of the votes in his race, a better showing than Libertarian presidential candidate Clark, who barely topped 1 percent nationally. Bolick's career as a candidate ended as it had begun—in the letters-to-the-editor column of the student newspaper. "There are now seven affirmed libertarians at King Hall," he wrote. "This is a 700% gain from 1978–79. . . . In brief, we are taking over. . . . Rejoice, ye downtrodden taxpayers and victims of government oppression. Liberty is on its way!" Signed, Clint Bolick, Living Libertarian Legend.

The lighthearted, silly tone of that letter suggested Clint was in better spirits during his second year of law school—and he was. During his political campaign, his photo and opinions were freqently featured in the local newspapers. His Democratic opponent (unlike his law school peers) treated him seriously in debates, and press coverage of his campaign was respectful. Also, a part-time job at a local law firm suggested to Clint that while he wasn't a good law student, he might become a good lawyer. The partners in the firm, where he mostly did nuts and bolts property law, praised Clint as a talented researcher and compelling writer.

BY HIS SECOND YEAR at King Hall, Bolick had gained enough confidence to step up his one-man battle against racial preferences. As always, the issue that fall of 1980 was whether all ethnic groups should be held to the same academic standards. Minority students across the country were beginning to protest the use of standardized test scores for admission, asserting that they were racially biased. At King Hall, students routinely demonstrated outside when the LSAT was administered, carrying such signs as, "Who Do Tests Benefit? (a) Women (b) Minorities (c) Low Income (d) None of Above. Answer—d." Enrollment figures also sparked protests, and that autumn, when only two blacks enrolled in the freshman class, dozens of students wearing black armbands picketed and boycotted classes.

In the law school newspaper, the *Advocate,* student Duane E. Bennett wrote a column answering the question "Why We Continue to Complain": "Minorities in America have always been subjected to some form of oppression, repression, and depression. We have been abused by racism, yet we have persevered. . . . We had to take the LSAT to get accepted into law school. The exam has been shown to be culturally and class biased. . . . Perhaps the name of the LSAT should be changed to the 'Nigger Weeder' since that is what it is used for." The bar exam, he added, was similarly flawed.

"We are constantly told," Bennett added, "that in order to pass a course we have to adopt the white middle-class male's way of thinking. We are told that we must learn to 'think like lawyers,' not as diverse people with different outlooks and experiences. As a consequence, many of us have had grade difficulties . . ." (Bennett's views mirrored the prevailing sentiment elsewhere on campus. The undergraduate newspaper routinely published the opinion that academic standards should be tailored to cultural differences. As one Hispanic student leader told the paper: "When [minorities] leave their own culture it's as different as night and day.")

Bennett, a self-described "ghetto kid" who had grown up in South Central Los Angeles, was a case of a young man for whom affirmative action programs had opened closed doors. Whatever Clint or other critics thought about the morality of racial entitlements, it was clear that affirmative action had enabled millions to move into the middle class. Bennett exemplified the gains of African-Americans:

During the 1970s, the percent of blacks who had attended college doubled from 10.3 percent to 21.9 percent (compared with 33.1 percent for whites); the percent of blacks with four-year degrees doubled to 8.4 percent (compared with 17 percent of whites). While the gap in median income between blacks and whites overall hadn't budged since the mid-1960s, it narrowed dramatically for black married couples, who by 1976 were earning 80 percent of their white counterparts.

Conservatives insisted that gains, if slower, already were being made in the 1960s, after discriminatory legal barriers began to fall, without lowering standards or granting preferential treatment. But that argument held little resonance for those enjoying the more tangible and immediate benefits of affirmative action programs.

Clint read Bennett's column and resolved to launch a debate with him through the pages of the *Advocate*. Sitting down at his electric typewriter, Bolick composed a lengthy reply:

"My main concern is that Mr. Bennett and his colleagues do in fact complain," he wrote, "but offer no suggestions to improve minority admissions. I have discussed the situation with the Admissions Office and learned that every conceivable resource was utilized to encourage minorities to apply, assist them with applications, and admit them whenever possible. Many were admitted. Only two black students enrolled. That is not the fault of the Admissions Office.

"Mr. Bennett's implied solution is to admit as many minority students as would be necessary [to boost enrollment], regardless of their qualifications. This, along with other plummeting quality standards . . . will destroy the educational integrity of King Hall, so that no one, including minorities, will want to attend. . . .

"Affirmative action programs based on race are . . . racist," Clint concluded, "because they assume that, by virtue of skin color, a person is 'disadvantaged' or 'inferior.' Conversely, they assume that minority groups have a monopoly on difficulties. Artificial social equalizers achieve little aside from racial polarization and the perpetuation of poverty. As a person who has had to overcome severe economic difficulties in order to achieve the grades, scholarships, and financial ability to reach law school, I resent those who refuse to help themselves, and who would impose artificial barriers against me because I am a white male."

Bolick didn't deny that racial discrimination was a barrier to achievement in America. His undergraduate thesis, the detailed indictment of Linden's Democratic machine, accused the mayor of behind-the-scenes racist remarks and of exploiting racial tensions to gain reelection. Clint was also acutely aware of the fact that he carried with him the baggage of the Right's history on civil rights—that "while most conservatives aren't racists, most racists have been conservatives," as he later said. He also was painfully cognizant of his own father's bigotry.

So in addressing King Hall's students through the paper, he articulated alternative approaches to promoting equal opportunity. "I support the concept of Jesse Jackson's PUSH program," he wrote during his ongoing debate with Bennett. "Before any group can succeed, it must resolve to do so. I also advocate an overhaul of the educational system that will allow greater access to quality education in disadvantaged areas (particularly through a voucher or educational tax credit program). But as for entry into the law profession, a student must be educated, or will ultimately fail."

"It was hard to debate Clint," Bennett recalled many years later. "He would say, 'we don't believe in discrimination.' That's a great argument. It's the argument Dr. King used. But people are always going to be judged by their race." As Bennett and Bolick debated back and forth in the pages of the *Advocate,* the faculty's Educational Policy Committee, chaired by Professor Rabin, voted to soften King Hall's policies for expelling students. Nevertheless, a handful of students still received failing grades and King Hall's annual spring rite—expulsions, followed by protests, followed by an unnerved faculty relenting when they could—continued. In the spring of 1981, eight students were expelled, six of them minorities. Another protest ensued, with charges of "institutional racism," and Clint was back in the *Advocate* with his own counterprotest.

"It is irresponsible to promote unqualified students," he wrote. "It is, further, a cruel hoax to send graduates into the legal world who cannot communicate effectively or represent clients competently. . . . The most effective way to inhibit disqualification is to screen applications more carefully.

"In our frenzy to increase the number of minority students, we should—in fairness to the applicants, community-at-large, and King Hall students—admit only those who are clearly qualified. King Hall must not, and cannot, be a remedial institution for those who have been disadvantaged. It is too late in the educational process for such an effort. . . . In order to reform a system, we must start at the beginning."

Over and over, Bolick tried to demonstrate to his peers that he wasn't a white male reactionary reluctant to share society's goodies with anyone who looked different. He was eager to engage in earnest debate about better ways to open doors, particularly school reform in disadvantaged neighborhoods. He wanted to be taken seriously. (Frankly, too, he wanted to be liked.) The problem was that he was a right-wing oddity inside King Hall, too impolitic to keep his out-of-fashion views to himself.

One day that second year, Clint was sitting, as usual, front and center in a lecture hall. The class was constitutional law, the subject that had inspired him to apply to King Hall in the first place. This time the discussion was not race or the Fourteenth Amendment. It centered on the First Amendment, the constitutional protection of free press and speech. Clint was making a libertarian case for the amendment's broadest reach, sounding no different from, say, an attorney for the ACLU—defending a radical's right to burn the American flag or a neo-Nazi's right to march in Skokie, Illinois. The particular subject didn't really matter because the feelings of King Hall's students toward Bolick had long ago solidified. This incident was merely a tidy summation.

Clint hadn't even finished answering the professor's question when out of the mouth of the student sitting behind him came the word that spelled out Bolick's place inside King Hall, the word that captured their hostility and his isolation, the word that would always ring in his head and remind him just how much he despised the Left. It ricocheted, forcefully and hatefully, through a lecture hall of some sixty students.

"*Fascist!*" the young man shouted at Clint.

CHAPTER 5

POL

"SCARCER 'N HENS' TEETH" was how real Georgians liked to describe the plight of the state's Republican Party in the years before Ronald Reagan's popularity undermined Democratic control of the South. Ralph Eugene Reed Jr. wasn't a real Georgian, having spent only three high school years in the Peachtree State, in Toccoa, a small town just shy of the South Carolina border where anyone born beyond the county lines qualified as an "outsider." He wasn't even a real southerner, unless loyalty to the literal caused one to count Miami—which looks more like New York City's sixth borough and where Ralph spent the longest stretch of his childhood—as part of the South. Ralph was, however, a real Republican. And by the time he enrolled at the University of Georgia in the fall of 1979, Ralph knew something about political power vacuums, and the art of filling them. "Scarcer 'n hens' teeth" also meant many mouths to fill.

Ralph would earn early fame (and infamy) at this Athens, Georgia campus, where he saw the Republican vacuum as an opportunity to promote hard-core conservatives like himself. A little more than a decade later, before he had even rounded his thirtieth birthday, he would make national history by transforming the anxieties of conservative, church-going parents throughout the United States into the Christian Coalition, a force feared and courted by Republican presidential and school board candidates alike. Ralph had an uncanny understanding of fear. He understood how to exploit the cultural fears propelling the Religious Right. He also understood how to assuage the political fears that activist evangelicals, in turn, inspired in outsiders. As leader of the Christian Coalition in the 1990s, Ralph would find a language to build common ground between the Religious Right and surburbanites worried about the nation's moral slide.

But as a young man, in the years before he found God, Ralph was less interested in soothing the majority than in shocking it. Reed was drawn to the offensive, the insulting, the extreme—and in that he wasn't far out of step with many fellow activists. Reflecting on his youth, he would later remark, in a regretful tone, that in those early years losing was not an option. "I never did anything that wasn't perfectly legal, but within the bounds of what I knew was legal I played to win." Legal, maybe. But by the end of his college years, Ralph would build a sizeable reputation as a hard-drinking hell-raiser who played dirty, a mark on his soul that nothing but an earthquake-size life change could erase.

Most of the public would come to associate Ralph with small-town southern values. But Ralph never did fit in with the small-town ways of Toccoa, Georgia, where he spent a rocky three years in high school. Dropping the adolescent Ralph into Toccoa was like flipping the handles on a pinball machine and watching the shiny metallic orb set off bells and ricochet off bumpers, never settling into a crook, announcing its loud racket to the world. He bounced off the quiet of the place, the long stretches of highway dotted by peanut stands and signs on wheels. He bounced off its southern civility, the soft accents of a townspeople instinctively following a centuries-long habit of proximate coexistence: Hold your tongue, because the same person you insult today might be the one tomorrow who is calling in your loan or grading your kid's school papers.

Nor did his delicate nose, slight build, and shock of brunette hair fully capture the aura that intimidated some classmates at the University of Georgia, and magnetically lured others. In Ralph there was an underlay of danger and aggression that, in a larger boy, might have been siphoned off into sports. But Ralph wasn't athletic (in fact he always resented all the attention accorded athletes), and so all this belligerence got pent up in his almost feminine features. His was a face tirelessly sizing up the opposition, readying for engagement, radiating an eagerness to confront the world. In yearbook pictures, Ralph is smaller than other boys, smaller even than many of the girls posing next to him. But it's the bigger teens who appear awkward, not quite sure where to put their hands or whether to smile into the camera. Hands in his pocket, head cocked, Ralph offers a self-assured expression that says, "Try me."

In the fall of 1979, Ralph arrived at the University of Georgia bursting with pent-up political zeal, freed from the claustrophia of small-town life on this campus of 23,470. Although antinuclear activists were visible, and registered Republicans were scarce, the Athens student body leaned conservative. Not many students, though, thought about politics: Their attention was riveted on the Sugar Bowl, the Gator Bowl, beer kegs, and rock bands. The football stadium stood squarely in the center of campus, where it was impossible to miss the ritual fuss over the Bulldogs' battle for the SEC championship.

If there was rightward political energy that year for Ralph to seize upon and spin into his own tornado, it emanated from the fears and hostility students felt as they came of age in an America suffering from a stagflated economy and losing its stature in the world. In November 1979, two months after Ralph's arrival on campus, Iranian revolutionaries seized the American embassy and its staff in Teheran, mocking U.S. power and prestige. Patriotic fervor in the country rose to fever pitch. A week after the taking of American hostages, a night-time protest erupted on the Athens campus, with about two hundred young patriots pouring out of their dorms to sing the "Star Spangled Banner." Chanting "Free Our Brothers!," they hung a crepe-paper Ayatollah Khomeini in effigy.

The night began as a natural, even healthy, outpouring against the hostage-taking by college students who had grown up watching a once proud nation surrender to the Vietcong, kow-tow to OPEC, turn a blind eye to Soviet aggression. But the scene quickly devolved into blood-thirsty xenophobia, as the crowd marched through the streets, calling for Iranian students living in America (twenty-nine of them at the University of Georgia) to quit "taking our places and go home." Marchers chanted "Nuke Iran!" "First Strike Now!" "Nuke 'Em 'Til They Glow!"

For many bystanders that night, the specter of scores of college students calling for nuclear war was a chilling one. Ralph, however, was entranced; two years later he would pass out buttons to College Republicans reading "First Strike Now" above a picture of a globe and a nuclear missile heading toward Moscow. While he was only a spectator at the campus protest, that night's scene burned in his mind. He would later cite it as the defining moment of his political development, cementing his desire to organize a third generation of conservatives. "Born in war and raised in scandal," he wrote of his generation's Vietnam-Watergate upbringing, "we were told as teenagers that the best days of our nation were over. . . . We are a generation hungry to feel good about our country."

One evening that same fall, sitting inside a campus theater that was showing the movie *Patton,* Ralph got caught up in the gleeful pandemonium that broke out when the bombastic World War II general suggested an all-out attack on the Russians. "Several hundred college students cheering a call to arms is something I shall not forget," Ralph recalled. "I became convinced at that moment that a political earthquake was taking place within my generation, a shift in values and attitudes that would have major consequences for the future direction of the nation." In short order, gruesome Patton-like guerrilla talk became Ralph's forte: "I paint my face and travel at night," he infamously explained to a reporter ten years later. "You don't know it's over until you're in a body bag."

Belligerence was the luxury of a generation young enough to have missed the prospect of being drafted into a jungle war, old enough to believe that America's desire for peace had created a nation of suckers who stood by and watched as the Soviets expanded their communist reach around the globe. Ralph embodied this sentiment, and topped it with the excesses of his own personality. Ralph, explained his college friend Sam Harben, was not a person attracted to moderation. "I think in Ralph's mind, he equates moderation with sin."

But moderation was what Ralph encountered when he began attending meetings of the university's College Republicans. Before Ralph gained control, the College Republicans at the University of Georgia—like the GOP apparatus elsewhere in the state—was mostly the province of the social elite, white fraternity boys whose interactions with the working class were mostly confined to greeting the household servants. Ralph's generation of activists never would have much use for these country-club Republicans. Ralph himself grew up comfortably middle class, but no one would mistake him for a member of the social elite. He drove a red Chevy Impala and had a jagged-edged personality that could hardly pass for ruling-class charm. Since Ralph didn't offer friends much personal history, one college buddy sized him up as blue collar, not the son of a doctor.

What Ralph Reed lacked in polish and smooth manners, he made up for in ambition. It was an ambition that keyed every muscle of his wisp of a being, as if the Marlboro smoke he inhaled contained some power-thirsty elixir. He was the sort of young man who, if the circumstances of his childhood were different, might have been on his way to becoming Hollywood's latest fast-talking, deal-cutting Sammy Glick, or joining in the parade of Gordon Gekko wannabes making fast millions on Wall Street in the 1980s. Instead, Ralph Reed ended his high school years a train-ride south of Washington. His game was politics, and he intended to win.

Ralph was only a freshman when he took one look at the frat boys controlling the sleepy College Republican chapter and saw the future, his for the taking. Members called themselves "closet Republicans" because together they could squeeze inside one good-sized closet. Ralph dutifully put in his time at a few meetings before using his already daunting powers of persuasion to convince a veteran group of fraternity brothers to back him as president in the spring 1980 elections, when he was still only a freshman. His opponent was another ideological freshman, Jay Hopkins (who also would later go on to become a figure in the conservative movement in Washington). Ralph had worked as an intern for Georgia's Democratic lieutenant governor, Zell Miller, so Hopkins tried to portray him as a liberal. But Ralph's backers scrounged up more fraternity brothers to turn out for the election, and he squeezed into office by just one vote.

For the students returning to class the following fall in 1980, passing the marble columns of Memorial Hall, it was hard to miss the self-assured new president. Standing in front of his College Republican table, Ralph's penetrating eyes would lock like lasers on a passing face. His voice, reverberating from a diaphragm deep inside his wiry torso, boomed his challenge: "Are you a Republican?" "Uh, y-y-es," replied an uncertain Tyllmann Wald, caught in Ralph's cross-hairs his very first day on campus. "Then you need to come right over here." Intimidated by this sophomore's towering force of personality, Wald did as he was told and signed the College Republican roster. "Five dollars, please," Ralph demanded. Wald had never seen a young person so confident of his own destiny.

Within months, Ralph Reed made himself the focal point of mounting conservative activism on the University of Georgia campus. To be sure, the excitement over Ronald Reagan's campaign juiced the Republican club. But it was Ralph—relentless, determined, wrapping his own ambition into theirs—who transformed them from "closet Republicans" into a vocal and visible student organization with some two hundred dues-paying members. To young Republicans on campus, accustomed to being isolated, perennial losers on the Georgian political scene, Ralph was a godsend. "We were looking for someone to make us look like winners and he did it," recalled classmate Harry Knox.

Ralph's instincts for tailoring a political message, and lighting rockets under it, were invaluable to building a political organization, especially on an apathetic campus. "He was always good at reading people," said college friend Robert O'Quinn. "He could talk to a professor at one level and Joe Lunchbucket at the other and still be compelling to both." While other College Republicans let African-American students pass by the recruitment table, assuming they were die-hard Democrats, Ralph approached them just as eagerly as he approached any white frat boy. He wasn't successful at recruiting blacks: At a university where, only twenty years earlier, the first two blacks were greeted by fellow students with rioting and shouts of "Two-four-six-eight, we don't want to integrate!," relations between the races remained polite but chilly.

If a student showed a glimmer of interest, Ralph wouldn't let him go without a commitment beyond a signature and the $5 dues. Can you put up some posters? Can you pass out some flyers? "He's an uncannily effective motivator of people," said Knox. Ralph incorporated into his organizing repertoire the techniques offered by the national College Republican "Fieldman Schools," two-day seminars designed to teach idealistic young conservatives the nuts and bolts of electoral politics. He knew that working the crowd and passing out flyers was far more effective than passively sitting behind a sign-up sheet. He knew that if you anticipated an audience of fifty, you could create the impression of a bigger crowd by setting up only thirty chairs, and leaving another twenty folded in the back.

Ralph took these smoke-and-mirror themes a step farther with a campus-wide "mock election" that purported to provide the state's news media with an accurate reading of political opinions among Georgia's students. Reed and fellow GOP activist Robert O'Quinn conspired to draft the campus's prominent debate club, the Demosthenian Literary Society, to sponsor a mock election a week before the 1980 Carter-Reagan showdown. Getting the Demosthenians on board was a no-brainer: O'Quinn happened to be president of the society at the time. But Demosthenian sponsorship was crucial because it assured the outside world that the election would be fair and unbiased.

And it would be. The catch was that both Reed and O'Quinn also knew that any election in which only 10 percent of the student body voted was easy to control. The young Republicans intended to out-organize their Democratic rivals, producing timely media stories that would inspire young people to turn out for Republican Mack Mattingly's struggling Senate campaign. Ralph's College Republicans went whole hog to win the mock election: They figured out how to exploit the Greek system, persuading fraternity friends to require new pledges to vote. They canvassed the dorms to identify potential supporters, skipping those identifying themselves as Democrats but passing out election materials to those leaning GOP. They plastered the campus with posters.

Mattingly was vying to become the first Republican Georgian elected to the U.S. Senate since Reconstruction, and Ralph brought him onto campus for a preelection rally. This time, Reed convinced the nonpartisan University Union to co-sponsor the event to lend it credibility. During the rally, Ralph's College Republicans passed out "Herman the Hermit" flyers attacking Mattingly's Democratic opponent, U.S. Senator Herman Talmadge, for his failure to appear. The flyers implied that it was the University Union that was denouncing Talmadge by failing to mention the fact that the literature was the handiwork of Reed's College Republicans. The University Union's president went ballistic, telling a campus reporter, "We are going to make it known we severely disapprove of the way things have been handled from [the College Republicans'] end."

The campus newspaper, the *Red and Black,* editorialized against the young Republicans' less-than-upfront tactics. But Ralph stood firm. The failure to put a disclaimer on the anti-Talmadge flyers, Ralph wrote, was "an error that we regret and for which we apologize. But the *Red and Black* took this error and used it to try to cloud the success of the rally." (After-the-fact apologies and explanations, issued too late to alter the victory that Ralph craved, would become a hallmark of his career—from College Republican shenanigans in the 1980s to the Christian Coalition's stealth campaigns and biased portrayals of opponents' political records in the 1990s.)

Predictably, the Republican candidates won the mock election and Ralph generated the publicity he wanted, with news media across the state proclaiming Georgian students in favor of the Republican ticket. In the real election, a losing Carter managed to carry Georgia, but Mattingly squeezed past Talmadge, a Senate veteran mired in an ethics scandal.

By his junior year, Ralph had transformed the College Republicans into winners at the University of Georgia. They had become a focal point of political activism on campus. So why was it that those young conservatives who benefited from Ralph's labors, activists in a position to see his maneuvering up close, harbored a nagging distrust of him? Why was it that when they read *The Prince* in political philosophy class, some of them couldn't help but think of Ralph? Why was it that a political ally such as Harry Knox would say of Ralph sixteen years later: "He is completely Machiavellian. He will do anything to win"?

RALPH BLEW INTO TOCCOA like Budd Schulberg's fictional Sammy Glick blew through his first job in a New York newsroom—"a little ferret of a kid" with spindly legs and a machete mouth. The teenage Ralph Reed made clear to everyone he elbowed past (as if anyone in that town of 8,800 could miss it) that he was on his way somewhere else.

His family moved to northeast Georgia in 1976, in time for Ralph to start his sophomore year at Stephens County High School. By then, the Reeds' three children—Ralph sandwiched between an older sister and a younger brother—had experienced the disjointed childhood of military life. Ralph Reed Sr. was an eye doctor and naval flight surgeon who had served two years on an aircraft carrier during the Vietnam War. Ralph was born in Virginia's Portsmouth Naval Hospital, across the street from the studio where a young Baptist minister named Pat Robertson was launching a small television ministry. But the family had lived in three other cities before settling in Miami in 1970, where Dr. Reed and his wife Marcy had grown up.

Eleanor Reed, Ralph's grandmother, hated FDR and the Democrats, and she let everyone know it. Ralph's parents, too, were rockrib Republicans. But beyond those two central facts, politics wasn't a major concern at the Reed family supper table. As a hyper-alert kid growing up in the 1960s and early 1970s, Ralph took most of his political cues from the chaos exploding outside his home. The unrest of the times alternately induced in the boy a sense of unease and thrill. He was wearing a P.O.W. bracelet and standing in awe of his father's naval aviator friends while older members of the baby-boom generation were marching in the streets shouting epithets at military recruiters. His mother was raising a family and serving with the Methodist Youth Fellowship while radical feminists were burning their bras in protest outside the Miss America pageant. But the activism Ralph watched unfold around him also suggested to this budding young politico that nineteen- and twenty-year-olds could shake up the world. Standing up to authority appealed to a brash youngster like Ralph.

Ralph spent six years, the largest chunk of his childhood, in the suburbs south of Miami. It was there that he was first bitten by the political bug, watching, as a wide-eyed eleven-year-old, the gavel-to-gavel coverage of the Republican and Democratic conventions the city hosted in 1972 (where city officials were consumed with the fear that "yippie" protesters would turn the event into a repeat of the 1968 Chicago Democratic convention). It was there that he ran his first campaign, for class president in the eighth grade (borrowing from the nickname that supporters garlanded on Stephen A. Douglas during the 1850s: "Vote for Ralph Reed. The Little Giant"). And it was there that he first volunteered on a congressional campaign.

But his parents also saw with unnerving clarity the warning signals of social change in Miami, for the city was a harbinger of the troubles that would later visit urban America. Miami hadn't yet become known as the murder and violence capital of America, as it would in the early 1980s. But serious crime in the city rose nearly 30 percent between 1970 and 1975, and drugs were beginning to pour in. By 1980, federal officials estimated that 70 percent of the nation's marijuana and cocaine business was being run through southern Florida. Ralph recalled his junior high school as a place infested with drugs, a war zone where the name of the game was survival, not learning. "It was difficult to keep children on the straight and narrow because of drugs and delinquency in the schools," his parents recalled.

The Reeds discovered Toccoa while shuttling the kids to and from a Methodist summer camp in North Carolina. In 1976, the town beckoned as a refuge from an America going awry. Set on the Piedmont plateau, with the southernmost foothills of the Blue Ridge mountains rising to the west, Toccoa was just big enough to host a county-wide high school, a couple of grocery stores, a two-block pedestrian mall downtown, and even a new McDonald's, where Ralph would later serve burgers, out on Big-A Highway.

Northeast Georgia was the Deep South, Bible Belt country. But it was not built on slave-holding plantations: Stephens County had been home to small farms, pig raisers, and whiskey producers before up-country cotton slowly emerged as a viable business in the early nineteenth century. Some of the nearby mountain counties had even resisted secession and supported the Union, giving Lincoln's party a few strongholds there a century later. But Stephens County remained solidly Dixie Democrat; Toccoa politics were Democratic, and tightly controlled. "To admit you were a Republican was almost like saying my mommy and daddy never got married," explained Dr. Arthur Singer, a Republican transplant from Philadelphia and co-founder of the town's medical clinic. As elsewhere in the South, it would take Ronald Reagan's presidency to give respectability to the Republican label. Eighty-one percent of county voters cast their ballots for Jimmy Carter in 1976.

The town's race relations in the 1970s were cordial, if distant. No one questioned the neat lines separating neighborhoods and the nineteen Baptist and two Methodist churches along race and class lines. That was just as natural as the fact that everyone—black or white, redneck or white collar—sat in the same classrooms and cheered at the same football games. The town celebrities were the high school athletes, black or white; the young cheerleader elected Miss Stephens County High School during Ralph's senior year was African-American. Toccoa had a history of electing black mayors and city commissioners.

When the Reeds moved into town in 1976, Toccoa was a tight-knit place with a history of looking askance at outsiders. The town's industry chieftains, principally thread producers and casket makers, were notorious for keeping out competition, commercial or political. But for all of its small-town insularity, its age-old rivalries, its library volumes cataloguing local family roots, Toccoa liked to think of itself as a bit cosmopolitan. That was largely because of the town's Toccoa Falls College, founded by a radio evangelist and his wife several decades earlier. And that, indirectly, was why Dr. Reed settled his family there. Northerners, many of whom would do missionary work around the world, passed through the college, and hence the town. In the 1940s, the college founder inspired two Philadelphia doctors—Arthur G. Singer and William H. Good Jr.—to leave their medical practices behind and come south to do the Lord's work serving patients regardless of ability to pay.

Singer and Good established a medical clinic in town, vastly improving the region's health care. In the 1970s, looking for a man of good Christian character to build the clinic's ophthalmology department, they hired Dr. Reed. His arrival was a blessing; before Ralph's father came to Toccoa, the townsfolk had to travel fifty miles, to Gainesville, just to get glasses or eye exams. Dr. Reed quickly built a stellar medical reputation, his surgical prowess saving the elderly Dr. Singer's sight.

Despite the influx of outsiders to the missionary college and medical clinic, this was still small-town Georgia when Ralph arrived. Toccoa was an ideal laboratory for Ralph to study the God-fearing, socially conservative, heartland values that would later form the foundation of his grass-roots Christian organizing. Churches dotted every corner, the local newspaper reprinted prayers and psalms, and businesses advertised Christmas with illustrations of the Virgin Mary and Son, not the secular tinsel favored by urban shopping malls. But Ralph never did, and never would, fit in with the ways of this Bible Belt town. "Ralph," said his best friend Donald Singer, "had no demeanor of civility."

This fast-talking Miami smart aleck, who thought he knew all the answers, especially rankled his teachers. "He was a pill," conceded one of his most loyal enthusiasts, Helen Sanders, a teacher of gifted students. The stories of Ralph mouthing off to teachers are legendary in Toccoa. "For Ralph, every adult had 'victim' stamped on his forehead," said Singer. There was the time he stood up in government class to correct the teacher (a coach, Ralph's favorite category of victim) about some fact relating to Georgian politics, snidely adding that all this guy knew about the subject could "fit on the head of a pin." There was the time he pointedly kept looking at his watch, asking "How long's this gonna take?" during a diversion that his history teacher, Diane Ramsay, was making to discuss the lives of George Washington's cabinet members.

Many of Ralph's teachers won't forget, or forgive. But Mrs. Sanders saw in the boy a promising future clouded mostly by immaturity. Born six weeks premature at a time when a lot of preemies didn't survive, Ralph was scrawny and impetuous, an overly eager child who used provocation to attract adult attention. "He was slow to mature," said Mrs. Sanders. "He was overly dominant because of his small size. He wanted everyone to hear him. As a youngster he would push his way in and yell. He was going to be seen and heard. He was not going to sit back quietly and mesh into anything. He was so gung ho: 'Watch out! Here I come! Katy block the door!' " Other teachers liked to point out that he wasn't as smart as he thought he was, either. He may have been the most articulate kid in high school, a star of the varsity debate team, but his grades didn't qualify him for honors.

There is, however, another way to look at Ralph's troubles in school: Some of his defenders point out that Toccoa was a town smug in its ways, enthralled by high school athletes, indifferent to college-bound kids, especially those who questioned or provoked. There were solid, dedicated teachers at Stephens County High, but others were provincial-minded and not particularly well-read. (One teacher allegedly boasted to his students that he had never finished a book.) A kid like Ralph, who dug up facts and figures from outside sources, could intimidate a not-very-well-informed teacher, and upset the peaceful equilibrium of classes in which students were expected to contain their curiosity to matters laid out in the state-approved text.

But given Ralph's insolent insouciance, channeling his considerable mental energies wasn't easy. His mother promoted Ralph and his talents, but teachers also saw her as a woman often at her wits' end. Marcy Reed hinted as much later on, when reporters called her seeking insights into the newly famous leader of the Religious Right: He was a "holy terror" at Sunday school, she said. "He was larger than life. He could argue with anybody about anything." "He was a wheeler dealer, he always wanted to have the upper hand." In written responses for this book, Ralph's parents were more cautious: "Toccoa was a small town," they explained, "and he yearned for a larger stage. He was very bright and worldly-wise for his age, and occasionally his youthful exuberance and youthful iconoclasm came forth."

Ralph's high school peers found him pushy, loud, obnoxious, willing to blurt out whatever happened to be on his mind. He would mock with a sarcasm that could border on cruelty, correcting the grammar of black kids, dismissing country kids as dim-witted cretins. Empathy was not his strong suit: He could be cutting in a way that was so sophisticated and overwhelming, it would crush some kids' spirits, enrage others. Mrs. Sanders was always amazed Ralph didn't get "knocked alongside the head" by the redneck crowd.

Ralph was elected junior class president a year after arriving at Stephens County High, but many of the kids recalled voting for him as a joke, all the time laughing at this brazen outsider behind his back. Donald Singer, son of Dr. Singer, who lived in a bookish house and loved to talk about world events with Ralph, appreciated what it meant to be an outsider in Toccoa. The pair became best buddies, but even that relationship was rocky at times. "It's hard to reach in there, very hard to reach," Singer said of his high school friend. "Now, there's steel there. There's a core there. There's a center. I know that and believe that. But it's hard to reach in."

Ralph saw himself, said Singer, as someone "who was on a mission. Maybe not on a mission from God at that point." (Indeed, regular church-goers among Ralph's classmates later remarked on the irony of his rise as a Christian leader: They didn't recall seeing him kneeling in church on very many Sunday mornings.) But Ralph had a wild streak tinged with danger, for himself and for others, that threatened to undermine his grand designs for his future. One time, he and Donald were at the Singer family cabin, which was equipped with rifles so they could shoot cans on the lake. They hopped into Singer's pickup truck, Donald driving and Ralph sitting in the truckbed. As Singer drove along, he recalled that Ralph would aim his gun at folks sitting on their porches and shoot blanks, laughing his hyena bark as his targets panicked. Another time, Donald, Ralph, and another friend were walking along Falls Road in the dark, carefully picking their way alongside a steep embankment that led to a creek below. Midway through one of his howling cackles, Donald recounted,

Ralph tossed himself over the rocky side, injuring himself just to shock his friends.

Ralph could have turned his last high school year into a dazzling success. He ran for senior class president with his first direct-mail political campaign, using the school computer and help from his geometry teacher to create individualized letters to each of his classmates. When the time came for campaign speeches, he faced off against a popular football player. The athlete had his say, then it was Ralph's turn. Ralph walked to the front of that lunchroom, facing two hundred hooting, howling teenagers who had nothing but disdain for this mouthy little kid with his irritating strut and plastered hair. Ralph sized up his audience (he could be remarkably self-aware when necessary), picked up his prepared remarks, folded them and slipped them into his pocket. Then he looked his audience in the eye, and with a savvy far beyond his years, offered an impromptu argument that won over the hostile crowd.

Toward the end of his senior year, his classmates voted him "most likely to succeed," but his name was still absent from the high school honor roll. Still, there was one spot of honor reserved for Ralph at the upcoming graduation ceremonies: He would write and deliver a commencement speech. It would be a triumphant moment to cap a rocky three years at Stephens County High, a chance to shine at the podium, where he always shined best. If only Ralph could keep his behavior in check.

One day, as graduation approached, Ralph's English teacher had to leave the room and go to the office on some business. She told the class to stay in their seats. Ralph defiantly left and wandered off to the library to work on a research paper. When the teacher returned, collected him, and confronted him, Ralph told her (in so many words) to take a hike. Enraged, she sent him down to the office, where the assistant principal meted out the worst possible punishment: He revoked Ralph's appointment to speak at graduation.

BY THE END of his sophomore year at the University of Georgia, Ralph didn't quite carry the celebrity status of star running back Herschel Walker (the Bulldogs, after all, prayed at the altar of football). But he had already made a name for himself as a student leader, no mean feat on a campus that was home to three times the population of Toccoa. He was a regular source, the campus' resident conservative mouthpiece, for the *Red and Black*'s young reporters. Need a quote about the election? Call Ralph. Need another side to the debate over student fee hikes? Call Ralph. He also wrote a regular op-ed column in the school paper, topped by his smiling mug.

But Ralph's ambition still gnawed, and the university's prestigious Demosthenian Literary Society beckoned. The 178-year-old society was the province of aspiring lawyers, politicos, and others drawn to the debate of public affairs. To step inside the society's stucco, two-story Federalist style building was to take a step back in time, when grand and florid oratory was a staple of lawmaking in the Old South.

Each Thursday evening at seven o'clock—just as future senators, judges, and Confederate leaders had done a century before—Demosthenians gathered on the hardwood floors of the downstairs parlor and library amid antique furniture, dusty rare books, and a bronze bust of Voltaire. A few minutes later they trundled up the staircase to a chamber designed as a nineteenth century state legislature. The society's officers, attired in coats and ties or dresses, would take their places at a dais at the back, the society's president seated in a high-backed, ornately detailed chair.

In contrast to more traditional debate clubs, the Demosthenian Society was based on legislative proceedings, rewarding quick thinking, fluid responses, and an ability to range across a continent of issues—ideal training for a budding pol like Ralph. The gathered students spoke extemporaneously and were required to follow Robert's Rules of Order. Once new business was announced, a roomful of hands would shoot up amid a chorus of "Mr. President! Mr. President!" The member who was tapped to speak first would head to the podium and offer a five-minute speech (just as U.S. House members do) concluding with a resolution offered for vote. The resolution might be a gravely serious one, drawn from the morning headlines: "Resolved, that the Demosthenian Literary Society supports the use of military action to rescue the hostages in Iran." Or, it might be a fanciful one, designed to entertain and provoke: "Resolved, that Santa Claus is a communist because he uses slave labor and hires the handicapped." Either way, rigorous debate ensued, followed by a vote.

When Ralph began attending Thursday night sessions as a guest in 1981, the once struggling society was enjoying a boom period as a haven for bright ambitious students, many of whom—such as Dan Mitchell, Nancy Mitchell, and Robert O'Quinn—would go off to make their own names in Washington's conservative circles. By the spring of that year, Ralph had every reason to believe he would be voted in as a formal member. He already knew many of the Demosthenian members; some were activists in his College Republican club.

He had a reputation as a persuasive and articulate orator; his earliest *Red and Black* columns, well-reasoned and compelling defenses of Reaganomics and other GOP initiatives, read like perfectly pitched five-minute floor speeches. The newspaper's op-ed editor, Alex Johnson, considered Ralph "one of the best writers there. He was good with language, with building an argument that, even if it wasn't plausible, sounded plausible. He brought depth and intellectual rigor" to the opinion pages.

Ralph had always had a keen interest in speechmaking; he was particularly intrigued by how powerful historical figures ranging from Adolph Hitler to Martin Luther King had used their oratorical skills to move crowds. He would write his senior history thesis, subsequently published in the *Georgia Historical Quarterly*, on a crucial election campaign of Thomas E. Watson, the turn-of-the-century populist firebrand who could lather up a Georgia crowd in less time than it took to draw a tub bath.

On May 21, 1981, Ralph petitioned for membership in the Demosthenian Literary Society. For his maiden speech, "Ralph Reed of Toccoa [spoke] on ideas about communication," the minutes recorded. "Mr. Reed was not considered. A motion to reconsider the vote failed." Ralph had been blackballed—literally, since Demosthenians voted on new members by the tradition of dropping black or white balls into a basket. Blackballing new members was rare enough; at a time when the society was trying to build up its membership it was practically unheard of.

Fellow College Republican Harry Knox had been the first to speak against Ralph's membership and, since he considered Ralph a friend, it was one of the most difficult moments of his life. But the question came down to trust. Knox stood at the podium and told the members that he worried Ralph would use their society to advance his own political agenda. His message struck a receptive chord. Others in attendance shared Knox's concern that Ralph might drag their esteemed society into partisan politics. Already, the Demosthenians' sponsorship of a mock election handily won by Ralph's College Republicans had caused some rancor within the ranks. Ralph was widely perceived as politically ruthless, recalled friend Jack Dominey; behind his back, some classmates called him "tricky Ralph," noted another friend. Ralph "was about winning at any cost," Knox later said, "and it didn't matter who got hurt in the process. We wanted to send him a message that he was out of control. We wanted him to get a conscience."

Elsewhere on campus, the "tricky Ralph" reputation was fed by his flip-flop over proposed state legislation to raise Georgia's drinking age from eighteen to twenty-one. During his freshman year, Ralph (despite his own considerable imbibing habits) pushed hard for the statehouse to pass the bill to raise the drinking age. He spoke at a student rally and submitted a letter to the *Red and Black* that argued, "If it can save lives on our highways and keep young people from needlessly abusing alcohol and ruining their lives and others, I am sure that we can all sacrifice a few beers at the local bar."

But by his sophomore year, Ralph's tune had changed. This time Ralph was trying to build support for the campus to join the Georgia Student Association, a lobby group on statewide issues. In an op-ed column, Ralph portrayed the drinking-age bill as an unfortunate, and avoidable, blow to students. "Young people scrambled to the phone to call their representative and voice their opposition to the drinking bill. . . . But it was too late. The student lobbying effort of 1980 . . . was a monument to political unorganization." Unfortunately for Ralph, his former opponents caught on. "I was one of the hundreds last year who went to a legislative hearing to protest raising the drinking age," one student wrote back. "If memory serves me correctly, Ralph Reed spoke in favor of setting the drinking age at 21."

On the night that Ralph's petition for membership in the Demosthenian Society was rejected, Knox walked down the stairs to the parlor, where Ralph was patiently awaiting the outcome of the vote and delivered the bad news. Stoically, Ralph thanked his friend for being honest, and for having the guts to tell him to his face. But he wasn't going to give up.

Eight months later, on January 21, 1982, Ralph was back in the chamber, petitioning for membership in the Demosthenian Literary Society. This time Harry Knox told the members he believed Ralph had learned his lesson. One by one, the Demosthenian members changed their minds. White balls filled the basket. Knox was correct about Ralph learning his lesson—almost. In the ensuing months, he proved himself a model Demosthenian who earned respect, and even fondness, from his peers. In debates, he was hard right, moralistic, and caustic. But not once during his year-and-a-half-long membership did he abuse his trust with the society's members; it was elsewhere on campus that Ralph's ethics would, once again, cloud his reputation.

WHATEVER ANYONE THOUGHT of the young man's character, or his politics, it was hard not to be awestruck by Ralph's extraordinary debating skills, which rivaled those of the society's other outstanding speaker, political leftist Rob Owen. These political opponents shared a kind of star quality at the society's Thursday night meetings—a couple of young thoroughbreds going at it was how the society's faculty adviser, Calvin Logue, described the scene. Demosthenian member Alex Johnson marveled at the ability of both Reed and Owen to "get up and speak extemporaneously for exactly five minutes, building to a perfect rousing crescendo at four minutes and fifty-nine seconds, speaking not just in complete sentences but in complete paragraphs."

In his early newspaper columns, as in his Demosthenian speeches, Ralph laced his conservative politics with an eloquent sense of history and calls-to-arms. In the *Red and Black* he quoted Plato in his missive on behalf of Poland's beleaguered Solidarity movement, climaxing with words to shame any American who would stand by and let the Soviets crush the workers' movement: "It is our heritage to accept nothing less than freedom." In a Demosthenian speech in support of America's arms build-up to achieve superiority over the Soviets, he quoted Winston Churchill's admonition that the free world should never befriend evil societies.

But Ralph was still Ralph, brazen and impetuous, sometimes nasty and invariably eager to shock (all character traits that his liberal-leaning editors at the *Red and Black* valued for sheer entertainment value). At one Demosthenian debate, he peppered his remarks supporting sodomy laws with references to "queers" and "faggots," startling one freshman who was offended enough to report the incident to the student paper. In his newspaper columns, Ralph dismissed supporters of the nuclear freeze movement as "freezeniks . . . unenlightened seekers of pseudopeace" whose movement was nothing more than "ignorance parading as intelligence." Taxes were "tyrannical confiscation," and he denounced the National Football League's executive director as a socialist.

Humorous sexual innuendo often filled the Demosthenian chamber. Ralph, who was never known to have a girlfriend during his college years, would issue his hyena bark of a laugh at his friends' carnal talk. But his own attempts at R-rated humor were mostly awkward, or inappropriate; women typically found him insulting. His lust seemed solely for the podium. "Mr. Reed stormed the podium in a patriotic fervor to demand the following resolution," the minutes recorded in words that captured Ralph's demeanor just about every other meeting.

Predictably for a young man passionate about President Reagan's vision for a strong America, Ralph regularly sought Demosthenian votes for the administration's initiatives on national security and the economy. But he could also surprise the members. In December 1982, he introduced a resolution opposing capital punishment: "One either respects the sanctity of human life or not; there is no gray area. Criminals are human beings. For those with an unqualified respect for the inviolability of human life, their execution is as distasteful as any ghetto murder or clinical abortion." At a January 1983 meeting he resolved to condemn the university for its "inadequate attempt . . . to attract blacks and other minority faculty and improve the positions of minority students."

You could almost hear the internal click of Ralph's brain as he sized up his audience, calculating ways to appeal to them—just as he sized up passing faces on Memorial Plaza, searching for the button that would turn this or that student into a dues-paying College Republican. His internal computer had to work overtime on difficult-to-sell social issues. He turned his anti-abortion stance into a civil rights issue, equating abortion with slavery in a Demosthenian speech and, in a *Red and Black* column, calling abortion "black genocide. . . . In one recent year more than 440,000 nonwhite babies were aborted." His defense of Bob Jones University, a Christian fundamentalist school in South Carolina that lost its tax-exempt status because of rules forbidding racial mingling, in Ralph's hands became a freedom of religion issue. "Bob Jones and I agree that the sun rises in the east and sets in the west. And that's about all we agree on," he allowed in the first sentence of his column on a controversy that would reignite political activism among religious conservatives. Nevertheless, he added, the rule was based on an interpretation of the Bible, just as Catholics prohibit female priests and women cannot lead prayers in Orthodox temples. All of these practices are in "disharmony with federal statutes. . . . But I respect their right to engage in such practices because it is their religion."

When religion and public policy crossed paths, he took positions on issues such as school prayer remarkably consistent with his later role as a Christian Right leader. But, on a personal level, the Holy Spirit still wasn't coursing through his veins: Politics was his faith. And yet, he increasingly appeared to be a young man in need of being saved. He appeared to drink to get drunk, and many of his friends would later regale each other with their favorite "drunk Ralph" stories—the time he passed out in a hotel lobby mid-sentence, the time he was "so deep in his beer cup," as one friend put it, he stood up through an entire football game screaming for the Bulldogs to "pass the ball to Herschel!" even though the running back was no longer on the team.

In every crowd of hard-drinking rowdy youth, there is one who pushes farther and harder, the lampshade guy. That was Ralph. Sam Harben recalled being part of a trio of friends, including Ralph, returning from a state College Republican meeting in Atlanta. Ralph wasn't driving—friends joked that no one would get in a car with Ralph behind the wheel unless they had a parachute in tow. So the other friend drove while Ralph hung his body out the car window, Harben holding him by the legs, so he could smash empty beer bottles against road signs.

So tightly wound was Ralph that many of his friends worried he was on a path to self-destruction—and drinking wasn't his only path downward. His twin demons—a hankering to win, and his arrogance once in positions of power—set him in the same direction. Twice in his last year of college those demons haunted. One incident resulted in a bitter split among the university's College Republicans. The second was far more humiliating because it was far more public: Ralph would be fired from his position as a regular *Red and Black* columnist, right there in the pages of the paper.

Unlike his libertarian pals like Dan Mitchell, Ralph didn't have any problems with government, when it suited his own ambitions. Just as he had supported the university's involvement in a statewide student lobby group, he also quietly used the College Republicans' influence to help bring student government back to the Athens campus not long after students had voted to eliminate it. Ralph devoted several columns to the importance of reviving student government, but otherwise he stayed in the background. "We didn't want Ralph to be too visible," Harben recalled. "So we had the fraternity groups control it."

Reed's front man was Harben, and as the campus-wide debate over whether to reinstitute student government raged on, Harben proved himself a reliable Reed loyalist. Ralph concluded that when he graduated in June, he wanted Harben at the helm of the College Republicans. There was only one hitch: Harben wasn't popular inside the CR chapter. Ralph would have to find some other way to get Harben elected president; if he didn't, Harben's opponent Lee Culpepper was a shoo-in.

Already a master at controlling organizations, Ralph understood the importance of bylaws and constitutions. By the spring of 1983, he had rewritten the chapter's bylaws to permit the registration of new club members right up to the day of a vote. In advance of the upcoming election, Ralph, Sam, and their allies spent weeks quietly recruiting one-time voters. Promising a keg party following the vote, they collected enough dues to cover 150 bodies who had never been to a College Republican meeting, and never would again. When potential partiers balked at paying five bucks, Ralph kicked in the money for them.

One hour before the meeting, Ralph called Tyllmann Wald, the CR treasurer, and told him to come over to his dorm room. There, Ralph handed him $750 and a list of registrations. Wald was stunned. Over the protests and, in some cases, tears, of CR veterans, a roomful of strangers poured into Memorial Hall that night to elect Sam Harben president. "We ran a dirty election," Harben later conceded with a laugh.

After the election, Culpepper wrote a letter to the national headquarters of the College Republicans in Washington protesting that the election had been a sham. The national committee investigated, while Ralph and his cohorts tried to make a persuasive case for themselves. "We never did anything illegal per se," recalled Harben. "But, look, everyone has a different perspective on something like that. So we'd get the people who knew all the good stuff and have them write a letter to the national office—vintage Bill Clinton." Ralph was reprimanded and a new election was set for the following fall. But by then, Culpepper had led an exodus of angry old guard members, who resigned and formed their own club, a county chapter of Young Republicans. Inside the CR chapter, only Harben supporters remained and he handily won the new vote. The price of winning had ratcheted up, but Ralph had gotten what he wanted. The price at the *Red and Black* proved steeper still.

As he neared graduation, Ralph's diplomatic side receded in his op-ed columns, and his tone grew more fiercely ideological. On April 14, 1983, under the headline "Gandhi: Ninny of the 20th Century," he launched a searing attack on the late Mohandas K. Gandhi, who was then drawing a new generation of admirers as a result of Richard Attenborough's Oscar-winning movie on the pacifist leader's life. "What would you say about a man who allowed his wife to die of pneumonia rather than be given a shot of penicillin that would have saved her life?" Ralph's column began. "What would you say about a man who urged the entire Jewish race to commit collective suicide, begged the British to surrender to Adolph Hitler, and spent his mornings rolling around in bed with naked teen-age girls to test his celibacy?"

The controversy that ensued wasn't over what Ralph wrote, but where those words first appeared. A graduate student who read Ralph's column realized he had seen it all before, just a few weeks earlier, in the March issue of *Commentary*, where film reviewer Richard Grenier had written a lengthy review criticizing Attenborough's favorable depiction of Gandhi. The student called *Red and Black* editor Chuck Reece and asserted that Ralph had plagiarized the column. Reece was shocked, and initially skeptical of the charges. He pulled Grenier's review from the library, and swiftly concluded that Ralph had lifted whole sections verbatim.

There were strong reasons to believe that Ralph had plagiarized Grenier. Each of the facts in Ralph's first sentence had appeared in Grenier's column. So did many of Ralph's sentences. Asserting that the Indian government provided financial backing and supervised Attenborough's screenplay, Grenier wrote that the movie should be preceded by the legend: "The following film is a paid political advertisement by the government of India." Making the same assertion, Ralph wrote that the movie "should begin with a disclaimer: The following is a paid political announcement by the Indian government.' " Grenier wrote that Gandhi had advised the Jews "when faced by the Nazi peril" to "commit collective suicide. If only the Jews of Germany had the good sense to offer their throats willingly to the Nazi butchers' knives and throw themselves into the sea from cliffs they would arouse public opinion, Gandhi was convinced." Ralph wrote that Gandhi urged the Jews "to commit 'collective suicide' rather than resist Hitler and save their lives. By cutting their own throats and hurling themselves from cliffs, Gandhi asserts, millions of dead Jews would 'arouse public opinion' against Hitler." Other similarities abound.

Reece later recalled that Ralph got "upset and really angry" when he confronted him. "The interesting thing was I don't remember any contrition on Ralph's part. It was just anger." Alex Johnson, the paper's managing editor at the time, took a more generous view of Ralph, saying that when he and Reece visited Ralph in his dorm, Ralph was "graceful about the whole thing. He didn't put up a fuss." In fact, though, the record shows that Ralph did put up a fuss—in print. Three days after his Gandhi column appeared, the *Red and Black*'s editors ran a letter-to-the-editor from the graduate student detailing the charges against Ralph. In a box next to the letter, a "note from the editors" confirmed the student's assertions and gave Ralph space for a six-paragraph response.

Ralph's response was the most memorable aspect of the whole

episode, providing a telling glimpse into how his mind worked. He opened by saying, "I sincerely apologize for not citing my sources . . . [which] was merely an oversight, not a deliberate attempt to deceive." Then, he went on to assert an elaborate sourcing for his short Gandhi column, saying he drew on the *Commentary* piece, another Grenier story appearing in the *American Spectator* (which included a tightly condensed version of the collective suicide comment), a *USA Today* story on the Indian government's involvement in the film, and volume 73, pages 253–255, of Gandhi's collected works, which Ralph said he "cross-referenced . . . while studying at the Library of Congress over spring break." "My column," he concluded, "was the culmination of two months of exhaustive research on Gandhi, as the aforementioned list of sources indicates. To imply otherwise is the most shocking, profane form of personal attack I can imagine." Later, legend would have it that Ralph's firing was the culmination of his ideological disputes with the paper's liberal-leaning editors. But that was a hard case to sustain given that the *Red and Black* regularly published columnists farther to the right than Ralph.

This time Ralph had gone too far, and he was left standing on a cold and unfriendly ledge. Readers wrote in thanking the editors for firing Ralph. Some of the letters were cruel, inspired by Ralph's own provocative rhetoric. One student wrote: "Dear Ralph: I believe you can accomplish your purposes more efficiently and a whole lot more honestly in the following way. Go stand on the corner of Broad and College and holler: 'Hey look at me, everybody. I'm Ralph Reed, and I'm small and scared. I need everybody's attention to make me feel like I'm really okay. Please pay attention to me."

Deep in his soul, Ralph must have known his life had to change. In the same month that the plagiarism incident occurred, Ralph was busily fulfilling his duties as secretary to the Demosthenian Society, lacing his recordings of the proceedings with his own humorous narratives. "In the backwoods of Georgia," he wrote, "they sing a song about a man who tried to crusade for the good of others. Eventually he became obsessed with dictatorial powers, and ultimately and tragically failed. The song was sung for Thomas E. Watson and Eugene Talmadge." Ralph penned those words as a teasing introduction for a fellow Demosthenian member he liked to call "the sage from Snellville." But he might well have penned them for himself.

PART TWO

*THE
REAGAN-BUSH YEARS:
REVOLUTION
FROM WITHIN*

CHAPTER 6

STREET THEATER

In THE SPRING OF 1981, Ralph Reed stood outside an elevator at a Chicago hotel, looking all of about seventeen years old though he was almost twenty, insistently asking the new chairman of the national College Republicans if he could join his war on the Left. It had been eighteen months since the chants of "Nuke Iran!" resounded on the University of Georgia campus and General George Patton's bellicose words on a movie screen ("All *real* Americans love the sting of battle!") gave texture to Ralph's life mission. He had served as president of the University of Georgia chapter of College Republicans for one year. Now, with Ronald Reagan in the Oval Office, Ralph wanted to join the national team of Jack Abramoff, chairman, and Grover Norquist, executive director, who were about to turn the College Republicans into a right-wing version of a communist cell—complete with purges of in-house dissenters and covert missions to destroy the enemy Left.

It was an easy sell. Charged by the voltage of this new recruit, Abramoff offered Ralph a summer internship on the spot, warning that he'd be working for a greater unpaid glory but offering his apartment couch as lodging. Thus would Ralph begin the Washington chapter of his life, a side not visible to most of his peers at the University of Georgia. From 1981 until early 1984—two years leading up to his college graduation and one year after—Ralph would shape (and be shaped by) the ideological extremes of Jack Abramoff's College Republicans. His tutor was Grover, a twenty-five-year-old Harvard MBA who saw himself at war, not just against communists abroad, but against Leftists and peaceniks at home, and against the scourge of disloyalty within his own ranks. With Ralph as his eager aide-de-camp, Grover intended to do his part to stop what he saw as the rolling tide of collectivist thought in America with a propaganda war launched from inside an organization run by post-adolescents being paid all of $12,000 a year.

In the summer of 1981, they joined thousands of other young conservatives descending on the nation's capital, harboring a certainty that the future was theirs, care of a seventy-year-old B-movie actor who offered sustenance for their patriotic hunger. These were young people who saw helicopters as a metaphor for America's position in the world during the 1970s—whirlybirds of defeat tipping with the weight of desperate humans escaping the fall of Saigon in 1975, exploding in the Iranian desert on a mission to rescue American citizens held hostage in Teheran five years later. In contrast, the newly elected Ronald Reagan promised an America of nuclear projection and supersonic stealth, a high-tech superpower calling its own shots. "The time is now," this president said, "to recapture our destiny, to take it into our own hands."

Ronald Reagan understood the value of clean plot lines, and he scripted the cold war as a morality play, America's struggle against a dark force. No more relativist talk of "spheres of influence," "detente," or "peaceful coexistence," as if communism and capitalism were two equally powerful, equally flawed economic systems competing for dominance in a complex world. He rejected the revisionist historians, who, with their blithe insistence on blaming the cold war on capitalists' hunger for economic hegemony, infuriated this generation of patriotic youth. This president (*their* president really, for he broadcast the thoughts many of them had been afraid to utter on liberal campuses) talked of freedom versus communism, of righteousness versus evil. "Must freedom wither in a quiet, deadening accommodation with totalitarian evil?" he would ask the British Parliament a year after taking office.

Reagan put the cold war in a moral context not much seen in Washington since Senator Joseph McCarthy discredited the cause of anticommunism in the 1950s. (Reagan's critics should recall Truman's regular references to "godless communism.") McCarthy's blacklists, trampling the civil liberties of American citizens in the name of anticommunism, represented the culmination of a decades-long right-wing delusion that "the entire Left was somehow part of a communist plot," as historian Richard Gid Powers has noted. In the years after McCarthy was discredited, political leaders increasingly shied away from even using the word "communist" for fear of being labeled a "McCarthyite." Now, three decades later, here was a president—once a friendly witness before the House Un-American Activities Committee—using the word at every opportunity, for the express purpose of drawing a line in the sand between the two incompatible ways of life.

The new wave of baby-boom conservatives took Reagan's cue, repeating to themselves over and over (as if to soothe any doubts about the rightness of their cause) that nine countries had fallen into the Soviet sphere in the past decade. That alone, they insisted, was evidence of Moscow's sinister global intent. The cause of anticommunism was a glue strong enough to bind a youth movement that stretched to include libertarians on one end, social conservatives on the other. It provided a bond, too, with the neoconservative movement, Bill Kristol's nesting ground, which had spawned during the Carter years the Committee on the Present Danger, Reagan's preferred source for high-level national security appointments. Anticommunism lent the Reagan youth movement a passion and moral authority that would prove hard to sustain.

The youthful swell of excitement in Washington following President Reagan's inaugural was reminiscent of the Draft Goldwater campaign seventeen years earlier. But with Reagan these young people were running behind a winner, so they told themselves they could forgive each other for their cocky irreverence, their certainty of truths. The president, meanwhile, seemed genuinely surprised by his youthful following; after all, said the man who once ordered National Guardsmen to dump tear gas on Berkeley students, "when I was Governor of California, they used to throw rocks at me."

AMONG ALL the conservative youth groups in Washington, and all the young people tucked away on Capitol Hill staffs and inside think tanks and within administration offices in that summer of 1981, the most energetic anticommunists could be found inside the first-floor cubicles of the Republican National Committee. This was the national headquarters of the College Republicans, which was about to become the hottest act in town.

The College Republicans had the ideological edge usually associated with the Young Americans for Freedom, which was founded at

William F. Buckley Jr.'s estate in 1960 and became a powerful campus movement in the early '60s. But by the Reagan years, internal strife was tearing at YAF's seams; it was the College Republicans who had energy and chutzpah—and a detailed plan to train a new generation of conservative activists by sending field teams to campuses to teach grass-roots organizing. Later, the most talented of the new activists would run Republican campaigns, build activist groups, or lobby Congress, forming the core of a formidable conservative network equipped to go toe-to-toe with the Left's powerful web of public interest groups.

The national CR office was a place for hard-core ideologues, not for bright-eyed college students who went weak at the thought of opening mail for some big-name senator or delivering coffee to a cabinet secretary. If Ralph had George Patton on his mind when he walked in that summer, Grover would remind him that their more immediate work drew on Stalin. "He was running the personnel department while Trotsky was fighting the White Army," Grover would explain to young acolytes such as Ralph. "When push came to shove for control of the Soviet Union, Stalin won. Trotsky got an ice ax through his skull, while Stalin became head of the Soviet Union. He understood that personnel is policy." Grover understood that, too. More, he understood that in 1980s America, personnel were recruited from college campuses, the turf of College Republicans.

Like a staunch Bolshevik, Grover preached that Reagan-era conservatives needed to move quickly to consolidate power by capturing positions of influence, and destroying organizations controlled by the opposition. "Defund the Left" was a central Norquist principle. Who cared if Congress cut the food stamps program 10 percent if liberal lawmakers could come in after the next election cycle and raise it 20 percent? Better to eliminate the program altogether. Better, too, to kill federal agencies that he considered house organs of the Left (chief among Grover's targets was the Legal Services Corporation, where he claimed that leftist lawyers spent more time lobbying to expand the welfare state than counseling poor people). Grover planned to cripple labor unions, too, because their leaders used member dues to promote a liberal agenda. And for the Right to secure permanent victory, he insisted, conservatives must infiltrate the media, academia, and other powerful liberal bastions.

During most of the 1970s, the College Republican clubs had operated like what they were—the youth recruitment arm of the Republican National Committee. College Republicans were, like the RNC, a big-tent operation, with room for anyone willing to accept the label

Republican and work on behalf of Republican candidates. Before the Abramoff-Norquist regime, the CR mission was party building (with the emphasis on "party," the Reaganite ideologues would later sneer, pointing to a 1970s CR recruitment poster featuring an elephant inside a champagne glass under the words, "Join the Best Party in Town!"). As Grover saw it, the Republican college clubs were the province of resumé-padding preppies and jocks. Rightist ideas were so irrelevant to the national organization that in the 1980 presidential election, independent John Anderson—a former Republican congressman who embodied centrist determination to stop Reagan—drew strong support from its ranks. Even Jimmy Carter attracted votes from the field, so horrified were many campus Republicans by the prospect of a Reagan victory.

But Grover, the Harvard MBA, looked over the College Republicans like a corporate predator sizing up a takeover target, and saw power in the making. Even before Reagan's election, nearly one thousand Republican clubs had formed on campus. The CR headquarters had access to GOP money and the GOP's top brass. Recast in a Reaganite image, the College Republicans offered a base from which Grover and his friends could push the national GOP rightward. All the place needed was some hard-core blood at the top, and Jack Abramoff filled the bill.

Abramoff, an Orthodox Jew, was a product of Beverly Hills and Brandeis. But his conservative views, dating back to age thirteen, readily qualified him as "hard-core." He had qualities that Grover lacked: Jack was a natural leader, the kind of can-do guy who could enthuse even the most phlegmatic gathering of college students. Grover had a tendency to ruffle the well-coiffed feathers of corporate sponsors; Jack had an innate ability to smooth them. Immersed in his own intellectual machinations, Grover lost sight of individuals. Jack shrewdly assessed their motivations. Jack had powerful connections and money to burn (which mattered, since he would spend $10,000 on his campaign for College Republican chairman). He was personally tied to Reagan through his father, who as president of the Diners Club franchises worked with Alfred Bloomingdale, the president's close friend and kitchen cabinet adviser.

Money and connections weren't the only reasons Abramoff had a clear shot at winning the national chairmanship. While Abramoff was at Brandeis, and Grover was finishing his MBA at Harvard, the pair had organized Massachusetts campuses in support of Reagan's 1980 campaign. When Massachusetts, so liberal that it was the only state to go for George McGovern in 1972, fell into Reagan's column, the Abramoff-Norquist team happily claimed credit for organizing the youth vote.

In the early months of 1981, Norquist launched Abramoff's campaign for CR national chairman. Abramoff's candidacy received a huge boost after they convinced their most serious contender, veteran CR organizer Amy Moritz, to drop out. They persuaded her in part by promising to offer her the title of executive director if Abramoff won. With Moritz out of the race, Abramoff's campaign, aided by funding from his father's well-heeled friends, unfolded without a hitch. By the time Ralph Reed showed up at the 1981 College Republican convention in Chicago, Abramoff had the election in the bag.

With one minor detail: Moritz was cut out of the deal before she could spell f-o-u-l. Later she would place the blame on a two-hour phone call from Grover in which he was clearly assessing her loyalty, issue by issue, tactic by tactic. Moritz was easily as staunch a Rightist as Norquist. But Grover decided that Amy had picked up a lot of the "bad habits" of the old guard (as Grover himself later put it); she was too resistant to bringing in new, and thus more hard-core, blood. She was reluctant to use protests to deliver a message (ironic since she would later run a group that earned the nickname "rent-a-riot" for its ability to deliver a placard-waving crowd at a moment's notice). Whatever the precise reasons, Grover questioned her loyalty and she was cut out of the deal.

Her consolation prize was the title of "deputy director," with no power. And no desk. Ralph, the perfect hatchetman, would reinforce the message that Moritz was not, and would not be, part of the team. He was assigned to Moritz's desk while her office workspace became a box full of belongings labeled "Amy's Desk." Angry as she was, Moritz (whose married name became Amy Moritz Ridenour) never took the episode personally—she later became good friends with Grover—because she saw the same pattern repeated over and over with others: "With Grover, you were either with him or against him. His view was, 'If you're not 150% with us, no matter what we're doing, then you're against us.' " David Ridenour, longtime CR activist and Moritz's future husband, was on the receiving end of similar treatment. But he shrugged it off as part of the Abramoff-Norquist-Reed war strategy: "Peace through superior firepower."

Superior firepower enabled the triumvirate to consolidate control of the College Republicans by revising the constitution to purge the old guard. They rewrote the document to eliminate entire structures, including regional committees, controlled by moderates. They changed the rules to give extra votes to chapters with more members and to states with more clubs, which effectively moved the entire organization rightward since ideologues were far more activist than moderates. Then, in an awesome display of political acumen, they persuaded the moderates to vote themselves out of office, convincing them the changes were a done deal and any attempt to mount opposition would prove futile.

Grover later said he wanted to inject a can-do attitude into the College Republicans, to eliminate the whiners who would complain that they couldn't meet goals because they didn't have enough money or bodies or resources. But the real impact of rewriting the CR constitution was to transform the organization into an organ of the Right, controlled out of Washington. "We probably made it very dictatorial," Abramoff later conceded. "But we wanted the College Republicans to remain conservative. That was our big concern."

There are those for whom politics is akin to professional sports: Just substitute party for team, electoral districts for players, voting margins for box scores. They believe deeply in their party and its success (who could be more loyal than a Red Sox fan? or hate the Yankees more than a Mets fan?), but they also appreciate the broader contours of the game. They understand how much they have in common with the opponent, and they see value in good sportsmanship, just as their political equivalents see value in bipartisanship. That was the sensibility that prevailed in the top echelons of the Republican Party in the early 1980s—and that was what the Abramoff-Norquist-Reed triumvirate was determined to change.

To this new generation of College Republicans, politics wasn't a sport, it was a calling. They had no interest in splitting the difference, no room for compromise. The young activists traded talk of their own political "conversion experiences," as if they were on some evangelical mission. They despised the moderates in their own party almost as much as any Ralph Nader–Jane Fonda–Tom Hayden type on the Left. With James Baker as chief of staff and Mike Deaver running communications, moderates controlled much of the Reagan White House. The Republican Party itself was populated with allies of Vice President (and one-time RNC chair) George Bush, many of whom still viewed the election of an ideologue like Reagan as some sort of fluke. The young hard-cores lumped the Republican moderates together as "Bushyites"—and derided them as sell-outs, "squishes" willing to cut deals with the Democrats on Capitol Hill, and with Soviet leaders at superpower summits.

The College Republicans generally avoided morality issues such as abortion and pornography, though one Florida CR chapter voted out its gay president when he came out of the closet, and a Berkeley chapter provoked the ire of Abramoff by trying to distance itself from the Moral Majority, which he considered a valuable ally. Mostly, the College Republicans were wickedly libertarian, and couldn't see anything (except of course the Pentagon and Ronald Reagan's White House) worth entrusting to the federal government. They plastered Washington with photos of the hefty House Speaker, Tip O'Neill, under the words, "Cut the Fat Out of Government." They supported a return to the gold standard, and sported buttons reading "There's no government like no government." They searched the nooks and crannies of daily news events for fresh anecdotes about the stupidity of government bureaucrats.

They viewed themselves as the nation's last line of defense for liberty and freedom, words they used regularly without a hint of self-consciousness. They believed, as Yale economics graduate and CR field organizer Paul Erickson put it, that America's hope for the future lay on the far Right, not in some mythical "vital center." The intensity of the place revealed itself to CR activist Sam Harben one day as he conducted a training seminar. A student in the audience asked why he had become a College Republican activist. "To save the free world," Harben replied, jokingly. No one laughed. They assumed he was serious, because they were.

And if you didn't believe in the calling, you shouldn't be there. Working for the Abramoff-Norquist-Reed triumvirate required slavish devotion. Otherwise, Grover would assume "you'd run wild and commit some unforgivable act of disloyalty," as Moritz put it—like talking to Jack's enemies or leaking the contents of some covert staff meeting. From his summer internship in the summer of 1981, to a stint as executive director two years later, Ralph rose quickly through the ranks, shuttling between Washington and his studies in Georgia. He glued himself to Grover's side with the religious zeal of a new convert, an evangelist in the Church of Holy Republicans. "Ralph was Grover's clone," recalled Erickson. He carried out Abramoff-Norquist orders with ruthless efficiency, not bothering to hide his fingerprints. It didn't take long for fellow CR activists to figure out that sharing a confidence with Ralph could be a dangerous thing indeed.

Ralph thrived in this circle of activists who liked their liquor straight and their politics high contrast. But even here, Ralph's extremes could provoke waves of anxiety; fellow activists recalled that he talked in crude obscenities ("bend over and take it—"), and would admiringly recount acts of violence by 1960s activists. "He didn't know how to go up to someone who was sitting on the fence over an issue and convince them to come with us by telling them what they wanted to hear," recalled Harben. "He would push them off the fence, calling them a sick party bastard or something."

Ralph and Erickson implemented their own hazing process for young recruits to assure that no one slipped in who might be squeamish about embracing their far-right positions. For laughs as much as for measure, they would ask recruits if they supported the death penalty for adultery, since their friend in the Senate, Jeremiah Denton, had a habit of complimenting foreign regimes that treated this particular sin as a capital crime. And before sending out field teams to teach grass-roots organizing on campuses, they required each recruit to memorize the movie version of Patton's searing warning against timidity, substituting the word "Democrats" for the word "Nazis": "The Democrats are the enemy. *Wade* into them! Spill *their* blood! Shoot *them* in the belly! . . . I don't want to get any messages saying we are holding our position. We're not holding anything. . . . We are advancing constantly . . . !" One year, the College Republicans' Christmas card featured a photo of Patton standing on a stone, binoculars in hand, under the words, "Merry Christmas from the Front."

Abramoff, who cultivated the image of a responsible adult, forswore Patton's gutter language (though he got a thrill out of the fact that screenplay co-writer Francis Ford Coppola had intended his audiences to be horrified by Patton's antics, when in reality young conservatives fell in love with the tyrannical general). But the CR chairman offered the same battle message to his troops in his own words: "It is not our job to seek peaceful co-existence with the Left. Our job is to remove them from power permanently. . . . This means removing Leftists from positions of power and influence in every area of student life: student newspaper and radio stations, student governments, Ralph Nader's Public Interest Research Groups, and academia. We are replacing these Leftists with committed conservatives."

Despite their heroic worship of Reagan, the young activists didn't enjoy access to him. The president's handlers never allowed Reagan to hold a private reception with the College Republicans, or even to speak at one of their events. The CR activists fumed with anger over the fact that they turned out hundreds of young people for a White House birthday party in honor of the president, and they weren't even accorded this small bit of recognition. When they repeatedly asked for a presidential appearance at their nineteenth anniversary dinner, they received as a consolation prize the embodiment of all they despised: Vice President George Bush.

But that was today. In tomorrow's political world, the College

Republicans saw themselves rising to power on the wings of three political friends—Jack Kemp, Phil Crane, and Newt Gingrich. Crane, the handsome, gladsome congressman from Chicago's upper-crust suburbs, had been the hard-core alternative in the 1980 presidential race, though his showing was unimpressive. After the election, he flattered his young fans in Washington by hanging out with them, sharing beers and laughs in Capitol Hill bars. But even twenty-year-olds could see that he wasn't presidential material.

Kemp and Gingrich, on the other hand, had staying power, and with these two members of the House, the CR activists were certain they were linked to the next generation of conservatism, one that would realign American politics forever. To Grover and Ralph and the other CR activists, Jack Kemp—not George Bush—was the rightful heir to Ronald Reagan's throne. (Asked to pull together an airport rally in Boston for Bush during the 1980 campaign, the ever impolitic Grover had shown up with a Reagan-Kemp sign in his trunk. Abramoff convinced him to leave it there.)

Kemp was a charismatic football star who appealed beyond the conservative base to the working class, to Jews, to blacks. He wasn't afraid to talk about free market solutions to racism and poverty, just as he wasn't afraid to propose massive tax cuts as a way to boost the economy (dubbed supply-side economics by its boosters, "voodoo economics" by detractors such as Bush). He was never a drinking buddy to the College Republicans, like Crane, nor a mentor, like Gingrich, but Kemp did what he could to help the group raise money and build support. They saw in him their Oval Office future.

But no politician connected with the young activists like Gingrich. Never a man lacking for vision or intellectual conceit, the former history professor from Georgia infused them with a certainty that they were a part of history in the making. The little-known backbencher was already plotting a conservative revolution. In his thirty-minute monologues to his young charges, he repeated the stages over and over: First, he would build a reform-minded, and confrontational, Republican minority in the House. Then this newly activated GOP would cast off its go-along, get-along leadership. In the end, these aggressive new Republican leaders would lead a takeover of the House, which had been controlled for decades by the Democrats.

Just as he built a supporting cast in Congress with his Conservative Opportunity Society, Gingrich understood the importance of grooming young activists, particularly the College Republicans, to pursue the revolution. He counseled these young people as if each was a political leader in the making—offering diet tips to one overweight young man, localized political strategy to another. He invited them to his office. They invited him to speak at CR events. And he showed, always. Never (like other politicians, they bitterly recalled) too busy practicing his golf swing or kowtowing to political donors. When Abramoff sent out invitations to House members and senators to join the CR advisory committee, the responses he received ranged from tortured excuses for declining to rambling, blowhard acceptances. Gingrich wrote simply, "Of course . . ." Gingrich taught the young activists how to think big, how to play to win, how to adapt to changing political environments. Grover spent hours under the congressman's tutelage.

Preparing for the next stage of the conservative revolution—Jack Kemp as president, Newt Gingrich as speaker of a Republican-controlled House—was a consuming mission. Grover and Ralph routinely pulled all-nighters on cigarettes and coffee as they organized street protests against the Soviets, plotted the destruction of liberal campus groups, and distributed rightist propaganda on colleges. Grover's clothes looked like he slept in them. Pretty soon, so did Ralph's. Even if they stepped out for an evening social event, Ralph would loudly proclaim sometime around midnight that he was returning to the office. Grover "hit the fritz point" more than once, friends recalled, and they would practically have to carry him to his apartment two blocks away. "He'd just collapse," said Erickson. "Lack of food. Bad diet. Mostly lack of sleep." At home, Grover would sleep for a day and a half and show up again, recharged.

There was never enough money for their ambitious campaigns, and they were always plagued by debts and unpaid bills. Even though both Jack and his father lent the organization money. And even though Jack didn't hesitate to exploit his family connections to solicit donations ("Alfred Bloomingdale, a close personal friend of my family, told me to contact you. . . ," he began one letter seeking funds.) "Neither Jack nor Grover were particularly administratively oriented and they'd run budgets over," recalled Amy Moritz. "They wouldn't pay much attention to how much they'd already spent because, of course, the way they looked at it was this: 'As long as we're spending it for a good goal, we'll spend it and get more later.' "

The GOP officials who oversaw the College Republicans and funded the bulk of their operations took a less generous view. "It was my first experience with the conservative movement and I came away with the impression that these were a bunch of hypocrites," recalled Republican National Committee deputy director Richard Bond, echoing other party officials from that period. "Here they are, spouting the conservative message, and they don't even pay their own bills. They were totally, totally irresponsible fiscally. They were spending money like water, with no accounting of it."

The money cycle became predictable: The Bushyites at the RNC would cut back their funding, and Abramoff would appeal their case to a more friendly Richard Richards, then the RNC chairman (named by the College Republicans as their "Man of the Year"). When that didn't work, Abramoff would ask prominent New Right leaders to make their case to the GOP purse-holders. Citing financial desperation, he also appealed to a New Right donor network that included the Coors Foundation, Amway mogul Richard DeVos, and Olin Foundation chair William Simon. And he hired a direct mail firm to raise funds. Still, the bottom line never seemed to add up: In August 1982, Abramoff told printers and other vendors to expect a thirty-day delay in payment due to an "interruption in our steady cash flow."

Abramoff was certain there was far more money to be mined in the world of nonprofits, where contributions were deductible but political operations severely restricted. Donors, Abramoff noted in one memo, were prepared to "shower money on us" once an "appropriate vehicle" was set up. In 1982, the appropriate vehicle became an outfit called the USA Foundation, funded by Coors and other New Right donors. Although billed as educational and nonpartisan, the foundation closely followed College Republican activities—pursuing its battle against Ralph Nader's campus Public Interest Research Groups, for example. For a time, Abramoff served as chair of both groups.

It wasn't just money that fueled tensions between the College Republicans and the moderates controlling the RNC. It was also the young activists' extremism. RNC communications director William I. Greener repeatedly counseled them to tone down their rhetoric. "Often, you choose your words carelessly," he jotted in the margins of an Abramoff memo detailing College Republican plans to "smash" the opposition. "The goal is to win, not to incite," Greener added elsewhere. But Greener and other RNC officials missed the point: The CR activists chose their words specifically to ring bells and sound alarms—and to demonstrate that they were not, and would not become, part of the Republican establishment.

When they needed to blow off a little steam, Paul and Ralph and Grover often went out drinking at Bullfeathers, a bar popular with the young Capitol Hill crowd. One cold night after ordering burgers and fries from the Little Tavern stand, they drove through the nation's capital, windows down, singing the anarchist hymn that Grover had taught them. To the tune of "America the Beautiful," they belted out their crusade for all the world to hear:

> " *'Tis time to right the great wrong done*
> *Ten thousand years ago.*
> *The state conceived in blood and hate*
> *Remains our only foe,*
> *So circle brothers, circle brothers*
> *Victory is nigh!*
> *Come meet thy fate, destroy the state*
> *And raise black banners high. . . . "*

UNTIL THE EARLY 1980s, conservative youth politics mostly had been a pretty straitlaced business. Morton Blackwell, middle-aged dean of youth training for the Republicans, shuddered at the thought of protests and demonstrations. There was too much potential for chaos, for arrests, for injuries. As Reagan's youth director in the 1980 campaign, he had encouraged young conservatives to take part in "Operation Rain on Carter's Parade" by turning out at Democratic party rallies, to be "very visible" but not "rude or discourteous. If you have a presence with sufficiently clever or unique signs you will be noticed." In the early 1970s, Blackwell had run an outfit called the Committee for Responsible Youth Politics.

Much as they would borrow from Blackwell's playbook in training their own generation of activists, Grover Norquist and Ralph Reed had no interest in pursuing "responsible youth politics." They were part of the Question Authority generation, weaned on a pop culture of irreverence, eager to shock and provoke. Barbed humor was their weapon. Though they didn't always take what they dished out: Impersonations of Reagan on *Saturday Night Live* prompted Abramoff to consider launching a boycott of the show. They preferred to set their own terms of humor for their generation. To drive home their ideological points, Norquist and Reed intended to smash mock Berlin Walls and burn Soviet flags and march in front of the Russian embassy. They were going to name-call and ridicule, despite the pleadings of RNC's public relations team. They were going to lift scenes straight from the screenplay of the 1960s Left.

And, in the end, they would repeat all the same mistakes, all the excesses, that undid their predecessors on the Left. Just as the 1960s Leftists turned much of the country against them by condemning American military leaders as "fascists," the 1980s Rightists undermined their own cause by labeling liberal student groups and peace activists as "communists." If the Left drew brown spider-web charts of right-wing conspiracies, the Right would use red to spin its own fantasies of leftist conspiracies. Like the 1960s Leftists, the 1980s Rightists would become polarizers rather than persuaders, leaving them ill-equipped to craft a message that could sustain a governing majority support.

They began with more promise than that, however. The College Republicans' nationwide effort on behalf of Poland's beleaguered Solidarity movement in the fall of 1981 revealed Ralph and Grover at their best. When Moscow cracked down on the Polish labor movement, the College Republicans launched their "Poland Will Be Free" campaign, a nationwide petition drive in support of Solidarity. With Grover as its mastermind, and Ralph as its field marshal, the Poland campaign was designed to demonstrate that if Soviet troops "move in to Poland and start shooting, people here aren't going to yawn," Grover said at the time. In between his studies in Georgia, Ralph flew to such Polish-American strongholds as Chicago, standing on street-corners and subway platforms to solicit signatures on anti-Moscow petitions. At his own University of Georgia, and on campuses nation-wide, the Solidarity cause helped Ralph boost the membership of College Republican clubs.

Grover saw in the events unfolding in Poland an opportunity to change the subject on American campuses, where Leftists were protesting right-wing atrocities in Central America. Solidarity was a workers' movement—led by the mustachioed electrician Lech Walesa—with the potential to shatter the Left's romantic notions about the Soviet Union as a worker's paradise. In meetings with his staff, Grover laid out his thinking: "You force the Left to reveal its pro-Soviet position, its anti-Americanism, its contempt for workers when they don't fit into a Marxist world view."

In December 1981, after a year of labor unrest and strikes, Poland's communist government declared martial law and arrested union leaders. Within hours, the CR staff was out demonstrating in front of the Polish embassy, tussling with police trying to keep them back from the entrance. That winter, Ralph became a master at street theater as he orchestrated a series of CR protests. He donated one of his suits for an effigy burning of Soviet leader Brezhnev. He calculated the exact dimensions for a mock Berlin Wall that would fit within the view of a TV camera lens as activists smashed it with sledgehammers. He counseled his activists on how to burn a Soviet flag: Soak it in kerosene first to get a robust, attention-getting flame. (Ralph understood that patriotic conservatives burning a flag was a surefire attention getter in the media.) He directed Republican activists to pass out bracelets on campuses with names and arrest dates of Polish prisoners—a reprise of the Vietnam-era P.O.W. bracelets.

But in the cold ideological eyes of the College Republicans, the Polish government wasn't the only Moscow dupe—so, too, were liberal student groups, the American media, leftist professors, and peace activists. In the reality of the CR activists, liberal media bias was "propaganda" directed by foreign agents. Leftist college professors were "Marxists" doing the Soviets' bidding. The nuclear freeze movement was controlled by Moscow. The College Republicans cranked out their own propaganda to counter what they called the "liberal establishment media." CR activists distributed on campuses nine hundred copies of *Target America: The Influence of Communist Propaganda on the U.S. Media,* James L. Tyson's book claiming the Soviets had planted four thousand journalist-agents in the American media to pursue a "massive secret propaganda campaign." (Tyson proposed government-appointed monitors to ensure that the TV networks follow "expert advice" on national security issues.) They used CR funds to buy a thousand copies of Arnaud de Borchgrave and Robert Moss's *The Spike* to distribute on campuses, never mind that this story of a journalist who exposes KGB infiltration of the American media and government was a novel. They used a contribution from William Simon to snap up and distribute copies of De Borchgrave and Moss's next novel, *Monimbo,* assuring their donor that "this will help us in our battles on campus."

Grover saw everyone, particularly reporters, as motivated by ideology. He explained to Abramoff that he was well acquainted with the media's "socialist" bias: When he was at the *Harvard Crimson* the arguments were not between Republicans and Democrats, but between Stalinists, Trotskyites, and Maoists. "Grover informs me that as he reads the names of reporters in the major media, he recognizes many of his friends' names," Abramoff wrote in one letter. Colorful as Grover's recollections of the *Crimson* were, they suffered from exaggeration. It was true that a handful of vocal Marxists of various stripes had populated the *Harvard Crimson*'s editorial ranks; it was also true that the paper had lent editorial support to the Vietcong and other communist causes. But among Grover's peers in the late 1970s, these leftover Leftists had gone into academia, the law, even Wall Street. The former *Crimson* journalists who had pursued media careers mostly had reputations as "neoliberals" who enjoyed disturbing the peace on both sides of the political spectrum.

After the 1981 attempt on Pope John Paul's life, College Republican headquarters issued a "Most Wanted" poster, charging Soviet leader Yuri Andropov with attempted murder. ("That's still conjecture!" RNC communications director Greener complained in a memo to Abramoff.) Ralph joined the Right's crusade against "yellow rain" by devoting a newspaper column at the University of Georgia to allegations that the Soviets were dumping toxins on Southeast Asia, leading to the gruesome deaths of scores of women and children, while the media establishment aided Moscow by ignoring the story. (Scientists later determined this "yellow rain" of fungal poisons had actually been pollen-laden excrement of honeybees, a conclusion that many on the Right rejected.)

Charged rhetoric also defined the College Republicans' assault on the United States Student Association, a group of student government leaders who described themselves as progressive or liberal. USSA had been a target of the Right for years. In the 1980s, the group drew the ire of Grover because of its vocal opposition to Reagan's student-loan cuts, as well as its liberal stands on social issues such as abortion, affirmative action, and military spending. Norquist and Abramoff asserted that the 350-chapter USSA was, in reality, a "pro-Soviet, pro-terrorist, Marxist-Leninist organization." Borrowing from a *Human Events* "exposé," they issued a report to CR chapters purporting to link USSA with Moscow. The report named the wrong USSA vice chairman, claimed incorrectly that USSA had not supported the Solidarity movement, and highlighted an appearance at a USSA conference by Tom Hayden (a lightning rod for the Right both as a visible Leftist and as Jane Fonda's then-husband) without mentioning the Reagan administration officials who had also attended.

It made political sense for the College Republicans to fight liberal control of college campuses by running conservative candidates for student government, as they did. It made political sense to stop the automatic dollar flow to student groups with overtly liberal political agendas, as they did in their campaign against Ralph Nader's Public Interest Research Groups, which pursued causes such as recycling and rent control. (Before the College Republicans took them to court to stop the practice, the PIRGs automatically received a "refundable" portion of student fees, but only the most motivated students sought such refunds.) It also made sense for young activists to highlight the liberal bias on university faculties by rallying around conservative professors in tenure battles and pressing for more balance in college appointments.

But the CR activists, certain that the system was rigged against them, preferred search and destroy tactics. So they denounced the USSA as a terrorist-supporting Marxist front, and the liberal PIRGs as "tyrannical," "radical," "a major threat to democracy on American campuses." College Republicans assigned to the anti-PIRG project would sit in an office facing a military-style map with pins locating the Nader chapters they intended to "take out." The CR training manual described leftist professors as traitorous Marxists who should be rooted out. "On many campuses there are professors who stray from teaching what Marxism is to teaching that Marxism is the only way to go," the manual advised activists. Rightist students should "(1) Launch a major boycott of the classes they teach. (2) Work with alumni and parent groups. . . . Many alumni are donors, so ask them to complain to the Dean's office or the Chancellor. Money talks. . . . (3) Pass a petition around in the local business community. Marx was against the ownership of private business and businessmen will be glad to sign on. . . ." (Intimidation tactics targeting leftist professors were adopted by a group affiliated with the College Republicans, called Students for a Better America. The president of SBA would later run Reed Irvine's Accuracy in Academia, cousin to the controversial Accuracy in Media.)

The CR manual that Ralph helped craft outlined similar attacks on student gay rights groups. "Over and over," the manual stated, "we have seen thousands of dollars of student activity fees given out indidcriminately [sic] to every liberal crusader and cause around. Some of the biggest users of activity fees on many campuses are the gay rights groups and the homoseual [sic] social clubs. If this is the case on your campus, . . . then try imitating the left. Form a 'Beastiality [sic] Club,' or 'Straight People's Alliance.' Charter the club and apply for student activity money. . . . If the student government refuses to give you money, hold a press conference and attack them for being 'sexist' and discriminatory. Complain to the Dean's office and make as big a stink as possible. Threaten a lawsuit."

THE COLLEGE REPUBLICANS considered the USSA a particular threat because of the huge numbers the group turned out to protest the Reagan administration's student aid cuts: seven thousand college students showed up at the U.S. Capitol in March 1982 to hear from Republican as well as Democratic supporters and to stage what the *New York Times* called "the most effective lobbying effort staged so far this year." But a larger menace to the Right and its agenda emerged that same year in the form of the nuclear freeze movement: One million people marched in New York City, calling for an immediate, bilateral halt to the testing, production, and deployment of American and Soviet nuclear weapons. Starting with town meetings in New England, hundreds of city councils began adopting freeze resolutions or declaring themselves "nuclear free zones." In May of 1982, more than 80 percent of Americans, including a majority of evangelical Christians, told pollsters they supported a freeze. Both of President Reagan's daughters signed freeze petitions. Reagan's planned military build-up was in deep trouble. To its critics, the freeze movement was the "greatest challenge to the West's ability to maintain strategic balance."

The movement dated back to the Carter years, when the Soviets began deploying triple warhead SS-20 mobile nuclear missiles aimed at Europe. Carter responded with a NATO plan of nuclear-armed Pershing II and ground-launched cruise missiles, but offered not to deploy them if the Soviets agreed to limit the SS-20s. With the heightened prospect of Europe becoming a battleground for an apocalyptic superpower nuclear war, peace activists there organized to halt the NATO deployment, led by the Dutch Interchurch Peace Council, the Italian Communist Party, the West German Green Party, and the British Campaign for Nuclear Disarmament. In late 1981 and early 1982, demonstrations in Bonn, London, Paris, Rome, and Amsterdam attracted hundreds of thousands of protesters.

After Reagan's election, the freeze movement caught fire in the United States and by the spring of 1982, its breadth was astonishing. Medical doctors and scientists figured prominently among freeze activists, as did teachers, clergy, and many corporate chief executives. Freeze petitions garnered 2.3 million signatures. From its inception on the Left, the movement reached rightward to encompass supporters among moderate Republicans and conservative Democrats. In its scope, but also in the casual attitude of some on the Left toward the Soviets, the movement also attracted communists. And that's what the College Republicans, and their allies on the Right, seized upon.

"You can't call an entire country subversive," *Washington Post* columnist Mary McGrory wrote in October, 1982. But the College Republicans figured it was worth trying. That fall, they passed out a poster depicting goosestepping Russian soldiers in Red Square, bordered by the words: "The Soviet Union Needs You! Support a U.S. Nuclear Freeze." They also funded "truth squads"—including De Borchgrave and John Barron, author of a *Reader's Digest* article asserting that the freeze movement was a Soviet plot—to speak on college campuses. College Republicans turned out at press conferences during a U.S. tour by European peace activists, armed with accusations that the freeze proponents were, in reality, unilateral disarmers toting the Moscow line.

In early 1982, when freeze proponent Ed Markey of Massachusetts stood up on the floor of the U.S. House of Representatives to condemn the College Republicans, Abramoff responded with a letter detailing his case that the freeze was Moscow-inspired. The Soviets, he said, have "long planned to export their insidious propaganda to our country in support of the 'freeze campaign.' " His evidence included a 1949 quote from a Soviet official urging his country to launch one of the "most spectacular peace movements the world has ever known. . . . The capitalist countries, decadent and stupid, will cooperate with joy in their own destruction."

"We don't say that everyone involved in this is a communist," Abramoff told *Post* columnist McGrory. "But they are supporting the Kremlin line." In this assertion, the College Republicans had plenty of company on the Right. A *Commentary* article from the period dismissed the movement as an "odd mixture of communists, fellow travelers, muddle-headed intellectuals, hypocrites seeking popularity, professional political speculators, frightened bourgeois, and youths eager to rebel just for the sake of rebelling. . . . There is also not the slightest doubt that this motley crowd is manipulated by a handful of scoundrels instructed directly from Moscow." Senator Jeremiah Denton stood on the Senate floor to assert that a freeze group called Peace Links was being advised by groups "either Soviet-controlled or openly sympathetic with" Moscow's foreign policy aims. In fact, Peace Links included a number of senators' wives and originated not in Moscow but at the kitchen table of Betty Bumpers, wife of senior Arkansas senator Dale Bumpers. President Reagan picked up on the same themes in October 1982, asserting that "Some who want the weakening of America . . . are manipulating many honest and sincere people." Later, he claimed that foreign agents were behind the freeze movement.

Congressional, CIA, and FBI investigations from the period concluded that the Soviets did try to "capitalize" on the American freeze movement, as one House committee put it. The movement suffered, moreover, by allying with communist-friendly groups such as the World Peace Council. But historians rejected the Right's claim that Moscow had somehow orchestrated the antinuclear sentiment. A 1983 FBI report concluded that despite their hopes, the Soviets did not "directly control or manipulate" the movement. Neither did they play a dominant role, the FBI concluded.

More objective observers attributed the rise of the freeze movement to widespread public fears induced by the global presence of 50,000 nuclear warheads, which combined held 1.6 million times the explosive power of the Hiroshima bomb; and to Reagan officials who told the public that there was a 40 percent chance of nuclear war with the Soviets, that casualties in a limited nuclear war could be contained to "only 10 to 100 million," that a "nuke war" was messy but not unmanageable. Since the first atomic bomb exploded in the New Mexico desert in 1945, Americans had lived with the ineffable reality that their leaders have the capacity to annihilate much of humanity. The peace movement gained momentum on American soil only after the ascension of a president publicly belligerent toward the Soviets, dismissive of arms control negotiations, and reliant on the advice of national security appointees who believed that a nuclear war could be won—and told the public as much.

Indeed, one historian of the period concluded that the freeze movement "faded from the public eye" as quickly as it had appeared in part because President Reagan "appropriated the language of the freeze" to build support for his Strategic Defense Initiative. After 1983 Republican polling revealed his reelection vulnerability on the nuclear issue, the president took other steps to ease public fears, including meeting with the Soviet foreign minister and "proclaiming his newfound concern about the existence of nuclear weapons and the immorality of nuclear war," David S. Meyer wrote in his history of the freeze movement.

But the College Republicans, confronted with mass opposition to Reagan's military buildup, saw only red when they looked at the protesters. The Right's activists also considered the "freezeniks" irrational and emotional, easily duped by the Soviets. Uncowed by images of missiles and mushroom clouds, the young activists reveled in their own realpolitik. In their minds, Soviet strategists—not foolish enough to launch a first strike—were exploiting the American public's fright to tighten their grip on East Europe and roll their tanks into third world countries such as Afghanistan. (Historians later revealed that Soviet leaders also harbored a terror of an American first strike: Believing Reagan's rhetoric, panicky Soviet leaders put their national security apparatus on heightened alert. "In his sometimes simplistic denunciations of the Soviet Union as the 'evil empire,' Reagan overlooked one dangerous Soviet vice: its tendency to paranoia in interpreting the West," remarked one historian of the KGB.)

In September 1983, three months after Ralph's college graduation, the Soviets shot down a South Korean jetliner that had strayed off course, killing all 269 passengers aboard. Hundreds of young

Washington activists painted signs accusing Moscow of murder, and Ralph, his tie knot loosened, his fists pumping, his face twisted in anger, led them in a protest through downtown Washington, landing his photograph in the pages of *U.S. News & World Report,* above the headline "Trigger-Happy Soviets—A Jolt in Relations with U.S." Ralph's followers marched with one martyr in mind, Larry McDonald, a Georgia congressman, friend and ally and one of the passengers killed on Flight 007. At the Soviet embassy, McDonald's son Tryggvi attempted to deliver a letter of protest but a poker-faced embassy official rebuffed him. In an emotional speech that Ralph helped write, Tryggvi told the crowd that his father's death had "sparked unanimous support for the things he fought for his entire life: defense of America and opposition to communist tyranny . . ."

McDonald had been a proud member of the national council of the John Birch Society, a group whose founder labeled President Eisenhower a communist. William F. Buckley Jr. once tried to distance the conservative movement from the John Birch Society and its fanciful red-web theories with the words, "There are bounds to the dictum, anyone on the Right is my ally." But the College Republicans didn't see those bounds, just as they saw no bounds to their own ordained future. "We believed," Abramoff later remarked, "that it was inevitable for conservatism to prevail." Reagan had made them believe. And for a while, as a conservative youth movement blossomed under the oldest president in history, they seemed to be right.

For a while.

CHAPTER 7

VANGUARD I:
IN THE AFRICAN BUSH

The Corinthian-columned U.S. Chamber of Commerce, catercorner from the White House portico, stood as a tribute to the strength of capitalism, not to the heavy-handed statism Grover Norquist saw each time he passed one of Washington's sprawling bureaucracies. Nonetheless, it was a staid place for this political radical to hang his hat; Grover's insurgent ambitions never would fit inside the confines of a nine-to-five job. In the months bordering President Reagan's 1984 reelection, Grover's resumé placed him inside the Chamber of Commerce building as a staff speechwriter, omitting the more important point that he was packing his off-hours with a budding assortment of revolutionary activities. Asked about the future of the conservative youth movement during this period, the twenty-eight-year-old market-Leninist straightened his tie and glanced across Lafayette Square to the White House before telling *Washington Post* writer James Conaway: "History is marching on our side. . . . I think the revolution is happening. It's going to stick. I don't see what could happen to move it back."

Grover's supreme confidence was shared by his peers in the Reaganite generation, who (in marked contrast to the sour tempers of older conservative leaders) refused to dwell on their many defeats during the president's first term. If they were to face facts (as their more seasoned elders were doing), they would have to admit that Ronald

Reagan did not turn out to be the revolutionary they had hoped. He had done little beyond his 1981 supply-side tax cut and military expansion to advance the Right's agenda. He hadn't eliminated government agencies or conducted a wholesale slashing of domestic spending—and he didn't appear likely to do so after his reelection. As conservative writer David Frum later noted, "Not one major spending program was abolished during the Reagan presidency."

Even on abortion, a matter of personal passion to the president, he seemed to be listening to the counsel of his kitchen-cabinet corporate friends who thought it best to steer clear of this messy matter. During Reagan's eight years in office only one of his three Supreme Court appointees, Antonin Scalia, would firmly stand against a woman's constitutional right to choice (another anti-abortion nominee, Robert Bork, would be rejected by the Senate). As Reagan's presidency progressed, moreover, so did his interest in pursuing arms control agreements with the Soviets "when there is overwhelming evidence the Soviets are violating the agreements we already have," complained conservative columnist M. Stanton Evans.

Evans was part of the Goldwater generation, and in the early 1980s he and fellow middle-aged veterans of the Right felt betrayed by Reagan and loudly proclaimed their disgruntlement. At a 1984 symposium, sponsored by the Heritage Foundation's *Policy Review* magazine, they vented their rage over the president's "unwillingness to do battle with the Washington establishment." *Policy Review* editor Adam Meyerson—at age thirty-one a member of the more sanguine baby-boom generation—was astonished by the older crowd's hostility toward Reagan, which he summarized this way: " 'We didn't spend twenty years organizing the grass roots,' they complain, 'so that we could end up with runaway entitlement programs and Henry Kissinger back in power.' " In that same symposium, Evans wrote off the Reagan presidency as "essentially another Ford administration" and noted that real budget growth was larger under Reagan than Carter: "The budget is now totally out of control." *

---

*Supply-siders asserted that Reagan's 1981 tax cut jump-started the economy, generating new jobs and additional government revenues to help balance the budget. But the national debt tripled during Reagan's term. Conservatives blamed this massive government debt on the unwillingness of Democrats in Congress to cut the budget. The reality is that Reagan never submitted a balanced budget to Congress; as columnist George Will noted at the close of the president's second term, the first six Reagan budgets constituted $13/14$ of the $1.1 trillion in deficits racked up over those years. Congress tinkered with the allocation, Will noted, but appropriated approximately the sums Reagan requested. As author and economic analyst Jeff Gates noted: "Rather than 'tax and spend' Democrats, American taxpayers endured a round of 'borrow and spend' Republicans."

But the generation of young conservatives who had arrived in Washington with Reagan held their tongues. Four years into his presidency, these activists remained in the throes of hero worship. More than dramatic words about facing down the Evil Empire, Reagan offered these young people—fresh from their campus battles in the 1970s—a profound sense of shared experience. From Hollywood to the California governor's mansion to the White House, he, too, had been bruised in hand-to-hand combat with the Left, the "beatniks" and "malcontents" of his world.

The baby-boom activists viscerally understood, as Reagan did, that they were engaged not so much in a policy war as a public relations war—to take liberalism out of fashion, to make the Left look uninformed, morally bankrupt, even loopy. The twenty-something Rightists overrunning Washington in the early 1980s were making more than a fashion statement when they drank Scotch and puffed cigars in their pin-striped suits, scoffing at the liberals with their jeans and mineral water and prissy no-smoking requests. As one activist said at the time: "It's boring to be a proletariat." They intended to prove that conservatism was no longer "the thankless persuasion" that scholar Clinton Rossiter claimed it to be a quarter-century earlier. They were determined to redefine the Right as the hip alternative, to reshape not just style but also the fashionable terms of debate.

Goldwater's trouncing two decades earlier had left the middle-aged New Right leaders with a brackish stench of defeat. Reagan's ascendancy, by contrast, produced a new generation stubbornly impervious to bad news. These baby boomers called themselves a third generation of American conservative, pursuing limited government, anticommunism, and traditional values. They intended to pick up where conservative intellectuals of the 1950s and 1960s, followed by the New Right organizers of the 1970s, had left off. Since early 1984, this third generation had been meeting fortnightly at the Heritage Foundation to share strategy, and more than a little attitude. ("Culturally speaking, surf's up in America," declared one.) Among the hundred or more young men and women who gathered to drink Coors beer in honor of Heritage's founding donor, few dwelled on Republican legislative setbacks. Ralph Reed stood before the group to share his vision that an impending Christian revival would rock the political world. Grover implored his peers to "do everything we can to institutionalize the conservative revolution and make it permanent in the minds of the people" by splintering the Left and building organizations within the Right.

While the baby-boom Reaganites kept doubts about their hero-president in check, they were openly disdainful of his accommodationist advisers. Norquist said his revolution had no room for "whores trying to jump on the bandwagon"; he and his allies already had their hands full combating the pernicious influence of the squishy advisers who crafted the the president's 1984 reelection campaign out of the syrupy theme "It's Morning Again in America." After the devastating 1982 recession, after loose talk of nuclear war had unnerved the public, the president's packagers were eager to soothe, not to fight. In their view, confrontation could only damage the president's popularity.

But confrontation was the calling card of the young Reaganites. They lived by a dictum that inverted Clausewitz's: Politics is a continuation of war by other means, a way to smash your cultural and ideological enemies. Compromise, caution, negotiation, anything that blurred ideological differences risked obscuring the mission that had drawn them to Washington in the first place. To the young Reaganites, the president's twenty-point lead over Walter Mondale going into the November 1984 election was political capital to be spent on clearing the brush that had sprouted in the firebreaks between the two sides. As Newt Gingrich, the new generation's mentor, put it: "Reagan should have prepared for [his second term in] office by forcing a polarization of the country. He should have been running against liberals and radicals."

Instead, the Gipper's handlers opted to play it safe. Left in the hands of party professionals—and the Right's twin nemeses, Michael Deaver and the president's wife, Nancy—the Reagan revolution that fall packed all the punch of a Hallmark commercial. The reelection team's ad-men even managed to transform Reagan the warmonger into Reagan the peacemonger. Veteran political reporters Jack W. Germond and Jules Witcover called Reagan's 1984 "Morning in America" campaign "the slickest, smoothest, most professional television commercials ever aired in a presidential campaign—and the most trite." For once, conservative activists found agreement with the conclusions of establishment reporters.

In October, frustrated young conservatives decided to mount their own campaign bid in support of the Reagan revolution. So while Deaver & Co. was selling the American people a president who made them feel good, Grover was among a group of activists trying to sell a president who had courageously toppled the communist regime in Grenada. They intended to accomplish this by reviving in voters' minds that vivid image from 1983, after the U.S. invasion of Grenada, when one of the American medical students rescued from the clutches of the island's communist regime stepped onto the tarmac at

Charleston Air Force Base, dropped to his knees, and kissed the soil of the United States of America.

Suspicions about Reagan's motives had run high during his October 1983 surprise invasion of a tiny Caribbean island that few Americans had heard of, and fewer still considered a national security interest. The president told the public he had sent in Marines and Army Rangers to rescue 800 American medical students from "a brutal group of leftist thugs" controlling the island-nation. But critics accused him of trying to divert public attention from the terrorist bombing of a Marine barrack in Lebanon two days earlier—a tragedy that killed 239 young Americans and fueled congressional criticism of the administration's Middle East policy. With the media blocked from independent investigation of the Grenada invasion, doubts about the administration's intentions were widespread. It took the TV images of returning medical students, one of whom kissed the ground, to reassure a dubious public.

A year later, and less than two weeks before voters were to choose between Ronald Reagan and former Vice President Walter Mondale, youth groups tied to the College Republicans orchestrated "Student Liberation Day" to commemorate the anniversary of the Grenada invasion. Their tutor in this enterprise was Gingrich, a former history teacher who had spent hours teaching Grover and other young activists the importance of producing commemorative symbols in the public's mind as one way to recapture America's story line from "biased" liberal academics. The USA Foundation, the group founded as a tax-exempt vehicle for the College Republicans, co-sponsored the anniversary event, despite prohibitions against engaging in partisan politics.

The activists tracked down eighty-nine of the rescued medical students, and brought them to Washington. The medical students had dramatic stories to tell—of huddling under their beds as gunfire rattled outside, of doors exploding open as U.S. Rangers stormed in, barking, "Identify!" For young Rightists, these scenes were *Rambo* and *Red Dawn* come to life, a public relations goldmine to counter campus Leftists then protesting U.S. involvement in El Salvador and Nicaragua. The Right's public relations mission was aided by the coinciding release of a Reagan administration report detailing the Grenada regime's ties to Cuba.

While pro-Reagan rallies unfolded on campuses around the country, the medical students gathered at Arlington Cemetery on a misty day in mid-October, forming a horseshoe around the grave of one of the Rangers who had died in the invasion. Even cynics could appreciate the visual power of the scene, as tearful students handed the Ranger's father a wreath, and he knelt down to kiss his son's gravestone. At the White House reception that followed, President Reagan performed with power and grace, warmly cradling one rescued woman. A wire service photo that went to newspapers around the country suggested an avuncular leader of the Free World protective of his nation's youth.

But the College Republican activists who had helped generate this favorable publicity for the president weren't in the room when that photo was snapped. They had stepped off their buses from Arlington Cemetery to discover that their names had been deleted from the White House security list. "We were barred entry at the gates to the White House," recalled Paul Erickson, who blamed Deaver, no fan of the young ideologues, for blocking their attendance. The lesson the activists took from that snub was clear: If Reagan was, as Gingrich said at the time, "the only coherent revolutionary in an administration of accommodationist advisers," the baby-boom conservatives would have to find their own means to let Reagan be Reagan.

HIS FRIENDS liked to say that Grover Norquist was becoming a "citizen of the world." He held down the Chamber of Commerce speechwriting job for two years. Before that, he did a brief stint with Americans for the Reagan Agenda, an ad-hoc group dedicated to Ronald Reagan's reelection. After the Chamber, Grover worked a few months for Citizens for America, financier Lewis Lehrman's new conservative lobby group. He was fired. Then he was offered the job of director of a new group called Americans for Tax Reform, which, ironically, a Bushyite—future Bush Attorney General Bill Barr—organized with White House prompting in 1985 to rally grass-roots support for the 1986 Tax Reform Act.

But Grover never seemed to be in the office. Beginning in 1985, he spent much of his time traveling to rebel base camps in Africa, pursuing his vision of building a worldwide anticommunist front to beat back what he saw as the advancing tide of communism. "He kept taking off and going to Africa and the [ATR] board of directors couldn't understand—'what the heck is he doing in Africa? He's supposed to be passing the Tax Reform Act!' There was a lot of pressure to get rid of him," recalled Peter Ferrara, the associate in Barr's law firm who recruited Grover, handled ATR's incorporation papers, and then spent the next two years running interference between the young director and his irritated board of directors. Ferrara, a hard-core libertarian and friend of Norquist's, was solidly in the Grover-as-a-citizen-of-the-world camp. "I didn't fully understand why he always had to go to Africa, but I figured if Grover thinks it's important, I've got to cover for him as long as I can," said Ferrara.

Norquist's wanderings were hardly out of the ordinary for the young Reaganites. In the mid-1980s, scores of aspiring Rambos were packing their Army surplus store fatigues, hopping on planes and into jeeps, carrying rattled nerves and outsized conceits to remote guerrilla camps in the jungles of Latin America, in the mountains of central Asia, in the African bush—wherever so-called "freedom fighters" were holding the line against communism. They slung AK-47 assault rifles over their shoulders and played the part of guerrillas with the contras in Nicaragua, the Mujahideen in Afghanistan, Renamo in Mozambique, UNITA in Angola, their tours funded by far-right businessmen and foundations, and encouraged by what the young activists tantalizingly called "our friends in the intelligence community."

Their role model was a Reaganite adventurer from California named Jack Wheeler, who pursued a Ph.D. in philosophy before making a career out of joining arms and cause with anticommunist insurgents. (Period piece letter from Jack Wheeler to College Republican President Jack Abramoff: "Jack: Just got out of Cambodia with the KPNLF—went to their 3 main command posts . . . almost got my ass blown away by a Vietnamese mortar barrage . . . Again, I realize it gets people in the door, but go lightly on this 'real life Indiana Jones' stuff. I've been doing these things for a quarter of a century now. . . . It is a better argument [perhaps true for all I know] to say that the character was based somewhat on my life, not the other way around. . . .") Wheeler was considered the "first conservative to formulate the notion of a third world anticommunist insurgency," as one writer put it. Just as important, he understood how to convince the Right's financiers to open their wallets to aspiring anticommunist Rambos.

Hooking up with guerrilla movements "was a rite of passage for a lot of conservative anticommunists," explained Dana Rohrabacher, a Reagan speechwriter who spent several months with the Mujahideen ("I disappeared," he recalled in a voice tinged with mystery) before being elected to Congress in 1988. "The feeling was that if we were not actually in the U.S. military, the least we could do was put our lives on the line for the freedom fighters, to verify ourselves for the cause. I was the inside guy for every freedom fighter group; I worked with Jack Wheeler, who was on the outside." When Reagan's foreign policy apparatus proved lukewarm to many of these guerrilla campaigns, the Right's activists dubbed themselves the "Freedom Underground" and focused their efforts outside official channels.

Marine Lieutenant Colonel Oliver North of the White House's National Security Council staff would emerge as the most famous figure of this underground network when he appeared as an unapologetic patriot during Congress's 1987 Iran-contra hearings. But North's end-run around a congressional ban on U.S. aid to the Nicaraguan contras was the most visible piece of a much larger and more diverse effort by the American Right, labeled a "right-wing diaspora" by one Reagan diplomat, to use unofficial channels to build their vision of a global anticommunist front.

Each time the Right's young free-lance warriors returned to Washington from their adventures, certain they were steeped now in the "realities" of far-flung regional wars, they stomped around Capitol Hill demanding U.S. military aid for their struggling comrades-in-arms. They wanted Stinger missiles for the Mujahideen; they wanted the ban on aid to UNITA lifted; they wanted Congress to fund the contras. The College Republicans managed to offend most of official Washington, and unnerve White House moderates, by peddling their "Adopt a Contra" campaign. Modeled on the "Save the Children" charity, their posters featured a contra wearing a crucifix and brandishing an M-16 rifle under the headline: "Only 53 cents a day will support a Nicaraguan freedom fighter."

The young Reaganites liked to think they generated the political force behind the "Reagan doctrine," a series of policy pronouncements that set in motion the administration's active support of anticommunist movements. "We got to see first-hand how the vacillation in D.C. [toward American aid for insurgent movements] affected people on the ground," said Michael Waller, a Norquist ally and one of the first young Americans to visit the contras. "We saw the human costs. It energized us, and had a profound effect: Here we were, helping guerrilla fighters, while the politicians on Capitol Hill were getting fat on greasy food at Bullfeathers."

Maybe the greasy food slowed their reflexes, but most Washington lawmakers, as well as experienced diplomats within the Reagan administration, entertained more sophisticated geopolitical calculations about the guerrilla groups enjoying the support of the American Right. They, too, were concerned about Moscow's expansionist aims, but they also recognized the indigenous roots of third world socialist movements: glaring economic inequalities, repressive political structures, centuries-old tribal and ethnic conflicts, histories that included Western colonialism and an absence of democratic traditions. This more nuanced worldview reigned at the Reagan State Department, making it the target of a powerful rightist network that tirelessly worked through back channels to undermine official policy.

"Conservatives were viscerally suspicious of any State Department strategy that appeared to rely on the arts of persuasion, seduction, conversion, cooption. . . ," recalled Chester A. Crocker, Reagan's assistant secretary of state for African Affairs, who was seeking negotiated solutions to the wars in southern Africa. A frequent target of the Right, Crocker asserted that in the Right's view "our failure to adopt simplistic, polarized definitions of good and bad Africans meant that we flunked the strategic exam. They had their own politics of righteousness; they were transfixed by a one-dimensional imagery of African Marxism, just as the liberal left was transfixed by a stereotype of racist South Africa. Grand strategy, for hard-right conservatives, entailed the discovery of enemies." In contrast, liberal and centrist lawmakers, like most of the American public, turned a skeptical eye on the character of the so-called "freedom fighters": the roots of Nicaragua's contra leaders in the repressive Somoza regime; the El Salvadoran government's tolerance of well-documented terror and assassinations of labor and human rights leaders by right-wing security forces; the documented slaughter of civilians by Mozambique's Renamo forces; the persistent rumors of murders ordered up by the leader of Angola's UNITA.

Despite the public's lack of support for many of the guerrilla groups, President Reagan's own heart lay with these so-called freedom fighters, whom he romanticized as modern-day George Washingtons. In his 1985 State of the Union speech, he breathed life into what became known as "the Reagan doctrine," proclaiming that America must not "break faith with those who are risking their lives on every continent, from Afghanistan to Nicaragua, to defy Soviet-supported aggression." Later, Grover would assert that without Reagan, "Central America would have been communist, and South Africa would have been communist, and they would have rolled up Africa, and they would have rolled up Latin America."

At age twenty-nine, Grover was the ideal candidate to join the Right's global anticommunist crusade. He hadn't acquired the bourgeois accoutrements—wife, children, mortgage on a suburban house—that had begun to tie down other aspiring revolutionaries. "He was so political he wasn't even thinking about whether he had a job or not," noted Ferrara. "He had his life organized so he didn't need a lot of money. He just had to pay the rent: He could probably eat going to receptions and stuff, he didn't buy fancy clothes."

For Grover, home in the mid-1980s was a group house on Capitol Hill that doubled as a museum displaying paraphernalia from his various escapades, political and military. He rented out rooms to fellow comrades, and lived, breathed, even entertained solely for the cause. Parties at Grover's pad were intended to keep the Right's activists out of the clutches of Washington's liberal social establishment, which might be intrigued enough by these right-wing oddities (their president was in the Oval Office, after all) to include them in their Georgetown dinner parties, seducing them away from the revolution with the lure of limelight and power.

In an age when a movie actor could be president, and Jack Wheeler could claim to be the real-life Indiana Jones, Grover could curry a reputation as the Hans Solo of the Freedom Underground—a "philosophical activist and political adventurer rolled into one," said Rohrabacher. During the second half of the 1980s, Grover visited the Pakistani border, returning to Washington to lobby for surface-to-air missiles for Afghanistan's Mujahideen in combat against Soviet troops who had invaded in 1979. He met with resistance leaders in Albania, which would emerge from totalitarian communism in 1991. He strategized with the Zulus in South Africa, trying, unsuccessfully, to convince Inkatha Freedom Party chief Mangosuthu Gatsha Buthelezi to open a Washington lobbying office. He camped with the Renamo in Mozambique. And he befriended Angola's Jonas Savimbi and his insurgent UNITA, the National Union for the Total Independence of Angola, which would become his most impassioned crusade. Over the course of a decade, Grover would make a dozen trips to UNITA's remote base camp in Jamba to share strategy, and to write articles promoting Savimbi's cause back in the States.

Grover first visited Jamba in June 1985, when he still held the title of field director for Citizens for America. CFA had been the brainchild of Lehrman, the drugstore mogul who narrowly lost election as governor of New York in 1982, and who was considering a run for president in 1988. Grover's immediate boss at CFA was Jack Abramoff, his close friend and former College Republican chair. Norquist and Abramoff convinced Lehrman to sponsor an international gathering of anticommunist guerrilla leaders. The summit was to be a grand public relations sweep for the Reagan doctrine, portraying Savimbi, contra leader Adolfo Calero, and resistance leaders from Laos and Afghanistan as anticommunist heroes who deserved the military aid Congress was reluctant to proffer. (The House had just voted down contra aid, and a resolution to lift a ban on assistance to UNITA was coming to the floor.)

For Grover, the event was an important link in the unfolding revolution, for it finally offered the Right, rather than the "liberal establishment," an opportunity to write history's first draft of the cold war. Grover helped craft a declaration of the "Democratic International," a communique that the guerrilla leaders would sign at Jamba: "We, free peoples fighting for our national independence and human rights, assembled at Jamba, declare our solidarity with all freedom movements in the world and state our commitment to cooperate to liberate our nations from the Soviet Imperialists." While the communique targeted Moscow, it did not condemn communism per se—fellow rebel forces in both Laos and Afghanistan enjoyed support from Communist China.

The summit required delicate planning. Oliver North paved the way for Calero's attendance, and Rohrabacher hand-delivered an invitation to the contra safehouse in Tegucigalpa; Wheeler invited the Afghans and Laotians. "These guys were all atop the Soviet hit list. We wanted media, but we didn't want to tell media where it was, didn't want the security risk," Abramoff recalled. After much negotiation, they settled on UNITA's base camp in Angola, where Savimbi, already a darling of the American Right, offered to play host. The State Department's Crocker concluded that support from South Africa intelligence agencies was crucial. Who else, he asked, could have "coordinated the logistics, communications, press coverage, and security of travelers from around the world into a military camp appearing on no published map in a war zone accessible only to South African military pilots and friendly air service contractors?" The white-minority Pretoria regime was one of the primary sponsors of Savimbi's war against the Angolan government and the 45,000 Cuban troops at its command.

News reporters and several guerrilla representatives flew in from Johannesburg on a Dakota DC-3 dubbed the "vomit comet" because it weaved so much during a low-level flight to escape detection by Cuban radar. They landed on a remote strip in southern Angola only to endure a rocky two-hour nighttime drive to Jamba. Surrounded by the region's bleak scrubland, the visitors slept on spartan metal beds, met inside thatched huts, and braved menacing spiders in the latrine. But the charismatic Savimbi tried to make it all worth the effort. Wearing his signature guerrilla fatigues, his pistol and ivory-handled swagger stick on his hip, he greeted the visiting dignitaries with a parade, a mock battle, and other displays of the discipline he was instilling in his twelve thousand followers.

The summit of rebel leaders unfolded as a queer meshing of cultures, with the multimillionaire Lehrman appearing at a mass rally in Jamba's stadium to present each of the guerrilla leaders with a framed copy of the American Declaration of Independence, along with an inscribed copy of a bowl used in George Washington's Mount Vernon home. The Reagan administration had refused to endorse the gathering, though Lehrman brought along a "Dear Lew" letter from Reagan offering tepid support. (Rohrabacher had tried to end-run the White House accommodationists and obtain a more hearty presidential endorsement, but failed.) Neglecting to mention that the letter had been addressed personally to him rather than to the rebels, Lehrman read the words to his audience, emphasizing its one heartening line: "Your cause is our cause." When the event wrapped up, Lehrman, who had arranged his own transportation, was swooped out of Jamba, while reporters spent twenty-four hours waiting for the arrival of the delayed vomit-comet. The event produced colorful news stories, but Lehrman's vaunted "Democratic International" was never heard of again.

Lehrman, a man of Park Avenue tastes, hadn't fared well in the spartan Jamba camp. So he was not in a good mood when he returned to the United States to learn how much of CFA's $3 million budget was already gone. Within weeks, he fired Abramoff, Norquist, and five other top staffers. A source close to Lehrman told the *Washington Post* the financier was livid about mishandling of funds and "lavish spending" (a telling replay of the College Republicans' controversies). Years later, Grover would describe the episode in ideological terms, arguing that Lehrman was "being manipulated by people [on the CFA board] who didn't like us doing all these sorts of conservative things."

BY THE TIME he lost the CFA job, Grover was back in Africa, this time to take part in a conference in Johannesburg sponsored by a youth group with close ties to the South Africa regime. The Republican approach to Pretoria was a conflicted one: Officially, administration policy resisted the growing call for economic sanctions against South Africa while pressing for internal reforms to loosen apartheid's grip. But a range of views wrestled for preeminence under that policy umbrella—from the State Department's alarm at P. W. Botha's draconian rule, to the hard-liners' embrace of Pretoria as a front-line ally against

Soviet influence in southern Africa. Grover and like-minded young activists allied with the second camp.

At a 1984 convention, the College Republicans had adopted a resolution of moral support for like-minded students in South Africa. In a preamble to the resolution, the College Republicans claimed that "socio-economic and political developments in South Africa are resulting in the betterment of the lives of all the peoples of South Africa." The resolution asserted that South Africa "suffers from deliberate planted propaganda by the KGB and their operatives," but nowhere in the resolution was apartheid condemned. (But, then, neither did their hero-president appear determined to transform South Africa's apartheid system into a democratic one: The State Department's Crocker recounted how, in a July 1986 presidential speech that White House hard-liners had a hand in drafting, "the words 'democratic' or 'democracy' did not figure in the President's vision for a future system." The speech triggered a bipartisan storm, and solidified support for sanctions.)

The National Student Federation, the South African youth group sponsoring the July 1985 conference, idolized the RNC's College Republicans. Its officers had studied fund-raising and organizational techniques at a CR training seminar in Florida; the NSF promotional brochure featured a two-page spread on the College Republicans, including a photo of Abramoff and a blow-up of his quote about the importance of "permanently removing the Left" from power. When the South African group decided to bring together freedom activists from around the globe, invitations went out to leading College Republicans. Twelve Americans accepted, including Grover, who still held a position as an officer with the USA Foundation, the nonprofit group established by the College Republicans to solicit tax-deductible contributions. The NSF, whose funding came from South African companies, footed the travel and hotel bill, estimated at $40,000, for all of the attendees.

The American activists viewed the NSF as a collection of white libertarians interested in peaceful change. But while the South African group portrayed itself as moderate, it defended the country's apartheid regime, campaigning in support of the South African Defence Force (the South African army) and against Bishop Desmond Tutu (recipient of the 1984 Nobel Peace Prize), the South African Council of Churches, and the United Democratic Front, the internal umbrella opposition group labeled a "terrorist" organization in NSF literature. (In 1985, Abramoff opened the Washington office of the

International Freedom Foundation, which promoted itself as an independent group fighting for worldwide democracy and run by a former NSF officer. Ten years later, news reports revealed that the group was in fact a front for the South African military, a fact that the American conservatives variously claimed not to know about at the time or dismissed as false.)

In 1985, American campus protests against apartheid were multiplying, with demonstrators demanding that their own universities divest from companies doing business in white-controlled South Africa. (This activism the NSF called part of a "very effective KGB disinformation campaign.") Young conservatives in both South Africa and the United States were eager to halt the growing chorus of support for economic sanctions against Pretoria. The threat to the apartheid regime was real: Congress was gearing up to pass sanctions. Meanwhile, some U.S. firms were pulling out of South Africa, as states and cities adopted measures refusing to invest their money in companies doing business with Pretoria.

The NSF's "Youth for Freedom Conference" was designed to shed some "enlightenment on disinvestment and the folly of disinvestment," one organizer said at the time. And Grover offered his own analysis of growing anti-apartheid activism in America: "The Left has no other issue [but apartheid] on campus. Economic issues are a complete loser for them. There are no sexy Soviet colonies anymore. [Apartheid] is the one foreign policy debate that the Left can get involved in and feel that they have the moral high ground to operate from."

Grover told a reporter at the time that the "best approach for conservatives is not to take the issue head on: It is not being debated in a rational form where you can sit down and make points. It takes too long, and the other side just yells 'racist' and nobody wants to put up with that." Instead, he counseled, conservatives should respond to anti-apartheid protests with their own campaigns encouraging people to divest from companies doing business with the totalitarian Soviet bloc. "Just as the Left in '81 wanted to make El Salvador the big issue, the College Republicans responded with a Poland campaign—same point made." By funding the NSF gathering, he added, South African companies were finally waking up to the importance of "sensitizing young political leaders around the world" to the "complicated situation" in their country, explaining to influential young Americans that "it's not all black and white and awful."

Grover believed that the terms of debate over right-wing

regimes had, once again, been captured by the Left, with its protests against El Salvador's death squads (a "passing fad," according to a College Republican newsletter) and South Africa's apartheid regime. ("Now Moscow has decided that South Africa is the fashionable topic," the newsletter continued, "and their legions of dupes at American colleges are falling in line.") What anticommunist regimes needed, Grover figured, was some astute media packaging to combat misinformation in the liberal press. Shortly before the fall of Philippine dictator Ferdinand Marcos in 1986, Grover told the same reporter: "The guys who do P.R. for the Philippines—do they go to the College Republicans and say, 'Here's some fact sheets: If we paid . . . would you mail it to all your chapter members'? Just so everybody would know something about the Philippines, so that they couldn't get fibbed to? No, they're not doing that, but it would make sense."

If one is to be judged by the company one keeps, the July 14–17, 1985, "Youth for Freedom" conference in Johannesburg shed some telling light on the Reaganite activists. The conference speakers included a Taiwanese military intelligence officer, a former NATO intelligence officer who served in Hitler's Navy, and a South African naval officer. Plans to invite South African Prime Minister Botha were dropped when European activists who condemned his repressive policies threatened to stage a walkout. "Everyone was really pissed off at the Europeans for that," one American activist explained. Instead, the conference attendees had to content themselves with a written greeting.

Later on, some College Republicans expressed regret about their alliances in South Africa: "In retrospect," said one, "we were on the wrong side of that issue. We were siding with the white libertarians, but they were very small and not in control. The National Party controlled things. But keep in mind, the Cold War was going on and everyone else in the ANC were bad guys [with ties to such figures as Cuba's Castro and Libya's Qaddafi]. . . . We had no idea Nelson Mandela was a Democrat."

"Yes," Rohrabacher conceded, "in a non–cold war period, we should have sided with one-man, one-vote. I have no problem with that today. But in those days, remember: We were fighting an atheistic, totalitarian system. We were fighting for the survival of the United States." Interestingly, Grover shared a critique of the Pretoria regime that his libertarian friend and *Wall Street Journal* editorialist John Fund once offered: Apartheid was a giant social engineering project, and the South African government was a backward, antebellum-style regime too unsophisticated to understand how apartheid limited its talent pool in a global economy. But in Grover's mind, the shortcomings of any single anticommunist regime paled in the context of a broader war against the totalitarian Soviets.

SOUTH AFRICA was also a crucial sponsor of Jonas Savimbi and his UNITA rebels in Angola, whose cause Grover adopted as his own. When Grover first met the guerrilla leader at the Jamba confab he took an immediate liking to him. He returned to Africa a few months later to ghost-write an article under Savimbi's name for the Heritage Foundation magazine, *Policy Review,* and his respect for Savimbi deepened. Savimbi was a former Maoist who (like Grover) was applying leftist revolutionary theory to the battle against Angola's Marxist government. "He walked me through several of the discussions he'd had with Che Guevara," Grover admiringly recalled.

In late 1985, Grover spent hours with the revolutionary leader, sometimes alone, sometimes with Savimbi lieutenants present, recording his words. After these sessions, the American activist would retire to his hut, feet up on a chair to avoid the scorpions, and translate those thoughts into words that would appeal to modern American conservatives. The *Policy Review* article that Grover produced during those months stressed UNITA's role in fighting to oust the Portuguese colonialists in the 1960s and early 1970s. When the Soviet-backed Popular Movement for the Liberation of Angola seized power in 1975, Savimbi reminded his readers, he was exiled to the jungle to wage a protracted war against the leftist Angolan government and the Cuban troops at its command. The article portrayed Savimbi as a serious revolutionary who understood the importance of instilling in his followers strict discipline and a sense of commitment, as well as the importance of international ties to curry military, political, and propaganda support. "From Mao and the communists, I learned how to fight and win a guerrilla war," proclaimed Savimbi, who wore a Mao-style cap.

In Washington's conservative circles, Grover's visits to Jamba lent him stature as a "freedom-fighter," a role he filled with gusto as he started wearing guerrilla fatigues to his office and regaling friends with stories from the front: How he would fly in on planes at tree-top level to avoid Cuban surface-to-air missiles; how he would sleep hearing termites eating the hut and rats racing across the roof; how he always had to worry about land mines and ambush attack. "One time I was at a forward base camp," he recalled, "and all of a sudden the sky lit up and there was a huge amount of shooting and heavy machine-gun fire. I was wearing a UNITA uniform, so I ran over and changed out of it to see if that would buy me [safety]." (As it turned out, the explosions came from a UNITA unit simulating a night fight before going off to battle.)

Africa also became a place where Grover could loosen up, taking long-delayed vacations, driving jeeps through the countryside or hoisting a few beers with visiting dignitaries (whom he would entertain by balancing a spoon on the end of his nose). He conducted lectures to UNITA troops on economics and American political philosophy, telling one American journalist he was surprised at their "knowledge of the American Revolution and its animating principles, and conversely their understanding of the failure of socialism, not only in East Bloc nations but in their African nations."

The American Right's free-lance diplomacy in Africa was a constant source of irritation to Reagan's diplomats, especially because it strengthened the hand of hawks in Pretoria. Grover and other American conservatives encouraged Savimbi's distrust of the State Department, making more difficult delicate negotiations to extricate the Cuban troops from Angola. Grover filled Savimbi's ear with advice on how to bypass the State Department and build political support among conservative groups and in Congress. "I was always stressing that the building blocks for his success were with the Republicans and the anticommunist movement in the United States," Grover recalled. "I would tell him he should speak about the Poles and the Afghans and others and show it as a seamless thread. If [his battle] was seen as just one country in Africa, it was less interesting to people. It had to be seen in the broader picture of rolling back the Soviet Union."

In 1986, Grover helped Savimbi author another article for American consumption, this time for the influential, and staunchly conservative, opinion pages of the *Wall Street Journal*. In this June 1986 article, Savimbi proclaimed himself an ardent capitalist, recounting the failures of African socialism and the destruction of his own country's self-sufficiency at the hands of a Marxist government supported by oil revenues from Chevron/Gulf operations in Angola. Savimbi called for a free market in agriculture, and in words that rang with the sound of Grover's logic (not that of a revolutionary leader whose war-torn territory lacked even a currency), the article stated: "I believe that in Angola the farmers must be exempt from all taxes. The state cannot claim the produce of a farmer's hard work. This would be theft." The article also called for the elimination of tariffs. "Grover was basically trying to turn Jonas Savimbi into a free market libertarian," noted his friend Peter Ferrara.

But even then doubts were beginning to surface about Savimbi's commitment to capitalism. In 1984 Savimbi had told a Portuguese magazine that "yes, UNITA is a socialist movement. . . . We are in favor of socialism because it is necessary to socialize production." One critic argued that the charismatic former Maoist "will dance to any ideological tune to get the foreign aid he needs." *New York Times* columnist Anthony Lewis, charging Savimbi with using terrorist methods, called him a politician "whose interest is in power, and is not choosy about who or what helps him."

The Right mostly rejected this cacophony of charges from the establishment press (in a 1986 letter to the *Wall Street Journal,* Jack Wheeler proclaimed Savimbi "about as much a Marxist as Margaret Thatcher")—and continued to tout him around Washington as the quintessential freedom fighter, able and ready to stand up to Soviet imperialism. Congress followed a 1985 vote to repeal a ban on aid to UNITA with a February 1986 gift of Stinger anti-helicopter missiles.

But rumors of murderous purges within UNITA's leadership ranks and of ferocious cult-of-personality practices continued to surface until even the Right could not ignore them. In 1989, the conservative *National Review* magazine published a piece by a Polish journalist who had visited Jamba. He called UNITA's officers "compulsive liars . . . traveling with UNITA is like touring a showpiece Soviet collective farm." He noted that every fifteen minutes UNITA's radio programming would blare the words: "Long live UNITA's great leader, staunchest patriot, the inspired commander . . . Comrade Doctor Jonas Malheiro Savimbi." He characterized UNITA's political structure as "overtly Leninist" and concluded that allegations of human rights atrocities were "too persistent and come from sources too well placed to ignore." One of those rumors pointed to thirteen people burned alive in 1983, just a hundred yards from where Savimbi later quartered his admiring international visitors.

Three years later, in 1992, Fred Bridgland, author of an earlier flattering biography of Savimbi, wrote a bone-chilling piece for the *Washington Post,* in which he concluded that scores of UNITA members had been killed in bloody leadership purges stretching over more than fifteen years. Bridgland recounted his own unwitting involvement in the murder of Savimbi's popular Washington representative, who apparently signed his own death warrant by confiding in Bridgland that UNITA troops had murdered members of his own family. That same year, Savimbi himself confirmed reports of human rights abuses, but blamed UNITA commanders who had since defected.

When Savimbi refused to accept the outcome of U.N.–supervised presidential elections in 1992, and then overran much of the country, criticism mounted, with journalists frequently referring to him as "bloodthirsty," the chief of an "Orwellian tyranny," a "monster." A U.S. diplomat from the period, however, described Savimbi in less sinister terms, describing him as a leader with "rare strategic vision" who suffered from being too isolated and surrounding himself with "third-rate people." This diplomat didn't blame Savimbi for ignoring the election results: "It was an election run by your enemy that your enemy wins. Savimbi was profoundly distrustful of the U.N. We shouldn't have permitted the election—the sides were not disarmed."

But even as staunch a freedom fighter as Rohrabacher later described Savimbi as "not a freedom fighter, but an ally. He had been a communist and there was every reason to believe that if he had won [Angola's civil war after the Portuguese left] he'd be a communist leader. But he was fighting communism at the time, so he was an ally." Grover, meanwhile, continued his staunch support of Savimbi, and was a registered UNITA lobbyist in 1996. Grover believed Savimbi's insistence that the purges had been the doing of others inside the UNITA ranks. And he blamed the communist-backed MPLA—not UNITA—for the failed election and renewed war in 1992. In discussing his support of UNITA, Grover stressed that, as in any guerrilla war, there were abuses on both sides. "Look, it's an African war," he later said. "It's extremely messy on both sides. Neither team takes prisoners. I'm not going to argue that UNITA conducts the war the way the United States would, but that has never been my point. To say I'm not going to help work for a democratic Angola because people on both sides are not Jeffersonians is an attitude that leaves Angola in the hands of people who don't wish it well."

DURING THE MID-1980s, Grover championed the cause of another African guerrilla movement, the Renamo in Mozambique. Mozambique was a drought- and famine-plagued southern African nation run by a self-described Marxist government. Nevertheless, the Reagan administration continued to work with the government and declined to place Renamo on its list of approved insurgencies. State Department officials considered Renamo "a group of undisciplined bandits supported by South Africa to destabilize Mozambique," as one *New York Times* reporter put it. Chester Crocker called Renamo "the African Khmer Rouge." If Grover was going to press the Renamo cause in Washington, he'd have to bypass the foreign policy experts and take his case straight to Ronald Reagan.

In July 1987, during one of Norquist's visits to Mozambique, he passed by an eighty-foot mural depicting a black man chained by another man. The oppressor was wearing a cap with a six-pointed star, which Grover assumed to be the Star of David. When he returned to the U.S., Grover initiated his own campaign against the Mozambique government by distributing photos of the mural as evidence of "outrageous" anti-Semitism. The mural, he asserted, was reminiscent "of the banners and portraits that once were displayed in the cities of Adolf Hitler's Germany." Among those receiving Grover's letter and photos were Secretary of State George P. Shultz and Rabbi Marvin Hier of the Simon Wiesenthal Center, who then launched a letter-writing campaign against the Mozambique government.

As fortune would have it, Grover was offered an opportunity to make his case to the president in person. In the fall of 1987, Grover led a group of ten conservatives to a meeting with Reagan in the Roosevelt Room, as speechwriter Peggy Noonan recounted in her memoirs. The meeting came just after Oliver North's widely hailed, patriotic, just-doin'-my-duty-ma'am testimony before Congress, and the conservatives were eager to re-energize their cause of supporting the world's freedom fighters. The contras were on the list of concerns at the meeting, and the group pressed the president to stand up to public resistance and provide needed support to the Nicaraguan rebels.

When it was Grover's turn, he steered the conversation to Mozambique—and to the offending mural. "He captivated the president with a kind of show-and-tell on Mozambique," Noonan wrote. Grover told the president that the State Department "tends to assume a black African is too dumb to be a communist, to think that's only for white Europeans." In fact, he said, the Mozambique government was quite serious about its socialist aims. And there is, Grover continued, a pro-democratic, pro-Western resistance movement that deserves American support.

Then he handed the president his eight-by-ten color glossy of the mural: "As you can see, this part of the mural shows a white man with a Star of David very prominent on his military cap. . . . The message is obvious: Zionism is the enemy." Captivated, Reagan asked to keep the photo.

As the meeting closed and everyone stood to leave, Noonan recalled, Grover walked over to the president and said: "Sir, when you meet with [Mozambique] President Chissanó in October, keep one thing in mind: Chissanó used to be the head of security. . . . He once had one of his lieutenants murder his own father in front of a thousand government troops to teach them what revolutionary discipline really means. Do you know how the man killed his father?"

Reagan shook his head, and Grover "drew an imaginary dagger from his belt, pointed it toward the president's abdomen, and traced up and over. The president winced and stepped back."

"So remember," Norquist continued, "when you meet with Chissanó: plastic cutlery."

It was a wonderful story, capturing Grover at his most colorful. The only problem was that Grover had been given wrong information by a Mozambique official and—in his zeal to tarnish the Marxists—passed it on without checking it out. After his allegations of anti-Semitism by Mozambique's regime touched off a small but fierce diplomatic contretemps, an investigation revealed that the star in the mural was not a reference to Jewish oppressors; it was a symbol worn by the Portuguese colonial police.

CHAPTER 8

VANGUARD II: IN THE BELLY OF THE BEAST

RONALD REAGAN had meant to close down the Department of Education. He said so enough times that conservatives took him at his word. To the president's supporters on the Right, the department was a Jimmy Carter creation intended to curry favor with the Democrats' teacher-union buddies, an object lesson in how Washington curls its tendrils into local matters. But as Reagan began his fifth year in office, there the loathed department stood, five thousand bureaucrats strong, faceless in the jumble of federal leviathans massed along Independence Avenue. And there, preserved within, was the secretary's expansive sixth-floor office. And there, preserved too, was the secretary's dining room, and the secretary's personal chef.

When Bill Bennett was offered the run of the place in 1985, he had to forswear any plans to kill the agency—otherwise, no Senate confirmation. But that didn't stop the combative new education secretary from transforming his taxpayer-funded lunchroom into a political war-room of the Right. And that didn't stop him from hiring as his aide-de-camp the young Bill Kristol, who had recently offered the mischievous theory that the more bombs a political appointee throws, the more success he shall enjoy.

At age thirty, Kristol, an assistant professor at Harvard's Kennedy School of Government, was not part of the third generation crowd populated by edgy enthusiasts such as Ralph Reed and Grover Norquist. While those young Reaganites were organizing street theater and hatching guerrilla plots in the early 1980s, Kristol was holed up in academia, though always with an envious eye on the events unfolding in Washington. At the University of Pennsylvania, where he taught political science for four years, his fellow Straussians jokingly called him "Public Man," a philosopher more prolific in political gossip than published work, his fingers ink-stained from the piles of newspapers he ravaged each day. Age and experience separated Bill from the Right's younger ideologues. But there was also a profound social divide: The Ivy League professors and assistant professors in Kristol's circle didn't cross tracks with activists such as the College Republicans. Rather, they read about their antics in the morning *New York Times* and groaned. (Grover, meanwhile, considered these Burkean conservatives a bunch of elitists who muddied up American history with European biases.)

Nor did Kristol share all of the third generation's libertarian enthusiasms for the citizenry's good sense, or its stock vitriol against government in any form. He brought a Straussian's moral yardstick to the Right's cause, measuring federal programs by their impact on the rectitude of the people they were meant to serve. While libertarians rejected most collective efforts as dangerous infringements on an individual's liberty, Kristol and his like-minded friends asked whether government programs warped the good character of the people, or the free market. As it happened, most fell into that category. But there were a few that didn't—Social Security chief among them. While Norquist's hard-core libertarian allies were busily denouncing Social Security as a "giant Ponzi scheme" that should be privatized, Kristol never questioned the entitlement program's right to exist. It's hard to make the case, he asserted, that this cherished safety net had corrupted the elderly.

But none of those distinctions altered the fact that Bill Kristol was a staunch Reaganite, as derisive of the Left and its do-gooder social engineering, as determined to turn back decades of liberal reform, as any third generation activist. Like them, too, he was a self-described troublemaker, not an accommodationist. "The attempt to 'manage' noncontroversially usually fails even on its own terms," Kristol opined in the January 1985 *Policy Review* article that landed him a job offer from Bennett. Political appointees who don't make waves, Kristol insisted, end up in more trouble than those who do: "They end up reacting to developments shaped by others, and fighting on others' terrain, at someone else's chosen time and place."

In an earlier era, young people came to Washington in the interest of "public service," a noble enough cover for baser motivations such as lust for power or the lure of charismatic leaders. The American political system, sociologist Daniel Bell observed in 1962, "with its commitment to deals and penalties, does not easily invite ideological—or even principled—political splits." For those who staffed the upper echelons of congressional offices and the executive branch, ideology formed, if at all, in reaction to scattershot events—economic depression, war, civil strife. "Bipartisan" was a positive adjective, and John F. Kennedy could be complimented for balancing his cabinet with appointments from both parties.

By the 1980s, though, ideology inflamed Washington, defining one's friends and one's enemies. Those who chose to live and work in the capital were drawn there less to pursue public service than to wage political war in pursuit of a cause. It had begun with the Left, to be sure—the feminists and environmentalists and all manner of self-described "public interest" activists who poured into town in the late 1960s and 1970s, on missions of reform. But in the 1980s, a parallel universe emerged on the Right, made up of young people marked "libertarian" or "neoconservative" or "Christian conservative" and credentialed with B.A.s and law degrees and Ph.D.s from the very same fine universities that had produced their liberal counterparts. They began to exhibit the same tribal loyalties as the Left, the same thickening networks of social and professional connections, the same thirst for battle.

Even during President Reagan's accommodationist second term—in many ways especially during those years—that spirit of ideological war was kept alive by a handful of tightly connected vanguards operating inside the administration. Kristol, who would later call the political center "boring" and ridicule leaders who shrunk from "big divisive issues," joined a determined group of young Rightists gathered around Bennett's sixth-floor suite. The Federalist Society, co-founded by David McIntosh and his friends, infiltrated the Justice Department, lending Attorney General Edwin Meese intellectual firepower for his siege against the American judiciary. And Clint Bolick joined a counterattack on the received wisdom of the civil rights community being waged by Clarence Thomas, chairman of the Equal Employment Opportunity Commission.

IF BENNETT couldn't shut down the Department of Education, at least he could put a face on a faceless bureaucracy. Unlike his low-key predecessor, T. H. Bell (whose calling card as a "lifetime educational professional" pretty much summed up his resistance to confrontation), Bennett understood the value of political warfare. He had raised his own profile as head of the National Endowment for the Humanities during Reagan's first term by assailing academia's embrace of multiculturalism, complaining that students were graduating ignorant of the great works of Western civilization. His critics lumped him together with Straussian author Allan Bloom and novelist Saul Bellow as the "three killer B's."

It was no accident that Kristol landed at Bennett's side. In January of 1985, he wrote to Reagan's personnel director seeking an administration job and citing his "admiration" for the education secretary, whose confrontational style he had praised in the *Policy Review* article. *American Spectator* editor R. Emmett Tyrrell Jr. lobbied on Kristol's behalf with a note to White House communications director and fellow conservative Pat Buchanan. Buchanan (who would face Kristol's ridicule when he ran for president eleven years later) wrote back that he'd keep Bill in mind: "Met him years ago. Takes after his old man which is A+."

Bennett already knew Bill's parents: Gertrude Himmelfarb and Irving Kristol had been instrumental in helping him secure the NEH job. He assumed he couldn't go wrong by hiring their Harvard-trained son. "We talked the same language," Bennett recalled of Bill. "We were trained the same. He was in government, but it was really political theory. I was in philosophy but it was really political philosophy. And given the gene pool, if he weren't smart as hell it would disprove evolution. Bea and Irving are two of the smartest people in the world." By the summer of 1985, Kristol had moved to Washington to join Bennett as a special assistant. Six months later, he was promoted to chief of staff. With this $77,500 job, Kristol was hooked: He and his wife Susan settled in Washington with their young child, both of them alarming Bill's professor-mother by leaving behind the security of tenure tracks for the vagaries of Washington politics.

Kristol and Bennett were both products of classical educations that connected their worldviews even if their interests diverged: Kristol was a Manhattan Jew with a Straussian's ear for high culture; Bennett, ten years older, was a Brooklyn Catholic who once played in a rock band and probably quoted Buddy Holly as often as Thucydides. Bennett claimed to never have read a word of Strauss. "I have no idea what the man ever wrote. All I was told was that I should never go to a Straussian party because all they do is talk," said the man who preferred to party to the beat of golden oldies.

The Bennett-Kristol alliance was sealed by a mutual certainty that the Left had compiled a dishonest version of America's tradition of tolerance and equality, using newfangled "moral truths" to raze educational standards. The classics of Western civilization, and its Judeo-Christian roots, had gotten trampled in the rush to make American education more "inclusive." Educators incessantly worried about children's "self-esteem" rather than their education. Teachers scrupulously skirted the reality of religion in American life, fearful even of discussing right and wrong in front of children (since even a discussion of values might offend someone). College officials fussily considered race and gender, rather than excellence, in considering whose works should form a core curriculum. Campuses were dropping traditional core requirements, displaying an ethic of "not passing judgment, [of] taking it easy on oneself and others," Kristol asserted at the time. "There's a kind of fecklessness about what goes on in higher education."

Bennett, with Kristol at his side, resolved to turn the Education Department into a traveling revival, a place to sermonize—loudly and provocatively—about the decline not only in education, but also in national character and morality. ("I got the chance and I oughta take it," Bennett liked to say, quoting Chuck Berry.) In doing so, Bennett would demonstrate to the Right the value of employing federal muscle to advance the conservative cause.

The top brains Bennett collected inside his department weren't dedicated as much to the Republican Party, or to the Reagan administration, as to their own crusade to overthrow entrenched liberal wisdom. Chester E. Finn, on his way to becoming one of the nation's leading education scholars, had been Democratic Senator Patrick Moynihan's legislative director. Bennett, personally loyal to Reagan, was still officially a Democrat, as was his communications director, Marion C. Blakey. One speechwriter, Columbia graduate David Tell (who would go on to become the editorial voice of Kristol's magazine the *Weekly Standard*), had voted for Mondale. Others on staff included Wendell Willkie, a grandson of the dynamic 1940 Republican presidential candidate, and Gene Scalia, son of the soon-to-be Supreme Court justice. The speechwriting staff was a nesting ground of young Straussians and neocons: John Walters, John Cribb, Bruce Carnes, and Peter Wehner, who became Bennett's right-hand man in the 1990s.

They dubbed their bureaucracy Fort Reagan, and raced through adrenaline-charged days on animated stop-and-start conversations that moved from the coffee table in Kristol's cubby of an office, to lunch in Bennett's dining room (where they rarely stopped talking long enough to notice how bad the food was), and back to the coffee table for late-night strategizing. The door between Bennett's office and Kristol's enclave was in perpetual motion, the hulking secretary diving through at predictably unpredictable intervals to hand his more diminutive chief of staff a press clipping on the latest liberal outrage.

Bennett's aides considered themselves intellectuals and were conscious of building on the thin reed of conservative social science then available to challenge liberal presumptions. Two decades earlier, scholar Clinton Rossiter had complained that the American Right "displayed an attitude of anti-intellectualism that goes far beyond . . . quizzical suspicion. . . . The American conservative has not merely distrusted the poet, professor, philosopher, and political theorist; he has scorned them, bullied them, and not seldom despised them."

But in the 1980s, the conservatives around Bennett considered themselves intellectuals whose presumptions rested on scholarly research. "You have to make the argument, find the ground, establish the intellectual credentials for your position," Bennett later said, echoing the same counsel he gave his staff in those years. "You ask to be taken seriously as an intellectual movement. And to do that you have to take other ideas seriously. It's not a matter of saying, 'Well, we're in the ascendancy. The country is going right, so everything on the Left is palaver.' " Bennett's staff read journals such as *Commentary* and the *Public Interest,* and books such as Allan Bloom's *The Closing of the American Mind* and Charles Murray's *Losing Ground.* As the staff gathered each day around Bennett's dining table, they often were accompanied by guest researchers on educational topics. They churned out reports on "what works" in schools, attempting to rejoin common sense and academic research (an effort that much of the press derided as simplistic nostalgia).

It was his first job in Washington, but Kristol had found his niche in this intellectual and political ferment. In his first months at Education, Kristol "came on as a smart guy, a hotshot, without question he had intellectual firepower," recalled Marion Blakey. But fellow staffers were dubious when Bennett promoted the young professor to chief of staff. "He hadn't managed anything, and this was a big ungainly department," Blakey recalled. Within months, though, Kristol—hardworking, an intent listener, a skillful player on the Washington court—had won over most of his skeptics. He always operated best at the helm of a tightly knit intellectual club.

There would remain, in Washington as in academia, a divide in opinion about Kristol: For his widening network of friends, he displayed a willingness to move mountains, plying his own considerable connections, through his father, to money and power to help them land jobs or launch conservative groups. To those outside his chosen circle, however, he often came off as an arrogant, if subtle, self-promoter. They saw mockery in the laughing eyes and crinkling forehead, the dancing eyebrows and under-the-breath quips. Kristol's Straussian training, which insulated him from the inflamed rhetoric of so many Reaganite activists, also lent him the aura of someone who looked down from above. "One of the main teachings" of Strauss, Kristol later explained, "is that all politics are limited and none of them is really based on the truth. So there's a certain philosophic disposition where you have some distance from these political fights. . . . You don't take yourself or your causes as seriously as you would if you thought this was 100 percent 'truth.' Political movements are always full of partisans fighting for their opinion. But that's very different from the truth.' "

Nevertheless, Kristol brought to his first Washington job a martial artist's instinct and an uncanny understanding of the concentration and care it takes to kick the board in order to break it, and not your foot. Even before he arrived in Washington, Kristol understood which arguments had a chance of breaking through the liberal establishment's sound barrier, and which would surely be written off as the unchecked passions of ideologues. Some of that came to him naturally. But family ties also provided him a close-up look at how to play the Washington game.

In the 1970s, a little-known journalist named Jude Wanniski began championing a little-known economist named Arthur Laffer and an obscure tax-cutting theory he called supply-side economics. A football star turned congressman named Jack Kemp took the idea national. "Jack Kemp embraced an economic theory that at the time had no academic backing to speak of, no popular support," Bill later explained to the writer David Frum. "And with one or two elected officials and the *Wall Street Journal* editorial page and Jude's book and six Capitol Hill staffers, [he] transformed the character, at least temporarily, of the Republican Party." Characteristically, Bill failed to mention that the man behind this clipped succession of events—and the one who orchestrated financing for Wanniski's supply side work—was his own father, Irving Kristol.

Bennett's combativeness landed him in trouble before Kristol arrived in Washington. At his first press conference, the secretary defended Reagan's college aid cuts by asserting that students who were harmed financially should "consider divestiture of a sorts—stereo divestiture, automobile divestiture, three-weeks-at-the-beach divestiture . . ." Bennett may have intended his remarks as a dig at liberal activists calling for university divestiture from South Africa, but the remark made the secretary—himself a product of Williams College and Harvard—look like an uncaring elitist. Critics called for his head.

When Kristol arrived four months later, his first job was to put Bennett's "divestiture" comment behind him by helping the secretary refocus the department on raising public school standards. Here, research was on their side, particularly in the alarming 1983 report *A Nation at Risk,* which could be used to appeal to parents and teachers uneasy about the demonstrated decline in children's academic performance. Kristol crafted a Bennett speech on bilingual education, using available research to argue that continuing to teach children in their native languages—then a gospel of the teaching profession—was leaving immigrant children bereft of critical English skills. In the fall of 1985, Bennett proposed giving local school districts more flexibility to use English-immersion strategies for immigrant students. By 1990s standards, the plan was a relatively modest one, but educators denounced the proposal as a "war on children." The Bennett approach proved prescient, however; a decade later, California scrapped its massive bilingual program because children were graduating without English skills.

Even more outrage ensued from Bennett's call for a debate on the role of religion in public life, and from his argument that the "fate of our democracy is intimately intertwined—'entangled' if you will—with the vitality of the Judeo-Christian tradition." Bennett's remarks were prompted by the Supreme Court's "fastidious disdain for religion" (as the secretary put it), the most recent example being a decision barring public schools from offering remedial and enrichment classes at parochial facilities. But Bennett also suggested a return to prayer, if only voluntary, in public schools. "Might not voluntary school prayer be an auxiliary to character in some places?" he asked. Fearful that Bennett was overstepping a carefully etched line between church and state, liberal groups denounced him as "outrageous," a man "bent on being the secretary of evangelism."

Eight months into Bennett's term, the *New York Times* proclaimed that the education secretary had "managed to stir up enough controversy for a full four-year term." None of these criticisms slowed down the Bennett team, and the Judeo-Christian theme would remain a hallmark of his tenure. But as Kristol and the other rookies on staff began to learn the dynamics of Washington, they helped their boss choose his targets more judiciously. The secretary stopped criticizing students, as he had with the infamous "divestiture" remarks, and was careful not to assail classroom teachers. Kristol even resisted assaults on liberal college professors. In 1985, when Reed Irvine's organization Accuracy in Academia was "monitoring" college professors for supposed left-wing bias, Kristol denounced the group and its harassment tactics. "Of course there is a bias on campus, but this kind of scrutiny by an external group isn't the way to attack it," he told a reporter. Kristol described his colleagues at Harvard as "predominantly liberal, but very tolerant. On the whole, professors try not to indoctrinate students."

If the baby-boom conservatives under Bennett's tutelage at Education could be criticized as bullies, at least they were learning to pick on opponents their own size—principally the teachers unions, college administrations, and the broader "educational establishment." Bennett began regular travels to schools, sidestepping union leaders in Washington to speak directly to teachers and even to teach in their classrooms. He publicly supported using taxpayer funds for private school tuition, and put forth a plan to "voucherize" the Chapter One program, taking money earmarked for disadvantaged children away from public schools and giving it to parents to apply toward remedial programs elsewhere. But the day-to-day efforts of Fort Reagan were focused on strengthening the public schools, which nearly 90 percent of the nation's children attended. Talking points that Kristol submitted for the president's 1988 State of the Union address emphasized merit pay for teachers, higher academic standards, and opening up public-school teaching to noncredentialed professionals.

Inside Fort Reagan, the educational establishment was known as "the blob" (for "bloated education bureaucracy"). Bennett directed his staff to put together a wall chart demonstrating the disconnect between spending and performance by the nation's school districts—a direct assault on liberal educators who claimed that troubled schools needed more money. He flew into Chicago and proclaimed its school system the worst in the nation. He accused colleges of being money-obsessed and treating students like pests. He flew to Harvard and attacked American universities for failing to give their students "the basic body of knowledge which universities once took it upon themselves as their obligation to transmit." He flew to Stanford to accuse administrators of bowing to leftist political pressure in broadening its basic curriculum to include works addressing race, gender, and class. He sat in budget hearings on Capitol Hill and militantly defended proposed cuts in federal education spending. "Our congressional solons are not used to someone fighting back," Kristol boasted about his boss in one note to the White House.

The joke around the Education Department was that the two Bills, Bennett and Kristol, were a pair of accelerators with no brake. But the dynamic was more complicated. Bennett taught Kristol—and the cadre of smart young conservatives around them—the art of political confrontation: how to use available research to challenge the Left's loftier position among intellectuals; and, most of all, how to choose battles that could reshape the national agenda. But it was Kristol, the less pugnacious of the pair, who often knew when to pull back or recalibrate a message with a gentler touch. He would pick up the phone to news reporters; he would traipse over to the White House to offer a heads-up before one of Bennett's crusades.

Kristol also understood the value of stealth. In the fall of 1986, Barbara Bush was promoting a national adult literacy campaign, which had become an object of derision among conservatives. Aided by well-intentioned TV network executives, Bush launched a public campaign to secure additional spending on adult remedial programs. But to conservatives critics, money wasn't the issue, standards were: There wouldn't be a mass adult literacy problem, they argued, if the public schools produced students with better reading and English skills. For Bill to be linked to critics of the vice president's wife would be politically foolhardy. But Kristol was happy to feed relevant facts and figures to Daniel Casse, then managing editor of Irving Kristol's *Public Interest* magazine. Casse then wrote a *Wall Street Journal* op-ed column attacking the adult literacy campaign, drawing a barrage of angry replies, including one from Barbara Bush.

Understanding that "talking about education is a license to talk about everything," as education aide John Walters put it, Bennett used his position to step into two other explosive cultural issues—sex and drugs. At the time, the nation was in a state of alarm over the emergence of AIDS and an explosion of inner-city violence fueled by a crack-cocaine epidemic. Bennett's point man on these issues was undersecretary Gary L. Bauer, who would become close friends with Kristol. Bauer, an odd man out among the urban elites surrounding Bennett, was the Kentucky son of a beer-guzzling laborer. A devout Christian, he held prayer meetings in his Education Department office each morning. Kristol was impressed by Bauer's quiet influence inside the Reagan administration, his courage in standing up for his principles, and his outreach efforts to African-American churches, typically hostile territory for Republicans. The unlikely friendship that sprouted between these two men ran deep, and their families began annual vacations together at a Delaware beach. Largely out of this personal connection came Kristol's staunch and public defense of the Religious Right (though in unguarded moments he sometimes slipped and referred to evangelicals as "those people"), a stance that sealed his divide from a broad Jewish community deeply committed to retaining clear lines between church and state.

Bauer and Kristol were drawn together by a mutual horror at society's open attitude toward sex. At the time, educators and public health officials were responding to a spike in teen pregnancies not by discussing "restraint" or "abstinence," as Kristol would have them do, but rather by offering birth control to children at younger and younger ages. In reaction to the AIDS scare, public health officials, including the well-respected Surgeon General C. Everett Koop, had advocated sex education for children as young as nine. Kristol fought back: "We do not think we need suddenly to have demonstrations of condoms for 9-year-olds," he explained to the *Washington Post* in January 1987. Within weeks, Bennett was waging a campaign against "condom-mania."

Kristol helped his boss wander far beyond matters of education, or even sexuality. In 1987, Bennett flew to Nicaragua in a display of support for the contras. That same year, both the education secretary and his chief of staff involved themselves in Reagan's judiciary appointments, orchestrating a public defense of the embattled Supreme Court nominee Robert Bork. And it was Bennett, concerned about the Reagan administration's moral message, who convinced the next nominee, Douglas H. Ginsburg, to withdraw his name after reports surfaced that he had used marijuana.

But for all of their talk about limiting the federal role in education, and all the alarm bells that educators sounded during the department's annual ritual of proposed budget cuts, Kristol's team didn't succeed in curtailing federal education spending. At the end of Bennett's tenure, the department was half again as big as it had been in 1981, mostly the result of spending hikes during Bennett's term. The spending trend was pretty much the same throughout the federal government: Conservatives lost Reagan's proclaimed war on Big Government without a shot being fired.

The moralists manning Fort Reagan, however, had never intended to give up their power—they wanted to use it to alter the nation's cultural zeitgeist. Bennett "taught conservatives the way to use government and the fruitlessness of simply being against government," Kristol said, "[how] to dominate the domestic policy agenda, not just be reactive, but positive." In that, Bennett and his team succeeded, even earning admiration in some unlikely quarters of the media, but not without making scores of enemies.

The 1980s were a time when state and local communities were heavily engaged in education reform. Critics accused Bennett of being divisive when he should have been supportive of those efforts. California school superintendent Bill Honig was among those who accused the secretary of setting the "cause of education reform back." But the Fort Reagan strategy was based on moving the national conversation forward by drawing lines in the sand, not blurring them. "We picked more fights than we needed to and we were probably a little harsher in rhetoric than we needed to be," Kristol later conceded. And maybe the department wasn't always a well-oiled machine, he noted, but the point was "not to hum quietly."

ANOTHER REAGANITE VANGUARD within the administration emerged during that second term—a group of young lawyers at the upper echelons of Attorney General Edwin Meese's Justice Department. They, too, considered themselves intellectuals: They had graduated from top law schools and earnestly debated the nuances of constitutional law at the Federalist Society's monthly Chinese lunches in downtown Washington. In Reagan's second term, they would attend the attorney general's high-minded weekend retreats on economic liberty or the separation of powers. Like the Straussians, who also formed an influential contingent of the Justice staff, and like the Religious Right, these young lawyers, too, were fundamentalists.

But theirs was a fundamentalism of law, applied not to the Bible, nor to Greek texts, but to the U.S. Constitution, a document they imbued with a patriotic air of sanctity. In their minds, the Founding Fathers—with their classical notions of governance, their belief that the most noble object of government was moral betterment ("the cultivation and improvement of the human mind," James Wilson asserted at the Philadelphia Convention)—had crafted documents suited for the ages. America had suffered, they asserted, from a Supreme Court that insisted on applying the spirit of the Constitution—rather than the Founders' "original intent"—to modern questions.

Conservatives faulted liberal judges who, in their eagerness to expand individual rights and produce a more egalitarian society, created new legal standards not found in the Constitution, nor often in statutes. Bill Kristol argued in his 1979 Harvard dissertation that the courts lost sight of their role as special "guardians of the Constitution" (Hamilton's words) once litigation ceased being a matter of dispute between two private parties and became a way of pursuing "grievance about the operation of public policy." "We have moved," Kristol wrote, "from an emphasis on the Constitution as a shield to the Constitution as sword."

In the summer of 1985, Attorney General Meese—a Reagan intimate known more for his law-and-order campaigns than for his grasp of constitutional law—launched a series of provocative speeches attacking sixty years of Supreme Court precedent. That a Reagan attorney general would criticize a Court that had blessed affirmative action and school busing, legalized abortion, and banned prayer in schools was hardly surprising. But Meese went further, asserting that the Supreme Court had erred in applying the Bill of Rights to curtail the states' authority in areas ranging from criminal justice to displays of religious faith. He called these precedents "politically violent and constitutionally suspect."

In rulings dating back to the 1920s, the Supreme Court rulings had created national standards on matters central to American democracy—in particular, free speech, freedom of religion, and equal protection. To suggest that the states—the source of Jim Crow laws, forced segregation, and other denials of fundamental rights—could abide by their own pronunciations of individual liberty was anathema to most Americans. What did Meese want to do, critics asked—go back to the days when black children weren't allowed in white schools, when public institutions could promote Christianity as the national religion, when legislatures could regulate the bedroom habits of married couples?

Liberals were eloquent in their condemnations of the attorney general. Supreme Court Justice William Brennan derided original intent as "arrogance cloaked as humility. It is arrogant to pretend that from our vantage we can gauge accurately the intent of the framers" on "specific, contemporary situations." Even Clint Bolick, a self-proclaimed originalist who would join Meese's Justice Department in 1987, argued that Congress clearly intended that the Fourteenth Amendment—with its "guarantee that no person be deprived of life, liberty, or property without due process of law"—should restrain the states from violating the Constitution's Bill of Rights. "States don't have rights," Clint asserted. "People have rights."

As a scholar at Harvard, Bill Kristol had made his own case for original intent. But as he looked across town at the attorney general's campaign he thought: Nice man, good intentions, ham-handed delivery—as bad a political backfire as Bennett's "divestiture" remarks. Meese's attack on sixty years of Supreme Court precedent had set off a tirade of criticism but convinced practically no one outside revolutionary circles. One prominent leader said the "extremism" of Meese's Justice Department "actually contributed to a sense of reaffirmation on civil rights" because it linked Republican moderates with liberals in opposing the attorney general's crusade.

Three thousand miles away, an intense young lawyer who would one day work for Kristol, and who also believed in original intent, had a different reaction. To David McIntosh, Meese's words came as a clarion call to quit his law firm job in L.A. and join the Reagan revolution. His Federalist Society friends were already there: After law school, Lee Liberman, Steve Calabresi, and Peter Keisler had settled in Washington to clerk for such movement heroes as Robert Bork and Antonin Scalia, and to put their rightist legal theories to work for Meese. While his friends were writing rattling the cages of the nation's legal establishment, David was handling real estate transactions on L.A.'s Westside.

In fact, there had been calculation behind David's move from the University of Chicago Law School to California. He was systematically following the plan, etched into his brain since youth, that laid out the first steps of a political career: One must pursue a private sector profession, church and family, and a settled life in a prospective congressional district. So as the revolution unfolded in Washington, David was living with three friends in an apartment near UCLA, biking along the Venice boardwalk in between his legal work. He stayed far enough away from mood-altering substances to earn a reputation among his roommates as "the saintly one," but neither was he considered a prude: David's humor, his friends recalled, was too biting, too barbed.

After his college years adrift from faith, David joined a church in L.A. But even that suggested a more complicated picture of McIntosh. His church, Brentwood Presbyterian, was a leading bastion of liberalism, a place where leaders of the sanctuary movement, which sheltered illegal immigrants, could count on a welcoming audience. David helped lead a church youth group to Tijuana, where 2,500 human beings were living off scraps of food in the city dump, to build homes for the homeless. His best friends included leftist missionaries such as roommate Mark Porizky, who went to Nicaragua to protest that country's civil war. (Years later, his church friends would see "Congressman McIntosh" in the news, blocking environmental efforts or supporting cuts in federal aid to the poor, and they would wonder: Hadn't Tijuana affected him, as it had them? But by then, David had his theories, and those theories, he was sure, were of more help to the people than the welfare state of his liberal friends.)

When the offer came to join Meese's team as a special assistant in the summer of 1986, the twenty-eight-year-old leapt at the opportunity. Despite the Justice Department's stern and echoey halls, there was no mistaking the ideological crusade taking place there during the Meese years. That summer David joined a group of committed young political appointees who, recalled Solicitor General Charles Fried, "thought of themselves as revolutionaries [and] did not trust the usual channels to deliver results." David quickly made his mark working on a case that became known to the Right's cognoscenti as the "Beck decision"—a court ruling that gave union members the right to withhold their dues from union political activities. Beck was an important victory in the Right's "defund the Left" crusade.

But the legal revolutionaries inside the Justice Department were so inflamed with cause, so certain in their righteousness, that they frequently underestimated the opposition and overestimated their standing with the American public. That became clear during the bloody 1987 nomination fight over Supreme Court nominee Robert Bork. Bork was a towering figure in the Right's legal establishment—combative, intellectually daring, fearless in his condemnations of three decades of legal precedent. As a professor in the early 1980s, he also had been a guiding light of the Federalist Society. McIntosh's Yale friend Peter Keisler, then in the White House counsel's office, was at Bork's side throughout the fight. Federalist Society co-founder Lee Liberman solicited support for the nominee from her new teaching post at nearby George Mason University. By then, McIntosh had moved to the White House, and he worked on preparing the nomination. At Justice, Clint Bolick, then enjoying his second year in Washington, was given the assignment of poring over cases Bork handled as Nixon's solicitor general for any hidden controversies.

Bork was a fat target for the Left. His youthful embrace of libertarian philosophy prompted him to write a 1963 *New Republic* article condemning sections of the proposed Civil Rights Act designed to integrate public accommodations—a position for which he later expressed regret but which nevertheless haunted him during his confirmation battle. As he evolved into a social and economic conservative, Bork inveighed against moral relativism and asserted that government attempts to root out natural inequalities in business and society lent the state tyrannical powers. His critique of a 1965 Supreme Court decision granting married couples the right to privacy against a state ban on contraception left no doubt about his willingness to permit states to outlaw abortion. "Most distressing in Bork's philosophy, from a liberal point of view, was his insistence that if legislatures passed intrusive laws, the laws had to be upheld if the Constitution did not specifically prohibit them," journalist Ethan Bronner noted in his comprehensive recounting of the Bork hearings. Adding to the nominee's notoriety was his willingness, under Nixon, to fire Watergate special prosecutor Archibald Cox after then Attorney General Elliot Richardson and his deputy had quit rather than carry out the order.

Whatever anyone thought of Bork's legal views, it was hard to ignore his lofty academic and judicial credentials. Nevertheless, the liberal opposition mounted a massive campaign of national advertising and grass-roots lobbying that ensured Bork was "demonized, caricatured, made to embody all they hated," according to Bronner. Speaking for his liberal allies, Senator Ted Kennedy laid out the terms of debate from which the nominee would never recover: "Robert Bork's America is a land in which women would be forced into back alley abortions, blacks would sit at segregated lunch counters, rogue police could break down citizens' doors in midnight raids, school children could not be taught about evolution, writers and artists could be censored at the whim of government." Even the *Washington Post*, which urged the Senate to reject Bork, condemned the "intellectual vulgarity and personal savagery" of his liberal opponents. Clint Bolick, who didn't always agree with Bork, who saw constitutional privacy protections where Bork saw none, nevertheless watched a "towering giant . . . being attacked by hordes of pygmies. . . . It was not just so much that they disagreed with what he'd done but they just really disliked the person." That fall, Bork was defeated on a 58–42 Senate vote.

For Bill Kristol, who aided the Bork forces publicly and behind the scenes, that defeat provided a telling lesson on how the Right, in an America largely shaped by liberal presumptions, was too often afraid of its own arguments. "I was appalled at the timid performance of the Republicans and the White House," he said. "They should have laid the groundwork, made the case why his positions were reasonable. . . . [The Bork nomination battle] was a terrible injustice and, really, he was treated badly. On the other hand, this *is* politics—you should fight intelligently and try to win. Conservatives sometimes like being martyrs more than winning. They have that sense of being unjustly persecuted."

For David McIntosh, the episode was a lesson in the importance of placing aggressive true-believers at the helm of the Right's political battles. Otherwise, he believed, the battle remains in the hands of those who "basically agree with [conservatives], but when their friends and neighbors and colleagues and people in the media say something is a bad idea, they become afraid of it. . . . Unless you stand up and fight, the issues get defined by the other side." Five months after his defeat, an embittered Bork found solace in the embrace of the Federalist Society's annual conference, where he would be treated to four standing ovations and the sight of audience members sporting "Reappoint Bork" buttons.

BY THEN, CLINT BOLICK was building his own relationship, deep and abiding, with a man who would step into Bork's shoes three years later. Although Clarence Thomas would succeed where Bork had not, he, too, would be subjected to an all-out assault by the Left that would scar those around him.

Back in 1985, when Clint first applied for a job with Thomas, then chairman of the Equal Employment Opportunity Commission, he was known in conservative circles simply as "the other Clarence." The more famous Clarence, also a black conservative, was Clarence M. Pendleton, chair of the U.S. Commission on Civil Rights, a man outspoken in his denunciations of such liberal icons as affirmative action ("immoral") and comparable worth, a feminist proposal to close the male-female wage gap by forcing companies to offer similar pay for similar-level skills ("probably the looniest idea since Looney Tunes"). Clint "worshipped at the altar" of Pendleton, former head of the Urban League's San Diego chapter, because he "was politically incorrect before there was a term, a no-holds-barred slashing revolutionary."

That (especially the no-holds-barred part) was precisely what Clint himself aspired to when he sent his resumé to Washington. After his grueling experience with leftist law students at U.C. Davis, Clint had joined Mountain States Legal Foundation in Denver, one of the Right's handful of "public-interest" law firms. But Mountain States turned out to be an inhospitable home for Clint, who believed its sponsors to be more interested in protecting business interests than in pursuing libertarian idealism. So he resolved to join the Reagan Revolution.

In the early months of 1985, Clint, who had been contributing to opinion pages to promote himself and his views since he was a teen, introduced himself to Washington with a column arguing that civil rights groups, by embracing the goal of equal results over equal opportunity, had abandoned any "claim to moral leadership in the field of civil rights." "The Left," he intoned, "learned all too well the lesson of the white supremacists it earlier had so bitterly opposed: that government's power to discriminate is awesome once unleashed, and that it can confer enormous tribute upon its beneficiaries. . . ." He submitted the piece to the conservative *Washington Times,* which sat on it for weeks. Until his words came back to haunt him.

Kristol's 1984 ode to political confrontation had landed him a job with Bill Bennett. But Clint's own diatribe a year later nearly cost him his first political job. Ricky Silberman, then Clarence Thomas's vice chair at the EEOC, was stunned when she opened the *Washington Times* to read Clint's impolitic words just days after she had offered him a position on her staff. Comparing civil rights leaders to white supremacists was bad enough. Worse (from a Washington standpoint) was the fact that Clint managed to leave out Thomas's name, and to include Pendleton's, in his list of intellectual leaders of a "new civil rights movement." Silberman called Clint at his home in Denver and told him to delay his trip to Washington. Clint was in a panic: He had already quit his job, sold his house, and had a wife and new baby to support. He begged and pleaded, and finally Silberman relented and allowed him to take the job—but only after Clint promised to keep his mouth shut.

Silberman had hired the twenty-eight-year-old because she thought conservatives (most of whom were "optimistically challenged," as she put it) could benefit from Clint's charged idealism. As she worked with him, as a mentor as much as a boss, Silberman saw in Clint a young man almost puppy-dog-like in his sentimentality, naive in his eagerness to convince the other side. "His enthusiasm and his openness and his almost inability to accurately gauge the depth of one's enemy's bad feelings toward you—that all made him strangely vulnerable," said Silberman.

Under Silberman's tutelage, Clint would build a vocabulary expressly designed to chip away at the considerable ground supporting the civil rights community. Silberman, a Washington veteran and wife of a prominent conservative judge, never allowed her staff to use words like "affirmative action," "goals," or "timetables." Instead, they relentlessly spoke of "quotas" and "racial preferences"—harsh words designed to "drive the opposition nuts," said Silberman. After a year at the EEOC, Clint would make recapturing the words "civil rights" from the Left part of his lifelong mission.

If Silberman was Clint's public relations guru, it was left to a man born in a wooden shack on the edge of a Georgia tidal marsh to lend Clint the vision. Clarence Thomas saw himself as a black man who had made it on his own, persevering in the face of racism and poverty to rise to the top of the Washington power structure. Affirmative action, he believed, had helped (and stigmatized) the black middle class, easing white guilt while leaving behind a burgeoning black underclass. "Man, quotas are for the black middle class," he said at the time. "Look at what's happening to the masses. They are my people. They are just where they were before any of these policies."

The EEOC was a federal agency created under Title VII of the 1964 Civil Rights Act and charged with rooting out discrimination in the workplace. During the 1970s, the agency focused on sweeping enforcement activities designed to produce more racial and gender balance in hiring. "Goals" and "timetables" were the operative words, as the agency sought to change the face, literally, of companies' workforces. Overt discrimination wasn't the only problem agency officials saw in the 1970s: There were also structural impediments to minority advancement. So the EEOC pursued "adverse impact" lawsuits, challenging the use of tests and other hiring requirements that might reduce the pool of qualified minorities.

Thomas reversed this trend, increasing the EEOC's caseload by focusing on individual claims of discrimination. Law enforcement, not social engineering, was the proper mission of the agency, Thomas argued. Politically, Thomas's strategy was a way of demonstrating that the Reagan administration was not, as its detractors claimed, soft on civil rights. Initially this worked. Civil rights leaders frequently expressed "disappointment" that Thomas's agency was "less vigorous" than it had been in the 1970s. Nevertheless, they distinguished him from other Reaganites, particularly their nemesis at Justice, the chilly and hard-edged civil rights chief, William Bradford Reynolds. Reynolds had made his mark in 1983 by fighting an IRS decision to remove Bob Jones University's tax-exempt status because of racist policies. Acutely aware that he could "easily be seen as an Uncle Tom coopted by these right-wingers" at Justice, Silberman recalled, Thomas attempted to forge an independent voice. One NAACP lawyer at the time expressed the belief that "Thomas has a commmitment to civil rights; there's no question about it."

Clint first encountered Thomas by way of his booming, raucous laugh, which sailed out of the chairman's office as Silberman guided her new recruit down the hall for an introduction. When Clint stepped inside to shake hands, Thomas good-naturedly mentioned the young recruit's offending *Washington Times* op-ed only to say he had borrowed one of Clint's lines for a speech. Clint, nervous but fast on his feet, this time came back with a politic reply: "Don't worry. If anyone asks, I'll tell them I stole it from you."

Thomas loved to discuss political philosophy with his growing following of young acolytes. Favored aides were treated to lunchtime showings of the movie version of Ayn Rand's *The Fountainhead*. Clint found excuses to wander into the chairman's office, and was frequently invited out to lunch to talk strategy and share in Thomas's passion for Southern food. Thus did Clint, a young man who had lost his father on the brink of adolescence, enter into a relationship that looked remarkably like his teenage adoration for Mr. Locascio, the Linden, New Jersey, city councilman who had fought a lonely battle against the Democratic machine. When his second son was born, Clint asked Thomas to serve as godfather.

Mentor and student both saw themselves as lone warriors against an entrenched—and yet widely admired—civil rights community that had long ago stopped being a movement and had, instead, become an establishment prone (as all establishments are) to corruption of mission, "complacent, elitist, patronizing, and increasingly detached from the needs of its claimed constituency," as Bolick would later write. Thomas believed that affirmative action was a disguised form of racism: These policies were premised on "some inherent inferiority of blacks . . . by suggesting that they should not be held to the same standards as other people." He complained about the media's "obsession with painting blacks as an unthinking group of automatons." "We certainly cannot claim to have progressed much in this century as long as it is insisted that our intellects are controlled entirely by our pigmentation," he complained. In one of his more provocative statements, Thomas accused black leaders of "watching the destruction of our race" as they "bitch, bitch, bitch, moan and moan, whine and whine."

Clint's one-on-one sessions with the EEOC chairman altered his political horizons: Don't focus your sights on the victims of "reverse discrimination," Thomas counseled him. Leave the cause of the Allan Bakke's to others. Instead, he encouraged Clint to turn his attention to the poor, who typically didn't benefit from the affirmative action programs in universities and corporations. Thomas shared stories of his grandfather, who had transformed a hand-built pushcart into a small but thriving coal, oil, and ice delivery business—only to face licensing authorities bent on putting blacks out of business.

Clint's thoughts about civil rights evolved into what he began to call "economic liberty." Everyone on the Right accepted the view that welfare, too readily offered, had undermined the poor's chance of success by promoting dependency on the state. Under Thomas's tutelage, Clint began asking another question: Could state and local laws and regulations be preventing people of color from becoming entrepreneurs instead of welfare dependents? Was Jim Crow still on the books, in subtler form?

Clint also emerged from these conversations with a perspective that in later years would distinguish him from some of his allies on the Right: Thomas reinforced his conviction that racism was a real and intractable force in American life, not just an exaggeration of Leftists eager to impose their own agenda on the nation. Later, in debates over the 1991 Civil Rights Act (denounced by Clint and others on the Right as a quota bill), Clint would dissent from conservative allies when he endorsed a provision to add punitive damages to Title VII as a disincentive to workplace discrimination. "It seemed to me," he said, "that if you didn't want quotas, you had to have tough remedies and punitive damages against recalcitrant discriminators. . . . That very much came out of Thomas."

Thomas also fed Clint's view that the Republican Party didn't really care about the plight of black America. Thomas complained that inside the Reagan administration, "indifference to the views of black appointees has been pretty prevalent. . . . You constantly have to prove your conservative credentials because it is assumed you are liberal." He said conservatives too often gave the impression that blacks were "tolerated but not necessarily welcomed." To be accepted, a black conservative must "become a caricature of sorts, providing sideshows of antiblack quips and attacks," he asserted.

Clint stayed at the EEOC for only a year before moving to the civil rights division of Meese's Justice Department in 1986 to gain needed courtroom experience. But Thomas's influence endured. During his off hours, Clint wrote his first book, ambitiously offering an alternative civil rights agenda for the nation. While it reached only a small audience, *Changing Course* was the first serious attempt by an activist on the Right to adopt the words "civil rights" as the underpinning of a conservative agenda. "Language is very, very important," Clint later said, "and there are certain terms we cannot cede."

Clint's book drew heavily upon the work of Martin Luther King, who extolled the notion of an individual's inalienable rights as expressed in the Declaration of Independence. Clint embraced the "rich legacy" of the civil rights movement while condemning the movement's modern leaders for reintroducing racial classifications to shift the agenda from equality of opportunity to equality of results. Drawing also on the work of Walter Williams, an economist who studied discrimination in public policy, Clint offered a detailed history of how state legislatures, backed until this century by the Supreme Court, had used government power to enforce discrimination. When Southern white supremacists failed to undermine emancipation in the free market, he argued, they resorted to coercion through law.

According to Clint, economic restraints against blacks arose in the form of Jim Crow laws, but also in less obvious cases, chief among them the so-called Slaughter-House Cases. In a narrowly decided 1873 decision, the Supreme Court upheld Louisiana's grant of a monopoly to slaughterhouses operating in and around New Orleans, saying authorities could restrict the location of cattle slaughtering. That ruling, Clint argued, set a precedent enabling states to impose arbitrary—and often racist or sexist—restrictions on entrepreneurs. He later made it his personal mission to convince the Supreme Court to overturn that nineteenth century ruling.

What Clint laid out as a "positive" approach for achieving civil rights—eliminating racial categories, breaking down state-enforced economic barriers—his critics dismissed as naive at best, insidious at worst, a compassionate-sounding cover for the Right's protection of racism. Liberal civil rights leaders worried less about continuing discrimination by government licensing authorities than by the free market and the white men who controlled it. Since the 1950s, the federal government had been an ally, not an adversary, of the civil rights movement. To civil rights leaders, race-based affirmative action was not state-enforced discrimination; rather it was reparation for past oppression, a way to bring minorities to the same starting line.

In 1984, Clint and his friend and former boss Chip Mellor had sat in Chip's Denver backyard, angry and near tears over their break from the Mountain States Legal Foundation. Together they forged a vision of building a libertarian public interest law firm that would be pure in mission, untainted by self-interested business donors. The dream at that point was nebulous, overly ambitious. Clint's discussions with Clarence Thomas, and the book that ensued, lent it clarity: Bolick and Mellor resolved to go to court, on behalf of disadvantaged people of color, to break down state-enforced economic barriers. They would build a new kind of civil rights movement, one based on what they called "economic liberty."

But it took several more years for that dream to become reality, and Clint made the first move alone. In 1989, he left government, took a grant from the conservative Landmark Legal Foundation, and set up practice as a "civil rights" lawyer in the basement of a Capitol

Hill townhouse. Shortly thereafter, he spotted a newspaper article about a Washington, D.C., shoeshine man named Ego Brown, whose curbside business had been shut down by city police enforcing a 1905 law forbidding stands on public streets. This was it: Clint's big break, a chance to imbue his legal theories with flesh and blood. The law was a relic of the Jim Crow era, the kind of insidious municipal overreach aimed at keeping blacks out of business. Ego Brown was the embodiment of the fictional taxi driver Clint had created in a magazine article on racist economic cartels. He was a reincarnation of Clarence Thomas's grandfather. It was time for a shine.

Clint found Brown at the small indoor stand he still maintained, and plopped himself into the chair. Brown's story was a compelling one, for judge or jury or TV audience (and Clint would always have a keen appreciation for the importance of currying a sympathetic media during his legal cases). Brown had expanded his business by hiring homeless youth, providing them with a shower, training, shoeshine kits, and a stand in return for a $10 share of their daily take. His business had been thriving until D.C. authorities stepped in, and now this dignified gentleman, natty in his black felt hat and argyle socks and spit-shined loafers, was steps away from the dole.

Clint told Brown that the city's action was not only unfair, but unconstitutional. He asked Brown if he'd be willing to file a lawsuit, with Clint as his pro-bono lawyer. Brown readily agreed and Clint filed *Ego Brown* v. *Marion Barry,* his first economic liberty case. In March 1989, a federal judge ruled the ordinance unconstitutional; later the city council repealed the law. ABC News named Ego Brown its "person of the week."

Yet (and this would stick with Clint for years to come) through the entire case, Washington's civil rights establishment remained hostile, or silent. One liberal attorney appeared on TV to argue that the District was operating within its legal police powers to regulate shoeshine stands. Another dismissed the suit as a relic of the nineteenth century. An activist attorney at the EEOC was overheard saying that collecting welfare was more dignified than shining shoes.

In Clint's mind, he had begun to forge an alternative strategy for securing civil rights in America, one that he believed held true to the country's founding principles. And all the Left could say (his friends thought, bitterly) was this: This guy Bolick is exploiting these poor people to advance his right-wing agenda.

CHAPTER 9

CO-BELLIGERENTS

No ONE BELIEVED IT, at first. Ralph Reed had come home to the Lord and all most of his friends could say was, "Must be another one of his scams." Ralph had burned so many bridges that his fellow activists figured his religious conversion was a way to wipe the slate clean, "to make people give him another chance," as Amy Moritz Ridenour recalled. Even those friends who accepted Ralph's account of being "born again" didn't buy the corollary about a metamorphosis of Ralph's character. "He didn't change his views," asserted University of Georgia classmate Jack Dominey, "he just found out that God agreed with him." "God should make you uncomfortable with your life, not comfortable," said fellow College Republican Sam Harben, who also became a committed Christian later in life.

But for those who eventually came to believe that Ralph had undergone a profound spiritual transformation (and there were plenty, like Moritz Ridenour, who did) the signs pointing to his dramatic new future had been evident for some time. At the University of Georgia, Ralph—who never went to church, who considered winning to be sacred and humility a vice—hardly appeared to be on firm ground with the Lord. Nevertheless, one night at the Demosthenian Society he walked up to the podium to proclaim that the three forces of history were knowledge, ignorance, and faith. Of the three, he asserted, faith was the most powerful. "Defy knowledge," he concluded, "rely on faith."

Another signpost was the sheer desperate way Ralph was living his life in the early 1980s. In Ralph's mind, he was merely "attacking life . . . and if you do that without a moral compass, you make mistakes." Looking back, he said his "mistakes" were no different from those made by other exuberant young men. But Ralph's friends, recalling in particular his excessive drinking, took a different view. His high school friend Donald Singer saw Ralph in the summer of 1982 and was deeply worried: "He looked wasted physically. His pallor was sickly." Ralph also seemed to be very lonely; he had drinking buddies, but few close friends. In a recollection that Ralph disputes, Moritz Ridenour said Ralph sometimes took off after work from the College Republican headquarters and drove aimlessly into the Washington suburban night, sleeping in his car and laughingly recounting the episode in the office the next morning. Those able to set aside their own pique at Ralph saw a young man hungry for something more than a political cause to believe in.

An early medical diagnosis may have played a part in Ralph's libertine ways. As a teenager, Ralph experienced joint pain and was diagnosed with juvenile arthritis, a condition that without treatment can lead to loss of muscle, crippling, even blindness. Ralph left the impression with at least one friend that he was deeply worried about his future physical condition. When he was a College Republican activist, Ralph's family doctor warned him to cut back on his constant travels and long work days. Later, though, Ralph said the arthritis symptoms never materialized, and he insisted the initial diagnosis hadn't seriously affected his emotional state. "Either [the doctor] missed the diagnosis or I grew out of it," Ralph recalled. "It was not a major factor in anything. I ended up being fine."

Ralph turned himself over to the Lord one Saturday night in September 1983, when he was sitting in Bullfeathers, the Capitol Hill bar-restaurant favored by Washington's young activists. "I had quit drinking," Ralph recalled ". . . and I just decided, 'I want to make a change. I'm not drinking with these guys anymore anyways. This isn't as fun as it used to be.' " He told Christian audiences that the Holy Spirit "simply demanded me to come to Jesus." Later, this story would evolve, as Ralph recalled that his change of life was reinforced by another scene he witnessed at Bullfeathers: A congressman, a friend and ally of the College Republicans, who clearly had "a little too much to drink, walked in with somebody he wasn't married to." To Ralph, this was "nothing you don't see in Washington on virtually a daily basis. But I just thought, 'You know, if I'm going to represent the values that I'm fighting for in my public life, I want to make sure that in my private life I exemplify those same values.' "

Regardless of the details of that particular night, Ralph experienced a change of heart. He walked outside to a phone booth, thumbed through the Yellow Pages under "Churches" and found, in Camp Springs, Maryland, the Evangel Assembly of God church, which advertised that "one visit could change your life." He resolved to attend services the next morning. When the pastor led an altar call, beckoning those who desired a closer relationship with Christ, Ralph raised his hand in affirmation and "began a new life of faith," joining (in his own words) those who believed in "the divinity of Christ, the achievement of eternal salvation through personal conversion, and the imminent and bodily Second Coming of Christ."

Even before that night in Bullfeathers, Ralph had begun to listen to voices urging him toward a life of faith: An evangelical college roommate had witnessed to him, and an intern at the College Republican office was nudging him toward a life committed to Jesus Christ. "I later found out that there was a group at the University of Georgia that was actually praying for me," Ralph recalled. "So there was groundwork." There was also groundwork in Ralph's high ambitions for himself. He was, after all, a young man who (encouraged by a resolute mother) had always believed he had been called to do great things in life. (How many mothers would, as Mrs. Reed did, try to get her precocious nine-year-old son's novel published, and then, when that failed, printed it herself?) "One of the reasons for the intensity of my rebellion," Ralph recalled, "was that I knew it was only youthful. I had this feeling that this was not what my life was going to be. I always felt, from the time I was a little kid, that I was called for greatness, that I was called to great and grand endeavors. I wasn't called to party and drink and chase women."

After accepting Jesus into his heart, Ralph knew his next step was to seek forgiveness—of the temporal sort. He issued apologies, some by letter, others in person, some direct, some more roundabout. However the apologies were delivered, his friends got the point, even if they didn't always accept Ralph's sincerity. One who did was Lee Culpepper, victim of Ralph's rigging of the College Republican election at the University of Georgia. "It was a heartfelt note," Culpepper recalled, "saying that maybe he had viewed politics as a tool to achieve certain ends and that now he saw it as an opportunity to do good."

Ralph later conceded that he "hurt some people and did some

things that were wrong. But it all turned out for the good because it forced me to come to grips with who I was and who I wanted to be." When he answered the pastor's altar call that Sunday morning, at age twenty-two, he chose a new road. "It was a choice that obviously dramatically changed my life," he said. "I wouldn't have married who I married, I wouldn't be who I am today, but for that one decision. Everything flows out of that decision." In turning to faith and seeking forgiveness, Ralph recalled that he looked at himself and said, "You know, I'll probably be powerful and I'll probably be rich but I'll look in the mirror and I won't like what I see. . . ."

To his parents back home in Toccoa, Georgia, Ralph's "faith experience in Washington was the thing that made a man of him. He is a better person . . . because of his faith in God." Surprisingly, liberal classmates from college were more willing than his conservative allies to accept Ralph as a changed man. "He wasn't at peace in college," said Chuck Reece, the editor of the University of Georgia student newspaper. "He was angry, self-righteous. Then he reached peace." But many in Ralph's circle of Washington-based Republican activists took months, sometimes years, to build trust in him.

In the end, most came around to accepting Ralph Reed as a deeply changed young man determined (if not always able) to leave his heedless ways behind. And then there was Grover Norquist's take on his friend and fellow hard-core activist: "Ralph got all mushy in the head. He wanted to love everybody."

In early 1984, Ralph celebrated his new direction in life by founding a political organization of campus evangelicals. The press release he sent out to introduce the group also announced his religious conversion to the world. The group, Students for America, actually was the brainchild of the old guard of the Young Americans for Freedom, including Marvin Liebman and M. Stanton Evans. Having watched YAF fall on hard times, they were eager to start a new, politically vibrant youth group with the same talent that had revived the College Republicans.

The SFA would use PAC money and young activists to support religious conservatives in key congressional and gubernatorial races. "I had recently become a deeply committed Christian," recalled Ralph, "and I basically said if you want a forum, a YAF of the 1980s, you've got to have a Judeo-Christian twist. . . . Also, YAF was kind of intellectual, highbrow, Manhattan. We wanted to make this more grass-roots." The initial plan was to base the group in Raleigh, North

Carolina, and to move the office every two years to build a regional network. Ralph's backers were determined to keep the headquarters away from what they saw as the seductive, corrupting influence of Washington, D.C.

As College Republican activists, Grover and Ralph had eyed the political potential of churches, figuring that conservative congregations could easily produce as many eager volunteers for the Right as unions had for the Left. With SFA, Ralph would have his first opportunity to test that theory. He began (as he would at the Christian Coalition five years later) by talking big: "Students for America is more than 7,000 students on approximately 200 college campuses in 41 states," the group's 1985 literature boasted. "We plan to register at least 20,000 new conservative and Christian voters in each of our ten target states."

Who could tell whether Ralph was exaggerating SFA's size and clout? Most likely he was. But he was also building something that was tangible, and potentially powerful. Amy Moritz Ridenour, herself a veteran organizer, was skeptical at first (not to mention reluctant to share mailing lists with a politico she still didn't trust). But what she saw of SFA was impressive: "They had real members, real activists. I know because when we were doing work in the field we came across their members."

The SFA offered talented young people—the group's "top guns"—a chance to fly to "targeted campuses on forty-eight-hour notice to tackle the Left on crucial issues." Field directors criss-crossed the country, recruiting thousands of new members. And at the SFA's first national convention, in Washington in January 1985, Ralph delivered such major conservative figures as Jesse Helms, Newt Gingrich, Jack Kemp, Bill Bennett, and Jeane Kirkpatrick.

Something else was happening behind the scenes at that 1985 convention that would affect Ralph's personal life. Three months earlier, at a Jesse Helms victory party, a bubbly young redhead named Jo Anne Young introduced herself to Ralph. Ralph, who was then twenty-three, already knew the girl had a crush on him. He also knew she was only sixteen years old, and he didn't share the infatuation. But Ralph did see in her a potential recruit. So he invited her to the upcoming SFA convention, taking place as part of the inaugural activities surrounding Reagan's reelection. Ralph assured Jo Anne's parents that their teenager would be supervised during the trip to Washington, and he assigned a young woman on staff to keep tabs on her.

Her supervisor turned out to be a "party animal," Jo Anne recalled, and soon the sixteen-year-old, caught up in the excitement of the inaugural festivities, was downing strawberry daiquiris in her hotel room. When their two other roommates—both strictly devout evangelicals—arrived, they began praying for Jo Anne's soul. "Later, they got me away from that girl and started sharing gospel with me. Because they thought I was older and in college, they started talking to me as if I was older. They scared me. I thought, 'Oh my God—I'm going straight to Hell!' " That weekend, Jo Anne turned herself over to the Lord (it would take another eighteen months for her to convince Ralph to turn himself over to her).

According to SFA's mission statement: "The Creator that gave us life also gave us liberty, and the sole duty of government is to protect both." Back at their Raleigh offices in the weeks following the group's opening convention, the SFA activists learned that a women's health clinic down the street was performing abortions, and they resolved to protect the Creator's work themselves. "There was this feeling that we should clean up our own backyard first," Jo Anne recalled.

In March, Ralph began leading his fellow activists in pray-ins and pickets at Raleigh's Fleming Center. While the protestors said they were careful not to hurt anyone or interfere with clients, the Fleming Center staff later recalled that the activists screamed epithets and intimidated patients with mock baby funerals. (Ralph, the veteran of street theater, rented a powder blue Cadillac to serve as the hearse.) Denise Moore, then the clinic's chief nurse, described the episode to a reporter: "We always had protesters. I don't remember it getting bad until [Reed] showed up. It was scary—every single day." Moore recalled that Ralph led picketers to the home of the Dutch-born doctor who founded the clinic, and demanded money from the clinic to fund a home for unwed mothers.

One day, Ralph entered the clinic's waiting room, opened his Bible, and began reading aloud. The arrest that followed was part of a calculated act of civil disobedience: Ralph went limp while police officers carried him out, and SFA issued a news release declaring that he planned a hunger strike in jail. When the police got wind of this, they released Ralph rather than assist him with his publicity ploy. Shortly thereafter, Jo Anne recalled, Ralph learned that a paper he thought he had signed to collect his personal possessions was actually a legal agreement to stay clear of the clinic.

Years later, as director of the Christian Coalition, Ralph would condemn the clinic confrontations orchestrated by Operation Rescue and other militant anti-abortion groups. But that turn in his life was still to come. In 1985, Ralph continued to struggle to move beyond his warmongering College Republican years. Jo Anne recalled that the Fleming Center incident left Ralph feeling "burned out" on political activism. "He thought, 'Is this what I want to be doing, for myself and my family, in the future?' " Perhaps with the abortion clinic protests, Ralph had, once again, gone to the edge, peered over, and stepped back, not liking what he saw.

Within months, Ralph's life took another U-turn: He resolved to become a college professor, certain that he could make a more fulfilling contribution to society on campus, writing books and teaching young people. In the fall of 1985, as his generational peers were pursuing the revolution in Washington, Ralph Reed simply checked out of politics. He entered Emory University in Atlanta on a full fellowship, to pursue a doctorate in history under the tutelage of Dan T. Carter, a prominent, and liberal, political historian.

RALPH WAS CHOSEN to enter Emory's graduate history program over some three hundred applicants, despite the fact that the department faculty was well aware (through the state's finely tuned academic grapevine) that Ralph had been accused of plagiarism at the University of Georgia. What Professor Carter saw when he looked at Ralph's application was not the young man's past mistakes, but his potential: Here was that rare graduate student who could write intelligent, persuasive, and eloquent prose.

For the next four years, Ralph threw himself into the largely liberal, secular world of graduate history studies at an elite university. He took courses in American and English and Russian history, studied American political movements in detail, and became convinced that American politics were shaped by demographic forces, a concept he would later apply to building his own social movement.

This was an isolating period for Ralph, though in later years he would reflect on the importance of taking that "walk in the woods," just as he often entertained periodic desires to leave the political fray and renew his perspective. Being virtually the only conservative student among liberal peers and professors added to his isolation. But his seclusion was also the result of academic demands he imposed upon himself: He maintained a stellar GPA while taking a full course load, and he embarked on a challenging dissertation that would require long hours in obscure historical archives.

To his professsors, who were aware of his activist background, Ralph appeared "intelligent, under control," recalled Carter. "His comments were not particularly ideologically driven." Indeed, the most telling chapter of Ralph's life at Emory was his last: His 515-

page dissertation on the South's nineteenth-century evangelical colleges was written in the critical voice of a secular historian, not in the passionate tones of a religious advocate. "It was an opening for him to write a special pleading for evangelicals," noted Carter. But Ralph not only avoided doing so, he was (in the considered opinion of his liberal dissertation adviser) overly harsh on his evangelical subjects.

"Fortresses of Faith: Design and Experience at Southern Evangelical Colleges, 1830–1900" is a crucial piece to the complex and evolving puzzle that is Ralph Reed. For those who would later come to fear this Christian Right leader, who would see in his piercing blue eyes designs for a Christian nation, Ralph's critique of moralistic evangelicals will come as a surprise. His dissertation dwelled on the miseries caused by the Christian colleges' strict regimen, intolerant and stern moral discipline, harsh punishments. Students suffered from widespread depression and occasional bouts of madness, Ralph wrote (with knowing sympathy for the "the prankster, the impious" for whom college administrators "made no provision").

His analysis did not sound like that of a man who would later publicly proclaim his faith in the inerrancy of the Bible. "Scientific findings that contradicted Scripture were dismissed as heresy," Ralph wrote in criticizing the evangelical colleges. Even ancient history, he noted, was cast in "stark religious terms." Physics students, he wrote, learned of the sovereignty of God as the creator of the universe, and astronomy students studied the star over Christ's manger and the solar eclipse that appeared upon Jesus' crucifixion. Religious witch hunts against suspect professors, he fretted, "produced a faculty that was as scholastically famished as it was spiritually sound."

In later years, Ralph would reassure his Christian Coalition membership of his belief in the Scripture's accuracy, writing: "We believe the Bible is the inerrant word of God. It is without error and it tells us the answers to life's problems." In the mid-1990s, those words served as a message to Ralph's members, a reminder that even as presidential candidates courted him, even as he was sought after by *Meet the Press* and *Face the Nation*, he was still part of their world. His dissertation, however, suggests that he also saw himself as part of another world, one seemingly at odds with faith-based politics.

Skeptics would claim that Ralph merely understood how to tailor his writings and remarks to his audience—demonstrating his evangelical credentials to religious activists, his scholarly detachment to faculty members, his tolerance and compassion to a broader public, his political instincts to national reporters. But "Fortresses of Faith" revealed something else about Ralph: He was a Christian evan-

gelical eager to operate in the modern humanist world. While his critics later would see a different image, Ralph clearly intended to steer
clear of the stern moralism that filled his story of evangelical colleges.
He was determined to draw distinctions between his own "persuade,
don't preach" strategy and the more judgmental messages of religious
right purists. "God gives each one of us a different way of witnessing
our faith," he once said. "John the Baptist was running around eating
locusts and screaming at people, and Christ went in and found a
woman by the well and said, 'Let me help you get some water.' They
were both perfectly legitimate witnesses."

In contrast to the pastors and ministers leading the Religious
Right in the 1970s and '80s, Ralph, a layman, frequently responded
"I don't know" when asked the details of his theological beliefs (a response common to fellow Christians who professed humility about
God's intentions). Asked to classify himself in the ongoing evangelical
debates about the timing and nature of the Lord's Second Coming,
Ralph answered: "I've never really gotten into that whole eschatology
thing because I really don't know when Christ is going to come back
and it's not my job to worry about it. I know that there are big debates
within evangelicalism about pre- and post-[millennialism] and all
that. I've never wasted an ounce of energy focusing on it. I mean, how
do I know [when Christ will return]? I really don't know."

Ralph's dissertation stands as a metaphor for his own life and
work: For the theme he repeatedly returned to in "Fortresses of
Faith" was the conflict between the Southern evangelicals' desire for
"protections from society's excesses" and their "hunger for prestige
and power" in the broader society. "On the one hand," he wrote,
"Southern evangelicals revered the accumulated wisdom and intellectual traditions of Western culture; on the other hand, they excoriated
society—particulary urban society—as wicked, sinful, and degenerate." In adopting the faith of a Christian evangelical, Ralph had put a
clamp on the social "excesses" in his own life. Yet his hunger for
"prestige and power" in academia and the national media was palpa-
ble. Could he deftly maneuver inside these two often conflicting
worlds, speaking both languages without tripping on his tongue? And
could he really lead modern day evangelicals out of their fortressses to
take a "place at the table" of the mainstream political establishment?

THE OFT-TOLD STORY of how Ralph Reed founded the Christian
Coalition begins at the Bush inaugural in January 1989, when failed
presidential candidate and televangelist Pat Robertson sat next to him

at a Students for America awards dinner and was so impressed he offered him a job. In truth, Ralph never intended to run Robertson's group. He planned to become a college professor, not a Christian activist. But Ralph had a wife, and a baby, and a need to make ends meet. Robertson, recalled Ralph's wife Jo Anne, simply "got to the finish line first," offering a paycheck before any university had.

Robertson was the son of a senator, graduate of Yale Law School and New York Theological Seminary, chief executive of a billion-dollar broadcast empire, and host of *The 700 Club*, a Christian-oriented TV news and commentary show. He was also a prominent figure in the charismatic wing of evangelicalism: He spoke in tongues, conducted healings, and once commanded a hurricane to depart from Virginia's shores. Fellow religious right leaders—such as Jerry Falwell, who pointedly did not invite Robertson to join his Moral Majority board in 1979—derided Robertson's style of faith.

Ralph didn't subscribe to Robertson's theology, either, nor was he a political supporter: Ralph had volunteered for Jack Kemp, not Robertson, in the 1988 presidential race. But both men had a keen appreciation for, and understanding of, grass-roots organizing. Robertson, who once said he had done "everything this side of breaking FCC regulations" to help elect born-again Baptist Jimmy Carter, felt (like other Christian conservatives) personally betrayed when the Democrat confessed "lust in my heart" to *Playboy* magazine and then went on to curry favor with his party's Leftists. So in 1980, he formed the Freedom Council to politicize evangelical Christians as well as Orthodox Jews and Roman Catholics. Sounding remarkably like his young hire nine years later, Robertson proclaimed at the time: "There are 175,000 political precincts in America. My goal was to have 10 trained activists in each precinct. . . ." In the years preceding his 1988 campaign for the Republican nomination, Robertson quietly built a grass-roots machine that was so effective it put the Bush campaign to panic in Michigan and produced a second-place showing for him in the all-important Iowa caucuses.

Even as Robertson retreated from the national political arena in 1988 to rebuild the shattered finances of his Christian Broadcast Network, he and his donors were loath to let all this organizational muscle waste away. In early 1989, moreover, Christian evangelicals were bereft of political leadership. The sex and money scandals then consuming the television evangelicals Jimmy Swaggert, Jim and Tammy Faye Bakker, and Oral Roberts had hurt the revenues and reputations of unrelated Christian evangelical organizations, including Robertson's CBN. Largely gone from the political landscape were the vocal

Christian Right groups of the early 1980s, including the Religious Roundtable and Christian Voice. The granddaddy of them all, Jerry Falwell's Moral Majority, had been folded into another group and was about to shut its doors for good.

As Robertson and Reed walked toward the elevators after the SFA awards dinner, Robertson said he knew donors willing to fund a new Christian political group. Would Ralph be interested in setting it up? The Emory graduate student, still at work on his dissertation, politely declined. But he did offer to outline how such a group might be organized. In February, Ralph mailed a memo to Robertson on how to form "a national political organization dedicated to mobilizing, educating and activating evangelicals" and their Roman Catholic allies. Ralph told Robertson that one of the most profound consequences of the 1925 Scopes trial, when humiliated evangelicals retreated from social and political action, was that "we have now had two full generations of Bible-believing Christians . . . with virtually no hands-on experiences in the political decision-making process." The outline of his plan to alter that balance of power boasted a membership base of 3 million, 350 chapters, and a $10 million budget—all by the 1992 presidential election.

Robertson never responded, and Ralph continued to work on his dissertation. Meanwhile, he and his wife Jo Anne struggled financially. In July of 1989, five months after he had sent his memo to Robertson, Ralph's stipend from Emory ran out. He still hadn't finished his dissertation. Jo Anne drew on savings to supplement her own income as a receptionist, as well as Ralph's meager fees from teaching American history survey courses at Emory and nearby Oglethorpe University. Still intent on pursuing a career as a historian, Ralph began the tortuous process of applying for academic positions in a tight job market.

By then, Jo Anne and Ralph had been married just two years. Though they had been friends since the 1984 Helms victory party, they didn't begin dating until the night of her graduation from high school in 1986. "I fell in love with him the first time I saw him," Jo Anne recalled. "I loved how funny he was. The stories he told might not be funny, but the way he told them was always funny. He was very smart." Jo Anne also saw Ralph as an extremely loyal person. "My parents are still married and I knew that once I got married, that was going to be it," she said. "We both had a committed relationship to the Lord. . . . There were just so many facets of our personalities that came together." Like Ralph, she was a military child whose family had moved every couple of years before settling in North Carolina.

While Ralph initially kept their friendship platonic, Jo Anne had more determined designs on him. In June 1986, she invited him to her senior prom, but then accepted another invitation while Ralph was mulling whether, at age twenty-five, he was too old to be donning tuxedos for high school soirees. Jo Anne followed her mother's old-fashioned advice to stand firm when he finally called back, telling him she was already booked. "My mom says that's when I got him—right then," Jo Anne recalled. Ralph did, however, show up for her graduation ceremony—late, as usual. That night the couple went on their first date; three months later, in October 1986, they were engaged. They married in July 1987.

Jo Anne's born-again experience hardly had the same personality-transforming effect that her husband's had. She said she had always been a "good girl." Even after their faith experiences, Ralph and Jo Anne Reed remained a young couple who appreciated a good time. Ralph was obsessed with golf, believed the Beatles had elevated rock music to an art form, and swapped bawdy wisecracks with friends. Jo Anne practiced tennis, turned up the volume on Garth Brooks on the car stereo, and charmed people with a bouncy personality that belied a shrewd business sense. (In the early 1990s, she would make a tidy sum for the family selling anti-Clinton paraphernalia.) While many in evangelical circles considered alcohol sinful, Ralph still drank beer, though now in moderation, and Jo Anne enjoyed her occasional wine or strawberry daiquiri.

When Robertson finally called in September, the young couple's savings were depleted and they had a five-month-old baby. Robertson invited Ralph to a gathering of leading political leaders from the conservative religious community. If the meeting had taken place in Dallas, as Robertson first intended, Ralph wouldn't have gone—he couldn't afford the air fare. But Robertson settled on Atlanta instead, and Ralph was able to drive across town to attend the meeting.

Ralph thought this was going to be an informal brainstorming session, and he would provide some outside counsel. Instead, to his dismay, Robertson introduced Ralph to the group—most of whom he didn't know—as the first staff member of his new political organization. To Ralph's further dismay, Robertson asked him to fly back to Virginia with him that very night to start work. On the second score, at least, Ralph resisted: He waited until the end of the week to head north and launch what would later become known as the Christian Coalition.

Pat Robertson had no intention of making Ralph Reed the public face of his new political machine. Ralph's job was to launch a viable organization so that Robertson could lure a more senior and states-man-like figure to run it. Ralph's title was "acting executive director." His salary was also unclear: After arriving in Virginia, Jo Anne re-called, Ralph had to phone his parents to borrow money. "Aren't you getting paid?" they asked, to which Ralph replied, "We haven't dis-cussed it."

But it was clear from the beginning who was boss: Robertson chose to call his organization the "Christian Coalition" without con-sulting Ralph. Ralph, who had written in his February memo that there should be "no spiritual litmus test for membership," preferred a secular name such as Citizens for a Better America. He worried that just as "Moral Majority" had become pejorative ("if you say you're moral, you're saying others aren't"), Christian Coalition would leave the group open to charges of sectarianism ("if you say, 'We're the Christian Coalition,' then what are they?"). But Robertson was deter-mined to keep the word Christian in the title. Later, the Coalition was criticized, as Ralph had predicted, by religious leaders disturbed by the implication that there was a "Christian" position on such earthly matters as the federal budget. Nevertheless, Ralph figured he could market an image that transcended the group's name. "We never be-came the Moral Majority," said Ralph, "we never became a curse word."

If Robertson saw Ralph as a glorified workhorse, Ralph didn't expect the televangelist's latest political project to turn into a perma-nent gig, let alone a path to national fame. Robertson, known as a cool and calculating executive, had a reputation for chewing up polit-ical organizers and spitting them out. Nearly all of Ralph's friends had counseled him to steer clear of *The 700 Club* host and his revolving-door political management. "I had one guy [advise] me to take the job, but demand my first salary in escrow," Ralph recalled. "I said, 'Yeah, right—that'll really work! That's a real confidence builder—first meeting, to tell Pat Robertson to his face that you don't trust him!' "

One person encouraging him to go forward, Ralph recalled, was Paul Weyrich, whose founding of the Free Congress Foundation and co-founding of the Heritage Foundation, and whose naming of the Moral Majority suggested more than a little political acumen. Weyrich told Ralph that Falwell had missed a historic opportunity with the Moral Majority, which, in the end, turned out to be more of a direct-mail list than an activist army. But with Robertson, Weyrich argued, Ralph could create something more lasting, something that could transform millions of conservative churchgoers into a powerful political force. And Ralph, never one to be plagued by self-doubt, agreed: "I could see the opportunity. I could see what it could do. If it didn't work out, I could move on. But if it took off, you could change the direction of American history. And I knew I could. I knew I could."

ROBERTSON'S OFFER would become the vehicle for Ralph's prophetic sense of destiny. It might have been something else: Imagine (as Ralph once mused) if Texas billionaire and 1992 presidential candidate Ross Perot had handed the reins of his Reform Party over to this scrappy and talented young politico. Ralph would have achieved a different kind of fame. His generation's movement might have looked different, too. But destiny tied Ralph to Pat Robertson, and Ralph would forever be defined by the words he had resisted—"Christian activist."

Ralph stepped gingerly into this role. When he followed Robertson to Tidewater, Virginia, he left Jo Anne and the baby behind, thinking he might be returning to Atlanta before too long. "We didn't want to uproot the family if it wasn't going to work out," Jo Anne recalled. But within months, Jo Anne was up in Tidewater, too, typing direct-mail donations into a rickety computer alongside another young mother as they took turns watching their two toddlers.

The soon-to-be exalted and reviled Christian Coalition of the 1990s began modestly: An aging warehouse office with one grimy bathroom; an undependable copying machine and angry calls from vendors demanding payment for past services to the Robertson '88 campaign; Ralph working the phones, and paying for them on his own credit card. But the direct-mail dollars began pouring in quickly. If Ralph's intention was to create a new kind of moral political voice, one that was positive and inclusive in its rhetoric and agenda, it wasn't evident in the Christian Coalition's first direct-mail drop. To generate a response, one historian of the Religious Right noted, "Reed relied on one of the Christian Right's most dependable ploys: outraging its constituency with sensational accounts of offenses against religion and morality committed by homosexuals, liberals, or the government." To be fair, though, the liberal community provided rich material: Ralph's direct-mail campaign solicited money from Christian conservatives by inveighing the handful of widely publicized sadomasochistic, homoerotic, and sacrilegious art that had been funded by grants from the federal National Endowment for the Arts. By the end of November, Jo Anne had inputted donations totalling $82,000.

The dollar flow freed Ralph to begin building something quite unusual in modern politics—a re-creation of the grass-roots voluntary associations that once drove American civic life. This model of connecting citizens—the Elks, the PTA, the American Legion—had been "upended since the 1960s," wrote Harvard Professor Theda Skocpol, a scholar on American civil society. By the 1980s, public policy debates were dominated by advocacy groups—on the Left and the Right—built on impersonal systems of direct mail and big donors, not on local federations of activist citizens. Examples included Greenpeace, the American Association of Retired Persons, Mothers Against Drunk Driving, or scores of other public interest groups. (Exceptions included the National Rifle Association on the Right and the National Education Association, a teachers' union, on the Left.)

Ralph was determined to avoid reliance on the direct-mail solicitations that had served as the rickety foundations of other groups on the Right, particularly the Moral Majority. Instead, he intended to construct a voluntary association with local chapters and leadership structures, one that offered grass-roots activists a clear path into Republican Party politics at the state and national level. "He reinvented a classic American form," said Skocpol.

Rather than campaigning to pass legislation or orchestrating high-profile events, "the end goal was to build the organization," said D. J. Gribbin, the Coalition's national field director in the 1990s. The national office in Virginia topped an organizational chart of state offices, local chapters, and church liaisons. "You didn't need all those boxes filled in every state, you just needed more boxes filled in than your competitor," said Gribbin. Ralph set out to build the Coalition—church by church, precinct by precinct—by training local activists to run their own show.

"At the peak," Ralph later said, "we had the largest grass-roots training program on the Right, maybe on the Left or Right, training fifteen thousand people a year." But in that first year, Ralph conducted the lion's share of a dozen training seminars—with a combined audience in the hundreds, not the thousands. He began each seminar by popping a video into the machine so that Robertson's familiar face could appear on-screen as he described an America in moral decline. Then Ralph followed up with the basics, teaching his pupils how to draw a crowd, how to build a base of volunteers, how to avoid sounding preachy, how to speak in public policy terms rather than "Christianese."

In fact, Ralph's field marshals never did preach. They counted. "Numbers, numbers, numbers," said Pat Gartland, Georgia's first

Coalition chairman. "You had to keep stuffing that front door with bodies." Fill rooms with volunteers, get them trained and assigned to an issue or a political campaign, anything to keep them on the roster. Then boast about your numbers (and Ralph would always be accused of inflating them): Rent small rooms to make crowds seem bigger; print a million voter guides (even if piles are left untouched); create a massive data base of churches and people (even if many were only voters who once signed a petition or called the office).

Ralph staffed the national office with savvy political and marketing people, and expected his workers to be fast on their feet. Anything less risked falling on the sword of Ralph's well-honed scorn: "What was that about?!" he'd ask, as his victim withered under his blue-eyed stare. "With Ralph, you have to get yourself up intellectually, be prepared for conversation with him because you're not going to have a relaxed conversation—it's going to be full speed ahead," recalled Marshall Wittmann, who later ran the Coalition's Washington office.

For the first three years, while he was organizing precincts, few outside the Coalition noticed what Ralph was up to. Reporters didn't call. Religious Right leaders, many hostile to the idea of competition, figured the Coalition was nothing more than a way for Robertson to keep his presidential hopes alive. When Jerry Falwell formally closed the doors of the Moral Majority the same year that the Coalition staff opened theirs, most figured he was passing the baton to James Dobson, the popular Christian psychologist and radio broadcaster. No one suspected that the fast-talking Ralph, then twenty-eight years old, would become the face of the Christian Right.

Certainly, Ralph was building on the work of others who had come before him: Morton Blackwell, whose training seminars taught the Right's young activists how to compete with the Left's; theologian Francis Schaeffer, who in the 1970s exhorted evangelicals to leave the social fortresses they had clung to since Scopes and engage in politics to break humanism's grip on society; Moral Majority founder Falwell, who by the late 1970s had set aside a self-imposed ban on mixing religion and politics to urge preachers to get people saved, get them baptized, and get them registered to vote (in that order); the Reverend Tim LaHaye, who, as chairman of the American Coalition for Traditional Values, had mapped out strategies for winning the battles for the "mind, the family, and the public schools." The Christian Coalition's controversial voter guides, which listed candidates' stands on its issues, updated the old Christian Voice scorecards from the early 1980s. The alliances Ralph would later make with conservative Jews and Catholics built on Schaeffer's then-radical notion that Protestant activists should set aside theological differences among themselves and become "co-belligerents" in a broad-based war against secular humanism.

But Ralph brought grander ambitions to the cause: To lead conservative religious activists out of their political ghetto, to mainstream their image and their ideas, to shape a new era of conservatism—just as liberal religious activists had shaped the civil rights movement in the 1960s. He took Schaeffer's theory of co-belligerency further by allying with libertarians and social conservatives, thereby providing the modern Right with an extensive grass-roots base. Grover Norquist, who in the 1980s was struggling with the problem of how to organize angry taxpayers, understood the Christian Coalition's potential. Churchgoers meet every Sunday, but "there's no special place where taxpayers meet on, say, Wednesday," said Grover. "That's the strength of the black community's organization—churches. That's what Ralph was doing, and that's why the Left was so terrorized—because they've seen the power of movements organized through churches."

But building a movement out of the rosters of church congregations was only part of Ralph's game plan. He also thought of himself as a marketing director, and he was politically astute enough to envision a broader pool of potential recruits than had the Religious Right leaders who came before him. Within months of setting up shop inside the Coalition's decrepit warehouse office, Ralph found a demographic survey of Robertson supporters amid the inflatable elephants, boxes of bumper stickers, and other detritus of a failed presidential campaign. The study, in all its eye-glazing glory, filled four three-ring binders. Ralph figured the campaign had probably paid some thirty or forty grand to the consulting firm that compiled it (the "typical extravagance" of a presidential campaign, he noted). Probably, too, no one had bothered to read the thing. He stuffed the binders in his car and took them home.

What he found would form the basis of Christian Coalition's recruitment strategy. The survey revealed two core demographics: One—empty nesters over fifty who were unnerved by changes in society since the 1960s—was predictable. But the second one was less obvious: young suburban couples with children. These were families who "probably went through a period of youthful rebellion, or youthful exploration, and drifted away from their church or synagogue and chased their career," Ralph explained. "Then they fell in love and they got married and they had babies. And then all of a sudden, one day they wake up and their kids are asking them questions about sex. And right then, their whole value system changed."

Ralph calculated there was an untapped market of 40 to 60 million nervous suburbanites. "Not every one of those people necessarily agrees with either our politics or our religion," he observed. "But that was neither here nor there. It was still a lot of people." How do you appeal to them? He could either "narrowcast" and preach a fundamentalist message, reaching the same one million people that Christian Right groups had been fighting over for a decade. Or, he could broaden the message by addressing social concerns as they—conservative, churchgoing, suburbanite families—articulated them. "You appeal to where the demographic is," Ralph explained. "You say, 'We're concerned about children, we're trying to strengthen the family, we're trying to reverse the coarsening of the culture, we believe that faith has a role in civic discourse.' You see, that's a totally different kind of marketing than saying, 'We're evangelicals and we're here to take over.' So I hop-scotched over the traditional [Christian Right] activist base that everybody else was feeding off of."

Ralph's vision crystallized: The Christian Coalition's membership base would be built on diverse suburbs being battered by social change, not on homogeneous Bible Belt towns resistant to change. Christian Coalition churches were the glassy modern fellowships ringing big cities—not the white clapboard Baptist congregations filling small towns like Toccoa. The prototypical member would be the thirtyish, college-educated, stay-at-home mother of three with a working knowledge of formica—not the pin-curl lady watching *The 700 Club* from her trailer park home. "You don't need a Christian Coalition in a Bible Belt town that has blue laws. I mean, you've sort of won," Ralph noted.

The people who were signing on to the Coalition's rosters and running its local chapters as the 1990s began tended to be college-educated with comfortable incomes. They were discomfited not by their socioeconomic status, but by the fact that the *Leave It to Beaver* childhoods they remembered and expected for their children were threatened by the upending of sexual and ethical mores since the 1960s: In public schools, fundamental values were no longer transmitted by adults, they were "clarified" as whatever the child thought right; sex was no longer a moral issue, it was an "education" issue; monogamous marriage was a choice among any number of equally legitimate lifestyles.

Among the tens of thousands who joined up, education issues were a top concern. Within a year of its formation, the Coalition was encouraging its activists to campaign for seats on local school boards. Victories by the Coalition and other Religious Right groups alarmed a broader public fearful of book banning, the institution of school prayer, and the forced teaching of creationism. But, as Harvard's Skocpol noted, "Local school politics was a classic American strategy to build voluntary associations. School issues were what got people passionate. The Left hasn't figured this out—it has such a hands-off attitude about schools."

The press could dismiss them as zealots, the Left could condemn them as fascists, Barry Goldwater could write them off as a bunch of "kooks," but Ralph was determined to portray Christian activists as bright, articulate, concerned citizens perfectly capable of speaking the jargon of the political establishment. The Christian Coalition was "an essentially defensive struggle by people seeking to sustain their faith and their values," he argued. Its activists were "far less interested in legislating against the sins of others, and far more interested in protecting their own right to practice their religion and raise their children in a manner consistent with their values."

Ralph himself was deft in fudging the contradictions between traditional Republicans—who cared mostly about lower taxes and smaller government—and the evangelical community he was leading into the ranks of the GOP. He argued that evangelicals cared about the same things as other Americans—schools, crime, lower taxes. He avoided openly calling for the teaching of creationism, and when he talked of school prayer, he dwelled on voluntary, student-led displays of faith—and described the absurdity of judges trying to root out any vestige of religion from public life. He argued that America's desperation to separate church and state had gone far beyond the intent of the Founders, producing public schools that were "religious-free zones," where the Bible was treated as "contraband." He routinely rattled off examples of how the courts had prohibited mentions of God in the classroom or in public meetings, saying this was indicative of the "culture's phobia of religion," its treatment of faith "as a form of pathology."

Ralph's careful tap dancing on the church-state issue didn't always achieve the desired results. When asked, for example, whether he supported the teaching of creationism in schools, he answered: "I think it's an issue of academic freedom. If a professor or a teacher wants to teach evolution, they shouldn't be prohibited from doing so because it is a theory. I think it should be taught as a theory." For his liberal critics, remarks like that were bad enough, but he confirmed their deepest fears about Christian-controlled school boards as he continued: "I do think that there are a lot of scientists who believe that there's a case that can be made, from science, not theology, for the idea of a created order. I think they ought to be allowed to teach that view. They shouldn't be forced to teach that view but they should be allowed to. . . . I think those kinds of decisions should be localized" and left to school boards.

On abortion, Ralph was politically astute enough to understand that a constitutional ban was unattainable in the current political environment. So he focused the Coalition on the more viable campaigns to curtail abortion, supporting restrictions such as parental approval requirements for teenage girls and, later, a prohibition on partial-birth procedures. True, abortion was the issue that animated the Coalition's core activists, those who regularly volunteered for duty and filled the audience at Coalition rallies. And Ralph would give these crowds what they wanted, usually in the form of vociferous demands that the GOP select pro-life candidates. But to a broader audience, he wrapped abortion inside his agenda for "stronger families"—"fewer divorces, fewer children born out of wedlock, more intact families, and more live births than abortions in even our largest cities."

Ralph was equally determined to free the movement of its racist past. He and his peers were only in elementary school when Jerry Falwell built a Christian school catering only to whites. Ralph was part of a new generation: He could quote Martin Luther King (as he did, often). He was free to extend (as he would, years later) an olive branch to the Jewish community, and to reach out to black churches. He would even claim to support "equal pay for equal work" for women, as well as tax breaks to make it easier for mothers to stay at home. Ralph's vision represented "not the values of an intolerant past . . . [but] the values of a vibrant future," insisted Bill Bennett.

Ralph would try to shape the Religious Right agenda along the lines set by the new wave of baby-boom conservatives. He intended to appeal to a mass audience—as Bill Kristol had learned to do under Bennett on education, and as Clint Bolick hoped to do with his alternative vision of civil rights. Ralph understood, as many of his generational peers did, that America was not an angry place. A worried place, yes. But anger only takes you so far in American politics.

Ralph knew that if he limited his appeal to resentful evangelicals, he would be back to that same one-million box of activists picked over by earlier Christian Right groups. He knew that even among those moral-minded suburbanites signing on to the Coalition's rosters, anger dissipated in the BMWs and Mercedes rolling out of the New South assembly plants, in the gated subdivisions cheerfully devouring Atlanta's Gwinnett County and the $300,000 fixer-uppers ringing Raleigh, in the satisfied roar of season-ticketed alumni crowds at college football games. Even in bad times, at the depth of the Depression, the Socialist Party barely registered as a major contender against the established parties: Americans buy the system, the protected pluralism of the place, its intrinsic hope and idealism—and Ralph would remember that longer than many on the Right.

Ralph also understood that purism was a paper-divide away from anger in a place as diverse as America. He wasn't a man built to sit inside a fortress. Even when he studied the 1960s, he was less interested in hippies fleeing to communes than the waves of feminists, environmentalists, and civil rights leaders who converted fringe opinions into mainstream politics by engaging the Washington game. But Ralph's decision to broadcast rather than narrowcast left him open to charges of selling out by purists on his right.

The reality was that the Coalition still would attract its share of separatists: The Iowa activists who pushed for a Republican platform calling for the registration of AIDS carriers and the mandatory teaching of creationism; the Washington state activists who sought a ban on gays in the health care, daycare, and teaching professions; the Montana vice chairman who asserted that God would reconstruct society along biblical codes and introduce capital punishment for adultery and homosexuality. Moreover, this was still Pat Robertson's organization, and Robertson had once likened non-Christians to termites: "The time has arrived for a godly fumigation."

ROBERTSON WASN'T the only problem. Although Ralph had matured, leaving behind his "politics as war" mentality to broaden the Right's appeal, he could occasionally slip back to his old ways. Despite the Ph.D. and inclusive rhetoric, he was still very much a product of the bloodthirsty College Republicans. He had been Grover's close lieutenant—Grover, who still divided the world into "us" and them," who still saw liberalism as a slippery slope to socialism and to communism. In the early 1980s, Ralph had memorized much of the dialogue of *Red Dawn,* a movie featuring Patrick Swayze leading a band of armed teenagers, the Wolverines, against a Soviet invasion of America, because the Left had sold out the country and no one else had the stomach to stand up to the Reds.

In 1990, Ralph slipped back into the role of a Wolverine, thereby risking the public support he needed if he was to achieve his vision of a mass movement. That year, the Coalition targeted Democratic congressional candidates for defeat with radio commercials that twisted votes on NEA funding into claims that the lawmakers had supported "pornography." That same year, the Christian Coalition counseled Religious Right candidates to target low-profile elections attracting few voters (recalling the University of Georgia mock elections Ralph had orchestrated), and then to conceal their views and avoid public appearances.

The use of these stealth tactics was a politically tone-deaf strategy, unnerving the same broad public that Ralph had hoped to assuage. But Ralph didn't understand that yet. Asked to comment on a Religious Right sweep of local San Diego races, Ralph pulled out his College Republican–*Red Dawn* script. "It's like guerrilla warfare," he boasted to a reporter. "If you reveal your location, all it does is allow your opponent to improve his artillery bearings. It's better to move quietly, with stealth, under cover of night."

Democratic elections as guerrilla warfare: Such was the American public's first introduction to Ralph Reed and his Christian Coalition.

10

UMPIRE
PAR EXCELLENCE

IT WOULD BE HARD, in 1989, to imagine a more delicious prospect for Bill Kristol than the chance to prove the liberal establishment wrong about Dan Quayle. Advising George Bush's vice president appealed to Bill's contrarian nature: Conventional punditry had pegged Quayle as a dolt, a political Bambi who had lucked into the VP slot simply because Bush thought his handsome Midwestern looks would add some youth and female appeal to an otherwise gray Republican ticket. To the media, Quayle was the "tinker-toy senator" turned "First Featherweight." "Can anyone be taken seriously who takes Quayle seriously?" asked historian Garry Wills, a question that aptly described the scale of the task awaiting Bill Kristol.

In fact, Indiana's former junior senator also represented everything the baby-boom conservatives professed to disdain—a frat-boy who was busy practicing his golf swing at an age when activists were doing scut work for the cause, a rich kid who sat out the Vietnam War with a posting in the Indiana National Guard. Quayle was midwestern whitebread, an especially odd project for Kristol, who explained to a reporter at the time that he had grown up under the prevailing view that "people who weren't from New York and Jewish were unfortunate: They ate Wonder bread and mayonnaise and had boring existences." But Kristol looked past Quayle's bland Rotary Club manner to his potential as a new-generation conservative leader. (Hadn't the press and political establishment always underestimated Reagan, too?) Kristol thought Quayle had astute political instincts. He was an eager learner who "likes ideas, likes agitation," as another aide noted.

Of such stuff can great statesmen be made—if you are, as a devoted Straussian, in the business of cultivating great statesmen. ("The political philosopher who has reached his goal," Strauss wrote, "is the teacher of legislators . . . the umpire par excellence.") Advising Dan Quayle promised a neat confluence of Kristol's philosophical aspirations and the vice president's burning personal ambition to rehabilitate his reputation just enough to slide neatly into the top slot of the 1996 GOP ticket. Bill brought to his new job a Straussian kit for grooming a national leader—reading lists filled with political biographies and think-tank treatises, a network of scholarly neoconservatives eager to offer advice, his own obsession with polls and the art of moving public opinion. And at his side was that intense young policy wonk, David McIntosh, who brought to the vice president's court his Chicago School blueprints for deconstructing the federal regulatory apparatus.

This was not a propitious time for the baby-boom Right. Their hero Reagan was gone, and the cold war, which had held together a diverse and potentially fractious movement, was winding down. The Republican in the White House was no friend: Even before Bush betrayed the Right by breaking his "no new taxes" pledge, true believers dismissed his administration as The Department of Surrender. Bush had catered to the Right's leaders long enough to get elected, and then ignored them as he filled his top jobs with detail men who believed in governance by tinkering, shaping an administration that promised to be all process and compromise. Inside an administration otherwise devoid of ideology (or a pulse, quipped the Right's baby-boom detractors), Kristol hoped to transform the vice president's office into a font of bold conservative ideas.

Kristol wasn't the only thinker in the late 1980s trying to prevent the movement from dissolving into a warm pool of Reagan nostalgia, or racing into the arms of a backward-looking, anti-immigrant trade protectionist like Pat Buchanan. On Bush's White House staff, another boomer intellect, James Pinkerton, was peddling a program he called "the new paradigm," a guiding principle for domestic policy that argued that the government should promote self-sufficiency—to empower individuals, not bureaucracies. ("Empowerment" was also a theme of conservative heroes Jack Kemp, now Secretary of

Housing and Urban Development, and House minority whip Newt Gingrich.) At the Heritage Foundation, another young intellectual, Adam Meyerson, was using his magazine, *Policy Review,* as a forum to debate proactive conservative approaches to historically liberal concerns, such as race and urban poverty. From his perch as a public interest lawyer, Clint Bolick was building his own conservative case for civil rights. And so it went, throughout the ranks of the movement.

Into the void left by Ronald Reagan, plenty of baby-boom conservatives poured plenty of ideas. But Kristol had the messenger, a man who was a heartbeat away from the presidency, who could someday (if all went according to plan) become a front-runner for the Republican nomination. Even from within a presidential administration that assiduously avoided vision, and division, Bill could hope to transform Quayle's operation into the nerve center of a reinvigorated, post-modern conservative movement. Just as Ralph Reed understood the importance of reaching beyond the one million activists forming the Religious Right's core, Kristol believed that modern conservatism needed to broaden its appeal. Reagan had built a majority coalition, including Democrats, with his massive tax cut, his stand-tall talk toward the Soviets, and his sunny disposition. Without Reagan, Kristol figured, conservative appeal topped out somewhere around 40 percent of the electorate.

But Kristol deeply believed that, even in modern America, a broader constituency could unite under a conservative vision of national greatness—a "politics of liberty, a sociology of virtue," as he called it. Bill could see the threads of a conservative reform agenda: Weren't most Americans, even those calling themselves pro-choice, troubled by more than a million abortions each year, by the prospect of their own teenage daughters undergoing such surgery without their knowledge or consent? Weren't most Americans ready to consider private alternatives to inner-city public schools rife with violence and graduating barely half their students? Wasn't America ready to acknowledge the links between rising numbers of fatherless children—a quarter of all births and nearly triple that among blacks—and rising crime, welfare dependency, drug use, and drop-out rates?

Couldn't the Right's case against big government also be vividly illustrated with McIntosh's laundry list of heavy-handed federal rules that cost the country jobs and economic growth? On foreign policy, wasn't the public—even in the post–cold war era—eager to hear about American values, not just strategic interests? Weren't Americans ready to stand behind a ballistic missile shield, the SDI, to protect their own country against rogue dictators or the unpredictable actions of a crumbling Soviet Union?

Kristol could see the message. He had the messenger. Conservatism *could* flourish without the soothing patriarchy of Ronald Reagan.

Only it didn't quite work out that way.

IF ANYONE UNDERSTOOD that the game of politics is one of real estate—location, location, location—it was Bill Kristol. "Kristol is always attracted to where the bright flame is," said his friend and GOP media consultant Mike Murphy. In 1989, his career prospects enhanced after his stint at Education, Bill might have signed on to work for weightier figures in the Bush administration; he might have joined Bill Bennett, who became drug czar, or accepted the top staff position for HUD Secretary Jack Kemp. Quayle's reputation was so sullied after the 1988 election that he had trouble recruiting staff. But the vice president's office offered the closest proximity to real power, especially if a White House job wasn't going to come Bill's way. Besides, Kristol was a sucker for long shots: He had just finished running the Maryland U.S. Senate campaign of his Harvard roommate, Alan Keyes, who was trounced by veteran Democrat Paul Sarbanes.

Quayle sought out Bill shortly before the holidays in December 1988 and the two men had lunch at a restaurant in Lafayette Square, a short walk from the White House. Kristol hadn't expected to be interested in the job. But he liked Quayle, and could see the potential— even if the job he was being offered held the minor rank of domestic policy adviser.

It wasn't long before colleagues in the vice president's office concluded that Bill didn't intend to remain a second-tier adviser to a third-tier politician. Kristol took care of the first matter within months, when it became clear that Quayle's initial chief of staff was on his way out the door. Bill artfully made himself the obvious replacement with his relentless presence, colleagues recalled. He was always around to give Quayle the smart answer, to offer the shrewd alternative strategy, to promote ideas to Quayle and Quayle to the media.

"Here are three articles you may want to read over the weekend," he wrote to the VP within weeks of coming on board, when he was still the domestic policy adviser. "The first, by Samuel Huntington, is a response to Paul Kennedy's decline of America thesis. The second, by Fred Barnes, speculates on your role . . . in the Bush Administration. The third . . . is a defense of 'democratic interventionism' in Central America."

"Before arriving in Venezuela, you might be interested in reading this eloquent tribute, by Jeane Kirkpatrick, to Venezuela's national hero, Simon Bolivar," he wrote in a January 30, 1989, memo to Quayle. That same day, he shipped out Quayle's first vice presidential speeches to two dozen major conservative commentators (including Irving Kristol). "Vice President Quayle has given three public speeches in his first ten days in office" on taxes, spending, budget reform, and religious freedom, Kristol enthused.

Despite his lightweight reputation, Quayle was an accomplished politician who, at age twenty-nine, had unseated an entrenched incumbent for a seat in the U.S. House of Representatives, and then beat veteran Democratic Senator Birch Bayh at age thirty-five. Perhaps because of these precocious successes, Quayle—never an intellectual—had developed a bad habit of winging it when he spoke, which was what led to his troubles. At a luncheon for the United Negro College Fund, for example, he garbled an aide's notation of the fund's slogan—"a mind is a terrible thing to waste"—ending up with this stammer: "What a waste it is to lose one's mind or not to have a mind is being very wasteful." Even when Quayle was not engaging in word gaffes, his demeanor was uncertain, awkward, untuned to his audience. By 1990, the vice president would be the butt of more late-night comic jokes than any other figure, including George Bush and Saddam Hussein.

The prevailing sentiment inside the administration was that Quayle should stay low and let time heal his image. Under this view, he should stick to his assignments—promoting a manned mission to Mars as chairman of the President's Space Council, and honchoing the administration's deregulation efforts as head of the Competitiveness Council. If he did his job well, and stayed out of the public eye, he would emerge with a reputation as a competent manager and a trusted adviser to the president.

But the thirty-six-year-old Kristol, Quayle's new chief of staff, had more ambitious designs for his new boss, and eventually his views would resonate with Quayle's own cheery ego. In October of 1989, three months after the Supreme Court ruled that states could impose some restrictions on abortions, Kristol urged the vice president to tackle that issue head on. "GOP panic about the political consequences of being pro-life is greatly overstated," he wrote to the VP. "What's needed, obviously, is a re-focusing of the debate on the extremism of the pro-abortion position (no parental notification, sex selection OK, pure abortion on demand, etc.); perhaps we can help on this." Two months later, he urged Quayle to articulate an "activist Bush economic agenda" to slash taxes and spending and counter budget director Dick Darman's pet project of a "deal of the century" with the Democratic-controlled Congress, which would accept tax cuts in return for budget reform and some spending restraints.

Kristol helped the vice president curry support within his two natural constituencies—the activist Right, and the Jewish community, both of which were distrustful of the Bush White House. Of the two, Quayle's courtship of the Jewish community, particularly Zionist and Orthodox groups, received the least notice. That was partly by design. "We should (quietly and informally) get this around," Kristol wrote to one colleague, attaching an article from a Palestinian publication attacking Quayle for "serenading" the "Israeli lobby."

Quayle, who had always been a strong supporter of Israel, gave a speech to Yeshiva University in New York in December 1989 that reflected Kristol's handiwork in its references to Albert Einstein and the Talmud. In that speech, Quayle spoke of his effort to persuade the United Nations to repeal its "zionism as racism" resolution. Kristol faxed the text to the *New York Times'* A. M. Rosenthal, with a "Dear Abe" note mentioning that Quayle had met privately with U.N. Secretary General Perez de Cuellar on the issue. Bill's efforts produced what one journalist called "the single most favorable piece of publicity Quayle has received since taking office." Rosenthal wrote that Quayle had "honored his country, himself, the supportive Bush-Baker diplomacy—and given the nations a chance to undo a great wrong."

In June of 1991, following the conclusion of the Gulf War, in which Iraqi forces were expelled from Kuwait, Bill helped draft a column for Minnesota Senator Rudy Boschwitz entitled "Dan Quayle Saved Jewish Lives." In the draft article, Boschwitz argued that in the Senate Quayle had helped to restore funding for the Patriot defense system, the weapon shield that had prevented Saddam Hussein's Scuds from strewing "death and destruction over Israel" during the war. Quayle and Kristol also worked closely with conservative Jewish groups in opposing the Democrats' version of the 1991 Civil Rights Act, which they viewed as a "quota bill."

Quayle's prominence with the Right was often useful to the Bush White House. In mid-1990, Bill was dispatched to Capitol Hill to cool the tempest over funding for the National Endowment for the Arts. House Republicans were responding to vocal groups on the Right—including Ralph Reed's Christian Coalition—who wanted NEA grants restricted, if not eliminated, because some of the funding had gone to artists who produced work they considered sacrilegious. But the White House resisted interference with federal funding of the arts. Kristol helped broker a compromise, and even drafted a soothing statement for the NEA's annual report proclaiming that the "debate over a few grants has raised larger issues on the proper role of the Federal government in supporting the arts. That debate has been vigorous and healthy. . . ."

Bill's reputation as a shrewd political thinker preceded him even at the White House, where other hard-core Rightists were viewed with suspicion. His input was sought by Bush chief of staff John Sununu and OMB director Darman. Even while he was still a policy adviser to Quayle, Bill was a regular at the 7:30 A.M. White House senior staff meetings. After he helped put out the NEA firestorm, White House memoirist John Podhoretz recalled, Kristol was rewarded with admittance to an even more select gathering—"Gnostic paradise, the informal pre–senior staff meeting with Sununu, aides Andy Card and Ed Rogers, and Darman, just before 7." Kristol, noted Podhoretz, "had many things in common with the Gnostics and therefore was accorded some respect by Sununu and Darman." That was, of course, until Bill's relentless courtship of the national press corps got the better of him.

George Bush hated leaks and leakers, and prized personal loyalty above all else (even hard-headed introspection), which didn't leave much running room for an iconoclast like Kristol. When the press began running accounts critical of the Bush White House, Kristol routinely clipped them and passed them on to his boss, as if they were in a Harvard seminar in government mismanagement rather than in a presidential administration under seige. Bill was not particularly discreet about his contacts with the press, nor about his disappointments with the Bush White House. "It was a fairly tight operation on the other side," one Quayle aide noted, referring to the West Wing. "When you look around at who's pissing on you . . . well, they pretty easily identified him." Bill was on the phone to reporters more often than Quayle's press secretary. Each week when the *New Republic* hit the newsstands, the joke around the VP's office was that its premier White House reporter, Fred Barnes, was, once again, "channeling Kristol."

Bill caught the blame for blind quotes critical of the Bush team, whether or not he was responsible. But then, responsibility in Washington is a fuzzy thing. Officially, Bill had nothing to do with a December 1990 *Washington Times* story headlined "Conservatives Say Sununu Must Go" and promoting Kristol as a leading candidate to replace Bush's chief of staff. Bill recalled being just as shocked as Sununu when he picked up the paper that morning. He didn't know the reporter, and considered it ludicrous that anyone would suggest him for the top White House job since it wasn't a secret that George Bush was no fan of his. But someone on Kristol's staff (communications director Jeff Nesbit) did have something to do with the story, and one is left to guess whether Kristol, who had a reputation for controlling everything that went in and out of his shop, knew about it.

Kristol showed up at the seven o'clock meeting of the Gnostics on the morning that the *Washington Times* story appeared and made a lame attempt at a joke about the article. Sununu wasn't amused. Kristol's standing invitation to Gnostic paradise ceased that very morning. Although Kristol and Darman continued their amiable relationship, the bad blood with Sununu ran deep. Quayle would often have to intercede to enable his chief of staff to attend strategy sessions.

Despite Kristol's proddings, Quayle opted to remain a loyal soldier to Bush in their first months in office. That began to change with a phone call from Bill as Quayle was rising in his Los Angeles hotel room on the morning of June 26, 1990. Kristol was calling from Washington with the news that Bush had just released a statement endorsing tax hikes as part of a budget deal with Congress. Quayle, who had been pressing for an actively conservative agenda of tax and spending cuts, was stunned: Darman's deal had prevailed.

Bush's about-face on taxes—breaking his famed "read my lips" pledge—would prove to be a fatal miscalculation (and would transform Grover Norquist into a movement celebrity as politicians from around the country rushed to capitalize on the president's blunder by signing the activist's no-new-taxes pledge). For Dan Quayle, it was like getting a new lease on his political life. From that morning on, noted Kristol, the vice president was "less willing to defer to Bush, and more willing to find his own voice."

Quayle emerged as a staunch pro-life advocate, a promoter of term limits for members of Congress, and a tireless defender of SDI. He made waves by decrying the explosive growth of litigation in a speech before the American Bar Association, and forwarding an ambitious tort reform plan. His growing independence bolstered his already strong standing in conservative circles and became a source of annoyance to his boss. "Sometimes," President Bush complained to a friend, "I think Dan has people in there who do not understand the role of the vice president. They aren't there to make policy."

But if Quayle was making policy, no one besides Bush seemed to notice, or care. By the spring of 1991, Quayle's popularity ratings remained in the tank; he was still Jay Leno's favorite target. In May, when the nation nervously watched as Bush checked into Bethesda Naval Hospital for an irregular heartbeat, "Quayle-bashing reached seismic levels," journalist Fred Barnes noted. One commentator predicted that if Quayle were to become president, the stock market would plunge six hundred points.

QUAYLE'S WASN'T THE ONLY reputation Kristol was attempting to resuscitate in 1991. On July 1, President Bush nominated Clarence Thomas, former EEOC chair and now appeals court judge, to replace the retiring Thurgood Marshall on the Supreme Court. Conservatives throughout Washington sprang into action, determined to protect their ally from being "Borked" (this was now a verb used by both sides in Washington's volcanic ideological wars). "This was the most harmonious I'd ever seen the conservative groups," Clint Bolick said at the time.

By contrast, the Left was fractured. Mostly white liberal groups, such as feminists and People for the American Way, the interest group founded by TV producer Norman Lear, vowed to fight the Thomas nomination. Thomas's feeble legal credentials—particularly when compared to courtroom titans such as Marshall, who had won several landmark civil rights cases before joining the Court—left the Bush administration vulnerable to charges of filling a "quota" spot for a conservative black. Still, civil rights groups were reluctant to oppose a black man for a seat on the nation's highest court, and an upcoming NAACP vote on that question was certain to be close. That disunity left an opening for a freelance public relations war orchestrated by Thomas's supporters on the Right.

By then, Clint had set up shop as a "public interest" attorney and was representing minority entrepreneurs who (like Thomas's grandfather) risked being put out of business by government licensing authorities. But Clint, as a teenager, had watched his beloved mentor Mr. Locascio destroyed by his hometown Democratic machine; as a law student he had felt personally smeared by the Left. There was no way he was going to stand by idly and watch as ideological opponents took a sledgehammer to his friend, mentor, and godfather of his son. So he mounted his own defense of the nominee.

Through an intermediary, Clint lobbied the NAACP by forwarding a packet of material to its chairman designed to show that Thomas "wasn't an enemy, that he had actually been the conscience of the Reagan administration." Then, when it appeared that Thomas would narrowly lose the NAACP vote, Clint helped orchestrate a media event designed to demonstrate that Thomas had strong support in the black community. On the day of the scheduled NAACP vote, a busload of "Pin Pointers," friends and supporters of Thomas from his hometown of Pin Point, Georgia, pulled into Washington. Georgia Democrats Sam Nunn and Wyche Fowler played host to this home-state delegation. The plan worked: On TV and in print, the NAACP vote was overshadowed by the images of the black nominee—who had risen from poverty to be nominated to the highest court in the land—being embraced by his grass-roots constituency. "The media was sensational," Clint told journalists at the time. "We were back to back with the NAACP."

But, as later revealed by journalists Jane Mayer and Jill Abramson, this outpouring of support wasn't quite as spontaneous as it appeared. The idea for the bus trip had originated with a White House aide, and was designed not only to show an alternative black position during the NAACP vote, but also to curry support from Southern Democrats such as Nunn and Fowler. Clint's legal organization, the Landmark Center for Civil Rights, covered most of the expenses of the bus trip, and a pro-Thomas group organized by Gary Bauer, the former Reagan aide and religious fundamentalist, chipped in for the Pin Pointers' hotel. The idea for Bauer's ad-hoc group—the Citizens' Committee to Confirm Clarence Thomas—arose in conversations he had with his close friend Bill Kristol, in which both men agreed that outside support for the nominee had to be "early and loud" in order to prevent the Left from seizing the high ground. In early July, as Kristol and Bauer were vacationing together at the beach, their kids and wives headed down to the beach each morning while the pair stayed behind to strategize on the Thomas nomination. Bauer spent most of his vacation on the phone to conservative donors, raising money to fund radio and TV ads in support of Thomas.

Officially, the Thomas nomination was handled by, among others, lobbyist Kenneth Duberstein, who was hired by the White House; Lee Liberman in the White House counsel's office; and Missouri Republican Senator John Danforth, Thomas's close friend. Kristol was a member of Duberstein's working group and helped Quayle lobby his former colleagues in the Senate. But the vocal support of outside activists would be critical going into the hearings. Ralph Reed huddled with other conservative lobbyists across town at the Heritage Foundation, counting Senate votes, knowing that (even before Anita Hill appeared on the scene) the vote would be razor thin. "At the time," he recalled, "many in the pro-family community expected Thomas to be the fifth vote in a decision overturning *Roe*, a hope that turned out to be groundless." But with abortion on the docket, no effort was spared. The Christian Coalition broadcast a $1 million radio and TV ad campaign in Georgia, Louisiana, and Pennyslvania, knowing that votes by senators in these states would be crucial to the outcome. In Pennsylvania, Coalition activists crammed into town hall meetings with Republican Senator Arlen Specter to demand his support for Thomas.

The previous year, Duberstein had escorted David Souter's Supreme Court nomination through the Senate with a "stealth" strategy designed to evade explosive issues such as abortion. He pursued the same strategy with Thomas, attempting to shift congressional and media focus away from the nominee's legal positions and toward his humble beginnings. The intent was to portray Thomas as someone sympathetic to the hard climb faced by women and minorities. In his confirmation hearings, Thomas would studiously (and awkwardly, as it turned out) avoid candor on such controversial matters as *Roe* v. *Wade* and natural rights theories. Indeed, the Bush White House appeared just as afraid of Thomas's views as the Reagan White House had been of Bork's.

Meanwhile, Thomas's supporters on the Right carried on their propaganda battle. With Thomas avoiding public appearances, Clint took it upon himself to patiently lead reporters through Thomas's record—his vigorous pursuit of individual discrimination claims at the EEOC, his opposition to racial categories but support for "affirmative action" aimed at opening doors to the disadvantaged, regardless of their color. To combat the Left's not-so-subtle portrayal of Thomas as an Uncle Tom willing to sell out his own people for power, Clint presented a picture of a maverick willing to stand up to the Republican establishment. Thomas's political philosophy, said Clint, could be summed up as "rugged individualism."

Clint's former boss and friend, Ricky Silberman, made it her job to crack the media's assumption that the feminist groups opposed to Thomas represented all, or even most, women. Silberman offered up alternative female voices, conservative women who knew and supported the nominee. (Silberman's efforts would later blossom into a postfeminist group aimed at professional women, the Independent Women's Forum.) As the confirmation hearings opened in September, Silberman and Bolick formed part of the pro-Thomas spin squad, making themselves available to reporters looking for opinions on the proceedings. "I think the nomination is solidly moving ahead," Clint would tell reporters. "I don't think the opposition scored any points today."

Thomas opened his testimony before the Senate Judiciary Committee triumphantly, bringing his audience nearly to tears with his moving description of his rise from an impoverished childhood. His performance soured, however, when the questions turned to his legal views; friends such as Clint were appalled to see that the White House's stealth strategy had transformed this fierce, opinionated man into a stiff, evasive replica of his former self. Nevertheless, the votes needed to confirm Thomas seemed to remain intact.

Then, thirteen days into the proceedings, as testimony was winding down and the Judiciary Committee was preparing to vote, a fax came clicking across the machine of committee chairman Joe Biden: After weeks of rumors, Anita Hill had signed a statement alleging that she had been sexually harassed by Thomas during her employment at the EEOC. Feminists and liberal activists were key players behind this revelation, first funneling rumors about Hill's allegations to Senate staffers, then helping a reluctant Hill draft a statement and assisting her during her appearance before the committee. The he-said she-said drama that unfolded during a weekend of extraordinary testimony, televised live, riveted an entire nation, everywhere stirring up complex and conflicting emotions over nettlesome issues raised by the massive influx of women into the workforce.

In Washington, this personal drama added fuel to an ideological war that had begun with the 1987 Bork battle, and was a portent of the divisive politics to come later in the decade. The Right rallied around Thomas; the Left around Hill; neither side was willing to suspend judgment until the truth might be ascertained. In a city where "to Bork" was a verb, the time was long past for moderation or reasoned consideration. On the Left, Anita Hill was canonized as the courageous feminist who stood forthright against abusive, foul-talking, pornography-loving men. On the Right, strategists worked tirelessly to undermine Hill's credibility, portraying her as a radical feminist, a spurned woman, a fantasizer.

Kristol, still carrying the lesson from the Bork battle that "you should fight intelligently and try to win," took part in the White House's determined defense of Thomas. Pouring over the documentation behind Hill's claim, he noticed that her friend, a key witness, had given the FBI a wrong date in describing Hill's early revelations of sexual harassment; Hill hadn't yet joined Thomas's EEOC on the date she supposedly confided in the friend. Kristol passed on the discrepancy to reporters and Republican senators. With this and other material, the Republicans were able to make this supporting witness look "nervous and vague" during her testimony, like someone who "failed to correct the impression that she herself had a history of concocting sexual harassment charges," according to the Mayer-Abramson account. From outside the White House, Clint and Ricky Silberman worked to discredit another witness who would support Hill's testimony, passing word to the press that the woman had been fired from the EEOC not because she rebuffed Thomas, but because she had called a co-worker a "faggot." If this woman's claims against Thomas—the second shoe to drop after Hill's—had sat in the press even one day without a rebuttal, "it could have killed Clarence Thomas," Clint said at the time. "We got across that she was a gay-bashing sewer mouth."

Other activists on the Right sought to undermine Hill's account. One was Ralph Reed, who faxed to the Senate Judiciary Committee a statement from the dean of Professor Hill's law school, in which he recalled that she had invited Thomas to speak on campus and had subsequently offered to drive him to the airport. This friendly exchange took place years after Thomas allegedly harassed her, and the dean's subsequent testimony before the committee suggested that Hill's behavior was not that of a woman who had been Thomas' victim. (A pro-Thomas account of the episode said Hill had opposed the choice of Thomas as speaker but was outvoted.)

On Tuesday, October 15, the Thomas nomination squeezed through the Senate on a 52–48 vote—but not before the nominee had sat through a public airing of charges that he liked to boast about his sexual prowess and penis size, that he once joked about pubic hair on a Coke can, that he regularly rented pornographic videos. For the Right, it was a bitter victory. The reputation of a friend and ally of the Right had, once again, been destroyed by the Left, by what Thomas memorably called "a high-tech lynching." Angry and bitter, the new Supreme Court justice would later condemn what he called the "new intolerance," the "systemic character assassination" of anyone who dared engage in "ideological trespass."

For Kristol, Thomas's victory demonstrated the expedience of all-out political confrontation. But for Clint, the episode left personal scars. One friend described the Thomas hearings as Clint's coming of age, his loss of innocence. "It was incredibly painful for him to see his friend suffer," this intimate said. "It embittered him. Clint would deny it, but I see the Lani Guinier episode [in which he almost single-handedly blocked President Clinton's top civil rights appointment] as encouraged by the awful treatment that Clarence Thomas received."

Media commentators, those first-draft historians, wrote up the Hill-Thomas confrontation as symptomatic of America's simmering gender conflicts. But the Right saw it as something else: Another chapter in an ongoing, and increasingly vicious, ideological war. "Conservatives felt that Thomas was a victim of left-wing McCarthyism and the target of an ideologically motivated witch hunt in which the feminists and the pro-abortion lobby would do or say anything to defeat a justice they feared might overturn abortion rights." Ralph Reed recalled. "I have always felt the vicious treatment of Thomas (and Robert Bork) by the radical Left helped inspire our movement." And so, the movement would Bork back.

DAVID MCINTOSH was fighting his own war that year—and losing, though he didn't know it yet, so deep was he in the bowels of the government's regulatory beast. In fact, in 1991, David had every reason to believe he was a winner: At age thirty-three, he was the top staff person for Dan Quayle's Competitiveness Council, which made him a very important man indeed. "In Washington's power stakes, Mr. McIntosh is hot," the *New York Times* would proclaim a year later.

The Competitiveness Council, a continuation of the deregulatory campaign George Bush had waged as vice president, wielded enormous power. It could short-circuit regulatory processes by overruling the decisions of such familiar authorities as the Environmental Protection Agency and the Food and Drug Administration. The council wasn't required to divulge its proceedings or its contacts with outside lobbyists as agencies were. Officially, the council was chaired by the vice president and consisted of half a dozen cabinet secretaries and agency heads. Its executive director, an Indianapolis car-wax mogul named Allan Hubbard, was David's boss. But Hubbard had other pressing duties as deputy to Kristol. The day-to-day operations of the Competitiveness Council were run by David, who served as deputy director, and a handful of staffers.

Congressional Democrats took one look at the Council and concluded it was a backdoor channel for business lobbyists who couldn't get their way with regulators: When developers complained to Quayle about President Bush's pledge that he would countenance "no net loss of wetlands," the Council set out to change the definition of wetlands, taking millions of acres out from under federal protection. United Parcel Service complained that a proposed Federal Aviation Administration rule to reduce airplane noise would hurt the company, and the Council went to work to relax the agency's timetable. Eli Lilly, a generous contributor to Quayle's Senate campaigns, complained that it needed more "operational flexibility" to meet new clean air standards, and the Council overruled the EPA and issued a rule that critics said would increase pollutant emissions by 245 tons a year.

In short order, the Council became the target of seven congressional investigations. Democratic House member Henry Waxman condemned the panel as a "nefarious, secret kind of government outside the constitutional and democratic processes for enacting laws." On the Senate side, Democrat John Glenn called on his colleagues to defund the Council and "restore public accountability, legitimacy, and integrity to the regulatory process." Soon, even the American Heart Association, the American Cancer Society, and the American Lung Association were joining in the denunciations.

None of this fazed David, who still loved a good fight, especially in defense of one of his cherished free market principles. Eight years after leaving the University of Chicago, he still clung to Professor Richard Epstein's theory that regulation constituted a "taking" of property. As McIntosh quipped in a March 22, 1991, memo to Quayle: "This land is your land (except as otherwise provided by government regulations). . . ."

David was still Eagle Scout–polite, his suits hanging off his thin frame even as specks of gray crept into his hair. But in meetings with career bureaucrats (whose work he was usurping) he could be stubborn and headstrong, refusing to budge even on minor issues. After these tense sessions, David's own aides would try to get him to yield, even if only around the edges. He hadn't yet married the vivacious young woman who would soften his public image. Neither had he faced defeat, so he had every confidence in his own bulldozer intellect (the one his sister complained would steamroll anyone in its path). His fondess for crisply reasoned debate, the family "Slough slayer" trait, had been shared with fellow ideological underdogs at the Yale Political Union, the Chicago law school, and other safe harbors for young Rightists in the 1970s. It was a trait that had been prominent among the cadre of young rightist lawyers, including David and his Yale friends, in Meese's Justice Department. And it was a trait that would nearly destroy the Right when its new generation of leaders— prideful young white men like David—took hold of the U.S. House of Representatives in 1995. For David and his ideological cohorts, it was how they said things—as much as what they said—that caused so many people to question their humanity.

For his part, McIntosh considered rulemaking bureaucrats the extremists—one side of an "iron triangle" that also included environmentalist groups and congressional staff. For years, he argued, this iron triangle had blithely swamped small businesses, farmers, and the economy. To McIntosh, Bush's "mindless" campaign promise of "no net loss of wetlands" constituted a "giant federal land grab," which, if taken seriously, "would have subjected huge areas of the country east of the Mississippi River to federal land-use permits in the name of saving wetlands." The wetlands rule was the most controversial issue of David's tenure. He waded into the esoteric language of hydric soils and hydrophytic plants and emerged with the conclusion that the EPA's definition of wetlands included land that was rarely wet—Indiana farms with spring puddles, California deserts flooded by seasonal storms. Environmental scientists dismissed that reasoning, noting that the wetlands were delicate ecological systems requiring connecting acreage that often was not wet.

After David and his staff rewrote the wetlands manual, even the federal Army Corps of Engineers—typically more sympathetic to development than the EPA—concluded that the Council's changes would remove federal protection from as much as half of the nation's 100 million acres of wetlands. In the face of widespread opposition, the White House was forced to back down. Reform efforts aimed at the Food and Drug Administration were more successful, and McIntosh's efforts to speed up the agency's drug approval process earned him grudging respect from upper-echelon bureaucrats.

Despite his loss on the wetlands and a number of other fronts, David's stature grew. His work on the Competitiveness Council transformed him (in the eyes of fellow Rightists) into a paragon of antigovernment virtue. When the thirty-four-year-old Indiana lawyer was promoted to executive director in 1992, the New York Times breathlessly catalogued his crusades:

"It was Mr. McIntosh who championed the Administration's move last week to give companies broad rights to increase their emissions of air pollution. . . .

"It was he who developed the legal and philosophical basis for the President's decisions in January to halt new regulations and rewrite old ones to make them friendlier to American industry. . . .

"Last month, the Competitiveness Council proposed easing restrictions on testing and marketing genetically engineered crops and organisms. . . .

"Mr. McIntosh was also at the center of a group of young White House aides who proposed removing restrictions on storing and disposing of 45 percent of the nation's hazardous wastes. . . ."

In the Washington power game, Kristol and his underling McIntosh were gaining reputations as seasoned pros. Among the press, they were recognized as masters in the art of the well-timed leak, the anonymous "backgrounder." By 1992, Kristol especially was getting what he wanted out of the press—glowing profiles of himself as Dan Quayle's "brain" (which raised his own stature at the expense of his boss's); stories precisely timed to advance his shop's bureaucratic battles; chronicles of battles with bureaucrats and the Democratic Congress that solidified the reputations of Quayle—and his staffers—as heroes in the conservative community.

And yet, the Kristol-McIntosh public relations crusade on deregulation, one of the Right's pet causes, flopped. The Competitiveness Council might have made a few big Republican contributors happy, but for all the press hype and critics' alarms, the Council was never able to do more than nibble around the edges of a vast federal regulatory apparatus. David approached his job like a committed ideological warrior, certain that there existed a vast public mandate for deregulation behind him. In fact, there was none, and the Council couldn't create one.

Conservatives assumed, correctly, that the public hated oppressive or overly costly or silly rules. But in their antigovernment zeal, these crusaders leapt to the conclusion that most Americans wanted to demolish bureaucracies that they credited for cleaner rivers, less smog, safer airplanes, air bags and child seats in cars, and health labels on food. (In one unguarded moment in 1998, McIntosh's wife Ruthie praised the Americans with Disabilities Act, signed by Bush and much maligned by the Right, as she rolled her baby's stroller up a smooth concrete handicap-access ramp.) In the early 1990s, at the height of the Competitiveness Council's battle against the EPA, for example, polls consistently showed that 70 to 80 percent of Americans considered themselves "environmentalists." By contrast, McIntosh and his friends traveled in political circles that frequently labeled environmental leaders "radicals" and called environmentalism "the new socialism."

Policy wonks such as David preferred to ferret out the costs of regulation; they liked to measure them and weigh them against a more difficult calculation of "benefits." But most Americans didn't relate to quality of life as determined by algebra. So the Right's wonks tried to make a personal connection with the public in a different way—by parading out anecdotes of regulatory outrages, illustrating the harm done to individual property owners, such as the farmer put out of business by a bug or the grandmother whose dream of a beach house was endangered because of federal protections on a neighboring swamp. In the 1990s, these anecdotes provided provocative material for talk radio and Capitol Hill speeches, but they weren't sufficient to build a majority support for large-scale demolition of cherished environmental laws.

Later, David would express regret at his strategies at the Council, but he had no regrets about his goals. "We were making an economic argument, that you maximize wealth in society by having reasonable regulations, by using cost-benefit analysis," McIntosh said. "Frankly, I think we should have adopted environmental protection as a moral imperative—but then say we have a different way of reaching it, that protecting the environment is best served through incentives to industry rather than a command and control regulation from Washington. We didn't make that argument at the time."

Ironically, for all the talk of the Bush administration catering to business interests, federal regulation actually increased at a rapid clip during the Bush years. Much of this was driven by the Americans with Disabilities Act and Bush's widely hailed reauthorization of the Clean Air Act. McIntosh argued that the agencies would have swamped the economy with more and harsher regulations if not for the Competitiveness Council's efforts.

Later in the 1990s, as the economy boomed and the Council's ideological wars receded from memory, property rights activists on the Right became the mirror image of extremists on the Left. Like wallflowers at a square dance, they were cut out of the real political action, which took place across a broad middle ground.

By the spring of 1992, Dan Quayle was, at Kristol's prodding, staking out a course cautiously independent from George Bush's reelection effort, which conservatives considered a message-less mess. The vice president had started listening to all of Kristol's entreaties that he address the breakdown of the family and its impact on American society. Kristol believed the Los Angeles riots—which had erupted in late April after an all-white jury acquitted police officers who had been videotaped beating a black man—aptly demonstrated his point. In White House strategy meetings to devise Bush's response to the riot, Kristol fought all suggestions of conciliation with the city's looters and argued for the president to graphically portray a city given over to social anarchy and lawlessness.

Quayle was scheduled to give a speech on May 19 at the San Francisco Commonwealth Club, and Kristol believed his boss should use the occasion to draw the connection between the riots and the nation's moral decline. The draft speech Quayle planned to deliver would make the point: "The lawless social anarchy which we saw [in Los Angeles] is directly related to the breakdown of family structure, personal responsibility, and social order in too many areas of our society." On the cross-country flight aboard Air Force II, the vice president took some time to further tinker with the speech. At one point, he leaned over to his chief of staff and asked, "You know, maybe I should take out that one sentence on *Murphy Brown*. It might get misinterpreted."

"Oh, don't worry," Kristol replied, "no one will pay attention to it." Of such offhand remarks are political legends made.

The Murphy Brown line, which Quayle himself inserted toward the end of a thirty-minute address, touched off an early summer electrical storm in the media. In his speech, Quayle criticized the producers of a popular TV sitcom called *Murphy Brown* for a plot twist in which the central character—a famous newscaster played by actress Candice Bergen—chose to have a baby as a single mother. Murphy Brown, Quayle asserted, mocks "the importance of fathers by bearing a child alone and calling it just another lifestyle choice." In the fracas that followed, everyone forgot that Quayle was not the first to make this point: Two major opinion pieces had already appeared in the Washington press criticizing the show's producers. Moreover, a handful of centrist policy groups, including the Institute of American Values, were raising their own concerns about skyrocketing rates of unwed births. But when the same concerns came out of Quayle's mouth, all hell broke loose.

From Washington, the Bush White House frantically tried to backtrack from Quayle's remark, as the president sputtered something about not wanting to take issue with a popular TV character. (Quayle press secretary David Beckwith later complained, "Bush could have just stated the obvious—that children are better off with a mother and father.") In the press, pundits were quick to condemn as trivial Quayle's attack on a fictional TV character; more serious critics accused the vice president of insensitivity to the plight of single mothers. (According to Kristol, the Murphy Brown reference was designed to make it appear that Quayle wasn't singling out single black welfare moms; his intent was to indict social standards encouraged by the nation's elite in general, and Hollywood in particular.) Some on the Left believed that Quayle's remarks about a "cultural elite" in New York and Hollywood were veiled references to Jews, and they accused Kristol of anti-Semitism. Even many of those who agreed with Quayle's concerns about the breakdown of the family asserted that the vice president, as a wealthy white male Republican, was the wrong messenger.

Searing as these attacks were, Kristol nevertheless loved all the attention and commotion he and his boss had stirred up. And eleven months later, he could flash his characteristic Cheshire cat grin when the respected bastion of intellectual liberalism, the *Atlantic Monthly* magazine, published research showing the links between out-of-wedlock births and a myriad of social ills under the headline "Dan Quayle Was Right."

In spite of, or perhaps in part because of, the Murphy Brown storm, Quayle's approval rating going into the critical summer of the 1992 presidential race remained a dismal 26 percent. Moreover, whatever progress Kristol may have made in transforming Quayle into a promising conservative leader was cut short one June afternoon at a New Jersey elementary school, when the vice president instructed a student in a spelling bee to add an "e" to the end of the word "potato." Back in Washington, Kristol and his staff went on emergency damage control: They blamed a misspelled cue card. They tried to think of other "o"-words that end in "e." They pulled out a Truman biography to highlight the bad spelling of that great president. But in the end, it was all to no avail. The "potatoe" incident crystallized everything Americans already believed about Dan Quayle. For years, it would be the first thing people thought of when they heard his name. Very possibly, it had ended his political career—and his staff knew it.

After "potatoe," it was all Kristol could do to prevent the dump-Quayle voices in the Bush campaign from growing loud enough to force his boss off the ticket. Bill managed to plug their efforts with a clever political maneuver: As rumors swirled that Bush might seek a new VP, Kristol convinced Quayle to walk over and ask the president himself—knowing full well that Bush was too loyal to personally fire his friend. The weekend before the Republican convention, Quayle followed Kristol's advice, and secured Bush's assurance that he was still on the ticket. Kristol leaked the whole businesss to the press—the rumors, the meeting, and the president's answer. That proved the end of the dump-Quayle effort. But Quayle still needed more than clever political maneuvers to rehabilitate his reputation.

PARTY CONVENTIONS are, by nature, quadrennial exercises in mass self-delusion, so maybe you couldn't blame the baby-boom conservatives for getting caught up in divisive rightist fervor that defined

Houston. And to be sure, the rhetoric of the baby boomers had been constructive going into the 1992 GOP convention. Kristol promised reporters that the nation would hear a string of uplifting speeches outlining a conservative reform agenda of school vouchers for poor children, tenant management and ownership of public housing, and incentive-based health care reform. For too long the GOP had "paid a price" for defining a "negative agenda," he told one reporter. Likewise, Ralph Reed, planning a national debut for his Christian Coalition, hoped to demonstrate that his group—unlike its predecessors—understood the importance of offering an inclusive message as it took its place on the national stage.

But shortly after the convention delegates were gaveled to order in the Astrodome, it became clear that this was not to be a celebration of the party that had ushered in the end of the cold war. Rather it would be a strange tribal outpouring of hostility, the war dance of the modern conservative movement. Even Kristol, beaten-down and cranky from his boss's continued ill fortune, couldn't resist joining in the wicked fun by telling reporters that Woody Allen, by romancing his stepdaughter, was demonstrating his credentials as a "good Democrat." But it was the evangelical group led by Ralph, the former brazen College Republican, which most pointedly demonstrated how out of touch the Right remained with mainstream America.

The media at Houston zeroed in on Ralph's fledgling Christian Coalition as a star of the show. Reed boasted to reporters that Coalition members constituted close to 20 percent of the convention's delegates, and that 42 percent of the delegates were self-described conservative evangelicals. About a quarter of the 107 members of the GOP platform committee were Coalition allies; under pressure from the Religious Right, the committee adopted a document "that you can take to any church on any Sunday morning," Ralph proclaimed.

With platform negotiations going his way, with Pat Robertson scheduled for a prime-time speech, Ralph knew things were good. They looked even better on August 17, with a Christian Coalition rally scheduled in a nearby hotel. Ralph had been worried all morning: He had secured one of the biggest ballrooms in the city, with a capacity of five thousand people, but he thought he'd be lucky if he could draw a crowd half that size. He had instructed his staff to set up popcorn and Coke stands around the room, hoping to give the illusion of an event filled to capacity.

But as Ralph and his wife Jo Anne reached the Sheraton, they saw "a line of hundreds of straw-hatted, sign-carrying Christian activists snaking across the hotel grounds." When Coalition organizers threw open the doors to the ballroom, "a mass of humanity surged toward the stage. Four thousand people toppled exhibit tables and nearly knocked over the popcorn machines." It was, said Ralph, like a Rolling Stones concert. Only the crowd wasn't clapping for Mick Jagger; it was clapping for Bill Kristol's prince, J. Danforth Quayle.

When the vice president, running late, finally arrived, Kristol and Secret Service in tow, the crowd chanted "We love Dan! We love Dan!" He might not be popular nationally, but here, in front of this all-white, God-fearing, abortion-hating crowd, Dan Quayle was the man of the moment, the embodiment of family values, a fearless warrior against the "cultural elite." Fans in the audience sported buttons reading "Dan Quayle Is Right," and "Murphy Brown Is a Tramp." "We got Quayle [as the rally's guest of honor] because we knew Quayle was key to those people," recalled Ralph. "Quayle was the reason why you were for Bush, because *he* was our guy."

Quayle stood at the podium and offered his audience words of political martyrdom. "The elites laughed at the reference to Murphy Brown and sneered at my defense of basic values," he told them. "But it wasn't just me they were laughing at, my friends. It was you, and your families, and your values." A chorus of "amens" and "praise Gods" erupted.

Down on the floor, those perceived as members of this "cultural elite" risked being personally targeted by the Rightists' wrath. As if the "Anita Hill: Feminist Fraud" buttons and the eerie displays of plastic fetuses weren't bad enough, some of the activists turned on reporters covering the event. They hurled angry accusations at a Canadian reporter who didn't put her hand over her heart during the Pledge of Allegiance. They shoved CNN commentator Bob Beckel and heckled his fiancée. Later, inside the Astrodome convention hall, other activists (Ralph insisted they weren't Coalition members) stalked National Public Radio reporter Nina Totenberg, calling her a "whore." Totenberg was one of a pair of reporters who first broke the news of Anita Hill's allegations against Clarence Thomas.

From the podium that week came charged jingoistic rhetoric. The Monday night invocation was given by a Presbyterian pastor who referred to those "atheists and secularists . . . that would lead us down . . . [the] godless trail to destruction." Pat Robertson, who told the Christian Coalition rally that homosexuality would destroy the country, used his prime-time convention spot to accuse Bill Clinton of harboring a "radical plan to destroy the traditional family." Marilyn Quayle implicitly dismissed working women and nonmothers as women who "wish to be liberated from their essential natures as

244 GANG OF FIVE

women." Pat Buchanan warned of a religious and cultural war going on for the "soul of America."

When it was all over, when the GOP's conventioneers had packed up and gone home, many in the media asserted that the Republican Party had fallen into the hands of the "crazies," and much of America agreed. But if Houston endangered their forward-looking conservative agenda, the baby-boom conservatives didn't pause long enough to notice that week. As Ralph enthusiastically told one reporter at Houston: "Politics is ultimately an intoxicant."

There was plenty of responsibility to go around for the failures of the conservative movement during the Bush years. First, there was the president himself, a man known to fear change and distrust crusades (though in Bush's defense it should be noted that this is the traditional definition of a conservative). Even if the conservatives had been able to craft a message that unified most of the country, George Bush was never going to be the leader to deliver it. In the Clarence Thomas episode, the Right's activists could blame their travails on the continued strength and ferocity of their Number One enemy, the organized Left. When the Competitiveness Council failed to stop the rising tide of regulation, they could blame that "iron triangle" of Democratic congressional staffers, environmental lobbyists, and agency bureaucrats.

But if the baby-boom conservatives were honest, they would have to look in the mirror. And if they did, they would have to acknowledge some hubris that prevented them from seeing how the Right's message at times scared mainstream Americans. America's connection to conservative ideas is there, to be sure, in the documents of the nation's founding, in its modern-day capitalism and populism and aversion to distant authority. But bereft of Reagan as hero, and Moscow as enemy, the new conservatives lost that connection. They tried packaging ("we need to work on our message," their pollsters would say, testing spin-words like "opportunity" and "choice" in focus groups). They complained about a biased press ("we can't get our message out!" they would grumble, incessantly). A few, like Kristol, searched for a new leader to come riding out of the crimson sun as it set over the old man's Santa Barbara ranch. And when none of that worked, they would fall back on that traditional standby of the Right: They declared war on anyone who didn't agree with them.

After the November election, when Bill Clinton squeezed just enough votes out of a three-way race with Bush and Ross Perot to lay claim to the presidency, the movement had its enemy.

PART THREE

*THE
CLINTON YEARS:
"WAR
WITHOUT BLOOD"*

CHAPTER 11

AN ENEMY'S
FATAL CONCEITS

THREE YEARS, and what a high they had been for Ralph Reed. Those white envelopes his wife Jo Anne began tearing open between baby naps in 1989 had, by the end of 1992, transformed the Christian Coalition into a $12 million–plus lobbying machine. The rickety PCs were gone, replaced with high-tech gadgetry that stored data on 250,000 dues-paying members, and another 1.6 million potential allies. In Jesse Helms's tight 1990 race for reelection, Ralph mobilized enough activists to help pitch the North Carolina senator over the top. In statehouse races in 1991, Ralph's forces surprised the voters of the Virginia Beach region with stealth campaigns to capture seven of nine seats. And in 1992, at the GOP convention in Houston, big-name reporters were awed and a little dismayed by the power of Ralph's political machine, which already dominated Republican Party organizations in as many as half a dozen states.

What a high.

And what a low.

As Ralph sat on the balcony of his Jamaica hotel room a few days after Clinton's victory in the November election, watching the sun dip over the glistening blue of Montego Bay, he weighed whether or not he should quit. Not that he hadn't considered leaving before; there had been plenty of moments of high frustration. But this time, even with the psychic distance of tropical surf and sand, he thought he might give up. "No amount of rest and relaxation could help me escape the magnitude of the setback we had suffered," he recalled. "We were being blamed for the Republicans' loss of the White House, the press was demonizing us, and our entire strategy seemed to be in jeopardy."

Not everybody was blaming the Christian Right for the fact that a Republican incumbent had fallen from a 90-percent approval rating just two years earlier to lose the White House. Many blamed the sluggish economy, or Bush's decision to break his tax pledge, or his idea-free reelection campaign. But Ralph heard (even as he rejected) those voices that asked: Had the Religious Right's saber rattling frightened moderates into the arms of Ross Perot, or even Bill Clinton? Had Ralph's boastful claims of power and influence inside the GOP backfired?

From the start, Ralph's grand ambition had been to lead the Religious Right out of its political ghetto, to take an unprecedented "place at the table" in mainstream politics. Yet he here was, three years later, sitting atop an activist base with cash stuffed in the bank, bodies stashed inside the GOP apparatus, but bearing the mark of Cain in the political world. For all his tweaks of the "liberal press," Ralph craved its respect. Yet the national media had tarred his movement as one filled with crazies, extremists, haters, demogogues. Instead of creating something new and far-reaching, had he just hung different faces on an old Religious Right message of hostility and intolerance?

He could have walked away after the 1992 election, but his faith provided a philosophical perspective on defeat. These were the trying times in which he would open his Bible to the words of Paul: "To keep me from being conceited . . . there was given me a thorn in my flesh, a messenger of Satan, to torment me. Three times I pleaded with the Lord to take it away from me. But he said to me, 'My grace is sufficient for you, for my power is made perfect in weakness.' " As he matured as a political leader, Ralph's friends saw in him an uncanny ability to weather the thorns in his own flesh. "Politics isn't about winning," he once said, "it's about surviving. People who don't understand that get burned out." You can't get too excited when you're up, or too depressed when you're down, he added. Conceit will blind you to the meagerness of victory, just as dejection can blind you to the short life of defeat.

Political commentators would argue about whether the activist Right in general, and evangelicals in particular, had been an asset or a liability to the Republicans in 1992. Less remarked upon was the fact that the image of conservatism presented at Houston was a rusty, outdated one. As conservative writer David Frum aptly noted, the convention reflected the Bush team's tone-deaf attempt to rally the Right. Like tourists who vainly try to communicate with foreigners by talking louder, the Bush organizers pandered to the Right by offering a microphone to divisive figures (just as they played to the center by offering prime TV time to visionless moderates). Failed presidential candidate Pat Buchanan received much of the attention, but he was a self-described paleoconservative who turned off most of the baby-boom activists with his isolationism, his aversion to free trade and immigration, his white-ethnic patriotism. (Bill Bennett once accused Buchanan of "flirting with fascism," and a quadrennial worry of many baby-boom conservatives was that Buchanan would hijack their movement.)

Phyllis Schlafly was the face of the anti-abortion forces, a key architect of the Republican platform. But it would be hard to imagine Ralph walking up to a podium, as Schlafly had done for decades, and claiming a woman who works is neglecting her family. Ralph never knew a workplace without women; he even had some quibbles with Quayle's Murphy Brown speech, believing that the vice president should have laid more guilt upon absent fathers. "Let's face it," he said, "the mother is left with a very difficult decision to make: Either abort the baby—which we don't agree with—or have the child and do what she can to provide that child with what it needs, materially, emotionally, psychologically."

A more contemporary conservative vision at Houston would have put flesh on Kristol's vision of "a politics of liberty, and a sociology of virtue." It would have centered on dramatic tax cuts, free trade, school choice, eliminating racial categories, injecting an element of private investment into Social Security, and promoting term limits to undercut liberalism's entrenched "special interests" in Congress. In this vision, cultural issues would be packaged as commonsense alternatives within mainstream America—a plank off which to walk for those on the Left who insisted on defending widespread abortion or calling fatherless families a positive lifestyle choice.

But even if the baby-boom conservatives could persuade most Americans to embrace their agenda—much of which was still quite radical at the time—they had their own public relations problems. The biggest obstacle was their own swaggering machismo, their insistence on being "hard-core." A decade after coming to Washington with Reagan, they continued to talk like insurgents, not like leaders.

For all his mainstream ambitions, Ralph was one of the worst offenders, promoting stealth "guerrilla warfare" in local elections and asserting that "what Christians have got to do is to take back this country, one precinct at a time. . . . I honestly believe that in my lifetime we will see a country once again governed by Christians . . . and Christian values." Bill Kristol jumped in, too, with his Woody-Allen-as-a-good-Democrat comment, his crafting of a Quayle stump speech that asked, "Would you trust Bill Clinton with your children?" And Grover Norquist would always turn off wavering moderates with his Manichaean division of the world.

Back in Washington a few weeks after Clinton's victory, Ralph swapped strategy over lunch with Kristol; the pair had become good friends when the latter brokered an agreement in the 1990 battle over federal funding to the arts. As they considered the future of their movement, Ralph was still locked in pessimism: "I wondered if our critics had not so thoroughly demonized conservatives that our effectiveness would be severely hampered." Kristol, by contrast, was looking forward to this upcoming time-out from power; he thought it would be healthy for conservatives, finally free of George Bush, to stop living off the intellectual capital of the Reagan years and to explore creative solutions to social and economic problems. "The conservative movement . . . in some respects has gotten, well, sectarian and bitter," he said at the time. "Other parts have become sort of fat and lazy. We need to regroup and think of a realistic agenda that isn't purely defensive. The conservative analysis of problems besetting us is very powerful. . . . The closing of the American mind we've analyzed. We don't know how to achieve the opening of the American mind."

Kristol's high hopes echoed the thinking of other movement conservatives eager to find a silver lining in the Bush defeat. "The argument runs as follows," Grover explained in his November 1992 *American Spectator* column: "Bill Clinton will raise taxes, overregulate, inflate the currency, cripple the economy, and champion his party's left-wing cultural values; while the Republicans unite in opposition, rediscover their Reaganite souls, and elect a truly principled president in 1996." Grover thought this theory was bunk and warned of a "coming Clinton dynasty." The Democrats, he insisted, would rig the system to stay in power, as they always had. "The Watergate babies and their left-wing allies in the Democratic caucuses have firmly controlled the House for eighteen years. How has that been possible in the face of the Carter failures, Abscam, the twin Reagan landslides, a Bush victory, Jim Wright's corruption, check bouncing . . . ? Simple.

They changed the rules. They stacked the deck. They cheated. And so will a Clinton administration."

Grover, who assumed that the Right naturally commanded the support of at least 60 percent of Americans, tended to view each of the Democrats' victories as evidence that they had "cheated." House Democrats, he asserted, had spent the two decades since Watergate entrenching themselves in power. "[A]lmost every Democrat in the House received his own subcommittee chairmanship, the better to extort campaign contributions from industries under his jurisdiction," he wrote. A Clinton presidency, Grover added, would "rescue organized labor from certain crack-up" by failing to enforce the Supreme Court's Beck decision, thereby allowing liberal union leaders to use compulsory membership dues to support the Democrats.

As the first Democratic president in twelve years stepped into the Oval Office, all this internal jostling among the baby-boom conservatives over the relative merits of being displaced from power receded to the background. The immediate reality was that they were, for the first time in their adult political lives, disconnected from the White House. For earlier generations of conservatives, this was a familiar sensation. For those who had come to Washington with Reagan, it was a jarring adjustment (even if the Bush years had provided an intermediate step into the wilderness). The faces of two older, and liberal, baby boomers—Bill Clinton and Al Gore—now filled TV screens and magazine covers and news pages. In victory, glamour had returned to the Democrats and their showy court of young advisers. The Democratic Party was the place to be for those fashion-conscious young Washingtonians whom John Podhoretz memorably called "the genetically endowed."

More than two hundred miles south of the glittering changes taking place in Washington, inside a first-floor office in a bland industrial park in Chesapeake, Virginia, Ralph wrote a postelection memo to local Christian Coalition leaders: "The pro-family movement now shifts to the loyal opposition. No more photo ops in the Roosevelt Room. . . . It will force us to do what we should have been doing all along: building a permanent presence at the grass roots, and returning to the state and local legislative issues that are closest to where people live, and where we are strongest. . . . It is awfully difficult to demonize individuals for their religious views if they have been elected to local political office and have served their community with distinction."

Ralph would always talk a good game about the importance of

local politics; in fact he was always drawn, mothlike, to Washington's klieg lights. In that, he was like many of his generational peers on the Right who yearned to walk the halls of the West Wing, calling the shots for their own Reagan. "If you grow up [playing baseball], what do you always dream of?" Reed pondered at one contemplative moment. "You dream for it to be the bottom of the ninth, the seventh game of the World Series, and you're at the plate, and there's a man at third, and all they need is a base hit. You want that moment. Would I like to have my own guy . . . what Clinton was to Carville, what Bush was to Atwater? Sure, I would love to have that. I'd love to be there helping him run the campaign. I'd love to be in the holding room telling him, 'This is what you need to say. This is how you need to say it.' But, it may not happen."

In the brief calm before the six-month storm that would define the debut of the Clinton presidency, Ralph could look enviously upon the young aide at the new president's side. George Stephanopoulos was about the same age as Ralph, and his charisma exerted approximately the same excitable effect on his fans as Ralph's exerted on his. As Clinton's senior adviser, George stood exactly where Ralph wanted to be. So there is some irony in the fact that Stephanopoulos's appearance at his first press briefing was what convinced Ralph to throw off his postelection blues and prepare to reengage the enemy.

By HIS OWN RECKONING, Stephanopoulos appeared at that press conference with the pallor of a corpse, the mark of a grueling week of putting out brushfires in between inaugural festivities. His face featured a five-o'clock shadow that made him look like "an adolescent Richard Nixon." He stepped to the podium inside the White House press room ready to fudge questions about attorney general nominee Zoe Baird and the brewing controversy over the immigration status of her nanny. But the first question was one that he was even less interested in answering: "How about all these stories on the lifting of the ban on homosexuals in the military?" a reporter asked.

As he sat in front of his TV in his Virginia office, Ralph watched the scene unfold: George's saggy look and saggier responses to a room full of hostile reporters. "I know how you feel, buddy," was what he thought as he watched Stephanopoulos stumble. What he smelled was blood: Here it was, opening day, and the Clinton administration was already under seige. Clinton's decision to fulfill a little-noticed campaign promise by drafting an executive order to repeal a ban on homosexuals serving in the armed forces was a political misstep of epic proportion, drawing the ire of even his own military advisers.

On the Right, the decision to lift the ban touched off a gleeful romp and the Christian Coalition jumped right in. Ralph knew this would be a hot-button issue with his members, so as he was driving home that night, talking to Pat Robertson on his car phone, he suggested that the televangelist flash the Capitol Building switchboard number on the screen while describing the Clinton policy on *The 700 Club*. "It is conceivable," Ralph told his boss, "that enough calls coming in at once would literally jam the switchboard." Robertson did just that on his TV show the following morning, and his viewers loyally added their voices to the record 436,000 phone calls swamping Congress that day. With the Clinton baby boomers stumbling out of the starting gate, Ralph was back in the game.

Ralph knew how to play the gay card with fellow evangelicals, and had never shied away from doing just that—whether the issue was NEA funding of homoerotic art or classroom materials presenting homosexuality as an alternative lifestyle. Yet within the gay community he was considered the least homophobic of the Religious Right's leaders. "Suprising many, Christian Coalition head Ralph Reed refuses to take a hard-line public stance against gay rights," the *Advocate*, a leading gay publication, would later state, adding that the Coalition's voter guides did not include candidate positions on same-sex marriage. Ralph's second book, *Active Faith*, would criticize such figures as Jerry Falwell for calling AIDS "God's judgment" on homosexuals, and referring to gays as "perverts" (though he didn't mention his own boss, Pat Robertson, who called it a "sickness").

Not that Ralph condoned homosexuality. He also would write that, from the Book of Genesis on, "the Bible makes it clear that homosexuality is a deviation from the normative sexual conduct and God's laws" (he noted also that adultery falls in the same category). Reed said he considered homosexuality a "wrong choice" but "on a public policy level our job is not to punish people who make wrong choices. Our job is to try to create a public policy environment that minimizes the damage of the wrong choices and doesn't encourage people who otherwise wouldn't make them to make them." Asked how he would react to having gay or lesbian teachers in his child's classroom, Ralph responded, "If it's not an issue for them, it's not an issue for me. If they make it an issue, it's an issue."

Despite the Right's condemnations of homosexuality, gay men were prominent within the movement's ranks. Inside the New Right, which defined the movement in the 1970s with aggressive pro-family, anti-gay rhetoric, closeted figures included Terry Dolan, the National Conservative Political Action Committee founder who died of AIDS, and former Republican Congressman Robert Bauman, a co-founder of Young Americans for Freedom and former chairman of the American Conservative Union. Bauman's political career ended in 1980 when he was arrested for soliciting sex from a male prostitute. Marvin Liebman, a central figure in the early conservative movement who helped found YAF and, later, Ralph's group Students for America, came out of the closet in a 1992 autobiography to denounce the "bigotry" of the Right.

Among the younger conservatives who emerged on the national stage during the Reagan years, gay friends tended to be more open and typically congregated in the movement's libertarian wing, where they turned a blind eye to the gay-bashing of religious fundamentalists and others. A handful of Ralph's College Republican friends were gay. "Typically, we were raised in suburbs, so we're natural Republicans," explained Tyllmann Wald, Ralph's ally at the University of Georgia. "Also, we were inspired by Reagan. . . . Just because we believe in being honest doesn't mean we're socialists."

Ralph argued that the gay-rights lobby had thrown a private morality issue into the public policy arena with demands for legal protection and equal consideration as "an alternative lifestyle" in schools and textbooks. It was the celebration of gay life as a "moral equivalent" to heterosexual marriage—not the prevalence of homosexuality—that bothered social conservatives such as Ralph. (New York City's addition of such books as *Daddy's Roommate* and *Heather has Two Mommies* to the first-grade curriculum activated the Christian Coalition in that city's heated 1993 school board race.) Even in libertarian circles, where a number of gay men occupied prominent positions, thinkers and activists vigorously opposed adding sexual orientation alongside race, religion, and gender in civil rights laws they already considered too liberal.

Kristol expressed far more alarm at society's tolerance toward homosexuality. History may well "record this revolution [in attitudes toward homosexuality] as the most fundamental social movement of the latter part of the century." In the preface to a book titled *Homosexuality and Public Life,* Kristol wrote: "More directly than almost any of the other liberation movements of the last thirty years—more than the attempt to secure the unbridled right to abortion, more than feminism—the homosexual rights revolution forces a consideration of whether there is any ground in nature for saying that certain human activities are to be preferred to others." Kristol allied himself with natural rights theorists writing esoteric treatises on the supremacy of heterosexual sex and marriage, with formerly gay psychologists working to free their clients from what they called SSAD or "same-sex attraction disorder," and with social scientists arguing that AIDS should be treated like other health epidemics, with mandatory testing programs. "It will be a political debate, so it will not be the kindest debate," he said of the issue, "but on our side we need to conduct that debate with civility."

Social conservatives claimed that President Clinton's decision to lift the ban on gays in the military put the government in the position of appearing to condone wrongful private behavior. "Clinton moved affirmatively to lift the ban," argued Ralph. "Nobody on our side ever brought it up. The military's position pre-Clinton was an eminently defensible legal position, [derived from a view that] this is deleterious to good order and morale and discipline in the military." Whatever nuance may have rounded Ralph's position on homosexuality, what mattered strategically in those early months of 1993 was that Clinton had handed him a talisman with which he could inspire and reinvigorate the Right's evangelicals.

The day after Coalition activists swamped the Capitol switchboard over gays in the military, a *Washington Post* writer blew on hot coals with a page-one story labeling followers of Robertson and other religious broadcasters as "poor, uneducated, and easy to command." In the eyes of conservative activists, the "liberal media" had revealed its true bias. "No other episode from the early Clinton administration so heartened and awakened our supporters," Ralph recalled. He immediately put in an order for buttons reading "Poor, Uneducated, and Easy to Command" that his staff could wear. Meanwhile, the Coalition's upper-middle-class staffers mobilized to fax their college diplomas and tax returns to the *Post*. The paper responded with a correction the next day, stating that "there is no factual basis for that statement."

Even without the *Post's* slur, Ralph knew his three-year-old Christian Coalition was in dire need of a makeover. In early 1993, he began an intensive effort to put the divisiveness of Houston behind him; he hired a polling company to help him broaden his message and recruited a Jewish former Leftist to lobby Congress on behalf of Christian evangelicals. Marshall Wittmann, a witty and worldly former Trotskyite from Waco, Texas, had met his wife on a United Farm Workers picket line. He had since swung to the Right, and was winding up his job as deputy assistant secretary for legislative affairs in

Bush's Department of Health and Human Services when he crossed tracks with Ralph.

Wittmann first decided to apply to the Coalition after the 1992 election, as he watched Ralph spar with major media commentators on NBC's *Meet the Press*. "I was just amazed at his skill," Wittmann recalled. "I thought he had outshined [Congressman Jim] Leach, [David] Broder, who was interviewing him, and [Tim] Russert. I was just stunned. He had a wisdom that wasn't always associated with that movement." He concluded that Ralph had the potential to lead a new generation beyond its yippies-of-the-Right self-image, eventually building an organization with the same staying power as liberal stalwarts such as the AFL-CIO and the NAACP. Wittmann wasn't the only one in awe of Ralph as his TV appearances mounted. Longtime friends couldn't believe how much the young politico had changed: His Emory Ph.D. showed, as the former College Republican responded to hostile questioning with calculated historical allusions and sentences filled with such soothing words as "plurality" and "diversity" and "balance."

As Wittmann came on board in early 1993, Ralph was studying the results of a national poll of evangelical Christians which reinforced his view that with recession worries still high, jobs and the economy topped the list of concerns, followed by taxes, the federal deficit, crime, and education. "Abortion was one of these voters' lowest priorities," he recalled. While not all evangelicals were staunch conservatives—more than a third had voted for Clinton, and many of those were pro-choice—the results nevertheless challenged the assumption that the Right's evangelicals were driven primarily by such volatile social issues as gay rights, abortion, and school prayer.

At the end of January, Ralph announced that the Coalition's top legislative priority would be to lower the tax burden on families by increasing the standard deduction. He later launched a $100,000 radio and direct-mail campaign opposing the Clinton budget plan because it failed to include a tax credit for children. As Ralph noted, the radio ads "marked the first time a religious conservative group had jumped into the fray on a purely economic issue, though our rationale was based on the need to strengthen the family."

But there was no getting around the fact that social issues drove Ralph's hard-core activist base and uncorked the flow on donations. Ralph's second priority in those early Clinton months was protecting the Hyde Amendment, legislation which outlawed federal funding for abortions under the Medicaid program. That summer, the Coalition ran a media campaign against the Clinton administration's attempt to repeal the law. The campaign centered on newspaper advertisements blaring "Al Gore Was Right," and publishing the vice president's statement as a senator that using taxpayer dollars for "the taking of innocent human life" was wrong. "The ad had the desired effect, demonstrating that taxpayer funding of abortion was unpopular even among many Democrats," Ralph recalled. In July, a vote to repeal the amendment was overwhelmingly defeated.

During those first months of the Clinton administration, Ralph resolved to tone down the Coalition's image by softening its language. "I became convinced that we had spoken sometimes . . . in the evangelical vernacular that the secular ear could not comprehend. And that it was really self-indulgent," he recalled. Christian political leaders, he added, should act more like ambassadors capable of translating the views of their community for mainstream media consumption. "You don't just show up at the meeting and speak in Hebrew if they speak Greek," he said. "You have to speak in their language. We weren't doing that—not because there was any philosophical or theological objection to it. We were just selfish."

In Ralph's makeover, the Religious Right was the "pro-family movement" (though even that nonreligious description left something to be desired, suggesting that people not of the same political mind were somehow "anti-family"). And the pro-family movement, Ralph argued, had, until now, "limited its effectiveness by concentrating disproportionately on issues such as abortion and homosexuality." Ralph wrote those words in the summer of 1993 in Adam Meyerson's influential magazine *Policy Review*, published by the Heritage Foundation. The article, "Casting a Wider Net," was a landmark in Ralph's career, signaling to fellow conservatives that he planned to be a very different kind of Religious Right leader.

In the piece, Ralph drew on historical analogies and compared movement conservatives to the Left's grass-roots organizers. "Cesar Chavez built the United Farm Workers union in the 1960s with hunger strikes and boycotts," he wrote. "But as he continued the same organizational tactics, membership in his union plummeted. . . . If the pro-family movement is not to suffer the same fate, the cluster of pro-family issues must now be expanded to attract a majority of voters." To broaden a movement that he called "policy-thin" and "value-laden," Ralph offered a proposal to alter the tax code to ease the time and work burdens on stressed families. He argued that the "only true solution to crime is to restore the family." He recommended reforming welfare to make it "more conducive to family formation," and he promoted school choice.

Perhaps Ralph's most radical supposition was that the Christian Right should—and could—appeal to a majority of Americans. That break with the evangelical past pushed Ralph toward the center, enabling more purist leaders to cast stones from the right (exactly where he wanted them to be). Just as Bill Clinton had distanced himself from Jesse Jackson and his party's left wing by condemning violent rap lyrics during the 1992 campaign, Ralph welcomed the attacks by hard-right activists such as Randall Terry, the former leader of Operation Rescue, the anti-abortion squad that gained notoriety for blockading women's health clinics. In the fall of 1994, as Ralph's prestige with the national media grew, Terry went on a tirade against the Coalition, accusing the group of treachery for embracing two GOP Senate candidates, Paul Coverdell of Georgia and Kay Bailey Hutchison of Texas, who supported restricted abortion rights. Helping "elect a child killer is nothing to brag about. . . . It is a deplorable act of treachery against heaven," Terry wrote in an op-ed that read more like a letter to Ralph. He described the Christian Coalition as a "mistress of the Republican Party."

As Ralph rowed centerward, there was always one figure clinging to his boat, weighing it down: his boss, Pat Robertson. If Ralph was telling the media, "We believe in a separation of church and state that is complete and inviolable," Robertson was calling this constitutional interpretation "a lie of the Left." If Ralph talked of America's "diversity and pluralism," Robertson argued that "non-Christians and atheistic people can use [the Constitution] to destroy the very foundation of our society." If Ralph talked of equal opportunity for women, Robertson condemned the feminist agenda as "socialist . . . encourag[ing] women to leave their husbands, kill their children, practice witchcraft, destroy capitalism and become lesbians." In 1991, Robertson authored *The New World Order,* a conspiratorial history that drew on rehashed anti-Semitic lore. The book sat largely unnoticed until a broad audience learned about it through a 1995 *New York Review of Books* article. (For Marshall Wittmann, the Coalition's Jewish lobbyist, revelations about the book contributed to existing family strains over his decision to join an organization founded by Robertson. Two years after joining, he resigned from the Christian Coalition.)

In the complex dynamic between Robertson and Reed, it was always clear who was the boss, and Ralph never strayed from his public posture as loyal soldier. "Ralph was very submissive and loyal to Pat

Robertson," explained his wife Jo Anne. "Ralph would share his opinion, but once that decision was made, he was loyal, even though it was frustrating at times, even if the Coalition was blamed for something that wasn't his idea. . . . He had to accept that blame. He would never divulge their disagreements, and I honor that. . . . Ralph would not be where he is if not for Pat."

In interviews, Ralph defended Robertson, saying he was the "opposite of his media caricature." Ralph described a man "with a sense of humor, a joie de vivre" and labeled him "one of the most significant figures in the history of twentieth-century evangelicalism." He considered it ludicrous for anyone to accuse Robertson of anti-Semitism given his staunch support for Israel. (Support for Israel is widespread among evangelicals who believe the Jewish nation figures prominently in the Second Coming of Christ.) And while he would refuse to publicly criticize *The New World Order,* one friend said Ralph "knew this stuff was kooky" and blamed Robertson's ghostwriter on the project.

Despite Robertson, Ralph accomplished a nearly complete makeover of himself and his Christian Coalition during the first two Clinton years. Kristol had been right: Defeat, at least for Ralph, had proven a blessing in disguise. This was the period when Ralph began to police his staffers and activists for signs of demogoguery, discreetly seeing that buttons reading "Exorcise the Antichrist from the White House" were removed before activists entered the Coalition's annual conference. This was when he began using legislative-style "whips" with walkie-talkies on the floor of Coalition rallies to hush the crowd's booing of (for example) Democratic National Committee Chairman David Wilhelm, who accused the gathered activists of scare tactics and distorting Democrats' records.

It was also during this period that Ralph began using a language that modern America understood best—the language of victimization. He criticized liberals and the media for bigotry in suggesting that "somehow it is dangerous" for evangelicals to participate in politics. He also recounted specific instances of "religious bigotry": The schoolteacher forced to remove a Bible from his desk; the staff psychiatrist suspended because he prayed with his patients; the forced removal of religious symbols from municipal public settings. As Marshall Wittmann described Ralph's argument: "People who came into the public square who were motivated by a devout religious interpretation, and were politically conservative, were not welcome. It was a sense of grievance, that they were victimized, that they were the last allowable victims in American political society." In the summer of

1994, when, once again, liberal attacks rained down upon the Coalition, this time from prominent Jewish quarters, Ralph would get a big boost from his friend, Bill Kristol.

CLINTON'S GAYS-IN-THE-MILITARY fumble wasn't the kind of issue that provoked Clint Bolick. In fact, when this eager libertarian considered the issue of homosexuality and public life, he mostly turned his anger inward, at his social conservative allies "who had a blind spot toward gays. . . . The gay bashing by some social conservatives drives me nuts," he declared in one interview. "It's repugnant." But in 1993, Clint was just as primed as any of his social conservative friends for attacks on the new Democratic president. Only his territory was civil rights, and there Bolick watched with a panther's eyes, ready to pounce. What he didn't expect was that the prey would appear so soon, or that her demise would be so swift and unequivocal.

At first, Bolick assumed that President Clinton would be a moving target on civil rights issues. Clinton ran for president as a New Democrat, a politician who forged his agenda through his role as chairman of the centrist Democratic Leadership Council, which had challenged traditional liberal reliance on racial preferences. While Clinton didn't fully embrace the DLC view of affirmative action, he didn't buy into Jesse Jackson's view of the world either. After his election, when the Democrats' diversity cops began demanding more appointments for women and minorities, President Clinton dismissed them as "bean counters" who were playing "quota games."

So it was with great interest that Bolick and his allies awaited the president's announcement of a nominee for civil rights chief at the Justice Department. The assistant attorney general for civil rights oversees a division of more than two hundred attorneys and is the point-person for any president's racial policies. Public employment, school desegregation, housing discrimination, prisons, voting rights— all fall within the division's enforcement authority.

Clint was an alumnus of the division under Reagan Attorney General Edwin Meese. But it was his friend, scholar Abigail Thernstrom, who learned from her Justice Department sources that the coveted appointment would be offered to C. Lani Guinier, a law school friend of both Bill and Hillary Clinton. Thernstrom knew Guinier as an intellectual opponent and considered her theories on the Voting Rights Act to be a radical interpretation of the law. Over dinner at the Jefferson Hotel, Thernstrom told Clint that it would be worthwhile for him to read her writings. "You're going to love her," Thernstrom said mischievously.

Guinier, a forty-three-year-old University of Pennsylvania law professor, was a jewel of the civil rights establishment: She had been a top lawyer in President Carter's civil rights division and a litigator at the NAACP Legal Defense and Education Fund during the Reagan years. She had specialized in voting rights since her days at Radcliffe; her father had pioneered Afro-American studies at Harvard. On April 29, President Clinton stood in the Justice Department's sun-dappled courtyard to announce his longtime friend's appointment, along with that of six other assistant attorneys general.

In his office at the Institute for Justice, the two-year-old public interest law firm he founded with Chip Mellor, Bolick was already studying Guinier's arcane writings. "It was really turgid stuff," he recalled. Since Clint hardly qualified as an expert on the Voting Rights Act, "it was like learning Latin in a week's time." But once he figured out what she was saying, he realized "it was wildly provocative. She's a creative thinker. But the implications were terrifying. It blew me away."

According to Guinier, voting rights had moved from first-generation efforts to ensure that blacks and other minorities weren't excluded from the polls, to a second-generation strategy in the 1980s of carving out safe districts to bolster minority candidates. Guinier questioned that second step and examined "third-generation" alternatives, posing this question: How should the law handle a southern community with a racially polarized power structure that entirely ignores the wishes of the black minority? Even the election of one or two black city council members wasn't going to alter that power structure. Guinier proposed a weighted system of voting—that is, voters in a city with five council members would get five votes, all of which could be cast entirely for one candidate or divided up among several. This, she theorized, would benefit a cohesive group, such as organized blacks, women, or Latinos. More tentatively, she also suggested ways to provide for a "minority veto"—such as requiring a two-thirds vote to pass community budgets. This, she contended, would foster consensus and force the majority to consider the wishes of the minority.

Her critics argued that instead of requiring minorities to build majority support for legislation or in elections, Guinier sought to guarantee equal outcomes by race. In a 1989 law review article, she argued that antidiscrimination laws mandate a "result-oriented inquiry, in which roughly equal outcomes, not merely an apparently fair process, are the goal." She wrote of "majority tyranny" and argued in 1991 that, "We ought to question the inherent legitimacy of winner-take-all majority rule." Her critics also accused her of calling for racial quotas in judicial appointments.

There was much in Guinier's writings to offend the sensibilities of conservatives and moderates: the social engineering aspect (one legal writer noted that, in her articles, "conceptions" and "models" do battle, not real people); the lumping of people together by ethnic groups with the underlying assumption that there is one united "black" or "Latino" political position; the political-correctness implicit in her references to "authentic" African-American leaders. But Clint honed in on the one aspect of her writings that would ring loudest with the public: Her challenge to the fundamental precept of one man–one vote. She "has a serious problem with American democracy," he insisted to one reporter.

Bolick crafted an op-ed piece for the *Wall Street Journal* explaining Guinier's "innovative radicalism"—which called for "abandoning not only the nation's one person–one vote principle but majority rule itself." As fortune would have it, the *Wall Street Journal* published the op-ed on April 30, the day after President Clinton announced Guinier's nomination, under the headline "Clinton's Quota Queens." (The other "quota queen" that Bolick criticized in his article was Norma Cantu, Clinton's choice for Department of Education's assistant secretary for civil rights.)

Just as the Left had defined Bork out of his Supreme Court nomination, so now the Right had slapped a label on Guinier from which she would not recover. "I earned my Ph.D. at the feet of Ralph Neas and Nan Aron," Clint once said with a chuckle, referring to the two civil rights leaders whose efforts had tarred Bork. "They were masterful teachers." Friends recalled there was another, fresher episode propelling Clint forward: the Left's destruction of the man who had guided him toward the life he was now leading as a public interest lawyer—Clarence Thomas.

In opposing Guinier, Clint resolved not to play dirty, so that he might look down from on high at the snoops who had dredged up Thomas's video rental records to document his alleged interest in pornography. When someone phoned Clint with a claim about the political pasts of Guinier's parents, he firmly told the informer he wasn't interested; the caller could take his tip to the Senate Judiciary Committee. Still, there was a rowdiness to the campaign against

Guinier. The quota queen label set a standard that the tabloids were eager to top; one paper labeled the prominent professor "Loony Lani." A conservative columnist called her the "Vicar of Victimization" and the "Czarina of Czeparatism."

To make a more substantive case, Clint undertook a time-consuming, painstaking effort to explain Guinier's writings to reporters on deadline—not an easy task given the density of the material. Media calls to Clint's office began the morning the *Wall Street Journal* piece appeared, and his staff responded by standing by the Xerox machine, copying, verbatim, her law review articles. For days, messengers on bikes ferried packages through the streets of downtown Washington to media offices, while Clint spent hours on the phone walking reporters through the material, a process that made him deeply respectful of journalists his fellow Rightists condemned as the "liberal media establishment." (One of the journalists credited with turning the tide against Guinier, National Public Radio's Nina Totenberg, also was one of the first to break the story of sexual harassment charges against Clint's friend Thomas.) To keep up with the media demands, the Institute hired a car equipped with a phone so that Clint could return calls to print reporters on his way to appearances on such TV shows as ABC's *Nightline* and CNN's *Crossfire*. "We became information central, in a way that we hadn't anticipated," recalled his partner Chip Mellor.

Clint was determined to be meticulous with his facts and able to back up each of his claims. But he also recognized that he was leading a public relations campaign: He laced the phrase "breathtakingly radical" through his interviews and he provocatively denounced Guinier's appointment as "the most frontal assault on majority rule in recent memory. Putting her in that job will throw gasoline on the smoldering race relations in this country." He claimed that her theories promoted the "tyranny of the minority . . . the most radical notion of government I've seen presented in my lifetime."

Liberal commentators condemned Bolick and his allies as racist and sexist, citing the "quota queen" label as Exhibit One: The term, they argued, evoked "welfare queen," an image expressly meant to denigrate African-American women. Guinier's supporters argued that the nominee was guilty only of "looking at civil rights issues in new and different ways," that her main interest was to "build multiracial coalitions and encourage full participation across the board by everyone." They accused Bolick and other conservatives of trying to marginalize Guinier by taking her words and theories out of context. As

William Coleman, a black Republican and President Ford's transportation secretary, argued, "Guinier was mainstream and pro-integrationist in the tradition of Thurgood Marshall." The attacks left her supporters with a "sense of Kafkaesque unreality," he added.

Bolick was aided by early opposition to Guinier from the president's own supporters, specifically the DLC and its think tank, the Progressive Policy Institute. DLC president Al From wrote to Clinton complaining that Guinier's positions undercut his own campaign rhetoric. PPI director Will Marshall argued that Guinier's writings call for "an unprecedented expansion of judicial supervision of state legislatures and county and municipal councils. . . . This pushes us further down the road toward racial entitlements and away from the broad inclusive view of national community Bill Clinton invoked . . . during the campaign." Representative Dave McCurdy of Oklahoma, a DLC leader, called Guinier's nomination "very distressing. . . . Her positions are inconsistent with the message of eliminating quotas and reaching out to the middle class." Thirty of the Senate's Democrats, including Senate Judiciary Committee chairman Joe Biden, who would oversee the nomination hearings, were DLC members.

Within three weeks of Clinton's glowing endorsement of Guinier in the Justice Department courtyard, the future of Clinton's nominee was in serious trouble. Even support for holding nomination hearings was eroding in the Senate, where the specter of white male senators throwing hostile questions at a prominent black woman was being dubbed "Anita Hill II." The White House did little to defend her: Guinier was kept away from the press and only began meeting with senators once her nomination was endangered. Just as the Reagan White House had appeared afraid of Bork's views, just as the Bush White House had tried to hide Thomas's views, now the Clinton White House was timid in its embrace of Guinier's views.

On June 3, just days after Guinier had begun making courtesy calls on key senators, President Clinton pulled her nomination, explaining that some of her theories were "antidemocratic." "At the time of the nomination, I had not read her writings," the president said. "In retrospect, I wish I had." But he also distanced himself from her critics on the Right, singling out Clint's April 30 op-ed in the *Wall Street Journal* as part of a "campaign of right-wing distortion and vilification."

The Left responded by accusing the president of betrayal. The Right was ready to party. Six months in, the Clinton administration had suffered two terrible and embarrassing blows: First, the president was forced to table his gays-in-the-military order (which would later be replaced by a "don't ask–don't tell" policy, which many on the Right also denounced). Now he was forced to withdraw the nomination of a woman who was not only a friend, but a pillar of the civil rights establishment.

At Clint's Institute for Justice offices, across the street from the Justice Department, the staff broke out champagne and cigars. Clint led his fellow lawyers in a little ditty, to the tune of the *Flintstones* theme:

> *"Lani, Lani Guinier*
> *She's a modern stone-age quota queen*
> *From the radical Left,*
> *She's a nightmare for majorities*
>
> *One day, Mr. Clinton called her up*
> *But he, hadn't read her stuff*
>
> *Now we, have no nominee*
> *But we don't have Lani Guinier*
> *No Lani Guinier*
> *We've got no quota queen"*

"The Lani Guinier episode was a defining moment and showed Clint at his best," said his partner Chip Mellor. "We never expected that outcome. I mean, who would? And much less so fast. We went in thinking we were going to give a good fight and do the best we could." By the end of the Guinier fight, Clint was firmly ensconced at the top of the Left's hit list. "You're a slash-and-burn killer and terrorist, and we're proud of you," one rightist ally wrote to him.

CHAPTER 12

REVOLUTION TIME

THE EX-TROTSKYIST in Gertrude Himmelfarb watched with bemusement as her son Bill Kristol turned his life over to composing political strategy memos that would land on the desks of party leaders via the fax machine. It reminded her of her communist friends from the 1930s, who mimeographed their broadsheets with clarion calls to unite the workers of the world (or at least of Brooklyn). Her son's new shoestring operation was so exquisitely insurgent that she could almost forget her distress that this forty-year-old father to three of her grandchildren had absented himself from the grand halls of academia for the low rent of politics.

It was November 1, 1993, almost exactly one year after Clinton's election, when Kristol hung the sign "Project for the Republican Future" on an office door two blocks from Farragut Square, creating a virtual think tank that mostly consisted of himself and two talented young cohorts, David Tell and Daniel Casse. Their product was a new political art form—a supposedly confidential strategy memo faxed to a list of hundreds and excerpted in the *Washington Times*. By offering unsolicited advice to Republican leaders, Kristol was implicitly anointing himself guardian of the GOP, which at the time, baby-boom conservatives complained, was in the habit of acting like some big dumb elephant that sits and sulks every time it gets hit over the head.

This time the hammer on the elephant's head was Clinton's health care plan, which most Americans believed they needed and which had left Republican lawmakers scrambling for a counteroffer that might save them from appearing indifferent to the plight of the sick and uninsured. Baby-boom conservatives were, once again, aghast at the timidity of their adopted political party. Kristol's self-described co-conspirator, GOP media consultant Mike Murphy (the pony-tail-wearing architect of the "big dumb elephant" metaphor), explained the frustration this way: "We were so intimidated by our cowardly Republican pollsters who were saying, 'Well, health care's important in the polls, Clinton's for health care, we can't be against health care.' Nobody [in the GOP] wanted to stand up and say the emperor has no clothes. It was like the old dime-store New Deal—be for everything the Democrats are for, but cheaper. Kristol was the one guy who had enough guts, and frankly the spare time and inclination, to stand up and scream 'fraud.' You know—to set the tinder box aflame."

Kristol's memo operation would soon make his opinion a permanent piece of the Washington narrative. More important, though, the advice he faxed out would help Republican lawmakers build a persuasive case against Clinton, one that would carry them to their historic 1994 victory in the mid-term congressional elections. "Nearly a full year before Republicans would unite behind the 'Contract with America,' Kristol provided the rationale and the steel for them to achieve their aims of winning control of Congress and becoming America's majority party," wrote political journalists Haynes Johnson and David S. Broder. "Killing health care would serve both ends."

Kristol's chutzpah wasn't nearly as charming to Republican regulars ("Who is this guy? What has he done for the Republican Party?" Bob Dole would later snarl). Bill was already on the outs with GOP leaders over a remark he made while promoting his friend Spencer Abraham in the January 1993 race for Republican National Committee chairman: If front-runner Haley Barbour won, Bill predicted to one reporter, "it's business as usual, and I think a lot of us will unfortunately have to look outside the party apparatus to find any kind of intellectual nourishment." As it happened, Barbour won and Abraham lost and no one forgot Kristol's snotty comment. (A year later, Abraham would win his long-shot bid for a Michigan Senate seat.)

So when Kristol used his father's connections to shake the trees of conservative foundations and New York investors, coming up with $1.3 million to launch his Project for the Republican Future, he was not exactly embraced by the RNC's paid strategists. Worse than his memos, as far as party regulars were concerned, was Kristol's insistence on broadcasting his advice to the media: Reporters topped his fax list, and he invited them to a series of conferences airing the party's dirty-linen debates over such prickly topics as abortion.

Even admirers of his political skills, such as Johnson and Broder, would accuse Kristol of Machiavellian intent. It was a natural conclusion to draw: The brainy Harvard Ph.D. who had scripted Dan Quayle, his witless prince, was now trying to pull the strings of party leaders. (And how effortless that task could be: "Bill understands the psychology of our leadership—it's very reactive and easy to lead around," explained one friend.) Strangely, though, Kristol's self-image was precisely the opposite. In the Straussian account of history, Machiavelli was brilliant—but a villain, the harbinger of modern political systems built on the manipulation of competing interests. As Strauss himself noted, Machiavelli believed that "one must lower the standards" to construct a desirable order, that leaders must shift the emphasis from "moral character to institutions." Call them cocky, call them arrogant (as many did) but Kristol and his Straussian peers considered it their moral obligation to involve themselves in a quest for a regime that aspired to cultivate virtue in its citizenry. Strauss, Kristol once wrote, concluded that "we could only ascend from the dead-end of Machiavellian modernity by returning to an earlier notion of 'the primacy of the good.' "

In the more pedestrian policy debates of the 1990s, this philosophical bent made Kristol a stern taskmaster who refused to allow the leaders of his party to lower their own standards. Republicans, he counseled, should stand firmly against Clinton's lofty promises, which would balloon a welfare state that had already wreaked dependency and entitlement on the good character of the American people. Kristol intended to "frame a new Republicanism by challenging not just the particulars of big-government policies, but their very premises." "The idea," recalled his colleague Daniel Casse, "was that the Republican Party actually stood for certain ideals and could be scolded into upholding them. Republicans would say, 'It's important to be positive.' We'd say, 'It's also important to be negative.' " And so, Kristol repeatedly counseled obstructionist tactics in his memos: Cede no territory. Don't go looking for a "least bad" compromise. Seek full surrender.

Kristol and Casse and Tell had raucous good fun producing new memos each time Republican leaders threatened to lose their spine. "They'd be jamming in the halls, ideas flying, outrageous laughs like braying donkeys," said their colleague Juleanna Glover Weiss. But there was no mistaking their seriousness of purpose. Despite his mother's déjà vu, Kristol's project was no proletarian cause. Insurgent, yes, but expressly elitist. Bill recognized himself as part of the intellectual elite (Nietzsche's "priestly aristocracy") which was duty-bound to rescue the nation from the wrong class of elites, the one represented by the Clintons and their pedigreed liberal friends. (Bill even expressed some regret for injecting the phrase "cultural elite" into Quayle's tirades against the decline of moral standards and the rise of Murphy Brown–style values; Kristol himself had no problem with cultural elites, as long as they were conservative and tradition-minded.)

This view of competing elites ran deep in the Kristol family: In the 1960s Irving Kristol had assailed the "new class" of liberal intellectuals. His historian mother had condemned Virginia Woolf and her Bloomsbury friends, the cultural elite of their day, for seeking moral and spiritual liberation from the remnants of Victorianism—celebrating love, beauty, and truth, but not virtue (engaging in tangled sex lives that were "not only homosexual but androgynous, near-incestuous and polymorphously promiscuous," she complained). Himmelfarb linked this rejection of old-fashioned values to Britain's decline from Great Power status: Bloomsbury member John Maynard Keynes propagated an economics emphasizing consumption and ridiculing saving, she insisted; the famed economist's ideas were "based entirely on the short run and preclude any long-term judgment," she wrote of the man who coined the phrase "In the long run we are all dead."

Likewise, in the early 1990s Himmelfarb's son drew connections between the state of a superpower nation and the state of its soul. The arrogance of liberal elites confident of their ability to engineer "solutions" to such complex problems as the nation's health care system was a flip side to their mindless embrace of the latest social fashion—sexual revolution, multiculturalism, moral tolerance, single-parent families—without bothering to consider the long-term consequences. Post-1960s liberalism, Bill wrote in 1992, was in "deep crisis," suffering "a hollowness at its core." A liberal nomenklatura continued to cling to power at the top of society's major institutions—government, academia, media, culture—even as it failed to win over the hearts and minds of the American people. "Beneath its smugness and self-righteousness," he insisted, "liberalism is undergoing a crisis of faith." A year later he concluded that Clinton's health care plan was the Afghanistan of liberalism—the overreaching that would expose its weakness and cause its collapse. Health care provided the ideal crucible for Kristol to prove that "unapologetic conservatism, deftly applied to political reality, was the best Republican path back to victory."

President Clinton had approached the real problems of spiraling health care costs and millions of uninsured Americans with stock liberal activism: large-scale, Washington-directed reform. The Clinton health care plan was devised by his policy wonk wife Hillary and longtime friend Ira C. Magaziner, a Rhodes Scholar and 1960s activist. This was a pairing of two people, noted one journalist, who believed that "no social problem, however complex and seemingly intractable, could resist his or her applied power to solve it." With its price controls on insurance premiums and a national health board overseeing newly created insurance alliances, the plan that President Clinton unveiled in the fall of 1993 left plenty of running room for conservative critics to denounce it as "socialized medicine," a plan to impose government control over one-seventh of the economy. Since the plan emerged from meetings not open to the public, critics also denounced its "secret" origins.

Even so, in the winter of 1993, when Kristol started issuing his faxed advice, many Republican leaders were inclined to find common ground with the White House. Systemic health care reform remained a hugely popular idea in public opinion polls. But opinion is not the same as truth, a Straussian would say. And so Kristol countered conventional Beltway opinion in his first memo, dated December 3, 1993, which argued that while close to 80 percent of Americans agreed that the system was in crisis and required fundamental change, about the same percentage of people were happy with their own health care. Inspired leaders could persuade the public that Clinton's plan would uproot "the entire U.S. health system, with disruptive and deleterious consequences" for their own care.

The Clinton administration had made the case, which the public believed, that the nation's health care system was in crisis. Kristol urged Republicans to reject that premise. The system had its problems, he conceded. But those could be addressed narrowly: tax code changes to make insurance more affordable, for example, and regulatory changes to make it more obtainable for people with preexisting health conditions. (He loftily called this approach a model for future conservative public policy—"a practical vision of principled incrementalism.") But first, Kristol counseled, the Clinton plan must be destroyed; its premise of a "crisis" undermined.

Party leaders weren't so sure. Even House minority whip Newt Gingrich, then a stand-firm man when it came to negotiating with

Clinton, believed that Kristol's no-crisis line sent "exactly the wrong signal to the American people. The average American seeing a Republican say there is no crisis . . . thought we were saying there was no health care problem." Gingrich accused Kristol of coining "a cute phrase which intellectually captured a moment but which reinforced a whole range of negatives about us. I thought it was very dangerous." In January 1994, Senate minority leader Bob Dole experienced firsthand the dangers of the Straussian shoals of truth when he adopted the no-crisis line for his televised response to the president's 1994 State of the Union speech. Dole's office "was flooded with indignant calls from people with family members facing illness and unpaid bills," according to Haynes and Broder.

Despite this public backlash, Kristol kept up the pressure to kill off Clinton's plan, firing off a new memo each time Republicans toyed with compromise. He was joined by other leaders on the Right, who threatened to deprive Dole of their support in the 1996 presidential primary if he surrendered even an inch. Grover Norquist was one voice in that chorus, warning that the sine qua non of Dole's nomination prospects would be his ability to block any government-run health care system. In February 1994, Ralph Reed's Christian Coalition launched its most ambitious lobbying effort ever, a national $1.4 million media campaign against the Clinton health care plan (which Reed condemned as a "bureaucratic, Byzantine, European-style syndicalist nightmare").

One of the biggest boosts to the Right's campaign against the Clinton health care plan came from a traditionally liberal source: the *New Republic*. In a February 7, 1994, piece under the ominous headline "No Exit," a then-obscure researcher for New York's conservative Manhattan Institute named Elizabeth McCaughey put the flesh of 4,400 words on the Right's claim that Clinton's health care system would eliminate personal medical choices and seriously endanger individual privacy. The White House challenged her facts and a range of journalists dismissed the piece as riddled with inaccuracies. Nevertheless, the Big Brother imagery she invoked gave Republican leaders and conservative activists exactly what they needed in their propaganda war against the Clinton plan. (McCaughey's crusade launched her to fame, and she was elected the Republican lieutenant governor of New York in 1994.)

By summer, sentiment on Capitol Hill began turning solidly against the Clinton health care plan, and Republican lawmakers were more willing to borrow Kristol's "no-crisis" argument. The mood shift in Washington also had a lot to do with the insurance industry's massive airing of television commercials featuring "Harry and Louise," a middle-class couple fretting about the prospect of "government-run" health care and "rationing" of services. But the Clinton White House faced another enemy front: the revival of hard-right activists ready for the kill, for this was the season that scandal returned as a plague on Clinton's house.

In the winter of 1993–94 onward, Troopergate and Filegate stirred the still air of Travelgate and Whitewater, two earlier Clinton scandals, and the Right played a pivotal role. First, in December 1993, came the controversial *American Spectator* magazine story alleging that Clinton had used state troopers to secure women when he was governor of Arkansas. Then, in February 1994, Paula Jones, who claimed to be one of his victims, used the support of conservative groups to file a sexual harassment lawsuit against the president. In between these two seminal events came the disclosure that files on the Clintons' personal finances, including the Whitewater investment, were missing from the office of Clinton friend and White House counsel Vince Foster. Foster had shot himself in a Virginia park the previous summer and despite an investigatory finding of suicide, conspiracy-minded Rightists on talk radio and beyond began promoting the theory that Foster had been murdered. With unfounded rumors such as these, noted one account, "Foster and Whitewater were joined, as salacious gossip from Troopergate was widely aired."

Four years later, when news of Clinton's affair with Monica Lewinsky emerged, Kristol would become a leader of the pro-impeachment forces against the president. But in 1994, he counseled the GOP to reject the scandalmongering of his allies on the Right:

May 4, 1994

MEMORANDUM TO: REPUBLICAN LEADERS
FROM: WILLIAM KRISTOL
SUBJECT: A WARNING ABOUT WHITE HOUSE
                              SCANDALS

So now comes a detailed sexual harassment charge against the president. . . . This development will no doubt further damage the president's already fragile moral standing, just as revelations about Mrs. Clinton's almost certainly improper commodities trading has undermined Democratic rhetoric about the "decade of greed." . . . But . . . no party should rest its hopes or base its goals on the weaknesses of its opponents. . . .

Sure, it's fun to watch Mr. Clinton's presidency in such terrible disarray. But it will be more productive (and satisfying) if Republicans work to ensure that this disarray is merely a precursor to the fundamental political and policy realignment that America needs and deserves. . . .

Although Kristol elected to take the high road on the Clinton scandals, he was eager to take advantage of his opponents' weaknesses to gain the upper hand on policy. By the time the White House introduced its first welfare reform initiative that June, Clinton was on the defensive. The Clinton plan mandated work for welfare recipients after two years but guaranteed them a government job if they couldn't find one in the private sector. As he had done with health care, Kristol urged a strategy of no retreat–no surrender. Republican leaders should kill Clinton's welfare plan, not improve on it, Kristol counseled. The president's plan, he argued, had ulterior motives:

June 13, 1994

MEMORANDUM TO: REPUBLICAN LEADERS
FROM: WILLIAM KRISTOL
SUBJECT: BOOB BAIT TIME

. . . The welfare reform PR campaign now underway is the Clinton Administration at its most cynical. What we are witnessing is a well-honed Clinton tactic: When the polls go south, reach for welfare reform. Today, with his approval rating below 50 percent . . . the Administration is only too happy to turn to tough talk on welfare—"boob bait for the Bubbas," in Senator Moynihan's evocative phrase. . . .

The president's plan, after all, does not merit serious consideration. . . .

To the many senators and members of the House phoning in to his PRF office for one-on-one consultation that June, Kristol offered the argument that Clinton's plan would *save* welfare as we know it, not end it," as the president had promised. But feeding catchy sound bites to the politicians on Capitol Hill was only the first stage of a more serious tutoring program he had in mind for Republican lawmakers eager to pursue their own plan to end welfare as an entitlement.

For the past decade, both Democrats and Republicans had approached welfare primarily as a jobs and spending problem—how to get recipients off the dole and into employment. Kristol was part of an intellectual cadre—including Bill Bennett and social scientist Charles Murray—actively pressing Washington lawmakers to consider a more fundamental argument: Welfare reform should be about marriage, not jobs. The economic pressure for husbands and boyfriends to stay in the household, and contribute to its finances, had eased once welfare checks became readily available, they argued. This contributed to a historically unprecedented rise in the number of children without fathers in their lives. By 1994, about a third of American children were born to unwed mothers each year; in black communities the rate was closer to 70 percent. Growing up fatherless was the leading indicator of whether a child would end up in jail, on drugs, pregnant as a teenager, unemployed, or on welfare. In other words, these conservatives argued, out-of-wedlock births, with welfare checks as an economic lifeline, were behind a whole range of social pathologies.

But ever since 1965, when Daniel Patrick Moynihan, then an assistant secretary of labor, was assailed as racist and uncaring for asserting that rising black illegitimacy rates would produce a "tangle of pathology" in the African-American community, political leaders had been loath to touch the subject. In October 1993, Charles Murray set off fireworks with a *Wall Street Journal* article—influential in conservative circles—warning of a "coming white underclass" and arguing that the mother-only family was not a viable economic unit. In April 1994, Bill Bennett and his co-directors at Empower America—former congressmen Jack Kemp and Vin Weber—denounced the House Republican alternative to Clinton's welfare bill for failing to address the spike in out-of-wedlock births.

That same spring, Kristol and peers such as the Heritage Foundation's Robert Rector made the case to Republican lawmakers that welfare reform must discourage poor women from having children out of wedlock, not guarantee them jobs and child care once they did. The issue was marriage before pregnancy, not jobs. (One could also make the argument that poverty was also about marriage as much as jobs, for there was then, and remains now, a yawning gap in the poverty rates of single-parent households—more than 35 percent in

1994—and families headed by married couples—6.5 percent). The effect of their lobbying was to fundamentally reshape the Republican case against the welfare state. In the 1980s, the Right had cast welfare mostly as a rip-off of taxpayers, a liberal pipe dream with high costs and low returns. (Recall Reagan's image of the Cadillac-driving "welfare queen.") Now, with these intellectuals making the argument, the focus shifted to the human costs of a welfare system that encouraged people to make choices that kept them locked in poverty. "This is not about a bigger welfare state or a cheaper welfare state," insisted Gingrich. "This is about replacing a system that is killing our children."

A year later, when the Republican-controlled Congress took up its own welfare plan, lawmakers would be drawn into heated debates over ways to discourage illegitimacy—including proposals to force states to withhold welfare checks from teenage mothers, and to cap payments to single women who continued having babies. Ultimately Congress and the governors rejected most of the specific proposals promoted by the Murray-Kristol-Bennett side: It was one thing to fret, in the abstract, about out-of-wedlock birth rates; it was quite another to cut off support to a child whose mother happened to be single, or to encourage women to have abortions, a prospect raised by some worried religious groups.

Instead, the welfare reform that Congress eventually adopted, and Clinton signed, relied on strict time limits to move recipients off the dole and ended welfare as a federal entitlement by folding it into state block grants. But as more and more public officials and media commentators began bemoaning the legacy of rampant illegitimacy, Kristol and his fellow moralists could claim one victory: They had succeeded in shifting the national zeitgeist over one of the most vexing social issues of our time. Murphy Brown wasn't a joke anymore.

FOR THOSE AMERICANS outside the Beltway who believed that Bill Clinton was a conniving liar whose administration was a leftist power grab at best, a criminal conspiracy at worst, talk radio offered a platform to vent and a community of like-minded citizens. For rabid Clinton haters fortunate enough to have an assigned position in the Washington power game, Grover Norquist's conference table provided the same outlet. Confrontation radio, with its protest politics and loose talk of revolution, was the civil disobedience of the 1990s. The activists who gathered weekly in Grover's conference room specialized in funneling all that populist anger into action, just as Leftists before them had escorted their causes out of the streets and into

Washington's budding special-interest-group sector. Grover called his widening circle of Rightists the Leave Us Alone Coalition (as in, that's what the government should do).

Perhaps no one in Washington was more perfectly attuned to the "angry white men" filling talk radio airwaves in 1994 than Grover Norquist. His words were theirs: "In 1994," he explained, "there was concern and fear. People believed that the government really *was* going to come out and steal your guns; that it really *was* going to take over your health care—and they came damn close. Had we lost in 1994, they would have socialized medicine and we would have been finished. We were playing for keeps; they were playing for lunch. . . . There is an advantage to being the guy who's scared—it concentrates the mind."

There was some precedent for this charged political atmosphere so expressively captured by Grover. Thirty-two years earlier, sociologist Daniel Bell described the emergence of a radical Right that could freely flex its muscles against the new Democrat in the White House after suffocating under a moderate Republican president. Then of course, the moderate Republican was Dwight D. Eisenhower, and the enemy reviving the Right was John F. Kennedy. Then, the hard Right was fueled by John Birchers and like-minded conspiracists. Now, the Right's theories hit closer to home, as the hard-core activists fretted not about a takeover by Moscow but about a power coup by corrupt Washington liberals.

Grover hardly sounded like a man who had grown up in the comfort of a posh Boston suburb, who had earned two degrees from Harvard, and who rarely used his gun to shoot anything but skeet. But Grover could talk the language of threatened Western survivalists as if he had been born in a rambler alongside a lonely highway. It came to him naturally after spending the past nine years splitting his life neatly between forays into Africa, riding jeeps through enemy territory with an AK-47 at his side, and his slightly more tame current profession as chairman of the Washington lobby group Americans for Tax Reform.

Grover, the son of a safety engineer, looked at politics through the interplay of systems. And as he saw it, the Left had spent the past three decades digging in, institutionalizing its position, even when Republicans controlled the White House: When Big Government grew, he asserted, so did the roster of government employees voting Democratic. The Clinton health care plan, Grover argued, was not about health care at all. "The purpose of Hillary Clinton's 1,300-page secret health care plan was the seizure and maintenance of political power," he theorized in a book he later published. "Remember, Bill Clinton won with only 43 percent of the vote. To get reelected, he needed something that would put at least ten percent of the middle class on the government payroll." Moderate Republicans wanted to cut government to save money. Conservative Republicans wanted to cut government to increase liberty. Grover wanted to cut government to destroy what he saw as a Clinton constituency dependent on taxpayer dollars.

Grover argued that agriculture subsidies should be eliminated to kill "the devil on one shoulder" of farmers who might be lured into thinking that the Democrat's Big Government was not so bad after all. He promoted a flat tax because if everyone paid the same rates the Democrats would be deprived of the "class warfare" arguments they used to recruit lower income workers. Ask Grover if he was concerned about a social problem such as rising divorce rates and he would answer, "Yes, because divorced women vote for Democrats." Ask him about the country's half-million children languishing in foster care, and he would answer that "of course" this was cause for concern: These tiny wards of the state most likely would grow up to bolster the ranks of Democrats; if adopted into two-parent families, they stood a good chance of becoming Republicans.

In 1994, Grover collected his forces for good under the umbrella of his Leave Us Alone Coalition and linked them to an important ally and mentor, Newt Gingrich. Longtime friends, Norquist and Gingrich had personalities uniquely suited to each other. In 1994, both men were certain they were riding white horses against a culture of corruption in Washington; they were certain, too, of imminent triumph. When conservative editor Tod Lindberg wrote this description of Gingrich in *Policy Review,* he might as well have been writing about Grover: "Naturally he explained things in ideological terms. An ideology is a closed system; there is nothing an ideology cannot explain. . . . And with the ability to explain, more often than not comes the urge to explain."

Much would be made of Gingrich's "urge to explain" via neat ideological systems. Grover exhibited the same tendency: His logic moved across a many-tiered terrain, always returning back to blame the government. He would, for example, explain that the controversy over gay marriage could be traced to World War II–era government-mandated wage and price controls, which led to private enterprise offering other benefits to attract workers, which led to employees passively accepting insurance from their companies, which led to the current battle over who should be covered, which led to gay activists pressing for legalized marriage so they could qualify for company benefits. "I don't particularly have an opinion on the subject [of gay rights]," Grover said. "I'm not in favor of what the homosexual lobby is trying to do in changing the nature of marriage because what they really want to do is to take existing contract law in employment and insert themselves into a benefits package, and that's cheating."

The upbeat single-mindedness that Grover brought to the cause made him enormously popular in activist circles. He was the "happy warrior," the "cheerleader," a staunch loyalist who kept everyone going when the chips were down. If Grover believed (as many of his rightist friends did) that Gingrich ultimately would be revealed as an opportunist with more commitment to power than cause, he never let on. Grover would remain faithful to the Georgia congressman through all the travails to come. His undying faith in this man, and the cause, made Grover an admired figure among the hard core. But nonbelievers, and even some within his chosen circle, saw in Norquist (like Gingrich) a curious emotional immaturity. There were no grays that came with age for Grover, nothing to soften his own clipped certainty about the way the world worked, one he had clung to since he was a teenager, in the cool of his basement, consuming the unmuddied political passions of Whittaker Chambers.

Nevertheless, this Harvard MBA was a shrewd strategist who understood how to move the Republican Party in his direction. Seven years earlier, Norquist had devised the simple but catchy idea of asking political candidates to sign a pledge not to raise taxes. In between forays to the African bush, he had peddled his no-new-taxes pledge around Capitol Hill. Within a year of inventing it, he had convinced 110 House members to sign on. In the ensuing years, hundreds of state and national candidates followed. Grover's pledge, combined with the conservative backlash caused by President Bush's 1990 decision to break his "read-my-lips-no-new-taxes" promise, fundamentally altered the terms of the tax debate within the Republican Party.

Throughout the 1980s, a significant portion of traditional fiscal conservatives—led by senior Senate Republicans Bob Dole and Pete V. Domenici—had been willing to accept tax hikes in order to reduce the deficit. By the early 1990s, the idea of raising taxes had been pushed off the table, and the only debate among Republicans was whether to cut taxes further. In 1993, not a single Republican in either chamber supported Clinton's tax-hiking budget bill; such rock-solid opposition to a new president's budget was nearly unprecedented.

Grover added to the theatrics surrounding his pledge by recounting stories of politicians who practically burst into tears at the thought of being bound to such a black-and-white commitment. He required that he, or his representative, be on hand to "witness" a candidate's signing. Recalling the boost his tax pledge received from Bush's misstep, Grover noted, "Knowing what poison it is to break the pledge makes the business of the pledge more valuable."

Grover hewed to the Gingrichian advice that every morning he should wake up and ask himself, "What am I going to do to move the revolution forward?" Despite his Leninist rhetoric, despite the Conan the Barbarian poster plastered above his desk, what Grover did to move the revolution forward in 1994 was remarkably establishmentarian. First, as he faced each day (still single, still living in his group house on Capitol Hill), he asked himself which candidates had not yet signed his pledge. Second, he asked himself what resources could be deployed where so that Republicans might gain enough seats to take over the House in the upcoming November election. At his disposal was his own Rolodex of some two thousand local activists around the country, and the strategists—representing hundreds of thousands of conservative citizens—who turned out at weekly meetings of the Leave Us Alone Coalition.

The coalition started out in 1993 as a tiny outpost of bitter, disgruntled Rightists. In the wake of the Bush letdown, followed by the humiliation of Clinton's election, Norquist offered them hope. He opened his doors to movement conservatives at a time when no one in the GOP seemed to be listening to them or their ideas. (No one, some Republican operatives snidely noted, probably listened to them when they were in high school, either. More than a few of the Norquist activists still looked like besieged and angry nerds, pasty-faced, with Neanderthal social skills. In some GOP circles, they were known as the "The Droolers.")

At first, a dozen seats filled constituted a decent turnout at these Wednesday morning meetings. But in the early months of 1994, Norquist's weekly meetings steadily grew in size, pulling together NRA lobbyists, Christian Coalition staffers, term limit activists, libertarian thinkers, conservative retirees, home schoolers, free market economists, property rights activists, Gingrich acolytes, Schlafly acolytes, GOP operatives, postfeminists, anti-liberal blacks, Orthodox Jews, pro-choice Republicans. This right-wing version of identity politics was a motley crew, not only in its potential splits on such issues as immigration and abortion, but also because of the differing passions each brought to the table. Norquist tied them together with anti-Washington rhetoric and assurances of imminent victory over the "Clintonistas." The Clinton health care plan, he preached, would become the Democrats' "Stalingrad, their Gettysburg, their Waterloo."

With the 1994 election on the horizon, RNC chairman Haley Barbour shrewdly understood the importance of motivating the Right's grass-roots base. He intended to bypass much of what the Right called the "liberal-media establishment"—mainstream newspapers and broadcasts—in favor of alternative messengers. Talk radio was one of his preferred delivery systems. The other was the conservative activist network, and Norquist's meeting was its Penn Central. Barbour began sending a high-level Republican emissary, Don Fierce, to Grover's weekly meetings. Initially Fierce played the role of punching bag, as Norquist's people unleashed their fury over the direction the party had taken under George Bush. But Fierce stuck it out, and he was able to energize the activists by giving them a sense of ownership in Barbour's new "party of ideas." He also gave many of them their earliest lessons in big league electoral politics: The activists in Grover's conference room learned the art of the sound bite—how to put their own spin on news stories whose meaning had once been the preserve of the hated liberal-media establishment.

Never before had the Right's activists been so closely tied to the party hierarchy and its professionals (later, that would come back to haunt Norquist's ATR and Reed's Christian Coalition as they faced charges of illegal partisan activities under tax and campaign finance laws.) The old Right had been a ragtag outer flank of the GOP's moneyed establishment, a noisy and bitter faction running on memories of resounding defeats, of Robert Taft passed over for Thomas Dewey and Dwight Eisenhower, of Barry Goldwater losing forty-four states. Even with the victory of Ronald Reagan, the Right had remained estranged from the party's central structure, as they spent the 1980s trying to outsmart the "squishes" who controlled the GOP. But this new generation of Rightists had come to Washington under the wing of a victorious leader, and so had acquired a taste for power. They didn't doubt their ability to govern (even if others did).

YEARS LATER, conservative activists would look back nostalgically on the cohesiveness of their movement in the months leading up to the 1994 Republican Revolution. When the Anti-Defamation League that summer released a report attacking the Christian Coalition, and Democrats began denouncing religious extremists in the GOP, the entire weight of the Right rose up in Ralph's defense. Norquist denounced the ADL report as a shoddy cut-and-paste job, and RNC officials vocally defended the role of religious conservatives in the party. But it was Kristol, as a leading Jewish voice in the Republican Party, who made the biggest media splash. And he did so using the language of his generation: conservative Christians as victims of discrimination. Kristol argued that when liberals applied the word "fervent" to evangelicals, it was a display of bigotry much like calling Jews "aggressive"—"a politely disguised expression of discomfort and disgust with the manners and mores of an entire social class."

"God is *exactly* the wedge issue [DNC Chairman David] Wilhelm and his colleagues have in mind for November," Kristol wrote in one of his trademark memos to Republican leaders. "Democrats, reeling from a long post-1992 string of federal, state, and local election defeats—and burdened by their own exhausted and collapsing liberal agenda (and presidency)—need something in November with which to scare voters into line. . . .

"More is going on here than an argument over coalition party building, of course. Sad to say, an aggressive effort is underway to demonize (and thus silence and disenfranchise) Christian conservatives—an effort radically inconsistent with the tradition of American political and religious tolerance. . . . Politically active conservative Christians, ADL concludes, are . . . well, 'extremist,' 'bogus,' 'conspiratorial,' 'fevered,' 'phony' 'flimflam,' 'bizarre,' and, yes, 'fervent.' In other words, Protestant evangelicals are simply *de trop*, an object of condescension and prejudice. . . ."

BY THE FALL OF 1994, Clinton's health care plan remained alive only as a scarlet letter for struggling Democratic candidates around the country. The president's much-heralded crime package likewise was under siege. The crime bill had begun as a serious effort to augment police forces and prison construction, but House Democrats transformed it into one of the most expensive social programs in years, offering billions of dollars to cities in a vague attempt at crime "prevention." Kristol and other critics denounced the bill as "social pork" designed to mollify key Democratic constituencies. Clinton's welfare reform was also going nowhere fast. But the president's approval ratings were on the move—downward.

On September 27, 185 Republican incumbents and challengers gathered on the grounds of the U.S. Capitol for a staged media event. Before TV cameras in the autumn heat, they awaited their turns to sign the "Contract with America," committing Republicans to vote on a series of conservative reform initiatives should they wrest control of the House from the Democrats in the upcoming election. Among the Contract's provisions: a balanced budget amendment, tax cuts, term limits, welfare reform, and deregulation. The Contract was bereft of favorite social issues such as abortion and school prayer, but Gingrich's decision to include a family tax cut promoted by Ralph had temporarily mollified the Christian Coalition, though other social conservatives felt shortchanged.

Gingrich promised that the Contract was only the first step in the impending revolution, and pragmatists such as Ralph appreciated the importance of consolidating conservative support on less controversial measures before moving on to more explosive matters such as abortion. Like Reed, Kristol too was dismissive of purists on the Right who criticized Gingrich's contract as overly modest. "This short-term Republican program is a more than sufficient general answer to that shop-worn, hostile question, 'What are you guys *for?*' " he wrote in a memo to Republican leaders.

The Right had always been saddled with a reputation for being mean-spirited and angry, hostile and isolated from mainstream America. So the Contract packaged its programs in positive words that a thirty-two-year-old pollster named Frank Luntz had tested and retested in focus groups—"accountability," "responsibility," "opportunity." Regulatory reform and cuts in capital gains taxes fell under "The Job Creation and Wage Enhancement Act." The balanced budget bill was called "The Fiscal Responsibility Act." Welfare reform was "The Personal Responsibility Act." The $500 per child tax credit was part of "The American Dream Restoration Act."

As the Republican candidates gathered to sign the contract, a first-time candidate for Congress could be seen weaving in and out among the tourists on the sidewalk leading toward the Capitol, bouyant and purposeful as he rushed to stand alongside his colleagues. David Martin McIntosh, candidate for Indiana's second district House seat, was the new generation's ideal of a reformist. Here was a candidate who didn't need the reading list that Gingrich, the former history professor at West Georgia College, was fond of offering young lawmakers. McIntosh was Yale class of 1980 and a product of the finest law school the conservative academy had to offer, the University of Chicago. He had his own reading lists (after the election, he would be absorbed in Gibbon's *The History of the Decline and Fall of the Roman Empire,* mining it for intriguing parallels to modern America). He came to the Capitol that day with his own ideas about how this revolution should unfold (he had already complained to Gingrich that the Contract's tax cuts weren't big enough).

Here was a candidate who not only wanted to deconstruct Washington's regulatory apparatus but understood the mechanics of how to do it, so the think tank libertarians loved him. He believed in the political import of "defunding the Left," so movement organizers such as Norquist loved him. Friends and colleagues knew him as a strong Christian, so Reed's Christian Coalition was doing what it could to get out the vote in his district. Campaigning in a year when the Right stood a solid chance of capturing the House, McIntosh came off as smart, connected, conservative, and, above all, electable.

He was also (his Indiana friends couldn't help thinking as they watched him on TV that day) one lucky fellow.

FORTUNE DID PLAY A ROLE in bringing McIntosh to the U.S. Capitol that September afternoon. But the same could be said of scores of Republican candidates that year, sailing toward Congress with a hearty anti-Clinton wind at their backs. And few could boast David's intellect or his prowess at fund-raising. Still, there was something uncanny about his luck that year, as he made his first run for political office.

After finishing his tenure at Quayle's Competitiveness Council in 1992, David and his new wife had settled in Muncie, not far from his hometown of Kendallville, so that David could plot a run for public office. Ruthie accepted a job as a fund-raiser for Ball State University while David commuted to his new position at the Hudson Institute, an Indianapolis-based think tank. The window to a political career opened earlier than either of the newlyweds had expected.

Muncie was in a district represented by Philip R. Sharp, a conservative Democrat who had served in Congress for ten years and showed no signs of vulnerability. Nevertheless, Ruthie shared her husband's political ambition and dragged him to a town meeting one night to see the congressman in action. The audience was packed with ditto-heads (as avid listeners of Rush Limbaugh's radio show described themselves) and they were throwing hostile questions at Sharp about his support of the Clinton budget and tax hike. The congressman "was being kind of flippant" toward the questioners, Ruthie recalled. "And I could see the wheels start to turn in David's head."

After that night, David started considering a run for Sharp's seat, studying the demographics of his new home district like a student cramming for the S.A.T. A bizarre string of luck followed. First, Sharp made the surprise announcement that he would retire, opening up the second-district seat. Then, the clear front-runner for the GOP nomination, Anne DeVore, the state's auditor and a darling of Indiana's GOP establishment, missed the deadline to file her candidacy papers, even though the filing office was down the hall from her own. If not for this staff error, according to local political analysts, McIntosh's odds of winning would have been slight. As it was, David had an uphill struggle against his other competitor, a perennial candidate against Sharp. He managed to secure an endorsement from a popular former governor and won the primary by a margin of only 473 votes.

Ruthie would chalk up this run of luck to divine intervention. But as her husband squared off in the general election against a rising star of the state Democratic Party, Joseph H. Hogsett, the secretary of state, Ruthie herself proved to be one of David's major assets. This daughter of a Navy captain and former aide to first lady Barbara Bush exuded red-white-and-blue good cheer. Watching Ruthie, you thought of home. Even though she had never lived in Indiana before, her presence mitigated the carpetbagger image Hogsett tried to hang on McIntosh—and made David look less like a rigid ideologue. "She lit up the camera," said one aide. "They put Ruthie on the air and his numbers jumped."

Ruthie also appreciated an important fact of political life: The path from her husband's Indianapolis think tank office to the U.S. Capitol would need to be paved, thick and early, with cash. Every spare moment had to be spent building a campaign war chest. All of David's plans for demolishing federal regulation, his meticulous understanding of the Washington game, his industry connections so doggedly cultivated, all were worthless if he couldn't make the sales pitch for himself, then close the deal with a check—and do it over and over and over, day in, day out, with the mulish determination of a telemarketer.

But in the early months of his 1994 campaign, "reminding" Dave to get on the phone and solicit donations became a near full-time occupation for Ruthie and their tiny campaign staff. Mornings when she stopped back home to take a break from her university job, she'd find her husband, the aspiring pol, still under the sheets, hiding from his own daily promises to work the phone. In the afternoons, annoyed staffers would come over to the house to usher McIntosh out of his beloved garden, where he was wasting his time raking in leaves rather than checks.

Most politicians don't enjoy calling up friends and strangers to plead for $1,000 checks; they see it as debasing, as vaguely sycophantic and intrinsically corrupting: At both ends of the phone line there lingers the unspoken awareness that the one who is giving wants—or will want—something from the one who is asking. Ruthie wasn't resigned to McIntosh's procrastination, but she understood it. This son of a widowed nurse had always paid his own way, through college, then law school; for David, soliciting money for his congressional campaign felt like asking for a handout. So she used her own university fund-raising experience to help script a sales pitch that gave donors, and David, the sense that he was soliciting money for a cause greater than himself. Being a movement conservative came in handy that way, allowing his personal ambition to be screened by his vision of a smaller, leaner, less intrusive government.

When he first started dialing, maybe three out of twenty calls cinched a donation; then it was five out of twenty; then close to a third. The hits were what really got Dave's juices flowing, what got him practically addicted to the game. "Hot dog!" he'd say out loud, thinking of Jimmy Stewart in his favorite movie, *It's a Wonderful Life*. He and Ruthie called their new vocation "Dialing for Dollars." Midway through the 1994 campaign they formed a major-donor circle called the Day One Club, an inside joke poking fun at all the contributors who had resisted their entreaties when David was a nobody, but later—after he had won the GOP nomination—insisted they had been supporters from "day one."

The cash was critical going into the fall campaign against Hogsett, who was arguably the better candidate on the stump. Both men were young and smart and tough. Both boasted major league political connections: Popular Democratic Governor Evan Bayh campaigned door to door with Hogsett, while McIntosh brought such conservative heros as Dan Quayle, Robert Bork, and Ed Meese to northeastern Indiana. But McIntosh, with his sleepy-looking eyes and a stilted stop-and-start speech pattern, was far less agile and smooth than Hogsett when the pair faced off in debates.

Luck, however, was again on David's side. For this was not a good year to run for office as a Democrat: Clinton's critics, crushing his vaunted health care plan, managed to tar the New Democrat as a big-spending liberal after all; his assault weapon ban had activated the gun lobby; and new and recycled Clinton scandals offered juicy material for the booming talk radio circuit. McIntosh poured his war chest into a run of TV commercials that "morphed" Hogsett's face into the visage of Bill Clinton, a video trick employed by scores of other Republican challengers that fall. In debates, David pinned unpopular Clinton initiatives onto his opponent as Hogsett dodged and ducked. Anti-Clinton activists turned out in full force at rallies for McIntosh, especially Christian Coalition activists and gun enthusiasts (euphemistically called "our Second Amendment friends" by Ruthie, who would later make encouraging women to overcome their fear of firearms a personal crusade).

FOR THE CHRISTIAN COALITION, a president who approved of gays enlisted in the military, carried on extramarital affairs, and threatened to "socialize" medicine proved a terrific boon to recruitment. During the 1994 campaign, the ranks of the Coalition mushroomed and multitudes of volunteers were put to work in 120 districts, such as McIntosh's, where they organized get-out-the-vote efforts with flyers and phone banks aimed at friendly voters, and distributed "voter guides" that implicitly endorsed candidates.

Ralph Reed had long ago made the tactical decision that his own power—and that of the Christian Coalition—resided inside the Republican Party. That was an expedient decision, but also a risky one given federal restrictions on the electoral activities of nonprofit citizen groups. Politically, too, this was a strategy that threatened the Christian Coalition's credibility, enabling critics from the Right and Left to accuse the group of being more interested in electing Republican candidates than enacting its legislative agenda. (Precisely for these reasons, many of Washington's most successful liberal-left citizen groups—including environmentalists and civil rights activists—had studiously avoided overt involvement in party politics.)

From 1994 until May 1995, when Ralph introduced his own legislative agenda in the form of the Contract with the American Family, the Christian Coalition's agenda was barely distinguishable from the Republican Party's. In the spring of 1994, the Coalition mobilized to help two friends secure Republican nominations: Lieutenant Colonel Oliver North, the Iran-contra figure, in the Virginia Senate race; and home school activist Michael P. Farris in that state's much-watched lieutenant governor's race. The critical margins provided by Christian activists in Republican races such as these lent them credibility with RNC chair Barbour, who was forced to fend off complaints from GOP old-timers about the Religious Right's influence in their party.

Technically, the Christian Coalition wasn't supposed to be aiding individual candidates. Most nonprofit citizen groups that involve themselves in elections do so by establishing political action committees, or PACs, which are monitored by the Federal Election Commission and required to disclose their finances. The Christian Coalition was organized in 1989 as a "social welfare organization" and applied to the IRS for tax-exempt status. While such nonprofits are permitted to lobby Congress, and may even advise their own members whom to vote for, they are not permitted to pursue campaigns as their primary work. By 1994, the Coalition's election activity had attracted the scrutiny of the IRS, which forestalled ruling on the tax-exempt application, and the FEC, which in 1996 would file a lawsuit seeking heavy fines against the Coalition for engaging in partisan election activities. "The problem was that Pat Robertson didn't want to pay taxes," said one knowledgeable insider. "He didn't want to render unto Caesar what was Caesar's. If we had been a PAC there would have been no problems."

A number of factors contributed to the Coalition's partisan reputation, including pro-Republican statements by Reed and Robertson and their acceptance of a $67,000 seed grant from the RNC at the group's launch. But the Coalition's voter guides fueled the allegations of partisanship. Using plus and minus signs, the guides listed candidate positions on issues of concern to the Coalition, ranging from tax cuts and the balanced budget amendment to federally funded abortion and NEA funding. In these tailored descriptions of candidates, Republicans fared best. In 1994, especially, a number of congressional Democrats witnessed a lethal drop in support from evangelicals as a result of the guides. Several accused the Coalition of distorting their records, charges backed up by a subsequent investigation into the voter guides by authors Larry J. Sabato and Glenn R. Simpson. In one case they cited, Representative Dan Rostenkowski, the powerful Democratic chair of the Ways and Means Committee, was portrayed as supporting the teaching of homosexuality to schoolchildren when he had voted for a measure designed to do the opposite.

But if there were complaints about the Christian Coalition voter guides, Ralph made sure there wasn't much time to air them. Boxes filled with guides arrived in churches and religious Christian bookstores, doctors' offices and employee lunchrooms only days before the election. "You want to hold [distribution] until that last Sunday [before the election] because if they start raising doubts about the voter guide, you're going to have a real skittish pastor that is just going to pull them," the Christian Coalition's voter education director counseled activists at one strategy session. As charities under IRS law, churches risked losing their tax-exempt status if they endorsed or opposed candidates.

All told, the Christian Coalition claimed it printed 33 million voter guides in 1994, one for every six voting-age adults. Later, insiders would say there was a smoke-and-mirrors element to this widely quoted number (as there was with the Coalition's membership numbers). Not all the guides were distributed; often boxes were tossed in the recycle bin or left on church tables. Still, millions went out to voters and "the effect was dramatic," noted Sabato and Simpson, "amounting to a multimillion-dollar advertising campaign for some candidates and against others."

WATCHING THE 1994 CAMPAIGNS of McIntosh and other Republicans unfold around the country that fall, Kristol could barely contain his excitement. Republicans stood a good chance of capturing both houses of Congress—and doing so with staunchly conservative agendas. "Eureka . . . An ideological campaign!" Bill gushed in a pre-election memo to Republican leaders. "Rest easy and keep on punching, GOP candidates. . . !" They kept on punching, and on Election Tuesday, GOP candidates officially led that big dumb elephant out of its funk and into the leadership of both chambers on Capitol Hill. For the first time in forty years, Republicans were a majority in both houses of Congress. The revolution's leader, Newt Gingrich, would become Speaker of the U.S. House. The earthquake reverberated beyond Washington: Republicans gained eleven governorships and 472 state legislative seats. Thirty governors were now Republican. No Republican incumbent congressman, senator, or governor was defeated.

Many would take credit for this historic sweep: Gingrich boasted about the Contract with America (which, it turned out, most voters had never heard of). Norquist stood in front Gingrich supporters on election night and admonished the new Congress not to forget the Leave Us Alone activists who had put them there. Kristol was granted the status of conservatism's "all-purpose seer" by the *New York Times*. And Ralph handed the media his own exit polls demonstrating that one-third of voters on Election Day were evangelical Christians, laying "to rest once and for all the myth that we are a liability rather than an asset in the Republican Party."

Gingrich, apparently seeking to reward the Christian right, immediately announced plans to put a constitutional amendment to permit prayer in school at the top of his agenda. But Ralph, eager to be the pragmatic team-GOP player, demurred. "I want to make it perfectly clear that this is not our top priority," he said, shocking Republican strategists. "I, for one, don't think we'll turn the country around by having public acts of piety." Instead, Ralph soon disclosed plans to spend $1 million lobbying for enactment of the GOP's Contract with America—a sum he would fail to match to push the Christian Coalition's own "Contract with the American Family" several months later.

David McIntosh won handily that November day, with 54 percent of the vote. In short order, the incoming freshman class would elect him as one of two liaisons to the House leadership. He would become that rare freshman to be offered the chairmanship of a subcommittee. He would become an undiluted voice in Congress for his generation of conservatives, "among the best and brightest of the famous class of 1994," as *Wall Street Journal* columnist Paul Gigot later wrote.

He would also demonstrate the limits of the movement that put him in office.

CHAPTER 13

WAR WITHOUT BLOOD

[U]ntil Communism began its collapse in 1989, American energies had been largely focused on fighting the Evil Empire, giving
statist Washington plenty of cover. . . . As in Eastern Europe five
years ago, the real work begins now.

GROVER G. NORQUIST
American Spectator
January 1995

I should have been thrilled, but my strongest emotion was a combination of exhaustion and foreboding. . . . In the days after the
1994 campaign, ebullient talk of "our turn" and "payback time"
filled the air. My deepest fear was that [we] could walk into the
booby trap of soaring expectations and negative press coverage
before the new Congress had a chance to find its sea legs.

RALPH REED
Active Faith

January 3, 1995

MEMORANDUM TO: REPUBLICAN LEADERS
FROM: WILLIAM KRISTOL
SUBJECT: '96 OR BUST

. . . Our current place in the American political cosmos is not so sure that we can, like some Scandinavian father, promptly hurl our newborn Republican electorate into the deep, undiluted ocean of conservative philosophy, supremely confident that the baby will swim (and not hate us for the lesson). . . .

Compromise is objectionable and unnecessary. But utopian overreach is a risk it would be a mistake to take. . . .

Beware delirium. . . .

ON JANUARY 4, 1995, day one of what America was calling "the Republican Revolution," David McIntosh took the oath of office wearing his lucky tie, dotted with gold silhouettes of James Madison, architect of the Bill of Rights. A fresh haircut made the thirty-seven-year-old freshman congressman look even more boyish than usual. As his former professor, Supreme Court Justice Antonin Scalia, administered the oath of office, David raised his right hand high, in an Eagle Scout salute. Tears welled in his eyes. The tears were for real, just like the salute, just like the talk of reform and helping average families. For David—like the seventy-two other members of the freshman class of 1994—entered Congress animated by righteous idealism.

They considered themselves purer than the party regulars, purer even than Newt Gingrich, their revolutionary leader. If the political world divides those motivated by ideas from those motivated by power, McIntosh once explained, then "Newt is much more on the side of acquiring and maintaining power. The average freshman wanted to preserve movement toward the idea." (Their chief opponents—liberals who had worked the Washington trenches far longer—saw something else in this freshman class. Mostly young, mostly male, mostly white dogmatists who had acquired their unified theory of justice from free-market textbooks, they were unhindered by the sort of life experience that might reveal to them a central truth: that bad things *do* happen to good people.)

The freshman lawmakers brought an evangelical intensity to the place. Whether you saw them as clean-up artists or dogmatists, Congress hadn't seen anything like this influx of lawmakers since 1974, when reform-minded young Democrats picked up the pieces left by Watergate. In 1994, the freshmen Republicans had run campaigns against a career Congress, that vast feudal system built up by forty years of Democratic control. They carried the torch of a burgeoning political movement to limit the terms of elected officials.

They insisted they weren't beholden to special interests, and, rhetorically at least, they could be as disdainful of big corporations feeding at the government trough as they were of Leftists constructing those government troughs. They came to Congress intent on dismantling Washington, sending power back to the states, to communities, to the people. If the first axe was to fall on liberal bastions like National Public Radio and the National Endowment for the Arts, there were plenty of new lawmakers who wanted a second axe to fall on corporate tax breaks and farm subsidies. The members of the class of '94 saw their natural constituents as small businesses and traditional families being crushed by taxes and regulation. McIntosh described his peers this way: "They visualize that they are working in Congress on behalf of a fairly young family with two kids and parents who work anywhere from a factory job up to middle management." They were themselves more middle class, and less wealthy, than the typical congressman.

The freshmen were also, by historical standards, short on the experience of give-and-take lawmaking, a deficiency that would come to define their revolution—and David's role in it. "Dave did not come from a legislative background," said his friend, Maryland Representative Robert J. Ehrlich Jr., who did. "He had a very different M.O. He was always chomping, biting, kicking at the leadership to move. He viewed his job as to push and push and push. I'm sure he was a pain in the butt to leadership." It was emblematic of the Republican Revolution that its freshman class elected David as one of its two liaisons to the House leadership: No one expected McIntosh to be a diplomat. "We thought that anyone who had had his salary deleted by Henry Waxman," when David was director of Quayle's Competitiveness Council and Democrat Waxman was his chief congressional foe, "was the type of person who could be a strong advocate," recalled freshman congressman Randy Tate of Washington state.

There were other dimensions to David's personality. In the 1990s he had settled outside Washington—in Muncie, Indiana—and traveled in a wider social circle than many hard-core Rightists who defined their friends (and enemies) by ideology. He had a strong sentimental streak. He was a pack rat who frequented antique stores and flea markets to fill his hundred-year-old colonial home in a college neighborhood near Ball State in a style his wife Ruthie laughingly labeled "Hoosier gothic." He was an avid reader of science fiction, drawn especially to romantic visions of space travel. His therapy was gardening, and passing neighbors often mistook him for the landscaper as he kneeled in his overalls and ball cap, planting daffodils and crocuses, daisies and cornflowers. (As a congressman, his image problem with the labor unions in his district extended beyond their pique over his failure to intervene when their factories closed; among the hardhats, David had a reputation as a sissy.)

As a young man with a range of close friendships, McIntosh appreciated the nuance of discussing matters of personal morality. David's view that "life begins at conception" crystallized when he was in his early twenties. But as he moved into his thirties, he adopted "an equally important view—that we must be loving toward those who hold different views." He came to this conclusion after "discussions with dear friends for whom my impassioned defense of the pro-life position was personally painful because they had chosen to have an abortion sometime in the past. I vowed never again to make the mistake of not being considerate enough to realize that something which, for me, is an abstract discussion . . . can be a very personal matter for the person listening." While he was part of a prayer group of freshman lawmakers, he didn't flaunt his faith. "God gave us the choice between right and wrong," he once said. "So you can't have government come in and force people to make moral choices. Compelled virtue is no virtue."

But this was not the side of David that revealed itself during the Republican Revolution as he pursued his pet economic causes—tax cuts and deregulation. He approached his first year in Congress as if he were still at the Yale Political Union, engaged in all-or-nothing verbal matches. As the revolution unfolded, the freshman class became a force to be reckoned with, especially when joined with forty-four equally hard-core sophomore Republicans. These novice politicians, McIntosh chief among them, would push House leaders toward a politics of confrontation. When Newt Gingrich, in his love of word trinities, called politics "war without blood," the freshmen took him at his word and brooked no compromise. "There was a sense that because we're there, everyone agrees with us. It was like drinking from a fire hose," recalled Randy Tate.

McIntosh would pay a price for his own role in this bloodless war: By year's end, he would be facing a House ethics investigation and polls showing mounting constituent concern that he might be protecting the interests of corporate polluters who aided his reform crusade and contributed to his campaign.

His OATH TAKEN, his emotions in check, David transformed back into "UniMac," the unstoppable machine, a politician who raced through each day as if he had been shot from a cannon, intent on pursuing every idea his fevered brain churned out, and at maximum speed. In the space of a few months, David put a year's worth of wear and tear on his young staff. "He's the most impatient patient person I've ever met," said one staffer. "He wears me out," complained Al Hubbard, his former boss and current close adviser. Added Representative Ehrlich: "He hates to lose. I know everybody says that about themselves, but with David, it's really true." For David, inept in sports, the policy debate was his football, his basketball, his golf.

As a young man David had called himself a liberal because he thought conservatives opposed change. But now, in the 104th Congress, conservatives were shaking up the entire House of Representatives with hurried reform. Even in a city that often confuses motion with movement, they resembled, in those first hundred days, a posse of speed freaks. During their fourteen-and-a-half-hour opening day, House members cast votes on a succession of Contract with America provisions designed to bring "openness" and "accountability" to the chamber. They adopted a House rule requiring a supermajority vote to raise taxes. They broke up entrenched legislative kingdoms by reducing committee staff, eliminating three full committees and twenty-five subcommittees, limiting the terms of committee chairmen and the speaker, and opening all nonclassified committee meetings to the public. They passed a law forcing Congress to abide by the same laws— from workplace discrimination to environmental rules—that had been imposed on other Americans. The 104th Congress, the revolutionaries proclaimed, would not be business as usual.

Or would it? Six weeks after voting to bring accountability to the House, Representative McIntosh was running a "war room" in a small office just off the House floor to secure the passage of a moratorium on new federal regulations. The legislation was written by a lobbyist for energy and petrochemical concerns. Inside the war room, sitting at a laptop computer tapping out responses to Democratic critics, was a lobbyist for the trucking industry, which had a direct financial interest in any environmental regulation the bill might halt. Also on hand was an airline lobbyist to tackle questions about transportation rules, and a United Parcel Service lobbyist to address workplace safety rules.

While his aides stood by ready to print and distribute these lobbyist-written responses, David appeared at a news conference to kick off the House debate. He brought along a three-foot-high stack of newly proposed federal rules, bound in scarlet ribbon, to symbolize red tape, and a bucket with holes in it, leaking confetti. The leaky bucket was there to demonstrate the absurdity of federal bureaucrats. The Consumer Product Safety Commission, he said, had proposed a rule requiring that "all buckets have a hole in the bottom of them, so that they can allow water to go through and avoid the danger of somebody falling face down into the bucket and drowning: The leaky bucket regulation."

It was a great story, a favorite of Republicans and talk radio that season. Too bad it wasn't quite true. In response to the deaths of an estimated forty babies each year who fall into five-gallon buckets full of water, the agency had examined ways to prevent these toddler drownings. One bucket manufacturer pointed out that some industrial buckets used for dry materials have holes, and this was mentioned in an advance notice of rule-making. But, as the agency chief wrote in a letter to McIntosh, the commission never seriously considered proposing it. Moreover, the CPSC had already reached a voluntary agreement with bucket manufacturers to place warning labels on their product.

But the Republicans were convinced that tromping out anecdotes about silly rules would solidify public support for shutting down Washington's regulatory apparatus. Behind them stood an array of industry interests. The lobbyists joining McIntosh in his war room were part of an ad-hoc industry group called Project Relief, organized largely by House whip Tom DeLay of Texas, a former pesticide company owner who was fond of saying he had never met a regulation he liked (even the pesticide DDT, which nearly caused the extinction of some bird species, should never have been banned, he argued). DeLay set the tone for the debate over regulatory reform by likening the EPA to the Gestapo.

McIntosh conducted combat in his own fierce, if slightly more tame, style from his post as chairman of an influential subcommittee on regulatory affairs, a congressional version of the Quayle Competitiveness Council. In March, Chairman McIntosh charged EPA officials with violating "criminal" law by publicly criticizing the Republicans' regulatory overhaul bill. McIntosh claimed the law precluded federal officials from influencing pending legislation through means other than official correspondence, and that EPA officials had broken that law when they issued a critical press release (the White House counsel disagreed with his interpretation).

As David was swinging his leaky bucket, Democrats were raising the prospect of lives lost if Congress adopted the Republicans' moratorium on regulation. Despite its exception for emergencies, Democrats argued that the legislation could prevent the EPA from finalizing, among others, a rule requiring water supplies to be tested for a life-threatening parasite. "Some would use the need for reform as a pretext to gut vital consumer, worker, and environmental protections—even things that protect business," President Clinton argued two days before the House debate on the moratorium. "They don't want reform. They really want rigor mortis."

But with the revolutionaries in control of the House, the moratorium easily passed. This wasn't the only legislative assault on Washington bureaucracy the House conservatives were pushing that season: At a time when 70 percent of the public believed the government was not doing enough to protect the environment, conservative House Republicans launched what one journalist called an "unprecedented assault on the nation's landmark environmental laws." In the Republican attempt to weaken the government's authority over areas ranging from water pollution to hazardous waste, industry lobbyists played a central role.

To McIntosh, this wasn't influence peddling. Rather, he saw it as a neat merger of interests between lawmakers philosophically committed to reducing taxes and regulation, and businesses eager to see both reduced. At the time, Republican lawmakers would point out that Democrats, in crafting bills, routinely used specific legislative language submitted by outside environmental and consumer groups. But that defense missed the point: Gingrich had come to power challenging Washington's cozy practices; he had promised the country a populist revolution. This wasn't supposed to be business as usual.

Kristol was one movement thinker worried about what he saw unfolding on Capitol Hill. "If [the Republicans] legislate for special interests," Kristol told the *Washington Post*, "it's going to be hard to show that the Republican Party has fundamentally changed the way business is done in Washington." John Fund, a *Wall Street Journal* writer whose editorials on Democratic corruption and the term limits movement had helped shape the 1994 revolution, echoed that sentiment four years later, with the advantage of hindsight: "I think the Republicans failed to properly distance themselves from business interests. They failed to distinguish between a pro-business and a pro-market agenda. To the extent that they identified in favor of corporations rather than freedom—even if these interests are often parallel—it hurt their moral case."

If McIntosh and his colleagues hurt their moral case, they didn't get much in the bargain. Even before any regulatory reform legislation could reach the president's desk, the far more baronial Senate put its foot down. (During those exhilarating first hundred days of the Republican Revolution it often seemed as if, with the teenagers running loose on the other side of the Capitol, the Senate's Republican leaders had decided that someone needed to play the responsible adult.) Sorry, Senate leaders told McIntosh and his colleagues in one meeting, your regulatory plan would certainly be filibustered. In March, the Senate ignored the House's deregulation plan and instead flaunted its bipartisanship with a unanimous vote on a far less severe bill, providing for congressional review of new rules.

In the House that spring, Republican moderates began distancing themselves from the deregulators, opposing one bill that would have opened parts of the Arctic National Wildlife Refuge to oil exploration and another that would have severely restricted EPA's authority to enforce water and air pollution laws. McIntosh told one reporter at the time that he was "surprised" by the level of support for existing environmental laws. Even Gingrich—an environmental moderate who at one point refused to cut funding for international wildlife protection—worried that the Republicans were mishandling the environmental issue. Jeffrey A. Eisenach, a baby-boom conservative who ran a think tank with close ties to Gingrich, faulted Republicans for attacking Washington's "command-and-control" system of regulation without first offering alternative ways to protect the environment. "The environment," he said at the time, "was one of the areas where the fact that the Republicans were not ready to be a majority has come back to haunt them."

But David continued in his single-minded quest to clear away what he called Washington's "choking fog of regulation." As summer approached, he began taking his subcommittee on the road, conducting field hearings to solicit regulatory horror stories. "Ordinary citizens" came forward. But so did corporate executives. Many months later, David's picture appeared alongside a *Wall Street Journal* article revealing that half of the eighteen corporations or business associations that met with McIntosh's committee in June of 1995 also contributed to his reelection campaign less than a month later. In addition, an analysis by one liberal activist group calculated that in his first campaign, David had received more than $36,000 from political action committees associated with Project Relief, the coalition of antiregulatory business interests organized by DeLay. This was "more than twice the average" intake of candidates, the study said.

In response to these disclosures, McIntosh's staff would point to equal amounts of money pouring in from individuals—housewives or teachers, small businessmen or farmers, often so inspired by McIntosh that they were making their first-ever campaign contributions. By the 1995–96 reelection cycle, moreover, so much money was rolling into David's reelection campaign that his aides could make the case that no single contributor carried particular weight. All the freshmen were riding a gravy train during their first year in office, raising more money than more senior colleagues.

Even during the jam-packed 1995 legislative session, David was an insatiable fund-raiser—"a freight train," as one of his advisers put it. Several afternoons a week, he would pack donor lists under his arm, head over to the National Republican Campaign Committee a few blocks away on Capitol Hill, and spend three to four hours in the suites set aside for the campaign activities of lawmakers. He was ruthlessly efficient, keeping two phone lines going so that when he hung up from one, his assistant would have another potential donor on the other. Two things were sacrosanct on his calendar: Bible studies and fund-raising. By the summer of 1995, he had raised $200,000, the beginnings of a war chest. His staff hoped the headline on this war chest, running in the local Muncie paper, would scare off potential competitors in his race for reelection. McIntosh would go on to raise $1.2 million for his 1996 reelection effort, the largest amount ever raised for an Indiana congressional race.

At 9:02 on the morning of April 19, 1995, a fertilizer bomb exploded underneath a federal office building in downtown Oklahoma City, and suddenly the "bureaucrats" who had borne the wrath of the Right were given a different public face. It was a face streaming with blood, or twisted in agony over the death of a child, or lost under the wreckage of concrete and steel. When the bomb went off, 168 federal office workers and their children were murdered in the deadliest act of terrorism ever to take place on American soil. It was also a tragedy with lasting political implications, for the terrorists in this case were products of a right-wing paramilitary movement that encouraged citizens to take up arms in "self-defense" against the U.S. government.

A crucial test for any political movement is its ability to police its outer fringes. Just as the antiwar and civil rights movements of the

1960s were forced to confront fringe radicals carrying out terrorist acts in the name of peace and social justice, so too the Right in the 1990s had to confront the emergence of antigovernment activists who viewed violence as a legitimate political tool. Oklahoma City occurred amid rising political violence on the Right: the bombing of abortion clinics and the murders of five medical workers; heavily armed militia members engaged in standoffs with federal officals attempting to enforce environmental, child support, and gun-control laws; the shooting of a Missouri highway patrolman in apparent retaliation for arresting an antigovernment activist.

One flashpoint for this brewing underground war had been the tragedy in Waco, Texas, two years earlier, when the authorities' attempt to seize illegal weapons from a compound occupied by the Branch Davidian cult led to a shootout and four dead ATF agents. The fifty-one-day-long siege that followed ended with a fire killing seventy-five men, women, and children. Eight months earlier, federal agents had engaged in a shootout with white supremacist Randy Weaver, who was hiding in a northern Idaho cabin to avoid a weapons charge. Weaver's wife and fourteen-year-old son were killed.

After these deaths, fatigue-wearing, gun-toting leaders of militia clubs began talking of armed revolution against the state. The National Rifle Association released a special report on Waco to its members with a photo of the Branch Davidian compound above the caption, "Your rights and your home next?" After the Oklahoma City bombing, the NRA tried to distance itself from the militias, but it couldn't escape the fact that its literature had likened federal agents to "storm troopers," and called ATF agents (not coincidentally, the nation's chief gun-control enforcers) "jack-booted government thugs."

On talk radio in 1994 and 1995, violent rhetoric was almost routine. G. Gordon Liddy described for his listeners how to shoot to kill federal agents who might storm through the door of one's home. Bob Grant told his one million New York drive-time listeners that he'd like to line up all environmentalists against a wall and shoot them. After passage of the 1994 assault weapons ban, Colorado Springs' Chuck Baker told his angry audience: "Am I advocating the overthrow of this government? I am advocating the cleansing. . . . Why are we sitting here?" Of Sarah Brady, the gun control activist and wife of the White House press secretary who was shot in the 1981 assassination attempt on Reagan, Phoenix talk radio host Bob Mohan said: She "ought to be put down. A humane shot at the veterinarian's would be an easy way to do it." Threatening rhetoric wasn't limited to talk radio. After the 1994 election (and on the anniversary of President Kennedy's assassination), Republican Senator Jesse Helms warned that President Clinton was so unpopular with American troops that if he visited North Carolina's military installations, he had "better have a bodyguard."

Oklahoma City, keyed to the anniversary of Waco, provided the Right's leaders with an opening to stand up and say "enough" to the threatening language pervading its ranks. Few stepped forward to do so (just as many leftist leaders failed to condemn violent acts and rhetoric in the late 1960s and early 1970s). Scores of lawmakers, including McIntosh, accepted money from the NRA but remained publicly silent about the provocations in its literature. While Bill Bennett condemned the NRA for sounding like the Weathermen of the 1960s— "the way they were talking . . . [that] cops are bad, cops are the enemy"—the *National Review* magazine dismissed as "slipshod reasoning" and "liberal paranoia" any suggestion that this kind of talk had created an atmosphere conducive to acts of violence. Twenty-five years earlier, reacting to the rhetoric of leftist militants, the same magazine had condemned pervasive talk of violence and revolution.

Ironically, the former cowboy of College Republicans, whose own edgy rhetoric and antics once frightened even his friends, later would take the strongest public stance against the Right's extremists. Ralph Reed, busily policing his own ranks against militancy that year, was at work on a book to be published in 1996 that called on religious conservatives to "forcefully condemn those who are guilty" of abortion clinic violence. He added that the Religious Right must "unequivocally disassociate" itself from the millennial-minded Christian Patriot movement and other groups seeking to "impose biblical law through direct political action." These Christian nation advocates, he wrote, believed in an "authoritarian ideology that threatens the most basic civil liberties of a free and democratic society."

But in the weeks after Oklahoma City, most commentators on the Right circled the wagons to deride the press for "demonizing" conservatives. "It's a sign of how weak and desperate the Left is that some of them are trying to exploit this tragedy for political gain," Kristol told a reporter at the time. While Kristol said conservatives should denounce hate-speech and hate-mongering, he dwelled on a history of ugly name-calling by the Left. "In the welfare-reform debate, you had people on the floor of Congress calling their opponents Nazis. That's about as bad as it gets."

It was reasonable to criticize the outrages of the Left, just as it was reasonable to condemn those Democrats and media commentators who irresponsibly suggested a link between the Right's anti-Washington legislative efforts and the authority-hating terror tactics of far-right paramilitary groups. It would have taken more foresight to forcefully distance the movement from these bad seeds, to display more interest in leading a nation than in defending the excesses of an ideology. But that would have revealed a movement at peace with its place in the nation, and the Right was not.

In 1994, the American people had handed its legislature over to staunch conservatives. They controlled the House and much of the Senate. Their words led the evening news and filled the headlines and could define an entire nation and its troubles. But in their cloistered, self-referring world, the Right's leaders still saw themselves as besieged victims of a liberal Goliath, even as hordes of reporters stood on hand to record their complaints that they couldn't get their message through the liberal-media establishment. They made much ado about words, the power of words, the search for the right words to describe their programs. Yet they exhibited an uncanny inability to comprehend the impact of their own unscripted words—the uneasiness provoked, for example, when the new Speaker of the House derided supporters of the president of the United States as "the enemy of normal Americans."

THE OKLAHOMA CITY BOMBING hung over the Republican Revolution like a toxic drip. A *Washington Post*-ABC poll taken after the tragedy found that voter satisfaction with government—the Right's bogeyman—jumped from 29 to 49 percent. Clinton, who condemned "purveyors of hatred and division," regained much of his lost stature with the public. The job approval rating for congressional Republicans, which began at 52 percent after the 1994 election, had dropped to 41 percent by June, and continued to slide into the 30s during the summer months that followed.

Such was the mood of the American people when House Republicans issued their plan to balance the budget—and David McIntosh conspired with like-minded colleagues to disarm the Republicans' opponents. In the first months of Republican control, the House had produced a budget encompassing two main goals of its conservative faction: It purported to be balanced in seven years while still handing taxpayers a massive rebate of $335 billion. To make this equation add up, the Republicans decided to squeeze Medicare, the medical entitlement plan that accounted for 11.5 percent of all federal spending and was growing at a rate of 10 percent a year due to spiraling medical costs and an expanding elderly population. Given the popularity of the thirty-year-old program, and the political power of the seniors it serviced, the Republican decision to cut Medicare's growth took a lot of nerve to defend. Many Republicans in the Senate, and even a few in the House, were losing theirs.

McIntosh often turned to his allies in the movement for input and advice: Get me Kristol on the phone. Get me Reed. "He likes the intellectual interaction," said one staffer. That spring, McIntosh and his allies were on the same page, as Kristol issued a memo to Republicans wobbling over the size of the tax cut. "Hey, fellas," Kristol wrote to lawmakers concerned about piling up more government debt, "You people are supposed to be *Republicans*. Taxpayers—also known as citizens—come first, not the government, remember? It's a crucial, maybe *the* crucial, distinction between the two parties."

If Kristol saw the primacy of tax cuts as good electoral strategy, Ralph Reed saw them as a necessary constituent service: Religious conservatives—who had agreed not to complain while House Republicans ignored their social agenda during the first phase of the revolution—expected something in return, and family tax cuts filled the bill. Grover Norquist and McIntosh, like other hard-core movement conservatives, viewed tax cuts in the context of a broader ideological war: This was not just a matter of putting more money in constituents' pockets, it was also about sucking the fuel out of a bloated welfare state, drying up its energy source.

But none of those ideological sentiments ran deep in the more moderate Senate, where veteran legislator and Senate majority leader Bob Dole was eyeing a run for the presidency. Many senators, Republicans included, had been around long enough to watch the national debt—and the interest payment on it—mount in the years following the Reagan tax cuts (an analysis rejected by supply-siders, who blamed a $4.5 trillion debt on increased spending by congressional Democrats and credited economic growth in the 1990s to the legacy of Reaganomics). More than their House colleagues, Senate leaders understood the dangers of curtailing a popular entitlement program for senior citizens. The instinct among many senators was to shrink the size of the tax cut, and limit any meddling with Medicare. But that would mean facing down the House, where McIntosh and like-minded freshmen were in no mood for compromise.

In May, with senators about to capitulate on the tax cuts, David organized eighty-five House conservatives who sent a letter to Gingrich warning that "you can count on our votes against any budget conference report that fails to balance the budget or significantly diminishes the tax relief passed by the House." In June, McIntosh and his colleagues circulated a second letter pushing for the full tax cut. On June 21, they leaned on Gingrich again, this time in a private meeting. The two chambers reached an eleventh-hour agreement the next day, reducing the House tax cut by $90 billion.

The Republican Congress produced a budget with a tax cut ($245 billion) that, to the average layman's ear, sounded close in size to the cut Republicans had proposed in the growth of Medicare spending ($270 billion). Since much of the tax cut would end up back in the pockets of upper- and upper-middle-class Americans, Democrats and their liberal allies began using this numerical approximation to make the argument that Republicans were "cutting" Medicare to pay for tax cuts for the "rich." Gingrich launched a campaign to convince reporters to stop using the words "cut" to describe the Medicare plan, arguing that the proposal only curbed the growth of spending. (Under the Republican plan, per-patient spending would rise over seven years from $4,800 to $6,700, though Democrats noted that it would cost $8,000 to maintain the current level of service.) "Only in Washington could someone say with a straight face that Republican proposals to increase Medicare spending . . . amounts to a cut," McIntosh wrote in an *Indianapolis Star* op-ed in May. That summer, lawmakers such as McIntosh were careful to employ the phrase that Gingrich's pollsters had devised to describe their Medicare reforms: "preserve, protect, and strengthen."

Even with this packaging, and even though Gingrich managed to neutralize a powerful potential opponent, the American Association of Retired Persons, the objections coming from Democrats and their liberal allies promised to be deafening. McIntosh had been around Washington long enough to appreciate the power of the city's vast network of liberal public interest groups. According to a detailed multiyear study by Tufts University professor Jeffrey M. Berry, these groups were better funded, longer standing, and had far more legislative success in Congress than their conservative counterparts. Even at a time when "liberalism" was supposedly in crisis, Washington citizens groups had allied with Democratic Senate staffs to destroy the Supreme Court aspirations of David's friend and mentor Robert Bork; they had stirred the pot of sexual harassment charges that forever tarnished Clarence Thomas's good name; they comprised one side of the "iron triangle" that had battled David tooth and nail at the Competitiveness Council.

The growth of this powerful liberal network since the 1970s could be traced directly to the growth in government during those years, Berry explained. "As new laws and programs were created, and new bureaucracies formed. . . , opportunities for citizen groups swelled," he wrote. "More programs meant more constituencies, more constituencies meant more opportunities for entrepreneurs to organize advocacy groups." Most of their activities were financed through private donations. But many liberal groups also received federal grants to administer various programs, ranging from education workshops for food stamp recipients to research on environmental problems.

From the Reagan years onward, the Right had been actively trying to drain money from these groups by cutting off these federal grants, without success. Liberal citizen groups enjoyed broad, often bipartisan, support in Congress, with "patrons on important committees and subcommittees," conservative analyst Michael S. Greve explained in 1987, after Reagan's failed attempt to defund the Left. "Support for public interest causes is remarkably broad."

Federal law already prohibited the use of public grant money for political work. Nevertheless, in the summer of 1995, when a coalition of labor unions and liberal advocacy groups made plans to target vulnerable congressional Republicans with a $2 million media campaign denouncing the GOP Medicare plan, McIntosh and a cadre of conservative allies asserted that the federal government was, in effect, subsidizing them. Money is fungible, the Republicans argued: Federal grants to liberal groups freed up other funds for use in political battles. McIntosh co-sponsored legislation to end this "welfare for lobbyists"; the bill would essentially prevent those groups which received government grants from engaging in any "political advocacy," a term far more broad than "lobbying."

McIntosh's legislation threatened to shut down much of the $40 billion a year in federal grants flowing to tax-exempt groups. "Dave came to Washington knowing who the enemy is, and now they know he's here," one conservative congressional staffer said at the time. But some 39,000 tax-exempt groups a year received government grants and only a handful were actively lobbying against the Republican budget plan. The bill would hurt not only liberal groups such as the AFL-CIO, which received $1.3 million in federal grants in 1994 and was spearheading an ad campaign against the Medicare reforms. It also threatened to cut funding to thousands of charities engaged in do-gooder work that federal agencies farmed out, such as the YMCA or the Indiana chapter of the Association of Retarded Citizens (representing "about 20,000 Hoosier families," as one columnist put it, aptly capturing McIntosh's public relations dilemma). Grants to those groups were at risk if they so much as issued a press release describing the impact of pending legislation on their members.

In the fall of 1995, as his liberal opponents were airing mass media attacks on the Republican candidates and the GOP Medicare plan, McIntosh and a colleague staged a dialogue on the House floor to drum up support for the "welfare-for-lobbyists" bill:

"In my district, they are running advertising, $85,000 in television ads and Medicare ads and telephone calling," proclaimed Washington state's Randy Tate, McIntosh's close friend and ally. "But it is the National Council of Senior Citizens that shows up as one of those groups" that receives federal grants.

"If the gentleman will yield," McIntosh cut in, "are you telling me this group—who receives 96 percent of its funds from the federal government—has bought television campaign ads in your district?"

"That is absolutely correct."

"That is incredible. No wonder it is difficult to get a balanced budget when you have all these federally subsidized lobbyists out there fighting us tooth and nail."

These floor theatrics made for an enticing open-and-shut case against the Republicans' opponents. The only problem was (like the leaky bucket story), the facts were more complex. The 96 percent McIntosh mentioned was actually a Department of Labor grant under which the National Council administered a nationwide workfare program for low-income seniors. So the money wasn't going to lobbyists, it was going into the pockets of poor, mostly black, mostly female, elderly citizens collecting minimum-wage paychecks instead of welfare checks.

David stepped up his rhetoric that fall. He accused the National Council and other groups of "money laundering" and ordered them to appear before his subcommittee. At one hearing he chaired, McIntosh repeatedly asked a liberal witness, "Are you taking the Fifth Amendment?" His critics accused him of engaging in "McCarthyism," of "paper rattling" and "intimidation tactics" reminiscent of Nixon's enemies list. During one debate on the welfare-for-lobbyists legislation that fall, Democratic congressman George Miller of California stood on the floor of the House, with McIntosh's family in the gallery, and proclaimed, "It is a glorious day if you are a fascist; if you are a fascist, it is a glorious day."

McIntosh could survive the name-calling; being called a fascist or a McCarthyite was nothing new to the Right. What tripped him up was his impetuous decision to take on a titan of the Left, a woman so steeped in the intrigue of Beltway politics that she knew—the minute she walked into David's hearing room on the afternoon of September 28, 1995—that victory was hers for the taking.

Nan Aron was president of the Alliance for Justice, an association of such familiar liberal groups as the NOW Legal Defense and Education Fund, the Women's Legal Defense Fund, the Children's Defense Fund, and the Center for Science in the Public Interest. She could also be credited with inventing "Borking," for it was Aron who had helped orchestrate the sinking of Robert Bork's nomination in 1987 and had quietly passed Anita Hill's name and story to key senate staffers in 1991. To the Right, she was Darth Vader: "Nan Aron's purpose in life is to savage Republican judicial nominees," a *Wall Street Journal* editorial proclaimed. "The Alliance for Justice is a liberal legal jihad."

Aron, in other words, was not an opponent to be taken lightly, and McIntosh's confrontation with her suggested that in Washington's high-stakes policy wars, the baby-boom conservatives were still amateurs. In response to a letter from McIntosh demanding information on the Alliance's funding, Aron had penned a made-for-media-consumption refusal that questioned his authority to "investigate" private organizations and accused him of casting a dangerous "chill" over the right to free expression. McIntosh responded by hauling her before his subcommittee.

Aron showed up at the hearing primed for a brawl. As she took her place at the witness table, she noticed that McIntosh's staff was distributing a chart purporting to list federal grants to her umbrella group. In fact, the Alliance received no federal funds, though some of its member groups did. The chart appeared on mock Alliance for Justice stationery—complete with the group's logo and membership roster—suggesting that Aron's group had prepared it. This was, Aron concluded, a "forgery" (a word she and her allies would use liberally and repeatedly).

When her turn came to testify, Aron pounced, consistently bringing the questioning back to the document and accusing McIntosh and his staff of a "dishonest and cowardly" act.

"[This] is not a fruitful use of your time," McIntosh cut in. "It would be much more beneficial to us to hear your arguments about the bill . . ."

"It's beneficial to me, Mr. Chairman," Aron responded.

And so it was. Any point that McIntosh wanted to make about the cozy, corrupt relationship between liberal activists and federal bureaucrats was lost in a tornado of charges about a document his staff had prepared as a prop. Aron's ally, Democratic Representative Louise Slaughter of New York, joined the chorus, charging McIntosh's staff with a "despicable act. . . . It is absolutely unscrupulous for the committee to put out a phony piece of paper here."

As the attacks mounted during the hearing, the gentleman from Indiana, sitting at the head of his own subcommittee, looked (his detractors thought) like a boy whose hand had been caught in the cookie jar. "We turned *his* hearing into *our* press conference," Aron would later gloat. "It was our finest hour." But the fun wasn't over yet.

That evening, McIntosh sent a letter of apology to Aron while his aides struggled to explain to reporters what had led to this "innocent mistake." Their efforts to end the matter were to no avail: On October 16, Democrat Luis V. Gutierrez filed a formal complaint to the House ethics committee on behalf of consumer advocate Ralph Nader, who labeled McIntosh a "thoroughly disreputable man. . . . If he did that in a company, he would be fired." On October 25, Slaughter offered a resolution on the House floor to sanction McIntosh; the resolution was defeated on a largely party-line vote. In December, Slaughter sponsored a complaint to the House ethics committee on behalf of Aron, who accused the lawmaker of distributing a "counterfeit" document and "fabricating" one of her quotes on the House floor.

If all of this seemed like a calculated overreaction to a screw-up by a congressman's overzealous, underexperienced staff, Aron and her allies could care less. If McIntosh wanted a war, he would have one.

WHILE ARON WAS MAKING David's life miserable, her liberal allies that fall were making the Republican leadership squirm with high-pitched denunciations of the GOP's Medicare plan. Activists from the National Council and other groups shuttled scores of senior citizens, grandmothers in jeopardy, to Capitol Hill so their photos might grace news stories on the Democrats' charge that the Republicans were engaging in a "historic betrayal" of the elderly.

David's friend Randy Tate was in particular trouble with the reelection season on the horizon. Labor unions—angry over his work on the welfare-for-lobbyists bill—ran a TV ad blitz against him throughout the fall. "You watch their ads and I wouldn't vote for me either," Tate recalled. "I felt like that 'Far Side' cartoon, with the two deer out in the woods, one with a bull's-eye painted on him. And the other deer says, 'Bummer of a birthmark, Hal—' "

Troubled by these liberal attacks on his friends, McIntosh tried to convince the Republican Party to open its wallet for its own media campaign—to no avail. McIntosh, the fund-raising freight train, "always believed we could raise more money," said one supporter. But party leaders, concerned about consolidating resources for the November 1996 election, still a year away, "were afraid they couldn't," said this supporter. David later argued: "If we had spent a million dollars at the end of 1995, then I think 1996 would have turned out differently."

On November 13, Clinton vetoed the Republican budget bill of tax cuts and Medicare reforms, prompting a six-day shutdown of the federal government—and a round of applause from the ranks of the Right. "The idea of a grand showdown over spending had long been a staple of conservative analysis," Gingrich later explained. Dramatic change, enough to bring down a welfare state five decades in the making, required dramatic confrontation, the theory went. The Right's activists were "all gung ho for a brutal fight over spending and taxes," Gingrich noted in his memoir of the period. "We mistook their enthusiasm for the views of the American public."

One of those activists was Grover Norquist, a regular recipient of weekend phone calls from the Speaker seeking support and input from a trusted friend. Grover thought shutting down the loathed bureaucracy was a good idea: Why not sell off a national park or a few monuments while they were at it? he counseled. You could show the public just how easy it would be to live without the heavy hand of Washington. "Only the establishment press would use the word 'blame' for closing the government," Grover later explained.

McIntosh, who approached legislative politics like a game of chess, was more interested in how to strategically exploit a government shutdown to trump the White House. Two months earlier, he had predicted that with Clinton and congressional Republicans heading toward a collision over the budget, a shutdown was a probability. Republicans, he argued in one leadership meeting, should prepare to insulate themselves from public indignation by defining the terms of a shutdown—enabling Social Security checks to continue to be issued, for example, but allowing "nonessential" services (and those the Right especially disliked, such as the IRS and public broadcasting) to languish. As he returned from the Thanksgiving break to watch the White House regain the upper hand in the budget battle, David was kicking himself for not having pushed that idea harder.

By then, the two sides had reached a broad agreement to temporarily reopen the government while budget negotiations ensued. The freshman class was fast losing faith in Speaker Gingrich, who, it appeared, was being seduced by Clinton's charm and the aura of the White House during personal meetings with the President. Publicly, David had been loyal to Gingrich all year, even though he disagreed with aspects of the leadership's Medicare reform plan. (Republicans, he argued, should have made a clear case that the Medicare program was facing bankruptcy; he also believed that a Republican proposal to increase out-of-pocket expenses for the elderly, without more comprehensive reforms, had handed Clinton a tactical advantage.) But he was growing annoyed with Gingrich's undisciplined leadership style, highlighted by the Speaker's public tantrum in November after President Clinton supposedly snubbed him on Air Force One during the flight back from Israeli Prime Minister Yitzhak Rabin's funeral.

In December, as Gingrich's resolve waivered, McIntosh joined a brigade of lawmakers pledging a bloodbath if the speaker compromised with Clinton. Budget negotiations between congressional leaders and the White House stalled midway through the month, and the government shut down again, this time for twenty-one days. The stock market dropped precipitously, and the media brimmed with stories of furloughed workers bereft of paychecks as the Christmas holiday approached. A year ago, polls had shown that only 30 percent of Americans had confidence in Clinton to deal with the nation's major issues, while 46 percent had more confidence in the congressional Republicans. Now, a year later, those numbers were reversed, with 49 percent favoring Clinton, and 35 percent favoring the Republicans.

As their popularity sank, Republican leaders broached an agreement with the White House on a limited interim spending bill that would reopen the agencies. A brigade of hard-core House Republicans, including McIntosh, resolved to oppose the agreement. "Newt's calculation was that in order for us to preserve power in Congress, we had to retreat because the president had beaten us," McIntosh later said. "The freshman view was that it's better to demonstrate to the public that we're going to stick to our principles—at the risk of showing that we're not powerful and the president can beat us."

On January 4, McIntosh proclaimed to reporters, "We will not reopen the government." But the next day, Gingrich issued an ultimatum to the Indiana freshman: You either vote with the leadership—and support its agreement with the White House—or you resign your leadership post. "Newt, you didn't choose me" for the leadership position, McIntosh recalled responding. Technically, this was true:

McIntosh had been elected by his classmates. But David knew that the speaker controlled whether the freshmen class had one spot or two or none at all on his leadership team. The threat was for real.

On January 5, when the votes were tallied on the leadership's plan to reopen the government, fifteen House Republicans withheld their support. David was not among them. He had suppported Gingrich and the leadership, voting in favor of a spending bill that just twenty-four hours earlier he had denounced as "bad for the American public." When he returned to his office, David told staffers he felt dirty.

Gingrich took note of the holdouts and punished two of them—both friends of McIntosh—by canceling appearances at their fundraisers. To McIntosh, that was the last straw. He called Gingrich to complain, warning that the Georgia congressman "might find people may not want him to come back in" as Speaker. He laid it on thicker at a press conference in Indiana, where he denounced Gingrich's "crybaby attitude toward people who may disagree with you"—a dig that recalled a favorite tabloid label for the Speaker after the Air Force One incident.

In the immortal words of Mick Jagger, you can't always get what you want. But in the bitter winter of 1995–96 the members of the freshman class didn't even get what they needed. In the first (and last) year of their revolution, they had succeeded in enacting internal reforms in the House. But on the big issues—slashing the welfare state and sending the proceeds home with a massive tax cut—they were left empty-handed. For David, it was an especially trying season: Regulatory reform and his welfare-for-lobbyists bill both died—the former a casualty of strong environmentalist sentiment in Congress, the latter a victim of the budget battle. When, in mid-November, the welfare-for-lobbyists provision had threatened to hold up a budget agreement that might reopen the government, McIntosh had meekly agreed to withdraw it. Other freshman-backed pillars of the revolution, such as eliminating the Commerce Department, died too.

In later years, David would not waiver from his position that shutting down the government was a winning proposition for the Republicans, and for the conservative movement. "I actually think if we'd followed our strategy and not reopened the government we would have eventually succeeded in getting more of the budget passed," he said. He asserted that public disenchantment with the Republicans would have receded—just as it had in states where governors initially were assailed for enacting stiff welfare reforms, only to be hailed as heros later.

WHEN IT WAS ALL OVER, when the conservatives couldn't bear to hear the words Republican Revolution "without cringing in embarrassment" (as one conservative put it), it was the freshmen who, fairly or not, would be targeted for blame. Among more senior House leaders, the freshman had developed a reputation for talking when they should have been listening, for shouting when they should have been organizing and legislating. As a class, they weren't experienced legislators, and many House veterans complained that the newcomers lacked the discipline to make things happen—to whip up votes or build coalitions or curry support for legislation in the media or among grass-roots groups. (Whatever happened to McIntosh's welfare-for-lobbyists crusade? one leadership source later asked rhetorically, noting that it takes years to patiently build support for such reforms.) Even David's friends thought he paid a price for his refusal to seek common ground with his opponents. "He wouldn't look across the aisle for votes and he learned this was a mistake," said Tate.

Most movement conservatives praised the freshmen for sticking to their guns. Bill Kristol was not among them. At the beginning of 1995, he had counseled "aggressive realism. If the choice is between winning with a philosophically acceptable half-loaf and losing with the whole, we say: go with the winner." A year after the government shutdown, his new magazine, the *Weekly Standard,* revisited the Republican Revolution, concluding that conservative lawmakers had lost the whole because they wanted "too much, too soon." "Clinton did support a balanced budget," one of his writers noted, "just not the balanced budget Republicans wanted him to support. The real miscalculation was the failure of the House and Senate Republicans to split the difference . . . declare victory, and go home. The blame for this does fall squarely on the shoulders of Gingrich and the 73 freshmen. . . ."

On January 23, 1996, Bill Clinton stood before a joint session of Congress, declared that "the era of big government is over," and embraced a trilogy of themes appropriated from the Republicans—a balanced budget, crime reduction, stronger families. Eight months later, he signed the most sweeping welfare reform legislation in sixty years, taking credit for "ending welfare as we know it." A year after that, he finally signed a tax cut, one far less ambitious than anything envisioned by McIntosh's freshman class. And a year after that, at a 1998 White House ceremony that excluded Republicans, Clinton celebrated the anticipation of the first federal budget surplus in three decades, a turnaround in Washington's finances that economists credited to the 1993 tax hike, budget cuts, and a booming economy. The Right would never forgive Bill Clinton, the baby-boom liberal they loathed, for stealing their show.

McIntosh ended his first term chastened and matured, a convert to incrementalism maybe, but no less committed to the cause of conservative reform, no less certain that the House freshmen had been right all along. As for his own political future, he could see it in the words of a favorite Gospel verse, Mark 9:23: "All things are possible for him who believes."

CHAPTER 14

ON RACE AND INTENT

LIKE MANY DEVOTEES OF AYN RAND, Clint Bolick began his political career as an atheist. But, like the label "libertarian," "atheist" was becoming a scratchy suit to wear as Clint rubbed up against the lives of his legal clients—people of color and low means and uncrushed spirit, people who never quite got over their pleasant astonishment at having a constitutional lawyer fly in from the nation's capital to plead their cases before the highest courts of the land. By early 1996, the Institute for Justice that Clint had founded five years earlier with friend Chip Mellor was representing cab drivers against local monopolies, African hair-braiders against licensing authorities, parents against social service agencies blocking their interracial adoptions. Clint was also the lead attorney for inner-city Milwaukee parents sending their children to private schools, at taxpayer expense, under a six-year-old experimental school choice program.

He was beginning to fall out of step with libertarian orthodoxy, which he considered cold and antiseptic and distant from his clients' lives (the ideological purists bristled when Clint publicly joked that he was a "big government libertarian"). To his friends, Clint was an incurable romantic, and it showed not only in his work, but also in his personal relationships. Since his divorce from his high school sweetheart years earlier, he'd been on an elusive quest to find the perfect female, suffusing even first dates with a rush of naive idealism. In his spare time, he was working on a novel, a psycho-thriller in which the hero-protagonist (who, a friend said, was reminiscent of Clint) triumphs over adversity.

As he approached his fortieth birthday, Clint was, too, reconsidering his lack of faith and would soon be describing himself as a "recovering atheist." So this somewhat mellowed libertarian-atheist might be forgiven as he stood at the head of a table in a cozy Milwaukee restaurant one February night in 1996 and invoked a spiritual scene to celebrate the cause of school choice. "I was doing some imagery today in preparation," he told the half dozen dinner guests assembled around him, "and the image that came together was one of crossing the frontier. With all the obstacles we've been through, I could see this group climbing the mountains. And now, we're looking out on the green valley, with a shaft of sunlight shining down on it and the promised land laid out before us. Tomorrow, the buses are going to roll down into that valley."

The shaft of light that Clint envisioned was shining down on the Wisconsin Supreme Court, where, the next day, he would deliver oral arguments in defense of the Milwaukee school choice program. And the buses he described would be packed with schoolchildren accompanying him down a long, flat interstate to the state capital of Madison. These were children attending private schools at public expense, escaping an inner-city district where the dropout rate for public-assistance students was 85 percent and the average grade of graduating black students was D-plus. Opposing Clint in court was an array of liberal groups, including the teachers' union, who insisted that school choice would doom the public school system by siphoning off precious resources and tax dollars. Critics asserted that school choice was designed to "rescue the best and warehouse the rest."

Milwaukee's school choice program was born out of the kind of strange-bedfellow political alliance that Clint regularly sought in his own legal work. In 1990, a black former welfare recipient turned Democratic state legislator named Polly Williams joined forces with Tommy Thompson, Wisconsin's white Republican governor, to enact the nation's first government-subsidized school voucher program. The program was billed as small and experimental, enabling the state to shift tax dollars to nonsectarian private schools for up to one thousand Milwaukee students. The teachers' union, backed by the NAACP, sued, but two years later, in 1992, a 4–3 majority of the Wisconsin Supreme Court upheld the program, calling it a "life preserver to those Milwaukee children caught in the cruel riptide of a school system floundering upon the shoals of poverty, status-quo thinking, and despair."

In 1995, the state legislature, again backed by Thompson, voted to increase the number of children participating in the voucher program tenfold, and to include Milwaukee's many religious schools in the program. That action brought the Wisconsin Education Association, the NAACP, and the ACLU back to court, arguing that the program constituted government sponsorship of religion, thus violating the constitutional separation of church and state. Just as he had in the first round of legal battles, Clint represented the parents' groups. And this time Governor Thompson rolled in a big legal gun to represent the state: former federal appeals court justice (and, later, Whitewater prosecutor) Kenneth Starr.

The outcome of this second Wisconsin Supreme Court case—deciding whether the inclusion of religious schools was constitutional—would be a critical juncture in the school choice battle. But even in the midst of such serious business, Clint believed in the value of celebration. When Clint represented shoeshine man Ego Brown's 1990 challenge against the District of Columbia's Jim Crow–era prohibition against outdoor stands, it killed him to watch his client nearly go out of business as the case dragged on. One of Clint's mentors, black community activist Robert Woodson, suggested a "rent party" and hosted a crowd of Clint's young white conservative friends to raise funds. The party also raised spirits. Clint knew these court battles could be like roller coaster rides. Victory never came in a straight line, if at all. So he made a habit of sponsoring dinners for his clients on the eve of important court battles. If nothing else, the dinners eased his own nerves and reminded him of why he was there.

As the dinner on this February night progressed, conversation turned to the logistics of the rally to be held in Madison before the oral arguments: Where to put six hundred schoolchildren and their parents ("overflow is a good thing visually," piped in one veteran activist); who should speak and what they should say. Each of the local activists around the restaurant table had done yeoman's work to guide Milwaukee's expanded school choice program through the legislature. But they also owed much to the legal advice provided by Clint, and, on the eve of his big court battle, they were eager to let him know.

"A toast!" chimed in the Reverend Bob Smith, a Milwaukee prinicipal whose private high school stood as a testament to the academic success possible in the inner city. "A toast to our attorney! A toast to our right-wing attorney!" Clint burst out laughing and turned red. This was a bit of a sore point: When he first came to Milwaukee to offer his legal services to parents, locals such as Reverend Bob had been skeptical. Sticking to Clint, like rotten gum on the sole of a shoe, was the paper trail of his "right-wing" past—the "quota queen" clips, his opposition to the 1991 Civil Rights Act, his alliance with Clarence Thomas. Clint's ideology was an issue he was forced to address with just about every client. But as he liked to say: "I am in the same business as Stephen King: Making people believe things they are not inclined to believe."

LIBERALS USUALLY WON'T ADMIT IT, but when they use the word "right-winger," they sometimes mean it as a euphemism for a more loaded word—"racist." This connotation has its roots in the 1950s and 1960s, when American conservatives—Goldwater followers, YAFers, the *National Review* crowd—claimed "states' rights" to oppose federal efforts to end racial segregation in the South. Clint's generation of conservatives, too young to have taken sides in these battles, liked to think it could escape the baggage of the Right's civil rights record. Many of these baby boomers even took inspiration from early civil rights leaders: They argued, for example, that Dr. Martin Luther King believed (as they did) in a color-blind society but that his successors were intent on dividing society along racial lines. "He drew constantly upon the principles and aspirations that unite us as Americans, black and white, rich and poor," Clint wrote. Unburdened by their own movement's legacy, these baby boomers didn't shy away from proclaiming that racial categories were no more American in the hands of affirmative action officers than they had been in the hands of Southern governors.

Goldwater-era activists, of course, also vigorously opposed affirmative action. But stalwarts of the Republican Party were more conflicted about whether special consideration should be granted to ethnic minorities. As Clint put it: "Guilt over being on the wrong side of civil rights during the 1960s motivated Republicans from Richard Nixon to George Bush to embrace racial preferences, even though it did nothing to attract minorities to the GOP." (Often overlooked is the fact that a far higher proportion of congressional Republicans than Democrats supported the century's most important piece of civil rights legislation, the 1964 Civil Rights Act, more than compensating for the defections of pro-segregation Southern Democrats. In this, the activist Right was far out of step with the GOP: Its national leader,

Senator Barry Goldwater, was one of only six Republican senators to vote against the act.)

But the younger conservatives carried their own baggage. Clint's libertarian philosophy initially stood in the way of his endorsement of the 1964 Civil Rights Act. That law prohibited, and punished, discrimination in employment and education, and outlawed segregation in public accommodations. He later came to embrace the 1964 law, "so great were the abuses of political power" by state authorities that Clint saw no other choice. But his new position drew the ire of orthodox libertarians who believed fervently in the right of individuals to associate with whomever they please.

Clint believed that categorizing people by their ethnicity, whether for motives good or ill, was immoral. Like other movement conservatives, he rejected forms of liberal programs to produce diversity because they judged individuals by type, not talent. Like his mentor Clarence Thomas, he also argued that the racial preferences—which he called "trickle-down civil rights"—were hurting the low-income people who formed his client base. "By taking cosmetic action to ensure proportional representation in certain institutions, it makes us think we are solving racial disparities, when, in fact, they are growing larger," he argued.

But making this case was an uphill battle, especially when the messengers came from the Right, and the Right's historical record on poverty, as well as on race, was not one to boast about. As the late theorist Russell Kirk admonished: "Conservatism has its vice, and that vice is selfishness." (The other half of that astute observation was: "Radicalism, too, has its vice, and that vice is envy.") Clint complained that conservatives were perceived, rightly, as "benignly neglectful or not so benignly neglectful" of race and poverty issues.

In the 1990s, the Right's opposition to racial preferences and support for welfare reform guaranteed catcalls from the Left. (After the 1994 election, Jesse Jackson went so far as to claim that the Christian Coalition had roots in Nazi Germany.) School choice, aimed at poor inner-city neighborhoods, was a way for the Right to address racial disparities and poverty while still staying within the bounds of conservative doctrine. Black students suffered a high school dropout rate three times that of whites, and were an average of two to four academic years behind. This educational disparity, Clint asserted, could not be cured by race-based affirmative action programs at colleges and universities. By then it was too late in the educational process.

In Cleveland, where Clint was defending another school choice program, the public schools were even worse than in Milwaukee. Cleveland's sad state left the numbers one and fourteen emblazoned on Clint's mind: "Children in the Cleveland Public Schools have a one-in-fourteen chance of graduating on time and proficient at a senior level; they also stand a one-in-fourteen chance each year of becoming a victim of crime in the schools." Bolick offered these kinds of numbers as "a wake-up call. The problem is not discrimination. The problem is the K–12 education system. Just as when you end welfare you have to begin really helping people find work and rebuild the family, so too if you end racial preferences you have to start asking the question: Why is it that universities are looking for minority students and they're not there? Why are they not graduating at higher rates? You need to ask those questions rather than gloss over the problem by adding points to kids' test scores."

WHEN CLINT FIRST CAME to Milwaukee in 1990 to offer free legal help to parents in the school choice program, locals were dubious. "Anticipation and skepticism filled the air," recalled Michael Holt, publisher of a leading local African-American newspaper. Many parents preferred a black attorney, he added, but efforts to secure one had fallen short: The candidates were either too expensive, unfamiliar with constitutional law, or unwilling to go up against a black establishment led by the local NAACP. Clint won over parents and community leaders not only with his constitutional arguments, but also with his frank description of political dynamics. School choice opponents "will do anything and everything to discredit [you]," he told a group of parents and activists. "They will paint pictures of choice supporters as pawns of the Right, of Republicans, of racists."

Behind the expanded school choice program sitting in front of the Wisconsin Supreme Court in 1996 was an alliance between the downtown business community and low-income parents distressed about the public schools. There was no way to categorize the politics of a pro-voucher coalition in which a leftist former Cesar Chavez activist (Milwaukee school board member John Gardner) taught a politically independent local businesswoman (Susan Mitchell) how to organize low-income, mostly black parents, while a neoconservative funder (Michael Joyce of the Bradley Foundation) poured money into the effort. The last thing Milwaukee's school choice supporters wanted was for their program to become an ideological football.

Instead of using free-market language—as pro-voucher libertarians such as Milton Friedman did—the local activists in Milwaukee spoke of parents' right to choose what was best for their children. Instead of berating "government schools"—as hard-core Rightists such as Grover Norquist did—they described their vision of a new system of publicly funded education that would offer a polyglot of charter, private, and public schools. The Wisconsin organizers argued, and believed, that choice would strengthen the public schools by shaking up entrenched unions and bureaucracies that appeared to have given up on disadvantaged children. Many of the Milwaukee parents in the voucher program also had children still in the public schools. (Likewise, Clint's two sons attended public schools in suburban Virginia.)

But the visible presence of such rightist groups as Clint's Institute for Justice, Joyce's Bradley Foundation, and the libertarian Landmark Legal Foundation prompted opponents to portray school choice as a right-wing conspiracy to destroy the public school system, the heart and soul of egalitarian America. The Institute for Justice, founded on seed money from libertarian energy moguls David and Charles Koch, also enjoyed funding from such conservative foundations as Scaife, Olin, and Bradley, and business interests such as Philip Morris, Chase Manhattan, and the Distilled Spirits Council. (William "Chip" Mellor, the institute's president and general counsel, built the group's $2.5 million–plus revenue stream, leaving much of the public work to Clint, who served as litigation director.)

The liberal critics almost got it right. There *was* a right-wing conspiracy of sorts, but it had a different goal: to demonstrate the dysfunction of institutions left in the hands of government. Milton Friedman had been promoting vouchers for three decades, but few listened to him until the public school system—particularly in the inner cities—decayed so precipitously, even in districts with high per-student spending. In the late 1980s, conservative education experts such as Chester E. Finn made the case that teachers' unions and urban administrations had become entrenched monopoly jobs programs for adults, not learning systems for children; editorialist John Fund wrote of the "culture of low expectations" in inner-city schools.

In the 1990s, some thinkers on the Right began looking at school choice as the silver bullet of their movement: Proving that the cherished public schools didn't work would open the door to deconstructing the hulking welfare state. A key figure in all this was Michael Joyce, whose Milwaukee-based Bradley Foundation had funded a wide range of conservative groups, including the Institute for Justice. "It is my opinion this will be a hot story," Joyce wrote to his friend Bill Kristol in 1990, when the latter was Vice President Quayle's chief of staff. "It pits poor, unorganized, urban minority parents against the established power of school bureaucracies, unions, old line civil rights organizations, and the advocates of special interests." During the 1992 election, Kristol tried repeatedly, and in vain, to persuade George Bush to talk about school choice as an empowerment issue for the middle-class and poor children who, without vouchers, didn't have a "choice" about which school to attend. He passed on to Bush campaign aides the message from his friend Finn that Republicans "should unabashedly become the party of education's consumers, not its producers"—the teacher unions and administration bureaucracies. "The producers are far better organized but less numerous."

The Bradley Foundation was founded on the fortune of an electronic and radio components manufacturer named Harry Bradley who had been an active member of the John Birch Society. But in many ways Joyce—who brought Clint to Milwaukee in 1990—reflected the thinking of a new generation of conservatives. Joyce was a former Democrat who insisted he was "not ready to repeal the welfare state." Instead, he wanted to "ameliorate [its] problems." He and Clint believed vouchers should be targeted at inner-city youth, at least initially, and remained at friendly odds with Friedman and other freemarketers who were pushing for universal vouchers, regardless of a family's income. "Clint and I [believe] that any attempt to do it universally will fail, and that the real tragedy is lack of opportunity for urban, lower income people," said Joyce. "As a matter of justice, this ought to be a high priority. The reality is that those who can make a choice in urban areas already have done so—by moving out or purchasing education in private schools."

After the Wisconsin legislature expanded the scope of the Milwaukee program to include religious schools in 1995, Joyce, Kristol, Bolick, and Governor Thompson met in Madison to discuss the legal challenge to it and the litigation's import on the national stage. Also in attendance was Starr, whom Joyce brought along to provide strategic advice. At the meeting, Kristol stressed the centrality of school choice to the conservative movement nationally. Bolick urged the governor to bring in an outside lawyer to represent the state; Wisconsin's attorney general was a Democrat who opposed choice, though he said he would support it in court. After the meeting, Thompson hired Ken Starr. "At that point," Clint recalled, "Starr's profile was not that high in the Whitewater case. Had it been, I would have opposed his involvement—it could have politicized the case, and our goal was to win the case, nothing else."

Despite Clint's sincerity about his cause (and the honest delight he felt when he visited the city's voucher schools and watched children standing in their uniforms to recite poetry, or plunging quietly and confidently into tests), his friends noted that he also understood the public relations value of representing low-income minority families. He was convinced that the children and parents sitting in the courtroom several years earlier at the first hearing on the Milwaukee program, had helped persuade a liberal judge, initially hostile to the program, to lend it her blessing. Voucher proponents lost on appeal, but the program continued to operate while the case progressed to the Wisconsin Supreme Court. During the oral argument before the state's highest court, courtroom seats were occupied by adults in suits, many of them educators who had taken the day off to hear the arguments. Most of the audience was white; the faces of children pressed up against the window panes of the courtroom door were black. Clint took one look at these "beautiful, innocent little faces" and wove the imagery into his oral arguments: Children were being shut out, left outside looking in on a decent education.

At another early and critical point in the battle, the state superintendent of education issued a blizzard of regulations governing private schools participating in the choice program. At Clint's prodding, John Fund—Clint's friend since his law school days—wrote a *Wall Street Journal* editorial that likened the superintendent to Orval Faubus, the Arkansas governor who called out the National Guard in 1957 to prevent black children from attending an all-white high school in Little Rock. The image plagued the superintendent and his efforts to strangle the program.

EVEN THOUGH THE FEBRUARY 1996 oral argument was Clint's second appearance before the Wisconsin Supreme Court, he fought butterflies as he took his seat at the counsel's table. The courtroom offered a familiar racial scene: The justices on the dais were all white, the attorneys speaking for both sides were all white, the courtoom audience, again, was nearly all white (parents and children were outside).

Starr led off the presentation: A nationally known constitutional lawyer, former federal appeals court judge, and, now, hired gun, he twirled constitutional nuances like a baton. He used words like "jurisprudentially" at every opportunity and was faintly condescending as he urged the court to "stay the course" and abide by precedent. "Not everything that affects religion in a way that could be viewed as beneficial . . . must be rooted out," he lectured the justices, adding that the correct constitutional standard for government action was "beneficent neutrality," not "hostility" toward religion.

The next defender of the school choice program, an attorney from the libertarian Landmark Legal Foundation with a crisp haircut and wire-rimmed glasses, offered a clipped enumeration of individual rights and the free exercise of religion. His arguments were bludgeoned by skeptical justices, and he gratefully took his seat when his ten minutes were up.

Then Clint rose to the podium to offer a very unusual kind of "right-wing" presentation. As a litigator, Bolick isn't every jurist's cup of tea, though many find him refreshing. He tends to write and talk in narrative, and he wears his heart on his sleeve. He can make strong arguments on precedent, but lawyers who have worked with him complain that he doesn't have enough grounding in, or patience with, the dreary mechanics of litigation, such as procedural motions and deposition taking. What he offers, instead, is a passion about the people he brings into court. He is incapable of lawyer-like separation of his feelings from his clients; in the school choice cases, he emotionally shoulders the weight of the children's futures. Dark moods, bitter and intransigent, frightening to his friends, descend after a court defeat.

Bolick nervously fingered his papers, looked across the line of six justices, and began: "Four years ago, I had the honor of appearing before this court to represent children whose educational horizons were expanded by the Milwaukee Public Choice Program. That decision . . . was the judicial equivalent of a ray of sunshine for those kids' lives. I appear today on behalf of their brothers and sisters. . . ."

Clint was deferential and attentive as justices interrupted his arguments with questions. He called them by name—"I'm glad you raised that question, Justice Wilcox"—and referred back to arguments they had made during his previous appearance before the court. He was acutely aware that the educational prospects for these kids would rest on a close vote.

The justices raised serious concerns that day, particularly over the potential breach in the wall between church and state. The Milwaukee program enabled voucher students to "opt out" of religious activities, but how was it possible to opt out of an entire curriculum that is infused with religious doctrine? The state's voucher reimbursements often exceeded the tuition charged by private religious schools: Didn't this mean the state was subsidizing religious schools? "Millions of dollars will be transferred from the state treasury to religious schools," argued one opposing counsel. And wasn't the Milwaukee program supposed to remain small and experimental, as described in the first state supreme court ruling? "Fifty-five million a year is not the experimental program you approved," argued the teachers' union attorney.

Clint tried to downplay the sweep of the program: No, this was still an experiment. Yes, the Milwaukee public schools had been helped, not hurt, by the competition. "One thing we do know that's *not* happening is an abandonment of the Milwaukee public schools," he argued, pointing to increased resources going into the district. The choice program simply makes aid "transportable" between public, private, and religious schools, he argued. Starr made the case that the government was not supporting religion because it was the parents who made the decision where to send their children: The voucher program was neutral and indirect.

Later that day, Milwaukee parents appeared at a rally outside the courthouse. As Clint stood quietly to the side, they offered testimonials about their struggles to send their children to private schools. "We as parents are the ones who should choose!" proclaimed one mother. Dr. Howard Fuller, former superintendent of the Milwaukee schools, asked the crowd if it was fair that Bill Clinton could send his daughter to private school, but these parents couldn't. "People who have money make choices everyday—" he pointed out to the gathered students. After the speeches, a teacher collected several children together to sing, a cappella, "We Shall Overcome." It was one of those moments (common with Clint, who was fond of quoting Martin Luther King) that set the civil rights establishment's teeth on edge: The hijacking of a hero's legacy on behalf of a right-wing cause.

But the Wisconsin choice program made an important political point: There was sometimes a wide gap in opinion between today's civil rights leaders and the people they purported to represent. The NAACP opposed the program, even though 90 percent of Milwaukee's blacks supported it. Parents using the vouchers were particularly pleased with the program, and demonstrated higher involvement and satisfaction with their children's educations than parents of public school students.

Academic achievements under the program were harder to measure because even research on its results had become mired in politics. A state researcher, appointed by a superintendent hostile to the plan, found no academic gains among children using vouchers. But when a Harvard researcher examined the program, he concluded that the state's study was seriously flawed, and found large academic gains beginning in the third and fourth years after students transferred out of the public schools. The findings of both studies contradicted the "rescue-the-best-warehouse-the-rest" argument: Those who applied to the school choice program tended to be among public system's poorest performers.

Two months after the oral arguments, the Wisconsin Supreme Court would deadlock in a 3–3 vote, sending the case back through another journey through the state's courts. It would take another two years before Clint could claim victory.

RALPH REED QUOTED Martin Luther King at least as often as Clint did. He embraced the civil rights movement as if it were part of his own history, as if it belonged to his generation. He even compared his evangelical movement, guardians of the church-going nuclear family, to the courageous seekers of racial justice. Some might wince at Ralph's audacity, but they had to admire the ambition of the sentiment; for on civil rights, Ralph's movement carried even more historical baggage than Clint's libertarians. Libertarians might be guilty of allowing textbook theories to obscure the racial realities—arguing, for example, that a rational free market will punish employers who limit their labor pool by engaging in racist hiring practices. But the Religious Right had a history of overt racist practices, of pro-segregation sermons and Christian schools formed to evade desegregation. "It is a painful truth that the white evangelical church was not only on the sidelines, but on the wrong side, of the most central struggle for social justice in this century," said Ralph.

Ralph cast himself as the racial conscience of the Religious Right, a man who by virtue of his generational standing and historical training could purge the movement of any remnants of discrimination. "The one thing he feels most strongly about is race," said one intimate. As a young man who had experienced rebirth himself, Ralph could envision a born-again "pro-family" movement, one that cast a wide net, was modern and diverse and inclusive. Ralph, who harbored a sense of chosen destiny, never doubted that he could be the leader to achieve that transformation.

But nothing was ever that simple with Ralph. His mind raced along two tracks, one high-minded and considered, the other spinning strategic calculations on the road to victory. Marketing always figured into his motivations. So that when, in 1995, he formed the Catholic Alliance to reach beyond Protestant evangelicals, he sounded like an ad exec pitching a client on how to reach a new audience. "You have a lot of citizens who are consumers of a niche-driven message. If you just take the abortion issue: Evangelicals are more likely to appeal to Scripture—Psalm 139, or John the Baptist leaping in his mother's womb—whereas Catholics are more likely to adopt a broader or more comprehensive ethic: to be a voice for the voiceless and a defender of the innocent."

When he began reaching out to the Jewish community that same year, he instinctively knew how to appeal to this new audience; he addressed, head on, Jewish fears about white evangelicals, fears which he said were "rooted in history." He recalled the emotional pain he felt when he visited the Holocaust memorial in Israel. When he took his message outside the Beltway, to suburban Jews in New Jersey, he pitched his message slightly differently, recalling his childhood in Miami, where "growing up, I attended more bar mitzvahs than baptisms." Even after a divisive debate preceding his visit—in which opponents portrayed him as a secret anti-Semite and hate-monger—he won over most of his audience.

As a historian who spent his formative years in the South, whose doctoral dissertation dwelled on the checkered racial history of southern evangelical colleges, it was natural for Ralph to put race relations high on his docket. And as a political leader looking to broaden his movement, reaching out to black leaders made strategic sense. As conservative strategist Thomas Atwood noted in 1990, just as the evangelical Right in the 1970s and 1980s missed opportunities to build strong relationships with the evangelical establishment—Billy Graham, *Christianity Today* magazine, the National Association of Evangelicals—so too had it missed a political opportunity by ignoring black evangelicals. On moral and social issues, white evangelicals were "closer to black evangelicals than they were to white non-evangelical Protestants," Atwood noted. If the evangelical Right were to become a movement with tens of millions, not millions, of members, it would have to seek out these allies, Atwood wrote.

But Ralph had his own problems as a messenger on race. He remained a staunch supporter of Senator Jesse Helms, leader of the campaign against a federal holiday honoring Martin Luther King and a politician widely viewed as a race-baiter. As a college student, Ralph had given a speech opposing the King holiday. And there was always the problem of Ralph's operative instincts—that still overweening desire to win at any cost—that threatened to choke off idealistic principles. That became evident when he refused to publicly defend a staunch Christian Coalition ally, South Carolina Governor David Beasley, who faced vituperative attacks in late 1996 after he announced his support for taking down the Confederate flag from the capitol dome in Columbia. Beasley believed that, for black citizens especially, the flag called to mind the state's racist past. Sources close to both men said Ralph advised the governor the issue was "too hot" to touch.

But publicly in 1996, Ralph's idealism shone through. He was certain he could bring conservative blacks into the fold (certain, too, that he could make his movement more righteous, and less self-righteous). Four months after Clint delivered his oral arguments on behalf of mostly black parents before the Wisconsin Supreme Court, Ralph was preparing to deliver a mea culpa to black preachers in Atlanta. By now, Ralph was a bona fide political celebrity: His face had filled the cover of *Time* magazine; he was a favorite of print reporters and TV talk-show bookers seeking an articulate spokesman of the Right. That year, an appearance by Ralph Reed at any event guaranteed a showing of TV cameras.

Ralph leveraged his fame to bring more public attention to a spate of violence against churches across the South. More than half of the sixty churches firebombed since January 1995 were black congregations, and the crimes were believed to be racially motivated. Already, Ralph had called on the Republican Congress to conduct hearings; he said the Christian Coalition would offer a $25,000 reward for information leading to the arrest of the perpetrators. In June, he invited a small group of pastors and civil rights leaders to meet at an Atlanta hotel, where he would announce (in front of the TV cameras that had trailed him) that the Christian Coalition planned to sponsor a special collection day at member churches to raise $1 million toward rebuilding the burnt churches. It was an ambitious fund-raising goal—but, then, Ralph always liked big round numbers.

He arrived at the hotel that morning armed with a short speech quoting W. E. B. Du Bois ("The problem of the twentieth century will be the problem of the color line") and, reminiscent of his remarks before Jewish audiences, offering apologies for white evangelicals' record on race relations. Walking toward the hotel meeting room, Ralph's eyes darted about nervously; the Southern Christian Leadership Conference had called on civil rights leaders to boycott the meeting and Ralph was worried the group might also stage a demonstration. But all he saw as he entered was a platform of cameras, scores of reporters, and the small group of invited pastors and community leaders taking their seats at the table. As he took his own place, he tried to recede into the background, demurring when the Reverend Earl Jackson—a prominent black pastor hired by the Christian Coalition to run its urban program—suggested he speak first. Instead, Ralph waited until the other guests had spoken before offering a moment of contrition.

"We come not in haughtiness but in humility," he told the gathering. "We come not in righteousness but in repentance. We come not to preach, but to listen—to those who bear the scars of the struggle for racial justice, a cause which in the past, the white evangelical church has failed to embrace to its great shame. . . . We come with broken hearts, a repentant spirit, and ready hands to fight this senseless violence." He had written these words the night before with help of a friend, David Kuo, an early architect of "compassionate conservatism." Ralph's insistence on turning projects such as this speech around on a dime, always operating on hyperspeed, could drive colleagues crazy. But Kuo never doubted his friend's sincerity on matters of racial justice: "There's a passage out of Galatians that says there is neither Jew nor Gentile, male or female, but all are one in Christ Jesus. Ralph very much subscribes to the belief that the kingdom of God is a colorblind kingdom." Moreover, said Kuo, if Ralph, with his soaring public profile, "had been silent on the church burnings, the silence would have been deafening." The day after the meeting, major newspapers featured a photo of Ralph, head bent in prayer, hands interlaced with those of African-American preachers.

While the SCLC's president dismissed the Atlanta affair as a cynical effort to boost the Christian Coalition's standing among blacks, several of the ministers who attended the meeting welcomed Ralph's words. Two political leaders in attendance, representatives of the Anti-Defamation League and the NAACP, were skeptical but polite. "We have to be wary of any Trojan horse," Nelson B. Rivers III, the NAACP's Southeast regional director, told reporters, "when the [church-burning] issue is used to get into our community to achieve other goals that may not be in our interest." During the meeting, Ralph had leaned over to Rivers and directly addressed his skepticism, telling him, "I've laid out before you what I want to try to do. The only way I can ever convince you is by doing what I say I'm going to do. You will have to be the judge of that."

The day of special church collections to raise $1 million proved to be a bust: It took seven months for the Christian Coalition to raise just half a million dollars from its members. The money was distributed to forty churches, according to the Coalition's Reverend Jackson. (Ralph would alternately cite the figures $750,000 and $850,000 to the press.) By contrast, the mainline National Council of Churches raised nearly $10 million to assist the rebuilding of firebombed churches. Undeterred by his membership's less than enthusiastic response, Ralph insisted that this "racial reconciliation" effort was "a spiritual agenda that I think, frankly, is more important than anything I've done politically."

On January 30, 1997, seven months after the Atlanta meeting, Ralph called a press conference in Washington to announce a new urban outreach program called the Samaritan Project, to be run by the Reverend Jackson. Standing alongside black and Latino clergy members as TV cameras rolled, he called on white evangelicals to make racial reconciliation the "centerpiece" of their legislative agenda. He urged Congress to adopt school vouchers for poor students, $500 tax credits for volunteers to poverty programs, and urban empowerment zones. At a "racial reconciliation" conference in Baltimore five months later, he expanded his policy agenda with a speech attacking redlining practices and racist cops.

"For too long, our movement has been primarily—and frankly almost exclusively—a white, evangelical, Republican movement, whose center of gravity focused on the safety of the suburbs," he proclaimed. "The Samaritan Project is a bold plan to break that color line and bridge the gap that separates white evangelicals and Roman Catholics from their Latino and African American brothers and sisters." Per Ralph's usual style, the numbers he attached to the Samaritan Project were enormous. He said the Coalition planned to raise $10 million for African-American and Hispanic churces in the inner cities, with cash grants going to one thousand urban churches working with young people, particularly at-risk youth. He promised to raise $1 million in 1997, the rest by the year 2000.

Liberal critics heatedly denounced the Coalition's new lurch in their direction, describing it as a plot by extremist right-wingers. People for the American Way, the liberal activist group founded by television producer Norman Lear, held a protest rally before the Baltimore conference. They needn't have expended so much energy. The Samaritan Project was no more than Ralph flying solo, and his membership was not to follow. (According to reliable insiders, Pat Robertson learned the details of the Samaritan Project from newspaper accounts and was livid that Ralph hadn't involved the Coalition's board.)

"It had not exactly bubbled up from the grass roots," recalled the Reverend Jackson, the pastor and Harvard law graduate hired to run the project. "Most state and local activists learned about it on CNN. There were even some at the highest levels of the organization who felt they were not given a sufficient opportunity for input. From the moment I floated the idea, the valid substantive question was raised of whether we were departing from the mission of the Coalition."

Jackson was right: He and Ralph were trying to add an alien component to an organization whose original direct-mail funding was built on anger over abortions-on-demand and taxpayer-funded art considered obscene and sacrilegious. Jackson recalled that many grass-roots Coalition leaders embraced the Samaritan Project as their own once they learned more about it, but the heart of the organization was never in it. Critics inside the Coalition asserted the Samaritan Project was emblematic of how Ralph was more interested in currying favor with the national media than with building a lasting political movement.

Less than a year after its founding, as the Christmas holidays approached, the Samaritan Project was abandoned by a financially struggling Christian Coalition, leaving Jackson with just $28,000, two computers, and a determination to stay afloat. Forget the $10 million: The Samaritan Project had raised barely $50,000 for its urban work. Nothing was heard from the Christian Coalition again about redlining or racist cops or empowerment zones. No white evangelicals moved into the inner city to help black families, as promised. Jackson was forced to struggle just to keep his project alive. The Catholic Alliance, which had already spun off from the Christian Coalition, received similar holiday tidings: Its annual $1 million grant from the Coalition grant was terminated.

IN JANUARY 1997, the same month that Ralph was launching his vaunted Samaritan Project, Clint was in California pursuing his own version of a conservative civil rights agenda. At a law professor's mission-style home on the north side of San Diego, a Sunday night celebration unfolded among core supporters of the California Civil Rights Initiative, or CCRI, a ballot measure to eliminate state-sponsored affirmative action programs that for years had given women and minorities a boost in the competition for everything from job offers to college admissions. California voters had overwhelmingly passed the anti–affirmative action measure in November 1996, producing a social earthquake that upended race relations in this important state. Now, however, the Clinton administration was challenging the new law in court.

Throughout the evening, the nearly all-white group of celebrants swapped stories of Asian and white friends who had been shut out of state and university programs because their skin color didn't qualify them as part of an "underrepresented" ethnic group. As the party wound down, the hostess ushered them into the living room to hear from Bolick, the evening's honored guest. Wine glass in hand, Clint took his place in front of the fireplace to offer his confidence that the courts would ultimately uphold the will of the voters. "This party is really about you," he said, sweeping his hand across the room of CCRI volunteers. "I never thought this day would come. . . . Let me quote my favorite revolutionary, Tom Paine: 'We have the power to begin the world over again.' "

The next night, Monday, Clint was seated in a Russian restaurant in downtown San Diego. Again, the talk was tinged with grievance. But this time nearly all the guests were African-American—five entrepreneurs who swapped stories about how a white-controlled state regulatory system had turned them into "outlaws." State law required these hair braiders to take $5,000 to $7,000 worth of classes to qualify for cosmetology licenses—even though the classes didn't teach their trade and emphasized chemicals shunned by the braiders, including straighteners to "correct" black hair. Unable to afford this training, many braiders operated their businesses out of their homes in order to avoid stiff fines and possible closure if they opened a public salon.

As caviar and blintzes, borscht and kabobs were placed on the table, Clint rose to propose a toast to honor the entrepreneurs seated with him—the next heroes, he declared, in the battle for "economic liberty." The following day, the braiders would be in court as plaintiffs in a lawsuit against California's Board of Barbering and Cosmetology. And Clint, a balding white male who joked that he knew more about African hair braiding than anyone who needed it less, would be their lead attorney.

These two sides of Clint's political life—his propaganda war against using affirmative action to help minorities, his litigation on behalf of minority clients—confounded his foes. Liberals familiar with Bolick's legal work regularly dismissed it as a publicity stunt, a man-bites-dog story ("Right-winger Helps Black People!") that the media couldn't resist. "Clint does a nice job of getting attention by doing things the press regards as counterintuitive," said Elliot Mincberg, general counsel of People for the American Way. "Economic liberty," he added, should not be categorized as a civil right alongside legal protections against "invidious discrimination" based on race, sex, or religion. President Clinton, fed up with Clint's many attacks on his civil rights nominees, at one point accused the Right of never having "lifted a finger to give anybody of a minority race a chance in this country."

But in Bolick's mind, these threads of his life were aimed at a single goal: "It's all about curbing the perverse power of the welfare

state," he said. "The state should not have the power to classify people on the basis of race, or erect barriers to entrepreneurs, or consign
kids to educational cesspools." Clint devised the phrase "grass-roots
tyranny" to describe the obstacles that bootstrap entrepreneurs confronted. At a time when most conservatives were arguing that govern-
mental power should devolve from Washington to the states and
municipalities, Bolick made the case that local authorities—more easily controlled by entrenched business interests—were often more oppressive than Washington bureaucrats. America's central cities would
have vibrant economies, he maintained, if regulators stopped protecting local monopolies by blocking street vendors, unlicensed cabbies,
hair salons, and a host of other tiny businesses that enable people to
gain a foothold in the urban economy.

When Clint and his partner Chip Mellor founded the Institute for
Justice in 1991, they began scouting out a client base of entrepreneurs
who had crossed state and municipal licensing authorities. Just as the
NAACP and ACLU lawyers made big law out of small people, so too
did the Institute for Justice, representing clients pro bono and training
young lawyers to pursue a rightist version of "public interest" litigation. Following the lead of liberal public interest lawyers, Bolick and
Mellor looked for sympathetic plaintiffs: Ego Brown, the black
shoeshine man nearly driven out of business by a Jim Crow–era law,
set the standard. "All of our cases share the theme of very heroic individuals engaged in occupations that are not only providing them with
a very good livelihood, but [whose legal cases] have the potential to
open up lots of opportunity for others," explained Mellor.

Even when the Institute for Justice lost cases in court, its media
operation, run by crack spinmeister John E. Kramer, usually exerted
enough pressure to force local politicians to throw out onerous regulations. In addition to hair braiders, the Institute's clients included jit-
ney drivers in Brooklyn and Queens who had been barred from
offering cheap rides to low-income commuters, and cab drivers in
Denver and Houston who were trying to break into government-
protected monopolies.

Each of these economic liberty cases made a compelling argument against the potential tyranny of bureaucracies. But as a group,
the Institute's lawsuits on behalf of entrepreneurs comprised a limited
and indirect assault on urban poverty: Critics would insist that they
were almost beside the point in cities where small businesses couldn't
obtain investment capital or insurance, where crime and drugs and
deindustrialization had driven out factories that once employed thousands. During the 1990s, it was the Clinton administration, which

drew mostly scorn from Bolick and his allies, that made great strides in reclaiming inner-city neighborhoods, block by block, by pumping in capital through federal support of community development corporations, and through stricter enforcement of federal laws requiring banks to lend to these communities.

But since the Institute for Justice's libertarian lawyers had philosophical objections to federal interventions, they designed a bottom-up legal approach. "You can't get capital if what you're doing is illegal," Mellor argued. Nearly five hundred occupations, covering 10 percent of all jobs in the country, are regulated by the states, he said, and about half of those require state licenses that often create a barrier to entry. (Bolick and Mellor didn't object to reasonable health, safety, and consumer protection rules imposed by states, though they acknowledged the difficulty of deciding which were reasonable.)

Politically, Bolick and Mellor were exploiting a potential political divide between middle-class members of ethnic minorities, who stand to benefit from race-based affirmative action programs, and those of the poor and working class, who are less likely to apply to a University of California campus, send a resumé to a *Fortune* 500 company, or secure a construction contract from the county. Typical of the Institute's clients was Taalib-Din Uqdah, the owner of a Washington, D.C., hair-braiding salon that faced fines and closure by regulators until Clint stepped in. "If you tell me affirmative action is trying to right some wrong, it hasn't helped me," said Uqdah, a largely self-educated man who describes himself as a "radical conservative." "Affirmative action has weakened an entire race of people. It's welfare for the educated." Eliminating racial preferences, he added, "will force people to find creative ways to make a living."

Unlike most liberals who battled Bolick, veteran civil rights leader Ralph Neas always believed Clint's efforts to help minorities were sincere. But he argued that Clint and his allies were blind to the subtle institutional obstacles—racial disparities in educational and employment testing, for example—that cannot be corrected without affirmative action. "On intentional discrimination," Neas said, "Clint is not that much different than me. But Clint is not willing to look at the hard stats. It's where you get into effects and results that we have the big battles."

Three years after helping to sink the Lani Guinier nomination, Clint again drew the scorn of liberals with his efforts on behalf of CCRI, arguably the largest civil rights battle of the decade. By then, the University of Texas and the University of California had already eliminated racial preferences—California by vote of its board of regents, Texas by court order. But the Republicans on Capitol Hill were far more reluctant to go down that road: In 1995, Clint helped craft legislation to abolish federal affirmative action programs but it languished in Congress.

The California measure, which appeared on the ballot in November 1996 as Proposition 209, shrewdly built on the language of the Fourteenth Amendment in outlawing the use of racial preferences by state and local governments: "The state shall not discriminate against, or grant preferential treatment to, any individual or group on the basis of race, sex, color, ethnicity or national origin in the operation of public employment, public education or public contracting." Clint offered creative political spin to CCRI organizers in a July 1996 memo, which argued that because "vocabulary matters greatly" they should avoid saying the measure would ban affirmative action. "Polls consistently show a large majority of Americans, spanning colors and genders, are opposed to racial preferences, but a slight majority favor 'affirmative action,' " he wrote. "We should argue that we *favor* affirmative action, in the sense of race- and gender-neutral methods to expand the pool of people capable of competing on an equal basis. That tends to translate into outreach and education, based on need, not color or gender. . . . We should not allow CCRI to be characterized as anti-affirmative action."

As the battle over CCRI raged in California through the summer and fall of 1996, Clint—eager to challenge that state's vast occupational licensing system—set out to find a hair-braiding client. Odds were that his position on CCRI would complicate his search—and it did. Through Uqdah, he met hair braider JoAnne Cornwell, the chairwoman of the Africana Studies program at San Diego State University. Unlike most of Clint's clients, Cornwell was a political sophisticate and a member of the academic elite. She was also a third-generation hair salon owner with grand ambitions for a hair-braiding technique she had trademarked under the name "Sisterlocks."

Cornwell's political views placed her far to the left of Bolick. As an educator, she was a vocal opponent of CCRI. As a black woman, she was a staunch critic of the Right's hands-off approach to business. "Extreme capitalism requires an underclass," she said of Clint's laissez-faire views, "and that underclass is going to look a lot like me." Baby-boom lawyer and baby-boom client stood on opposite sides of their generation's ideological divide. Where Bolick talked of oppressive bureaucracies and struggling individuals, Cornwell talked of racist power structures and struggling peoples. She organized her thoughts around ethnic groups; he organized his by personal rights.

To Clint, hair braiding was a matter of entrepreneurial freedom. To JoAnne, hair braiding was a matter of ethnic identity. "African-American women have a unique relationship with our hair," she said. "We are judged by whether our hair is straight or straight-looking. The damage that has been done is rooted deeply in our cultural psyche."

Nevertheless, Clint needed a hair-braiding client, and JoAnne needed Clint's free legal services if her business was to thrive. The pair would have to carve out a common language. What emerged in the early, slightly strained, conversations between JoAnne and Clint was a shared willingness to challenge the establishment, and a common comfort in employing a word popular among both liberals and conservatives in their generation: empowerment. She described her cause as one of people of color versus a white-created and controlled licensing authority. He described her cause as one of individual economic rights versus regulators interested in protecting the commercial status quo. Despite her concerns about his politics, JoAnne said, she "liked the fact that Clint's ultimate goal is to see people empowered."

On the morning of Tuesday, January 28 (the borscht and blintzes of the previous evening but a pleasant memory) Clint, JoAnne, and three other hair-braiding clients arrived at a press conference in downtown San Diego to announce the filing of their lawsuit, *Cornwell* v. *California Board of Barbering and Cosmetology*. In the months of strategy meetings preceding that day, Clint and JoAnne had adopted each other's language—and another strange-bedfellow political team was born.

"When you stifle the entrepreneurial urge in any community, you are doing violence to that community," Cornwell told reporters, her long lush locks flowing past her petite shoulders.

"This is not only economic suppression," asserted the balding Bolick as the TV cameras rolled, "but cultural suppression as well."

CHAPTER 15

THE SEARCH: 1996

I T WAS TO BE the election to seal the second millennium and make way for the third, swayed by a tectonic shift of American politics toward a new era of conservative ethics and morality. As a man of abiding Christian faith, who professed belief in the inerrancy of the Bible, Ralph Reed naturally thought in terms of great happenings infusing meaning in milestones of time. (Likewise, as a political animal, Ralph scripted his own life in four-year increments that coincided with the presidential election cycle.) The closing of the millennium was an important event, even in secular humanist America, where Reed now held a position somewhere between brilliant political strategist and dangerous demogogue. Stretching out each word as if to span the ages, Reed reminded his evangelical audiences as the 1996 presidential election approached: "We are choosing a new leader, not only for a new destiny, not only for the twenty-first century, but for the third millennium!"

Bill Kristol's faith in the upcoming presidential election, if not wrapped in millenarianism, was equally boundless as the campaign approached. "1996 is key," he wrote in a "Memo to Republican leaders" one year before the first primary. "The proto-realignment of 1994 needs to be confirmed and deepened by bigger Republican wins in 1996—extending control of Congress and gaining the Presidency.

All GOP decisions *this* year should be made strictly in the context of—even subordinated to—that goal." Whatever doubts Kristol had about the Republican Revolution still unfolding on Capitol Hill, he believed it demonstrated the emerging strength of conservatism in America—and the delicious possibility of recapturing the White House.

In Kristol's mind, as in Reed's, controlling Congress was insufficient to solidify conservatism as a majority position in America. To achieve that, the Right needed a popular president, and in early 1995 these two politicos had every reason to believe the movement could reinvent Ronald Reagan, a conservative who nevertheless looked gladsomely forward, a budget cutter trusted by the most skeptical Medicare patient, a nationalist who emboldened even young people to flaunt their respect for authority. In those first months of 1995 and the celebrated Republican Revolution, the Clinton presidency was shriveling before the nation's eyes ("hard to see how the President can recover in time for '96," Kristol wrote then) and the GOP had finally rid itself of the Bushyites. Here, at last, was a Republican presidential campaign that looked like it was the Right's to define, even win: Reagan II.

In the end, this presidential contest would alter the lives of both Kristol and Reed in ways they hadn't anticipated. Instead of finding the next Reagan, Kristol in late 1995 would make the startling shift from insider kingmaker to outside agitator, publishing a magazine that would become notorious among the party faithful for its assaults on the GOP and its nominee. Reed would collide against the confines of the movement he led, discovering the contradictions inherent in playing mainstream politics—securing a place at the table, as he put it—while leading an evangelical crusade.

And the man chosen to lead the Republican ticket—not a Ronald Reagan nor a creature of the Right, but a veteran politician who believed he needed the Right's support—would learn the dangers of dancing with revolutionaries.

AT THE TIME, Kristol and Reed were leading voices in a political movement at the height of its power and influence. That remained true even after the debacle of the government shutdowns: The 1995 budget confrontation demonstrated the limits of a movement intent on dismantling the Great Society and even the New Deal, but it didn't alter the fact that the nation was shifting rightward. Conservatives had set in motion the chain of events that would soon lead to the historic reform of welfare and an agreement to balance the budget for the first time in three decades. By transforming Clinton's promise of universal health care into an ideological debate over Big Government, they had demonstrated public intolerance for new programs (a sentiment that would constrain the Democrats' policy making for the rest of the decade). Inside the Republican Party, they had spawned an environment where any serious GOP presidential candidate would need to promise a major tax cut.

With the nation moving in their direction, Kristol and Reed, New York Jew and Southern evangelical, enjoyed reputations as two of the sharpest strategists on the political scene. Bill Bennett thought these two friends should hang out a shingle as political consultants, team up to demonstrate to all those third-rate professional hacks how a truly visionary campaign should be run. If the pair had taken Bennett's advice, it would have been the merger of two very different men, united in political cause but divided by far more than the ten years between them.

It would never occur to Bill, a man who grew up in the womb of the eastern intellectual elite, to advertise his Ph.D. with the title "Doctor Kristol." He had absorbed that studied (if false) modesty of Harvard graduates who, when asked where they went to college, respond simply "Boston." Ralph—"Dr. Reed" to his staff—yearned for the respect of the establishment press even as he bashed big-name reporters in front of activist audiences. (He once sent an aide scurrying for his copy of David Broder's latest book so the esteemed political journalist could sign it.) Reed flaunted his command of political history in talks to editorial boards and in press club speeches with titles such as "The New Great Awakening and the Role of Faith in Public Life," as if to demonstrate his bona fides to the national media. Kristol, on the other hand, talked to the press in shorthand and half-sentences, the way one might communicate with former classmates from prep school.

But in the game of electoral politics, Reed was subtle where Kristol was almost playfully blatant. Reed operated feline-like; his modus operandi was deniability. In the 1996 primaries, he planned to quietly deliver the evangelical vote to Senate Majority Leader Bob Dole— hardly a card-carrying member of the Christian Right, but the candidate he (and his boss Pat Robertson) believed stood the best chance of winning the White House for the Republicans. Kristol, by contrast, was like a big St. Bernard, barking his intentions to the world. He couldn't move voters, as Reed could, but he could move opinion makers at the highest levels of the GOP and the media. To Kristol, Dole was a candidate without a clear conservative vision, a disaster for the

Right's goal of shaping the Republican Party. More important, Kristol harbored serious doubts that Dole could win. He intended to block this front-runner by finding and promoting an alternative candidate, one who could win and who (willingly or not) would plant the Right's flag in the Oval Office.

But Kristol and Reed were united in their determination to prevent the Old Right—embodied in the candidacy of Patrick J. Buchanan—from capturing their movement. A genial but reactionary populist, Buchanan represented that side of the Right that was racially divisive, anti-immigrant, protectionist, and isolationist. Not only did these qualities precisely sum up what the baby-boom generation was trying to shed from the movement, they also added up to a losing combination in a general election. Buchanan was part of the Goldwater generation, which saw honor in losing on behalf of conviction. The baby-boom generation—which came to Washington in the shadow of a winner, Ronald Reagan—wanted to reclaim power and assumed it was within their reach. Buchanan's emergence as a presidential candidate threatened to relegate the baby boomers to the back of the bus in American politics.

Kristol was searching for a winner, but one with vision. Like others in the movement, he divided successful politicians into two broad categories: (1) idea-driven statesmen in the Ronald Reagan–Margaret Thatcher mold who knew precisely where they wanted to take the country, and (2) plodders, politicians like George Bush and John Major, whose personal ambitions ensured they would be at the right place at the right time, but whose leadership skills stopped at making hard decisions, not inventing the choices. The baby-boom Right categorized Bob Dole as a plodder, and that meant there was room in the race for a true conservative visionary.

Kristol had begun shopping for a candidate back in 1994, when he tried to convince Bill Bennett—whose best-selling *The Book of Virtues* granted him the role of nation's chief moralist—to seek the nomination. Bennett, then co-director of the Washington-based think tank Empower America, had heard the exhortation from Kristol (and Reed, too) before, and frequently. "It's almost funny, like he can't stop himself," the former education secretary said of his former chief of staff. Despite renewed lobbying by Kristol and others, Bennett opted out in the summer of 1994.

Over the next eighteen months, Kristol searched in vain for the next Ronald Reagan. There was Texas Senator Phil Gramm, whose credentials on paper should have made him the odds-on favorite of the conservative movement. Gramm was a smart, well-funded, visionary candidate. But his large and insular ego turned off conservative opinion makers and suggested a fatal weakness in his prospects for victory. Once, when Pat Robertson and Ralph Reed paid a call, Gramm sat at his computer terminal, eyes locked on the screen, engaged in a pedantic monologue about the mechanics of raising money for a presidential race. As they left, Robertson told Reed to cross the Texan's name off the Christian Coalition's most-favored-candidate list.

Then there was General Colin Powell, Reagan's national security adviser and a Gulf War hero who was drawing huge and enthusiastic crowds in the fall of 1995 as he peddled his best-selling autobiography. At every stop, the African-American general was asked if he would run for president; media pundits had practically canonized him. In Kristol's mind, Powell embodied the two necessary sides of a winning Republican candidate: He was a tax-cutter whose own life embodied the vision of an America rooted in morality and personal responsibility. There was also a visceral cultural connection between Kristol's neoconservative forebears, children of New York's Jewish European immigrants, and Powell, son of West Indian immigrants who grew up in the South Bronx. To both, education and boot-strap effort had been the escape hatch from poverty, and neither put much stock in racism (Powell's case) or anti-Semitism (the neoconservatives') as rationale for failure.

When Kristol launched his new magazine, the *Weekly Standard,* in the fall of 1995, he also launched a personal Powell-for-President campaign. Noting Dole's downward trajectory in the polls, Kristol argued that the moderate Powell could win the nomination, "especially if [he] throws a few bones to conservatives by saying the right things about personal responsibility, no new taxes and limited government." Powell was far too centrist to be a candidate of the Right. Kristol reasoned, however, that a Powell presidency would leave the Republican Congress free to steer domestic policy rightward.

But Powell was everything that the hard-core Right despised, a pro-choice Republican who proclaimed he was not "knee-jerk antigovernment," and who vigorously defended Social Security and Medicare. Powell had attacked the "extreme right who seem to claim divine wisdom on political as well as spiritual matters," and he called the Contract with America "a little too hard, a little too harsh, a little too unkind." Grover Norquist, still director of Americans for Tax Reform, resolved to put an end to Kristol's romance before it got out of hand.

Together with leaders of a dozen other rightist groups, Grover booked a room at the National Press Club one November morning in 1995 to issue a formal denunciation of Powell. The line-up of critics at the podium that morning fulfilled every stereotype of the ill-mannered right-winger. Veteran conservative strategist Paul Weyrich set the tone by likening the former chairman of the Joint Chiefs of Staff to a Gilbert and Sullivan figure who had become "ruler of the Queen's Navy by polishing the handles on the big brass front door." The activists didn't confine their attacks to Powell's policy positions, with Weyrich raising doubts about his "character" and other leaders threatening to turn over every rock in the general's military and political past if he chose to run.

Kristol dismissed the press conference as "chest-thumping childishness by portly conservatives." It was classic hubris, Kristol said, for the Right's activists to assume they could intimidate a nationally beloved figure such as Powell. Kristol wasn't the only conservative leader appalled by Grover's press conference. "This was the one event where I felt most ashamed being associated with religious conservatives," recalled Christian Coalition lobbyist Marshall Wittmann. "I thought it was one of the most despicable events ever held. Here you have an African-American general, a hero, considering becoming a Republican candidate and here was a group of people trashing him with the most personal invective."

The one figure visibly missing from this fracas on the Right was Ralph, who—unlike Kristol—was not a man eager to make public enemies. Ralph's penchant for shaving the jagged edges off policy positions extended to his relationships with public figures. So he sent word to the press conference organizers that he was on vacation, but insiders said his absence was no accident of timing: Ralph didn't want to take sides. (On the question of Powell, moreover, the history was more complicated than anyone knew at the time: In 1993, Pat Robertson, with Reed in tow, had met with Powell and urged him to unite the party by running for president.) But by dodging this particular ball, Ralph would later set off a barrage of attacks from his right flank that never let up.

After Powell bowed out of the race on November 8, Kristol—again using the *Weekly Standard* as his megaphone—flirted briefly with the idea of a Newt Gingrich candidacy. Millionaire publisher Malcolm Forbes, a wooden figure, appealed to tax activists such as Grover with his flat-tax proposal, but turned off social conservatives. Over the holiday season, Kristol threw his media weight behind former Tennessee Governor and Bush Education Secretary Lamar Alexander, a long-shot whose talk of the need to reinvigorate "civil society"—family, neighborhood, churches, schools, civic groups, private charities—appealed to modern-day Tocquevilles in the movement. But Alexander's star sank in the early primaries, and Bill Kristol's last shot at riding a conservative candidate into the 1996 presidential campaign was gone.

BETWEEN 1993 AND 1995, Kristol had positioned himself as a cheerleader and strategist eager to help his chosen party recapture the White House. (Though Bill's own West Wing lust was so conspicuous that friends joked his fax operation was actually a well-financed "Kristol-for-White House-Chief-of-Staff" campaign.) But in 1996, as Bob Dole emerged as the front-runner, Kristol used his new magazine, the *Weekly Standard,* to pillory his own party and its likely nominee. "Bob Dole is likely to lose," Bill wrote in April, a full seven months before the general election. "He may lose badly. . . . [C]onservatives must not subordinate all their efforts to the Dole campaign, must not succumb to the siren song of 'teamwork,' and must not defer to Dole." He also freely aired his complaints to reporters, calling the staff-heavy Dole campaign "witless" and likening it to the Politburo: "They sit around reassuringly saying, 'Tractor production's up 400% Mr. General Secretary. . . .'"

Generally, when Bill's name was heard inside Dole headquarters, it was attached to a choice epithet. Kristol "constantly crapped on us," growled a key Dole operative. What Dole and his inner circle didn't know was that their nemesis had the gall to try to shape their campaign even as he assailed it. In July, three months after predicting Dole's defeat, Kristol worked through his good friend, Dole policy adviser Kevin Stach, to promote Bennett as a candidate for the vice president slot. Kristol primed the pumps during his increasingly regular appearances as a commentator on ABC-TV. On July 21, he told viewers of the Sunday talk show *This Week with David Brinkley* that a Bennett VP candidacy was a "long-shot possibility. He and Dole have not been close, but if you wanted a pick that would energize . . . the Republican Party and conservatives, but would also speak to lots of Americans out there . . ." Bennett was the man. Dole apparently agreed, though Bennett bowed out before Dole could formally extend an invitation.

Then Kristol fixed his attention on former congressman Jack Kemp, who had served as secretary of housing and urban development under Bush and was now Bennett's co-director at Empower America. Baby-boom conservatives were drawn to Kemp's Reaganesque, forward-looking demeanor and tax-cutting ideas, though they gulped when he occasionally embraced liberal solutions in his eagerness to aid the urban poor. He also suffered from a reputation as an undisciplined candidate. Nevertheless, Kristol believed Kemp would bring vision—and the prospect of victory—to the ticket. Like Bennett, Kemp had the national stature, and star quality, to give a much needed jolt to a ticket that was 20 points down.

On August 6, two days after Bennett preemptively rejected the VP job, Kristol was back on ABC's *Good Morning America,* in his role as political commentator, floating Kemp's name. Later that day, Kristol called Dole campaign manager Scott Reed to congratulate him on the warm reception Dole's economic plan had received, and to apologize for the dead-end run on Bennett. Then, as a gentle prod, Kristol asked the Dole campaign manager what he thought of that morning's mention of Kemp. Did Scott think the idea was totally hopeless? Would Kristol be whistling in the wind if he repeated Kemp's name again the next day on the morning program? "No," said Scott, "I don't think it's totally hopeless."

BACK IN 1995, Bob Dole—not a man known for insurgent temperament—had mostly remained in lockstep with the Republican Revolution unfolding in the House. It was a political calculation based on fear as much as anything else—fear that conservative activists, who now dominated much of the GOP, could deny him the Republican nomination, and fear that a candidate like Gramm might swamp him from the Right. What wouldn't become clear until much later was the price he would pay for that calculation when he had to face moderate voters in the general election. Until late 1995, Dole had been running neck and neck with Clinton in the polls. After the two government shutdowns (during which Dole repeatedly sought an "exit strategy"), he dropped behind Clinton by double digits. That gap wouldn't narrow until the last weeks before the election, when the first allegations of a Democratic fund-raising scandal surfaced, driving down Clinton's numbers.

Dole wasn't the only presidential candidate courting the Right. In September 1995, nearly all of the GOP hopefuls showed up to woo four thousand Christian Coalition activists at Ralph's annual "Road to Victory" conference. The turnout of presidential candidates put Reed in a millennial mood. It was clear to the political world that he had, at last, arrived. ("I used to be in awe of these guys," he boasted to friends. "Now I got them eating out of my hand.") Just two years after the *Washington Post* had described the Religious Right as "poor, uneducated, and easy to command," the political press corps was not only offering Ralph a place at the table, it was setting out the silverware: "Christian Coalition Wields Conservative Clout," asserted *USA Today.* "Christian Group Flexes Newfound Muscles," blared the *Washington Post.*

Money was rolling into the Christian Coalition, and just as quickly rolling out—for expensive direct-mail campaigns; for a burgeoning staff; for the cutting-edge technology underlying its rapid-fire data banks. The Coalition claimed to have a computer base of 1.7 million religious conservatives nationwide—their names, addresses, phone numbers, precincts, congressional districts, contributions to the Christian Coalition, issue interests, volunteer histories. But that number, routinely reported in much of the media as the Coalition's "membership," actually was a compilation of everyone who had had even the most minimal contact with the group, including petition signers and callers to the Coalition's 800 number. Reliable insiders put the true membership of the Coalition—at its peak in 1996—at just shy of 600,000. According to U.S. Postal Service records, the Coalition's magazine—mailed to anyone who sent in the $15 annual membership fee—went to just over 300,000 households. Even among insiders, Ralph was notorious for his opaque and overly boastful claims about the size of the Coalition. As reporters pressed him at one impromptu news conference, he finally blurted out: "If anything, we're probably underestimating the number of people involved in the organization. It's really closer to 3 million. . . . I've got to go now—"

Still, the Christian Coalition's ability to get out the vote in close elections was real, and had been demonstrated in several House and Senate contests in 1994. That year, the magazine *Campaigns and Elections* credited the Christian Coalition with being dominant in Republican Parties in eighteen states and substantial in thirteen more. So the Republican presidential hopefuls who showed up to court the four thousand Christian activists at the "Road to Victory" conference were acutely aware that they were tapping into networks of voters back home capable of pulling a candidate over the top in early primary states. Also, the Christian Coalition was grooming hundreds of activists to run as delegates to the Republican convention the following summer, so these evangelicals would be a powerful force in shaping the party's platform on abortion and other issues.

Pat Robertson boasted that the Coalition planned to expand its dominance over the GOP to all fifty states and to elect "a conservative president." But Ralph, keenly aware of the Federal Election Commission's thickening file of allegations that the Coalition had violated federal law by campaigning on behalf of candidates, intended to wield the Coalition's muscle with the subtlety of a Navy SEAL. He also wanted to make sure that when the election was over, no one could blame "the Christian Right" for costing the GOP the White House, as had happened in 1992. In speaking to reporters, he boasted of the Coalition's power—"42 percent of all Republican primary voters are self-identified born-again evangelicals and about 22 percent are members of the Coalition"—but he steered the conversation away from descriptions of how that power might play out in a particular primary race. Instead, he'd tell the press, coyly, "I would rather have a thousand school board members and two thousand state legislators than a single president."

Out of the media spotlight, Reed was quietly warming up to the likely front-runner, Bob Dole. Two, three times a week he was on the phone with his good friend, Dole campaign manager Scott Reed. Privately, Ralph was generous with advice to the Dole campaign; publicly he was fulsome in his defense of the candidate. To political reporters, he touted Dole as the likely nominee. Regardless of Reed's protestations that he didn't endorse candidates, activist leaders interpreted his steadfast loyalty to Dole as an implicit endorsement.

Ralph hedged his bet, though. He kept one foot in the camp of Dole's most likely challenger, Phil Gramm, when key Coalition state officials joined the Texan's campaign. He remained on good terms with Lamar Alexander, too, giving him a thumbs-up on abortion in Iowa, both in the Christian Coalition voter guide and on national TV, even though Alexander's position wasn't sufficiently pro-life to satisfy purists. And Ralph was always chummy and publicly effusive toward Buchanan, even though, as one Christian Coalition insider put it, "We didn't build up this movement so that Pat Buchanan could come along and hijack it."

Buchanan was certain to get trounced in the general election, leaving Christian conservatives to shoulder the blame. Even his appearance in the primary field was a setback to Ralph's diligent makeover of the Christian Right. Reed's version of social conservatism appealed to those evangelicals eager to demonstrate that wanting to protect the unborn and defend traditional values didn't make them racist or intolerant or hateful. Buchanan's social conservatism appealed to evangelicals' fears and anxieties. Reed's was inclusive; Buchanan's was divisive. Reed spoke best to suburbanites who had a relatively secure place in America's economy; Buchanan spoke to the economically distressed facing a rapidly changing international market. (His protectionist stance was especially anathema to an international mogul like Pat Robertson.) Buchanan was the past; Reed's eye was on the future.

But saying any of this publicly would be risky for a Religious Right leader. (Colleagues recalled Ralph's stray remark, made in one meeting as the primary season approached—"I'm gonna break Buchanan's neck and leave him in the snow, without any fingerprints"—suggesting that Reed hadn't lost his penchant for colorful guerrilla rhetoric.) Among Christian Coalition members in 1995, Buchanan polled slightly higher than either Dole or Gramm. More to the point, it was Buchanan, a Catholic, who invariably lit up gatherings of Protestant evangelical activists. With his emotional and heartfelt anti-abortion pitch, he got them stomping and cheering and standing on chairs. For those who believed that abortion, at any stage of pregnancy, was tantamount to infanticide, Buchanan left nowhere else to go. He proposed defining life as beginning at conception and favored an abortion ban that provided exceptions only to save a mother's life. Dole, who supported a ban that would provide exceptions for victims of rape or incest, never appeared to have his heart in the issue (his aides frankly wished the whole messy subject would just go away).

If Buchanan was to be stopped, it would have to be a no-fingerprints job. Even then, the strategy almost blew up on Reed and Robertson, right out of the starting box. When the Christian Coalition sent out invitations to the September 1995 "Road to Victory" rally, the cover featured a collage of photos of invited speakers; conspicuously missing was Buchanan's picture. Inside, Buchanan's name appeared toward the end of a list of featured speakers. The Buchanan campaign went ballistic—here was proof that Reed and Robertson intended to sabotage their campaign. Buchanan threatened to cancel his planned appearance, and only after much negotiation in the final days before the event did he commit to come. For Ralph, a Buchanan no-show would have meant certain mutiny among most diehard activists.

In early 1996, less than five months after the "Road to Victory" rally, Ralph put his strategy for delivering the evangelical vote to Dole into action. But it took just two states to prove how difficult this mission would be. In the Iowa caucuses, Buchanan's strong second-place finish to Dole was largely underwritten by conservative Christians, 41 percent of whom offered their vote to the Old Right candidate—even though the president of the state's Christian Coalition had personally endorsed Dole. In the New Hampshire primary, Buchanan won with the help of 51 percent of self-described evangelicals, four times as many as Dole and Alexander drew. (Since evangelicals constituted only one-tenth of the vote in New Hampshire, it was mostly Buchanan's economic populism that fueled his victory there.)

South Carolina's March 2 primary, the first southern vote of the season, was critical to all of the presidential candidates. In the South, where evangelicals comprised 40 percent of the vote, Buchanan's moral message had the potential to find a large and receptive audience. But Reed, who spent his high school years across the border in Georgia, was convinced that he understood South Carolina better than Buchanan, a northern Catholic. For all Buchanan's eagerness to push Confederate hot buttons, the candidate (Ralph was sure) would fail to connect with modern South Carolina voters. Buchanan defended flying the Confederate flag on the state capitol as "a symbol of defiance, courage, bravery," but Ralph didn't see any political gains to be made from tackling that issue head-on: He knew that modern evangelicals felt great ambivalence about the legacy of segregation, which was just as woven into that flag's stars and bars as memories of slavery. Buchanan offered a protectionist message to textile workers who had lost their jobs because of foreign competition, but Ralph had watched the rise of the New South economy, aided by infusions of international investment. Even abortion wasn't as much of a hot-button issue as Buchanan hoped it would be: According to exit polls, abortion ranked fourth, behind economic issues, as the subject that most influenced Republican primary voters in that state.

The Christian Coalition chapter in South Carolina, led by veteran politico Roberta Combs, was probably the strongest in the country. Publicly, Combs remained neutral, but Dole supporters boasted to the media of help she provided. Moreover, her husband endorsed Dole. But here the story, like the state, has a more complex subplot. The state's Republican governor, David Beasley, an evangelical Christian who was an important bridge between religious activists and the party establishment, supported Dole, and he planned to deliver both ends of that bridge to his candidate. But local Christian Coalition activists supporting Buchanan almost ambushed him.

For the Thursday night before the state's Saturday primary, the Christian Coalition had organized a much-heralded "God and Country" rally in a downtown Columbia hotel. In the hours leading up to the event, which would draw nineteen TV cameras and every bigfoot political reporter in the country, it was becoming clear to Beasley's staff that the ballroom would be laden with Buchananites. If that were true, the event would produce major media stories portraying the state's evangelicals as embracing Pat Buchanan, not Bob Dole. Word went out to the event's organizers: Beasley would recommend that Dole stay away.

Negotiations between the Christian Coalition and Beasley's staff ensued, and a last-minute compromise was reached: Dole would show, but only if a large contingent of his supporters were allowed to enter the ballroom early so they could sit up front. The Dole campaign culled volunteers from Columbia and nearby Lexington. They even brought in van-loads of supporters from other parts of the state. When the candidates arrived at the rally, the screams of "Go Pat Go" were offset by shouts for Dole. The room was so packed because of the doubled crowd that fire marshalls descended to shut the doors.

Buchanan predictably set off the most sparks, even with the watered-down crowd. But Dole, surrounded by the state's Republican establishment and introduced by Beasley as "a man who loves God," offered a moving rendition of his struggle to regain his life after the traumatic injuries he suffered as a GI in World War II. The crowd was enthused, and the press coverage glowed. When Dole handily won the South Carolina primary two days later, Dole campaign aides privately gave Ralph less credit than they gave Beasley. But the national media credited Ralph with the whole victory. "Bob Dole owes Ralph Reed, big time," journalist Eleanor Clift told *McLaughlin Group* viewers.

Mutiny began to fester inside the ranks of the Christian Coalition. From the field came threats of resignations and calls of complaints that Ralph was locked in a behind-the-scenes alliance with Dole. The heat became so great that on Monday, March 18, Reed sent a fax to state and chapter leaders around the country, denying that he or the Christian Coalition had taken sides in the race. "I made no effort to encourage or dissuade any of our state or local leaders to become involved in any campaign or endorse a given candidate," Reed wrote. Media reports alleging otherwise "are inaccurate." But Robertson didn't help his employee's case when he asserted April 2 on *The 700 Club* show that without the Christian Coalition, "probably Bob Dole wouldn't be the nominee, they've helped him."

In fact, troop restlessness about Ralph's loyalty to Dole fed a festering unease about a more central concern: Ralph's position on abortion. In early 1995, the Coalition spent $1 million lobbying for the Contract with America, which didn't even mention abortion. That May, when Ralph released his Contract with the American Family without comparable financial backing, the document noted the Coalition's support for "constitutional and statutory protection for the unborn child." However, its legislative action plan stopped at calling for a ban on partial-birth abortions, which are rare, and ending taxpayer subsidies to organizations that promote and perform abortions. Six major pro-family groups denounced the Coalition for failing to propose any type of ban on early abortions, which account for nearly 97 percent of all terminated pregnancies. One pro-life leader said the Coalition's position was the equivalent of "closing one-third of Nazi death camps."

Abortion was also at the heart of the matter when James C. Dobson, president of Focus on the Family, one of the groups that had denounced the Christian Coalition, issued a searing indictment of Ralph in October of 1995. Dobson's family-advice radio show, carried on 1,500 radio stations nationally, attracted 5 million loyal listeners; his organization maintained a mailing list three times the size of the Christian Coalition's. Dobson wasn't very visible in Washington circles, preferring to leave his public policy work in the hands of Gary Bauer, one of Bill Kristol's closest friends and the head of the D.C.-based Family Research Council. And until he ran for president four years later, Bauer never achieved the same celebrity status accorded Ralph. At pro-life rallies in 1996, swarms of TV cameras dogged Reed while Bauer sat quietly off to the side, like the unpopular kid at a school dance. But these looks were deceiving. When an issue the Family Research Council cared about surfaced on Capitol Hill, Dobson and Bauer could—and did—inundate the place with phone calls and postcards.

Dobson was angry because Ralph, appearing on a Sunday news talk show, refused to condemn Colin Powell for supporting legal abortion. Dobson splayed his rage across a four-and-a-half-page single-spaced letter to Ralph. "Lord help us, Ralph!" Dobson exclaimed. "Is power the motivator of this great crusade? If so, it will sour and turn to bile in your mouth. . . . Who cares whether or not you or I have a place at the table? . . . There is temptation in all of us to bend to the pressures of pragmatism and personal ambition. . . . I have seen the warning signs in your recent appearances."

Friends encouraged Ralph to lob a bomb back at Dobson—certainly that was what Bill Bennett, also a target of Dobson's scourge, had done. Reed was all fired up to do just that, friends recalled. So they were surprised that Ralph's reply was as polite as a choirboy's. "You suggest that I should have attacked Colin Powell more aggressively. That is an honest disagreement. My own view is that he is unlikely to run. . . ." Eager to demonstrate his ideological credentials,

Reed recalled arriving at one speech and being forced to use the back entrance because of "two hundred [leftist] protesters waving signs and screaming my name like an epithet. Jim, if you do now know this, they surely do: I will never retreat, I will never quit, I will never falter in my struggle for these values."

Dobson was an unbending purist prone to shrill denunciations of his opponents. But his presence on Reed's right had the effect of making the Christian Coalition director look—to many activists—like someone a little too chummy with the enemy, a little too eager to be popular with the national media. There was also overlap in the membership of Dobson's and Reed's organizations, making Dobson a leading figure within the Christian Coalition.

Like other baby-boom conservatives, Ralph had a strong pragmatic streak and understood that most Americans supported legal, if restricted, abortion. Congress was nowhere close to adopting an outright ban. A number of conservative thinkers—among them Kristol, Bennett, and George Weigel, president of the Washington-based Ethics and Public Policy Center—had made the case that opponents of abortion should shift their focus from seeking a legal ban to changing a culture that produced 1.6 million abortions a year. This "moral suasion" strategy would focus on abstinence programs to curb unwanted pregnancies and the promotion of domestic adoptions, while seeking incremental legal restrictions on abortion such as parental consent statutes, waiting periods, and a ban on partial-birth abortions.

But to activists in the field, Ralph's maneuvering on abortion looked suspiciously like part of a master plan to boost Dole's candidacy. In May 1996, with the publication of Ralph's second book, *Active Faith* (for which he had received a $400,000-plus advance), Reed's anti-abortion allies saw confirmation that the young Christian Coalition leader was a Judas in the making, ready to betray their cause for a seat at Bob Dole's conference table. On Saturday morning, May 4, a *New York Times* headline blared: "Top Conservative Would Back Shift on Abortion Issue." And below that, "Seen as Dole Supporter." A few days later an excerpt of the book in *Newsweek* highlighted Ralph's central argument: "The Religious Right must give ground—or risk irrelevance."

"Giving ground" was not part of the anti-abortion movement's vocabulary in 1996. Hewing to the most extreme position—a Constitutional amendment to outlaw abortion—was a testament to the strength of one's convictions, to one's resilience against the worldly temptation of political relevance. Four years earlier Phyllis Schlafly, who had crafted the unyielding Republican platform plank on abortion, proposed updating it into a statement of "principle" rather than law. Even she was forced to back down in the face of grass-roots opposition. So, the plank remained intact: "The unborn child has a fundamental individual right to life which cannot be infringed. We support a human life amendment to the Constitution, and we endorse legislation to make clear that the Fourteenth Amendment's protections apply to unborn children."

Dole had to walk a fine line on abortion: To gain the nomination, he needed to avoid angering powerful pro-life forces. But against Clinton in the upcoming general election, he would need to appeal to centrist voters. A handful of moderate Republican governors were pressing him to soften the party's abortion plank. At first, the pragmatic Ralph Reed looked like a promising broker, someone who could persuade evangelicals to support the effort. But could he deliver? The reaction to the May 4 *New York Times* story suggested he could not.

The morning the story appeared, angry calls started pouring into Ralph's office. He issued a statement denouncing the story as "totally inaccurate" and placed a call to the *Times*. In a second interview with the *New York Times*'s James Bennet, Reed explained that while he might accept an exception for rape and incest in legislation banning abortion—but only if that's what it took to get it passed—he wasn't referring to exceptions in a constitutional amendment, as Bennet suggested. He also rejected the implication that he would support efforts to weaken the abortion plank at the GOP's upcoming convention in San Diego. In a second front-page story, Bennet made another attempt to explain Reed's highly nuanced position. The *Times* reporter could be forgiven for the confusion: Following the skips and shuffles in Reed's abortion position, whether it was laid out in interviews or in his new book, was a little like trying to learn the zydeco step backward.

In *Active Faith*, Reed appeared to back away from his prior support for a human life amendment, arguing that "it has become apparent that amending the Constitution may be the least practical and most remote weapon at our disposal." But he also wrote that he would "personally support" all legal and constitutional remedies to protect innocent human life. He criticized Kristol's "moral suasion" argument, yet he wrote that "until public opinion shifts on a political solution to abortion, outlawing all abortions by constitutional fiat would create the same dilemma for pro-lifers that the prohibitionist movement faced. . . . [We must] pour our greatest efforts into education, persuasion and prayer—not politics alone."

Did he support a revised Republican platform, or not? Did he endorse the pro-life movement's current course, or not? Was he promoting the "moral suasion" argument, or not? Did he mean it, or not, when he wrote in the *Newsweek* excerpt: "As a community of faith, we stand at a crossroads. Down one path lies . . . irrelevance and obscurity. It is a path defined by its spiritual arrogance"? If he meant it, why the timidity with the *New York Times?* Why didn't he step up to the plate and lay out a bold new direction for the anti-abortion movement, as his book suggested he intended to do?

The answer could be found in those phone calls to his office from irate leaders of the anti-abortion movement chastising him, like nuns taking the ruler to an errant schoolboy. "Nobody agreed with him," Schlafly recalled, "so he was left out on a limb and had to backtrack. . . . People were very upset with Ralph. Everybody was very upset." After the *Newsweek* excerpt, Gary Bauer privately told Reed his words were damaging to the movement. Others took their grievances public. "It's tragic," said Judie Brown of the American Life League. "He's taken the child in the womb and that baby has become a political football to him, and that is sad." Angela "Bay" Buchanan, Pat's sister and campaign manager, said Ralph had lost his credibility inside the pro-life movement. "There is no question," she said, "that [Reed] no longer represents those of us who feel very strongly about family values and life and the importance of the Republican platform."

For the second time that campaign season, Ralph was forced to protect his right flank with an "urgent statement" faxed to the field: "The Christian Coalition opposes abortion in every case except when the mother's life is in danger. We will oppose with every fiber of our being any effort to include a rape and incest exception in the pro-life plank or to drop a call for constitutional and legal remedies such as an amendment to the Constitution."

The boy-genius and master politician suddenly looked like a rank amateur. His timing was off: He hadn't anticipated that the growing chorus of pro-choice governors and senators eager to soften the abortion plank would make pro-lifers especially prickly that spring. He hadn't calculated that the price he would have to pay for his quiet alliance with Dole was a no-holds-barred defense of the GOP abortion plank. And he failed to intuit that he was the wrong person at the wrong time to lead the movement in a more pragmatic direction. Even if the pro-life community was ready to hear a new message, it would have to come from a purist, not a darling of the national media.

Later, it would all become clear to Reed: The Christian Coalition's activist members hadn't turned their lives over to campaigning for delegate seats and school boards and county councils because they felt passionately, deeply, powerfully about big government, tax cuts, and the plight of black America. What fueled Reed's activist base was raw emotion over the decline of national morality, symbolized by 1.6 million abortions a year. As the leader of a political movement, Ralph knew that if he lost his base, he'd lose everything. Was he risking his core supporters in his quest for a seat at the table?

In the unfolding presidential campaign, Ralph tried to shore up his own pro-life credentials. A month after the fracas over his book, when Dole did his own flip-flop on abortion, Reed held the candidate's feet to the fire, threatening a floor fight at the upcoming GOP convention. But the purist posturing came too late. While many Christian Coalition activists still adored Ralph and appreciated the favorable media he brought to their movement, others were growing uneasy. Said one insider: "Once doubts started to arise in the field as to whether the Christian Coalition was there to call the nation back to God, or whether there was a political agenda being pursued, designed to feather the nests of certain people—once those questions are put in people's minds, they never go away."

That year, 1996, contributions to the Christian Coalition peaked and a downward slide began.

THE 1996 REPUBLICAN CONVENTION that opened in San Diego in August was going to be Bob Dole's show. The Right's ideologues weren't going to steal his thunder, as they had with George Bush four years earlier in Houston, when talk of a "cultural war" filled the air. This convention was going to be as spritely and telegenic as its host city.

Dole lost a major battle with the Right the week before the convention opened, when a "fearsome foursome" alliance of Schlafly–Bauer–Bay Buchanan–Reed used their delegate strength on the platform committee to squelch his attempt to soften the abortion plank and add language expressing "tolerance" for Republicans with different opinions on the issue. Though Ralph was publicly part of that alliance—pushing the purist position as if paying a penance—the Dole campaign had privately concluded that he could not deliver delegate votes on a compromise; any agreement would need the blessing of the three hard-liners. So while campaign officials mostly negotiated with Schlafly, Ralph stood outside in the hall, offering commentary and sound bites to the reporters surrounding him.

For Dole, the headlines that followed—variations on "Dole Camp Retreats on Abortion"—were an embarrassing distraction from the unveiling of his much-hyped 15 percent tax cut plan, announced the same day. But at least the divisive abortion battle had been laid to rest, leaving GOP regulars free to choreograph San Diego as a convention with ambitions squarely in the middle, with moderates dominating the podium and the Right relegated to a sideshow. But what a sideshow it was: Ralph intrigued reporters with talk of his "war room," operating from a "secret" location somewhere in the city (actually it was inside a twenty-first-floor suite in the Marriott tower next to the convention center, and reporters who checked in with the Coalition's P.R. man were treated to a grand tour). Mimicking White House control centers established for key legislative battles, this war room consisted of staffers sitting at computers, and wall charts of the group's elaborate system of 102 floor whips, equipped with minicomputers that relayed e-mail on the convention floor.

It was an impressive (and expensive) setup, even though—with the abortion platform settled and pro-life Jack Kemp on the ticket—the closest thing to military action that Ralph's soldiers would see that week was outside the window, where a U.S. Navy warship sat docked in the diamond waters of the San Diego bay. But Ralph knew, instinctively, that a good bit of politics was showmanship, and the digital equipment and the staffed-up war room fluffed his plumage, reminding everyone that the Christian Coalition was a modern electoral machine, able to organize and deliver votes. "We're just going to be doing some dry runs for 2000," Reed spinned reporters. "This thing [the convention] is really put to bed, which is fabulous."

The '92 and '96 Republican conventions were like night and day for Reed and Kristol. Both were now bona fide media celebrities. On the convention floor, a pack of reporters and photographers hovered by Ralph, hoping for a stray sound bite on the opening morning of a convention designed to avoid making news. When he sat, they waited. When he rose, they stirred. When he walked out, they followed. Only one other person on the floor drew comparable media attention, and that was Newt Gingrich.

Kristol's pundit skills were in high demand that week, his pancake makeup wearing thin as he balanced early morning commentaries on ABC's *Good Morning America* with appearances on PBS's *The NewsHour with Jim Lehrer* and a host of other interviews in between. Despite his new life as magazine publisher and news commentator, reporters still labeled Bill a "Republican strategist," enabling him to move in a narrow corridor between insider and outsider. Had he pushed a Colin Powell candidacy, in his *Weekly Standard* magazine and on air, to save the GOP or to fuel magazine subscriptions? When, on ABC, he had dropped the names of Bennett and then Kemp as vice presidential possibilities, was he offering viewers the inside scoop, or pushing his own agenda with the Dole camp, or both?

That week in San Diego, the baby-boom conservatives were in a mood that editorialist and fellow traveler John Fund aptly described as "cautiously giddy optimism." With Kemp on the ticket, Dole's poll numbers had bounced upward, and, for the first time, the prospect of a Republican victory in November looked like more than just a hallucination. Even Kristol, for all his sour prognostications, was beginning to wonder if he'd been wrong: Maybe the Dole campaign *had* found a path to victory. "It's depressing because they may be right," he told one reporter.

The image of a President Dole was almost enough to take the edge off Ralph's morning on the third day of the convention, as he paced the colonnaded breezeway of Balboa Park's Organ Pavilion, where a crowd of 4,500 was gathering under a searing sun. His cell phone crunched to his ear, Ralph was trying to convince the Dole campaign to send over one of the candidates—if not Dole, at least Kemp—to address his "Faith and Freedom Celebration." He was enough of a political realist to know that with the primaries over and the general campaign in full swing a Dole appearance before the Right's evangelicals could hurt the candidate by reviving the specter of Houston and divisive culture wars. Still, Ralph figured that Dole would be astute enough to come by and "lay a little lipstick on the collar" of activists who had figured prominently in his nomination victory.

So as the heat beat down on his black suit, Ralph busied himself with dressing up his event for mainstream consumption. This was a looser crowd than the middle-aged matrons who had dominated Schlafly's pro-family event the day before (and larger too, Ralph noted to himself). His soccer moms and athlete dads were joined by the biker who found Jesus after a bad acid trip and the Rastafarian who folded a newspaper into a hat to top off his dreadlocks. In contrast to Phyllis's brass band, Ralph offered a hip young woman in black who sang Christian pop. But the hard-core anti-abortion forces turned out in full force too. Looming as backdrops to Ralph's rally were six-foot-tall posters showing aborted fetuses, compliments of Operation Rescue activists. Ralph got on his cell phone to direct an aide to remove the offending propaganda. When the Operation Rescue squad refused, threatening to let themselves be arrested on trespass charges, Ralph dropped the issue, knowing that arrests would create even more of a scene.

When the rally began, Ralph stepped to his microphone at center stage and offered glowing introductions to a series of speakers that included not only loyal Rightists like Dan Quayle and Newt Gingrich, but also a former leader of the Jewish (and generally liberal) Anti-Defamation League, who proclaimed that he, too, believed that "liberalism was leaving our country in tatters." Ralph issued his own message of inclusion, asserting that the Republican Party "stood for people who had been left behind because of a different color and a different ethnic background. Today it must stand for marginalized people. It must stand for the unborn. It must stand for the minority adolescent in the inner city who is walking through a metal detector. . . ." (As he spoke, he faced a huge white cross, held aloft in the center of the audience alongside a sign reading: PRO-LIFE WITHOUT COMPROMISE. WITHOUT EXCEPTION. WITHOUT APOLOGY. Was this a message meant for him?)

As Ralph finished speaking, word trickled through the crowd that the Republican Party honchos had agreed to send over an emissary. But it wouldn't be Bob Dole, nor his wife Elizabeth. Jack Kemp wasn't coming either. Instead, the party regulars had settled on Joanne Kemp, wife of the vice presidential nominee—a great woman, a solid Christian, but, to be honest, the bottom of the GOP ticket's food chain. Ralph had just been offered a pointed reminder of his new place inside Bob Dole's Republican Party.

"I'M GONNA POP 'EM . . . I'm gonna pop 'em . . ." One month after the Republican convention, Ralph was backstage at the Hilton ballroom in Washington, D.C., doing his part to resuscitate the presidential candidacy of Dole, to whom his own fortunes were tied. His audience was five thousand evangelicals, the cream of the Christian Coalition, those activists who cared enough to drop at least a grand on a trip to Washington to attend the 1996 "Road to Victory" conference. The high of the San Diego convention was long gone; now, in mid-September, Dole trailed Clinton by 20 points, and Ralph was going crazy over the campaign's refusal to throw anything more harmful than a spitball at the Clinton White House.

Ralph was still too much of a loyalist to go public with his frustrations (unlike Pat Robertson, who told the activists "it would take a miracle from Almighty God" for Dole to win, adding another item to Reed's lengthy damage control to-do list: Call Scott Reed and apologize for his boss's faux pas). Instead, Ralph would do what he could to energize his own people, hoping they could bring Dole back from the dead. But to reach this core activist crowd, Ralph would have to put aside his message of tolerance and inclusion, and fall back on the rhetoric of his days as a hard-core ideologue. This crowd, Ralph knew by now, didn't respond to messages of gray.

"I'm gonna pop 'em! . . . I'm gonna pop em!" Reed uttered the words under his breath like a morning prayer as he worked the rooms backstage, greeting the dignitaries who arrived to speak. Less than four months earlier, he had published a book asserting that the Right's hatred of Bill Clinton had gotten out of hand, with Jerry Falwell marketing a video claiming the president had ordered the murder of political opponents, and other religious conservatives coming "dangerously close to defining themselves in purely anti-Clinton terms." "If Bill Clinton is a sinner, then he is no worse or less than you or me," Ralph wrote. "Has our version of the gospel become so politicized that we no longer believe that His grace extends to Bill Clinton?"

But that was then, and this was now. Over the summer, Ralph had learned some hard lessons about the limits of temperance. For weeks, he'd been nagging the Dole campaign to "go negative" and run scathing commercials against the president. Now he could barely contain himself, his body a live wire in the holding tank. Ralph planned to go out in front of that audience and "pop 'em" good, Clinton in particular.

"We are on the brink of the most important election of our lifetime . . . ," Reed called into the microphone after he reached the podium and the clapping of the audience fell into rhythm with the marching music that proclaimed his arrival.

"*We* don't say it takes a village to raise a child, *we* say it takes a family to raise a child! When *we* talk about the institution of marriage, *we* are talking about a man and a woman united in holy matrimony under God!"

The crowd jumped to its feet. Outside, across from the hotel entrance where Ronald Reagan was shot in 1981, feminist, gay, and other leftist activists walked in protest. They waved placards likening Ralph and Robertson to Nazis. A circle of Christian Coalition delegates counterdemonstrated by joining hands a few feet away, singing "Amazing Grace," praying for the souls of these wayward protestors.

"So, let's review that record . . . ," Ralph continued inside the hotel. "This president, who recently has gotten so upset about tobacco, appointed as surgeon general of the United States the highest ranking medical officer in the nation, Joycelyn Elders, who called for the legalization of drugs!" (She said the subject should be studied, a position no different from that of Ralph's libertarian allies. But Ralph wasn't interested in nuance this day.)

"This president promised a sweeping tax cut for middle-class families with children. . . . He gave us the largest tax increase in American history!" (Actually, the 1982 tax hike, signed by Reagan, was the largest in U.S. peacetime history.)

"This president had a unique opportunity to sign the first ban on abortion procedures since *Roe* versus *Wade*—the partial birth abortion, a procedure so gruesome and so inhuman and so horrific that even the American Medical Association called on the president to outlaw it. . . . A child is two-thirds of the way out of the womb and is systematically executed. . . ." Reed's last words were swallowed in the riptide of cheers and applause as the activists sprung to their feet and stood on their chairs. Abortion, Reed knew from experience, always put this audience into overdrive.

"This president went before a national audience of young people and when asked, 'Mr. President, if you had the chance to do it over again, would you inhale?' and he answered, and this is a direct quote, 'Shuurrr, if I could!'

"Now, I ask you—is that the kind of moral leadership that we need in the White House?"

"No!" the crowd responded in unison.

"This president slashed the drug czar's office by 83 percent and during his watch monthly cocaine use among American teenagers has skyrocketed 166 percent. That means that since Bill Clinton took the oath of office, there are forty thousand more teenagers using drugs *every single day.* Now, I ask you, is that moral leadership for America?"

"NO!!!"

"This president has even been forced to take a step that no president in history has had to do, and conduct the first random drug testing of White House employees in American history because some of those who report to him had admitted that they used hard-core drugs in the last few years. . . .

"Mr. President, Mr. President, we have a message for you. Before you tell us to get tobacco out of our house, you need to get illegal drugs out of the White House!"

And with that, Ralph Reed wrapped up his lesson on how to run a proper Republican campaign.

Two months later, Bill Clinton summarily defeated Bob Dole, and the baby-boom conservatives faced four more years of exile from the White House.

CULTURE CLASH

To GROVER NORQUIST, American politics divided neatly between the good guys, who allied with his "Leave Us Alone Coalition," and the bad guys, who were part of the "Takings Crowd." The Takings Crowd wanted to steal your money (taxes), indoctrinate your children behind Berlin Walls (public schools), appropriate your property (wilderness protection laws), and confiscate your weapons (gun control). The Leave Us Alone activists who gathered every Wednesday in Grover's conference room at Americans for Tax Reform represented *real* Americans, people who wanted to be left alone, free from the communal conceit that government could create a better society.

Grover often used socialist rhetoric to express this dividing line, no doubt an instinct encouraged by his regular visits with former Maoist Jonas Savimbi in the African bush. Indeed, Grover—like Savimbi—had much in common with the far Left (and was an avid reader of the *Nation,* a favorite magazine of the Left). He analyzed events through power structures and institutions—bureaucracies, media, unions—and assumed monolithic ideological motivation on the part of the people inside them. Just as Leftists drew their webs purporting to demonstrate control of the economy by a capitalist few, so too did hard-core Rightists use diagrams to demonstrate how a small but devious liberal elite controlled government and culture.

This clipped division of the world, devoid of a center, pervaded the ranks of the hard-core Right, fostering a code of loyalty that forbade public criticism of the movement or its comrades-in-arms. Even some stalwart Rightists complained about the movement's "Manichaean view of the world," as one leading thinker put it. "Conservatives have a paranoia about being betrayed." The activists in Grover's Leave Us Alone Coalition kept close tabs on who qualified as a "friend" and who might be an "enemy," and they dealt harshly with anyone perceived as a collaborator with the "liberal media." "I spend a lot of time working with the conservative press to make sure that we're all thinking alike and talking alike," Grover said.

In Grover's circle, conservatives treated warmly by the establishment press were suspect (here, Bill Kristol treaded the line). Those embraced by the establishment press when they criticized fellow conservatives were off the team (here, Bill Kristol crossed over the line). Loyalty to comrades and cause was not an ethic Kristol fostered at the offices of his new *Weekly Standard* magazine, two blocks south and one block east of Wednesday Group central.

The second-generation neoconservatives Kristol enlisted for the *Weekly Standard* office were intellectual iconoclasts, eager to criticize, willing to veer off the party line. (Apostasy had a lineage in the Kristol family: Bill's father switched to the GOP in the 1970s after deriding his fellow Democrats, then had the effrontery to offer sweeping advice to his new political home in an article titled "The Stupid Party.") As editor of the *Weekly Standard,* Bill Kristol infuriated the hard-core Right with his disloyal attacks on Dole during the Republican race (for by then, the Right had tied its fortunes to the GOP) and, later, his traitorous support for aspects of Clinton's foreign policy. Worse, Kristol and his fellow intellectuals publicly ridiculed Grover's libertarian philosophy. "Wishing to be left alone isn't a governing doctrine," Kristol and his colleague David Brooks wrote in a not-so-subtle slap at Grover's umbrella group. "[S]ome conservatives' sensible contempt for the nanny state has at times spilled over into a foolish, and politically suicidal, contempt for the American state."

From late 1996 onward, a bitter rivalry between the Norquist and Kristol camps threatened to split the movement wide open. That rivalry stemmed, in part, from philosophical differences that have plagued the Right for decades: Libertarians such as Norquist cherished an unregulated free market and believed people should be allowed to live their private lives as they choose. Norquist was rabidly anti-Washington, once describing the American government as "tyrannical and overbearing," a regime that "steals too much of people's money and violates rights and murders people in Waco."

Social conservatives were more concerned about the nation's moral climate and more skeptical about the effects of a completely unfettered market. The traditionalists around Kristol were free-marketers who wanted smaller government, too. But they didn't automatically denounce all government as evil—nor all commerce as good, as they inveighed against the prevalence of violent conspiracy-talk on an unregulated Internet and the prurience of Hollywood's entertainment offerings. "As a nation, we are concerned about pollution, about pure air and water. Is there no such thing as moral pollution?" noted a *Weekly Standard* article which appeared under a headline that made the libertarians bristle: "The Case for Censorship."

Rather than completely destroy Washington's bureaucracy, Kristol believed that government could be used to propagate long-lost conservative social values, as he and Bennett had done at the Education Department in the 1980s. The *Weekly Standard* thinkers yearned for a past of great statesmen in the mold of Winston Churchill, a time when citizens believed in something more noble than themselves—family, country, community—an era when traditional morality was compatible, not at odds, with rigorous intellectualism.

In contrast, Norquist was a "dynamist" who embraced modern culture, to borrow a label used by libertarian thinker (and philosophical ally) Virginia Postrel. While Kristol listened to Mozart and opera, and fretted endlessly about the nation's moral compass and which contemporary cultural genies to put back in the bottle (divorce? nihilist rock? Internet sex?), Norquist hung a Janis Joplin poster in his office and fixed his gaze jauntily ahead: "This modernity thing is a European problem. When the Europeans get all weepy-eyed about the good ol' days, they're talking about some stupid king. The tradition of American conservatives is the Revolution. This is the United States of America: We *are* the future. . . . What is it we have a problem with? The telephone? Computers?"

Since the 1960s, conservative thinkers trying to mesh these two competing philosophies had taken their cue from the "fusion" theory of *National Review* columnist Frank Meyer, who argued that most people would naturally choose to lead moral lives if freed from the pernicious meddling of government, particularly liberal-activist judges and bureaucrats. "Libertarian means," he contended, "will achieve traditionalist ends." This was the theme that Grover adopted to hold together the social conservatives and libertarians in his Leave Us Alone Coalition.

But Kristol, less trusting of the common man than was Norquist, was more doubtful that personal freedom would necessarily produce virtue. Meyer's fusion theory was easier to swallow in the early 1960s, when most Americans still aspired to conservative lifestyles and values, than it was in the 1990s, the age of Jerry Springer and obscene gangsta-rap lyrics and one-in-three children born without fathers, noted David Frum, a regular contributor to Kristol's magazine. "Today," Frum wrote, "it's not so clear that American people, left to their own devices, will behave in ways that a conservative would consider 'virtuous.' "

But the rivalry between Norquist and Kristol ran deeper than philosophical differences, for theirs was also a clash of personality cultures. Even if the thinkers around Kristol didn't openly call themselves "intellectuals" (as Irving and Bea Kristol's generation had done), that's certainly how they thought of themselves. The hard-core activists around Norquist, by contrast, were populists who shared with their historical predecessors on the Right a distrust of "intellectuals" and "experts" who, after all, make it their business to raise doubts and elucidate social problems.

Like the first generation of neoconservatives, Bill Kristol's circle of friends embraced bourgeois values. They married and had children; wives—typically intellectuals, too—stayed home or worked part time as mothers. (Among these traditionalists, one member conceded, women who combined full-time professions with motherhood were "suspect.") Many of them former New Yorkers, these urban sophisticates relished city life but were willing to give it up to raise their families in the suburbs. Enjoying a generous income as the *Weekly Standard* editor and, until early 2000, a commentator for ABC-TV (boosting his earnings by $250,000 in 1999), Bill lived a tame life in an elegant new home in a Virginia suburb. His three children attended public schools ("government schools," in Grover's ideological parlance), where his wife Susan, a former classics professor, put in time as a PTA president.

By contrast, a striking proportion of Norquist's activists stayed away from family life, despite all the talk about "family values" pervading the Right. Like Grover, still a bachelor living in his group house on Capitol Hill, many of these fierce ideologues stayed single well into middle age. A number of the older Wednesday Group regulars were divorced (their mentor, Newt Gingrich, would divorce a second wife in the 1990s). The ambitious young women who sat in

Grover's conference room each Wednesday morning didn't yearn to be stay-at-home mothers; the young men didn't expect them to. Certainly, many Wednesday Group attendees were tradition-minded (and married), including Christian evangelicals or Orthodox Jews, but a good portion of the regulars were libertarians who didn't pursue particularly conservative personal lifestyles.

Grover himself believed "people should organize their families the way they wish to." He was often dismissive of issues such as the breakdown of the family that so animated Kristol's circle of thinkers. "There have been studies that suggest that in the old days you lost parents to death and desertion," he once explained, "and one of the reasons the divorce rate is higher today than it was last century is that people back then didn't get divorced, they just left."

On political strategies, too, Kristol and Norquist diverged. Even in the face of electoral setbacks for the Right, Norquist stubbornly clung to his belief that more than 60 percent of the country agreed with him (a view that Kristol derided as "Grover's inevitability thing"). The problem, in Grover's mind, was that a hostile media and political establishment had blocked the Right from getting its message out. For all of the dynamism and stubborn optimism of the hard-core Rightists, this distrust of the establishment made them separatists from the mainstream political culture, "more counterculture than the original counterculture," said one Wednesday Group regular.

Kristol rejected the view that most of America instinctively embraced the Right's vision. "Conservatives can win the fight in America. But you can't simply make America a bunch of *National Review* readers," he said, referring to the magazine that had been a house organ of the Right for thirty years. "It's a big diverse country. . . . There's a kind of hubris to the argument that, 'If only everyone would see our stuff, then of course they would agree with us.' That's not true. The movement is never going to be 51 percent of the country. So the question is: How do you take the country—which is a little more conservative than liberal or Left, with a lot of moderates—and move it in the direction we want to go? If you asked Grover how to win, he'd say, 'We put all of my constituencies together to make 51 percent, then we pass what we want and win.' We would say you gradually convince people."

And to accomplish that, Kristol and his fellow thinkers traveled the top echelons of the media establishment that Grover so virulently distrusted—the TV networks, National Public Radio, the op-ed pages of the *New York Times* and the *Washington Post*. They weren't afraid of using their media platforms to criticize fellow conservatives, nor taking positions that brought them in line with what Grover labeled "the enemy."

Later, when the intellectuals around Kristol and the populists around Norquist found common ground, it would be to promote the demise of a shared enemy: Both men would call for the impeachment of President Clinton and his removal from office. But even that crusade could not mend the rift between the two camps.

"IT'S THE BRIGHT PINK SHEET, not the pale one. If you want to bring someone who's hard-core and friendly, that's fine. But do R.S.V.P."

After three and a half years, one-hundred-eighty-odd meetings (meetings that proceeded on schedule each week, vacations or not, never losing momentum), Grover Norquist moved in perfect sync with the rhythms of the Wednesday Group sessions he chaired. He knew, as did the four-score rightist souls who frequented his conference room that fall of 1996, that if you planned to pass out anything, it paid to call attention to it.

This passing of paper—flyers and reports, issue papers and op-eds, magazines and invitations—was part of the weekly ritual in Norquist's Wednesday morning strategy sessions with Washington's leading right-wing activists. The paper was as central to the ambiance as the bagels and vocal digs at a clueless "liberalmediaestablishment." Every twenty minutes or so, when Norquist ceded the floor to a different slice of the Leave Us Alone Coalition he had painstakingly stitched together, the room filled with the sound of fingers meeting pulp, as pages from the latest handout were passed. Here's a handout on a congressional candidate being pummeled by the unions—can anyone help with a fund-raiser? Here's a list of tax-cutting ballot initiatives—Who's got reliable troops in these states they can mobilize?

The handouts papered over the latent conflicts in a coalition that included pro-life and pro-choice Republicans, gay free marketers and Christian evangelicals, libertarians favoring legalization of drugs and social conservatives favoring school prayer. Even as they allied with moral police such as Paul Weyrich, many of the groups represented in Grover's conference room enjoyed funding from Richard Mellon Scaife, the reclusive Pittsburgh billionaire who funded rightist efforts to discredit the Clintons—and a man who "supports abortion rights and is friendly with the gay community," as one profiler noted.

Keeping this far-flung coalition together wasn't always easy. In the mid-1990s, one of the most fractious disputes centered on whether the government should restrict online pornography. The

Christian conservatives under Grover's umbrella supported the Communications Decency Act, which Clinton later signed. Grover and other libertarians contended that laws restricting Internet content violated free market principles. Arguments erupted at the Wednesday meetings, and Norquist's standing as a purist was briefly shaken when the *Wall Street Journal* later disclosed that he was receiving a $10,000-a-month retainer as a consultant for Microsoft, a leading opponent of the bill.

But mostly Grover presided over these weekly strategy sessions with avuncular good humor. (Grover's engineer father had been so fearful of public speaking that he forced his son to recite speeches over and over; as a result Grover was quite comfortable in front of groups.) He reminded his diverse group of their common goals—cutting government and taxes, and destroying congressional Democrats, labor unions, and the "Clintonistas." When divisive social issues threatened to rip at his coalition's seams, Grover would chide aggressors with a gentle, "Let's play nice, now." The Wednesday morning sessions included representatives from activist think tanks such as the Heritage Foundation and Citizens for a Sound Economy, from public interest law firms such as Clint's Institute for Justice, from single-issue groups such as the National Rifle Association and U.S. Term Limits, and from lobby groups with broader social agendas, such as Schlafly's Eagle Forum and Reed's Christian Coalition.

These groups tapped into a formidable army of grass-roots activists around the country. When conservative Republican candidates for state or national office visited Washington, they usually made it a point to stop by the Wednesday meeting to make a pitch for help with their campaigns. The Wednesday Group also served as an informal national headquarters for rightist ballot initiatives around the country, including measures to cut taxes, impose term limits on elected officials, and ban affirmative action. Grover solicited grass-roots support for these measures at his meetings and conducted regular conference calls with organizers in the field. Just as important, the Wednesday group discussions shaped much of the commentary in the conservative media. Reporters from the *National Review, American Spectator,* the *Washington Times,* and *Human Events* regularly culled stories from the sessions. And Grover recruited articulate volunteers from his group to promote the Right's positions on the talk radio circuit.

But for all the Left's alarms about a well-financed "right-wing conspiracy," and the tangible grass-roots power of the NRA and pro-life groups, Norquist's groups remained outgunned in the congressional battles of the 1990s. The agenda of the Republican Revolution—from eliminating federal environmental protections to cutting Medicare growth—faced a firewall of resistance from powerful liberal activists allied with veteran lawmakers from both parties.

Most of the proposals in the Christian Coalition's 1995 Contract with the American Family went nowhere, including a constitutional amendment to permit prayer at public events, and the elimination of the Education Department and the National Endowment for the Arts. A $500 child tax credit passed Congress (and was vetoed as part of the budget fight), but that was part of Gingrich's Contract with America. The Coalition supported the restriction on Internet pornography but that legislation had broad bipartisan support "and was helped by *not* being identified as a bill of the Religious Right," one analyst noted. Congress's adoption of a ban on partial birth abortions, vetoed by Clinton, was the group's major victory.

Liberal groups not only outnumbered their conservative counterparts, they also tended to be more stable and better financed, according to scholar Jeffrey Berry's study of citizens groups. Groups such as the Sierra Club and the Environmental Defense Fund, the ACLU and NOW, and Ralph Nader's network of consumer lobbies remained on the scene for decades while a number of supposedly powerful rightist groups, such as the Moral Majority and National Conservative Political Action Committee, flamed out.

True, liberal groups had enjoyed early advantages in fund-raising by soliciting government grants and collecting attorneys fees for public interest litigation against the government. Moreover, as Berry noted, their membership base tended to be in higher income brackets than that of such conservative groups as evangelicals. Conservatives relied on expensive direct-mail campaigns and consistently overfished their own fund-raising waters, he concluded. Still, the Right benefited from the generous backing of determined corporate friends—the Koch family, Scaife, the Bradley Foundation, the Olin Foundation, and others—so the relative weakness of the Right's citizen groups couldn't be blamed entirely on the Left's funding advantages.

Likewise, one could make the case that the media was biased in favor of liberal groups. But that didn't explain Berry's finding that in 1991, for example, conservative groups actively lobbied on just 4.5 percent of primary domestic legislation before Congress whereas liberal groups lobbied on 66 percent. Why were the conservative groups so often AWOL? Berry concluded that liberal groups had developed mainstream reputations by building information machines, making themselves indispensable to lawmakers and the press. "Mother was right: Hard work pays off," he wrote. "The numbers indicate that conservative citizen groups don't put nearly as much energy or money into lobbying the Hill or hiring policy experts. . . . The greater visibility and credibility of the liberal groups can be explained by the large bureaucracies they have built, the policy experts they employ, the research they fund and the long-term stability of their organizations."

But there was one aspect of the Washington game these rightist groups *were* especially skilled at—scandal-mongering against their political foes. In the mid-1990s, well before Monica Lewinsky's name ever surfaced, the Wednesday group was a clearinghouse for every rumor and tip on the scandals plaguing the White House, from Travelgate and Filegate to Democratic fund-raising at a Buddhist temple. This was a place where Representative Dan Burton, the Indiana congressman who shot a pumpkin in his backyard to "prove" Vince Foster's death was not a suicide, found warm support against sallies by the mainstream press. It was a place where Grover organized large orders of urine cups from medical suppliers to be passed around at rallies as a reminder of accusations of drug use by White House staffers. Congressional staffers stopped by the Wednesday sessions to brief activists on the progress of various Republican investigations against the White House. Grover was a contributing columnist to the *American Spectator* magazine, home to the Scaife-funded $2.3 million Arkansas Project, which was aimed at digging up dirt on Clinton (starting with the 1994 Troopergate story). While Grover's own writings focused on politics, much of the rest of the magazine was routinely devoted to uncovering the one revelation that might bring down the Clintons. In 1996, the magazine accused Hillary Clinton of engaging in "an obstruction of justice at the highest level since Watergate" by spiriting incriminating files out of Foster's office, and editor R. Emmett Tyrrell Jr. asserted, without foundation, that the president refused to release his medical records because he had used drugs heavily and "may have been treated for a drug overdose."

But even if Clinton fell, Grover knew that Washington's entrenched liberal establishment would remain intact. So he spent considerable effort constructing a competing conservative establishment, starting with social networks. The annual Dark Ages Weekend, launched in 1995 by young right activists as an alternative to the liberal establishment's annual New Year's gabfest, The Renaissance Weekend, was "extremely important as a revolutionary act," said Grover, who served on its advisory board. From its rules banning "group hugs" and encouraging the use of chlorofluorocarbon sprays to its hard liquor supply and skeet-shooting sessions, Dark Ages (later renamed The Weekend) also provided a platform for the Right to mock the prim political correctness of liberals.

In the mid-1990s, a number of conservative groups attempted to displace Harvard University as the chief sponsor of orientation sessions for newly elected members of Congress. This postelection training enabled conservative lawmakers to "resist becoming collaborators," Grover explained. "You make your decision: Our team or their team. If you want to come to Washington and join the establishment, take the plane to Harvard. If you want to join the revolution, join us." Likewise, Grover mounted quixotic campaigns to "smash" the state societies—organizations that attempted to foster a bipartisanship spirit between lawmakers from the same state—and to kill the bipartisan National Governors Association. The aim of all these efforts was the same—to make sure "nobody on our side gets seduced by the dark side into joining their team."

Washington journalist and social doyenne Sally Quinn missed the point when, in early 1996, she wrote a *Washington Post* essay bemoaning the reluctance of Norquist and other conservatives to join the capital's established social scene, which in an earlier era had nurtured an air of civility between Democrats and Republicans. Grover didn't want to knock on Quinn's door; she represented "them," the hostile liberal establishment. Neither did he want his troops fraternizing with the enemy; they might go soft on him. "We came here to displace their Washington," Quinn quoted him as saying.

You could almost hear Norquist's derisive snort when, unswayed, Quinn confidently asserted, "Today's conservatives, if they stay, will join" the Washington establishment. This was a war, no mistaking it, and Norquist wasn't going to be lured from the trenches with fine linens, expensive cabernet, and a dinner seat next to a cabinet secretary. The Wednesday Group was not a home for Republicans who worried about finding common ground with the Democrats, or receiving friendly treatment in *Time* magazine, or getting invited to Quinn's dinner parties. "It's important for the revolutionary party not to say that our measure of how successful we are is if [the mainstream media] say nice things about us and want to have lunch with us," Norquist explained.

This counterculture style, the swaggering attempts to be "in" by being "out," pervaded Grover's Wednesday sessions. Grover kept mice named David Bonior (the House Democratic whip) in a cage, each awaiting its turn to be fed to the office pet, a boa constrictor named after the turn-of-the-century anarchist Lysander Spooner.

When GOP strategists showed up at Wednesday meetings to air their campaign commercials during the 1996 contest, the activists loudly groaned at positive ads extolling a candidate's virtues—but whistled and applauded and murmured "v-e-e-ery good!" at attack ads accusing Democrats of paroling murderers or being too chummy with "big labor bosses."

Grover's own lobby group, Americans for Tax Reform, was created as a tax-exempt organization declaring that its "purposes shall be pursued wholly without partisanship." In fact, by the mid-1990s Grover and his coalition allies were deeply loyal to the Republican Party—an overtly partisan spirit that also distinguished the Right's activists from many of their more long-standing liberal foes. The head of the National Republican Congressional Committee named Norquist first when asked to list the "most important people or groups behind the Republicans' effort to maintain control of the House" in 1996, and the RNC offered Grover as a "Republican surrogate" to offer commentary to reporters during the Democratic convention.

So loyal was Grover that the RNC channeled $4.6 million to his tax-reform group during the final weeks of the 1996 campaign, a sum more than four times ATR's total income the previous year. Grover used the contribution on a direct-mail and phone bank operation targeting voters in 150 congressional districts, primarily to defend the GOP's Medicare plan. Later, that contribution came back to haunt Norquist when Senate Democrats launched an investigation and concluded that the RNC had "improperly and possibly illegally" funneled campaign spending through ATR. This soft money was the "single largest dollar transfer from a national political party to a tax-exempt organization in the history of American politics," Senate Democratic investigators noted. (With the Republicans in charge and focusing the panel's attention on allegations of illegal fund-raising by Clinton and Gore, the congressional investigation of ATR ended with the publication of a report.)

The Leave Us Alone activists were skeptical of the news sources that most Americans relied upon for political information. "The idea that the establishment press was going to give you a fair break was whistling Dixie, just silly," Grover insisted. He and his allies continued to maintain that Clinton was a "friend" whom the liberal press intended to protect, even as reporters from the *Los Angeles Times,* the *New York Times,* the *Washington Post,* and other mainstream news organizations ferreted out new information that fed the Clinton scandals. It often seemed as if the Right's distrust of the press was predicated on an assumption that there were no "facts" untainted by ideological motivation. That being the case, it was always safer to turn to "friends" to interpret reality.

In the fall of 1996, rightist pollsters and analysts appeared at Grover's Wednesday meetings claiming that—contrary to the predictions of the establishment press—Dole could win and Republicans would gain substantial ground in the House. "If the election were held today, we'd gain six to twelve [House] seats. And I'm not being Pollyanna. It's very honest," a coalition favorite, twenty-nine-year-old Kellyanne Fitzpatrick, assured her allies. Of course, when voters went to the polls, Dole was trounced and the Democrats gained nine seats in the House. But in the collective mind of Norquist's Wednesday Group, the 1996 elections were evidence of a neat conspiracy between a president who lied about his intentions, labor unions who used $35 million in coerced membership dues to mount duplicitous attacks on GOP freshmen, and a liberal media establishment determined to keep its friends in power. (In advance of the 1998 congressional elections, Grover wrote a column on "why the Republicans will win very big this fall" for the *American Spectator.* "If there is one strong argument that Republicans will fail to strengthen their grip on the House . . . it is that Clinton will do everything he can to prevent it. He knows that if he recaptures the House, he can stop congressional investigations into his scandals." Instead, the Democrats defied historical odds that year to pick up five House seats.)

Although Norquist's tent was big enough to hold a raft of policy disagreements (sales tax versus flat tax? stop Internet porn or let free information flow?), he imposed a litmus test on attitude—only the hard-core need apply. His conference room was not a place for the faint-hearted who might cringe at references to Medicare as "socialized medicine" and Social Security as a "Ponzi scheme," or who might object to strategy sessions on how to impeach the president of the United States. More than a year before the public was introduced to former White House intern Monica Lewinsky, Norquist and his Wednesday Group discussed how to lobby lawmakers to open impeachment proceedings against President Clinton, even though independent counsel Kenneth Starr's Whitewater investigation had not produced any evidence of criminal wrongdoing by the Clintons (and never would, though others would be implicated).

In the conspiracy-dominated reality of the Wednesday Group, there was mounting certainty that after the November 1996 election Clinton planned to issue presidential pardons to key Whitewater figure Susan McDougal—then in jail on contempt charges for her refusal to testify against the president—and to the first lady and, lastly, to himself. In the fall of 1996, with the election two weeks away, Norquist encouraged fellow activists to write op-eds and make talk radio appearances asserting that, if reelected, Clinton was likely to hand out pardons.

"I think the discussion has to start: Did you know that the president has the power to pardon himself?" Norquist told a group of about eighty activists at his October 16 meeting. "Do you really want to elect a guy who's capable of pardoning himself?" His associate, Peter Ferrara, shared conclusions from his research examining the president's power to pardon. Then Norquist peppered Ferrara with questions about the breadth of congressional impeachment powers.

"You could theoretically impeach the president because you're mad at him, right?" Grover asked. "You don't need to prove that he robbed a bank?" That's right, Ferrara answered, before setting forth his argument that the Constitution should be amended to restrict the use of presidential pardons.

At the following week's Wednesday Group meeting, Norquist invited an attorney from the rightist Landmark Legal Foundation to further explore the intricacies of the presidential pardon. "My feeling is if [Clinton] feels someone close to him is going to be indicted," the lawyer explained, "he has to decide if he's going to pardon, then they have to decide when. He's free to pardon them today, though that would be insanity." The hundred-odd activists gathered in Grover's conference room seemed enraptured with the idea of impeaching Clinton.

"I think it makes sense for the House Republicans to say, 'If he pardons, we will impeach, if he pardons in a way that obstructs justice,' " offered Norquist.

"On a political level, should we be saying people should be taking a closer look at Al Gore because this president might be impeached?" proposed one woman.

"This is a criminal conspiracy taking over the federal government, that's what we have today," Ferrara piped in, as the group murmured its assent. "We cannot allow him to pardon all these people who might incriminate him and then just walk off." It was time, Ferrara concluded, for movement activists to press Senate Judiciary Committee Chairman Orrin Hatch and House Judiciary Committee Chairman Henry Hyde to issue a stern, and very public, warning to the president: "If he pardons people we will impeach him."

With the adrenaline of impending war so thick in that room, the Landmark lawyer did not receive a warm response to his insistently cautious conclusion that, "I don't think we ought to go around impeaching presidents lightly."

In fact, Clinton pardoned no one, and impeachment proceedings would have to await revelations of a new scandal fanned by the Right.

WHEN BILL KRISTOL CONVINCED Australian media mogul Rupert Murdoch to finance the *Weekly Standard* in 1995, he intended to build a magazine that served as a mirror on a political movement unaccustomed to self-introspection. Other conservative magazines mostly served as vehicles to shore up the faithful by publishing precisely the kind of loyalist tracts that passed through the hands of the Wednesday Group regulars. (Like father, like son: Irving Kristol had founded the *Public Interest* in 1965 as an alternative to the *National Review,* which he said was too right-wing in those days, not sufficiently analytical or intellectual.)

Bill believed that airing self-criticism was healthy; Grover believed it was dangerous, like handing ammunition to the other side. Bill believed movement conservatives could be their own worst enemies; Grover had no doubt *who* the enemy was—and it wasn't fellow activists. As Kristol took more and more positions at odds with the Right, hard-core activists concluded that he was an opportunist more interested in promoting himself and his magazine than the conservative cause.

Bill modeled the *Weekly Standard* on that neoliberal stalwart, the *New Republic;* he had hired the *New Republic*'s Fred Barnes— one of the nation's premiere political reporters—as executive editor. The *Standard* showcased the work of Barnes and a handful of other talented reporters, and its editorials were exhaustively researched. But compared to the thick and wide-ranging reportage of the *New Republic,* Kristol's new magazine was often thin, favoring wry commentary and opinion over investigative research. Like the *New Republic,* the *Weekly Standard* was a money loser. In the first four years after its founding, its circulation still hovered around 60,000 (compared to 98,000 for the *New Republic*), a number that temporarily dropped each time Kristol angered his rightist subscribers with fresh evidence that he might be a turncoat. One subscriber summed up the *Weekly Standard* publisher's standing in the movement when he recalled wondering "whether you were actually a liberal mole. I had become convinced that sixty new Democrats are registered for every minute you spread your anti-populist message on ABC News and PBS."

Kristol didn't consider himself beholden to the Republican Party, or its prospects for victory. His digs at Dole during the 1996 presidential campaign earned him the label "the first rat" from the nominee's communications director John Buckley (Buckley's jab, though, was also an unwitting acknowledgment that the campaign was a sinking ship). Even if Norquist's crowd initially had reservations about Dole, who had a history as a tax-hiker, they faithfully embraced him once he became the GOP nominee and they abhorred Kristol's constant carping about his campaign. "It doesn't help," a visibly angry Norquist snapped one afternoon as he examined a *Weekly Standard* editorial headlined, "Saving the GOP from Dole-Kemp 96." (Like Speaker Gingrich, Norquist reserved his "it doesn't help" response for the actions of wayward comrades. The comment, intended to work its way back to the targeted person, was meant to serve as a temperate but pointed reminder that this might be a good time to fall back in line.)

Plenty of Republicans played on Washington's media-establishment game turf, and still remained loyalists, at least on the record. Not Kristol, who eagerly broadcast his attacks on Dole and other Republicans. In 1996, *New York Times* reporters quoted Kristol fifty-four times; *Washington Post* reporters, forty-five times; *Wall Street Journal* reporters, twenty-two times. At times, though not often, Kristol even worried himself. "I have to sort of watch myself to make sure that I'm saying what I believe, not what the press might want to hear," he confessed to one reporter.

Bill and his peers were part of an elite and never quite comfortable with the Right's embrace of the word "revolution." In 1996, when Pat Buchanan, referring to his supporters, warned that the "peasants are at the gates" of the Republican establishment, Kristol revealed more than he probably intended when he quipped that he and his friends were on the side of the "lords and barons. We at the *Weekly Standard* are pulling up the drawbridge against the peasants."

The original *Weekly Standard* staff included John Podhoretz, son of neoconservatives Norman Podhoretz and Midge Decter and one of the originators of the idea for the magazine; senior editor David Brooks, a University of Chicago graduate who spent most of his childhood in Manhattan as the son of liberal academics; editorialist David Tell, who studied Chinese language and history at Columbia University; senior writer Christopher Caldwell, a Harvard graduate who developed a reputation around the office for reading French novels, in French; foreign policy expert Robert Kagan, son of a prominent neoconservative and a graduate of Yale and Harvard's Kennedy School of Government; managing editor Claudia Winkler, who earned a master's degree in medieval history from the University of California, Berkeley; and co-managing editor Richard Starr, whose resumé included stints at two other bastions of the conservative elite, the *National Interest* and the *Public Interest*.

They shared with their editor an eagerness to challenge the comfortable suppositions of the Right even as they ridiculed the Left. "We are comfortable in the faith," explained Podhoretz, who later left the magazine to become a *New York Post* columnist. "It doesn't have to be shored up all the time. . . . I'm not here to get Republican politicians elected." Brooks called the magazine "post-conservative—it assumes we're no longer in the wilderness, no longer a beleaguered front against a powerful liberal elite. So we don't adhere to the eleventh commandment: Thou shalt not attack a fellow conservative."

Just about any of the *Weekly Standard* writers would make a sparkling contribution to a Sally Quinn dinner party. The conversation that started among Straussian graduate students at Harvard in the 1970s, and continued inside the education secretary's lunchroom in the 1980s, culminated in the 1990s with Monday morning editorial meetings that were contests of wits—where "you had to be very fast, and very guy" to fit in, as former staffer Juleanna Glover Weiss put it. The caustic collective also included senior editor Andrew Ferguson, a self-described journalistic hit-man who once wrote an essay in which he dubbed Republican strategist David Gergen "a goggle-eyed melon head," and reporter Tucker Carlson, whose profile of Ross Perot raised the simple question, "Is he nuts?"

These journalists were adept at bashing the liberal media establishment. But unlike Norquist's circle, they were also quite comfortable traveling inside it. Kristol was witty, learned, and—like a good Washington talking head—spoke fast enough to compress intelligent and trenchant analysis into ten-second sound bites. Kristol and Kagan co-authored foreign policy articles for *Foreign Affairs*, published by the Council on Foreign Relations, the headquarters of the eastern foreign policy establishment that sent much of the hard Right into paroxysms over the prospect of a world government. Barnes, like Kristol, was a familiar face on the TV talk show circuit. Senior editor Brooks was a commentator on National Public Radio, which the hard-core Right considered a taxpayer-subsidized liberal propaganda outfit.

The writers who congregated around the *Standard* had been weaned on the writings of Straussians such as Allan Bloom, who called rock music a "a nonstop commercially prepackaged masturbational fantasy," and neoconservatives such as Norman Podhoretz, who called baby-boomer grief over John Lennon's murder a "posthumous orgy of self-congratulation and self-pity." Yet these same conservatives came of age in an era pounding to the beat of rock 'n roll. While most young Rightists in the 1990s tried to demonstrate their bona fides as pop culture hipsters, the traditionalists at the *Weekly Standard* were more conflicted (though Kristol, the Mozart devotee, never gave in).

Determined to make a conservative case for rock music, contributor Mark Gauvreau Judge argued against the notion that "we are somehow betraying the cause because we like pop music." Maybe, he wrote on a tormented note, one can stay true to conservative values by distinguishing the "high and low achievements" within the idiom of pop music; dismissing the "solipsism and spoiled-brat ethic" of some bands and celebrating the "joyful, innocent, hook-drenched" songs of others. But later, in a controversial *Weekly Standard* cover story, freelance writer Diana West prudishly concluded that rock music undermines "the essential ideals of bourgeois culture—responsibility, fidelity, sobriety."

On high culture, *Weekly Standard* contributors debated the nature of "conservative art": Should conservatives continue to dismiss abstract art? No, said Yale computer science professor David Gelernter, arguing instead for a rejection of today's "hateful art, art that dirties the soul, [that] vicious circle of spite in which artists parade their angry contempt for the public. . . ." Should Republicans support the arts? Yes, argued Joseph Epstein: "The arts are nothing if not an elitist enterprise, but they are elitist in the best American sense. They represent elitism detached from social class and privilege; they represent democratic elitism."

The *Weekly Standard* writers liked to think of themselves as modern cosmopolitans who embraced the "vigorous virtues"—merit, self-sufficiency, adventurousness, and high aspiration. "People [should] be treated as captains of their own fate, not the victims of social forces so huge that only government can ameliorate them," wrote Brooks, who also condemned the "prissy etiquette" of liberals fretting about fur coats and the rain forest. Other *Weekly Standard* writers criticized America's elevation of "feminine" values in American culture.

The voices in the *Standard* were overwhelmingly male. One could thumb through weeks of back issues without spotting a female byline. A symposium on worldwide conservatism that solicited contributions from twenty-eight authors included only one woman, Noemie Emery. But Emery did write some important pieces for the magazine, including a cover story on abortion, and occasionally the

Standard offered a forum for the postfeminists who congregated around the conservative *Women's Quarterly*. One such contributor was Danielle Crittenden, who argued that men were the winners and women the losers in the sexual revolution, and that the feminist ideal of career-driven women had made strong marriage, fulfilling motherhood, and individual happiness more elusive.

Shades of Irving Kristol's "Two Cheers for Capitalism" could be heard as these new neoconservatives raised alarms about the lurid entertainment culture the market produced—though the position was complicated by the fact that their salaries were paid by Rupert Murdoch, a media mogul who marketed the sensational in his tabloid newspapers and whose Fox television network courted the lowest common denominator with sexually explicit prime time shows and reality fare featuring the world's "scariest" police chases and "sexiest" TV commercials. Was Bill Clinton really more responsible for the decline of the nation's morality than capitalists such as Murdoch? Bill Bennett and Senator Joe Lieberman, both of whom sharply criticized Clinton's behavior during the Lewinsky affair, offered their own answer to that question when they handed a "Silver Sewer Award" to the media mogul and denounced the sexually explicit content of the Fox network, noting its "tireless, tasteless, and ongoing efforts to drag down network programming standards." Asked about the conflict between the values his magazine promotes and the entertainment fare offered by his owner, Kristol responded simply that it was unfair to single out Murdoch, owner of a large and diverse conglomerate. He added that he was grateful for the support of Murdoch, who had never interfered with his magazine's editorial content.

The *Weekly Standard*'s coverage of Washington politics was imbued with a knowing, smart-alecky tone that often turned off older conservatives. Kristol's writers and editors were very much a product of the Question Authority culture—*Mad Magazine* and *Spy, Saturday Night Live* and MTV—of their youths. But in between the irony, the satire, and piercing parody, Kristol and his writers wrestled with the big questions facing modern conservatives: Was the decline of American character and culture the result of liberal activism, or of a nihilism that the free market had helped produce? Had America, and the movement, lost the sense of national pride and unity that Reagan had once instilled? Wasn't there more to being a conservative than opposing government programs?

In early 1997, Kristol, Kagan, and Brooks began a long-running, oft-interrupted conversation about the direction of American politics, and American conservatism. Out of those conversations emerged a cover story, "A Return to National Greatness," in which Brooks debuted the theme of a "limited but energetic government" that would nourish the sense of ideal and purpose the country embraced when it supported such grand public works as the Library of Congress. "You can't lead a great nation if you don't have an affirmative view of the public realm," Brooks wrote. (In the piece, Brooks also extolled many of the same grandiose Washington buildings that Norquist once condemned as reminiscent of something produced by Nazi architect Albert Speer.)

On foreign policy, Kristol carved out a position at odds with much of the Republican Party. Since the fall of the Berlin Wall, isolationist sentiments had spread on the right, particularly among conservatives who viscerally distrusted Clinton's motives overseas. Likewise, Republican business interests were more interested in opening markets, particularly in China, than in exercising American military might against potential adversaries. By contrast, Kristol and Kagan argued for a strategy of "benevolent hegemony" and promoted the idea of a militarily strong America willing to promote freedom and democracy around the globe.

The *Standard* supported an expanded NATO and the Clinton administration's intervention in Bosnia. In 1999, Kristol allied with Senator John McCain in calling for the United States to send in ground troops to Yugoslavia "to defeat Serb forces and stop the slaughter and ethnic cleansing of Kosovar Albanians." McCain, wrote the *Standard*'s editors, "had the guts to get out in front of public opinion and make the case that the moral and strategic stakes in Kosovo are high, and that when America starts a war it needs to win it—even if that means using ground forces." (The Clinton administration, concerned about loss of American lives, relied on air strikes against the Serbs.)

That editorial, like early *Weekly Standard* endorsements of foreign interventions, drew a slew of angry replies from readers. Subscribers were particularly livid that Kristol had lent aid and comfort to an enemy of the Right (President Clinton) by supporting any type of military action by his administration. The nation's commander-in-chief is a "draft dodger who loathes the military" (said one reader), his administration is "treacherous [and] anti-American" and its "immoral ends . . . are bluffs, lies, cover-ups, and death" (said another).

Toward China, the *Weekly Standard* supported an aggressive hard-line stance. The magazine became a megaphone for what would later come to be called the Blue Team—an informal network of lawmakers, think-tankers, and journalists in Washington, "all united in the view that a rising China poses great risks to America's vital interests," as one account put it. Kristol forcefully argued that the U.S. policy of engagement toward China—pursued first by the Bush administration, then by President Clinton—was, in fact, a policy of "appeasement" that ignored the dictatorial practices of the Chinese regime toward its own people and the dangers inherent in its military buildup. Kristol was among those conservatives (including his friend, 2000 presidential candidate Gary Bauer) who allied with liberals in pressing the Clinton administration to withhold trade privileges from China because of human rights and religious rights abuses.

IF THE RIGHT'S ISOLATIONISTS didn't trust the American government to intervene overseas, there were those at home who didn't trust the American government, period. In the 1960s, neoconservatives had stood up to the anti-Americanism that infused the counterculture Left; in the 1990s, Kristol and other successors watched the rise of anti-Americanism on the Right, and resolved to put a stop to it.

In November of 1996, Catholic priest Richard John Neuhaus, editor-in-chief of the religious academic journal *First Things,* sponsored a forum ominously titled "The End of Democracy?" In it, he asked whether the American government was an illegitimate regime that "no longer governs by the consent of the governed. . . . America is not and, please God, will never become Nazi Germany, but it is only blind hubris that denies it can happen here and, in peculiarly American ways, may be happening here." The symposium, whose contributors included Robert Bork and Charles Colson, suggested civil disobedience and "morally justified revolution" to combat "laws that cannot be obeyed by conscientious citizens." Neuhaus had previously used the journal to broadcast concerns about liberal courts. But now he took his cause to the precipice: Apocalyptic talk of "revolution" had spread from militia men to middle-aged intellectuals.

In some ways what followed was an incestuous debate—Kristol's mother, Gertrude Himmelfarb, and Podhoretz's mother, Midge Decter, sat on the *First Things* editorial board—and Kristol later concluded the whole brouhaha was spawned by Neuhaus's hunger for publicity. But the episode shed telling light on the gaps between Washington's baby-boom conservatives and more alienated Rightists. David Brooks wrote for the *Weekly Standard* a piece sharply criticizing the Neuhaus argument and asking whether the Right was about to go anti-American. He quoted a letter from Himmelfarb, who resigned from the *First Things* board after calling the Neuhaus tirade "absurd and irresponsible." And he quoted Norman Podhoretz, who compared Neuhaus's argument to the Left's outburst of anti-Americanism in the 1960s. What amazed the *Standard* editors was that most of the response from its readers was sympathetic to Neuhaus. As one Colorado reader wrote: "When government all but outlaws religious expression, officially sanctions infanticide, legitimizes homosexuality and promotes illegitimacy, is it any wonder that we think government has become illegitimate?"

GROVER WAS ANNOYED by Kristol's brash disloyalty toward fellow Republicans, and by his magazine's criticism of libertarians. ("There is no doubt that life under [a libertarian] regime would be more uncomfortable, less stable, more risky, and require more effort from ordinary citizens," one *Standard* writer wrote). He thought the Kristol crowd, a bunch of "thumb-suckers," should drop all their high-minded virtue talk and go man the trenches for the rightist insurrection against big government. "Some conservative writers are saying it's not politics, it's all civic virtue," he once complained. "Okay, but when somebody is done listening to your speech or reading your column, what do they do? What are you asking them to do? You need a legislative agenda."

But it wasn't until Kristol's writers turned their sights on Grover's friend, speaker Newt Gingrich—and then on Grover himself—that the rivalry really turned ugly. Kristol's magazine had staunchly defended Gingrich through the ethics investigation into whether he had used tax-exempt organizations for partisan political goals. But in the spring of 1997, the *Weekly Standard* began adding its voice to a chorus of critics asking whether Gingrich was up to the job of leading the House and the conservative movement. A March 10 editorial encouraging a rebellion against the House leadership was followed by an Andrew Ferguson piece skewering the speaker with an exposé of the "bizarre diagrams . . . empty buzzwords . . . [and] endless train-wrecks of verbiage" that Gingrich sketched in notebooks to describe his political vision. Then reporter Major Garrett wrote the March 31 cover story, "Newt Melts," giving voice to his Republican critics on Capitol Hill. Gingrich counterattacked in an April 6 appearance on a Sunday talk show: "I don't know of any conservative, who's a serious person, who isn't frankly worried about what's happening at the *Weekly Standard* and Kristol's passion for destroying Republicans."

The speaker's interests were uppermost in Grover's mind one spring day when he sat down, uninvited, at a restaurant table where *Weekly Standard* reporter Tucker Carlson was eating. "His hands shaking with anger," Carlson recalled, "he accused me of being the instrument of a conspiracy to 'destroy the speaker.' How typical of the speaker's enemies, he hissed at me, to 'get a movement conservative [me] to attack movement conservatives [Norquist and Gingrich].' "

It happened that at the time Carlson was writing a profile of Grover—not for the *Weekly Standard* but for the *New Republic*. The June 9 story, "What I Sold at the Revolution," revealed that Grover was a $10,000-a-month lobbyist for the Seychelles, an island paradise off the East Africa coast run by a former Marxist dictator named France-Albert René. René first came to power in a 1977 military coup, but then triumphed in democratic elections conducted sixteen years later.

The Seychelles had been on Grover's plate since the late 1980s, when he tried to turn the deposed president, Sir James Mancham, into a cause célèbre of the American Right. (A photo of Grover and Mancham hangs on the activist's office wall, one of the few from his freedom-fighting days in which he is not holding an automatic weapon.) In 1992, after the regime agreed to open elections, Grover visited the island with Mancham, René's chief opponent in the race. Grover told Carlson that the environment during this visit was "very hot," for he was a marked man with the René regime. Mancham "had six bodyguards," Grover recalled. "I wore a vest. It was jumpy, edgy."

Elections were held in 1993 and René won, though Mancham returned from exile to head the opposition party. Justice Department records show that Norquist represented the René government as a lobbyist between September 1995 and March 1999. (His initial twenty-four-month contract called for half of his $10,000 a month fee to be paid in American dollars deposited in a U.S. bank, and the other half in Seychelles rupees wired to an island bank "to be used only to purchase real and/or personal property in the Seychelles" during that period.) In 1997 and 1998, Grover met with a number of senators and members of Congress "to discuss the possibility of increasing U.S. visibility" in the island nation. He now defended René—once portrayed as a ruthless dictator by the American Right—telling Carlson he was merely "a guy who preferred not to have elections for a number of years."

In a later interview for this book, Grover stressed that "my effort with the Seychelles was not to lobby for foreign aid, but to get more military presence in the region, which we ought to have." At the time, the Seychellois government was trying to dissuade the United States from closing its embassy and radar tracking station there. As the *Wall Street Journal* noted, the government was also "fighting accusations that a recently passed law to encourage foreign investment is an open invitation to money launderers."

Carlson's article portrayed Grover as doing the bidding of an authoritarian regime, citing a State Department report concluding that René continued to "wield power virtually unchecked." Grover maintained that the country was a democracy, noting that the State Department had concluded that the election was fair, parliamentary sessions were televised, and that, in Grover's words, "more of the Seychellois economy has been privatized in the past four years than any other nation." He said he was "proud that both political parties in the Seychelles asked me to work to strengthen the American presence in the region."

In fact, the picture in the Seychelles was more complicated than either Norquist or Carlson suggested—and demonstrated the dangers of Grover's insistence on fighting the battles of countries and causes with few democratic roots (like Jonas Savimbi's UNITA). The same 1998 State Department report that concluded René wielded unchecked power also found that the government "generally respected the rights of its citizens." But in contrast to Grover's assertion, the report stated that "progress toward privatization has been slow," and that while citizens can generally "speak freely," the government exercised a "near monopoly over the media."

Grover was livid when Carlson's *New Republic* article called his Seychelles lobbying "a remarkably cynical reversal, even by Washington standards." In a letter to the editor, he accused Carlson of making seventeen errors (though aside from describing the Seychelles' progress toward democracy, he neglected to cite these mistakes). The article, Grover asserted, dripped "with venom": Carlson's "friends and co-workers told me that his goal was to write critically of a conservative so that he could escape the conservative writers' ghetto and make himself desirable to *Esquire* and *Vanity Fair.*"

Grover did raise one salient issue: Carlson had failed to disclose that his father, Richard Carlson, had served as ambassador to the Seychelles during much of Grover's work there. In his letter, Grover implied that Carlson's father was soft on communism, asserting that the Republican ambassador had refused to aid Norquist's pro-democracy efforts, and had later betrayed conservatives by accepting a job presiding over the taxpayer-supported Corporation for Public Broadcasting (a popular target of the Right). "I won't forgive him," Grover wrote of Carlson's father in his letter to the editor. "When our team holds the cold war version of the Nuremberg trials, I will testify against [Richard] Carlson as a collaborator."

So angry was Tucker Carlson that when he next encountered Norquist at a Washington social event, he threw a drink at him. But more lasting was Carlson's written response, because it invoked words that many of the thinkers in Kristol's orbit shared among themselves but usually didn't voice in the company of liberals: "It is hard to know which to point out first," Carlson wrote to the *New Republic*'s readers, "Grover Norquist's dishonesty or his authoritarian impulses."

CHAPTER 17

LEGACIES

F OR ALL THE THUNDER and flash emanating from the Right in the last years of the millennium's last decade, a quieter enterprise held the deepest meaning: The Ronald Reagan Legacy Project, brainchild of Grover Norquist. Grover intended to memorialize the fortieth president (and hence the movement he had inspired) by placing Reagan's name on parks and highways and buildings. His first mission was the capital's chicly refurbished airport, which, by act of Congress, became known as Reagan National. That done, Grover planned to work with governors in each of the fifty states to "get other things named. . . . Liberals went out and named things after JFK, King, Roosevelt. People look back and say 'they must be great— look at all the stuff named after them.' " He even hoped to see Reagan's faced carved on Mount Rushmore, alongside those of Washington, Jefferson, Lincoln, and Teddy Roosevelt. And he planned to lobby Eastern European countries to name squares and monuments in honor of the American commander-in-chief who had faced down the Evil Empire.

Grover's campaign to memorialize the president who had inspired his generation was an important symbol of the state of modern conservatism in the late 1990s, for it alluded to the fundamental questions facing the movement:

What do you do after you've fought Big Government to a stalemate? What do you do after the federal budget is balanced for the first time in thirty years—when Americans resist new programs but aren't clamoring for cuts in the ones they have? What do you do when hardly anyone anymore questions the value of work over welfare but still supports a safety net for the neediest? When a sustained economic boom has transformed even diehard Leftists into ardent capitalists, but capitalists who nevertheless want the government to protect them—and their environment—against corporate excess? What do you do when, across the political spectrum, Americans applaud a court and law enforcement crackdown that has produced plummeting crime rates but also support gun control and worry about police brutality?

What do you do when the politicians who favor flaunting American military muscle around the world are the Democrats, and it's the Senate Republican leader who proclaims that we should "give peace a chance"?

What do you do after liberal elites declare that "Dan Quayle was right" about the importance of two-parent families, after rates of teen pregnancy and out-of-wedlock births and divorce fall—but the days of 1950s-style families and G-rated entertainment remain firmly locked in the attic of nostalgia? What do you do after megastates like California and Florida abandon affirmative action—but the nation won't give up on diversity as an ideal?

What do you do, in other words, when the nation has shifted toward your worldview, but stubbornly resisted embracing it?

If you're Grover, you believe that "the lessons of the past are taught every day. It's not like the past is fixed." You believe that memorializing past victories is every bit as important as securing future ones: "Marx spent a lot of time explaining the past in order to explain today. Stalin kept rewriting the past to justify the present." History is malleable. The plot line depends on who's doing the telling, so conservatives have a duty to recapture America's story. Leave Reagan's legacy in the hands of liberal academics, and inevitably he will be subjected to ridicule. (Predictably, liberal critics of Grover's legacy campaign asserted that Reagan's real legacy to the nation was a $3 trillion national debt.)

As Grover set out to rescript the nation's history, his fellow activists looked to a future that wasn't always as rosy as the past he sought to memorialize. Representative David McIntosh crafted a softer version of conservatism even as he battled in vain to preserve one remnant from the Republican Revolution, major tax cuts, and in doing so turned against onetime guerrilla leader Newt Gingrich. Clint Bolick continued his slog through the courts on behalf of school choice and urban entrepreneurs, and Ralph Reed gave up his struggle to bring a reluctant Religious Right to the table of mainstream American politics.

Meanwhile, Bill Kristol waged a crusade against the most conspicuous legacy of the 1960s—the belief that (as philosopher Richard Weaver put it) any individual can be "his own priest, his own professor of ethics." And he did so by fixing his cross-hairs on the one baby boomer most representative of this dangerous relativism—the president of the United States.

ON THE AFTERNOON of April 23, 1997, Ralph Reed, having wrapped up a whirlwind visit to Texas—which included a Christian Coalition fund-raiser and a private meeting with Republican governor George W. Bush, son of the former president—settled into a seat on his chartered Lear jet and closed his eyes. He appeared to be napping during most of the flight back to his headquarters in Virginia. Only later would the real motive behind this uncharacteristic rest become apparent: It enabled Ralph to fortify himself for the difficult moments that would surely follow once he broke the news of his impending resignation to the two top staffers traveling with him, D. J. Gribbin and Bishop Earl Jackson.

Ralph broke the news as the Lear approached the Norfolk airport. He and Pat Robertson had already met, and his resignation would become effective several months hence, providing transition time for a new leader. Gribbin and Jackson were stunned; thoughts of unfinished business filled their minds. Gribbin was still busy building a permanent membership base. Jackson was running the two-month-old racial outreach initiative, the Samaritan Project, which had the support of Ralph but not of Robertson and the rest of the Christian Coalition board.

When the jet landed, Ralph's wife Jo Anne was waiting. She joined the trio for the twenty-minute ride to the Coalition's offices, where another dozen top staff members had been called together to hear the news. In the morning Ralph would fly to D.C. and, after calling Coalition leaders in the field, make his announcement before scores of reporters and TV cameras.

Ralph orchestrated the media coverage of his departure brilliantly. By springing the news on everyone at the same time, he avoided early news leaks that might have spawned speculations beyond his control—about rumored conflicts with Robertson, about the IRS investigation and FEC lawsuit into whether the Coalition had violated campaign finance laws, about the grand jury probe into a former employee's allegations against Ralph. Instead, the press coverage of his resignation billed Ralph as a boy-genius, off to pursue a promising new career as a political consultant, leaving the Christian Coalition to face an uncertain future. Even Jo Anne was pleasantly suprised at the glowing reviews of his tenure. "I didn't want him to leave at that time," she recalled. "I didn't want people to think he was leaving under a cloud with the Judy Liebert thing, or that he was being forced out because of it. He wasn't."

In fact, the "Judy Liebert thing" had been one more hairpin turn in Ralph's roller-coaster life. A year earlier, Liebert, then the Coalition's chief financial officer, had gone to the U.S. Attorney's office with concerns about Ralph's dealings with the Coalition's direct-mail vendor, Benjamin Hart, a close friend with whom Ralph regularly golfed and vacationed. Liebert suspected Hart's firm was regularly marking up the Coalition's bills. She alleged that a former Hart employee had shown her evidence of overbilling—$85,000 on one order alone. She also charged that Ralph turned over, free of charge, the Coalition's entire mailing list—the group's most valuable asset worth an estimated $900,000—to Hart's firm, Hart Conover Inc. Hart allegedly used the list to solicit contributions for two rival groups he formed, the Christian Defense Fund and the Center for American Values.

Liebert had raised questions internally about Hart Conover's bills and the passing of the Coalition's mailing list, but failed to get satisfactory answers. On April 18, 1996, she took her concerns to the U.S. Attorney's office. A grand jury subpoenaed Hart Conover's records shortly thereafter. Alerted to the investigation in May, the Christian Coalition board, with Ralph sitting at Robertson's side, demanded that Liebert recant her charges. Asked if she believed Ralph had engaged in any wrongdoing, she answered: "I don't know." By the end of that week she had been suspended with pay. She was fired six months later.

During subsequent negotiations over a severance package, the Coalition board offered Liebert a letter of recommendation, a year's salary of $80,000, and another $25,000 to cover legal expenses, provided she agreed not to publicly disparage the Coalition. She refused. "I would never have been able to tell the truth," she said. At the request of investigators from these agencies, Liebert also turned over internal memos to the FEC and IRS suggesting possible ties between the

Coalition and individual Republican campaigns. When news of Liebert's charges reached the press, a Coalition lawyer labeled Liebert a "disgruntled employee."

But Liebert, who worked at Ralph's side for six years, was not someone easily dismissed. Four other former Christian Coalition employees went on the record with *Virginia Pilot* reporter Bill Sizemore to back up various aspects of Liebert's story. Documents also raised issues about the Coalition's dealings with Ralph's friend Hart. The Coalition's marketing director wrote a memo expressing concern about the " 'closed circle' of business that provides Hart-Conover with an extraordinary income stream. . . . It doesn't give us the benefit of a competitive bidding environment. Consequently, our 'above the line' cost for direct mail fundraising is astronomical (somewhere in the 50–70% range)."

In response to the overbilling allegations, the Coalition hired an outside auditor and a settlement was reached under which Hart Conover repaid the Coalition an undisclosed sum. A Christian Coalition attorney told reporters the audit confirmed that "no coalition employee or officer personally benefited from the organization's relationship with any outside vendor." A lawyer for Hart Conover said the audit found no pattern of overcharging, only invoicing errors on both sides. No criminal charges were brought against the Coalition or any of its officers as a result of the grand jury probe. Ralph declined to discuss the charges publicly, though in an affidavit he denied turning over the mailing list.

But in December of 1997, after Ralph's departure, the Christian Coalition filed a lawsuit against Hart Conover, accusing its former direct-mail vendor of fraudulently obtaining its mailing list and using it to entice donors away. (The Coalition blamed the slide in its own donations partly on Hart's use of the list.) In March 1998, the two parties reached an out-of-court settlement, but the details remain secret.

Liebert's charges were not the result of personal animosity toward Ralph. Indeed, it was Liebert who had often defended Ralph around the office when fellow staffers accused him of hypocrisy—a man who claimed to follow Christ but whose imperious ways with staff were hardly those of a charitable Christian. Liebert, seventeen years older than Ralph, merely considered him immature and too new to his faith to have changed his hardball ways. She often tried to coach him on people skills, feeding him books and advice on how to treat others with kindness. Even after she was fired, Liebert said in an interview that she considered him "brilliant . . . I loved Ralph Reed like a son."

Ralph's Washington staff, in particular, also considered their boss a shrewd strategist and an articulate spokesman who had built a promising movement largely on the strength of his own media appearances. "A lot of people who weren't regular churchgoers would send in checks after seeing Ralph on TV," said one Coalition officer who remained a booster. But among other Coalition staffers, especially within the Chesapeake headquarters, a less charitable view of Ralph took root. These insiders recalled that Ralph could be dismissive and arrogant in his dealings with staff, often berating employees in front of others and establishing a power imbalance with visitors by needlessly keeping them waiting or conducting meetings while watching CNN. "I'm just amazed that no one in the media picked up on the petty, small side of Ralph," complained one insider.

Some staffers said Ralph's inflated vision of himself led him to an equally outsized sense of paranoia. He checked into hotels under assumed names and kept a bodyguard on staff. But his wife Jo Anne said security measures were necessary because the troubled husband of a former employee had stalked Ralph and made threats against him. Security for the Reed family included escape drills at their Virginia home for Ralph and Jo Anne and their four small children. "They made it like a game but it was still nerve-racking for a mother," Jo Anne recalled. Robertson also coached Reed on how to avoid entrapment, knowing that with Ralph preaching a message of morality, political foes might be eager to catch him in a compromising position.

Critics inside the organization saw his resignation as evidence that "Ralph was looking out for Ralph," as one put it, that he knew the Coalition was crumbling from within. He had bought low and was selling high, getting out while the going still looked good, said one insider. Ironically, if the Coalition was crumbling, it was for the same reasons that had killed earlier New Right organizations whose mistakes Ralph had intended to avoid—namely high operating costs, especially on direct mail. "We never built up a major donor base" that would provide the organization with more financial stability, said one person knowledgeable about the Coalition's finances.

Insiders also portrayed Ralph's management style as too often "seat-of-the-pants." He never executed a formal contract with Hart Conover, relying instead on purchase orders, a decision that spawned suspicion even if there was no basis for it. The failure to build internal support for the Samaritan Project, the racial outreach program, was another lapse in management. Neither did Ralph lay the groundwork for his own departure by first grooming a viable successor. This lack of follow-through was evident, too, in the 1995 Contract with the American Family, most of which was languishing in Congress when Ralph announced his departure.

But Ralph had built the Coalition on the premise that lasting influence required changing politicians, not the minds of politicians already in the system. The Christian Coalition was more an electoral machine than a lobby, and as such it could claim spectacular success, especially in turning out voters in close races. Yet the Coalition was not organized as a political action committee, subject to taxes and disclosure laws, and so IRS and FEC investigations dogged the organization from early on. Intent on helping Republicans win, Ralph tied the Coalition's star to the GOP and, in 1996, to its front-runner for the presidential nomination. It was a calculation that cost the Coalition membership at the grass roots.

Ralph's most lasting legacy was showing Religious Right activists a path out of their political ghetto and into mainstream politics. He turned them into a force feared and courted by candidates for local and state offices, for Congress, and for the presidency. He had been their voice—educated, articulate, inclusive—on the Sunday morning talk shows and in the pages of the *New York Times*. But in casting his wider net, he never quite figured out how to avoid losing those who first knit it—the Coalition's core activists, to whom politics was a Godly mission, not a temporal game.

Those left behind after Ralph's resignation insisted his brainchild would thrive without him. "Ralph slaps a happy face on the movement," Gribbin said, reflecting on his boss's imminent departure. "Instead of one voice, there will be fifty voices. We'll have to work harder on visibility, but we're not going to let the media write our obituary." Unfortunately for Gribbin and others who slaved to build the Christian Coalition into a permanent fixture on the political landscape, that happy face proved to be ephemeral.

After Ralph's departure, the Christian Coalition went into a steady and swift decline. Two years later, the organization was crippled by layoffs, management shakeups, and a $2.5 million debt. The Coalition was forced to reorganize and pay back taxes after the IRS indicated it would deny the organization tax-exempt status because of the partisan cast of its voter guides and officers' remarks. The only bit of good news was a federal judge's rejection of most of the charges in the FEC lawsuit. But the same judge also ordered the Christian Coalition to pay a civil penalty for advocating the election of Gingrich in 1994 and improperly sharing its mailing list with Senate candidate Oliver North.

☐

LIKE OTHER REPUBLICAN LAWMAKERS, David McIntosh was beginning to see the limits of the Right's government-is-evil theme. Instead, he adopted a more conventional conservative line of promising to reduce "the unnecessary bureaucracy that wastes taxpayer money." In 1994, McIntosh's instrument of attack in campaign commercials had been the morphing machine—transfusing his opponent's face into that of the enemy, Bill Clinton. In his successful 1996 bid for reelection, it was the oboe, played low and plaintive behind campaign commercials designed to portray the congressman as a caring Hoosier who rescued children by cutting through the FDA's red tape to obtain critical drugs:

"My name is Molly Dailey," a sweet-faced college student told viewers, as the oboe played on, "and I'm surviving cancer thanks to a treatment that David McIntosh helped me get. . . ."

"My son's alive because of David McIntosh," the mother of a boy with a genetic liver disease told TV viewers. "David made me a believer in people again. And it's been a long time coming."

The man who had counseled his wife to "put your faith in ideas, not in people," was shaving off the rough edges of his ideology, and listening more to his constituents. As a midwestern congressman, much of his job entailed running interference for the mundane and sometimes life-or-death dealings his constituents had with the same federal bureaucracy that rightist theory said should disappear. His voters would shuffle up to him after the speeches and the rallies and the glad-handing—not Republicans or Democrats, but constituents, their faces lined with worry, their heads holding in precarious balance the crabbed details of this Medicare service not covered or that student loan denied.

After one campaign debate in 1996, an elderly factory worker stood at David's elbow, his blue windbreaker covered with pro-union and "Vote Democrat" buttons, his bony trembling hands holding an envelope containing the news that his disabled son no longer qualified for SSI payments under a newly slashed budget. As union leaders stood by, waving signs that taunted McIntosh as a coldhearted extremist, David tipped his head and listened to the man's story, took a few notes, and pretended not to notice the Democratic campaign buttons. Then he promised to help.

His tumultuous first years in Congress, David later said, had given him "a greater understanding that the public values programs in government—programs that, as a pure philosophical or ideological matter, you could say we could get rid of." Acutely aware that the public wasn't as eager as he was to eliminate scores of health, safety, and environmental protections, McIntosh lowered his sights on regulatory reform, seeking incremental rather than sweeping change. "We've shrunk back from trying to restructure the system," he told a reporter in his second term.

Union leaders in his district still opposed him, but he began earning even their respect: In response to a series of plant closings, the congressman orchestrated annual job fairs that successfully connected hundreds of unemployed workers with training programs and companies with openings. In Washington, he signed on with a group of lawmakers calling themselves "the renewal alliance" and promoting government incentives to businesses and charities to aid the poor. During his second term in Congress, from 1997 through 1998, McIntosh's flagship themes were hardly revolutionary: eliminating the tax penalty for married working couples and improving public education.

But there was one legacy of the otherwise failed Republican Revolution that David believed was still worth a no-holds-barred fight: sweeping tax cuts. The promise of massive tax reduction had been the crown jewel of the 104th Congress. But, as 1997 opened, the Republicans controlling Congress, locked in budget battles with the White House, still hadn't been able to deliver on that promise. In McIntosh's mind, Gingrich was too willing to give away sharp tax reduction in order to reach a budget deal that the president would sign. In the spring of 1997, the Indiana congressman was part of an emerging mutiny by conservative House Republicans against the speaker, egged on by Bill Kristol's *Weekly Standard,* which described McIntosh as a "rebel with a cause," a lawmaker who is "building a record of principled opposition to the budget deal and to the GOP's general quiescence. . . . [This] mutiny pleases conservatives."

Suprisingly, as hard-core House members gathered in each other's offices that spring, swapping gripes about the speaker's latest foible, the Right's outside activists were far more gentle toward their onetime mentor. In April, Grover invited the speaker to a meeting with outside activists. "Gingrich explained his tax strategy and I can't think of anyone who objected," said one frustrated participant. "It was so strange: The House conservatives were in more of a revolt than the activists. The outside groups were placid."

One reason for the polite reception accorded Gingrich was the speaker's close friendship with Grover. Always respectful of Norquist, the Right's activists kept their emotions in check (though that didn't prevent a handful of them from offering anonymous barbs at Gingrich to reporters after the meeting). Another reason was the move-ment's hunger for a leader. In the past, conservatives had been able to look to Robert Taft, then Barry Goldwater, then Ronald Reagan. If now not Newt, then who?

McIntosh believed that without a change in the House leader-ship, the Republicans risked losing their majority in the November 1998 elections. But he had qualms about unceremoniously dumping Newt, who had been the face of the conservative revolution at least as long as David had been in Washington. McIntosh preferred a slow and steady transition, allowing Gingrich to save face by moving on to another endeavor, such as running for president. David wasn't so much driven by personal loyalty as by process loyalty: He feared that a precipitous dump-Newt effort might weaken the House Republi-cans, endangering their beloved tax cuts.

But there were other lawmakers far more determined to secure Gingrich's immediate ouster, and by summer these rebels—furious over reports of another impending Gingrich compromise on the budget—were secretly broaching the possibility of a coup d'etat. One afternoon in July, David joined the ringleaders for a meeting inside the Capitol office of House majority leader Dick Armey of Texas. For the first time, the rebels considered the actual mechanics of removing the speaker. One member described the House rules: If enough Republicans crossed the aisle to vote with Democrats, they could "vacate" the speaker's chair. That accomplished, House Republicans could then elect a new speaker.

The rebellion came to a head on Thursday night, July 10, when seventeen lawmakers, including McIntosh, met with majority whip Tom DeLay, also of Texas, the Number Three leader in the House. The meeting ended with the rebels declaring they were ready to vote to vacate the chair, provided they had support from others on Gin-grich's leadership team. "I think I'd be ready to do it . . . ," DeLay re-sponded. "And I think the others would too."

McIntosh continued to favor a strategy of allowing Gingrich to script his own exit but his was a minority voice among the rebels. By then, too, events were spiraling beyond anyone's control. As two top Gingrich lieutenants who harbored personal ambitions for the speak-ership, Bill Paxon of New York and Dick Armey of Texas, weighed whether to join the dissidents, Gingrich caught wind of the plotting. Divisions within the leadership ranks enabled Gingrich to swiftly re-gain the upper hand. Within four days, he had snuffed out the coup and forced the resignation of Paxon, the only House leader appointed by Gingrich rather than elected by GOP members. Rumors of further retaliation swept through the Capitol, and McIntosh, as class leader, considered ways to defend the core coup plotters against Gingrich's wrath.

On Wednesday night, July 23, the full House Republican conference gathered behind closed doors to hear apologies from Gingrich's lieutenants. Gingrich reasserted his authority and, quoting a Bible passage, indicated that all was forgiven, if not forgotten: "Bless those who persecute you; bless and do not curse." Gingrich was firmly back in charge, but McIntosh, for one, saw the revolution that the speaker professed to lead slipping further away.

In David's mind, the troubling surrender was not that of the coup plotters but that of the Republican budget-makers. Within weeks, House Republicans cut a deal with the Democrats on a budget that included only a third of the tax cuts they had sought. The bill also established a new, $25 billion entitlement program to provide health care for needy children. After a divisive two-year battle over the budget, this was the endgame: Gingrich called on House Republicans to support legislation so moderate that even Washington's liberal activists were applauding it.

McIntosh cast his vote against the budget deal. "The fight's not over," he told his downcast colleagues. But he also had choice words for the speaker: "Newt still has a tin ear" for the concerns of the conservatives, he said in an interview at the time. "We said, 'we don't want to get into a [leadership] fight now, we're in the middle of this budget.' " But the rebels' willingness to back down "wasn't about personal loyalty" to Gingrich, he added, it was about "loyalty to issues and a cause."

CLINT BOLICK would look back on the summer of 1997 as his Valley Forge period, knowing that victory must be somewhere on the horizon but unable to see its fine sheen. On May 1 of that year an Ohio appeals court had ruled that Cleveland's school choice program was unconstitutional. The Cleveland program was an important national test case because it was the first one to allow children to use tax-funded vouchers to attend religious as well as secular private schools. The court ruled that the program violated both the First Amendment of the U.S. Constitution and the Ohio constitution's religious establishment clause.

To Clint, who was representing parents in the case, the ruling was a personal blow. The Cleveland public schools were among the worst in the nation, worse even than those in Milwaukee, where Clint had successfully argued his first school choice case. This court ruling was a decisive roadblock for some three thousand poor students who had planned to attend private schools in Cleveland that fall. The day the decision came down, Clint was settling back in his office after a trip to Arizona, where legislators were discussing a school choice plan for that state. He received word of the court's decision just after lunch and for the rest of the afternoon, and the weekend that followed, he was haunted by self-doubt. He felt personally responsible for "letting these kids down."

The next week he and partner Chip Mellor sent a memo to supporters that sounded like they were trying to convince themselves, as much as their readers, of the prospects for ultimate victory: "As at Valley Forge, it's time to bunker down before the ultimate triumph. The movement has come a tremendously long way, against overwhelming odds, in a very short time. It is clear that no victory will come easily. But it is even more clear that the real-world payoff, in terms of brighter educational prospects for children who desperately need them, is greater than many of us dared to hope. The course ahead may prove difficult, but undoubtedly it is the right one, and well worth the fight."

Clint began reconsidering his legal and public relations strategy and recruited several of the Right's most prominent legal minds for a day-long brainstorming session. Out of that strategy session came heightened efforts to work with prominent liberal academics and journalists supportive of school choice. But it would take another year for the tide to turn again.

In June of 1998, the Wisconsin Supreme Court upheld the use of tax-funded vouchers for religious schools, and five months later the U.S. Supreme Court let that ruling stand. One year later, the Ohio Supreme Court upheld the constitutionality of the Cleveland program but invalidated it on a technicality that the state legislature moved quickly to correct. Nevertheless, a federal judge, disagreeing with the Ohio Supreme Court, ruled that the program violated the First Amendment, and the battle continued into 2000.

In 1999, Florida adopted the first statewide school choice program, offering taxpayer-financed vouchers to students in failing schools. That same year, the U.S. Supreme Court upheld the constitutionality of a related approach to school choice, Arizona's program of offering state income tax credits for contributions to private scholarship programs.

On August 19, 1999, a federal judge handed Clint a victory in his economic liberty litigation by upholding the San Diego African hair braiders' constitutional challenge to California's cosmetology regulations. The state declined to appeal the decision.

THE POLITICS OF SCANDAL can be tricky business, especially if the side throwing the mud is already struggling to overcome a reputation for being "mean-spirited." America's culture of tolerance has made the country a forgiving place when it comes to the personal foibles of political leaders. Managing sex scandals is especially risky with all those glass houses standing atop the political landscape: Who could have known that Speaker Gingrich was having his own dalliance with a young staffer (a relationship that would lead to a bitter divorce from his wife Marianne) during the months he was halfheartedly leading the House Republican charge to punish Bill Clinton for the Lewinsky affair?

During Clinton's first six years in office, Kristol had counseled conservatives against relying on the weapon of scandal against their liberal foes. True, Kristol had publicly attacked Clinton during the 1992 campaign for the candidate's alleged "womanizing." True, his magazine—with editorialist David Tell setting the tone—had repeatedly hammered Clinton as a liar, a compulsively disingenuous president who operated his administration like a "used-car dealership." But, until January of 1998, Kristol and his staff had steered clear of much of the scandalmongering infecting the Right. Occasionally, *Standard* writers even parodied the Right's loonier conspiracy theories—such as those surrounding the suicide of White House counsel Vince Foster and Commerce Secretary Ron Brown's death in a plane crash.

Kristol claimed he wasn't an avid Clinton hater; he would point out that he had made enemies on the Right by supporting the president's military interventions overseas. (Even during the impeachment phase of the Lewinsky affair, Kristol would support Clinton's decision to bomb Iraq, while most conservatives asserted the military action was a calculated diversion from Clinton's domestic troubles.)

But in early 1998, when Monica Lewinsky's name hit the headlines and Bill Clinton claimed—under oath in legal proceedings for the Paula Jones sexual harassment case—that he never had sexual relations with the young intern, Kristol declared war. In the scandal that ensued, the *Weekly Standard* editor would emerge as one of the most vociferous figures in Washington calling for Clinton's ouster. If not for Kristol's obsessive marshaling of the pro-impeachment forces, said a number of conservatives, independent counsel Kenneth Starr's investigation might have petered out, and House Republicans might have allowed the public's disapproval of their course to dissuade them from voting to impeach the president.

Like his fellow conservative leaders, Kristol was thinking about legacies—in this case, a liberal vestige of the baby-boom generation. It wasn't just that Clinton had had a sexual affair with a young White House intern and was now (Kristol was certain) lying about it. Nor was the issue just Clintonism's "self-satisfied nonjudgmentalism, a soft relativism, . . . easygoing nihilism," though those were certainly important factors behind Kristol's crusade. What peeved Kristol was what the Lewinsky episode said about the nation's changed attitude toward sex since the liberation movements of the 1960s. Clintonism (Kristol's a.k.a. for liberalism) "specifically exempts one sphere of life from all moral judgments: sex. . . . Sex, and sex alone, must be free of constraint, and of judgment." Lying about sex is *the* permissible form of lying, he noted: "Just as the right to abortion is the one right that can never be abridged; just as homosexuality is the one practice that can never be criticized; so consensual sexual behavior is the one realm of human activity about which any sort of moral judgment is illegitimate."

For twelve months, *Weekly Standard* writers rooted for impeachment with a zeal that suggested they almost believed this constitutional action would, at last, purge the nation of the cultural detritus left behind by baby-boom liberals. If the Clarence Thomas–Robert Bork–Murphy Brown episodes were skirmishes in the struggle for the soul of a generation, impeachment was Armageddon. The Lewinsky affair, the *Standard*'s traditionalists argued, was emblematic of the lax morality of their generation. The Clinton White House, Peter Collier told *Standard* readers, was "a place where denatured New Left politics meets denatured New Age therapeutics"; "1968: A Revolting Generation Thirty Years On," one cover of the magazine declared. A *Standard* editorial asked, "Where's the Outrage?" Clinton was shameless, a liar, the big he, the top narcissist of a narcissistic generation.

Within days of Clinton's televised denial of the affair in January 1998—when the public was still making up its mind about the veracity of his story—Kristol made his weekly roundtable appearance on ABC's *This Week* and assured millions of Sunday morning viewers that "the president of the United States is lying. Everyone knows he's lying. He's inducing others who work with him and for him to lie. Lies beget lies. Washington is now, I think, drowning in deceit and it cannot go on." In the following Sunday roundtable discussion, he proclaimed: "If we have a culture that mocks honesty, we're not going to take lying seriously. . . . This president has done a very good job of defining public morality down. . . . To let him stay now, I think, is fundamentally corrupting."

If attempting to shame his TV audience was one part of Kristol's impeachment crusade, another was coaching Republican leaders to stand against the tide of public opinion, just as he had done in the health care and welfare debates. Throughout the Lewinsky episode, a solid majority of Americans told pollsters that, regardless of Clinton's misdeeds, they preferred to see the whole matter dropped. As a Straussian, though, Bill believed political leaders should mold public opinion, not be molded by it. ("In politics, the first of the virtues is courage," Bill once wrote.) In early 1998, he began assuaging nervous Republican leaders with assurances of Clinton's ultimate demise. In February, when the president's future seemed uncertain, he predicted that Democratic leaders would convince him to resign. A week later, he predicted Starr would issue a report alleging that Clinton had committed "impeachable offenses."

Even in May, when it became clear that Clinton had dug his heels into his mound of public approval, Kristol wrote: "President Clinton is doomed. . . . I know, I know. His approval rating is sky-high. The American people don't want to hear about his sex life. Ken Starr has a tin ear for politics. Republicans in Congress are afraid of taking Clinton on. All more or less true. But all, ultimately, more or less irrelevant. . . ." What Republicans need now, he proclaimed three weeks later, "is the nerve to fight" for impeachment. With it, "they will win big in [congressional elections in] November. And their victory will be more than a rejection of Clinton. It will be a rejection of Clintonism— a rejection of defining the presidency, and our public morality, down."

That summer, Kristol played cheerleader to a besieged Ken Starr, and later to members of the House Judiciary Committee pursuing impeachment. After running a magazine cover headlined "Clinton Must Go" on August 31, he greeted Starr's long-awaited investigative report on September 21 with the cover "Starr's Home Run." Even some long-term Clinton-bashers considered the report inappropriately salacious, a leering invasion of privacy. But the *Weekly Standard* hailed Starr's document for revealing Clinton to the public as "a lout and liar and criminal."

All of this noise had a modest effect on nervous congressional leaders. In April, Gingrich had finally spoken out against the president, asserting that he would never again make a speech without commenting on the Lewinsky matter. But by August, Kristol was condemning the Speaker's go-slow approach as a "simulacrum of statesmanship. The truly statesman-like thing to do under the circumstances is to address the question of Clinton with dispatch." Members of Congress, however, were facing hard political facts: Even after the Starr report, even after the release of Clinton's videotaped testimony in the Jones case, even after most people said they believed that Clinton had lied under oath, 63 percent of the public didn't believe he had committed an impeachable offense. Moreover, large segments of the public were coming to the conclusion that Clinton's deplorable behavior was outmatched by that of his political enemies.

Like others on the Right, Kristol was learning a difficult lesson in how far out of sync his views were with those of the American public. "In the Reagan years," he later said, "conservatives took cheap comfort in the claim that, 'The public's right, and we're right—so we're the public and it's the liberals who are out of touch.' Now, I guess it's payback time."

THE SOUND COMING from the Right during the summer and fall of 1998 seemed to have one pitch—a bullhorn screech calling for Clinton's head. The first lady, White House aides, and Clinton supporters decried a menacing "right-wing conspiracy" to bring down a Democratic president. In fact, though, there was considerably more nuance within the ranks of the baby-boom Right.

Ralph, in his new role as founder and head of the Atlanta-based political consulting firm Century Strategies, sent a memo to Republican leaders in September arguing that "if we rely entirely on the scandal, we will come up short on Election Day." (By contrast, the Christian Coalition's new leadership team of Donald Hodel, a sixty-two-year-old businessman who had served Reagan as energy and interior secretary, and former U.S. congressman Randy Tate made impeachment a top priority. Later, Hodel would resign in frustration when Pat Robertson stalled the Coalition's pro-impeachment direct-mail drive by urging Congress to "get on with something else.") It wasn't that Ralph didn't consider Clinton's transgressions impeachable—he did, though he never believed they rose to the level of a scandal like Watergate. Mostly, Ralph was worried that impeachment threatened the prospect of Republican victory in November.

For those on the Right looking for victory in their own policy battles, the Lewinsky affair was like a tornado that soaked up all the energy and light from the atmosphere. No one hated Bill Clinton more than Clint Bolick, who considered the president "arrogant, filled with cloying self-righteousness, the sort of guy who will do anything he needs to do to protect his presidency." Bolick's contempt stemmed in part from the president's refusal to apply his "third way" approach to racial issues. On welfare, on regulation, on spending, on crime, the Democratic president had carved a pragmatic middle ground, a "third way," between Right and Left. But on affirmative action, the president had elevated liberal constituency politics over innovation, appointing defenders of the status quo to key civil rights positions. It was Bolick who in 1997 had put together a coalition of senators to block the confirmation of the Justice Department's civil rights chief Bill Lann Lee, who was then forced to serve out his term as an "acting" assistant attorney general. It was Bolick who constantly badgered the administration over affirmative action and its court battle against the California Civil Rights Initiative, which barred the use of gender and racial preferences in state programs.

Nevertheless, Bolick worried that "every minute that we spend on the Clinton [impeachment] is wasted capital, and drags us deeper and deeper into the quicksand." His libertarian instincts also made him wary of joining a crusade against the president's sexual misdeeds. "There is a sacrosanct realm of privacy and a lot of people are just offended that Starr and others have delved so deeply into the inner sanctum of [Clinton's] life," he said. "There's something dirty about it. . . . It seems to me that the people who set out to get Clinton, set out to get Clinton. And it flat-out didn't matter what was going to happen along the way."

Unlike Bolick, Grover didn't worry about the privacy issue. He argued that the president had made the Lewinsky affair a public matter when he lied about it under oath. Members of Grover's Leave Us Alone Coalition had been licking their chops at the prospect of a Clinton impeachment since well before Lewinsky's name surfaced. But as the year of the sex scandal wore on, consuming the nation's attention, Grover sometimes found himself wishing it would just go away. "No one would talk about anything else," he complained. And Grover—a man known for issuing "no sex talk, please" requests to fellow activists who dwelled on matters of private behavior—didn't have much to say about the scandal. Other activists in Grover's Leave Us Alone Coalition worried that Clinton's departure would leave the Oval Office to Al Gore, who, they believed, was more liberal and politically stronger than Clinton.

McIntosh had tried to carve out his own piece of Clinton scandal in 1996, when he demanded that the White House turn over its

200,000-name data base so that he could investigate possible fund-raising abuses. But during the Lewinsky affair, David held back, repeatedly saying the president deserved the "benefit of the doubt until the facts proved otherwise." Ultimately he supported three out of four articles of impeachment. But in the months leading up to that historic House vote, McIntosh mostly viewed the scandal as a way for Republicans to regain the upper hand in budget negotiations. With the federal budget under negotiation that August, McIntosh began lobbying GOP leaders for another budget confrontation with the White House, arguing that they should shut down the government until Clinton agreed to their tax and spending cuts. With the president bogged down in scandal, McIntosh told a reporter, "I think we win this time around." McIntosh claimed broad support from fellow members for this strategy, but moderates quickly doused the idea. "It's false bravado . . . it's ridiculous," said one. "If history has shown anything, it's that Clinton is better at P.R. than House Republicans."

WITH CLINTON ENGULFED IN SCANDAL and facing the possibility of impeachment, many conservatives were certain that November 1998 would bring triumph. But on Election Day, the extent of their wishful thinking became painfully clear. When the votes were counted, the Democrats had picked up five seats in the House—a stunning outcome, the first time this century that a president's party gained seats in the middle of his second term in office. Although the Democrats failed to pick up seats in the Senate, Republicans Al D'Amato of New York and Lauch Faircloth of North Carolina, two of Clinton's most determined pursuers, both lost their bids for reelection.

For Ralph, election night was darkened by personal defeat. In his debut as a campaign consultant, he lost most of his major races—including those of the controversial Alabama governor, Fob James, whose reelection loss marked the first time in twelve years that a Republican had failed to capture that state's governor's mansion, and two congressional challengers, Gex Williams in Kentucky and Gary Hofmeister in Indiana. The 1998 campaign also took a toll on Ralph's public image. Even as much of the national press continued to treat him as a brilliant strategist, southern journalists covering his candidates condemned him for running "some of the more vicious and racist campaigns in this election season," as one commentator put it.

Grover faced his own losses in 1998. In June, Californians had voted down the so-called Paycheck Protection Act, an initiative designed to prevent union leaders from spending member dues on political activities without their consent. The California initiative, and similar measures in other states, were central to Norquist's strategy of breaking the electoral strength of organized labor. He had spent $441,000 on a petition drive to secure a ballot spot for the California initiative, and quickly became the poster boy of what union leaders described as a right-winger fronting for big business.

Initially, a strong majority of California voters had favored Norquist's initiative, believing that unions should be required to get permission from members before spending their money on politics. (While most labor leaders support liberal Democrats, some 40 percent of union members often vote Republican.) But the unions fought back with a $12 million media campaign aimed at demonstrating the imbalance between economic classes certain to occur if Proposition 226 passed. They argued that corporate PACs—whose expenditures don't require shareholder approval—spent $11 for every $1 spent by unions, and that union political activities were designed to protect workers on wage, health care, and safety policies that affect their lives and livelihoods. By the time of the June election, opinion polls had flip-flopped on the initiative, and it was defeated. Grover then turned his attention to a similar initiative in Oregon. On election night in November, Grover not only watched the Republicans get battered in the House, he also watched the Oregon initiative go down in a narrow defeat.

David McIntosh had little trouble winning reelection, but he faced defeat inside the House. In October, the House had approved a spending bill that lacked the tax relief he had sought yet included new increases in spending. The vote prompted *Wall Street Journal* columnist Paul Gigot to quip: "Democrats depressed that President Clinton has been diminished by scandal can relax. If he gets any weaker, Republicans may pass Hillary's health care plan." McIntosh, whom Gigot described as "a member of the class of '94 who still remembers why he was elected," complained that "a lot of members are furious that [Clinton] was able to browbeat our leadership to get what he wanted."

Days after the devastating election results came in, Newt Gingrich formally ended the Republican Revolution by stepping down as speaker. The man who emerged as the leading contender to replace Gingrich was Bob Livingston, the appropriations committee chairman who had cut all the tax-and-spend deals with the White House. In other words, he was considered a traitor inside the House's hardcore conservative faction. McIntosh publicly condemned Livingston as an "old-style pork caucus kind of guy who would lead us back to the minority." Livingston lasted just long enough to confess to his own adulterous affair, step down, and issue a challenge to Clinton to do the same.

Clinton stayed on, through the impeachment hearings in November, through the House vote to impeach him in December, and through the Senate's vote to acquit him in February. By then, Kristol had long given up his belief that (as his editorialist David Tell put it): "Impeach him, explain it, and they will come." Most of the public had soundly rejected Kristol's contention that President Clinton was no longer worthy of remaining in office. Instead, Kristol extolled congressional Republicans as honorable and courageous with a magazine cover labeling the House impeachment vote "Their Finest Hour."

NINETEEN NINETY-NINE OPENED with much of the Goldwater generation ready to throw in the towel. Shattered by the public's refusal to support impeachment, New Right leader Paul Weyrich sent a memo to fellow conservative leaders on February 16: "We probably have lost the culture war. What we have been doing for thirty years hasn't worked. I no longer believe there is a moral majority."

But the generation of conservatives who came to Washington with Reagan had no intention of "quarantining" themselves from the mainstream, as Weyrich had suggested. Whatever setbacks they had suffered in the late 1990s, the baby-boom conservatives always saw victory on the horizon. They remained certain they were running with the tide of American culture, not against it. Even Kristol retained his optimism about America's direction: "I don't despair," he said in early 1999. "I think the public is ambivalent" about morality and public life, and in need of guidance from leaders less skittish about raising these thorny issues.

As the presidential election of 2000 approached, the baby-boom conservatives toted up their victories—Republicans still in control of Congress, still holding on to three-fifths of the nation's governor's mansions, still enjoying the huge gains made in statehouses over the past decade—and assured each other of triumphs still to come. Ignoring more purist Rightists running for the Republican presidential nomination, Reed and Norquist opted instead to check their futures with a winner, Texas Governor George W. Bush, a candidate who would try to broaden the movement's appeal with the label "compassionate conservatism."

But in promoting this reformist conservative, Ralph and Grover both reverted to type, borrowing the hardball tactics they had perfected twenty years earlier in the College Republicans, as they waged war on Bush's chief rival, Arizona Senator John McCain. Even before McCain's presidential bid, Grover had denounced the senator as disloyal, saying his campaign finance reform initiative would shield organized labor's electioneering while hurting Republicans and the Right's grass-roots lobbyists. During the New Hampshire primary in early February 2000, Grover's group, Americans for Tax Reform, ran a series of TV ads accusing the Republican senator of "helping Democrats."

Despite the attack ads, McCain achieved a stunning upset over Bush in New Hampshire. To stop McCain, Reed and Norquist joined a pro-Bush carpet-bombing campaign against him in the all-important South Carolina primary. The Bush campaign's "slashing tactics"—attacking McCain's character, his abortion stance, and his commitment to the conservative cause—were "ferocious even by South Carolina's down-and-dirty standards," according to one account. Ralph delivered his own anti-McCain pitch in media appearances, denouncing the senator as a chameleon and questioning his credentials as a Republican. Reed organized negative phone calls and mailings to the state's 400,000 Christian conservatives. Grover's ATR was one of a number of outside organizations to blitz the state with anti-McCain radio and TV ads. McCain's campaign chairman, former New Hampshire Senator Warren Rudman, called Ralph "a baby-faced assassin. He's silky smooth, butter wouldn't melt in his mouth, but he's a vicious guy." Rudman dismissed Grover as a Washington lobbyist who represented authoritarian foreign regimes.

The 2000 primary season also revealed what the Christian Coalition had become without Ralph's determined makeover work. By now his successors Hodel and Tate were both gone. Most of the Washington office, once the province of savvy politicos, had quit. So many state leaders were resigning each week that one former Coalition organizer kept a running "fatalities list." The Coalition was now Pat Robertson's personal fiefdom, and Robertson jumped into the fray with comments meant to divide, not to unite. In one case, he labeled Rudman, McCain's Jewish campaign co-chairman, an anti-Christian "bigot."

McCain counter-punched against this and other Religious Right attacks by flying into Virginia in early March, on the eve of that state's primary, to denounce two of its homegrown evangelicals, Robertson and Jerry Falwell. McCain's attacks on the Christian Right (he later offhandedly called Robertson and Falwell agents of "evil") was probably a strategic mistake that cost him Republican votes. But the whole episode also offered a pointed reminder that the Religious Right remained locked inside a political ghetto. With Ralph busy playing hardball behind the scenes, the public face of the Religious Right was Pat Robertson, Jerry Falwell, and Bob Jones University, the fundamentalist South Carolina school that denounced Catholic theology and, until early 2000, barred interracial dating. This was an image that frightened many moderate voters, even in the Republican Party. To compete against Democratic Vice President Al Gore in the general election, George Bush would have to mend the damage caused by his visible alliance with Robertson and his February visit to the Bob Jones campus.

Kristol had avoided overtly picking sides until his friend, Christian Right leader Gary Bauer, dropped out of the presidential race in February before the South Carolina primary. Then he packed up with the self-proclaimed rebel against the Republican establishment, John McCain. For those who believe that the GOP is still the "stupid party"—that the "conservative movement in many ways has become an obstacle to achieving conservative goals . . . then you're likely to have rallied to John McCain," Bill wrote in February. Supporting McCain, he added, was less a matter of ideology than of temperament, a display of one's willingness to challenge the Republican status quo. Supporting McCain also gave Kristol a place to park his ambitions as a court adviser: The Bush camp, viewing him as an opportunist and self-promoter, steered clear of the *Weekly Standard* publisher.

In that same piece, Kristol tweaked his old friend Ralph Reed. When Ralph reads that Bush, as the establishment choice, is the inevitable nominee, he "nods his head and works to ensure a seat for religious conservatives at the establishment table," Kristol wrote. Kristol, by contrast, insisted he was looking to foment a rebellion, not join an establishment. (Fellow rebel Mike Murphy was already on board with McCain as the campaign's chief strategist.) To the Kristolites, McCain had the potential to put forward a new kind of conservatism of "limited but energetic government" and a renewed sense of patriotism, a call to "national greatness." Unfortunately for them, McCain didn't survive the Super Tuesday primaries in early March, and Kristol was left on the sidelines again, watching (for the third time) a Republican establishment candidate not of his own making attempt to plant the conservative flag on the White House lawn.

But the revolution progressed in fits and starts beyond the presidential campaign and the confines of Washington. Grover was peddling a plan around the country to enlarge America's pool of ardent

capitalists (and therefore Republican voters) by pushing a pension reform proposal that would transform more state employees into stock-
holders, and at the same time gin up support for privatizing Social
Security. He was also busily forming mini–Wednesday Groups in the
states, providing a rightist strategic base for tax cutting, tort reform,
and school choice initiatives. In 2000, Grover was elected to the
board of the National Rifle Association, where he now sits next to
singer Ted Nugent. In 2001, he played a key role in the drafting of
President Bush's massive tax cut. Once that legislation passed Congress, Norquist continued to lobby for deeper cuts, still hoping to cut
the size of the federal government in half.

David McIntosh was running his own campaign—for governor
of Indiana, challenging the incumbent Democrat on tax and school
reform issues. It was a revealing move: While the Rightists on Capitol
Hill had hit the wall in their dreams of transforming Washington, Republican governors were making steady progress transforming conservative ideas into public policy. With a willingness to compromise,
they had built reputations as strong and pragmatic leaders, not divisive ideologues. In 2000, McIntosh looked to Indiana's statehouse as
the place where he might fulfill the political ambitions he had nurtured since he was eight years old. But facing a popular incumbent
Democrat and controversy surrounding his own record as on of Congress's most hard-core conservatives, McIntosh lost his race for the
governor's seat.

Clint Bolick had never been a GOP activist, and even the horse
race of the 2000 campaign couldn't inspire him toward party politics.
His mind that year was on the courts, where his battles on behalf of
school choice and against "grass-roots tyranny" continued. Ten years
after embarking on a career as a rightist public interest lawyer, Clint
was growing accustomed to bit-by-bit progress, knowing that, for all
the setbacks and defeats, those bits would add up to something big,
just as they once did for the Left. He still eagerly awaited the day
when he could walk up the steps of the U.S. Supreme Court, prepped
to argue the case that (he was certain) would change the world.

IN EARLY 2000, Bill Kristol, shaken by the ferocity of the Christian
Right assaults on Republican John McCain, declared a "conservative
crack-up." Historians, he asserted, "will look back and say, 'This was
the end.' I think the Christian Right, which I've defended, is finished
because of what Ralph Reed and Pat Robertson have done in South
Carolina, because of the meanness of the assault."

But wasn't this the nub of it all, the vulnerability of an entire movement, not just Reed, that insisted on pursuing politics as war? As the new millennium opened, the baby-boom conservatives had much to celebrate: They had shifted the nation's cultural and political landscape away from the legacy of the 1960s. They had transformed American conservatism with new levels of intellectualism, and broadened its reach by crafting a language of inclusion rather than division. They had held positions of power their precedessors on the activist Right could never dream of, helping to reshape not only the Republican Party but also the policies of the entire nation. In January 2000 their ally George W. Bush stepped into the Oval Office, insisting that he was bringing a new, more forward-looking brand of conservatism to the presidency.

Yet too often in the past, these one-time campus pariahs had displayed an ever-present thirst for blood, resorting to battle cries when their efforts at conservative reform came up short. In the overreach of the Republican Revolution, in the clipped division of the world between "our team" and "theirs," in the rejection of a political center, in the moralistic crusade to bring down Clinton, a perpetual question lingered. It was the same question that their friend President Bush would wrestle with in the early months of his administration: Do you intend to be leader of the whole, or remain at war with half?

NOTES

This book is based on dozens of tape-recorded interviews with the subjects over the course of four years, as well as on-site reporting of their activities. In addition, more than two hundred interviews were conducted with parents, other family members, friends, fellow activists, intellectual mentors, and leading conservative thinkers. Most of the interviews were conducted on the record, and quotations are attributed in the text. Anna McCollister participated in preliminary interviews with Bolick and Norquist; conducted the interviews with Ann Stone, Phyllis Schlafly, and Paul Erickson; and provided on-site reporting of the school choice case from Wisconsin. I also conducted extensive archival research, and owe particular thanks to these institutions for granting access to their files: the Ronald Reagan Library, the George Bush Presidential Library, the Harvard University Archives, Hargrett Rare Book and Manuscript Library at the University of Georgia, the Demosthenian Society, the Yale Political Union, U.C. Davis's King Hall Library, the College Republicans, People for the American Way, and the U.S. Public Interest Research Group.

Part One: THE 1970S: CAMPUS REBELS WITH A CAUSE

Chapter One. Contrarian

24   "a radical mood in search of a radical program": Irving Kristol, "What's Bugging the Students," *Atlantic,* November 1965, pp. 108–110.

25   "sullenly resentful": Irving Kristol, "Why I Am for Humphrey," *New Republic,* June 6, 1968, p. 21.

25   Barry Goldwater prediction: Frank S. Meyer, "Principles and Heresies: Why Goldwater Can Defeat Johnson," *National Review,* July 14, 1964, p. 581. Actually, a more complicated scenario lay behind Kristol's memory as a twelve-year-old: According to William F. Buckley's biographer, John B. Judis, the *National Review* founder was far more skeptical about the candidate's prospects than the Goldwater cheerleaders on his staff, including Meyer and William Rusher. In contrast to Meyer's prediction of victory (most likely the one that Kristol remembered), Buckley wrote

that it "is not helpful . . . to assert apodictically, and pridefully, that he *will* win." That fall Buckley stunned a Young Americans for Freedom conference by predicting "the impending defeat of Barry Goldwater."

26   "more than stupid": William Kristol, "Points of Rebellion," *Alternative,* November 1970, p. 6.

26   holiday wish list: William Kristol, "The Christmas Gift List That Was," *Alternative,* January 1971, p. 7.

26   "facile ideological self-gratification": William Kristol, "Uncharitable Students," *Alternative,* February 1973, p. 3.

26   "As we rush off": David N. Hollander, "Remember the Strike," *Harvard Crimson,* September 1970 preregistration issue.

26   font of socialist wisdom: The *Harvard Crimson's* editorial, "Support the NLF," first appeared in the paper on October 15, 1969, the first Vietnam Moratorium Day, and was reprinted for the benefit of incoming freshmen in the paper's 1970 preregistration issue, p. 11.

27   Muller: Jim Muller, letter to the editor, *Harvard Crimson,* March 30, 1971.

27   Pusey: Former Harvard President Nathan Pusey's comparison of the tactics of antiwar activists to those of Senator Joseph McCarthy were laid out in detail in his June 9, 1970, baccalaureate address before the class of 1970.

29   "argue the world": This phrase is borrowed from producer/director Joseph Dorman's evocative film documentary of the period, *Arguing the World,* First Run Features, 1998.

29   "a mob": Irving Kristol quoted in Alexander Bloom, *Prodigal Sons: The New York Intellectuals and Their World* (New York: Oxford University Press, 1986), p. 343.

29   "cool and critical": Michael Oakeshott, *Rationalism in Politics and Other Essays* (London and New York: Methuen, 1961), p. 412.

30   "coherent argument": Irving Howe quoted in Gary Dorrien, *The Neoconservative Mind: Politics, Culture, and the War of Ideology* (Philadelphia: Temple University Press, 1993), p. 69.

30   "planned to be emissaries": Bloom, *Prodigal Sons,* p. 51.

30   Kristol's youth: Irving Kristol describes his youth, including his Army experience, in his book *Neoconservatism: The Autobiography of an Idea* (New York: Free Press, 1995).

31   "it would never have occurred to us": "Memoirs of a Trotskyist," as reprinted in Kristol, *Neoconservatism,* p. 471.

31   "unregenerate prig": Himmelfarb, *On Looking into the Abyss: Untimely Thoughts on Culture and Society* (New York: Knopf, 1994), p. xii.

32   Victorian women: Himmelfarb's views on women and their condition during that era can be found in her collection of essays, *Marriage and Morals Among the Victorians* (New York: Knopf, 1986). Her other books on the Victoria era include *Poverty and Compassion: The Moral Imagination of the Late Victorians* (New York: Knopf, 1991); *The Idea of Poverty: England in the Early Industrial Age* (New York: Knopf, 1984); and *Victorian Minds* (New York: Knopf, 1968), which was nominated for a National Book Award. As a graduate student, she authored *Lord Acton: A Study in Conscience and Politics* (London: Routledge & Paul, 1952).

32   "equality rather than liberty": Himmelfarb, *The Demoralization of Society* (New York: Knopf, 1995).

33   "to lay bare the pretensions": Roy Porter, "Poverty and Compassion: The Moral Imagination of the Late Victorians," *New Republic,* November 25, 1991, p. 34.

33   Darwin's legacy challenged: Himmelfarb, *Darwin and the Darwinian Revolution* (Chicago: I. R. Dee, 1959).

33   Kristol and McCarthy: Irving Kristol, "Civil Liberties, 1952—A Study in Confusion," *Commentary*, March 1952, pp. 228–236. This episode is also discussed in detail in Peter Steinfels's *The Neoconservatives: The Men Who Are Changing America's Politics* (New York: Simon & Schuster, 1979), and Gary Dorrien's *The Neoconservative Mind*.

33   Glazer and McCarthy: Nathan Glazer discusses the McCarthy era in the previously cited film, *Arguing the World*.

36   No Tracks: *No Tracks on the Ground but the Ones He's Making* was produced by Collegiate students Jeffrey Daniels and Michael Owen, 1970.

38   "beginning of wisdom": Milton Himmelfarb, "On Leo Strauss," *Commentary*, August 1974, pp. 60–66.

38   "great minds are great": Gertrude Himmelfarb, "Political Thinking: Ancients vs. Moderns, The New Battle of the Books," *Commentary*, July 1951, pp. 76–83.

38   "Strauss had disciples": Milton Himmelfarb, ibid.

39   "souls of students": Werner J. Dannhauser, "Leo Strauss: On Becoming Naive Again," *American Scholar*, Autumn 1975, pp. 636–642.

39   rot of modern thinking: It should be noted that Strauss himself was not concerned with modern-day politics; his own studies focused on classical antiquity, medieval Judaism, and early European political philosophers. (Milton Himmelfarb noted in his essay that Strauss "despised" laissez-faire economic thought.) Strauss's disciples arrived at their policy perspectives through their Straussian intellectual training.

39   "noble dream": Strauss, "Why We Remain Jews: Can Jewish Faith and History Still Speak to Us?" 1962 lecture reprinted in Kenneth L. Deutsch and Walter Nicgorski, eds., *Leo Strauss: Political Philosopher and Jewish Thinker* (Lanham, MD: Rowman & Littlefield, 1994).

39   "incompatible claims": Strauss, "Jeruselum and Athens: Some Introductory Reflections," *Commentary*, June 1967, pp. 45–57.

39   "religion to be a good thing": Milton Himmelfarb, ibid.

41   "radical elitists": Shadia B. Drury, *Leo Strauss and the American Right* (New York: St. Martin's Press, 1998) and *The Political Ideas of Leo Strauss* (New York: St. Martin's Press, 1988).

41   "neither wise nor good": Drury, *Leo Strauss and the American Right*, p. 18. Drury also details Strauss's religious views.

41   "Religion can": William Kristol, "Americans and Indians in *Democracy in America*," Harvard College, March 1973, pp. 65–67.

41   "an invitation": Milton Himmelfarb, ibid.

43   "Once democracy is established": Harvey C. Mansfield, "Democracy and Populism," *Society*, July/August 1995, pp. 30–32.

46   "appreciated . . . that republicanism": Gordon S. Wood, "The Fundamentalists and the Constitution," *New York Review of Books*, February 18, 1988, pp. 33–40. Wood also, however, argued that the Straussians made a fatal scholarly mistake by rejecting the reality that America and its founding documents were produced amid a morass of contradictory intentions and interests.

47   "satisfying their desires": Kristol thesis, ibid., p. 21; "natural inclination": p. 36.

47   "sacred maxim": William Kristol, "The American Judicial Power and the American Regime," 1979, Harvard University Archives, p. 213.

47   "people's liberty": p. 207.

CHAPTER TWO. WONK

48   "Can Capitalism Survive?" *Time*, July 14, 1975, pp. 52–63.

53   Description of Liberman quoting Shakespeare: Amy Singer, "A Federalist in the White House," *American Lawyer*, October 1991, p. 87.

54   liberal orthodoxy: William F. Buckley Jr., *God and Man at Yale: The Superstitions of "Academic Freedom"* (Washington: Regnery Gateway, 1986).

54   "signs of declining commitment": *Report of the Committee on the Freedom of Expression at Yale,* Yale University, January 8, 1975.

55   The Vincent-Socrates dialogue appeared in the *Political Forum,* the union's newsletter, in September 1979. McIntosh's editorial appeared on page 2 of the same issue.

58   Indiana as older America: James H. Madison, *The Indiana Way: A State History* (Bloomington: Indiana University Press, 1986); Indiana and the KKK described in Madison, pp. 289–295.

64   "If there's a position": Steve Chapman, "Takings Exception: Legal Theorist Richard A. Epstein," *Reason,* April 1995, p. 36.

65   whiz kids: David Halberstam, *The Best and the Brightest* (New York: Random House, 1969).

65   "terms which have no content": Posner quoted in Paul M. Barrett, "A Movement Called Law and Economics Sways Legal Circles," *Wall Street Journal,* August 4, 1986, p. 1.

66   "They would genuinely welcome a politics": Jedediah S. Purdy, "The Chicago Acid Bath; The Impoverished Logic of 'Law and Economics,' " *The American Prospect,* January–February 1998, p. 88.

67   "The more outlandish": Ron Grossman, "Conservatism with a Smile; U. of C. Law Professor Richard Epstein Is the Rightist that Liberals Hate to Love," *Chicago Tribune,* June 17, 1993, p. 1.

67   "The liberal philosophy of government": Grossman, ibid.

68   "one of the few reactionary groups," Mark Holmes, "Federalists Invade Yale," *The Phoenix,* May 10, 1982, p. 1.

68   First Federalist Society meeting: The proceedings of this meeting are recorded in the *Harvard Journal of Law and Public Policy,* April 1982.

69   booklet: "How to Form and Run a Federalist Society Chapter," informational brochure.

69   Michael Horowitz: quoted in *Justice for Sale,* a 1993 report by Alliance for Justice, Washington, DC, p. 83.

CHAPTER THREE. HARD-CORE

72   1978 tax revolt: Other states besides California voting to restrict tax or spending powers of legislatures in 1978 included Alabama, Arizona, Hawaii, Illinois, Massachusetts, Missouri, North Dakota, South Dakota, Texas, and Michigan.

72   "No one wore war paint": Grover Norquist, "86,000 Endorse Tax Revolt," *Harvard Chronicle,* February 15, 1978, p. 1. This was the debut issue of the libertarian paper, which proclaimed its ideology as thus: "We believe that the only social interactions between people which are moral are those based on their *voluntary consent.* . . . A government is an institution with a legalized monopoly on the use of force."

74   "Neo-American fascism": Norquist quoted in Thomas Edsall, "Right in the Middle of the Revolution; Activist Rises to Influence in Conservative Movement," *Washington Post,* September 4, 1995, p. A1.

79   Weinstein: Allen Weinstein, *Perjury: The Hiss-Chambers Case* (New York: Knopf, 1978).

80   "prevailingly toward socialism": Whittaker Chambers, *Witness* (Washington, DC: Regnery Publishing, 1952), pp. 471–472.

80   "impeccably pedigreed": Chambers, ibid., p. 476.

81   Trilling: Lionel Trilling, "Whittaker Chambers and the Middle of the Journey," *New York Review of Books,* April 17, 1975.

81   "little fat man": Chambers, ibid., p. 769; "conspiracy of gentlemen," pp. 89–90.

82   "two shibboleths": Susanna McBee, "Nov. 7 Shaping Up As Series of Prop. 13 Look-Alike Contests," *Washington Post,* September 10, 1978, p. A3.

83   New Right funders: Described in Alan Crawford, *Thunder on the Right: The "New Right" and the Politics of Resentment* (New York: Pantheon Books, 1980), pp. 1–41; and Dan Morgan, "Conservatives: A Well-Financed Network," *Washington Post,* January 4, 1981, p. 1; and listed in Crawford.

83   Scaife description: "Citizen Scaife," *Columbia Journalism Review,* July-August 1981, p. 43.

83   Committee for the Survival of a Free Congress: Crawford, ibid., p. 15.

83   "stir up hostilities": Crawford, ibid., p. 51.

84   Conservative Caucus: Crawford, ibid., p. 39.

84   "resort to biblical law": Crawford, ibid., p. 271.

84   Phil Crane and NCPAC letter: Elizabeth Kastor, "The Cautious Closet of the Gay Conservative: In the Life and Death of Terry Dolan, Mirror Images from the Age of AIDS" *Washington Post,* May 11, 1987, p. 1.

85   "The Good Guys," "squish": Crawford, ibid., pp. 112–113.

85   New Right attacks on Goldwater: Crawford, ibid., pp. 115–116; on Reagan, pp. 117–118 and pp. 270–271.

CHAPTER FOUR. WHITE MALE

89   American Bar Association: In August 1980, the American Bar Association decided to require all U.S. law schools to adopt affirmative action to improve minority enrollment figures.

92   only 27 percent of California's students: State officials quoted in Carolyn Friday, "Minorities Remain Underrepresented Despite Affirmative Action," *California Aggie,* March 12, 1980, p. 1.

92   FIGHT NATIONAL OPPRESSION: Chris Johnson, "Students Demonstrate Against Standardized Tests," *California Aggie,* December 3, 1979, p. 1.

93   "delightful improvement": Karen G. Johnson, "Law School Admits More Minorities," *California Aggie,* September 5, 1979, p. 1.

93   "not just equality as a right": Lyndon B. Johnson commencement address at Howard University, 1965.

94   "dubious distinction": *King Hall Advocate,* September 4, 1979, p. 1; Karen G. Johnson, "Law School Reinstates Students," *California Aggie,* September 27, 1979, p. 1.

96   Stanley Mosk comments: Joel Dreyfuss and Charles Lawrence III, *The Bakke Case: The Politics of Inequality* (New York: Harcourt Brace Jovanovich, 1979), p. 71.

96   "diminishing minority representation": Gene Girard, "Fireside Chat: LSA Recruitment Plan," *King Hall Advocate,* September 18, 1979, p. 4.

96   "unimpressive GPA's": Girard, ibid.

96   Student platforms for election contest: "Candidates for Faculty Recruitment Committee," *King Hall Advocate,* September 18, 1979, p. 11.

101   Bolick's views/activities as adolescent: Reports are drawn from a scrapbook of newsclips which appeared in the *New Jersey Hillside Times,* the *Daily Record* (northwest New Jersey), and his high school newspaper, the *Hiller,* between 1971 and 1975.

104   "apathy, arrogance": Clint D. Bolick, "Hooray for Me, to Hell with You: The Contemporary Suburban Political Machine: John T. Gregorio and Linden, N.J.," Drew University, April 15, 1979

105   "society of liberty": David Boaz, *Libertarianism: A Primer* (New York: Free Press, 1997).

106   "The real scoundrel": Bolick quoted in "Libertarian Announces Assembly Candidacy," *California Aggie,* February 22, 1980, p. 3.

106   "noose around my neck": Bolick quoted in Peter Adamco, "Assembly Candidate Cites Foes," *California Aggie,* October 23, 1980, p. 1.

106   "Living Libertarian Legend": Bolick letter to the editor, *King Hall Advocate,* November 30, 1981, p. 2.

107   Bennett: Duane E. Bennett, "Why We Continue to Complain," *King Hall Advocate,* October 21, 1980, p. 2.

107   Bennett's views mirrored: The cultural differences and "psychological shock" faced by minority students entering college is detailed in a series of articles in the *California Aggie,* particularly Karin Fox, "Minorities Face Subtle Racism at UCD," April 28, 1980, p. 1.

109   Bolick response to Bennett: *King Hall Advocate,* November 3, 1980, p. 2; Bennett response same issue.

109   "It is irresponsible to promote" Bolick letter to the editor, *King Hall Advocate,* October 20, 1981, p. 2.

Chapter Five. Pol

113   Anti-Iran rally: Brian O'Shea, "200 Students Protest Against Iran," *Red and Black,* November 14, 1979, p. 1, and subsequent editorials and letters to the editor, November 15–17, 1979.

113   "Born in war and raised in scandal." "Several hundred students." Record of Reed's comments to Heritage Foundation gatherings, collected in *The Third Generation,* edited by Benjamin Hart (Washington, DC: Regnery Books, 1987), pp. 67–70.

114   "I paint my face": Reed quoted in Mark O'Keefe, "Robertson's Phone Corps Boosted GOP; Local Democrats Claim Network Ambushed Them," *Norfolk Virginian-Pilot,* November 9, 1991, p. A1.

117   "We are going to make it known": Tom Lee, "Howard Baker Praises Mattingly During Candidate's Visit to Campus," *Red and Black,* October 30, 1980, p. 1. The *Red and Black* editorial "Bad Idea and No Issues" appeared October 31, 1980, p. 4. Reed's letter in response appeared November 5, 1980.

120   Toccoa Falls College: *The Heritage of Stephens County,* Vol. 1 (Stephens County Historical Society, 1996), p. 26.

120   History of medical clinic recounted in an interview with Dr. Arthur G. Singer by Patrick Neal, publisher of the *Chieftain and Toccoa Record,* October 22, 1996, p. 2.

122   "holy terror": Jill Lawrence, "Ralph Reed heeds a new political calling," *USA Today,* April 14, 1998, p. 8A.

122   "larger than life": "The Might's Right Only 33," by Gayle White, *Atlanta Journal and Constitution,* January 15, 1995, p. 1.

122   "wheeler dealer": Kim Hubbard, "The Religious Right's New Leader

Loves His Political Enemies; They're Afraid His Affection Is Deadly," *People,* February 27, 1995, p. 60.

125   "Mr. Reed was not considered": Quotes from all Demosthenian proceedings cited drawn from the minutes of the Demosthenian Literary Society (with acknowledgment to the Hargrett Rare Book and Manuscript Library), and from notes on the proceedings recorded by Dr. Calvin M. Logue, faculty adviser to the society during this period and professor of speech communication at the University of Georgia.

126   flip-flop over drinking-age bill: Hope Dlugozima, "Hundreds Gather at Capitol to Debate Legal Drinking Age," *Red and Black,* January 29, 1980, p. 1. "If it can save": Reed letter to the editor, *Red and Black,* January 25, 1980; "Young people scrambled": Reed column, "University Needs Lobby Rep," *Red and Black,* January 20, 1981, p. 4. The student's response to Reed appeared January 27, 1981.

127   "It is our heritage to accept" Reed, "A Parallel to Poland," *Red and Black,* January 19, 1982, p. 4.

127   " 'queers' and 'faggots,' " Robert Niedermeyer letter to the editor, *Red and Black,* April 7, 1983, p. 4.

127   "freezeniks": Reed, "Nuclear Freeze the Wrong Step in Achieving Peace," *Red and Black,* April 15, 1982, p. 4.

127   "tyrannical confiscation": Reed, "Flat-rate Tax Scale Needed," *Red and Black,* May 14, 1982, p. 4.

127   NFL executive director: Reed, "Football Wage Proposals Socialistic," *Red and Black,* September 23, 1982, p. 4.

128   "black genocide": Reed, "Abortion Is the Ultimate Discrimination," *Red and Black,* January 29, 1983, p. 4.

128   Bob Jones University: Reed, "Bob Jones, Voltaire and Freedom," *Red and Black,* October 21, 1982, p. 4.

130   Reed, "Gandhi: Ninny of the 20th Century," *Red and Black,* April 14, 1983, p. 4.

131   Richard Grenier, "The Gandhi Nobody Knows," *Commentary,* March 1983, pp. 59–72.

131   The graduate student's charges and Reed's response appeared in the *Red and Black* on April 19, 1983, p. 4. Letters to the editor regarding the incident appeared on April 20 and 21, p. 4.

PART TWO: THE REAGAN-BUSH YEARS: REVOLUTION FROM WITHIN

CHAPTER SIX. STREET THEATER

136   "The time is now": Ronald Reagan's speech accepting the Republican nomination, July 17, 1980.

136   "Must freedom wither . . . ?" Reagan's speech to the British Parliament, June 14, 1982, *Weekly Compilation of Presidential Documents,* pp. 764–769.

137   delusion that "the entire Left": Richard Gid Powers, *Not Without Honor: The History of American Anticommunism* (New York: Free Press, 1995), p. 41. Powers's exhaustive history of the subject demonstrates how, from the Palmer raids to McCarthyism, the extremism of the countersubversive undermined respectable anticommunism in America.

137   Committee on the Present Danger: President Reagan appointed thirty-two of the organization's members to key staff and advisory positions. Ronald Brown-

stein and Nina Easton, *Reagan's Ruling Class: Portraits of the President's Top 100 Officials* (New York: Pantheon, 1983), pp. 532–533.

137 "when I was Governor of California": College Republican National Committee, 1983 *Annual Report*, p. 2.

138 "Trotsky was fighting": Norquist quoted in *The Third Generation*, edited by Benjamin Hart (Washington, DC: Regnery Books, 1987), p. 160.

143 Denton: Jeremiah Denton's views on adultery are described in Myra MacPherson, "The Militant Morality of Jeremiah Denton," *Washington Post*, December 7, 1980, p. L1.

143 "It is not our job to seek peaceful co-existence": Abramoff interview in College Republican National Committee, 1983 *Annual Report*, p. 8.

145 "Of course . . .": Gingrich letter to the College Republicans, October 19, 1981, files of the College Republicans, National Archives, Washington, DC (hereafter "CR files").

145 "Alfred Bloomingdale": Abramoff letter to Roy Cohn, July 8, 1981, CR files.

146 "interruption in our steady cash flow": Abramoff letter to Weadon Printing and other vendors, August 4, 1982, CR files.

146 "shower money on us": Abramoff memo to Randy Dwyer, November 25, 1982, CR files.

146 "Often, you choose your words carelessly," "The goal is to win, not to incite": William I. Greener memo to Abramoff in response to March, 13, 1983 Abramoff memo to RNC Chairman Frank Fahrenkopf, CR files.

147 "Operation Rain on Carter's Parade": The October 13, 1980, memo was cited in Charles R. Babcock and Howard Kurtz, "Democrats Stepping Up Charges of Harassment," *Washington Post*, September 25, 1984, p. A3.

148 "move in to Poland": Norquist quoted in Greg Helms, "Past Campus GOP Leader Petitions for Polish Rights," *Red and Black*, October 21, 1981, p. 1.

149 "this will help us with our battles on campus": November 12, 1983 Abramoff letter to William Simon, CR files.

149 "Grover informs me": Abramoff letter to Clint Wilkes, August 17, 1983, CR files.

150 "That's still conjecture!": Greener's marginal notations on February 9, 1983 Abramoff memo to RNC Chairman Frank Fahrenkopf, CR files.

150 Pope John Paul: Among those disputing KGB involvement in the assassination attempt on the Pope is Jonathan Kwitny, author of *Man of the Century: The Life and Times of John Paul II* (New York: Henry Holt, 1997), though in 1998, Italian state security archives revealed KGB plans to discredit and possibly assassinate the Pope ("KGB contemplated assassinating pope," *Washington Times*, April 8, 1998, p. A13). A Turkish gunman was convicted of the murder attempt.

150 "yellow rain": Scientific skepticism about the existence of so-called "yellow rain" in Indochina was encapsulated by Harvard biochemist Matthew Meselson in the September 1985 issue of *Scientific American* (p. 128) and was followed by similar conclusions by scientists in Britain and Canada. (Eliot Marshall, "Yellow Rain Evidence Slowly Whittled Away," *Science*, July 4, 1986, p. 18.) Newspapers covering the investigations included the *Washington Post* (Philip J. Hilts, "U.S. Reports Disputed 'Yellow Rain' Charges," August 30, 1987, p. A1). Despite these conclusions, the conservative *American Spectator* in March 1998 continued to repeat the allegations that the Soviets had dropped yellow rain on Laos and Afghanistan in the early 1980s. Reed's column on yellow rain appeared in the *Red and Black*, May 7, 1982, p. 4.

150 "pro-Soviet": Allegations of USSA as Marxist group appeared in *CR Report*, April 1, 1982. The *Human Events* article appeared December 12, 1981, and March 21, 1982.

151   the liberal PIRGs: Abramoff regularly referred to PIRGs as tyrannical and radical in fund-raising correspondence. PIRGs as "threat to democracy" appeared in Joseph B. Treaster, "College Republicans Open a Drive Against Student Activist Groups," *New York Times,* March 13, 1983, p. 28.

151   the manual advised: Advice on how to respond to "Marxist" professors, gay rights clubs, and other liberal/leftist people and activities on campus is contained in an undated *College Republican Technology Manual.*

151   Students for a Better America: Saul Landau recounted his run-in with Students for a Better America in "Dress Rehearsal for a Red Scare," *Nation,* April 5, 1986, pp. 482–483.

151   Student protest against Reagan budget cuts: Marjorie Hunter, "Students Lobby in Capital Against Cuts in U.S. Loans," *New York Times,* March 2, 1982, p. 22.

152   American public's support for a bilateral nuclear freeze: Detailed in David S. Meyer, *A Winter of Discontent: The Nuclear Freeze and American Politics* (New York: Praeger, 1990), pp. 86–87.

152   "greatest challenge to the West's ability": Powers, *Not Without Honor,* p. 397.

152   From its inception on the Left, the nuclear freeze movement: Meyer, *A Winter of Discontent,* p. 113.

152   "You can't call an entire country subversive": Mary McGrory, "In the Senate, Echoes of McCarthy Over Issue of Peace," *Washington Post,* October 5, 1982, p. A3.

153   Abramoff letter to Rep. Ed Markey: March 31, 1982, CR files.

153   "We don't say that everyone involved in this is a communist": Abramoff quote in McGrory's October 5, 1982, column.

153   "odd mixture of communists, fellow travelers": Vladimir Bukovsky, "The Peace Movement and the Soviet Union," *Commentary,* May 1982, p. 19.

153   "either Soviet-controlled or openly sympathetic with": Denton's remarks quoted in McGrory column.

153   "Some who want the weakening of America": President Reagan made this remark in commenting on nuclear freeze protesters outside a veterans gathering he addressed in Columbus, Ohio. Herbert H. Denton, "Reagan Coolly Received on Midwest Swing," *Washington Post,* October 5, 1982, p. A1.

153   Reagan claim on foreign agents: cited in Leslie Maitland, "FBI Rules Out Russian Control of Freeze," *New York Times,* March 26, 1983, p. 1.

154   Soviet attempts to manipulate freeze: Detailed in John Vinocur, "K.G.B. Officers Try to Infiltrate Antiwar Groups," *New York Times,* July 26, 1983, p. 1.

154   FBI report: This report is dated March 1983 and titled "Soviet Active Measures Relating to the U.S. Peace Movement."

154   Reagan officials' comments regarding nuclear war: Detailed in Meyer, *A Winter of Discontent,* pp. 70–74. "Only 10 to 100 million casualties" comes from confirmation hearings of Eugene Rostow, appointed as director of the Arms Control and Disarmament Agency. Richard Pipes, member of the president's National Security Council, estimated the chances of nuclear war at 40 percent. Louis Giuffrida, director of the Federal Emergency Management Agency, said a "nuke war" would be messy but not "unmanageable."

154   panicky Soviet leaders: This heightened, and unprecedented, state of intelligence alert is detailed in Martin Walker, *The Cold War: A History* (New York: Henry Holt, 1993), pp. 275–277, and in Andrew and Gordievsky, *KGB,* pp. 583–85.

154   "In his sometimes simplistic": Andrew and Gordievsky, *KGB,* p. 582.

155   landing his photograph: Joseph Fromm, "Trigger Happy Soviets," *U.S. News & World Report,* September 12, 1983, pp. 22–25.

155   Tryggvi McDonald comments: Lawrence Feinberg, "Soviet Embassy

Won't Accept Letter from McDonald's Son," *Washington Post,* September 8, 1983, p. A25.

155   "There are bounds to the dictum": John Judis, *William F. Buckley, Jr.: Patron Saint of the Conservatives* (New York: Simon & Schuster, 1988), p. 199.

CHAPTER SEVEN. VANGUARD I: IN THE AFRICAN BUSH

156   "History is marching": James Conaway, "Young and Restless on the Right: The Under-30 Conservative Movement: Rooting for Reagan & Challenging the '60s Generation," *Washington Post,* January 25, 1985, p. C1.

157   "Not one major spending program": David Frum, *Dead Right* (New York: Basic Books, 1994), p. 38.

157   Even on abortion: Ibid., p. 65.

157   M. Stanton Evans remarks and Adam Meyerson's summary of the Right's disgruntlement: "What Conservatives Think of Ronald Reagan: A Symposium," *Policy Review,* January 1, 1984, pp. 12–19; "unwillingness to do battle": from Meyerson's introduction.

157   Will: George Will, "Another Muddy Message," *Newsweek,* November 21, 1988, p. 30.

157   Gates: Jeff Gates, *The Ownership Solution* (Reading, MA: Addison-Wesley, 1998), pp. 26–27.

158   "boring to be a proletariat": Conaway, "Young and Restless on the Right."

158   "the thankless persuasion": Clinton Rossiter, *Conservatism in America: The Thankless Persuasion* (New York: Random House, 1955).

158   "surf's up": The third generation meetings are summarized in the book *The Third Generation: Young Conservative Leaders Look to the Future,* edited by Benjamin Hart (Washington: The Heritage Foundation, 1987). Reed's comments appear on pp. 88–91. Norquist's comments appear on p. 160.

159   "whores trying to jump on the bandwagon": Conaway, "Young and Restless on the Right."

159   "Reagan should have prepared"; "the only coherent revolutionary": Gingrich remarks appear in the January 1984 *Policy Review* symposium.

159   "slickest, smoothest": Jack W. Germond and Jules Witcover, *Wake Us When It's Over: Presidential Politics of 1984* (New York: Macmillan, 1985), p. 337.

159   Details of Grenada ceremony: Drawn from interviews and from Lou Cannon and Karlyn Barker, "Grenada Remembered; Reagan, Students Hold Ceremonies," *Washington Post,* October 25, 1984, p. A1; Howard Kurtz and Charles R. Babcock, "Two 'Nonpolitical' Foundations Push Grenada Rallies," *Washington Post,* October 4, 1984, p. A1.

162   "first conservative to formulate": Sidney Blumenthal, "Reagan Doctrine's Passionate Advocate; North, Rallying the Right, Forged a Political Base for Contra Aid," *Washington Post,* December 17, 1986, p. A1.

163   "right-wing diaspora": Two books that detail the struggles between the hard Right and centrist foreign policy veterans during the Reagan years are: Thomas Carothers, *In the Name of Democracy: U.S. Policy Toward Latin America in the Reagan Years* (Berkeley: University of California Press, 1991); and Chester A. Crocker, *High Noon in Southern Africa: Making Peace in a Rough Neighborhood* (New York: W.W. Norton, 1992).

163   "Adopt a Contra" campaign: Criticism by officials of GOP, and Save the Children charity noted in Jacqueline E. Sharkey, "Republicans Raising 'Contra' Funds Complain of White House Muzzling," *Washington Post,* March 22, 1985, p. A8.

164 "Conservatives were viscerally suspicious": Crocker, *High Noon,* p. 450.

166 Grover helped craft: "Declaration of the Democratic International," Jamba, Free Angola, June 2, 1985.

166 "coordinated the logistics": Crocker, *High Noon,* p. 289.

166 Jamba summit: In additions to interviews, details about event were drawn from: Alan Cowell, "Reporter's Notebook: Angola's Children of War," *New York Times,* June 10, 1985, p. 2, and "4 Rebel Units Sign Anti-Soviet Pact," *New York Times,* June 6, 1985, p. 16; "A Fledgling Alliance," *Time,* June 17, 1985, p. 30; Walter Shapiro and Peter Younghusband, "Lehrman's Contra Conclave," *Newsweek,* June 17, 1985, p. 29.

167 "lavish spending": Sidney Blumenthal, "Staff Shakeup Hits Conservative Group; 7 Fired at Lehrman's Citizens for America," *Washington Post,* July 27, 1985, p. A10.

168 adopted a resolution: The 1984 College Republican resolution on South Africa read in full:

> Whereas the pretense of Soviet proxy forces in Southern Africa threatens not only the interests of the RSA and the USA but all western interests in the region;
>
> Whereas the Soviet-backed terrorists in Southern Africa are a vital link in the world-wide chain of Soviet aggression and furthermore that aggression is a continual re-affirmation of long standing communist designs for world domination;
>
> Whereas the socio-economic and political developments in South Africa are resulting in the betterment of the lives of all the peoples of South Africa;
>
> Whereas the RSA suffers from deliberate planted propaganda by the KGB and their operatives, concerning its action in the region;
>
> Whereas it is important for visionary student leaders to co-operate insofar as they are the moderating factors in the moulding of our future;
>
> Be it resolved that: We as College Republicans offer our moral support and cooperation to the Student Moderate Alliance [an NSF branch] of South Africa for the general pursuit of our common world security interests.
>
> Be it further resolved that we join in solidarity with the peoples of the RSA in their struggle against Soviet expansionism in that region and that we place a primary emphasis on supporting the South African initiative to better their situation.

168 International Freedom Foundation: Dele Olojede, "D.C. 'Think Tank' Was Front for S. Africa; Foundation Was Funded to Protect Apartheid," *Newsday,* July 17, 1995, p. 1.

169 "KGB disinformation campaign": National Student Federation, *The Standard,* second quarter, 1985, and NSF brochure, 1985.

169 "no sexy Soviet colonies": Notes from free-lance reporter Allan Nairn's interview with Grover Norquist, conducted after July 1985 "Youth for Freedom" conference in Johannesburg, South Africa.

169 "best approach for conservatives": Nairn interview, ibid.

170 "passing fad": College Republican newsletter, February 1986.

170 "the guys who do P.R. for the Philippines": Nairn interview.

170 "really pissed off": Notes from reporter Nairn's 1985 interview with College Republican officer Dennis Kilcoyne.

171 "From Mao and the communists": Jonas Savimbi, "The War Against Soviet Colonialism: The Strategy and Tactics of Anti-Communist Resistance," *Policy Review,* January 1, 1986, pp. 18–25.

172   "farmers must be exempt": Jonas Savimbi, "Don't Sacrifice Angola on the Alter of Socialism," *Wall Street Journal,* June 2, 1986.

173   Savimbi as socialist and comments to Portuguese magazine: Williamson M. Evers, "Will the Real Jonas Savimbi Please Stand Up?" *Wall Street Journal,* February 11, 1986; Robert S. Greenberger, "Right-Wing Groups Join in Capitol Hill Crusade to Help Savimbi's Anti-Communists in Angola," *Wall Street Journal,* November 25, 1985. Evers also cites a 1982 Savimbi interview with the *New York Times* in which he says, "I don't want to be a capitalist. To exploit who? My own people?"

173   Lewis, other critics cited (and rebuffed): Peter Worthington, "Can We Trust Savimbi?" *National Review,* May 9, 1986, p. 28.

173   Wheeler's defense of Savimbi appeared in a March 6, 1986, *Wall Street Journal* letter to the editor.

173   "compulsive liars": Radek Sikorski, "The Mystique of Savimbi," *National Review,* August 19, 1989, p. 34. From the other end of the ideological spectrum, charges against Savimbi were elaborated in Victoria Brittain, "Savimbi, bloody Savimbi," *Nation,* July 11, 1994, p. 50.

173   Bridgland: Fred Bridgland, "Angola's Secret Bloodbath: Jonas Savimbi and His Hidden War Against Unita's Leaders," *Washington Post,* March 29, 1992, p. C1.

174   Renamo: Renamo's human rights record is recounted in Kathi Austin, *Invisible Crimes: U.S. Private Intervention in the War in Mozambique* (Washington: Africa Policy Information Center, 1994), which draws its conclusions from eyewitness accounts and a 1988 State Department report.

174   "undisciplined bandits": Neil A. Lewis, "A 6-Pointed Star and Mozambique," *New York Times,* November 30, 1987, p. 8.

175   Norquist's meeting with Reagan: Former Reagan speechwriter Peggy Noonan recounts this meeting in her book, *What I Saw at the Revolution: A Political Life in the Reagan Era* (New York: Random House, 1980), pp. 245–249.

176   diplomatic contretemps Norquist set off over Mozambique mural recounted in Lewis, "A 6-Pointed Star."

CHAPTER EIGHT. VANGUARD II: IN THE BELLY OF THE BEAST

178   "The attempt to 'manage' noncontroversially": William Kristol, "Can-Do Government: Three Reagan Appointees Who Made a Difference," *Policy Review,* January 1, 1985 pp. 62–66.

179   "with its commitment to deals and penalties: *The Radical Right,* Daniel Bell, ed. (New York: Doubleday, 1963), p. 1.

179   "boring," "big divisive issues": Kristol quoted in Deborah Tannen, *The Argument Culture: Stopping America's War of Words* (New York: Ballantine, 1998), pp. 116–119. Tannen was analyzing a Kristol appearance on National Public Radio.

180   Kristol job search: Kristol letter to John. S. Herrington, Assistant to the President for Presidential Personnel, January 29, 1985; R. Emmett Tyrrell Jr. letter to Pat Buchanan, February 18, 1985; Buchanan undated handwritten response. The Ronald Reagan Library, Simi Valley, California.

181   "a kind of fecklessness": Barbara Vobejda, "William Kristol: The Education Secretary's Fired-Up Office Engineer," *Washington Post,* March 16, 1987, p. A7.

182   "anti-intellectualism": Rossiter, *Conservatism in America,* p. 213.

182   "what works" reports and "nostalgia": Robert Pear, "Rooting a Domestic Policy in the Past," *New York Times,* December 21, 1986, p. 5.

183   "Jack Kemp embraced an economic theory": Kristol quoted in David Frum, *Dead Right,* p. 8.

184   "divestiture" remarks: Quoted in Keith B. Richburg, "Bennett Backs College Aid Cuts," *Washington Post*, February 12, 1985, p. A1.

184   "war on children": Keith B. Richburg, "Plan to Change Bilingual Aid Rekindles Debate," *Washington Post*, January 25, 1986, p. A3.

184   " 'entangled' if you will": August 7, 1985, speech before the Supreme Council of the Knights of Columbus.

184   "fastidious disdain for religion": Bennett quoted in Keith B. Richburg, "Bennett Assails Parochial School Ruling," *Washington Post*, July 3, 1985 p. A4.

184   "Might not voluntary school prayer . . . ?" March 27, 1985, speech before the National Press Club.

184   "outrageous," "secretary of evangelism": Critics quoted in George Will, "Protectors of the 'American Way,' " *Washington Post*, August 15, 1985, p. A21.

184   "managed to stir up enough controversy": Edward B. Fiske, "Do Schools Need an Official Language?" *New York Times*, September 29, 1985, p. 6.

185   Accuracy in Academia: Kristol quoted in Alison Muscatine, "Group Monitoring Academia Stirs Support, Concern on Campus," *Washington Post*, November 3, 1985, p. D1.

185   "congressional solons": Kristol undated note to Patrick J. Buchanan, Ronald Reagan Library.

186   Casse then wrote: Daniel Casse, "Reading and Writing as an Entitlement," *Wall Street Journal*, September 2, 1986. Letters to the editor in response by Jonathan Kozol, Assistant Secretary of Labor Roger D. Semerad, Barbara Bush, and Capital Cities/ABC Vice President John E. Harr appeared on October 6, 1986.

187   "condoms for 9-year-olds": Kristol quoted in Vobejda, "Koop and Bennett Issue Joint Advice on AIDS; Schools Are Urged to Teach Abstinence," *Washington Post*, January 31, 1987, p. A3.

187   the department was half again as big: Department of Education spending rose 47 percent between 1981 and 1989; three-quarters of the rise occurred under Bennett, Frum, p. 43.

187   "taught conservatives the way to use government": Kristol quoted in Barbara Vobejda, "Bennett Leaves Post He Endowed with New Visibility, Influence," *Washington Post*, September 30, 1988, p. 4.

188   setting the "cause of education reform back," Honig quoted in Vobejda, September 30, 1988, p. 4.

188   well-oiled machine: Kristol quoted in Vobejda, March 16, 1987, ibid.

188   fundamentalism: The intersection between the Straussians and Constitutional originalists was captured by Gordon S. Wood in "The Fundamentalists and the Constitution," *New York Review of Books*, February 18, 1988. Wood wrote: "More than any other single group the Straussians are attempting to set the agenda for public debate over the Constitution." Among the books he reviewed, released in connection with the Constitution's bicentennial, was one co-edited by Irving Kristol and another by Gary L. McDowell, a Straussian and the Justice Department official credited with crafting Meese's "original intent" campaign.

189   "Constitution as a shield": Kristol, "The American Judicial Power and the American Regime," Ph.D. dissertation, Harvard University, May 1979, p. 57.

189   "politically violent": An adaptation of Meese's original intent theories can be found in *Policy Review*, Winter 1986, p. 332. Speeches by Meese, Brennan, Bork, Justice John Paul Stevens, and Ronald Reagan on the subject are reprinted in *The Great Debate: Interpreting Our Written Constitution* (Washington: The Federalist Society, 1991). A comprehensive overview of conservative legal theories in the mid-1980s can be found in Michael W. McConnell, "The Counter-Revolution in Legal Thought," *Policy Review*, Summer 1987, p. 18.

189   "arrogance cloaked as humility": William J. Brennan Jr., "The Constitu-

tion of the United States: Contemporary Ratification," speech at Georgetown University, Washington, DC, October 12, 1985.

189   "States don't have rights": Clint Bolick, *Grassroots Tyranny* (Washington, DC: The Cato Institute, 1993), introduction.

190   "reaffirmation on civil rights": Ralph Neas, then director of Leadership Conference, an umbrella of 180 civil rights groups, quoted in Ethan Bronner, *Battle for Justice: How the Bork Nomination Shook America* (New York: W.W. Norton, 1989), p. 50.

191   "thought of themselves as revolutionaries": Charles Fried, *Order and Law: Arguing the Reagan Revolution—A Firsthand Account* (New York: Simon & Schuster, 1991), p. 51.

191   "Most distressing in Bork's philosophy": Bronner, *Battle for Justice,* p. 75.

192   "demonized, caricatured": Bronner, ibid., p. 107.

192   "intellectual vulgarity and personal savagery": Bronner, ibid., p. 312.

193   "immoral," "Looney Toones": Clarence Pendleton quoted in Jacqueline Trescott, "Pendleton in the Hot Seat," *Washington Post,* April 21, 1986, p. B1.

193   "claim to moral leadership": Clint Bolick, "Recharting the Course of Civil Rights," *Washington Times,* March 6, 1985, p. 4D.

195   "quotas are for the black middle class": Thomas quoted in Juan Williams, "A Question of Fairness," *Atlantic Monthly,* February 1987, p. 70.

195   Thomas reversed this trend: The EEOC filed 526 discrimination suits in 1986, an all-time high for the commission since its creation. Lena Williams, "Equality Employment Opportunity Commission: Harnessing the Horses on Job Discrimination," *New York Times,* February 8, 1987, p. 54.

195   "Thomas has a commitment": NAACP attorney quoted in Lena Williams, ibid.

196   "some inherent inferiority of blacks": Thomas quoted in Bolick, *Changing Course: Civil Rights at the Crossroads* (New Brunswick, NJ: Transaction, 1988), p. 63.

196   "obsession with painting blacks": Bolick, p. 90.

196   "bitch, bitch, bitch": Juan Williams, "Thomas and the Isolation of the Liberal Establishment, *Washington Post,* September 9, 1981.

197   "indifference to the views of black appointees": Robert Pear, "Blacks and the Elitist Stereotype," *New York Times,* September 29, 1987, p. 30.

197   Bolick's views of early civil rights movement: Bolick, *Changing Course,* pp. 31–51; discussion of Slaughter-House Cases, p. 32.

CHAPTER NINE. CO-BELLIGERENTS

201   "Defy knowledge": Reed remarks at Demosthenian Society, April 27, 1982.

201   "a little too much to drink": Recounted in Jill Lawrence, "Ralph Reed Heeds a New Political Calling," *USA Today,* April 14, 1998, p. 8A.

202   "new life of faith": Ralph Reed, *Politically Incorrect* (Dallas: Word Publishing, 1994), p. 26.

205   "We always had protesters": Clinic nurse Denise Moore quoted in Anne Sake, "Christian Leader Was Firebrand in Raleigh," *Raleigh News & Observer,* July 16, 1995, p. B1.

207   dissertation: Ralph Eugene Reed, "Fortresses of Faith: Design and Experience at Southern Evangelical Colleges, 1830–1900," Department of History, Emory University, 1991.

207   "the prankster, the impious": Reed, "Fortresses of Faith," p. 103.

207   "heresy": Reed, ibid., p. 209.

207   "scholastically famished": Reed, ibid., p. 202.

207   "inerrant word of God": Ralph Reed, "Priorities," *The Christian American*, May/June 1997.

208   "protections from society's excesses": Reed, "Fortresses of Faith," p. 4.

208   "accumulated wisdom": Reed, ibid., p. 63.

209   "everything this side of breaking FCC regulations": Robertson quoted in William Martin, *With God on Our Side* (New York: Broadway Books, 1996), p. 259.

209   "There are 175,000 political precincts": Martin, ibid., p. 177.

210   Reed's memo to Robertson: Excerpted in Reed's book *Active Faith: How Christians Are Changing the Soul of America* (New York: Free Press, 1996), p. 2.

213   "most dependable ploys": Martin, *With God on Our Side*, p. 303.

214   Christian Coalition as voluntary association: Interview with Theda Skocpol and excerpted from her study, "Advocates Without Members: The Recent Transformation of American Civic Life," in *Civic Engagement in American Democracy*, Skocpol and Morris Fiorina, eds. (Washington, DC: The Brookings Institution Press and the Russell Sage Foundation, 1999).

218   "religious-free zone," "contraband": Reed, *Active Faith*, pp. 42–43.

219   stronger families: Reed, ibid., p. 29.

220   "godly fumigation": Michael Kramer, "Are You Running with Me, Jesus?" *New York*, August 18, 1986, pp. 22–29.

221   "guerrilla warfare": Barry Horstman, "Christian Activists Using 'Stealth' Campaign Tactics," *Los Angeles Times*, April 5, 1992.

CHAPTER TEN. UMPIRE PAR EXCELLENCE

222   "tinker-toy senator" turned "First Featherweight": Maureen Dowd, "The Education of Dan Quayle," *New York Times*, June 25, 1989, p. 18.

222   "Can anyone be taken seriously": Garry Wills, "Late Bloomer," *Time*, April 23, 1990, p. 28.

223   "likes ideas, likes agitation": David Beckwith quoted in Dowd, "The Education of Dan Quayle."

223   "umpire par excellence": Leo Strauss, *An Introduction to Political Philosophy* (Detroit: Wayne State University Press, 1989), p. 62.

225   "Here are three articles": Memos in this chapter were drawn from the George Bush Library, Office of Vice President collection, College Station, Texas.

226   butt of more TV jokes: The Center for Media and Public Affairs calculated 162 late-night jokes for Quayle, 147 for Bush, and 137 for Saddam Hussein in 1990; Burt Solomon, "War Bolsters Quayle's Visibility . . . But Hasn't Increased His Stature," *National Journal*, March 2, 1991, p. 523.

227   "serenading" the "Israeli lobby": Muhammad Hallaj, "Dan Quayle Serenades the Israeli Lobby," *American-Arab Affairs*, Fall 1989, p. 52.

227   "single most favorable": Jacob Weisberg, "The Veep's keeper: meet Dan Quayle's brain; chief of staff Bill Kristol," *New Republic*, March 12, 1990.

227   "honored his country": A. M. Rosenthal, "This Infamous Act," *New York Times*, December 19, 1989, p. 27.

228   "Gnostic paradise": John Podhoretz, *Hell of a Ride: Backstage at the White House Follies 1989–1993* (New York: Simon & Schuster, 1993), p. 115.

229   Vice President Dan Quayle's tort reform plan was presented in a speech before the Annual Meeting of the American Bar Association, Atlanta, Georgia, August 13, 1991.

229   "Sometimes, I think": Bush quoted in James Gerstenzang and David Lauter, "Quayle Set on Getting Last Laugh," *Los Angeles Times*, December 2, 1991.

230   Quayle-bashing, stock market will plunge: Fred Barnes, "Quayle Alert," *New Republic*, May 27, 1991, p. 11.

230   "the most harmonious": Bolick quoted in Jane Mayer and Jill Abramson, *Strange Justice: The Selling of Clarence Thomas* (New York: Houghton Mifflin, 1994), p. 198.

230   "wasn't an enemy": Mayer and Abramson, ibid., p. 179.

231   Pin Point bus trip: Mayer and Abramson, ibid., pp. 185–186.

231   "early and loud": Mayer and Abramson, ibid., p. 193.

231   "At the time": Reed, *Active Faith*, p. 135.

232   "rugged individualism": Bolick quoted in David Brock, *The Real Anita Hill: The Untold Story* (New York: Free Press, 1993), p. 64.

234   "nervous and vague": Mayer and Abramson, *Strange Justice*, p. 317.

234   "gay-bashing sewer mouth": Bolick quoted in Mayer and Abramson, ibid., p. 326.

234   Hill outvoted on law school invitation to Thomas: Mayer and Abramson, ibid., pp. 280–281.

235   "left-wing McCarthyism": Reed, *Active Faith*, p. 135.

235   "Mr. McIntosh is hot": Keith Schneider, "Washington at Work; Administration's Regulation Slayer Has Achieved a Perilous Prominence," *New York Times*, June 30, 1992, p. 19.

235   Eli Lilly efforts: Detailed in Michael Weisskopf, "Rule-Making Process Could Soften Clean Air Act," *Washington Post*, September 21, 1991; United Parcel Service efforts detailed in Bob Woodward and David Broder, "Quayle's Quest: Curb Rule, Leave 'No Fingerprints,' " *Washington Post*, January 9, 1992, p. A1. Other connections between corporate campaign contributors and Council actions are detailed in Bob Davis and Jill Abramson, "Many of Competitiveness Council's Beneficiaries Are Firms That Make Big Donations to the GOP," *Wall Street Journal*, October 13, 1992, p. A22.

236   "This land is your land": McIntosh memos cited here were drawn from the George Bush Library, Vice President's Office collection.

237   "It was Mr. McIntosh": Schneider, "Washington at Work."

239   federal regulation increased in Bush years: Jonathan Rauch, "The Regulatory President," *National Journal*, November 30, 1991, pp. 2902–2903.

240   Two major opinion pieces: Two articles criticizing the *Murphy Brown* plotline—and its implication that fathers are expendable—appeared in the *Washington Post* days before the speech, and likely planted the seed for Quayle and his speechwriters: "What Is Murphy Brown Saying?" by Barbara Dafoe Whitehead, May 10, 1992, p. C5; and "Murphy, Where's My Pa?" by Judy Mann, May 15, 1992, p. E3.

240   raising their own concerns: See Nina J. Easton, "Life Without Father," *Los Angeles Times Sunday Magazine*, June 14, 1995, pp. 15–46.

241   *Atlantic Monthly*: Barbara Dafoe Whitehead, "Dan Quayle Was Right," *Atlantic Monthly*, April 1993, pp. 47–84.

241   In spite: Even after the Murphy Brown speech, Quayle's ratings slid. A *New York Times*/CBS poll showed him slipping from 33 percent in March to 20 percent in June, cited in Andrew Rosenthal, "Quayle's Moment," *New York Times*, July 5, 1992, p. 11. On August 2, distressed over Quayle's continued troubles, Bill wrote to a friend: "The last few months have been frustrating though, in a way, educational. I'll survive, I hope, through the election and then figure out what I want to do when I grow up."

242   "negative agenda": Kristol quoted in E. J. Dionne Jr., "Framing a New Agenda; GOP Attempts to Recast Conservatism," *Washington Post*, August 18, 1992, p. A1.

242   "that you can take to any church": Ralph Reed quoted in Steve Daley, "GOP Platform Veers Right," *Chicago Tribune*, August 13, 1992, p. 1.

242   "straw-hatted, sign-carrying": Reed, *Active Faith*, p. 139.

243   Canadian reporter: Linda Diebel, "God-fearing Republicans Give Democrats Hell," *Toronto Star*, August 22, 1992, p. D1.

243   Bob Beckel and Nina Totenberg incidents: Recounted in Ralph Reed, *Active Faith*, pp. 140–141.

244   into the hands of the "crazies": Garry Wills, "George Bush, Prisoner of the Crazies," *New York Times*, August 16, 1992.

244   "Politics is ultimately an intoxicant": Ralph Reed quoted in Anne Groer, "GOP Religious—They're No Sheep," *Orlando Sentinel*, August 30, 1992, p. A1.

PART THREE: THE CLINTON YEARS: "WAR WITHOUT BLOOD"

CHAPTER ELEVEN. AN ENEMY'S FATAL CONCEITS

248   "No amount of rest": Reed, *Active Faith*, p. 151.

249   tone-deaf Bush team: David Frum, *Dead Right*, pp. 17–18.

250   "what Christians have got to do": Reed quoted in Religious News Service, May 15, 1990.

250   "thoroughly demonized": Reed, *Active Faith*, p. 152.

250   "sectarian and bitter": Kristol quoted in Henry Allen, "Dan Quayle's Gray Matter," *Washington Post*, October 21, 1992, p. B1.

250   "The argument runs as follows": Grover Norquist, "The Coming Clinton Dynasty," *American Spectator*, November 1992.

251   "genetically endowed": John Podhoretz, "Dole, the GOP, and the Genetically Endowed," *Weekly Standard*, May 27, 1996, pp. 18–20.

251   "loyal opposition": *Active Faith*, p. 156.

252   "adolescent Richard Nixon": George Stephanopoulos, *All Too Human: A Political Education* (New York: Little, Brown, 1999), p. 108.

253   "It is conceivable": Reed, *Active Faith*, p. 164.

253   Reed's views on homosexuality and the Christian Right's response: Detailed in Reed, ibid., pp. 263–267.

253   "Surprising many": J. Jennings Moss, "Soft Sell," *Advocate*, April 30, 1996, p. 25.

254   "record this revolution": William Kristol introduction to *Homosexuality and American Public Life*, Christopher Wolfe, editor (Dallas: Spence Publishing, 1999), pp. xv–xx.

255   "It will be a political debate": Kristol remarks at The American Public Philosophy Institute conference on "Homosexuality and American Public Life," June 19–21, 1997.

255   "poor, uneducated": Michael Weisskopf, "Energized by Pulpit or Passion, the Public Is Calling," *Washington Post*, February 1, 1993, p. A1; correction appeared February 2.

255   "No other episode": Reed, *Active Faith*, pp. 164–165.

257   "The ad had the desired effect": Reed, ibid., p. 172.

257   *Policy Review* article: Ralph Reed Jr., "Casting a Wider Net," *Policy Review*, Summer 1993.

258   "child killer": Randall Terry, "Selling Out the Law of Heaven," *Washington Post*, September 18, 1994, p. C9.

258   "a lie of the Left": Reed's words are contrasted with Robertson's statements in "The Two Faces of the Christian Coalition," published by People for the American Way, September 1995.

258   Robertson authored: Pat Robertson, *The New World Order* (Dallas: Word Publishing, 1991); revelations about book: Michael Lind, "Rev. Robertson's Grand International Conspiracy Theory," *New York Review of Books,* February 2, 1995, pp. 21–25.

260   "repugnant": Clint Bolick later said he "never got more grief" from the Right than he did after he supported the 1996 Supreme Court decision *Evans v. Roemer,* which overturned a Colorado initiative that would have prevented municipalities from adopting gay rights ordinances. In a June 4, 1996, article for the *Los Angeles Daily Journal* (headlined " 'Roemer' Court Struck a Blow for Individuals Against Government") Clint wrote: "An individual's sexual orientation is a private matter, and properly outside the scope of government concern. But I also cherish the freedom of association and believe that people should be free to indulge their moral judgments about people's lifestyles and proclivities, even though I do not share those [moral judgments]." Clint opposed adding sexual orientation to the list of groups protected by civil rights laws. But the Colorado initiative had singled out gays for hostile treatment, he wrote, "rendering them alone incapable of attaining protected-category status through the democratic process."

261   "going to love her": Thernstrom quoted in Michael Isikoff, "Power Behind the Thrown Nominee: Activist with Score to Settle," *Washington Post,* June 6, 1993.

261   Her critics: In their assault on Guinier, conservatives such as Bolick focused on two major articles: "The Triumph of Tokenism: The Voting Rights Act and the Theory of Black Electoral Success," *Michigan Law Review,* March 1991; and "No Two Seats: The Elusive Quest for Political Equality," *Virginia Law Review,* November 1991.

262   "conceptions" and "models": David G. Savage, "Paper Trail Could Block Nominee for Justice Post," *Los Angeles Times,* May 22, 1993, p. 1.

262   "serious problem with American democracy": Savage, ibid.

262   the *Wall Street Journal* published: Clint Bolick, "Clinton's Quota Queens," *Wall Street Journal,* April 30, 1993.

263   "the most frontal assault": Bolick quoted in Tony Mauro, "Two Clinton Nominees Face Tough Sledding," *USA Today,* May 14–16, 1993.

263   "welfare queen": NAACP lawyer quoted in Karen Branan, "Lani Guinier: The Anatomy of a Betrayal," *Ms.,* November 9, 1993.

263   "looking at civil rights issues in new": Mauro, "Two Clinton Nominees."

264   "Guinier was mainstream": William T. Coleman Jr., "Three's Company: Guinier, Reagan, Bush," *New York Times,* June 4, 1993, p. A31.

264   Will Marshall criticism: Quoted in Lally Weymouth, "Lani Guinier: Radical Justice," *Washington Post,* May 25, 1993.

264   "Anita Hill II": Branan, "Lani Guinier."

264   "right-wing distortion and vilification": Clinton quoted in R. W. Apple Jr., "President Blames Himself for Furor Over Nominee," *New York Times,* June 5, 1993, p. 9.

CHAPTER TWELVE. REVOLUTION TIME

267   "Nearly a full year before": Haynes Johnson and David S. Broder, *The System: The American Way of Politics at the Breaking Point* (New York: Little, Brown, 1996), p. 234.

267   "Who is this guy?": Bob Dole, responding to Kristol's assertion that

his presidential candidacy was hurting the party, *Face the Nation*, CBS, April 21, 1996.

267   "it's business as usual": Kristol quoted in Gerald F. Seib, "GOP Hopes to Pick a Party Chairman Who Can Help Calm Troubled Waters," *Wall Street Journal*, January 28, 1993, p. A16.

268   "one must lower the standards": Leo Strauss, *An Introduction to Political Philosophy* (Detroit: Wayne State University Press, 1989), p. 47.

268   "we could only ascend from the dead-end": William Kristol, "Good and Evil in Littleton," *Weekly Standard*, May 10, 1999, p. 8.

268   "frame a new Republicanism": William Kristol memo to Republican leaders, December 2, 1995

269   Himmelfarb observations on Bloomsbury: "A Genealogy of Morals: From Clapham to Bloomsbury," an essay republished in her book, *Marriage and Morals Among the Victorians* (New York: Alfred A. Knopf, 1986).

269   liberalism in "deep crisis": William Kristol, "A Conservative Looks at Liberalism," *Commentary*, September 1993, p. 33.

269   liberalism's Afghanistan: Kristol quoted in Adam Meyerson, "Kristol Ball; William Kristol Looks at the Future of the GOP," *Policy Review*, Winter 1994, pp. 14–18.

270   "unapologetic conservatism": Kristol memo to Republican leaders, May 1, 1995.

270   "no social problem, however complex": Connie Bruck, "Hillary the Pol," *New Yorker*, May 30, 1994, pp. 58–96.

270   "entire U.S. health system," "principled incrementalism": Kristol memo to Republican Leaders, December 2, 1993.

271   "exactly the wrong signal": Gingrich quoted in Dan Balz and Ronald Brownstein, *Storming the Gates* (New York: Little, Brown, 1996), p. 252.

271   "flooded with indignant calls": Johnson and Broder, *The System*, p. 363.

271   sine qua non of Dole's nomination prospects: Johnson and Broder, ibid., p. 385.

271   "bureaucratic, Byzantine": Reed quoted in Dan Balz, "Christian Coalition Launches Effort Against Clinton Plan," *Washington Post*, February 16, 1994, p. A6.

271   *New Republic*: In addition to the *New Republic* piece, Elizabeth McCaughey criticized the Clinton health care plan in a series of *Wall Street Journal* columns, chief among them "Health Plan's Devilish Details," September 30, 1993, p. A18, and "Price Controls on Health Care," November 22, 1993, p. A14.

272   "Foster and Whitewater were joined": Johnson and Broder, *The System*, p. 261.

274   "*save* welfare as we know it": Kristol-Bennett-Murray efforts on welfare reform detailed in Nina J. Easton, "Merchants of Virtue," *Los Angeles Times Magazine*, August 21, 1994, p. 16.

275   "not about a bigger welfare state": Gingrich quoted in Balz and Brownstein, *Storming the Gates*, p. 271.

276   "The purpose of Hillary Clinton's": Grover Norquist, *Rock the House* (Ft. Lauderdale, Fla: VYTIS Publishing, 1995), p. 143.

277   "the devil": Norquist quoted in Rick Henderson and Steven Hayward, "Happy Warrior," *Reason*, February 1997, pp. 28–34.

277   "An ideology is a closed system": Tod Lindberg, "Gingrich Lost and Found," *Policy Review*, April–May, 1999, p. 10.

281   "God is *exactly* the wedge issue": Kristol memo to Republican leaders, June 16, 1994.

282   "more than sufficient": Kristol memo to Republican leaders, September 16, 1994.

282   weaving in and out: George Stuteville, "Deficit Widens Despite Leaders' Intentions," *Indianapolis Star,* October 9, 1994, p. D1.

287   Rostenkowski case: Larry J. Sabato and Glenn R. Simpson, *Dirty Little Secrets: The Persistence of Corruption in American Politics* (New York: Random House, 1996), p. 128. Sabato and Simpson provide an in-depth examination of charges that the Christian Coalition guides manipulated the political positions of candidates, particularly Democrats.

287   "if they start raising doubts," "the effect was dramatic": Sabato and Simpson, ibid., p. 128

288   "Eureka": Kristol memo to Republican leaders, October 19, 1994.

288   "all-purpose seer": Robin Toner, "The Right Thinkers: Some Voices in the New Political Conversation," *New York Times,* November 22, 1974, p. 7.

288   "to rest": Reed quoted in Michael Shanahan, "Religious Conservatives Are Taking the Credit for Big Republican Landslide," Newhouse News Service, November 19, 1994.

288   "public acts of piety": Reed quoted in Catherine S. Manegold, "Some on Right See a Tactical Misstep on School Prayer," *New York Times,* November 19, 1994, p. A1.

289   "among the best and brightest": Paul Gigot, "Class of '94: Go Midwest Young Man," *Wall Street Journal,* June 25, 1999.

CHAPTER THIRTEEN. WAR WITHOUT BLOOD

291   McIntosh's first day in Congress: Recounted by George Stuteville, "Opening Day—GOP Style," *Indianapolis Star,* January 5, 1995, p. A1.

293   "war without blood": Michael Weisskopf and David Maraniss, "Republican Leaders Win Battle by Defining Terms of Combat," *Washington Post,* October 29, 1995, p. A1.

294   "wears me out": Hubbard quoted in Donna Cassata and Bob Benenson, "Government Operations: McIntosh at the Cutting Edge of Cutting Back," *Congressional Quarterly,* January 14, 1995, p. 155.

294   "war room": detailed in Michael Weisskopf and David Maraniss, "Forging an Alliance for Deregulation; Rep. DeLay Makes Companies Full Partners in Movement," *Washington Post,* March 12, 1995, p. A1

295   leaky bucket: Background on controversy in correspondence from CPSC Chairman Ann Brown to Rep. David McIntosh, February 24, 1995.

295   EPA as Gestapo of government: DeLay quoted in Alan Fram, "House Rejects GOP Effort to Blunt EPA Pollution Enforcement," The Associated Press, July 29, 1995.

295   violated "criminal" law: McIntosh quoted in Alan Greenblatt, "Worth Watching: David M. McIntosh, R-Indiana," *Congressional Quarterly,* October 28, 1995, p. 3270.

296   "Some would use": Clinton address, February 21, 1995.

296   70 percent of public supporting environment laws: *Washington Post*–ABC News Poll, May 1995.

296   "unprecedented assault": Paul Rogers, "Environmental Acts Endangered Laws' Future Uncertain as Debate Heads into Senate," *San Jose Mercury News,* September 4, 1995.

296   "If [the Republicans] legislate for special interests": Kristol quoted in David Maraniss and Michael Weisskopf, *"Tell Newt to Shut Up!"* (New York: Touchstone, 1996), p. 14. Similarly, in an October 1, 1992, memo outlining his idea for a new think tank, Kristol worried that the Republican Party was the "party of business—still reactive and me-too. . . ."

297   "surprised": McIntosh quoted in Allan Freedman, "Republicans Concede Missteps in Effort to Rewrite Rules," *Congressional Quarterly,* December 2, 1995, p. 3645.

297   "mishandling the environment": Gingrich quoted in Freedman, ibid.

297   "not ready to be a majority": Eisenach quoted in Freedman, ibid.

297   McIntosh fund-raising efforts: Detailed in Gerald F. Seib and Greg Hitt, "McIntosh Campaign Donations, Meetings Show Pattern," *Wall Street Journal,* March 21, 1996, p. A20; 1994 contributions by Project Relief firms in "Special Access for Special Interests," a report by Citizens for Sensible Safeguards; other contribution figures drawn from Federal Election Commission reports. The typical freshman raised $123,000 in the first six months in office compared to the average lawmaker, who raised $110,000, according to Karen Tumulty, "The Freshmen Go Native," *Time,* November 20, 1995, p. 70.

298   Oklahoma City: For a comparison of the violence on the Left and Right, see Nina J. Easton, "Their Politics Are Light Years Apart, but the Bombers of the '60s and '90s Share Volatile Rhetoric, Tangled Paranoia, and a Belief that Violence Is a Legitimate Weapon," *Los Angeles Times Sunday Magazine,* June 18, 1995, p. 8.

299   Liddy: G. Gordon Liddy's full quote can be found in Renee Graham, "Talk Radio's Tough Talkers," *Boston Globe,* April 19, 1995; Mohan quote, ibid.; Baker quote, ibid.; Bob Grant quoted in Philip Gourevitch, "Dial Hate," *New York Magazine,* October 24, 1994, pp. 29–34; Senator Helms's remark "better have a bodyguard" contained in interview with the *News & Observer* of Raleigh, November 22, 1994; apology described in John Monk, "Senator's Bluntness Angers Some, Cheers Others," *Charlotte Observer,* November 23, 1994, p. A1.

300   "slipshod reasoning": Easton, "Their Politics Are Light Years Apart."

300   "forcefully condemn those who are guilty": Reed, *Active Faith,* pp. 261–263.

300   "It's a sign of how weak": Kristol quoted in Rod Dreher, "Right Feels Sting from Mainstream Media," *Washington Times,* April 26, 1995, p. A14.

301   "enemy of normal Americans": "Sayings of a Revolutionary," *Newsweek,* November 21, 1994, p. 40.

301   congressional job approval ratings: Pew Research Center for the People and the Press, Washington, D.C.

302   "Hey, fellas": Kristol memo to Republican leaders, March 30, 1995.

302   "you can count on our votes against": McIntosh letter quoted in *Congressional Quarterly,* May 27, 1995, p. 1490.

303   "Only in Washington": David McIntosh, "Taking the Lead to Protect Medicare," *Indianapolis Star,* May 24, 1995, p. A11.

304   "opportunities for citizen groups swelled": Jeffrey M. Berry, *The New Liberalism: The Rising Power of Citizen Groups* (Washington, DC: Brookings Institution, 1999), pp. 28–31.

304   "patrons on important committees": Michael S. Greve, "Why 'Defunding the Left' Failed," *Public Interest,* Fall 1987, pp. 91–106.

304   "knowing who the enemy is": *National Review,* December 11, 1995, p. 92.

305   "In my district they are running advertising": *Congressional Record,* House floor debates, September 29, 1995.

305   "glorious day if you're a fascist": Rep. George Miller quoted in "Vanishing Liberals," *Wall Street Journal,* August 7, 1995, p. A12.

306   "Nan Aron's purpose in life": "Nan Cries Foul," *Wall Street Journal* editorial, October 5, 1995, p. A14.

306   "casting a dangerous 'chill' ": Nan Aron letter to Rep. David McIntosh, September 26, 1995.

306   "not a fruitful use of your time": Hearing on the Istook-McIntosh-Ehrlich proposal before the Subcommittee on National Economic Growth, Natural Resources, and Regulatory Affairs, September 28, 1995.

308   "The idea of a grand showdown": Newt Gingrich, *Lessons Learned the Hard Way: A Personal Report* (New York: HarperCollins, 1998), pp. 49–50.

309   December 1994/December 1995 polls: Yankelovich Partners Inc. on behalf of *Time/CNN*.

310   "bad for the American public": McIntosh quoted in Jackie Koszczuk, "Dole and GOP House Rebels: An Uneasy Relationship," *Congressional Quarterly,* April 27, 1996, p. 1151.

310   "crybaby attitude": McIntosh quote and description of his own conversation with Gingrich described in George Stuteville, "Gingrich No Pal to Hoosiers," *Indianapolis Star,* January 14, 1996, p. C1.

311   "without cringing in embarrassment": Tod Lindberg, "Gingrich Lost and Found," *Policy Review,* April–May 1999, p. 8.

311   "aggressive realism": Kristol memo to Republican leaders, January 25, 1995.

311   "blame for this does fall squarely": Matthew Rees, "Too Much Too Soon," *Weekly Standard,* November 18, 1996 p. 26.

CHAPTER FOURTEEN. ON RACE AND INTENT

316   Bolick's views of Martin Luther King Jr. and the civil rights movement he led are detailed in his book *The Affirmative Action Fraud: Can We Restore the American Civil Rights Vision?* (Washington, DC: Cato Institute, 1996), pp. 23–38.

316   "Guilt over being on the wrong side": Clint Bolick, "Made to Order Issue Missed by GOP?," *Washington Times,* July 7, 1996.

317   "Conservatism has its vice": Russell Kirk, editor, *The Portable Conservative Reader* (New York: Viking Penguin, 1982), p. xxiii. In the 1990s, the Right's attempts to improve its standing on racial issues suffered further setbacks on the publication of two books by conservatives. The first, Dinesh D'Souza's *The End of Racism: Principles for a Multiracial Society* (New York: Free Press, 1996), prompted the resignation of two prominent black conservatives from the think tank that funded it. The conservatives, Robert L. Woodson and Glenn C. Loury, objected to the book's "derogatory" portrayal of blacks. The second book, *The Bell Curve: Intelligence and Class Structure in American Life* by Richard J. Herrnstein and Charles Murray (New York: Free Press, 1994), suggested a link between IQ and race.

317   "benignly neglectful": Bolick often cited a 1992 poll by the liberal-leaning Joint Center for Political and Economic Studies. The poll found that 33 percent of blacks label themselves conservative, 28 percent liberal, and 31 percent moderate. Joint Center officials, however, cautioned that these self-labels should be viewed skeptically, since the same poll showed that overwhelming majorities of blacks favored various forms of government aid and support.

317   Jesse Jackson's blast at Christian Coalition: Laurie Goodstein, "Jackson Offers No Apology for Blast at Christian Right," *Washington Post,* December 9, 1994, p. A2.

318   "Anticipation and skepticism": Michael Holt, *Not Yet "Free At Last": The Unfinished Business of the Civil Rights Movement* (Oakland: Institute for Contemporary Studies, 1999), p. 90.

318   "will do anything": Clint quoted in Holt, ibid., p. 93.

319   "pits poor, unorganized": Michael S. Joyce, memo to William Kristol, May 31, 1990, George Bush Presidential Library, Office of Vice President collection, College Station, Texas.

320   "party of education's consumers": Chester E. Finn, "Memorandum for my fellow Republicans," June 1992, Bush Library.

321   Orval Faubus: "Blocking the Schoolhouse Door," *Wall Street Journal*, June 27, 1990, p. A12.

323   research mired in politics: Bob Davis, "Dueling Professors Have Milwaukee Dazed Over School Vouchers," *Wall Street Journal*, October 11, 1996, p. 1; an overview of research on the Wisconsin school choice program can be found in Howard L. Fuller, "The Real Evidence," *Wisconsin Interest*, Fall/Winter 1997.

325   When he began: When Ralph took his message to the Jewish community, the central obstacle he faced was his boss Pat Robertson's book *The New World Order*, which drew on anti-Semitic global conspiracy theories. In remarks before the Lautenberg Family Jewish Community Center in New Jersey, Ralph defended the book by saying Robertson "never intended to refer to Jews or Jewish bankers," and tried to fend off charges that Robertson was anti-semitic by noting that the first banker named by Robertson was not Jewish, but Scottish. Reed's remarks were reported by Matthew Fleischer, "Slaying the Christ Killer: Ralph Reed Woos Jews in Jersey," *Village Voice*, December 26, 1995, p. 27.

325   "rooted in history": Reed speech to ADL recounted in Gustav Niebuhr, "Olive Branch to Jews from Conservative Christian," *New York Times*, April 4, 1995, p. A1.

325   "more bar mitzvahs than baptisms": Fleischer, "Slaying the Christ Killer."

325   "closer to black evangelicals": Thomas C. Atwood, "Through a Glass Darkly," *Policy Review*, Fall 1990, pp. 44–52.

328   "spiritual agenda": Ralph Reed interview, Black Entertainment Television, March 30, 1997.

328   "not exactly bubbled up": Earl W. Jackson, "Samaritan Project Becomes Independent," *Ethnic Newswatch*, March 31, 1998.

331   "grass-roots tyranny": The phrase is also the title of Bolick's 1993 book, published by the Cato Institute, Washington, DC.

332   Clinton administration strides: Ronald Brownstein, "Clinton Seeks More Private Funding for Inner Cities," *Los Angeles Times*, January 19, 1994, p. 1; Brownstein, "Minorities' Home Ownership Booms Under Clinton but Still Lags Whites'," *Los Angeles Times*, May 31, 1999, p. 5.

333   "vocabulary matters": Confidential memo from Clint Bolick to Victor Porlier, July 15, 1996.

333   hair-braiding client: The hair braiders' stories are recounted in detail in Nina J. Easton, "A New Civil Rights Story," *Los Angeles Times Magazine*, April 20, 1997.

CHAPTER FIFTEEN. THE SEARCH: 1996

335   "proto-realignment": William Kristol memo to Republican leaders, " '96 or Bust," January 3, 1995.

336   "hard to see": Kristol, ibid.

339   "throws a few bones": Kristol, "President Powell?," *Weekly Standard*, September 18, 1995, p. 16.

339   "a little too harsh": General Colin Powell quoted in "Colin Powell: 'I Don't Fit Neatly into Either Party,' " Reuters, May 21, 1995.

340   "chest-thumping childishness": Kristol quoted in Paul Taylor and Dan Balz, "Conservatives Fire Away at Powell's Possible Bid," *Washington Post*, November 3, 1995, p. A18.

341   "Bob Dole is likely to lose": William Kristol, "A Dole Defeat and the Conservative Future," *Weekly Standard,* April 29, 1996, p. 22.
343   Robertson's ambitions toward the GOP: Thomas B. Edsall, "Robertson Urges Christian Activists to Take Over GOP State Parties," *Washington Post,* September 19, 1995, p. A24.
348   "one third of Nazi death camps": Judie Brown, president of the American Life League, quoted in *The Hotline,* May 23, 1995.
348   "Lord help us, Ralph!": October 9, 1995, letter from Dr. Jim Dobson to Dr. Ralph E. Reed.
348   "honest disagreement": October 11, 1995, letter from Ralph Reed to Dr. Jim Dobson.
349   "moral suasion" strategy: The "moral suasion" argument is set forth in Kristol's *Weekly Standard* magazine, December 25, 1995, in Noemie Emery's cover story, "Abortion and the Republican Party: A New Approach," pp. 26–31.
349   On Saturday morning: James Bennet, "Top Conservative Would Back Shift on Abortion Issue," *New York Times,* May 4, 1996, p. 1; "Leader of Christian Coalition Denies Shifting on Abortion," May 5, 1996, p. 1. A month later, Reed further angered pro-life forces by supporting Texas Senator Kay Bailey Hutchison as a delegate to the GOP convention. Hutchison supported restrictions on abortion, but favored legalized abortion until the fetus is viable.
349   "risk irrelevance": Ralph Reed, "We Stand at a Crossroads," *Newsweek,* May 13, 1996, p. 28.
350   Reed discussion of abortion: This appears in Reed, *Active Faith,* pp. 269–270.
351   "It's tragic": Judie Brown quoted in Thomas Edsall, "Conservatives Win First Conflict Over GOP's Antiabortion Plank," *Washington Post,* May 12, 1986.
351   "no longer represents those of us": Angela "Bay" Buchanan quoted in Edsall, ibid.
354   "it's depressing": Kristol quoted in Thomas Edsall, "Revolutionaries on Back Bench," *Washington Post,* August 15, 1996, p. A33.
356   Reed's discussion of Falwell and Clinton-bashing: Reed, *Active Faith,* pp. 259–261.
358   "get tobacco out of our house": It should also be noted that a few weeks before the Road to Victory conference, a more conciliatory Reed had considered joining the Clinton crusade against tobacco marketing aimed at children.

CHAPTER SIXTEEN. CULTURE CLASH

360   "The Stupid Party": Irving Kristol, "The Stupid Party," essay republished in *Neoconservatism: The Autobiography of an Idea* (New York: Free Press, 1995), pp. 349–353.
360   "isn't a governing doctrine": William Kristol and David Brooks, "What Ails Conservatism," *Wall Street Journal,* September 15, 1997, p. A22. See also David Brooks, "Up from Libertarianism," *Weekly Standard,* August 19, 1996, p. 28.
361   "moral pollution": David Lowenthal, "The Case for Censorship," *Weekly Standard,* August 23, 1999, pp. 21–26. In the same issue, William J. Bennett rejects Lowenthal's censorship proposal, arguing for "flushing out" rather than silencing Hollywood producers of "senseless violence and sex."
361   "dynamist": Virginia Postrel, *The Future and Its Enemies: The Growing Conflict Over Creativity, Enterprise, and Progress* (New York: Free Press, 1998). Postrel is editor of the leading journal of libertarian thought, *Reason.*
361   "Libertarian means": Frank S. Meyer's theory detailed in his book, *In Defense of Freedom: A Conservative Credo* (Chicago: Henry Regnery, 1962).

362   "left to their own devices": David Frum, "The Libertarian Temptation," *Weekly Standard*, April 21, 1997, pp. 19–24.

364   Scaife description: Judy Keen, "First Critic: Richard Scaife Is Thorn in Clinton's Side," *USA Today*, May 28, 1998, p. 1A.

365   Norquist as Microsoft consultant: Phil Kuntz, "Head of Antitax Group Has It Pursuing Issues Benefitting the Computer Industry," *Wall Street Journal*, April 8, 1996, p. A20.

366   Success of Contract with the American Family: Detailed in Berry, *The New Liberalism*, pp. 104–107.

366   press bias in favor of liberals: A frequently cited polling number on the Right came from a 1996 Freedom Forum survey of 139 Washington reporters and bureau chiefs, which found that 89 percent had voted for Bill Clinton in 1992; only 7 percent for George Bush. Only 4 percent said they were registered Republicans, and a tiny 2 percent share of the journalists described themselves as conservative. For the Right, this was, at last, irrefutable proof that the national press corps was enemy No. 1.

366   AWOL: Berry, *The New Liberalism*, pp. 88–91.

366   "Mother was right": Jeffrey M. Berry, "Liberalism's Transformation," *Washington Post*, July 11, 1999, p. B3.

367   "obstruction of justice at the highest level": James Ring Adams and R. Emmett Tyrrell Jr., "The Case Against Hillary," *American Spectator*, February 1996, pp. 22–27.

367   "may have been treated for a drug overdose": R. Emmett Tyrrell Jr., "Clinton on Cocaine," *American Spectator*, November 1996, p. 16.

368   "We came here to displace": Norquist quoted in Sally Quinn, "Guess Who's Not Coming to Dinner?," *Washington Post*, February 4, 1996, p. C1.

369   ATR founding statement and details on $4.6 million RNC contribution: Senate Governmental Affairs Committee, *Final Report of the Investigation of Illegal or Improper Activities in Connection with 1996 Federal Election Campaigns*, Additional Minority Views, Chapter 11, March 1998.

370   Grover wrote a column: Grover Norquist, "Calling the House: Why the Republicans Will Win Very Big This Fall," *American Spectator*, September 1998.

372   "liberal mole": Letter to the editor from David R. Zukerman, *Weekly Standard*, March 24, 1997, p. 8.

373   "first rat": Howard Kurtz, "Kristol Brings Out the Animal in Dole Aide," *Washington Post*, October 21, 1996, p. C1.

373   "I have to sort of watch myself": Kristol quoted in James Bennet, "Iconoclastic Weekly Grabs Attention on Right," *New York Times*, May 23, 1996, p. B12.

373   "lords and barons": Lloyd Grove, "The Castle Strikes Back," *Washington Post*, February 23, 1996, p. C1.

374   "goggle-eyed melon-head": Andrew Ferguson, *Fools' Names, Fools' Faces* (New York: Atlantic Monthly Press, 1996), p. 3.

374   "Is he nuts?": Tucker Carlson, "Temperamental Tycoon," *Weekly Standard*, April 8, 1996, pp. 19–23.

375   conservative case for rock: Mark Gauvreau Judge, "The Miracle of Pop," *Weekly Standard*, October 14, 1996, p. 37.

375   undermines "the essential ideals": Diana West, "Against Conservative Cool," *Weekly Standard*, August 5, 1996, pp. 20–24.

375   abstract art: David Gelernter, "What Is Conservative Art?," *Weekly Standard*, September 23, 1996, pp. 32–36.

375   Should Republicans support the arts?: Joseph Epstein, "Why, Despite Everything, Republicans Should Not Abandon the Arts," *Weekly Standard*, June 3, 1996, p. 29.

375   "prissy etiquette": David Brooks, editor, *Backward and Upward: The New Conservative Writing* (New York: Vintage Books, 1991), p. xviii.

375   "feminine" values: See Christopher Caldwell, "The Feminization of America," *Weekly Standard,* December 31, 1996, pp. 14–19; and James Webb, "The War on the Military Culture," *Weekly Standard,* January 20, 1997.

376   Crittenden: Danielle Crittenden's views, put forth in her book, *What Our Mothers Didn't Tell Us: Why Happiness Eludes the Modern Woman* (New York: Simon & Schuster, 1999), provide an important piece of conservative postfeminist thinking.

377   "limited but energetic government": David Brooks, "A Return to National Greatness," *Weekly Standard,* March 3, 1997, p. 16.

377   "stop the slaughter": Robert Kagan and William Kristol, "Win It," *Weekly Standard,* April 9, 1999, pp. 9–10.

377   "draft dodger": Letter to the editor from Nell Williams; "treacherous [and] anti-American": Letter to the editor from Patricia P. Greenhood, *Weekly Standard,* April 26, 1999, p. 4.

377   Blue Team: Robert G. Kaiser and Steven Mufson, " 'Blue Team' Draws a Hard Line on Beijing," *Washington Post,* February 22, 2000, p. A1.

378   *First Things* debate: The "End of Democracy?" forum unfolded in two issues of the New York–based journal: November 1996 and January 1997.

378   whether the Right was about to go anti-American: David Brooks, "The Right's Anti-American Temptation," *Weekly Standard,* November 11, 1996, pp. 23–26.

379   "more uncomfortable": Daniel Casse, "The Murray Manifesto: Trying to Make a Case for Libertarianism," *Weekly Standard,* January 20, 1997, pp. 34–37.

379   "bizarre diagrams": Andrew Ferguson, "The Collected Works of Newt Gingrich, Vol. 1," *Weekly Standard,* March 17, 1997, pp. 18–20.

379   "Newt Melts": Major Garrett, "Newt Melts," *Weekly Standard,* March 31, 1997. The article also provoked angry responses from the hard-right side of the magazine's audience.

380   "hands shaking with anger": Tucker Carlson, "What I Sold at the Revolution," *New Republic,* June 9, 1997; letters to the editor from Norquist and Carlson appeared August 11 and 18, 1997.

380   $10,000-a-month contract: The contract was detailed in filings with Justice Department's Foreign Agent Registration Unit.

381   "open invitation to money launderers": Kuntz, "Head of Antitax Group."

381   The same State Department report: *Seychelles Country Report on Human Rights Practices for 1997,* U.S. State Department, Bureau of Democracy, Human Rights, and Labor, January 30, 1998.

Chapter Seventeen. Legacies

385   "his own priest": Richard Weaver, *Ideas Have Consequences* (Chicago: University of Chicago Press, 1948), p. 2.

386   "I would never have been able to tell": Liebert quoted in Bill Sizemore, "Fired Official Is a Key Player in Christian Coalition Troubles," *Virginian-Pilot and Ledger-Star,* Norfolk, VA, July, 27, 1997, p. A1. Sizemore interviews with other Christian Coalition staff, response from Coalition lawyers, and marketing memo also quoted.

391   "We've shrunk back": McIntosh quoted in Allan Freedman, "GOP's Secret Weapon Againt Regulations: Finesse," *CQ Weekly,* September 5, 1998, p. 2314.

391   "mutiny pleases conservatives": Matthew Rees, "Rebels with a Cause," *Weekly Standard,* June 23, 1997, pp. 26–29.

392   "I think I'd be ready": DeLay quoted in Ceci Connolly, David S. Broder, and Dan Balz, "GOP's House Divided," *Washington Post,* July 28, 1997, p. 1.

395   "used-car dealership": David Tell, "Where's the Outrage?," *Weekly Standard,* January 12, 1998, pp. 7–8.

396   "self-satisfied nonjudgmentalism": William Kristol contribution to "Clinton, the Country, and the Political Culture: A Symposium," *Commentary,* January 1999, p. 34.

396   "Sex, and sex alone": Kristol, ibid. See also David Frum, "Putting Sexual Liberation First," *Weekly Standard,* October 25, 1999, p. 21.

396   "denatured New Left politics": Peter Collier, "From the Sixties to the Nineties," *Weekly Standard,* February 16, 1998, p. 23.

396   "1968: A Revolting Generation": *Weekly Standard* cover, September 7, 1998; David Frum, "A Generation on Trial," *Weekly Standard,* February 16, 1998, pp. 19–23.

396   Clinton as narcissist: David Tell, "The Big He," *Weekly Standard,* February 2, 1998, p. 7.

396   "The president of the United States is lying": William Kristol remarks on *This Week,* ABC, January 25, 1998.

397   "first of the virtues is courage": Kristol contribution to "Clinton, the Country, and the Political Culture."

397   "President Clinton is doomed": William Kristol, "Clinton is the Issue," *Weekly Standard,* May 25, 1998, p. 18–20.

398   "simulacrum of statesmanship": William Kristol, "Impeach Now," *Weekly Standard,* September 21, 1998, p. 8.

400   "we win this time around": McIntosh quoted in Ethan Wallison and John Breshahan, "Conservatives: GOP Can Win Shutdown Fight," *Roll Call,* August 10, 1998, p. 1.

400   "some of the more vicious and racist": Cynthia Tucker, "Voters Offer Reed a Sermon on Race-baiting," *Atlanta Journal and Constitution,* November 8, 1998, p. 5G; see also Tom Baxter, "Ralph Reed's Tough Day Holds Lessons for Right," *Atlanta Journal and Constitution,* November 5, 1998, p. 1. Among the incidents Ralph's critics cited: a Hofmeister commercial showing the face of his opponent, black Democrat Julia Carson, dissolving into prison doors and the image of a syringe and a drug addict, with voice-over accusations that Carson was soft on crime. His candidate for Georgia's lieutenant governor, Mitch Skandalakis, was criticized for the tone of his repeated attacks on Atlanta's mostly black city administration. Political analysts concluded that Ralph's candidate was defeated largely because Skandalakis energized the black community against him.

401   "Democrats depressed": Paul Gigot, "Three Strikes and Republican Leaders Are Out," *Wall Street Journal,* October 16, 1998, p. A14.

402   "Impeach him, explain it": David Tell, "Grow Up—and Impeach," *Weekly Standard,* October 5, 1998, pp. 7–8.

402   "Their Finest Hour": *Weekly Standard* cover, December 28, 1998.

403   "slashing tactics": Eric Pooley with James Carney, John F. Dickerson, and Maggie Sieger, "Read My Knuckles," *Time,* February 28, 2000, p. 28.

403   "baby-faced assassin": Rudman quoted in Frank Rich, "Are You Ready to Rumble?," *Austin American-Statesman,* February 29, 2000, p. A9.

404   "you're likely to have rallied to John McCain": William Kristol, "The Rebellion Has Just Begun," *Washington Post,* February 21, 2000, p. A21.

405   "conservative crack-up": Kristol quoted in Melinda Henneberger, "McCain Fits Quite Well Among His Attackers," *New York Times,* February 19, 2000, p. 11.

BIBLIOGRAPHIC NOTE

THIS IS A SELECT BIBLIOGRAPHY, meant to provide readers with some points of departure for further reading on the subject. With that in mind, I begin with histories that illuminate the antecedents of today's Right. Indispensable to understanding the historical intellectual roots are two books, Clinton Rossiter's *Conservatism in America: The Thankless Persuasion* (Vintage Books, 1962) and George H. Nash's *The Conservative Intellectual Movement in America* (Intercollegiate Studies Institute, 1976). Several other books examine the rise of the American Right as a political movement during the 1950s and early 1960s, in particular Daniel Bell, ed., *The Radical Right* (Doubleday, 1963); Mary C. Brennan, *Turning Right in the Sixties: The Conservative Capture of the GOP* (University of North Carolina, 1995); and John A. Andrew III, *The Other Side of the Sixties: Young Americans for Freedom and the Rise of Conservative Politics* (Rutgers University Press, 1997). In the twentieth century, anticommunism has been a fundamental piece of the American Right. Critical to understanding this dynamic is Richard Gid Powers, *Not Without Honor: The History of American Anticommunism* (Free Press, 1995).

Other notable histories of the Right include John B. Judis's excellent biography, *William F. Buckley, Jr.: Patron Saint of the Conservatives* (Simon & Schuster, 1988); William A. Rusher's insider's account, *The Rise of the Right* (William Morrow, 1984); and Lee Edwards's *The Conservative Revolution: The Movement that Remade America* (Free Press, 1999). The Right in the 1970s is examined by Alan Crawford in *Thunder on the Right: The 'New Right' and the Politics of Resentment* (Pantheon Books, 1980); the conservative institutions and leaders that flourished in the early 1980s are the subject of Sidney Blumenthal's *The Rise of the Counter-Establishment: From Conservative Ideology to Political Power* (Times Books, 1986). David Frum's *Dead Right* (BasicBooks, 1994) provides a pointed and concise understanding of how and why the Right failed to achieve its goals during the Reagan and Bush years.

For more on the history and ideas of the neoconservatives, these books are especially helpful: Peter Steinfels, *The Neoconservatives: The Men Who Are Changing America's Politics* (Simon & Schuster, 1979); Gary Dorrien, *The Neoconservative Mind: Politics, Culture, and the War of Ideology* (Temple University Press, 1993); Alexander Bloom, *Prodigal Sons: The New York Intellectuals and Their World* (Oxford University Press, 1986); and Irving Kristol, *Neoconservatism: The Autobiography of an Idea* (Free Press, 1995).

INTELLECTUAL INFLUENCES

To understand today's Rightists, it helps to sift through the canon of literature that lines their personal bookshelves. Among the most important sources of early inspiration were: Richard M. Weaver, *Ideas Have Consequences* (University of Chicago Press, 1948); Russell Kirk, *The Conservative Mind: From Burke to Eliot* (Regnery Publishing, 1953); Whittaker Chambers, *Witness* (Regnery Publishing, 1952) and the biographical *Whittaker Chambers* by Sam Tanenhaus (Random House, 1997); F. A. Hayek, *The Road to Serfdom* (University of Chicago Press, 1944); and William F. Buckley Jr., *Up From Liberalism* (Honor Books, 1965) and *God and Man at Yale* (Henry Regnery, 1951). More recently, Charles Murray's *Losing Ground: American Social Policy 1950–1980* (Basic Books, 1984), Myron Magnet's *The Dream and the Nightmare: The Sixties' Legacy to the Underclass* (William Morrow, 1993), and Marvin Olasky's *The Tragedy of American Compassion* (Regnery, 1992) profoundly shaped the Right's case against the welfare state during the late 1980s and early 1990s. James Q. Wilson's work, particularly *The Moral Sense* (Free Press, 1993), offered social conservatives powerful moral language with which to challenge the premises of liberal justice.

Scholars can, and do, spend decades studying Leo Strauss, whose more esoteric works include *Natural Right and History* (University of Chicago, 1950). But for those who aren't students of political philosophy there are two relatively accessible volumes: *What Is Political Philosophy?* (Free Press, 1959) and Hilail Gildin, ed., *An Introduction to Political Philosophy: Ten Essays by Leo Strauss* (Wayne State University, 1975). A critical and highly readable perspective on Strauss is set forth in Shadia B. Drury, *Leo Strauss and the American Right* (St. Martin's Press, 1998) and *The Political Ideas of Leo Strauss* (St. Martin's Press, 1988).

IN THEIR OWN WORDS

Three of the subjects portrayed in these pages have written their own books, providing insights both into their corners of the movement and into their personal intellectual development. Ralph Reed's makeover of the Christian Right is evident in *Active Faith: How Christians Are Changing the Soul of America* (Free Press, 1996); and *Politically Incorrect: The Emerging Faith Factor in American Politics* (Word Publishing, 1994). Grover G. Norquist's ode to the Republican Revolution is titled *Rock the House: History of the New American Revolution* (VYTIS Press, 1995).

Clint Bolick is the most prolific of the group. His criticism of race-based policies and visions for a new civil rights agenda are woven through five books: *Transformation: The Promise and Politics of Empowerment* (ICS Press, 1998); *The Affirmative Action Fraud: Can We Restore the American Civil Rights Vision?* (Cato Institute, 1996); *Grassroots Tyranny: The Limits of Federalism* (Cato Institute, 1993); *Unfinished Business: A Civil Rights Strategy for America's Third Century* (Pacific Research Institute, 1990); *Changing Course: Civil Rights at the Crossroads* (Transaction, 1988).

For other contemporary libertarian voices, see Virginia Postrel's *The Future and Its Enemies: The Growing Conflict Over Creativity, Enterprise, and Progress* (Free Press, 1998); David Boaz's *Libertarianism: A Primer* (Free Press, 1997); and Charles Murray's slim volume, *What It Means to Be a Libertarian* (Broadway Books, 1997). For social conservatives, two of Gertrude Himmelfarb's works are especially relevant: *The Demoralization of Society* (Alfred A. Knopf, 1995) and *On Looking into the Abyss: Untimely Thoughts on Culture and Society* (Alfred A. Knopf, 1994). William J. Bennett's *The De-Valuing of America: The Fight for Our Culture and Our Children* (Touchstone, 1992) and *The Index of Leading Cultural Indicators: Facts and Figures on the State of American Society* (Touchstone, 1994) are also important. For books that capture the personality of the baby-boom conservatives, see David Brooks, ed., *Backward and Upward: The New Conservative Writing* (Vintage Books, 1995); and Benjamin Hart, ed., *The Third Generation: Young Conservatives Look to the Future* (Regnery Books, 1987).

CONSERVATIVES AND RACE

On the racial politics of the past thirty years, I found these volumes particularly helpful: Stephan Thernstrom and Abigail Thernstrom, *America in Black and White: Race in Modern America* (Simon & Schuster, 1997); and Thomas Byrne Edsall and Mary D. Edsall, *Chain Reaction: The Impact of Race, Rights, and Taxes on American Politics* (W. W. Norton, 1991). The reaction against affirmative action in the 1970s, when Bolick began attending law school, is chronicled in Joel Dreyfuss and Charles Lawrence III, *The Bakke Case: The Politics of Inequality* (Harcourt Brace Jovanovich, 1979); and Terry Eastland and William J. Bennett, *Counting By Race: Equality from the Founding Fathers to Bakke and Weber* (Basic Books, 1979).

THE REAGAN YEARS

Of course, scores of books have been written on the Reagan, Bush, and Clinton administrations. I list here a few that were helpful in understanding the role of the Right during those years. In the Reagan years, two books that discuss the Right's attempts to subvert the administration's foreign policy are Chester A. Crocker, *High Noon in Southern Africa: Making Peace in a Rough Neighborhood* (W. W. Norton, 1992) and Thomas Carothers, *In the Name of Democracy: U.S. Policy Toward Latin America in the Reagan Years* (University of California Press, 1991). Former Reagan Solicitor General Charles Fried describes the Right's influence on the Justice Department in *Order & Law: Arguing the Reagan Revolution—a Firsthand Account* (Simon & Schuster, 1991). Jane Mayer and Doyle McManus provide an excellent overview of Reagan's second term in *Landslide: The Unmaking of the President, 1984–1988* (Houghton Mifflin, 1988); and a comprehensive accounting of Robert Bork's failed Supreme Court nomination can be found in Ethan Bronner, *Battle for Justice: How the Bork Nomination Shook America* (W. W. Norton, 1989). Former White House speechwriter Peggy Noonan provides a lively view from the Right during those years in *What I Saw at the Revolution: A Political Life in the Reagan Era* (Random House, 1980).

THE BUSH YEARS

Two baby-boom conservatives who worked for President Bush offer jaunty perspectives on their disappointments in his administration: John Podhoretz, *Hell of a Ride: Backstage at the White House Follies 1989–1993* (Simon & Schuster, 1993) and Charles Kolb, *White House Daze: The Unmaking of Domestic Policy in the Bush Years* (Free Press, 1994). Accounts of the Clarence Thomas episode can be found in two books that approach the subject from opposite perspectives: Jane Mayer and Jill Abramson, *Strange Justice: The Selling of Clarence Thomas* (New York: Houghton Mifflin, 1994) takes Anita Hill's side, while David Brock weighs in from the pro-Thomas Right with *The Real Anita Hill* (Free Press, 1993). The emerging divisiveness in American politics during that period is described by E. J. Dionne, *Why Americans Hate Politics* (Simon & Schuster, 1991).

THE CLINTON YEARS

Books on the early Clinton years that are especially helpful include Haynes Johnson and David S. Broder, *The System: The American Way of Politics at the Breaking Point* (Little, Brown, 1996); Bob Woodward, *The Agenda* (Simon & Schuster, 1994); Elizabeth Drew, *On the Edge: The Clinton Presidency* (Simon & Schuster, 1994) and *Showdown: The Struggle Between the Gingrich Congress and the Clinton White House* (Simon & Schuster, 1996); and George Stephanopoulos, *All Too Human: A Political Education* (Little, Brown, 1999).

Washington Post reporters David Maraniss and Michael Weisskopf offer a compelling inside account of the Republican Revolution in *"Tell Newt to Shut Up!"* (Touchstone, 1996), while the political dynamics surrounding the historical 1994 congressional elections are explained in Dan Balz and Ronald Brownstein, *Storming the Gates: Protest Politics and the Republican Revival* (Little, Brown, 1996). Newt Gingrich lays out his political vision in *To Renew America* (HarperCollins, 1995) and later reflects on its failures, and the Right's role in them, in *Lessons Learned the Hard Way: A Personal Report* (HarperCollins, 1998). The importance of talk radio in fueling rightist discontent in the early 1990s is chronicled in Howard Kurtz, *Hot Air: All Talk All the Time* (Times Books, 1996). For more on the Right's role in the 1996 election, see Elizabeth Drew, *Whatever It Takes: The Real Struggle for Political Power in America* (Viking, 1997).

People for the American Way, the Anti-Defamation League, and Americans United for the Separation of Church and State track the Religious Right and have released numerous studies with useful information. For a more balanced perspective, there are a number of scholarly books on the Religious Right, including William Martin's *With God on Our Side: The Rise of the Religious Right in America* (Broadway Books, 1996); and Justin Watson's *The Christian Coalition: Dreams of Restoration, Demands for Recognition* (St. Martin's Griffin, 1997).

For an objective, quantitative study of the relative strengths of citizens groups on the Right and Left, see Jeffrey M. Berry, *The New Liberalism: The Rising Power of Citizen Groups* (Brookings Institution, 1999). This important study challenges the myth of an omnipotent right wing at work in Washington.

ACKNOWLEDGMENTS

The idea for this book grew out of spirited conversations over lunch with Anna McCollister, then a young public relations director at the Cato Institute (and the most stylish libertarian I had ever encountered). It was 1995, the year of the vaunted Republican Revolution, and the media was fascinated with the Right. I myself was at work on one of several pieces about the conservative movement for the *Los Angeles Times Sunday Magazine*. Most of that media coverage treated the Right as a potent political force, an intriguing or worrisome development, depending on the writer's bias. Anna suggested a different story, a social history that might illuminate the soul of the movement—its personality and personalities—in the same way that the 1960s Left had been examined. She was instrumental in the launch of this book and assisted in the preliminary research. To her, I am deeply indebted.

I owe many thanks to the subjects of this book and their spouses, who were willing to open their lives, sitting through anywhere from six to a dozen extensive interviews, as well as patiently answering follow-up e-mails and phone calls: Clint Bolick, Grover Norquist, Bill and Susan Kristol, David and Ruthie McIntosh, and Ralph and Jo Anne Reed. I also want to thank the parents of these men, as well as the friends and other family members who kindly gave of their time to share personal histories.

At Simon & Schuster, Alice Mayhew lived up to her reputation as an inspiring editor who always demanded and encouraged excellence. Her associate, Roger Labrie, is among the finest editors I've ever worked with, bringing to his task intelligence, care, and an impeccable talent with words. Victoria Meyer and Elizabeth Hayes did yeoman's work on publicity. To my agent and lawyer, Robert Barnett, who was enthusiastic from the start and always available to smooth the way, I am deeply indebted.

Two others were especially instrumental to the writing of this book: Maloy Moore, a researcher with an uncanny talent for searching news archives, and Olwen Price, who quickly and carefully transcribed dozens of interviews. I also want to thank Robin Cochran and Aleta Embry, who provided additional research assistance along the way, as well as photographer and friend Debbie Accame.

Thomas Edsall and David Kuo read the full manuscript and offered comments that vastly improved the final work. Over the years, both of these friends have been generous with their help and support, and I am in their debt. David Maraniss helped me conceptualize the narrative in its earliest stages. As the project took shape, it benefited from Adam Meyerson's historical wisdom, John Fund's encyclopedic memory, David Carmen's gimlet eye, Lee Berg's dissertation, and the thoughtful insights of E. J. Dionne, David Brooks, Marshall Wittmann, D. J. Gribbin, and Peter Wehner. Joe Klein, Adam Nagourney, Dan Balz, Janet Hook, Mary Boyle, Jane Mayer, Gary Ross, Patricia Zohn, Ron Klain, Monica Medina, Michael Duffy, Demetra Lambros, Bruce Reed, and Bonnie Lepard offered both creative counsel and enthusiastic support along the way. Chloe Mantel and Bill Taylor were kind enough to open their home to me during my research in Boston.

While space doesn't permit me to mention everyone I interviewed, I do want to offer special thanks to Joseph P. Locascio, Michael Joyce, William Bennett, Daniel Casse, Gary Bauer, Kay James, Theda Skocpol, Ralph Neas, Nan Aron, Jeffrey Eisenach, Jeffrey Bell, James Higgins, Patrick Pizzella, Chris Jones, John Kramer, William Mellor, Donna Matias, Ricky Silberman, Dan Mitchell, Mike Murphy, Don Fierce, Scott Reed, Kevin Stach, Bill McInturff, Kevin Kellems, John Walters, Marion Blakey, Jeff Nesbit, David Beckwith, Juleanna Glover, Tucker Carlson, David Tell, John Podhoretz, James Warren, Dana Rohrabacher, Randy Tate, Robert Ehrlich, Chuck Cunningham, Earl Jackson, Frank Luntz, Morton Blackwell, Mark Kimpel, Richard Thrapp, Scott Stroman, Dr. David Rind, Andrew Zydney, Robert McTiernan, Donald Singer, Dr. Arthur Singer, Helen Sanders, James P. Lucier Jr., Larry Krakauer, and Peter Ferrara.

Harvey Mansfield, Stephen Rosen, Mark Blitz, Jim Muller, and Eliot Cohen were especially patient and generous with their time in explaining Straussian political philosophy. Richard Epstein characteristically provided a lively and informative tour through his libertarian views. Gertrude Himmelfarb and Irving Kristol kindly offered their evocative personal accounts of the neoconservative movement. Milton Friedman helped me place today's libertarians within a historical context. Chester Crocker provided important insights on the Reagan administration's Africa policies.

Eugene Meyer, Lee Liberman Otis, Steven Calabresi, and Peter Keisler offered insights into the Federalist Society as well as their friend's life. My reporting on the College Republicans was greatly enhanced by conversations with Jack Abramoff, Amy Moritz Ridenour, David Ridenour, Robert O'Quinn, Sam Harben, Jay Hopkins, Tyllmann Wald, Jack Dominey, Harry Knox, and Frank Lavin, as well as Anna McCollister's detailed interview with Paul Erickson.

In my research on campus, I also want to thank Dan T. Carter at Emory University, Ed Rabin at the University of California, Davis, and Calvin Logue and Gilbert Head at the University of Georgia. Officers of the Yale Political Union—Louis Tompros, David Buchwald, Christopher Thacker—opened their files and invited me to sit in on their proceedings. Former national College Republican chairman Adam Brohimer helped me obtain access to his organization's historical files. Gene Karpinski opened his archives at the U.S. Public Interest Research Group. I also owe thanks to the helpful staffs of the Hargrett Rare Book and Manuscript Library, the George Bush Library, and the Ronald Reagan Library.

During my ten years at the *Los Angeles Times,* I was fortunate in having editors who not only enabled me to pursue new creative paths, including this one, but also encouraged me, even when it wasn't in their immediate interests to do so. In particular, I want to thank Shelby Coffey and John Lindsay. While both have since moved on to their own new endeavors, I will always treasure their formative influences.

Support on a project of this scope comes in many forms. I am fortunate to have in my life dear friends whose loyalty and support smoothed my life during these often arduous years combining family demands with writing a book. Among them: Lillian Linz Mason, Alina Tugend, Helenanne Hirsch and Philip Recht, Carolyn Breen, Beth Frerking, Catherine Gewertz, Allison Thomas, Marti and John Sutton, Ann Gradowski, the Kearns family, Mary Leslie and Alan Arkatov, Pam Carmen, Nancy Balz,

Susan Montgomery, Anne Swindale, Gina Hass, Ulla Hafeez, Claire Lerner, Jenny Holmqvist, Victoria Klein, and Wanda and Will Yeatman.

I also want to thank my loving parents, who have been patiently wondering for the past four years why it always took me so long to return their phone calls: Here, at last, is the answer. My two sons, Taylor and Danny, probably learned more than they ever wanted about the virtues of independence during the years that their mother's life was consumed by these pages. For their endurance, but mostly for being a boundless source of joy and inspiration in my life, I am forever grateful.

INDEX